BOSTON BRUINS®

BLOOD sweat & 100 YEARS™

1924 2024

RICHARD A. JOHNSON RUSTY SULLIVAN

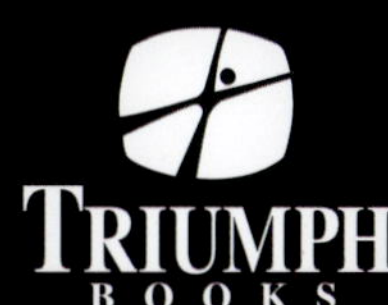

TRIUMPH BOOKS

Library of Congress Cataloging-in-Publication Data available upon request.

This book is available in quantity at special discounts for your group or organization. For further information, contact:

TRIUMPH BOOKS LLC
814 North Franklin Street
Chicago, Illinois 60610
(312) 337-0747
www.triumphbooks.com

Printed in China
ISBN: 978-1-63727-474-3

Design and editorial production by Alex Lubertozzi

CONTENTS

Foreword by Jeremy M. Jacobs iv

1920s
FOUNDING FATHERS 3

1930s
OLD-TIME HOCKEY 25

1940s
DYNASTY DASHED 45

1950s
A FLAGSHIP FRANCHISE 63

1960s
THE RISE OF THE BIG BAD BRUINS 87

1970s
CUPS & LUNCH PAILS 115

1980s
STANDARDS OF EXCELLENCE 145

1990s
HELLO GOODBYE 173

2000s
A BLACK & GOLD REBOOT 201

2010s
RETURN TO GLORY 225

2020s
SOMETHING SPECIAL 257

Afterword by Charlie Jacobs 275

Acknowledgments 276

Appendix: Boston Bruins All-Time Roster 277

FOREWORD

by

JEREMY M. JACOBS

HOCKEY IS PERHAPS the only sport in which the postseason becomes an entirely different game.

Skates dig deeper, shots land harder, and gloves come off like they're on fire. Every minute is played with such desperation and intensity that it makes you wonder how a team could possibly sustain this momentum across four consecutive seven-game series.

In my tenure as owner of the Bruins, I have watched Boston's beloved team reach the hockey afterlife 40 times, including 16 trips to the Conference Finals and seven appearances in the Stanley Cup Final. When we raised Lord Stanley's cup in 2011—after a heart-stopping seven-game series that had us crisscrossing the continent—it was never more evident that hockey players are the most impressive athletes in the world.

In times of both victory and defeat over the last 100 years, the Boston Bruins have always played with a grit and heartiness that helped put hockey on the map in the United States and inspired subsequent generations of players. The U.S. national team that donned Olympic gold in 1980 grew up in households cheering for all-time hockey greats such as Bobby Orr, Phil Esposito, Johnny Bucyk, and Gerry Cheevers—all of whom sported our fabled Black and Gold sweaters.

You can imagine my surprise when the Boston Bruins hit the market in the mid-1970s with little fanfare. Storer Broadcasting was looking to sell the Original Six team and its home ice, the legendary Boston Garden, and I couldn't sign on the dotted line fast enough.

Fortunately for me, hockey ownership was not an entirely new venture. My father, Louis Jacobs, owned the Buffalo Bisons of the American Hockey League from the team's inception in 1940 until 1955. He hired former NHL player Eddie Shore—a legendary Bruin and four-time Hart Trophy winner—to lead the front office.

Shore told my dad: "Louie, here's what I want you to do. I will take care of the team and run it. I want you, if you have a question, to take out a notebook and write it down. At the end of the year, we'll talk about it."

That's how my dad approached ownership: hire the right people and get out of their way. I adopted this philosophy when I bought the Bruins, and it has guided my nearly 50 years of ownership. I owe a great deal to my friend and hockey mentor Harry Sinden, who, much like Eddie Shore, kindly told me to move out of the way and let him manage the team.

Of course, the word "ownership" is a bit of a misnomer in professional sports. While I may have the economic investment in the Bruins, our fans and the city of Boston have the emotional investment and are the true owners of the team. In fact, the city and the Bruins are inextricably linked, and it's impossible to separate one's identity from the other. That's why, when Boston Garden reached the end of its useful life, we knew it was critical to keep the team playing in the heart of Boston.

We were told we would never be able to build a new arena on the same site as the Garden because the conditions weren't suitable for new construction. Twenty years later, I watched as the final steel beam was raised on today's TD Garden. That's not to say it was easy going, as we overcame obstacles from the city and state that would have driven many owners into the suburbs. But we knew that the Bruins belonged in Boston, so we never gave up.

Two decades after opening the new TD Garden, we undertook a major renovation to keep pace with the state-of-the-art venues popping up in sports towns across the country. I dare say we have exceeded the nicest of the new arenas, because our Bruins and Celtics fans deserve the very best.

When I had the honor of being inducted into the Hockey Hall of Fame, I shared in my speech that owning the Bruins has been incredibly meaningful to my family. For me, it is particularly gratifying to watch the next generation carry on the stewardship of this great franchise.

My wife, Peggy, and I take great joy in how the Bruins bring together my children, grandchildren, and great grandchildren. In fact, opening night and playoff games are sometimes the only events where we can count on seeing all of them in one room at the same time. I know the same is true for families across New England for the past 100 years of Bruins hockey.

Here's to 100 more.

Jeremy M. Jacobs is the owner of the Boston Bruins and chairman of Delaware North, one of the world's leading hospitality and food service companies.

BOSTON BRUINS®

BLOOD sweat & 100 YEARS™

1924 2024

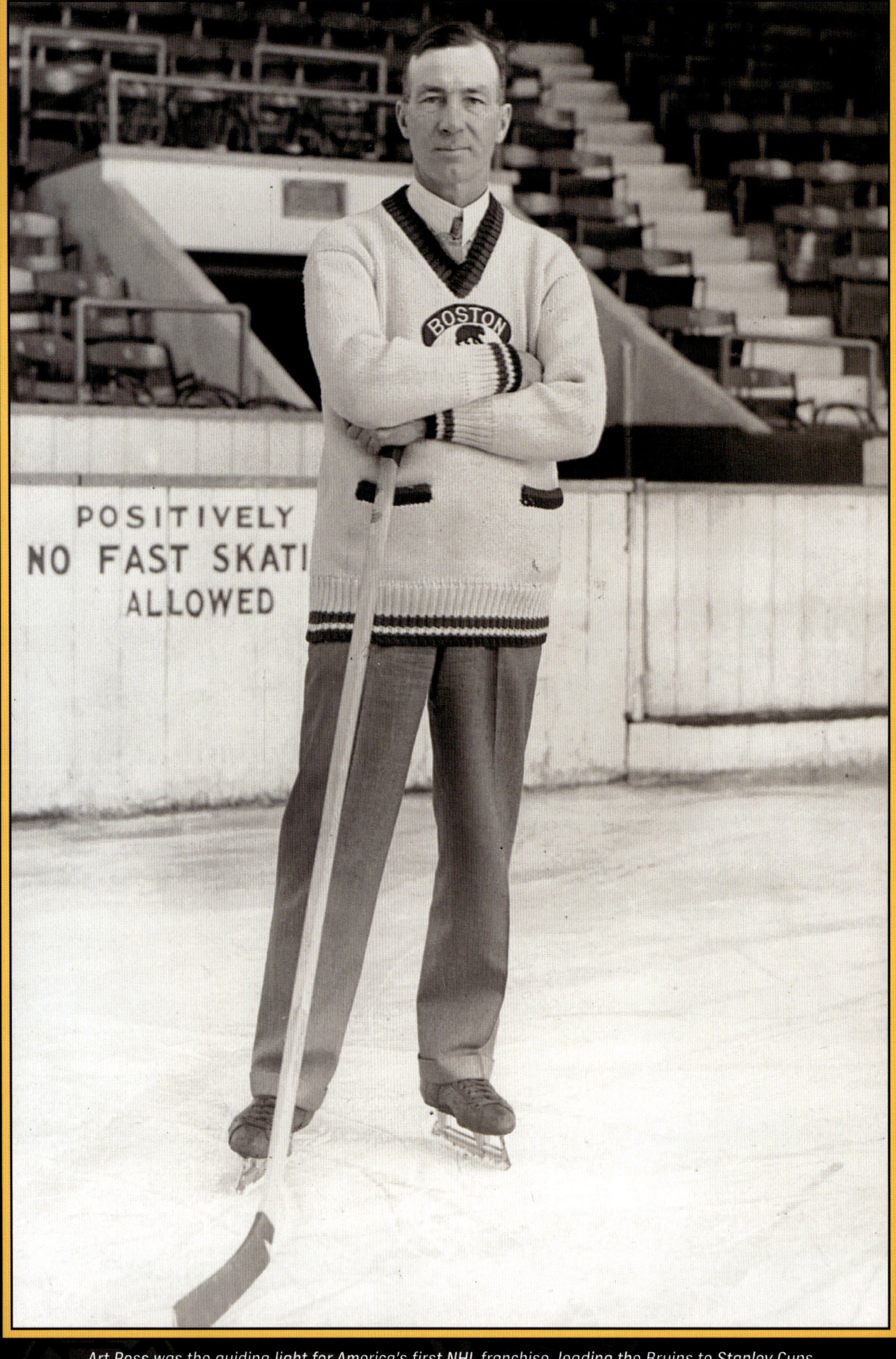

Art Ross was the guiding light for America's first NHL franchise, leading the Bruins to Stanley Cups as head coach and general manager in 1929 and 1939 and then again as general manager in 1941. He was known to one and all as simply "Mr. Ross." (Collection of The Sports Museum)

FOUNDING FATHERS

The Bruins are an untamed animal whose name is synonymous with size, strength, agility, ferocity, and cunning.

—Charles F. Adams, Bruins founder

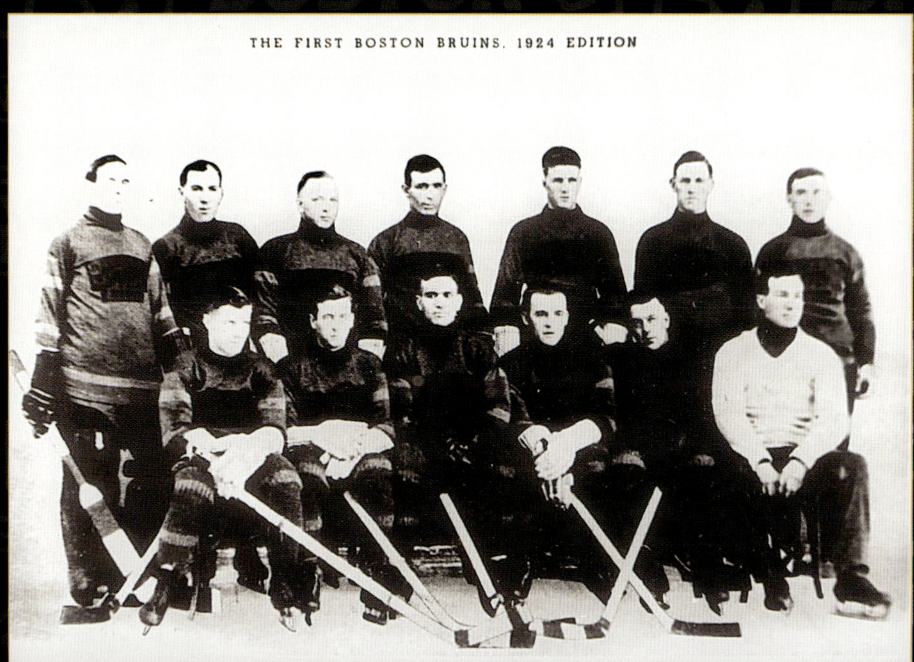
THE FIRST BOSTON BRUINS, 1924 EDITION

The inaugural Bruins team in 1924–25 went 6–24 and finished in last place. Brighter days lay ahead. (Collection of The Sports Museum)

The Bruins were a perfect fit for sports-mad Boston in the middle of the Roaring Twenties. In the two decades prior to their arrival in 1924, the city had achieved great success on all levels. Not only had its two baseball clubs, the Red Sox and Braves, won five world championships from 1912 to 1918, but Harvard's football team scored a 7–6 victory over Oregon in the 1920 Rose Bowl.

By the mid-1920s, the sport of hockey had already sunk deep roots in the region, with the formation of the first interscholastic hockey league in America as well as the presence of many pioneering collegiate programs. Boston Arena, built in 1910, was home ice for a wide array of high school, college, and amateur club teams. Players such as the great Hobey Baker of St. Paul's School and Princeton attracted overflow crowds to the arena that would soon host the Bruins.

Against this general backdrop, the stage was set perfectly for professional hockey in Boston.

The Bruins' first squad was hastily assembled in November 1924, within a month of the National Hockey League approving Boston's entry as the league's first American franchise. The players on that inaugural team were a motley and colorful collection of blue-collar sportsmen. Included on their roster were a Great Lakes deckhand (center Jimmy "Sailor" Herberts), a practicing dentist (goalie Charles "Doc" Stewart), an automobile salesman (defenseman Billy "Red" Stuart), and a Royal Canadian Mounted Policeman (defenseman Lionel Hitchman).

By the time the team played its first game on December 1, 1924, fans had already embraced the game on every level and were eager to adopt the franchise founded by Vermont-born grocery magnate Charles F. Adams.

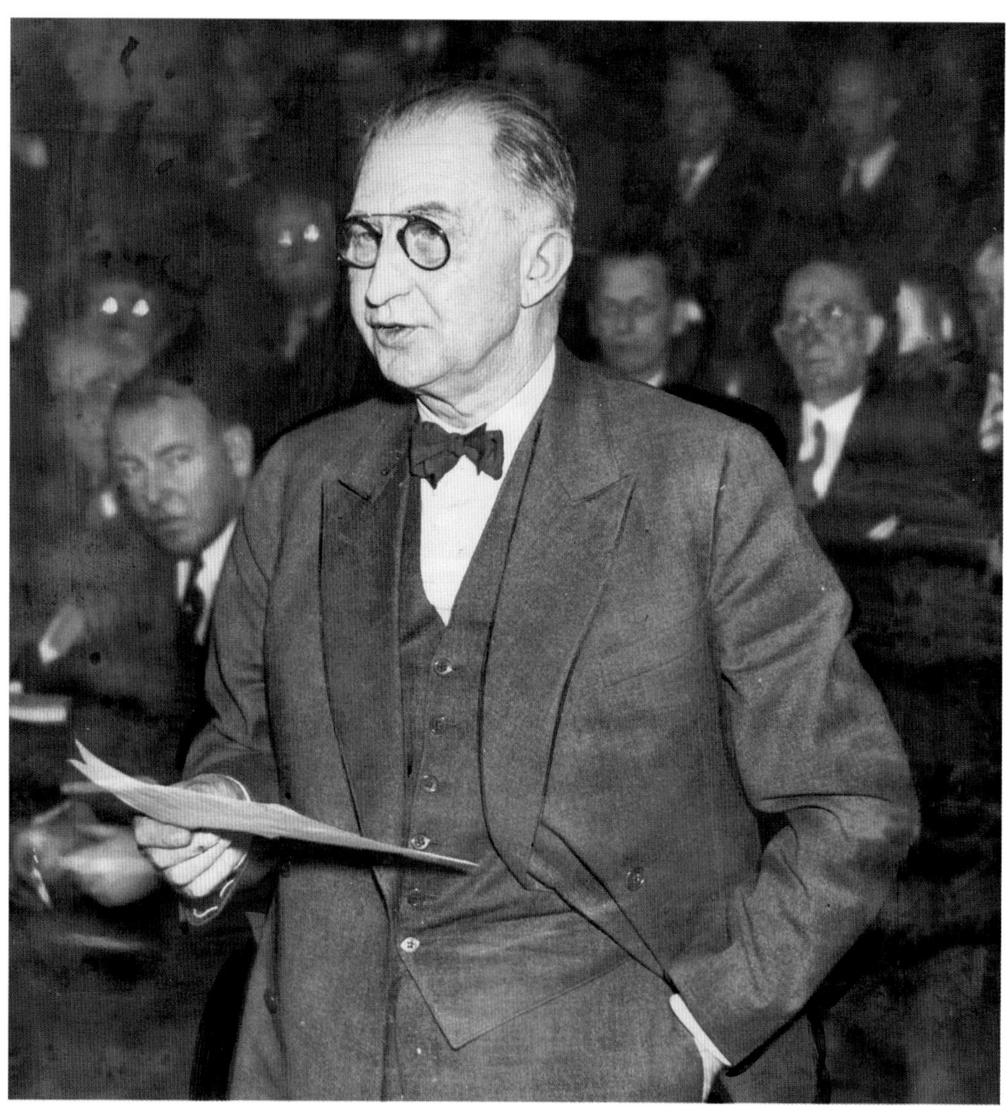

Self-made grocery magnate Charles F. Adams paid the NHL $15,000 for the rights to the first franchise in the United States. (Collection of The Sports Museum)

Within four seasons, Adams and coach/general manager Art Ross built a franchise that rose to the top of the NHL.

In their first decade, the Bruins elevated both the league and the game itself, as they showcased the talent of defenseman Eddie Shore, a drawing card worthy of comparison to baseball counterparts Ty Cobb and Babe Ruth. They also partnered with sports promoter extraordinaire Tex Rickard to build Boston Garden, the Hub's equivalent of New York's newly opened Madison Square Garden. The building in Boston opened in 1928 to overflow crowds and was christened with the winning of the franchise's first Stanley Cup on March 29, 1929.

CHARLES F. ADAMS

There is no doubt that Boston Bruins founder Charles Adams shared certain core traits with the best of Boston's professional franchise owners. Like Robert Kraft, he was a devoted fan of his sport long before he developed any interest in purchasing a team. Like John Henry, he was a self-made magnate. And like Jeremy Jacobs, he built a state-of-the-art arena that became a hub of sports and entertainment in the city. Moreover, similar to his more recent championship-pedigree compatriots, Adams attracted the best executives and coaches in the business and simply left them to their own devices. The prime example of this was Adams hiring Art Ross in 1924—including cutting him in as a limited partner—which led to the Bruins winning their first Stanley Cup in only their fifth season.

Born into poverty in Newport, Vermont, in 1876, Charles Francis Adams was a classic rags-to-riches story, working his way up from grocery clerk to achieving success as a lumber broker and eventually parlaying his retail experience to serve as treasurer of the New England Maple Syrup Company in Cambridge, Massachusetts.

Following a move to an executive position in banking, he returned to the retail food business, eventually becoming chairman and principal owner of the First National grocery store chain.

Though not a member of the world-famous Adams political dynasty that began in the late 1700s and extended well into the next century, Charles gave his own burnish to the Adams name in Boston with several significant achievements, especially in the realm of sports. His first and most lasting legacy was founding the Boston Bruins in the fall of 1924. Strangely enough, the team came about in the wake of a scandal involving the Pittsburgh Yellow Jackets and Boston Athletic Association (B.A.A.) of the United States Amateur Hockey Association, in which the Pittsburgh team threw a playoff game against Boston in order to secure an additional home game at Duquesne Gardens.

The resulting controversy opened the door for a group, initially led by Montreal horseracing executive Thomas Duggan, to place an NHL team in the United States, with New York City being the desired landing spot. For various reasons, however, New York backed out of its deal. Adams quickly stepped in and completed negotiations for a deal that placed a team in Boston and also allowed Duggan to start a team in Montreal, the Maroons, to compete with the Canadiens.

Boston Arena, long a home to a host of school, collegiate, and top-flight amateur competition, was more than happy to reserve Monday nights for the home games of America's first NHL franchise.

According to legend, Adams held a contest to name his team, and general manager Art Ross's secretary, Bessie Moss, came up with the Bruins name.

The *Boston Globe* reported as follows: "An interesting item is connected with Pres. Adams' partiality towards brown as the team color. The pro magnate's four thoroughbreds are brown, his fifty stores are brown, his Guernsey cows are of the same color, brown is the predominating color among his Durco pigs on his Framingham estate, and the Rhode Island hens are brown, although Pres. Adams wouldn't say whether or not the eggs they lay are of a brown color."

After suffering through two dismal seasons, Adams secured an influx of talent with his purchase of the Western Canada Hockey League from the Patrick brothers in 1926 for $300,000. Included in the deal were such future Hall of Fame players as Duke Keats, Harry Oliver, Frank Boucher, and Eddie Shore. Soon after, Adams invested $500,000 for the construction of Boston Garden. Within three years, Shore would lead the Bruins to their first Stanley Cup, with the team selling out the Garden as well as opposing arenas throughout North America on a regular basis.

Adams soon expanded his sports portfolio beyond the Bruins. He founded a minor league hockey team, the Cubs, which shared space in the Garden and charged fan friendly prices in the depths of the Depression with a top ticket price of $1. As head of the Eastern Racing Association, Adams led the effort to build Suffolk Downs, a facility that routinely attracted more paying customers than the Red Sox and Braves combined. He also bought a minority share in the Boston Braves National League baseball team in 1927, remaining a board member until 1935, when his ownership stake in Suffolk Downs forced the commissioner of baseball, Kenesaw Mountain Landis, to request the sale of his shares.

Elected to the Hockey Hall of Fame in 1960, Adams later had a division in the NHL's Prince of Wales Conference named in his honor. The Adams Division enjoyed a run of two decades from 1974 to 1993 before the NHL renamed it (first as the Northeast Division and then with its current name, the Atlantic Division).

Adams occupies a singular place in Boston sports, having been the owner and partner of two local pro franchises simultaneously while also building one of America's legendary thoroughbred tracks.

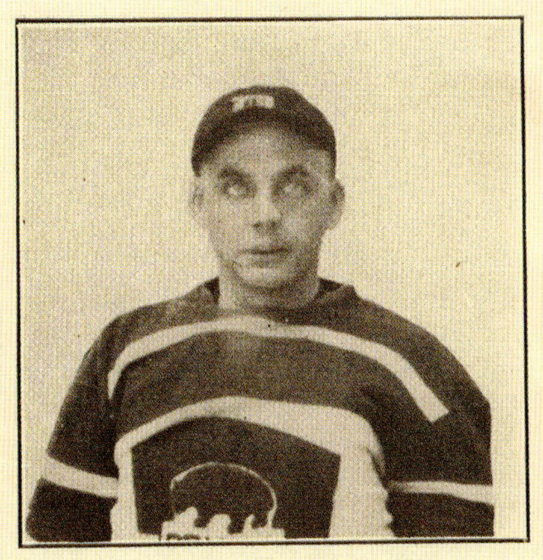

CHARLES STEWART

Goal

CANADA made a great "save" when Dr. Charles Stewart entered the world at Carleton Place, Ontario, in 1895. Charlie has played hockey for 14 years. He has played with Kingston Collegiates, Frontenacs, Argonauts, Toronto Dentals, Aura Lees and Hamilton Tigers. This is Stewart's third year with the Bruins. "Doc" is one of the best goalies in hockey. He is a dentist and answers to "Doc." He is No. 11.

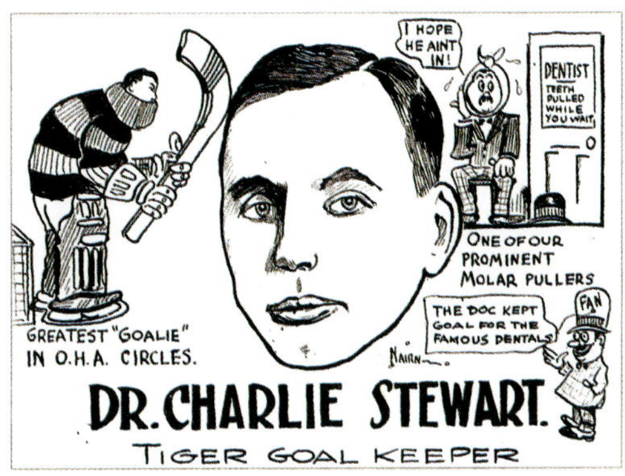

One of the goaltenders on the first Bruins team, Charles Stewart, was a dentist.
(Collection of Richard A. Johnson)

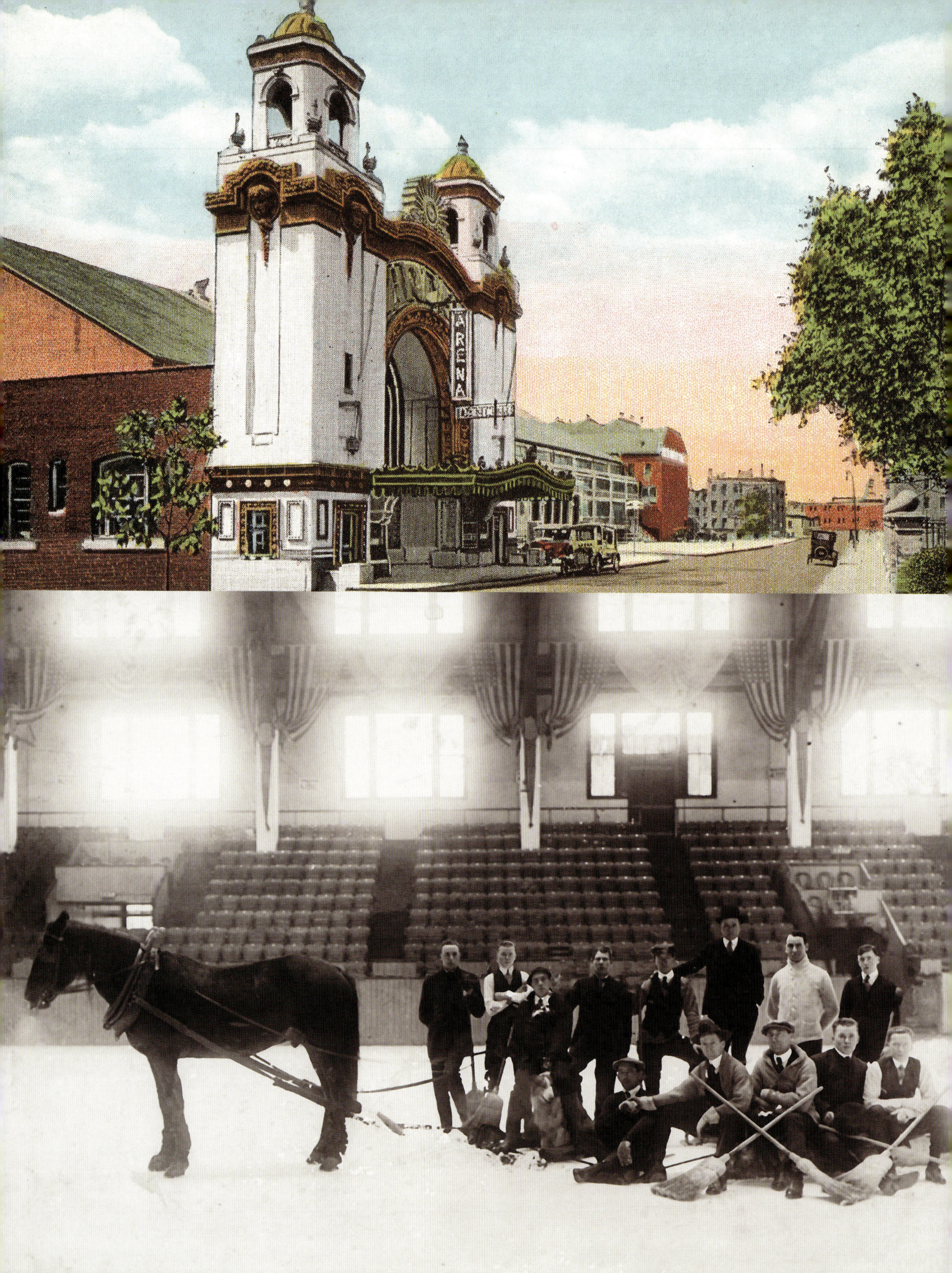
ARENA

Boston Post | November 1, 1924

BOSTON WILL WATCH BIG LEAGUE HOCKEY DURING COMING WINTER AT ARENA

Seattle Team Will Be Brought Here Intact—Local Club Will Be Sole American Representative in Pro Game

Boston will have professional hockey to look at this winter. The Seattle team of the Pacific Coast League will be brought here to represent Boston in the National Hockey League of Canada and this city will have the only United States team in the big pro circuit. Home games will be played Monday nights at the Boston Arena.

This was announced last night by President Charles F. Adams of the new "pro" club and Manager George V. Brown of the Arena.

The change of attitude of Manager Brown was prompted by the refusal of New York hockey interests to promote the professional game.

Boston Arena (opposite page, top) was the Bruins' home for their first four seasons. The arena, which opened in 1910, is now known as Matthews Arena and is home to Northeastern University's hockey and basketball teams. (Collection of Richard A. Johnson)

Boston Traveler | December 1, 1924

BRUINS FACE MONTREAL TONIGHT IN FIRST LEAGUE BATTLE

Contest Should Be Fast, as Both Teams Want Win at Start of League Race

MONTREAL TEAM STRONG AGGREGATION, WITH SEVERAL FORMER STAR AMATEURS—BRUINS ARE IN GOOD CONDITION

by Ralph Clifford

The Boston Bruins, with a practice game under their belts, set sail tonight for National Hockey League honors when they tackle the new Montreal team at the Arena.

Plenty of Action Looked for Tonight

All the speed and dash that characterizes the professional game will be in evidence tonight, for both teams will be out to start the season with a win. There will not be the over-zealous defensive play, for there is something at stake for both aggregations in this case, which was not true in the exhibition game.

Manager Art Ross of the Bruins has stressed the three-man defense and the need for better team play in all practice sessions, with the result that there should be great improvement in this department of the local team's play.

To date he has avoided any set combinations, either on the offense or defense, in order that all players may familiarize themselves with the play of the other individual members of the squad. In this way, there will be no loss of effectiveness in the team play when substitutions are made and no player will feel that his best work is dependent upon the fact that any other particular player is paired up with him.

Prior to the invention of the modern-day ice resurfacer, ice maintenance at Boston Arena was performed with a plow-like ice scraper pulled by a horse followed by broom-toting workers (opposite page, bottom). (Collection of The Sports Museum)

Boston Post | December 2, 1924

BRUINS BETTER IN ROUGHHOUSE GAME

Chase Montreal Maroons, 2–1, in League Clash— Players Constantly Put Off for Roughing It.

by Burt Hoxie

The Bruins, so called, Boston's representatives in the National Professional Hockey League, won their opening league game at the Arena last evening. At the expense of the Maroons of Montreal did they get away to a pleasing and flying start, the score being 2 to 1.

The dyed in the wool hockey fans who previous to tonight's professional hockey's visit to this city arose to remark that the pro game was yards faster than the amateur didn't say enough. It is faster as last evening's show went to prove. But it has all the characteristics of football, and football at least half of last evening was the game played on the Arena surface.

It may be rubbing it in a trifle to state that the pros don't stick to the game of the puck and shinny. It was to be expected with both teams anxious to prove their ability to the fans that discretion would be thrown to the winds and a few outside elements make their debut.

It was 60 minutes of as rugged indoor ice stuff as hockey fans have seen here for many a day. There was hardly a time during the game when someone, sometimes two, three in fact occupied the penalty box. Sticks flew dangerously about the heads of the contestants, body checking was at its height, and the sideboards lost some of the new paint through the constant contact of the entertainers.

When matters reached a fever height toward the close of the game, it looked as though all hands would indulge in a free for all at close quarters. At least half the players piled up at one end of the rink seeking each other's scalp with a minute left to play.

But fortunately the quarters were too close for any damaging blows. At least it looked so from the side lines. If a few more minutes had remained, some of the fight managers present might have located a new white hope on the "pure" surface.

Hub Team Improves

Speaking of the game itself, it wasn't so bad, considering real pro hockey from these teams seems still to be somewhat in its embryo state. The Bruins, to be sure, showed that they have divested themselves of certain rough spots since Thanksgiving. Team work to a better extent has been developed. Their eyes have also located the target. And with a whale of a defense offered, the Bruins' claws are getting quite keen.

Montreal in the opening period showed a keener nose for the puck and through following the scent scored their first and only goal. "Dinny" Dinsmore, remembered by fans as a persistent puck pest when a member of the Aura Lees, caged it. It took nine minutes for the curtains to be dented, and it was rather a lucky goal, too. "Dinny" made a shot with steam attached from the defense from the beginning. Heck Fowler stopped the disc all right, but his underpinning went out from under him afterwards. Dinsmore pounced on the Para and sent it home. The Bruins played tit-tat on Benedict's pads in the opposite cage, but their efforts went unrewarded till early in the second period. Bullet Cooper, and Harris, both of whom played a whale of a game, offensively and defensively speaking, tied it up in less than four minutes of play.

Show Pretty Team Work

It was the prettiest piece of passing of the evening; quick in its execution and true as a die from center ice to the goal's entrance.

It was Cooper who was responsible for the winning tally less than three minutes later. Two goals before half the period was over indicates that the Bruins were doing things this session. Bill Cook had a finger in the scoring pie by the way. Bill made a solo trip down the right lane, went beyond the goal and made a nifty pass out, hoping some hound would pounce on the rubber. Cooper was that canine. With a back-hand flip, goalie Benedict was hoodwinked, the Bruins took the lead and held it ever after.

The third period contained the better hockey, the better scoring chances, as well as the stuff of the rough sort. Both teams frequently had but four men on the ice. The odds shifted from one side to another with the chances excellent of the score being tied, or of the Bruins going into a safe lead.

It was, as stated, some game and had some wind-up. If some of the amateurs who recently turned pro have to take it as they did last evening under the professional rules, they're likely to wish themselves back in the ranks of the "pures" before long.

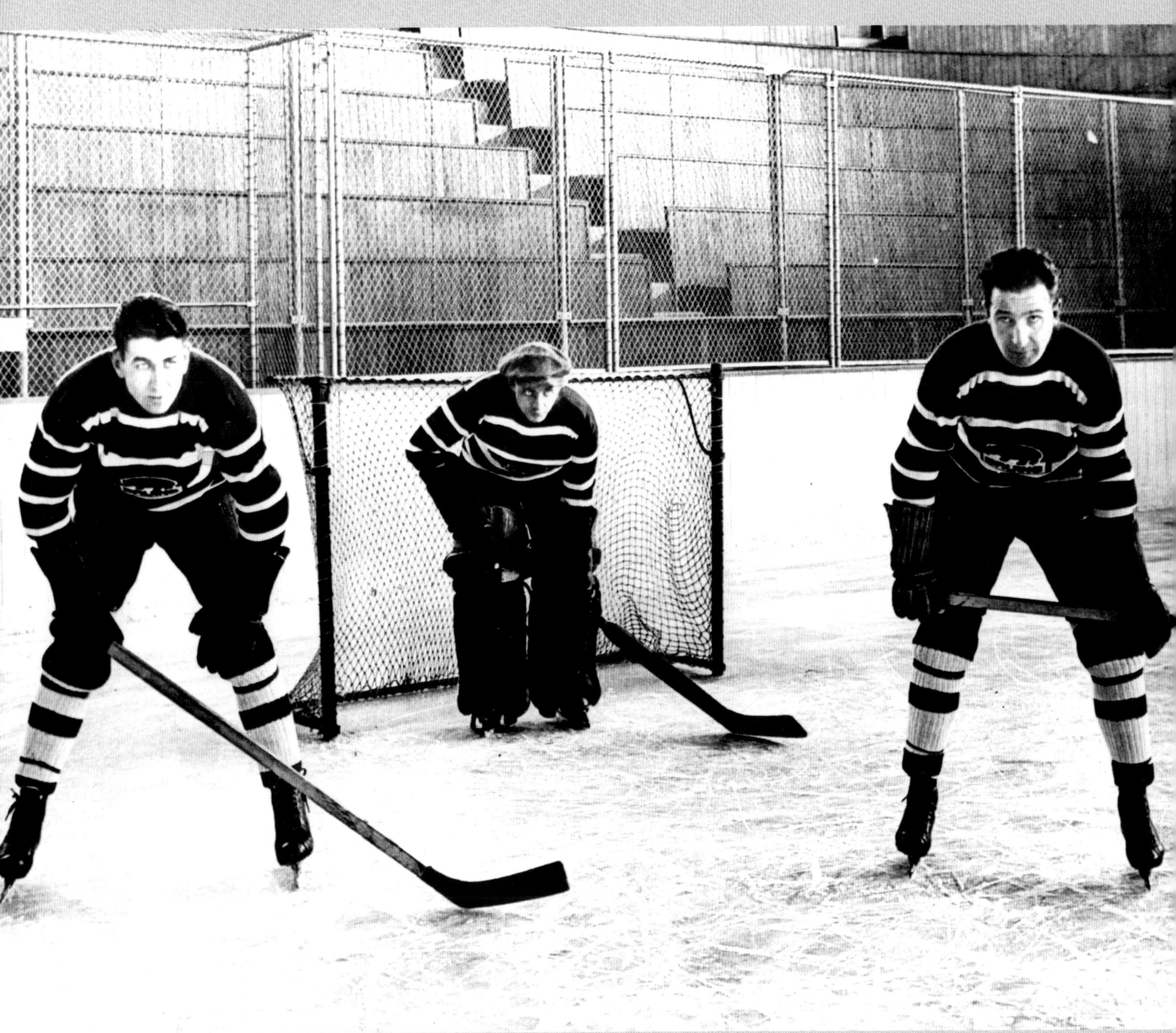

Lionel Hitchman, Charles "Doc" Stewart, and Sprague Cleghorn form a defensive wall in November 1925. Cleghorn was considered one of the toughest players in hockey and helped establish the Bruins' rugged identity.

(Collection of The Sports Museum)

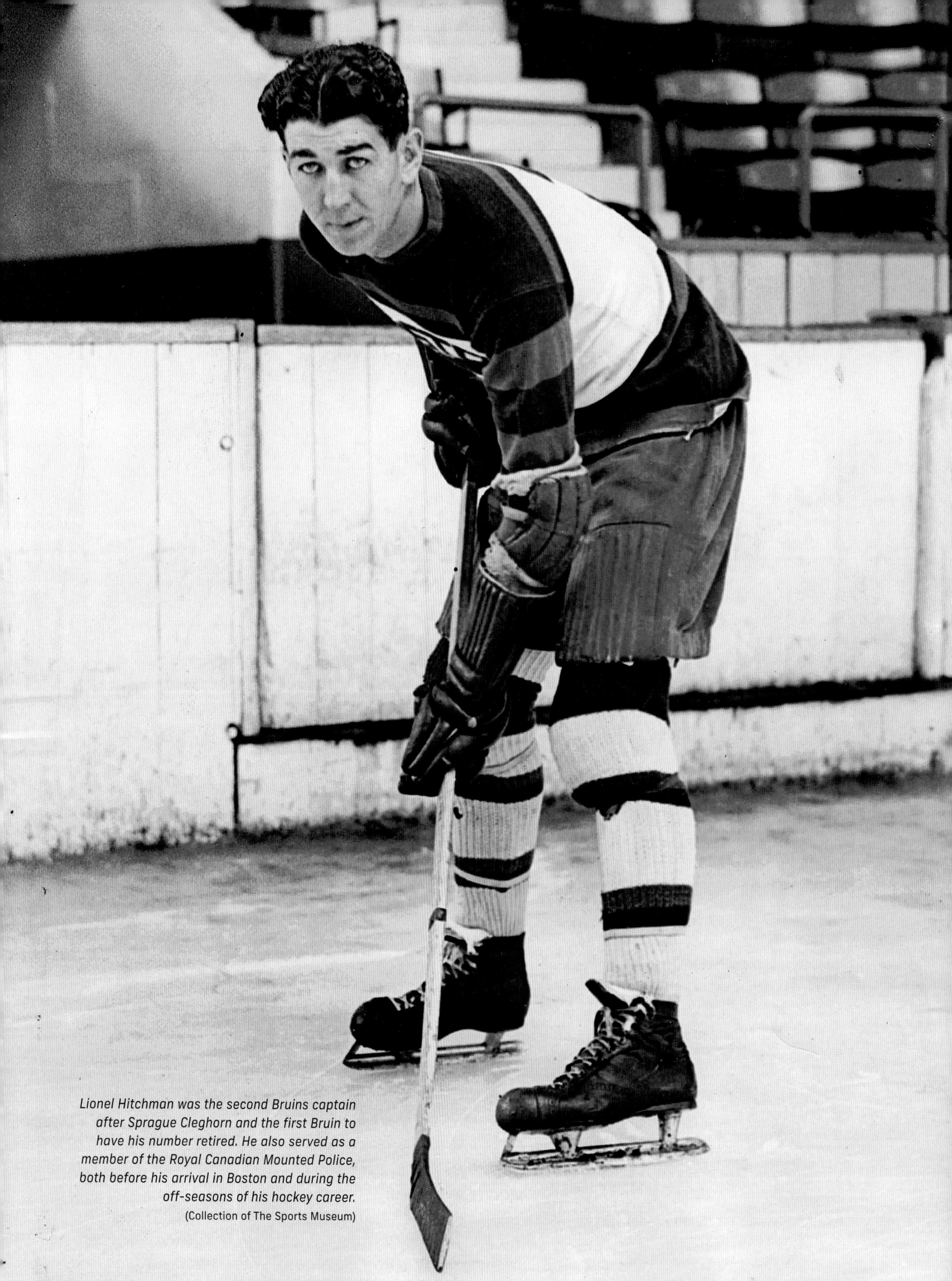

Lionel Hitchman was the second Bruins captain after Sprague Cleghorn and the first Bruin to have his number retired. He also served as a member of the Royal Canadian Mounted Police, both before his arrival in Boston and during the off-seasons of his hockey career.
(Collection of The Sports Museum)

Boston American | December 14, 1924

OTTAWA'S PRO HOCKEY TEAM TO PLAY BRUINS AT ARENA

World's Best Defense Sextet Booked Against Boston Team at St. Botolph Rink Tomorrow Night

Professional hockey has made a tremendous hit in Boston and its suburbs. It's the wow in sport.

The game last Monday in which the Canadiens featured so sensationally, was one of the best exhibitions of athletic skill ever seen in this city. The speed displayed by Aurele Joliat, the way he manipulated his stick, the rapidity with which he went through the defense and the accuracy he displayed when he propelled the disc for the cage, proved such an entertainment that spectators sat enthralled.

If all professional hockey games are so intensive, it's no wonder the people in Canada are so keen for them.

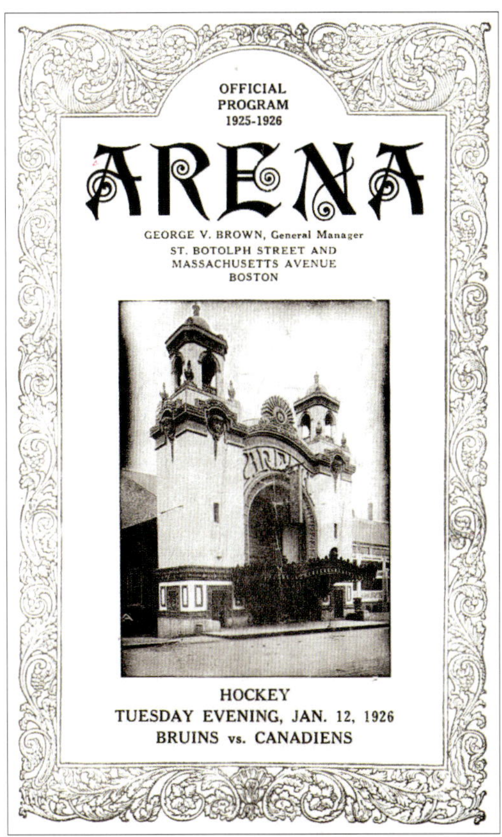

Boston Arena served as the nerve center for Boston and New England hockey prior to the opening of Boston Garden in November 1928. It was also the first home for both the Bruins and Boston Celtics. (Collection of The Sports Museum)

LIONEL HITCHMAN

LIONEL HITCHMAN was the first of the great Bruins defensemen to anchor the franchise. The part-time Canadian Mountie joined the first Bruins team in 1924, having already won a Stanley Cup with Ottawa the previous year in his first NHL season. During his decade in Boston, Hitchman was regarded as the best pure defenseman of his era, rated ahead of his more famous and flamboyant teammate, Eddie Shore.

Unlike Shore, famous for his rink-length rushes and infamous for his bruising play, Hitchman was a classic "stay at home" defenseman, known for both his poke checks and ability to play tough while staying out of the penalty box.

"When Les Canadiens play the Boston Bruins, I keep away from that fellow Hitchman," said Aurele Joliat, the legendary Montreal Hall of Fame player. "That long stick can break up any play and I don't go down his side if I can help it."

Hitchman and Shore formed one of the great defensive pairs in NHL history and helped lead the Bruins to their first Stanley Cup in 1929 and to the NHL's all-time best regular season winning percentage the following season (38-5-1, .875).

Named team captain in 1928, Hitchman was the first Bruin ever to have his jersey number retired, in 1934. It marked only the second time a North American professional athlete was so honored, following the Maple Leafs retirement of Ace Bailey's No. 6 in 1933.

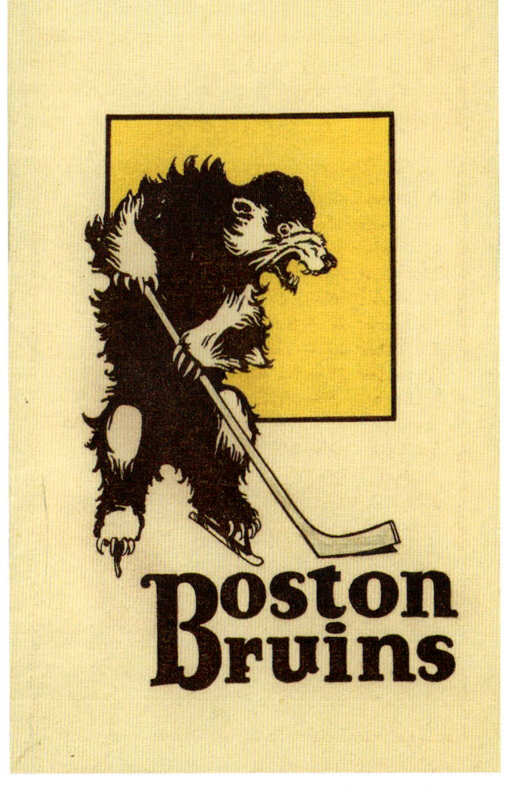

Above: Boston Bruins 1927–28 Yearbook. Left: Boston Bruins 1926–27 Yearbook. (Collection of Richard A. Johnson)

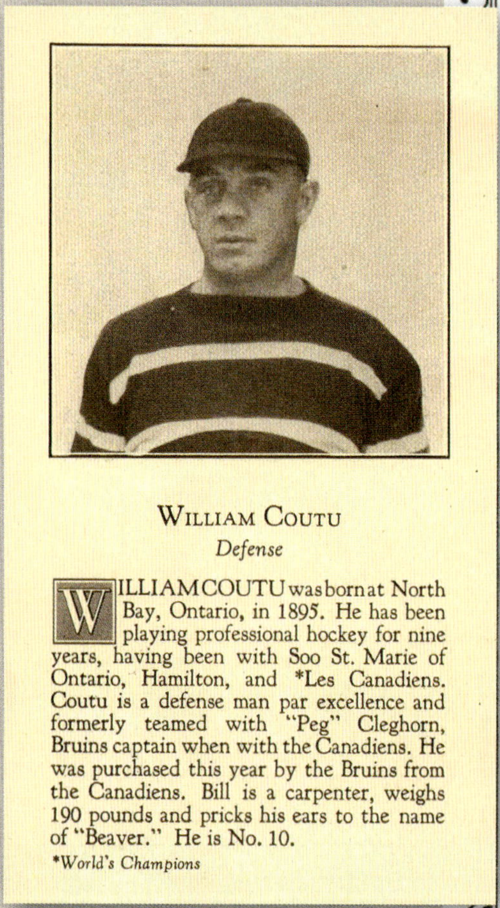

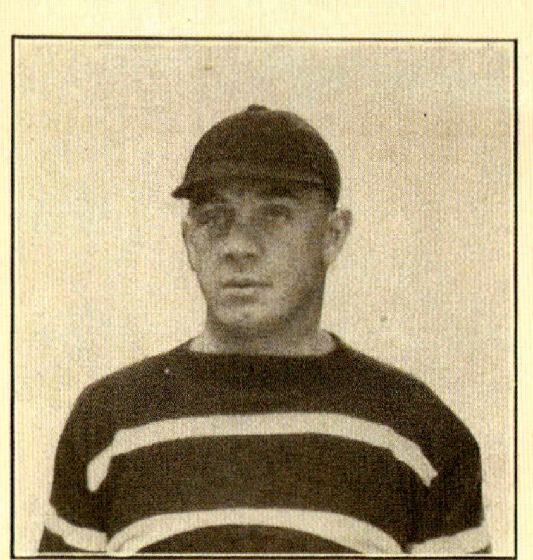

WILLIAM COUTU

Defense

WILLIAM COUTU was born at North Bay, Ontario, in 1895. He has been playing professional hockey for nine years, having been with Soo St. Marie of Ontario, Hamilton, and *Les Canadiens. Coutu is a defense man par excellence and formerly teamed with "Peg" Cleghorn, Bruins captain when with the Canadiens. He was purchased this year by the Bruins from the Canadiens. Bill is a carpenter, weighs 190 pounds and pricks his ears to the name of "Beaver." He is No. 10.

World's Champions

Defenseman Billy Coutu (above) earned a lifetime suspension from the NHL for his postgame attack on referee Jerry Laflamme following the Bruins' 3–1 loss to the Ottawa in the 1927 Stanley Cup Final. (Collection of The Sports Museum)

POSITIVELY NO SMOKING DURING GAME

OFFICIAL PROGRAM 1927-1928

ARENA

GEORGE V. BROWN
General Manager

ST. BOTOLPH ST.
AND
MASSACHUSETTS
AVENUE
BOSTON

BOSTON BRUINS
vs.
CANADIENS
TUESDAY
EVENING
DEC. 6, 1927
at 8.30 o'clock

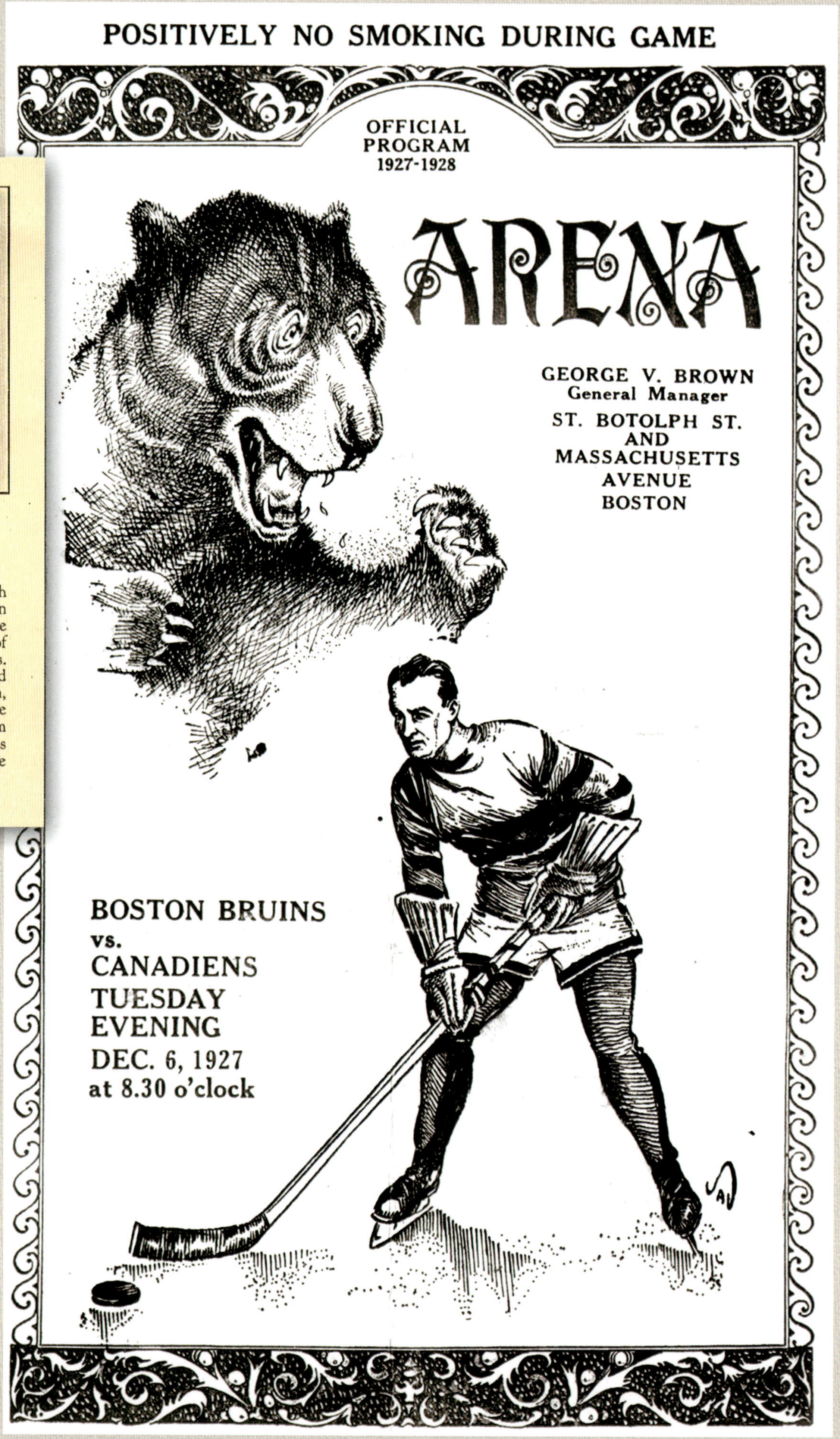

The graphic depiction of the early Bruins more than matched the ferocity of a team led by the likes of Sprague Cleghorn and Billy Coutu. (Collection of The Sports Museum)

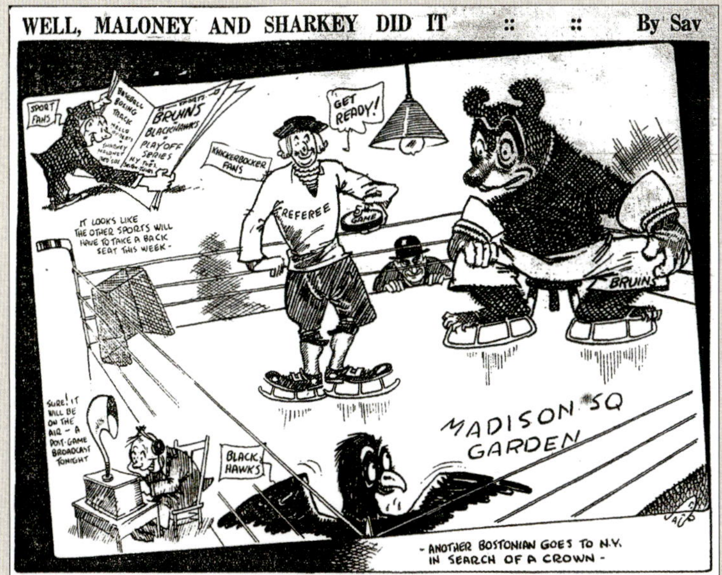

The Bruins' very first playoff opponents in 1927 were the Chicago Black Hawks. The opening game of the series, a 6–1 Boston victory, was played at Madison Square Garden in New York due to a scheduling conflict at Chicago Coliseum. (Collection of Richard A. Johnson)

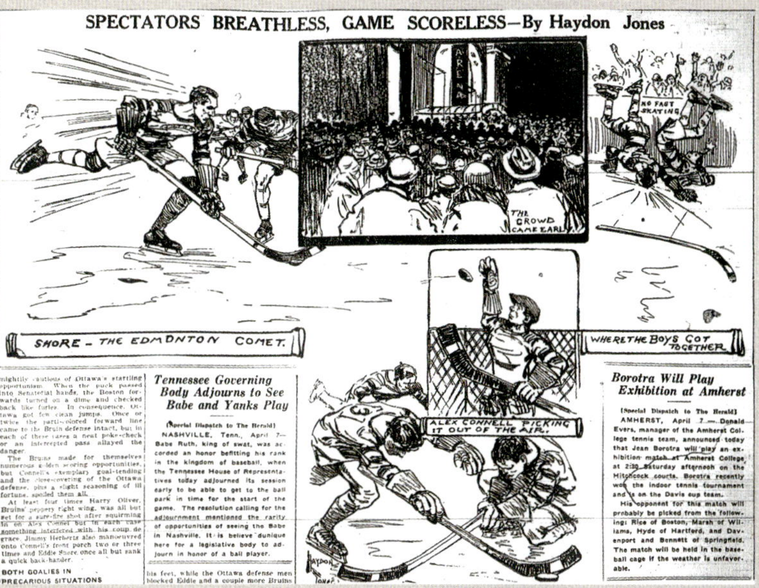

SPECTATORS BREATHLESS, GAME SCORELESS—By Haydon Jones

mightily cautious of Ottawa's startling opportunism. When the puck passed into Senatorial hands, the Boston forwards turned on a dime and checked back like furies. In consequence, Ottawa got few clean jumps. Once or twice the parti-colored forward line came to the Bruin defense intact, but in each of these cases a neat poke-check or an intercepted pass allayed the danger.

The Bruins made for themselves numerous golden scoring opportunities, but Connell's exemplary goal-tending and the close-covering of the Ottawa defense, plus a slight seasoning of ill fortune, spoiled them all.

At least four times Harry Oliver, Bruins' peppery right wing, was all but set for a sure-fire shot after squirming in on Alex Connel but in each case something interfered with his coup de grace. Jimmy Herberts also manoeuvred onto Connell's front porch two or three times and Eddie Shore once all but sank a quick back-hander.

BOTH GOALIES IN PRECARIOUS SITUATIONS

Tennessee Governing Body Adjourns to See Babe and Yanks Play

[Special Dispatch to The Herald]

NASHVILLE, Tenn., April 7—Babe Ruth, king of swat, was accorded an honor befitting his rank in the kingdom of baseball, when the Tennessee House of Representatives today adjourned its session early to be able to get to the ball park in time for the start of the game. The resolution calling for the adjournment mentioned the rarity of opportunities of seeing the Babe in Nashville. It is believe dunique here for a legislative body to adjourn in honor of a ball player.

his feet, while the Ottawa defense men blocked Eddie and a couple more Bruins

Borotra Will Play Exhibition at Amherst

[Special Dispatch to The Herald]

AMHERST, April 7 — Donald Evers, manager of the Amherst College tennis team, announced today that Jean Borotra will play an exhibition match at Amherst College at 2:30 Saturday afternoon on the Hitchcock courts. Borotra recently won the indoor tennis tournament and is on the Davis cup team.

His opponent for this match will probably be picked from the following: Rice of Boston, Marsh of Williams, Hyde of Hartford, and Davenport and Bennett of Springfield. The match will be held in the baseball cage if the weather is unfavorable.

The Bruins faced the Ottawa Senators in the 1927 Stanley Cup Final, the first contested by teams exclusively drawn from the NHL. The first game ended in a 0–0 tie after three full periods plus an overtime and was called off due to excessive heat at Boston Arena. (Collection of Richard A. Johnson)

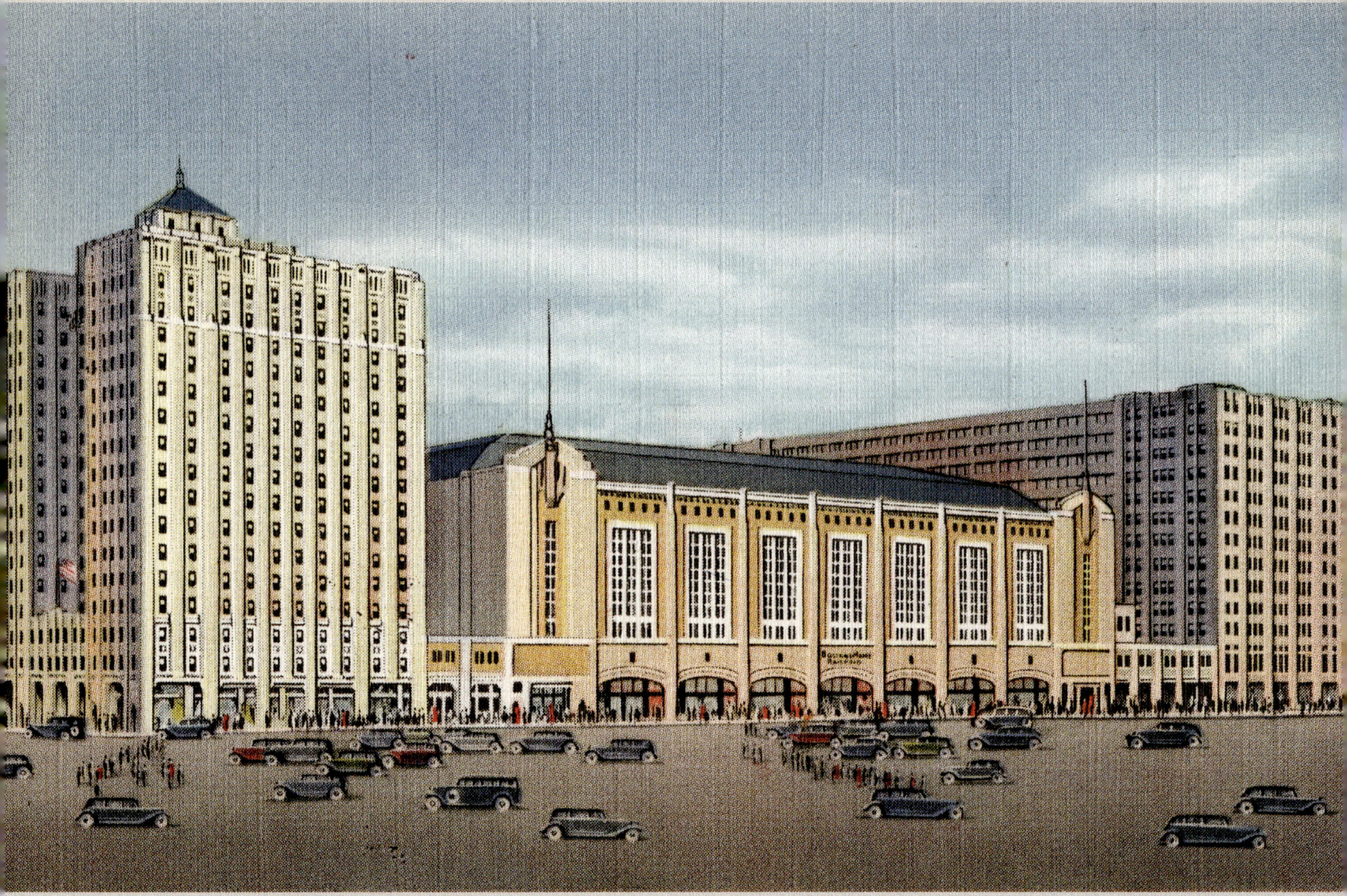

Built atop Boston's North Station, Boston Garden opened in November 1928 to sellout crowds for both hockey and boxing. (Collection of Richard A. Johnson)

FIRST-EVER GAME AT BOSTON GARDEN

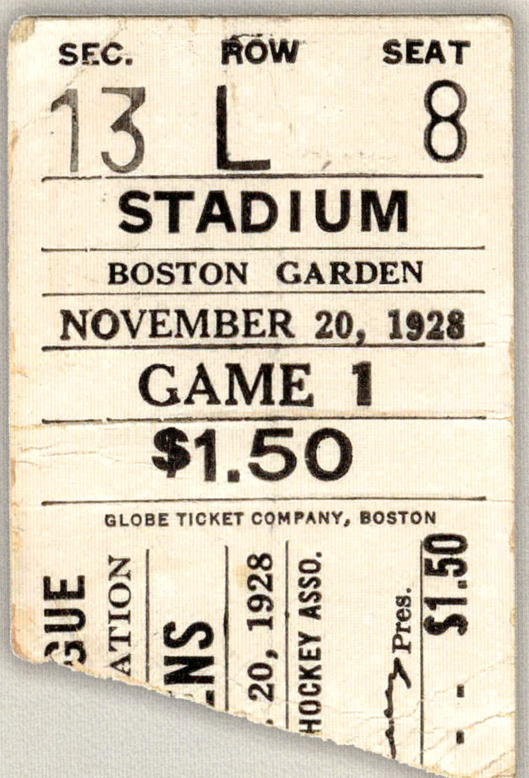

A ticket stub from the Bruins' first-ever game at Boston Garden, a 1–0 loss to the Montreal Canadiens on November 20, 1928.
(Collection of The Sports Museum)

Boston Traveler | November 21, 1928

BRUINS LOSE, 1–0, BEFORE 17,500

Packed Boston Garden Goes Wild as Mantha Scores Lone Goal in 2d

CROWD FIGHTS WAY IN DESPITE POLICE

by Stanley Woodward

Les Canadiens, the dazzling French of Montreal, more dazzling, more furious than ever in reaction to the biggest crowd that ever saw a hockey game, defeated the Bruins, 1 to 0, last night on the occasion of the opening of the National league season and of Boston Madison Square Garden as a setting for hockey.

It was more than a hockey game. It was a riot, a mob-scene, a reenaction of the assault on the Bastille. It is estimated that 17,500 persons, 3,000 in excess of the supposed capacity of the Garden, saw the game.

The surplus were the shock troops who, in the front rank of a mob that swept before it police lines, ushers, doors and windows by force of numbers and tremendous pressure in the rear, came into the building ticketless, perhaps even against their will.

Once inside, the crowd spread like rushing waters to every corner of the Garden, blocking the aisles, overflowing in every direction. Seat holders who came late were walled out by packed humanity and had to go over the top or stay out.

It is estimated that 10,000 persons were turned away, or better, perhaps, forced away by reorganized police lines and rebarred doors. Fifteen hundred seats in the second balcony were sold in a few minutes.

Five hundred standing room admissions were sold in a few minutes more and when the last legitimate space had been disposed of the crowd still pressed forward, waving money, pleading for admission, eventually demanding it.

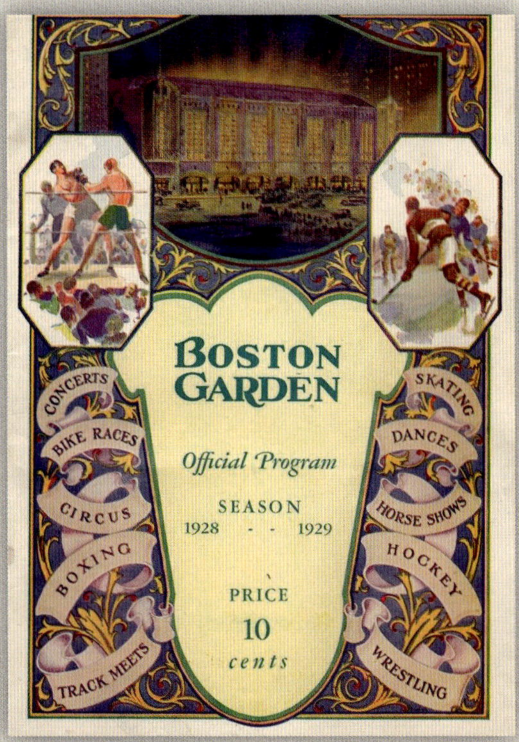

Program cover for the first Bruins game at Boston Garden on November 20, 1928.
(Collection of The Sports Museum)

Season Ticket Agreement Nº 1466
BOSTON BRUINS 1928-29
OWNER R. C. Lorine
ADDRESS 333 Wash
Telephone No. Hub 3150
If the owner desires season tickets delivered to any other person, this card must be presented by such person to secure tickets.
SECTION ROW SEATS

Bruins season ticket from their first season at Boston Garden. On the reverse side, ticket takers punched a number corresponding to the game attended.
(Collection of The Sports Museum)

BRUINS WIN STANLEY CUP; BEAT RANGERS AGAIN, 2–1

Deciding Goal by Carson on Pass from Oliver Two Minutes from End.

GIVES WORLD HOCKEY CROWN TO BOSTON

by Stanley Woodward

NEW YORK, MARCH 29—Dr. Bill Carson, Bruin center, struck the blow that gave Boston the hockey championship of the world and the Stanley Cup, a minute and 58 seconds before the end of time in Madison Square Garden tonight.

Skating like a fury down the left lane, he took a pass from Harry Oliver, clear for the moment of the pachydermic defense men of the New York Rangers, and like a flash whipped the puck into the far side of the cage, past the small but competent John Ross Roach.

The score was 2–1.

In the second period Harry Oliver, who must be regarded as the main hero of the evening, had scored a brilliant single-handed goal for Boston. In the third period Butch Keeling had tied it for the Rangers with a shot from the blue line, one of the few of this category of shots which has passed Tiny Thompson, Cerberus of the Boston nets, this season.

The play of the game, the play, in fact, of which a continent will be talking tomorrow, was the 11th hour combination of Boston's two big little men, Oliver and Carson.

It was a play which crowned with success pioneering efforts in professional hockey which were begun five years ago, which turned to reality the fondest dreams of a hockey-mad Boston sporting public.

Furthermore, it was a play which culminated fittingly a great hockey game and rewarded fittingly one of the hardest fighting and gamest hockey teams ever assembled. Tonight, they were fighting as ever, but they were opposed by a Ranger team that was roused from the neo-lethargy it had displayed in Boston 24 hours before, that was skating like mad, checking desperately, pressing in constantly, dangerously.

But all its meteoric speed was wasted against the "money" play of the Bruins, fast as meteors themselves, keen as grey-hounds, game as terriers. It was a battle all the way, but a result that was shaded in a different way would have been unjust before the fates.

The 1928–29 Boston Bruins, the franchise's first Stanley Cup championship team.
(Collection of The Sports Museum)

Many Vacant Seats

Needless to say, from first to last, Madison Square Garden was in an uproar. Strange to say, Madison Square Garden was not full to capacity. There was a large crowd, but several thousand seats were unoccupied throughout the game.

Those who stayed away missed the crowning achievement of the unparalleled team of hockey. Straight through the play-offs to the cup the Bruins have gone, brushing aside the blazing Canadiens and the dogged Rangers on the road. Five games in a row they took on their way to the title, scoring nine goals to three for the combined opposition.

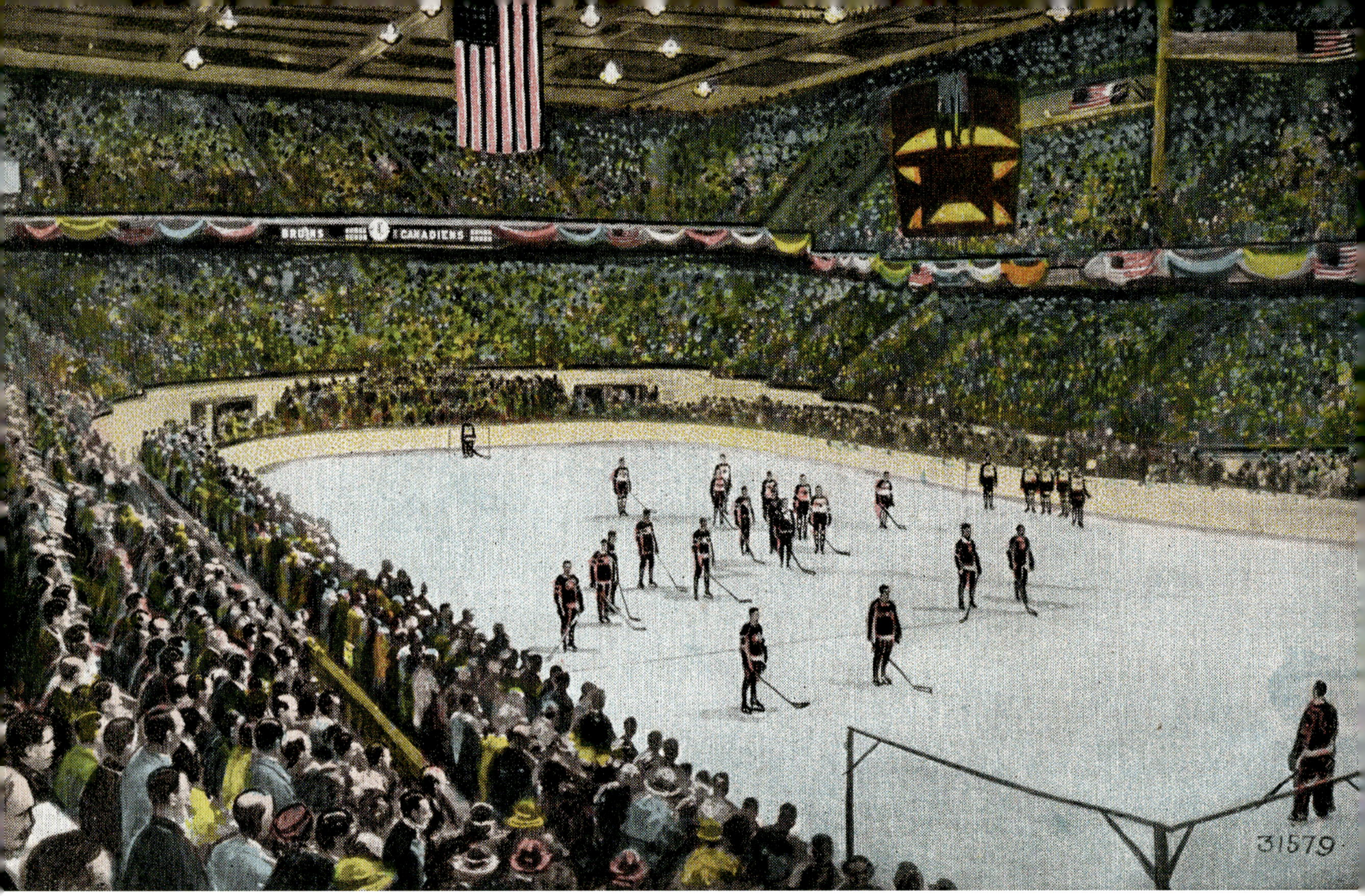

Postcard depicting the first-ever Bruins game at Boston Garden. Note the wood and chicken-wire protective barriers at each end as well as the lack of a central scoreboard. (Collection of Richard A. Johnson)

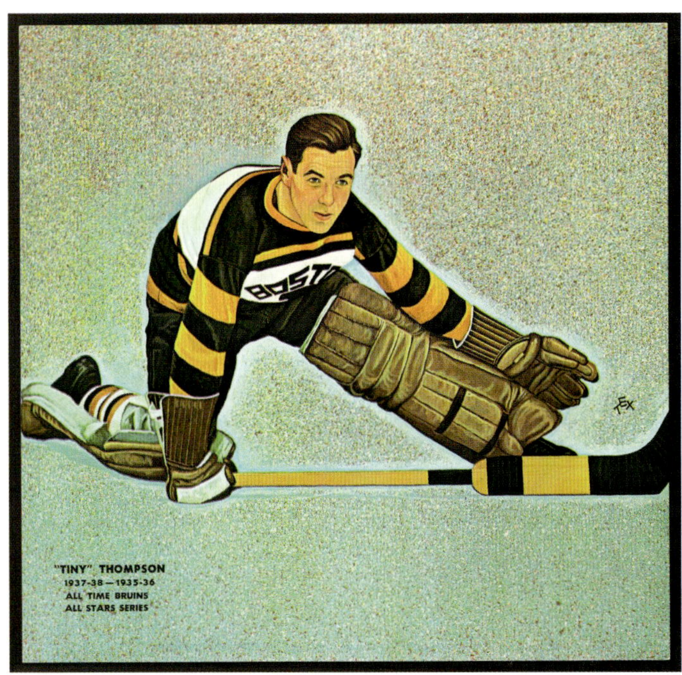

In his rookie season of 1928–29, goaltender Cecil Ralph "Tiny" Thompson recorded a shutout in his first NHL game and led the Bruins to their first Stanley Cup, posting 12 shutouts and a 1.15 goals against average. (Collection of The Sports Museum)

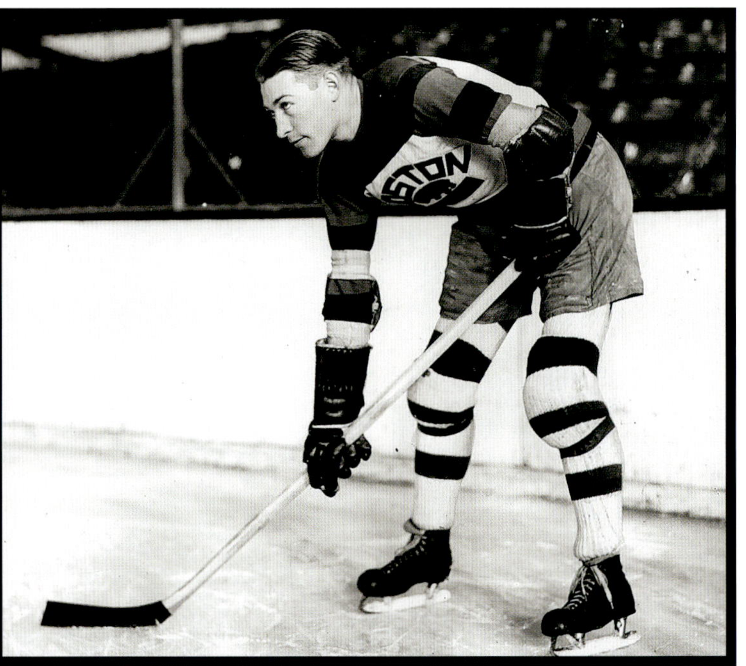

Dit Clapper began his Hall of Fame career with the Bruins in 1927. He would remain a fixture in the lineup for the next 20 years. (Collection of The Sports Museum)

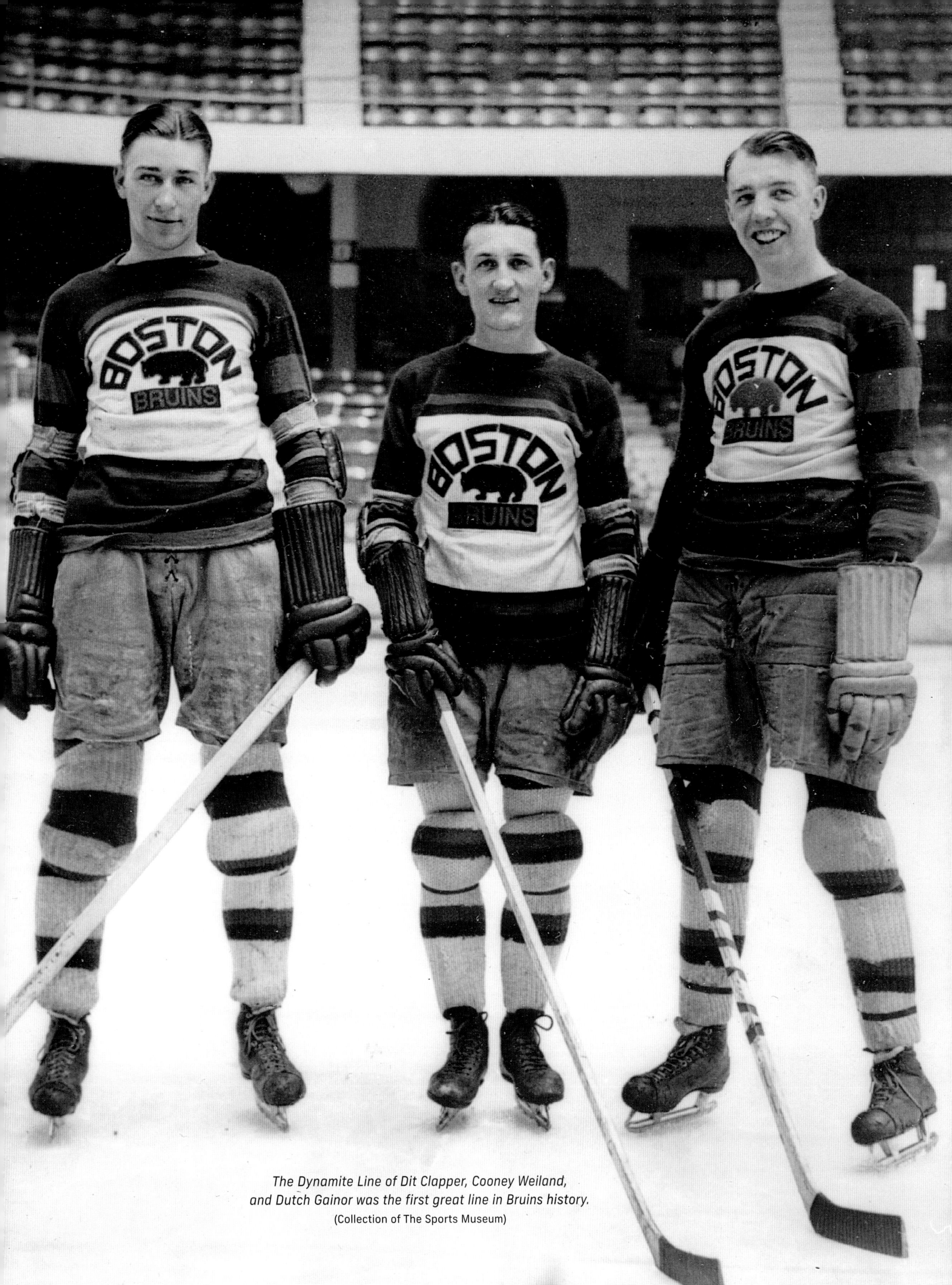

The Dynamite Line of Dit Clapper, Cooney Weiland, and Dutch Gainor was the first great line in Bruins history.
(Collection of The Sports Museum)

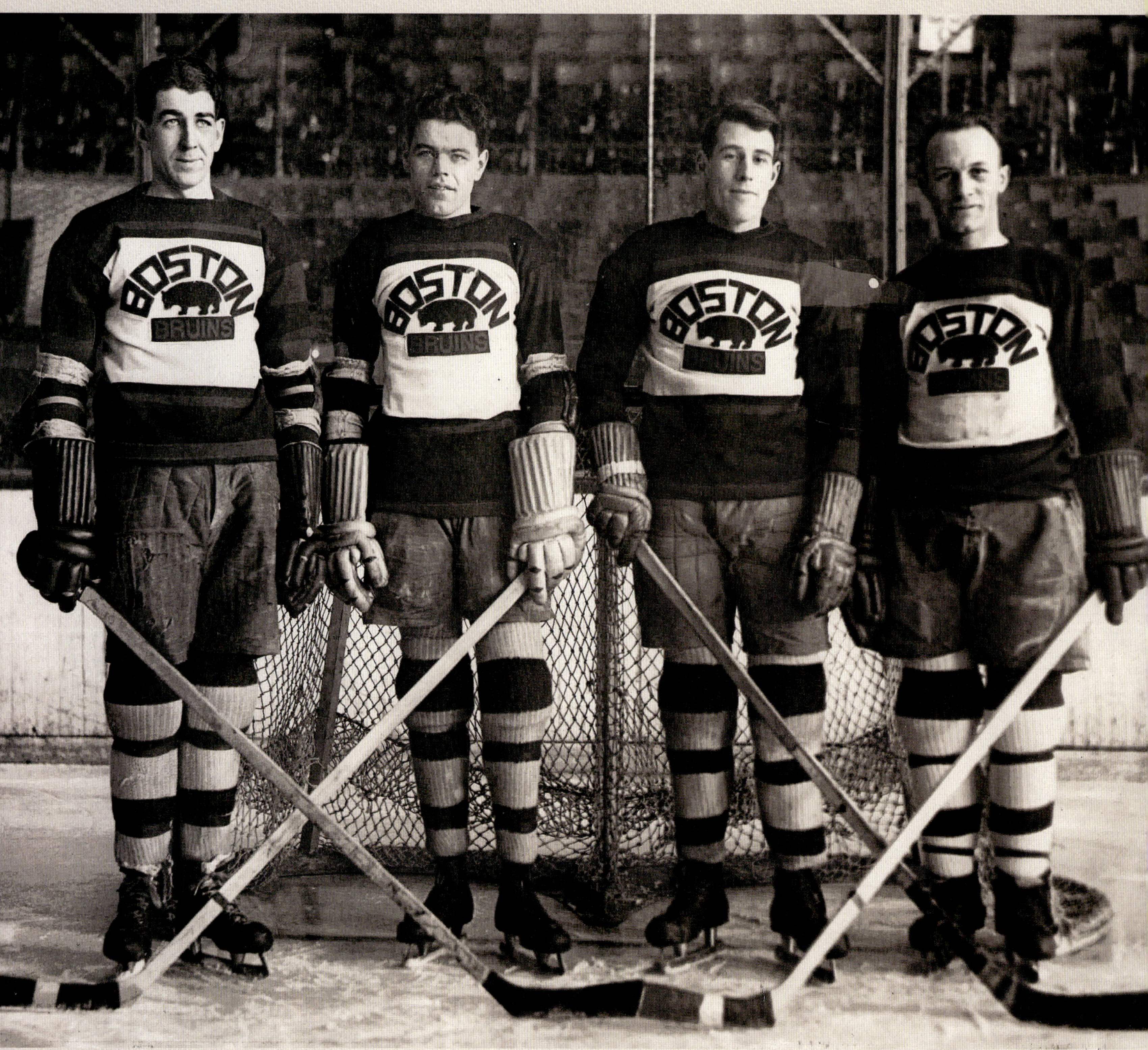

The Bruins defensive corps in their championship season of 1928–29 featured (left to right) Lionel Hitchman, Myles Lane, George Owen, and Eddie Shore. Prior to acquiring Lane halfway through that season, the Bruins, somewhat incredibly, played NHL games with just three defensemen (Hitchman, Owen, and Shore) in uniform.

(Collection of Richard A. Johnson)

IN HIS OWN WORDS...GEORGE OWEN

BRUINS DEFENSEMAN George Owen is remembered as one of New England's great all-around athletes. As a nine-letter man at Harvard (Class of 1923), he epitomized the F. Scott Fitzgerald ideal of the gentleman as scholar and athlete, while taking several pages from the tales of Frank Merriwell at the same time.

A product of Newton High School, Owen was only the second graduate of an American high school to play in the NHL, following Melrose native and Dartmouth star Myles Lane into the new pro hockey league. Owen was a mainstay on the first Bruins Stanley Cup championship team in 1928–29, joining forces with the legendary Eddie Shore and Lionel Hitchman to anchor the Bruins defense. Owen would later be named captain of the Bruins in 1931.

Set forth below are excerpts from an exclusive interview that Richard A. Johnson, the coauthor of this book, conducted with Owen several years before he passed away in 1986 at the age of 84.

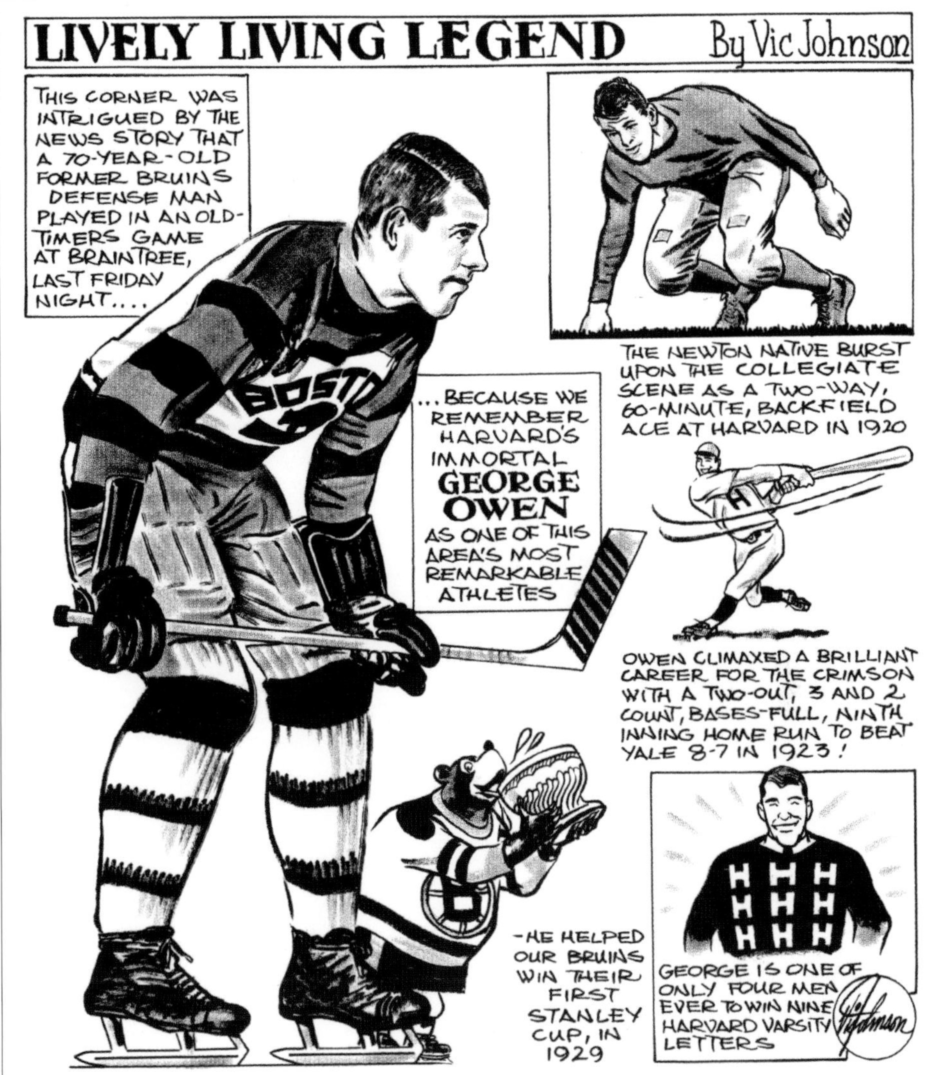

George Owen is regarded as one of the greatest all-around athletes in Harvard history, outslugging Lou Gehrig of Columbia in baseball, having a Hall of Fame career as a fullback/linebacker in football, and winning nine varsity letters in all. He joined the Bruins in 1928 at the relatively advanced age of 27.

(Collection of Richard A. Johnson)

On signing with the Bruins in 1928

Connie Smythe, the Maple Leafs owner, was an old friend of our family, having known my father when my dad was designing yachts for the Royal Canadian Yacht Club [Owen's father was subsequently named head of the Naval Architecture Dept at MIT]. I remember Smythe coming to our house on his visits to Boston when he was hockey coach at the University of Toronto.

When he became owner of the Leafs, he asked me to consider professional hockey as a career. He then made me a pretty substantial offer. In fact, it was the highest sum offered to an amateur until Jean Beliveau was signed by Montreal in the '50s. Smythe offered me $25,000, and therefore persuaded me to try the National Hockey League. His offer was made on a Sunday, and we agreed to get together on the upcoming Tuesday when the Leafs would visit Boston and iron out details of the deal.

On Monday, my father was in Boston getting some plans for one of his boats, and who should he run into but Art Ross, the Bruins coach and general manager. Ross asked my dad how I was doing, and my father told Ross that I was about to sign a contract with Toronto the following day. Ross then exclaimed, "Why didn't you tell me that before?"

To make a long story short, Ross made contact with me that afternoon. I visited his office at Bruins headquarters, which were located across Post Office Square from the brokerage house where I was working at the time. First, he told me that the Bruins had always wanted me to play for them, and then he asked what Toronto had offered. Ross then said that he would top Smythe's offer. By Monday evening the deal was set and on Tuesday the ink dry on my contract.

On debuting with the Bruins

I broke in with Tiny Thompson, Cooney Weiland, and Dit Clapper, and was especially fortunate to work with the great Eddie Shore. I loved playing with those guys and was lucky to get out of the bond-selling game before the Great Crash in 1929.

On Eddie Shore

No question about it, he was the greatest. When Shore rushed up the ice, the crowds in every rink in the league would stand to watch the spectacle of this runaway train on skates taking control of the game. Once my sister remarked that after watching one of our games that she was more tired than I was because of the constant ritual of standing and sitting and standing again for Shore. The lack of any significant forechecking at that time in the NHL allowed Shore to gain tremendous momentum in his rink-length rushes.

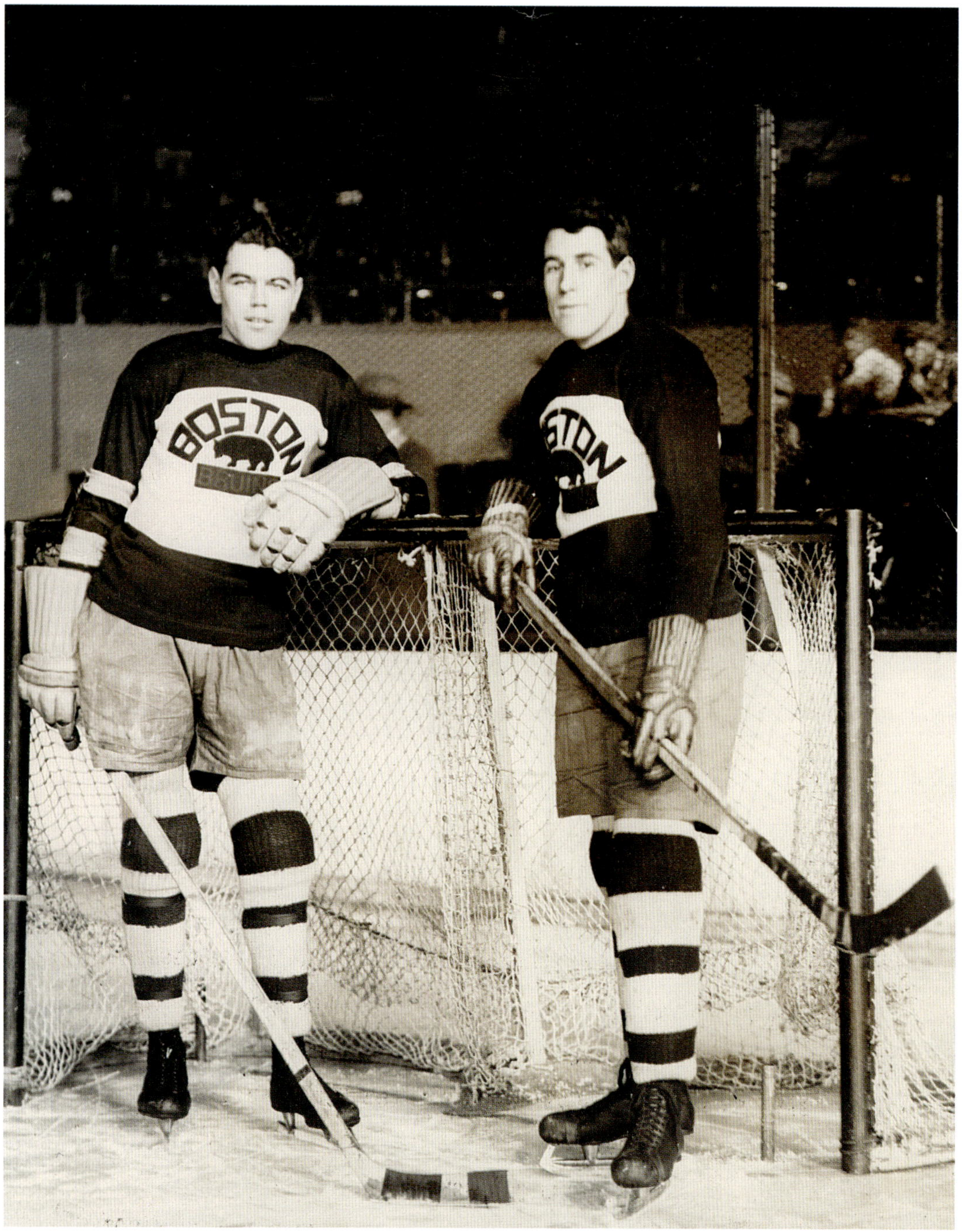

On the 1928–29 Bruins carrying only three defensemen for the first half of the season

Well, Shore had more ice time than either myself or Lionel Hitchman. However, Shore and I were both built along the same lines and could skate indefinitely. We just played long shifts.

Bruins defensemen Myles Lane (left) and George Owen strike a pose at Boston Garden in January 1929. Lane and Owen hailed from the Greater Boston Area and played their college hockey at Dartmouth and Harvard, respectively, before skating with the Bruins. (Collection of Richard A. Johnson)

WHY BOSTON FIRST?

by Stephen Hardy

ON DECEMBER 1, 1924, the Boston Bruins—the NHL's first American franchise—opened their inaugural season against the Montreal Maroons, the league's other rookie club. The game was held in the "New" Boston Arena, a multipurpose facility with 4,000 seats and a narrow concourse that could pack in an additional 2,500 "standing room" patrons. The prior year some 300,000 fans had attended 72 evening games of college and senior amateur clubs, an average of 4,166 per game. A Bruins' November 27 exhibition against the Saskatoon Sheiks had drawn less than capacity. The *Boston Globe* reported that "thrills were almost lacking" in the Sheiks' 2–1 victory. How would the real season debut pan out?

Not very well, wrote veteran *Boston Herald* sportswriter Stanley Woodward. Despite "the most rugged body checking that Boston fans ever have seen," the stands were not filled. It was a "scattered and rather chilly gathering." The lack of crowd noise was "deadening." It looked, Woodward concluded, "as if Boston will have to be educated to the professional game."

So why did the NHL Governors tap Boston first among American markets? Why not New York, Pittsburgh, Chicago, or Detroit, all of which had arenas and decades of hockey experience? Canadian teams had been touring south ever since the wave of new-technology, artificial-ice rinks appeared in America's northern tier in the mid-1890s. On February 29, 1896, Montreal's *Daily Herald* announced an "Invasion of U.S." just before the Shamrocks and Montreals squared off in Baltimore, Washington, D.C., and New York—fifteen years before Boston had a reliable venue. The first avowedly professional league—the International Professional Hockey League (1904–1907)—included a team in Pittsburgh's 6,000-seat Duquesne Gardens. The Pacific Coast Hockey Association (PCHA, 1911–1924) had rinks, plus teams in Seattle and Portland.

More SPORT this evening

—a National Hockey League Game

at the Boston Arena between the BOSTON BRUINS the United States Champions, 1926-1927, and the DETROIT COUGARS, is well worth seeing, as it will show this premier ice game developed to its highest standards.

Reserved Seats may be secured at all down-town agencies, or at the BOSTON ARENA.

BOSTON PROFESSIONAL HOCKEY ASS'N., Inc.
CHARLES F. ADAMS, *President*

Bruins advertisement from the 1927 Harvard-Yale football program.
(Collection of Richard A. Johnson)

But the NHL came first to Boston for three main reasons: its long standing as a sports market, the Boston Arena, and the characters associated with it.

While Boston's rank in the U.S. Census list of most populous cities fell from No. 3 in 1790 to No. 7 in 1920, its place as an intellectual, commercial, and industrial hub was still secure, built on book and newspaper publishing, early telegraph and telephone lines, and strong transportation networks, especially railroads. When the B&M's opulent North Station opened on Causeway Street in 1893 and South Station opened in 1899, the terminals aggregated existing rail options north, south, and west.

All this fueled Boston's place as a big-league sports market, symbolized most notably by its plank holder status in both National League (1876) and American League (1901) baseball. By 1915, the Braves and the Red Sox had new, state-of-the art venues with steel, concrete, brick, and mortar. Close by, Harvard had built its reinforced concrete Stadium in 1903, reinforcing its position as a national leader in football. For a while, Boston lacked a modern hockey venue—that is, until 1910, when the Boston Arena opened, spawning the cast of characters who brought the Bruins to Beantown in 1924.

First and foremost was lifelong Brookline native and MIT graduate George C. Funk, the Boston Arena's principal architect who *Popular Science Monthly* later described as "Boston's ice engineer who built the first modern rinks in that and other large American cities" and who was "largely responsible" for hockey's American advance. Funk's Boston Arena included an "administrative" building, with a grand arched entrance and a magnificent 60′ x 50′ lobby. The main building featured 4,000 "polo chair" seats and a 90′ x 244′ ice surface—the largest of its day and bigger than NHL rinks today.

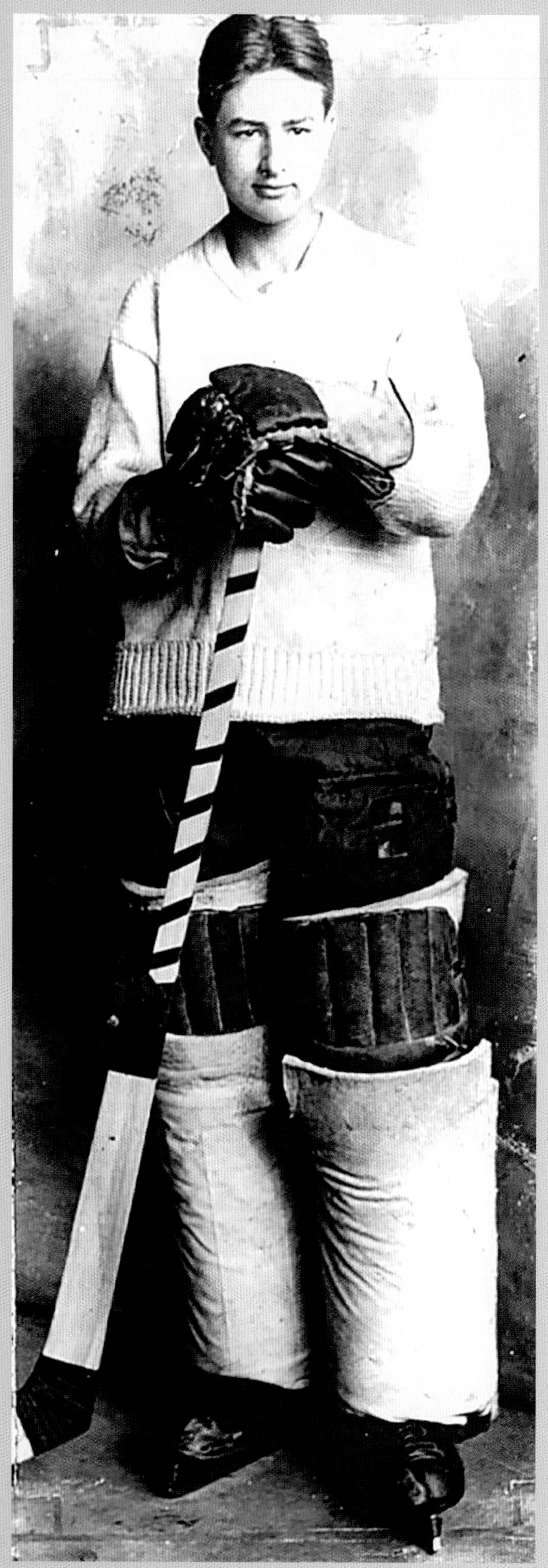

The Boston Arena opened in April 1910 with skating and hockey exhibitions. High school and college teams were excited about reliable practice and game schedules the next winter. But the Arena's investors needed paying customers in the seats. And that meant bringing in Canadian teams to show off the game's best players. On December 29, 1910, 4,000 fans watched Toronto's St. Michaels earn a tough 5–3 decision over the Boston Hockey Club, which was well-stocked with recent Harvard stars. Mayor "Honey Fitz" Fitzgerald attended with his son Tom and his daughter Rose. It was, crowed the *Boston Post*, "the largest gathering that ever watched a hockey game in this part of the country."

Other Canadian teams visited the Arena that first season, which culminated in late March 1911 with a two-game, $2,500 stakes showdown between what the *Post* called the "Premier Teams in the Universe"—the Montreal Wanderers and the Ottawa Senators, who were fresh off capturing the Stanley Cup. The Senators featured Fred "Cyclone" Taylor, a "locomotive-like skater." The Wanderers matched him with "clever" Art Ross, who would later give Boston a long career of managerial cleverness. Taylor and Ross led their teams in two hard-fought games of a series split. Both men, said the *Post*, thrilled the "6,000 wildly enthusiastic followers," as they gathered the puck "time and again, and by clever dodging and hurdling" stickhandled "through their opponents the entire length of the rink."

On January 31, 1912, a *Boston Traveler* headline announced that Arena management had floated an offer to host the champs of the PCHA and National Hockey Association (NHA, soon to morph into the NHL) for a Stanley Cup showdown. The story emphasized that Boston's financial guarantee was "considerably higher than any rink in Canada is willing to pay." Nothing happened, but Canadian teams kept visiting, rumors about pro hockey in Boston continued, and money kept talking.

Meanwhile, the Arena relied on high school, collegiate, and senior amateur draws like Hobey Baker when he came to town with Princeton (1911–1914) or New York's St. Nicks (1914–1916). Boston's top amateur side was the B.A.A. (Boston Athletic Association) Unicorns, managed by George V. Brown, the B.A.A.'s director of athletics and a leading figure in amateur sports. Harvard alum Ralph Winsor coached the Unicorns, who were well-stocked with Crimson grads. Rival teams rose and dissolved over time, all hoping to knock off the B.A.A. Those clubs featured local talent like Cambridge's Raymie Skilton, who led a 1912 mash-up called the Intercolonials in a best-of-five series with the B.A.A. Boston papers trumpeted the games with no-byline stories that were probably written by Arena publicist

Future Bruins President Weston Adams Sr. played goalie for Philips Exeter Academy in 1923. He later played varsity hockey at Harvard. (Collection of The Sports Museum)

and longtime hockey writer Fred Hoey, who later recalled that Skilton's team manager was a "hustling" young grocery executive named Charles F. Adams. Both teams brought in ringers. The Adams-Skilton franchise won the series but dissolved within two years.

Boston Arena hockey expanded steadily from this base until the main building burned to a rubble the evening of December 17, 1918. Fire marshals determined the cause to be a cigarette, left smoldering after a boxing event. Two years later, a "new" Boston Arena opened under new ownership and a new board of directors which included Charles F. Adams, who with his colleagues appointed George V. Brown as manager. This made the two men partners in growing Boston and American hockey. Brown focused his attention on building a national circuit of senior amateur teams. He was a founder of the U.S. Amateur Hockey Association (USAHA) in 1920 and its playoff between three regional loops extending from Boston and New York through Pittsburgh and Cleveland out to Michigan and Minnesota. From the beginning, however, the USAHA was plagued by the use of non-resident (especially Canadian) ringers and allegations of under-the-table salaries. In February 1924, the *Herald*'s gossipy "Bob Dunbar" column complained of "this mercenary side of 'amateur' hockey that is one of the many reasons why some of our leading sportsmen and clear thinkers want to hurry the arrival here of pro hockey of the honest and above-board stamp."

Charles F. Adams might have written that line himself. While serving on the Boston Arena board, he kept his eye on the NHL, which had limped through the World War, rink disasters, and legal challenges. By 1923, however, the four-team circuit was stabilized and looking south, partly in reaction to rumors of new rival leagues. In February of that year, NHL President Frank Calder made a deal with Tom Duggan, a Montreal sports promoter: $2,000 for options on two franchises to be placed among Boston, New York, and Brooklyn. Duggan traveled extensively over the next year and a half, holding press conferences to announce he was on the cusp of something big. But Brooklyn lacked an adequate venue. New York's existing Madison Square Garden had no ice and was soon to be replaced in 1925 by a "new" MSG, whose ice systems were designed by George C. Funk. So New York would have to wait until 1925, when it would be forced to accept "Second City" designation.

That left Boston as the lone "First City" possibility for the 1924–25 season. A *Boston Post* writer linked Duggan with Adams, who worked hard to dissolve the reluctance of George V. Brown and the Arena's board of directors to give ice time to a pro team that might undercut support for the senior amateurs. All the while Funk funneled inside information back to Duggan, who along with Adams agitated publicly and privately about new pro leagues, a new arena, and "shamateurism." The Arena directors finally relented. For this help, Duggan gave Adams the Boston franchise at cost. In November 1924, the NHL approved Adams' new team for $15,000. Adams' first big move was to hire a manager: Art Ross, whom the *Herald* called "an old fox at the game." After a miserable inaugural season (with a win-loss record of 6–24), Ross steadily built a stronger roster. In October 1926, newly acquired Eddie Shore played his first game as a Bruin in the Boston Arena, newly expanded with a balcony. He spent two seasons there before the Bruins moved in November 1928 to a new "Garden" on Causeway Street, where they surged in late season to win their first Stanley Cup in the spring of 1929.

BOSTON BRUINS ™

Stephen Hardy retired from the University of New Hampshire as professor of kinesiology and affiliate professor of history. He has written numerous articles, reviews, and book chapters that explore the history of hockey. His book *Hockey: A Global History*, coauthored with Andrew C. Holman, was published in 2018. He is a founder of the Charles Holt Archives of American Hockey, which are located at UNH's Dimond Library. His work may be found at stephenhardywriter.com.

BOSTON BRUINS (1924–1929)

Season	W	L	T	PTS	PTS%	Finish	Playoffs	Coach	Division
1924–25	6	24	0	12	.200	6th of 6		Art Ross	
1925–26	17	15	4	38	.528	4th of 7		Art Ross	
1926–27	21	20	3	45	.511	2nd of 5	Lost Stanley Cup Final	Art Ross	American
1927–28	20	13	11	51	.580	1st of 5	Lost NHL Semifinals	Art Ross	American
1928–29	**26**	**13**	**5**	**57**	**.648**	**1st of 5**	**Won Stanley Cup Final**	**Art Ross**	**American**

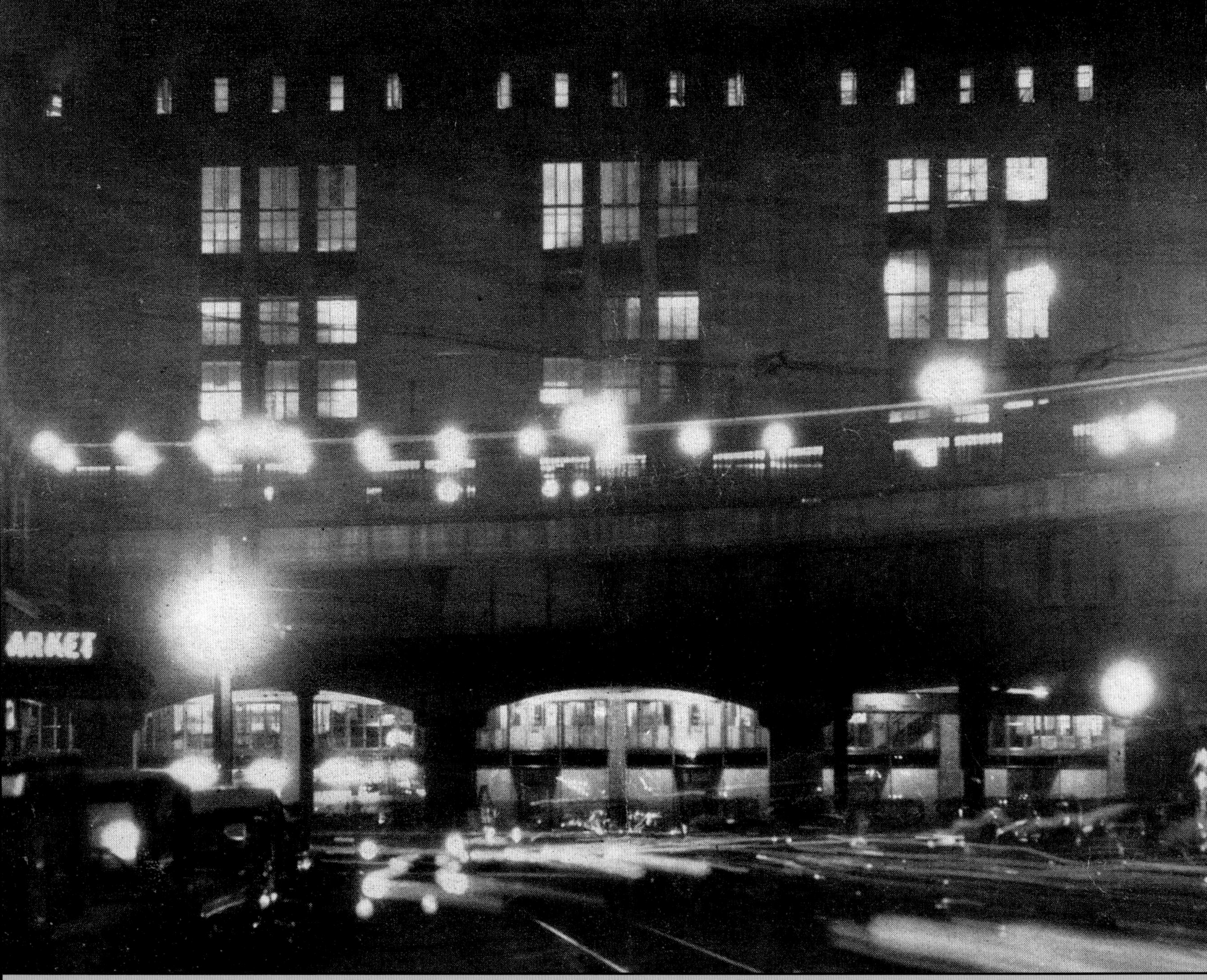

Boston Garden, built partially atop North Station, was home to the Bruins from 1928 to 1995.
(Collection of The Sports Museum)

1930s

OLD-TIME HOCKEY

"As goes Ruth, so go the Yankees. As goes Shore, so go the Bruins."

—Dave Egan, *Boston Globe* columnist

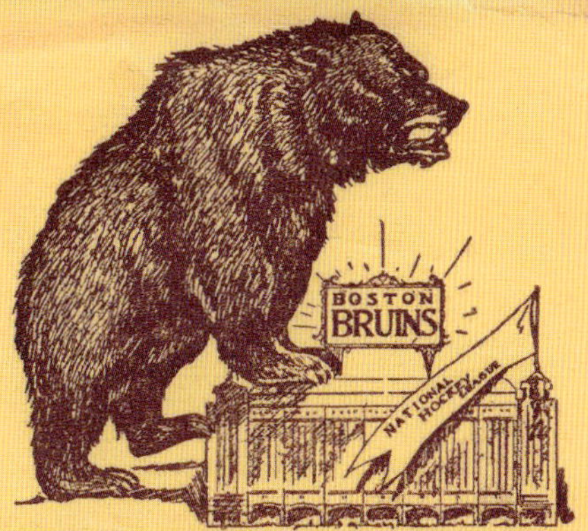

Bruins letterhead from early 1930s. (Collection of The Sports Museum)

The seeds sown by the Bruins in 1924 as America's first NHL franchise blossomed in the late 1920s and into the Great Depression as the league expanded to New York, Pittsburgh, Chicago, Detroit, Philadelphia, and St. Louis. And though the franchises in Pittsburgh, Philadelphia, and St. Louis were short-lived, falling victim to hard times, the league flourished with

THE 1929–30 BRUINS

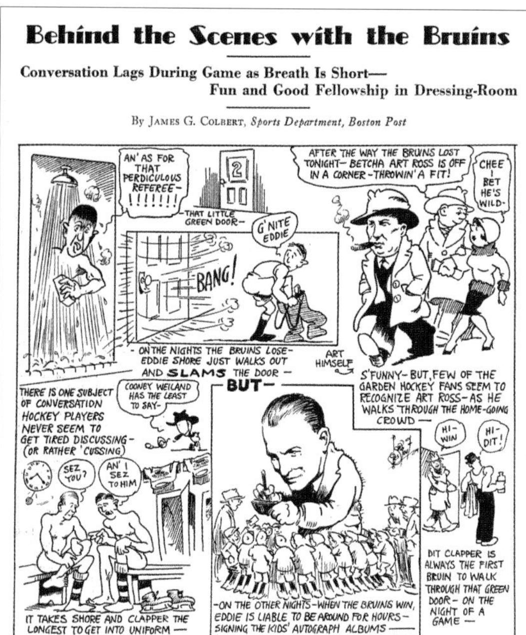

This Boston Post *cartoon takes us inside the Bruins locker room of the 1930s.* (Norbert Quinn illustration, Collection of The Sports Museum)

THROUGH THE YEARS, the Bruins have had several teams that would easily qualify as a juggernaut, including the 1970–71 squad (which scored 399 goals to set a new NHL record) and the 2022–23 team (which set new NHL marks for most wins and points in a season).

For sheer regular season dominance, however, it's hard to beat the 1929–30 Boston Bruins.

This team was stacked. Its offense scored 179 goals in just 44 games to set a new NHL record, with Cooney Weiland and Dit Clapper leading the way with 43 goals and 41 goals, respectively. The Bruins were equally talented on the blueline, with George Owen, Hall of Famer Lionel Hitchman, and the incomparable Eddie Shore. And they got superb goaltending from Tiny Thompson, who won the first of his four Vezina Trophies as top netminder in the NHL.

The Bruins won on opening night and never looked back, leading the league from wire-to-wire. They had a 14-game winning streak toward the start of the season and another 11-game winning streak toward the end of the campaign. They lost just five times all season—and three of those five losses were by one goal.

At season's end, the Bruins had compiled a breathtaking 38–5–1 record, setting new records for most wins in a single regular season (38), most regular season wins on home ice (20), and the best single-season winning percentage in NHL history (.875). The latter is a record that still stands today, nearly 100 years later. So do two other marks set by the team—fewest losses in a season (5) and fewest ties in a season (1). They, too, are records that are unlikely ever to be broken.

Alas, the season did not end with a championship, as the Montreal Canadiens stunned the Bruins in the Stanley Cup Final, winning two games to nil. The Bruins were thus deprived of the fitting capstone for their season of dominance as well as a second consecutive Stanley Cup championship.

While the 1929–30 Bruins may not have won the Cup, however, they were still a team for the ages.

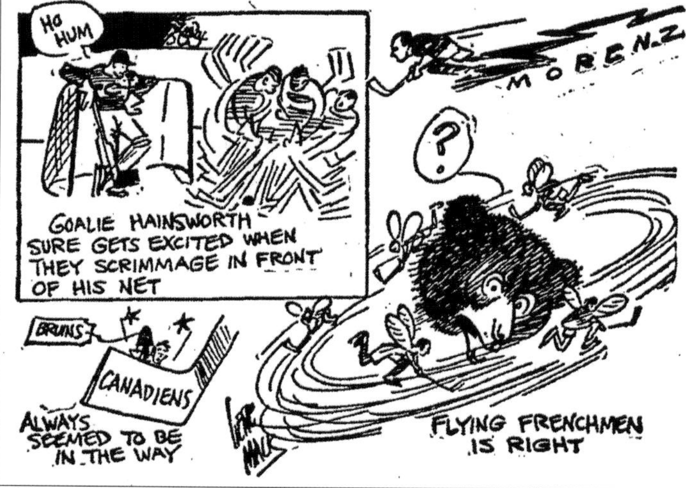

Boston's playoff frustrations at the hands of Montreal began in 1930, when the Canadiens upset Boston in the Stanley Cup Final after finishing 26 points behind the Bruins in the regular season. (Gene Mack illustration, Collection of The Sports Museum)

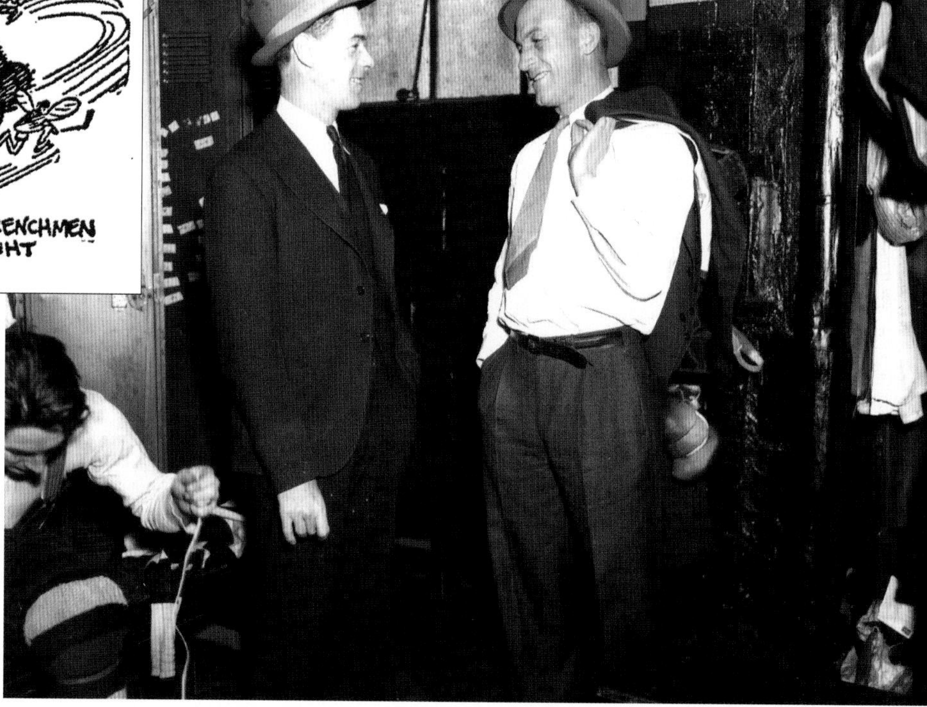

Tiny Thompson (left) and Eddie Shore are dressed to the nines following a game in the 1930s. Both were instrumental in making the Bruins the toast of the NHL during the Depression Era. (Photograph by Leslie Jones, courtesy of the Boston Public Library)

COONEY WEILAND

PERHAPS THE BRUINS' most underappreciated single-season feat was the scoring record set by center Ralph "Cooney" Weiland in 1929–30. Centering the famed Dynamite Line that included right wing Dit Clapper and left wing Dutch Gainor, Weiland scored 43 goals in 44 games while adding 30 assists to set a new NHL single-season scoring record with 73 points. Weiland would leave Boston in 1932 only to return three years later for a second stint with the Bruins. In his final season, he helped anchor the 1938–39 Stanley Cup champions.

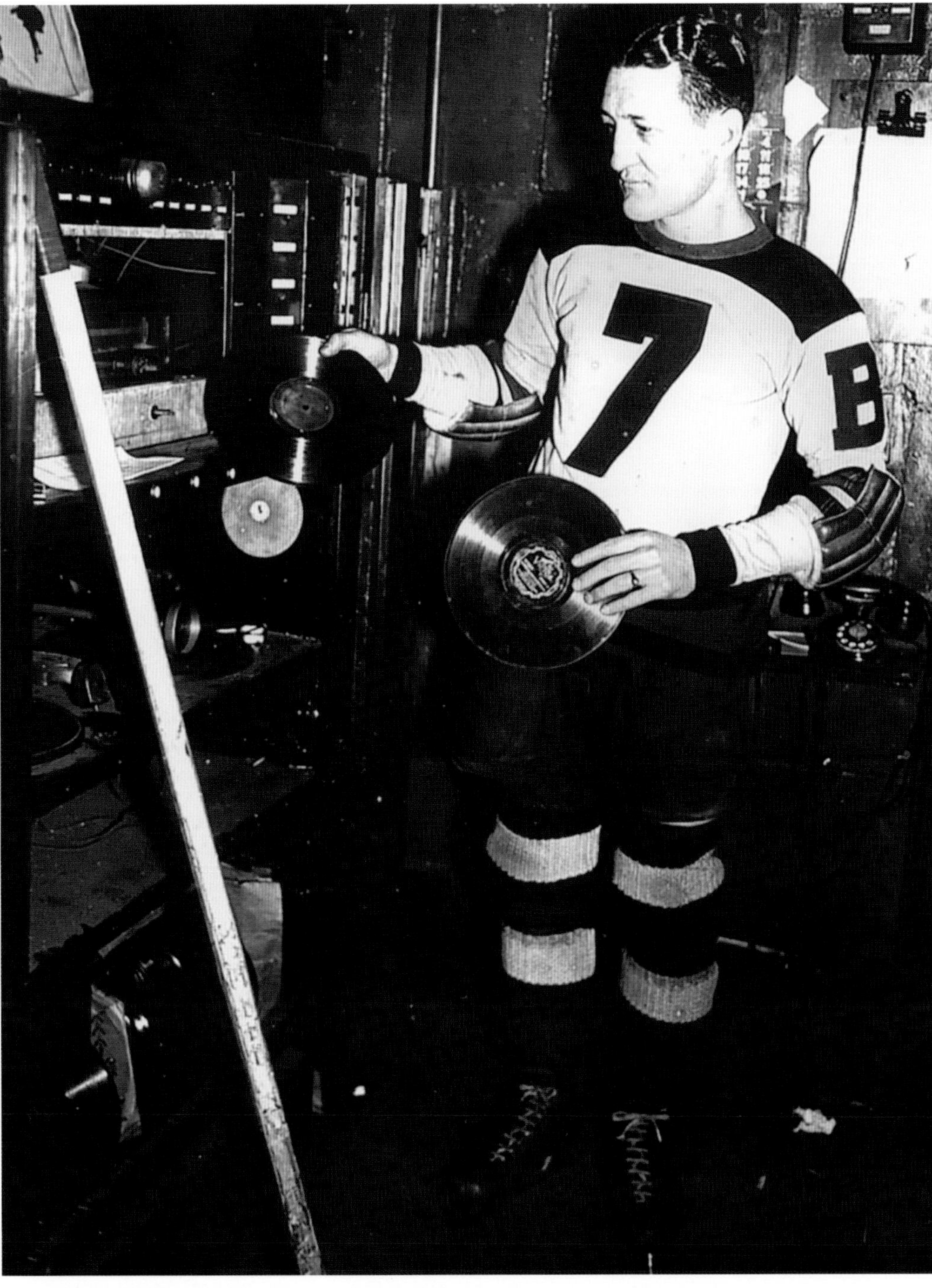

Cooney Weiland spins some records at Boston Garden. Weiland scored 43 goals in 44 games in 1929-30 and played on Stanley Cup championship teams in 1929 and 1939. He later coached the team to a third Stanley Cup in 1941. (Photograph by Leslie Jones, courtesy of the Boston Public Library)

Following his retirement as a player in the spring of 1939, Weiland replaced Art Ross as head coach, leading the Bruins to a Prince of Wales trophy in his first season and a Stanley Cup in his second and final year as head coach in 1940–41. He would later serve as head coach at Harvard, where he led the Crimson to a sterling record of 157–88–5 over the course of 21 seasons while mentoring players such as 1960 Olympic gold medalists Bob and Bill Cleary.

ART ROSS

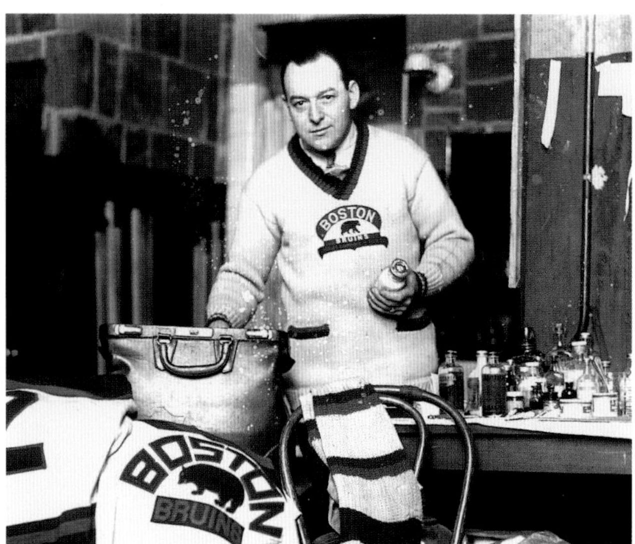

Bruins trainer Win Green wore many hats, treating player injuries, looking after their equipment, and sharpening their skates. He also served as trainer for the Boston Red Sox. (Collection of The Sports Museum)

ARTHUR HOWE ROSS was hockey's first true Renaissance Man. Fluent in French, English, and several First Nation languages, Ross wore many hats in the business world. For a time, the ardent motorcyclist was even the Canadian distributor for Harley Davidson. He was also an inventor of some note.

But it was in hockey that Ross made his lasting mark, initially as a player (as a two-time Stanley Cup champion who was credited as the first defender to rush rather than just merely pass the puck) and then later as the founding coach and general manager of the Boston Bruins. As a head coach and general manager, Ross built his first championship squad in just five seasons. Fellow Hall of Famer Frank Selke said of Ross, "He's the best judge of a hockey player I've ever seen. He can take one look at a player, and tell you whether he's got it or not. He's almost infallible in his judgment." To that end, in 1928 when Rangers chairman Colonel John Hammond suggested that Ross trade him Eddie Shore straight up for a local hero, Melrose native Myles Lane, Ross made the now legendary reply of, "You're so many Myles from Shore you need a life preserver."

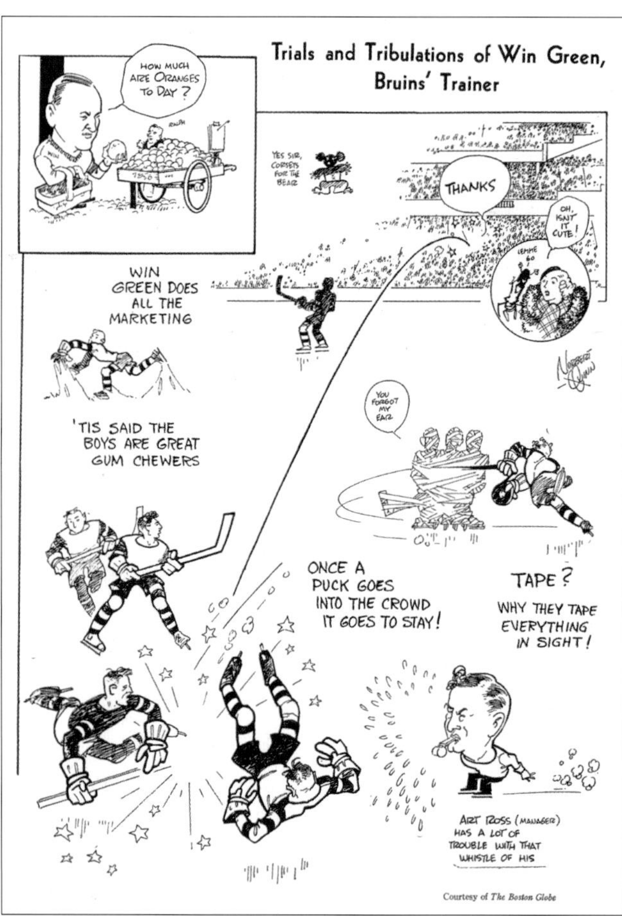

Trainer Win Green as depicted by Boston Post *cartoonist Norbert Quinn.* (Norbert Quinn illustration, Collection of The Sports Museum)

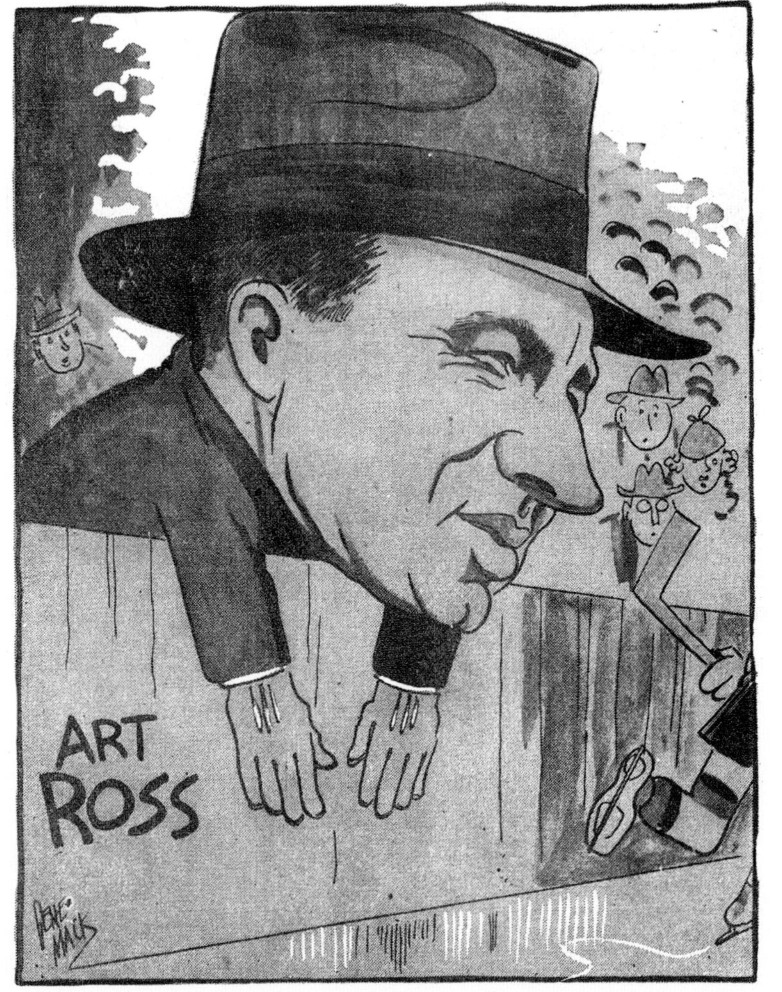

Bruins general manager and head coach Art Ross was known for his sartorial style and animated demeanor behind the bench. He often pounded on the boards to get the attention of the on-ice officials. (Gene Mack illustration, Collection of The Sports Museum)

DECEMBER 12, 1933—TOLL ON ICE

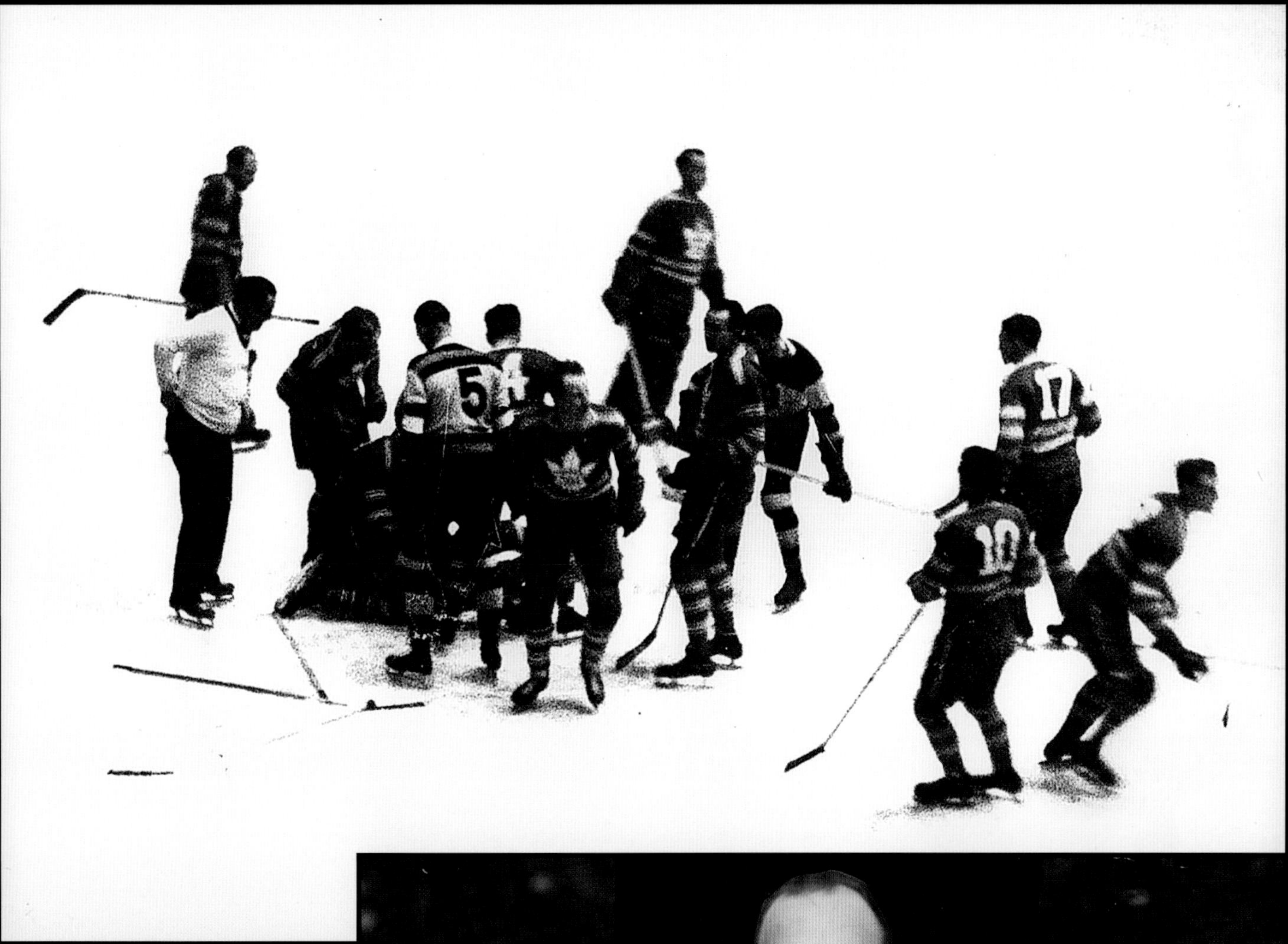

Players gather around Maple Leafs forward Ace Bailey (above) in the aftermath of the vicious hit applied by Bruins defenseman Eddie Shore (who mistakenly thought it was Bailey who had just tripped him seconds earlier). Suffering a skull fracture, Bailey hovered near death for days. While he eventually recovered, he never played hockey again.
(Collection of The Sports Museum)

Following the Ace Bailey incident, Shore was taken to task in the media, including this image (right) from the files of the Boston Advertiser *that depicts him as Public Enemy No. 1.*
(Collection of The Sports Museum)

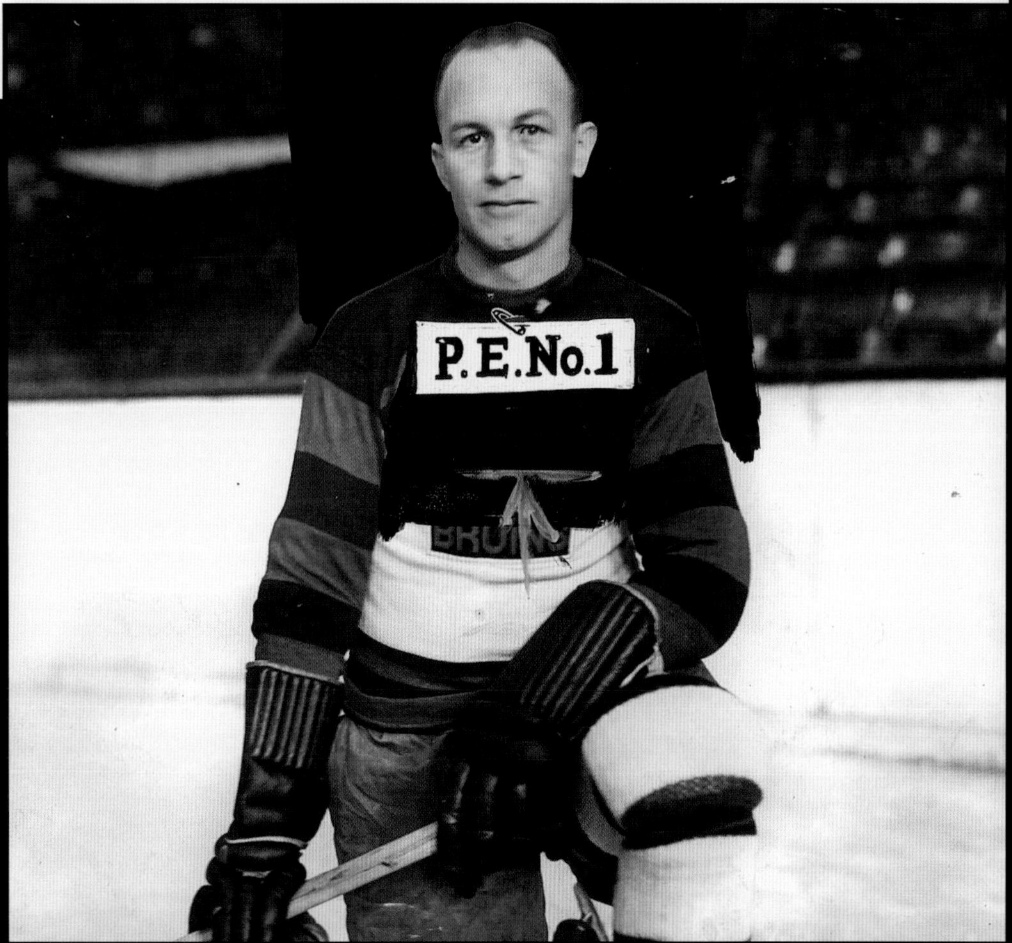

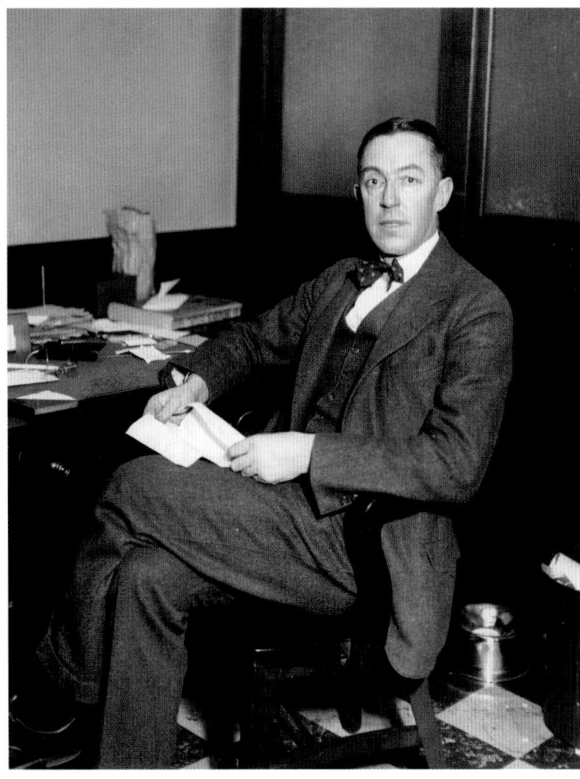

In 1931, Brookline native and 1913 U.S. Open golf champion Francis Ouimet briefly worked for the Bruins as president of their Boston Cubs farm team at the behest of his good friend, Bruins owner Charles F. Adams. (Collection of Richard A. Johnson)

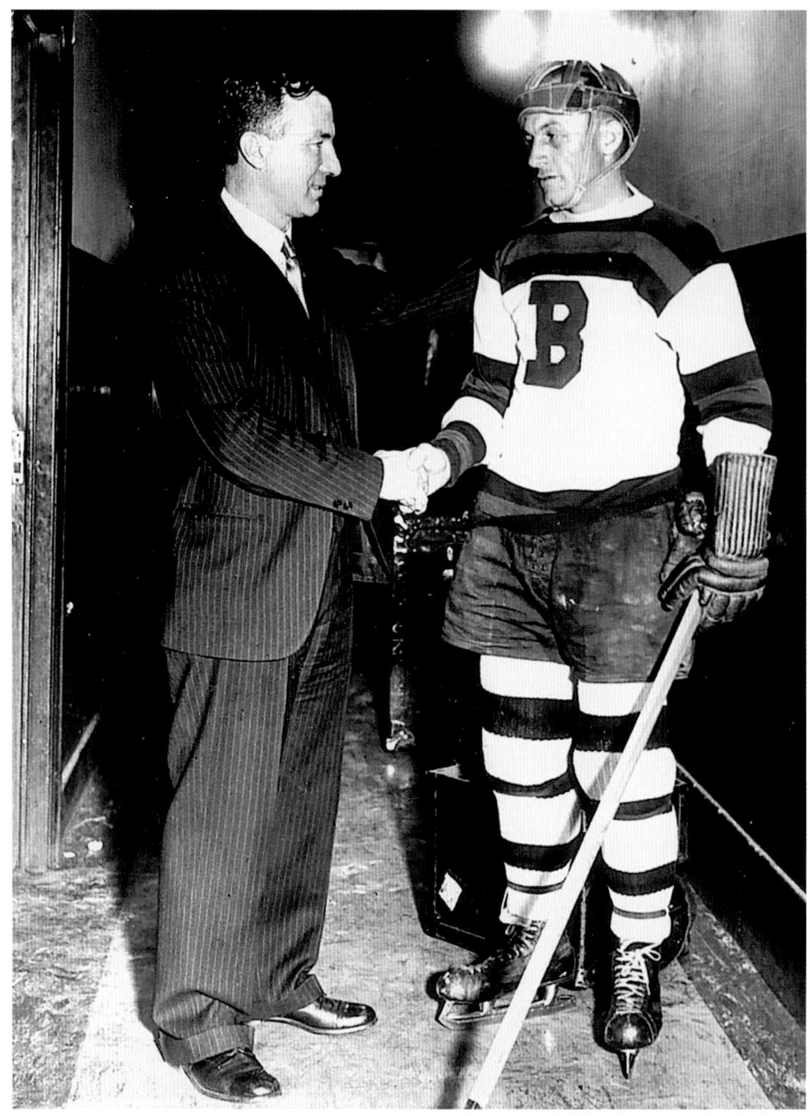

Art Ross greets Eddie Shore following Shore's 16-game suspension for his career-ending hit on Maple Leafs forward Ace Bailey in December 1933. Shore and many of his teammates began wearing helmets after the incident. (Photograph by Leslie Jones, courtesy of the Boston Public Library)

As a strategist, Ross owns the distinction of being the first NHL coach to pull his goalie for an extra skater when behind late in games. He was also an early advocate of analytics who, according to his biographer Eric Zweig, explored the use of a points system accounting for both offense and defense to judge the performance of every player on the ice. In addition, Ross was instrumental to the growth of both the NHL and the game itself as an inventor, owning the patent on both the puck and net design. He also experimented with many helmet designs as well as a slew of metal and composite sticks.

A large share of his legacy resides with the Art Ross Trophy, so named because he donated the award to the league. Originally slated to honor the NHL player of the year as voted by his peers (as opposed to the Hart Trophy, voted by journalists), it has been awarded to the league scoring champion since 1947.

Following a banquet in 1949 at which the Bruins honored Ross for 25 years of service, writers made mention of his many inventions and innovations, including the loose netting that backed his net (for which he always regretted not seeking a patent), his development of the Achilles tendon guard, and his unorthodox strategy of line shifting that so baffled Detroit Red Wings coach Jack Adams in a 1945 playoff series that he called for the referee to declare it illegal.

All grist for the mill for a gentleman who players referred to respectfully simply as "Mr. Ross."

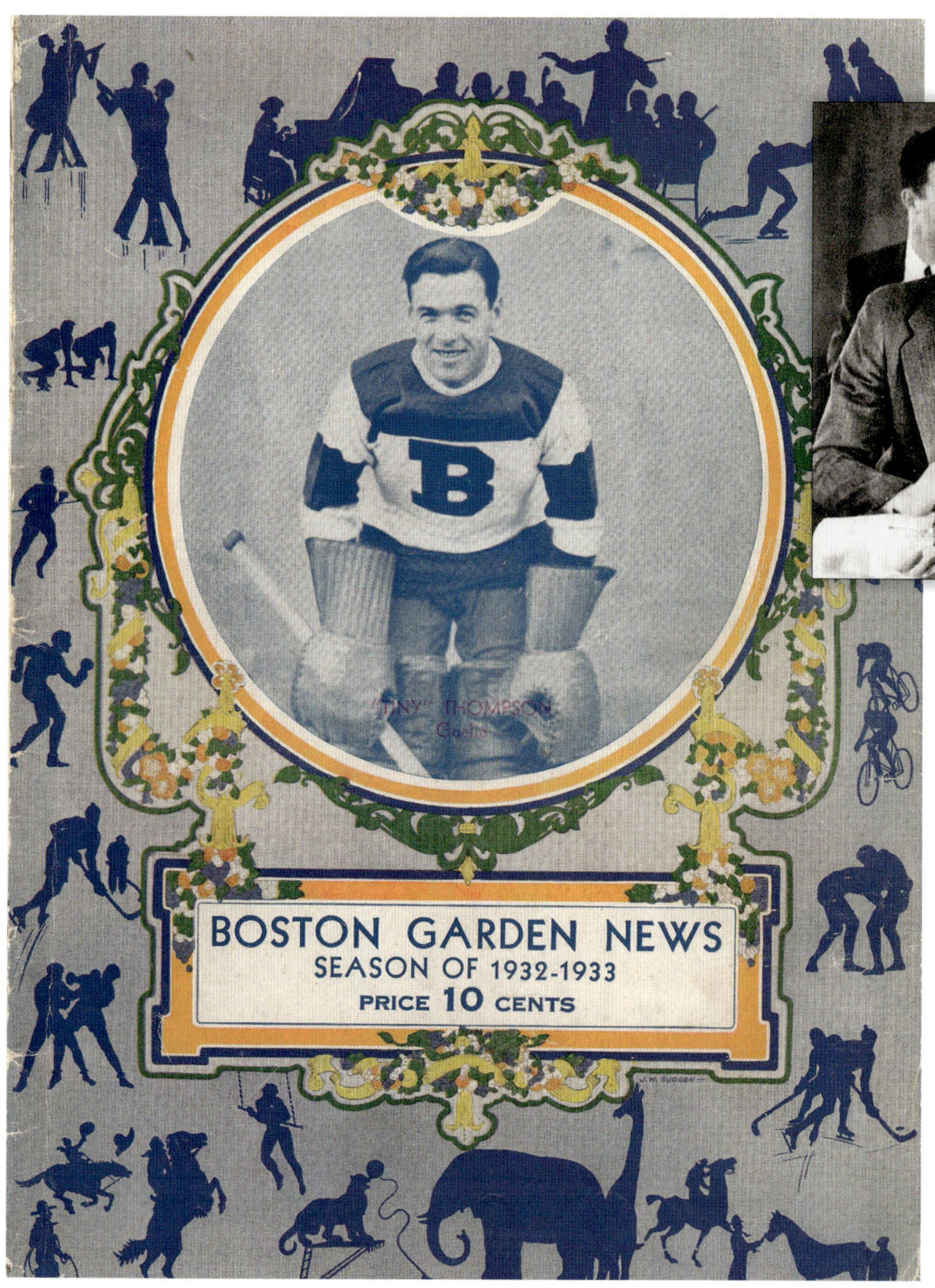

Goalie Tiny Thompson backstopped the Bruins to a Stanley Cup title in 1929 while also winning Vezina Trophies as the league's top netminder in 1930, 1933, 1936, and 1938. (Collection of The Sports Museum)

Bill Cowley, Woody Dumart, Dit Clapper, and Flash Hollett (from left to right) relax in a dining car while on a Bruins road trip in the 1930s. For the first four decades in team history, the Bruins traveled almost exclusively by train. (Collection of The Sports Museum)

TINY THOMPSON

BOSTON'S FOUR-TIME Vezina Trophy winner Cecil Ralph "Tiny" Thompson was cited by renowned hockey historian Stan Fischler as having once remarked about his craft, "I wasn't crazy about it as a kid, but I had to agree to go between the pipes or the other kids wouldn't let me play."

Arriving in Boston in the fall of 1928, Thompson beat out Hal Winkler for the starting goalie's job despite the fact that Winkler had tied a league record with 15 shutouts the previous season. Thompson would play every regular season and playoff game in 1928–29 while helping lead the Bruins to their first Stanley Cup. In five playoff games, he allowed only five goals while recording three shutouts. Over the next decade, he set the standard for NHL goaltending while playing in all but seven of the Bruins 508 regular season and playoff games prior to his trade to the Red Wings for Normie Smith and $15,000 in cash on November 28, 1938.

1939 STANLEY CUP PLAYOFFS

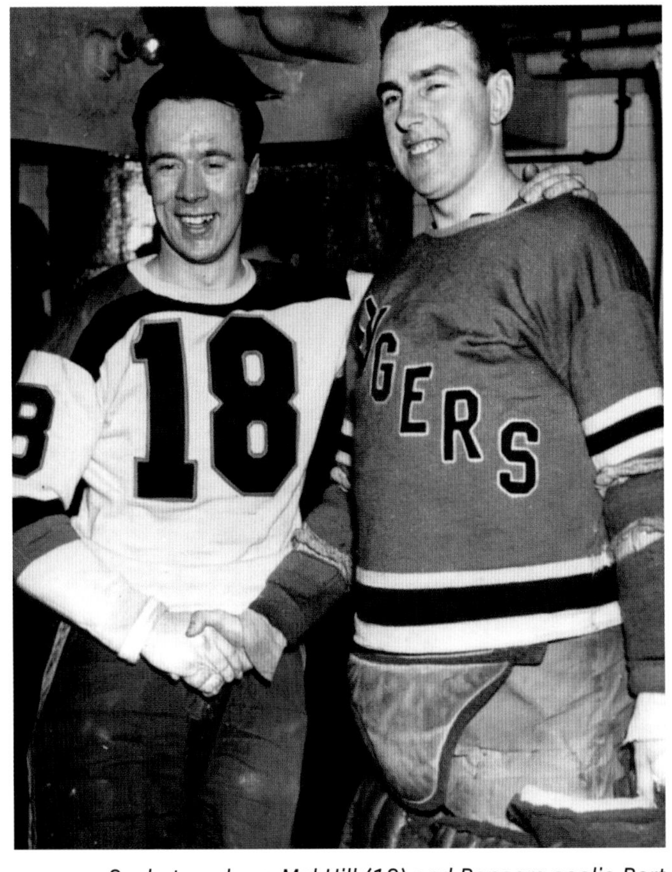

Saskatoon boys Mel Hill (18) and Rangers goalie Bert Gardiner shake hands after Hill's overtime goal won Game 7 of the 1939 Stanley Cup Semifinals. (Collection of The Sports Museum)

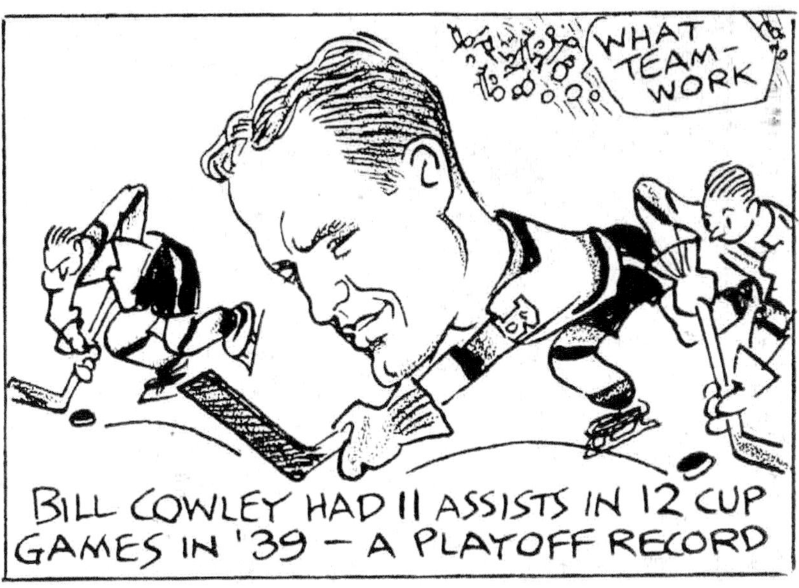

In 1939, playmaking Bruins center Bill Cowley helped the team win the Stanley Cup, pacing the team in playoff scoring with three goals and 11 assists. (Gene Mack illustration, Collection of The Sports Museum)

Head Coach Art Ross (right) hugs right winger Mel Hill following Hill's remarkable feat of scoring three overtime goals, including the Game 7 winner, against the Rangers in the 1939 Stanley Cup Semifinals. It remains an NHL record for overtime goals by one player in a single playoff series. (Collection of The Sports Museum)

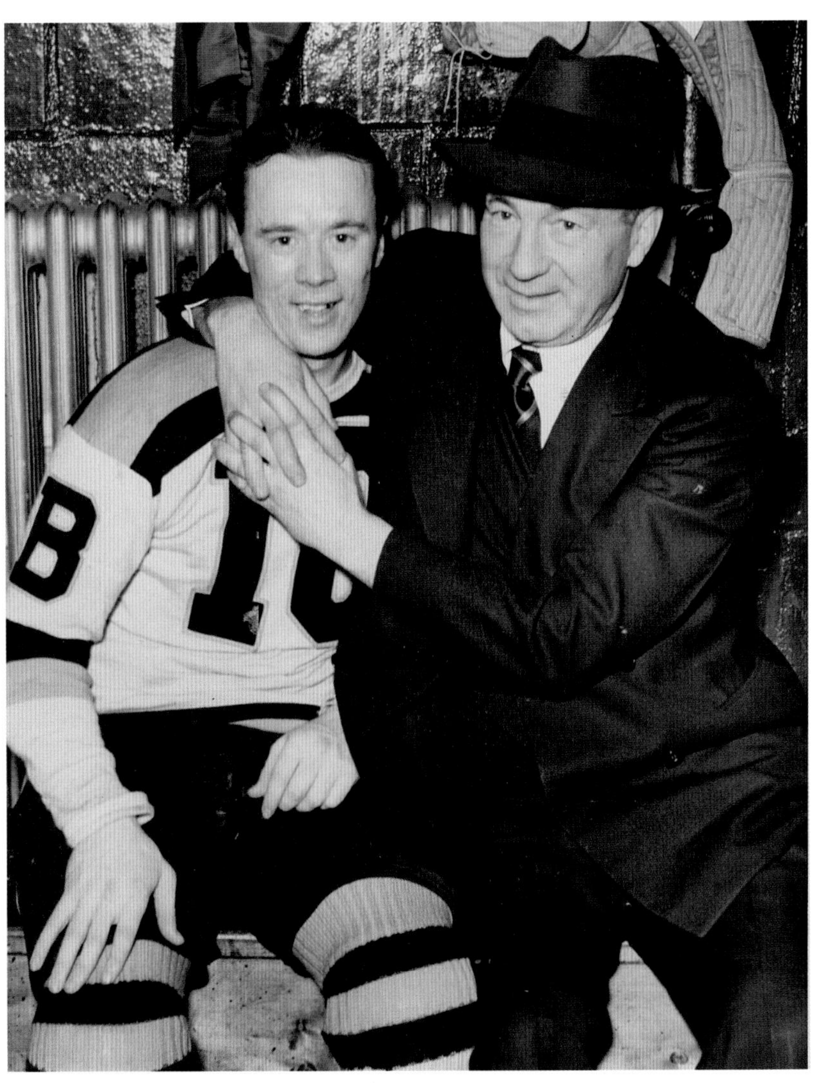

Boston Herald | April 17, 1939

STANLEY CUP TO BOSTON

Bruins Win Stanley Cup as 16,891 See Leafs Lose Third Straight, 3–1
Boston Takes Series, 4–1; Hill, Comacher, Hollett Share Scoring

CLINCH FIRST TITLE FOR B'S IN 10 YEARS
THE STANLEY CUP! WORLD CHAMPIONS!

Ten years of dreaming, hoping and wishing were realized in one short hour last night at the Garden when the Bruins, the greatest hockey team in Boston's history and probably of all time, won the beautiful silver Stanley Cup for the first time since 1928–29, by taking their fourth and deciding game from Toronto's Maple Leafs, 3 to 1.

Winning their third straight from the Leafs to give them the vital series, four games to one, the Bruins were led to the pinnacle of hockey supremacy by Roy Conacher, 21-year-old Toronto lad who fired the winning goal at 17:54 of the second period to break a 1–1 deadlock.

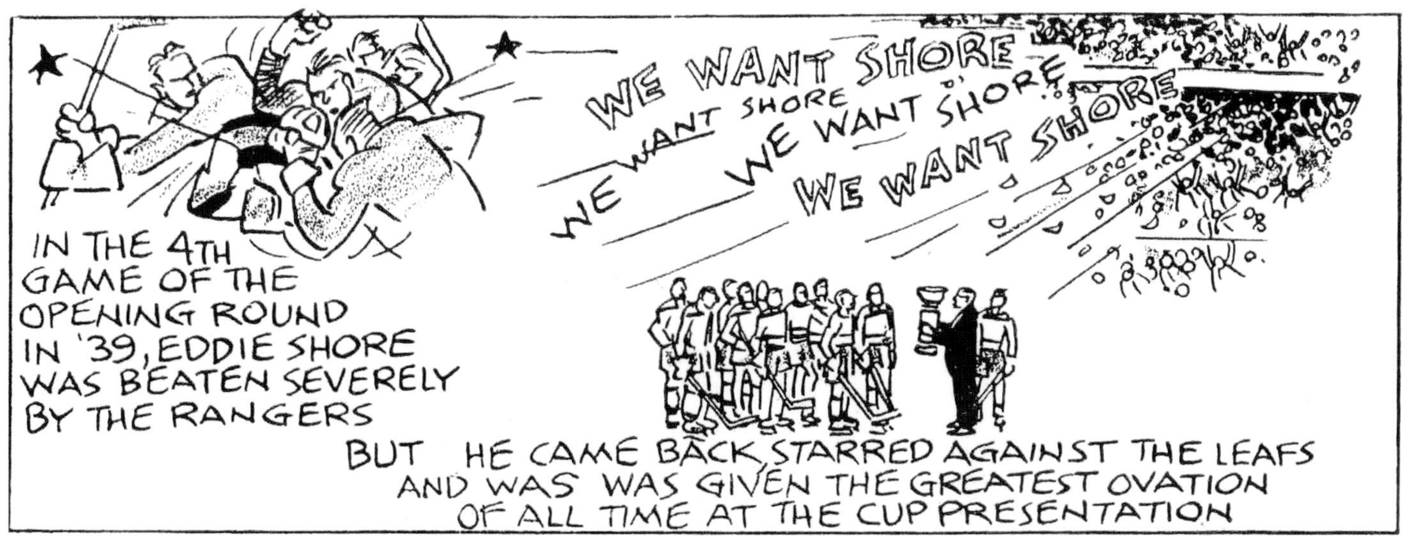

Following the Bruins' home-ice Stanley Cup victory over Toronto on April 16, 1939, the ovation for Eddie Shore was reported to be the longest and loudest in Boston Garden history. (Gene Mack illustration, Collection of The Sports Museum)

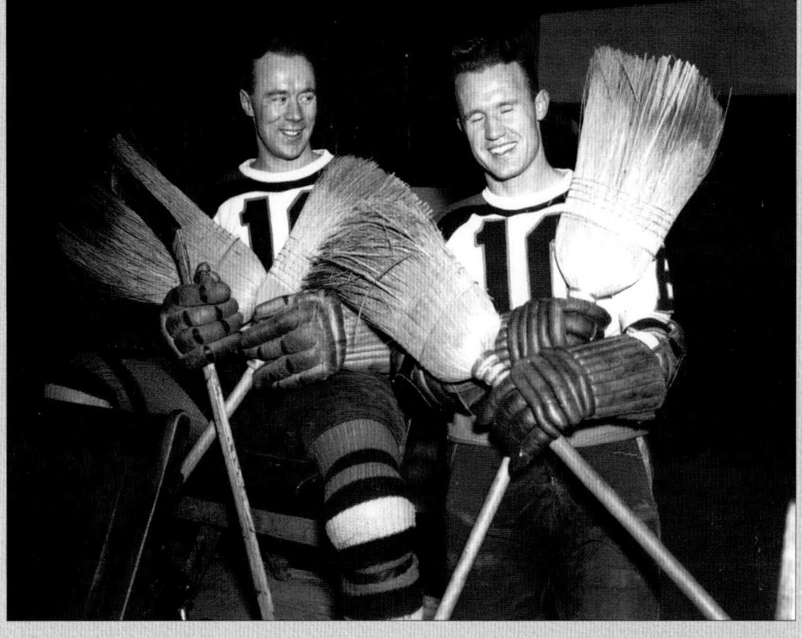

In the 1939 Stanley Cup playoffs, Mel Hill and Bill Cowley helped lead the way, combining with linemate Roy Conacher to score 15 goals as the Bruins beat the Rangers and Maple Leafs to become champions. Here they are seen in the Boston Garden locker room after the Bruins defeated the Maple Leafs in Game 1 of the Stanley Cup Final, 2–1, with the brooms representing the hopes of a four-game sweep. While that didn't end up happening, the Bruins ended up prevailing in five games to bring the Cup back home to Boston. (Photograph by Leslie Jones, courtesy of the Boston Public Library)

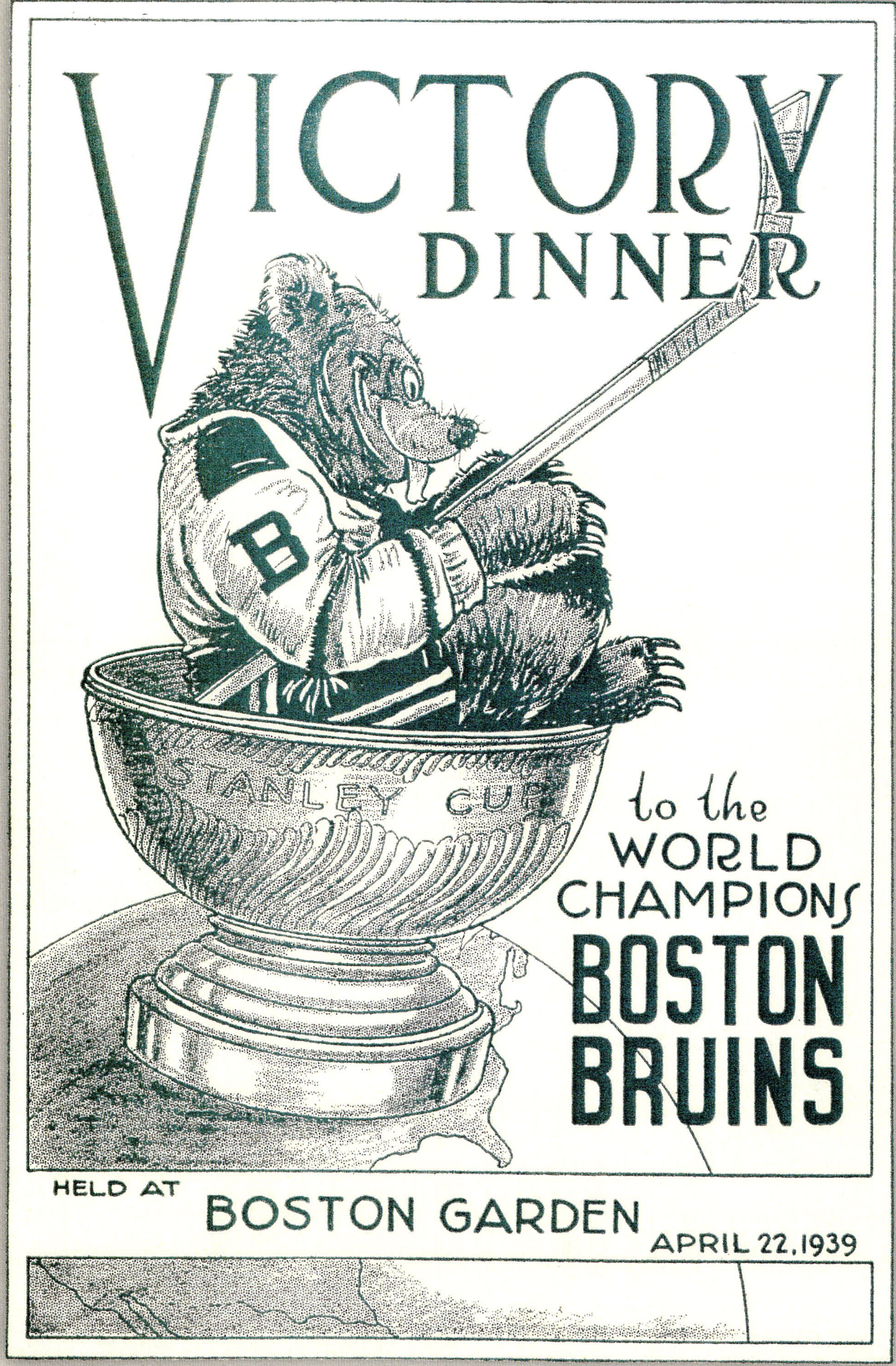

The 1939 Stanley Cup champions celebrated their victory with a gala banquet held at Boston Garden less than a week after clinching their title on home ice. (Collection of The Sports Museum)

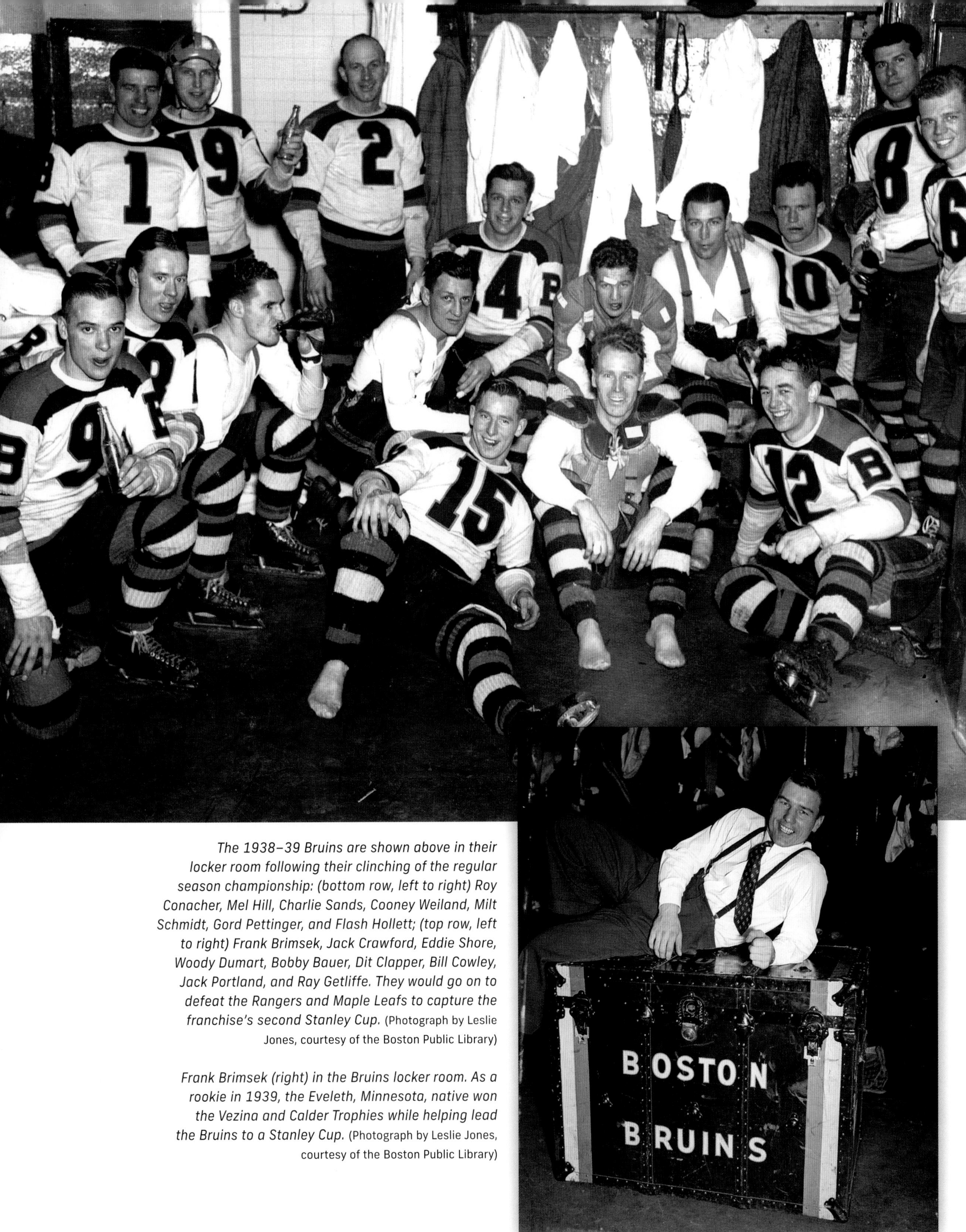

The 1938–39 Bruins are shown above in their locker room following their clinching of the regular season championship: (bottom row, left to right) Roy Conacher, Mel Hill, Charlie Sands, Cooney Weiland, Milt Schmidt, Gord Pettinger, and Flash Hollett; (top row, left to right) Frank Brimsek, Jack Crawford, Eddie Shore, Woody Dumart, Bobby Bauer, Dit Clapper, Bill Cowley, Jack Portland, and Ray Getliffe. They would go on to defeat the Rangers and Maple Leafs to capture the franchise's second Stanley Cup. (Photograph by Leslie Jones, courtesy of the Boston Public Library)

Frank Brimsek (right) in the Bruins locker room. As a rookie in 1939, the Eveleth, Minnesota, native won the Vezina and Calder Trophies while helping lead the Bruins to a Stanley Cup. (Photograph by Leslie Jones, courtesy of the Boston Public Library)

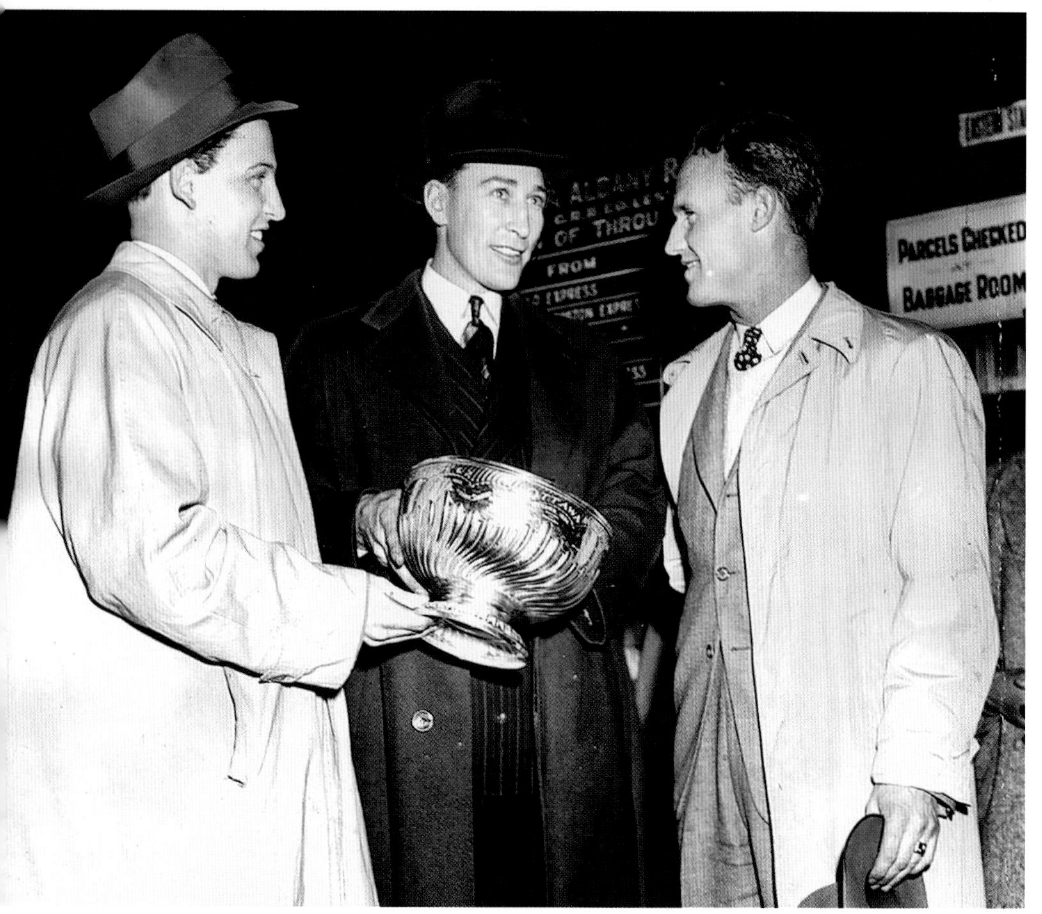

Jack Crawford, Dit Clapper, and Bill Cowley (left to right) hold the Stanley Cup as they prepare to greet fans. The trio were teammates on the Bruins Stanley Cup championship teams of 1939 and 1941. (Collection of The Sports Museum)

DIT CLAPPER

IF EDDIE SHORE was the Babe Ruth of the NHL, then Aubrey V. "Dit" Clapper was most assuredly the Lou Gehrig of the fledgling league.

Indeed, despite the fact that he was one of the elite players of his era, Clapper was content to toil in the shadow of his more famous teammate. His physical presence (at 6′2″, he was one of the league's tallest players) as well as his easygoing demeanor served as a counterbalance to the often overbearing Shore.

Milt Schmidt considered Clapper his mentor and recalled an incident where Clapper tricked Shore by sawing through a couple of his hockey sticks. When they broke in the midst of practice, Clapper was the first to respond with laughter, much to the delight of his teammates. Even Shore joined in.

Clapper would go on to become the NHL's first 20-year player, evenly dividing his career between playing right wing and defense. As a member of the famed Dynamite Line in 1929–30, he was the prototypical power forward, scoring 41 goals. He remained a top producer at wing until making the switch to defense in the late 1930s.

Named as player/coach in 1945 toward the end of his distinguished playing career, Clapper was the ideal choice to lead a postwar Bruins squad that included many of his teammates from the two Stanley Cup championship teams of 1939 and 1941. On February 12, 1947, he announced his retirement as a player on a night he helped lead Boston to a 10–1 victory over the Rangers. The Bruins marked the occasion by announcing that his No. 5 would be retired, and the Hockey Hall of Fame immediately inducted him as an Honoured Member. At the time, it marked the only time an active player, and the first time a living member, had been inducted. Following the end of the 1948–49 playoffs, Clapper resigned as Bruins head coach in order to care for his wife.

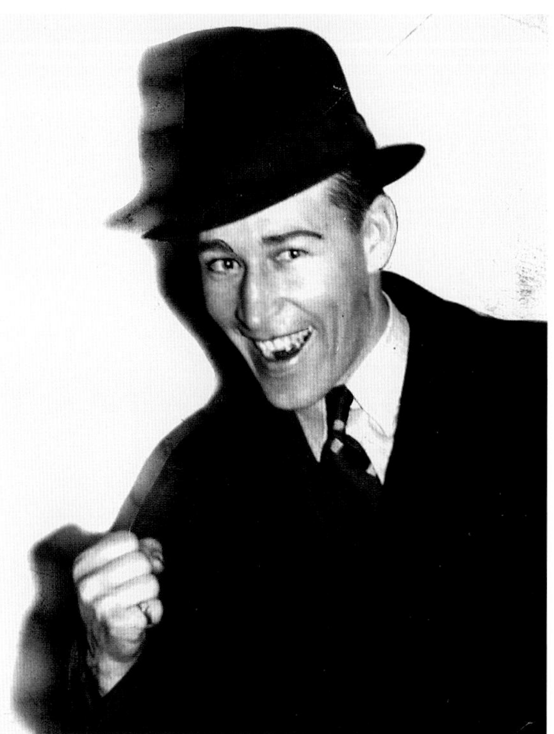

Versatile forward/defenseman Dit Clapper was the beloved heart and soul of the Depression Era Bruins, helping lead his team to three Stanley Cup championships. He was especially helpful in shaping the careers of young stars such as Milt Schmidt and Woody Dumart. (Collection of The Sports Museum)

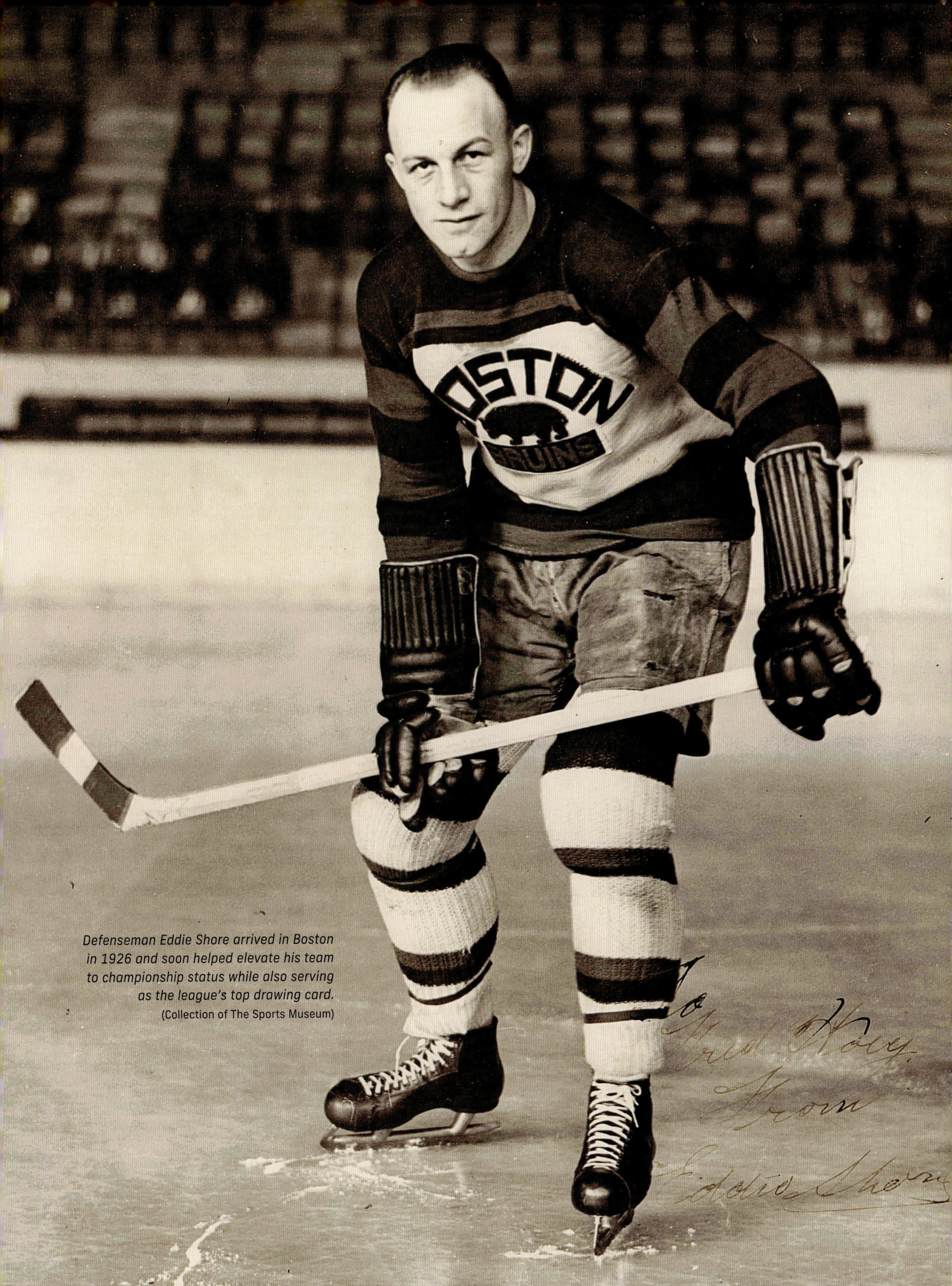

Defenseman Eddie Shore arrived in Boston in 1926 and soon helped elevate his team to championship status while also serving as the league's top drawing card.
(Collection of The Sports Museum)

IN HIS OWN WORDS… MILT SCHMIDT

MILT SCHMIDT first came to Boston as an 18-year-old phenom from Kitchener, Ontario, in 1936. Skating alongside linemates and fellow Kitchener natives Bobby Bauer and Woody Dumart, Schmidt would soon captivate the fans of New England and become one of the greatest centers in Bruins and NHL history. "Milt Schmidt was one of the best skaters you ever would see," teammate Ed Sandford said in a 2022 interview. "How he would glide."

Through the years, Schmidt served the Bruins as team captain, head coach, assistant general manager, and general manager. He was also the first Bruin to have his name inscribed on the Stanley Cup four times, twice as a player and twice as an executive. His clever playmaking helped the Bruins win two Stanley Cups, in 1939 and 1941. A quarter century later, Schmidt's shrewd engineering of the "Deal of the Century," which brought Phil Esposito, Ken Hodge, and Fred Stanfield to town, provided the Bruins the necessary ingredients for their Cup triumphs in 1970 and 1972.

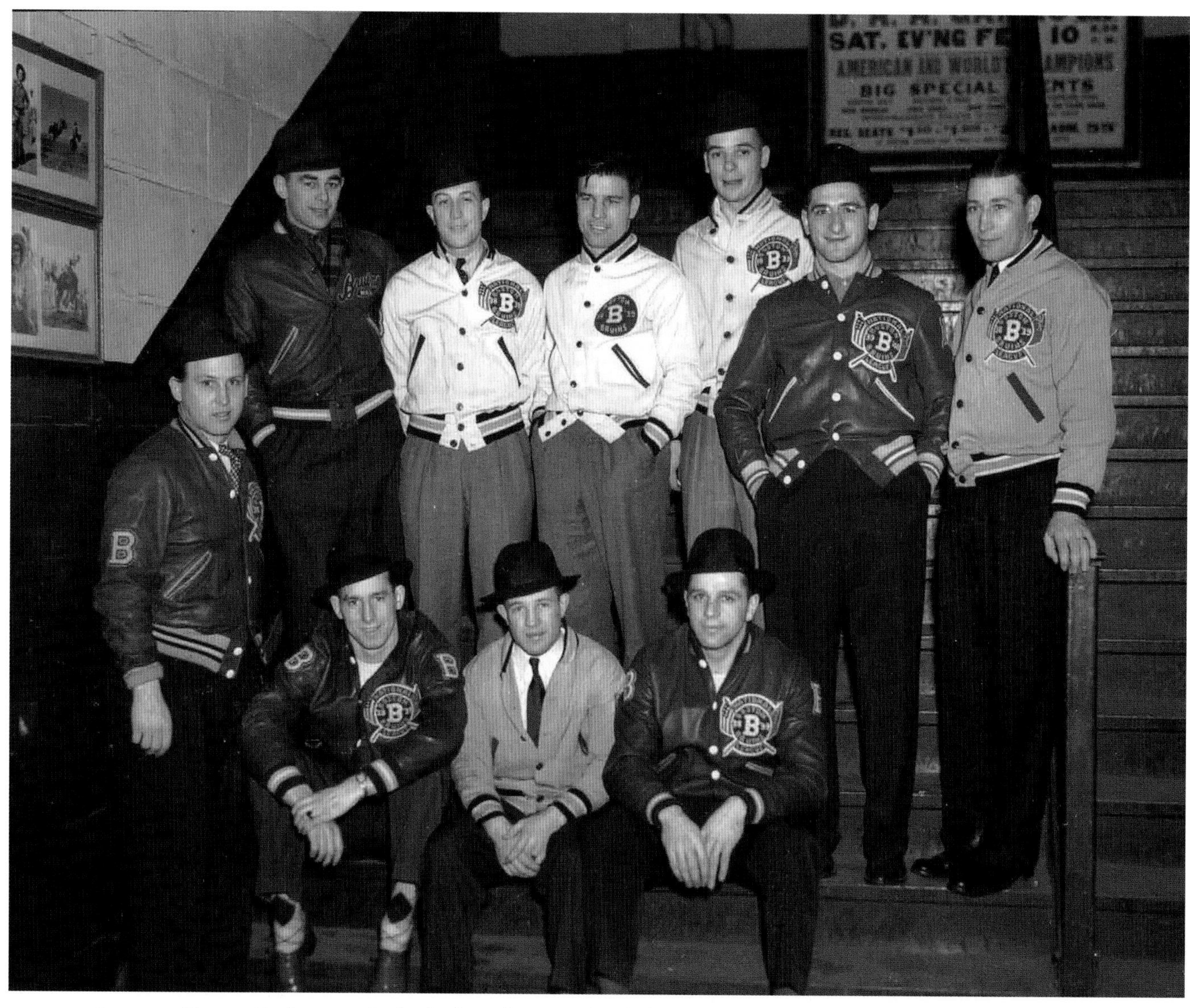

A group of happy Bruins pose in the jackets they won for their successes during the 1939 and 1940 seasons: (front row, left to right) Jack Crawford (standing), Milt Schmidt, Bobby Bauer, and Woody Dumart; (back row, left to right) Flash Hollett, Art Jackson, Frank Brimsek, Roy Conacher, Jack Shewchuk, and Dit Clapper.

(Photograph by Leslie Jones, courtesy of the Boston Public Library)

Set forth below are excerpts from an exclusive interview that Richard A. Johnson, the coauthor of this book, conducted with Schmidt several years before he passed away in 2017 at the age of 98.

On joining fellow Kitchener, Ontario, natives Woody Dumart and Bobby Bauer on the Bruins

Bauer was obtained from the Maple Leafs organization by Art Ross in 1934. Following Bobby's arrival at training camp he suggested that Ross scout both Dumart and myself. Both Woody and I were invited to the Bruins training camp in 1935. I was only 17 at the time and was offered a contract for $2,500. To which I politely said, "No thank you." I went home and played another year of junior hockey and made a lot more than $2,500. The following year I was invited to the Bruins camp in Boston, and I'm not ashamed to say that I signed for $3,500. As the saying goes, word of mouth advertising is very important, and Bobby's suggestion to Ross was the reason that Woody and I became Bruins. Woody was originally a defenseman and was moved to left wing. Our line, soon to be known by the nickname of the Kraut Line, given to us by a writer, first played together in the NHL beginning in 1937.

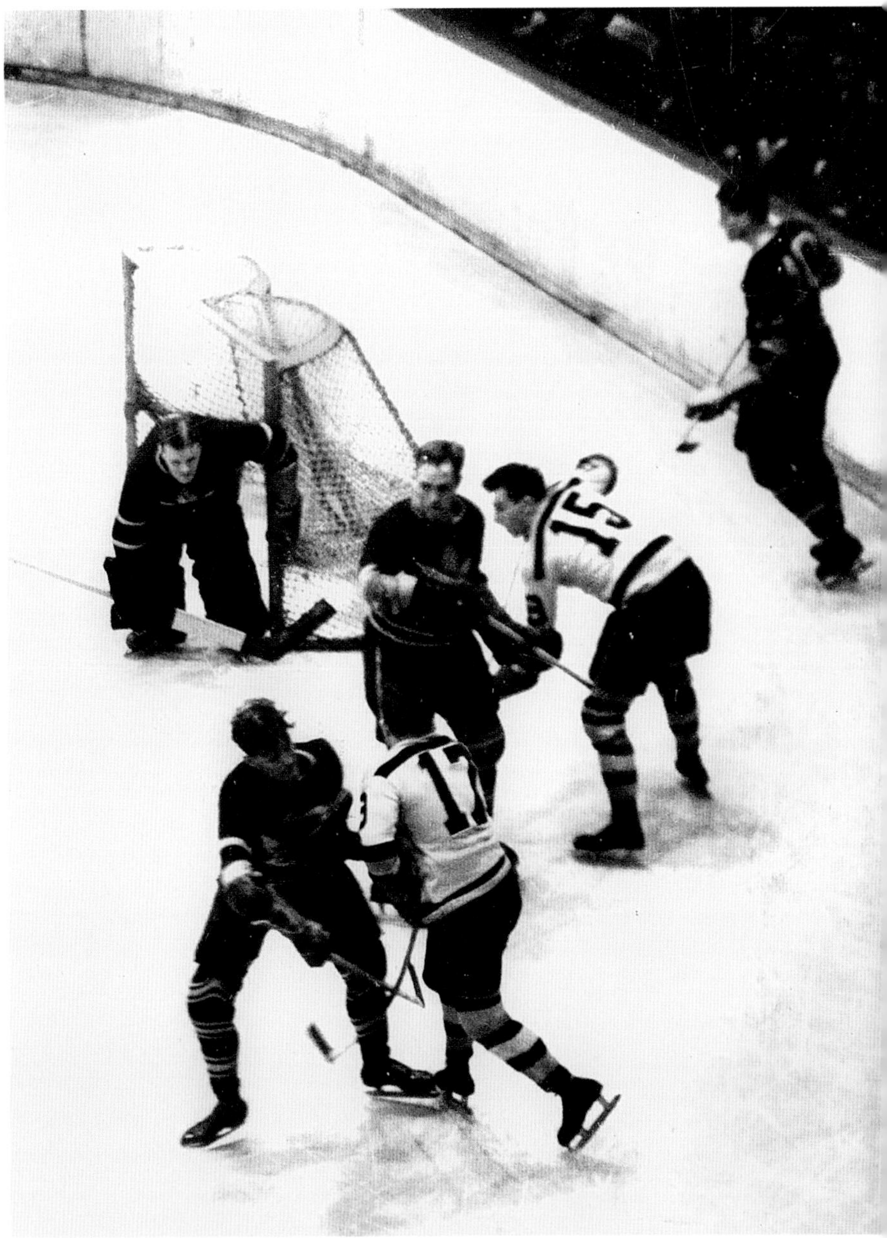

Linemates Milt Schmidt (15) and Bobby Bauer (17) press the attack against the Maple Leafs and goalie Turk Broda at Boston Garden in 1939. (Photograph by Leslie Jones, courtesy of the Boston Public Library)

On the Kraut Line players requesting identical contracts

During the years we played together as a line, we did in fact ask for and receive identical contracts. What one got the other got—no more, no less. The only time we asked for separate contracts was after Bauer retired and Woody and I got separate pacts. Following the '38–39 season when Bob, Woody, and I finished 1-2-3 in the NHL scoring race, we were rubbing our hands in anticipation of training camp and signing our new contracts. Well, Ross saw fit to offer us the same contracts [as] the previous season. We finally received a $500 raise but didn't sign our contracts until three hours before our opening game in Montreal. At one point during our impasse, we had attempted to leave training camp and meet with the president of the NHL, and waiting for us at the train was Hammy Moore, the Bruins assistant trainer, who told us that Ross wanted us to reconsider and stay. Let me tell you that our team had been successful primarily because of 10 or 12 players, and I'll guarantee you that nobody in the NHL played for less money than we did.

On the Kraut Line's final game before enlisting in the Canadian military for World War II

If I remember correctly, we were playing the Montreal Canadiens at the Garden and thrashed them pretty badly. Our line scored 11 points; but what we did on the ice was secondary to the reaction of the fans. We'll never forget the ovations we received that night. The fans were and continue to be the greatest. Despite the 8–1 score, the Canadiens saw fit to carry us on their shoulders for a few strides around the ice.

EDDIE SHORE

by C. Michael Hiam

EDWARD WILLIAM SHORE arrived in Boston in early November 1926, one of several spoils of the collapsed Western Hockey League that the canny Art Ross had managed to acquire that summer. Ross assigned Shore to his minor-league Cubs, but by the end of the two-week training camp, the Cub emerged a Bruin. The home opener at Boston Arena against the hated Canadiens was November 16, days away from Shore's 25th birthday. The obscure player from the Canadian prairies impressed a reporter at the game as being "tall [5′11″] yet sturdily built. His speed for a man weighing 190 pounds is exceptional and he handles both his body and his stick well. He is aggressive and quite agreeable to giving and taking the body bumps." With just minutes left in the tied game, Shore took one of those body bumps from Auréle Joliat and landed on his back, but not before passing the rubber to Carlson "Dead Eye" Cooper who broke the tie and won the game. Shore, the reporter concluded, had caught the "fancy of the fans."

Team practices at Boston Arena were casual affairs, Ross believing that his Bruins could work it out themselves. During one of these practices on a morning in December 1926, Billy Coutu, new to the Bruins but in his 10th NHL season, decided to work it out with Shore. The veteran had disliked the upstart since the first day of camp and "seized every chance he got to rough me under cover," Shore recalled. "I took what I had to take for a long time. Then it was a fight to the finish between that old-timer and myself." Shore and Coutu began bumping each other good and hard, Coutu repeatedly lining Shore up for a smashing charge and Shore repeatedly repaying the favor. Couto's final charge started at the far end of the rink and ended when at the last second Shore crouched down and met his adversary with all his weight and might. Coutu was sent flying backward, fell to the ice, and then, Shore said, "got up and sank down, got up again, and went down again. This time he stayed there." Although still standing, Shore was not unhurt. In the collision, Coutu's head "had smashed into my ear and torn it off. There was just a little piece of skin holding it on."

The team physician, Dr. Joe Shortell, said the ear could not be reattached, but Shore had the trainer tape it to his neck and apply some ice, and then went looking for a second opinion. Doctor after doctor repeated Shortell's words, but just before office hours ended for the day, Shore explained, "I ran across a fellow who was more encouraging. He asked what type of anesthetic I wanted. I told him just to give me a small mirror. That way, I could watch the kind of stitching he did. I made him change the very last stitch. If I had not done that, he'd have left a scar."

Mysteriously wearing a large bandage over his ear, Shore immediately returned to action. Having recently been moved by Ross from wing to defense, he proceeded to display an independent streak that delighted Boston fans. Ignoring the well-oiled combination play preached by Ross, Shore would gain the puck in Bruins' territory and, in a solo effort, dash straight up ice and, if not score—which he occasionally did—at least end up as a spectacular train-wreck, often taking opposing players with him. Equally spectacular to fans was Shore's penchant for revenge, such as when Nels "Poison" Stewart of the Montreal Maroons lunged at the Bruins goaltender for the crime of having just caught a shot. A wild fight ensued in which Shore, aided by teammates who pinned Stewart down, pounded the Maroon mercilessly (and got a major penalty and a $15 fine for his exertions).

Thanks to some astute mid-season trades by Ross, the 1926–27 Bruins went all the way to the Stanley Cup Final but ultimately lost to the Ottawa Senators. By season's end, Shore ranked second in the NHL in penalty minutes, trailing only the aforementioned Nels Stewart. "There is no finer kid in the league," the *Boston Herald*'s Stanley Woodward wrote, "but he's still a little crude."

Ross was always prepared to pay his players as little as possible, and Shore's salary that season had been so meager that he had to frequent the pool halls of Boston to win some extra cash. However, delighted by his team's first Cup appearance, Charles Adams sent each Bruin back to Canada $10,000 richer. Shore used his bonus to buy a farm in Alberta, and there he would return at the end of all his subsequent Bruins seasons. And Shore would never again arrive at training camp without a lucrative contract in hand. If Ross failed to send him one, he was content to stay on his farm while Bruins fans fretted that the season would start without their beloved Eddie.

While the paying customer fixated on Shore's human-cyclone style of hockey, his devotion to the art of skating went unnoticed. Shore practiced solo at the Boston Arena for hours on end and learned from closely watching the other greats in the league like his favorite, Howie Morenz. "When you start to play hockey," Shore advised in a youth magazine, "use every opportunity to see the good players and study them. Observe how they lift their feet, how they set them down, how they shove them forward, how they sway their bodies, the spring of their legs, the angle of their knees and their body bend; all these things are important and count in playing the game." Perhaps too shy to admit it to the boys, Shore also studiously watched and learned from ladies' figure skating.

For the Bruins, the 1928–29 campaign would prove to be "the year," and it began on November 20, 1928, at the enormous Boston Garden. Despite their brand new home, the Bruins performed poorly during the first half of the season. To salvage the remainder, they had to turn things around. Shore would become a key part of that salvage effort.

Two days into January 1929, though, Shore missed the last train to Montreal the night before an important meeting with the Maroons (he had been helping a friend fix his car). Shore called the Boston airport to see about hiring an airplane. The Montreal airport, he learned, was snowed in. "There was a cab line outside the station," Shore later explained, "and I talked one cab driver into driving me the 340 miles for $100." It was a lot of money, but Shore knew Ross would fine him easily twice that much if he didn't show.

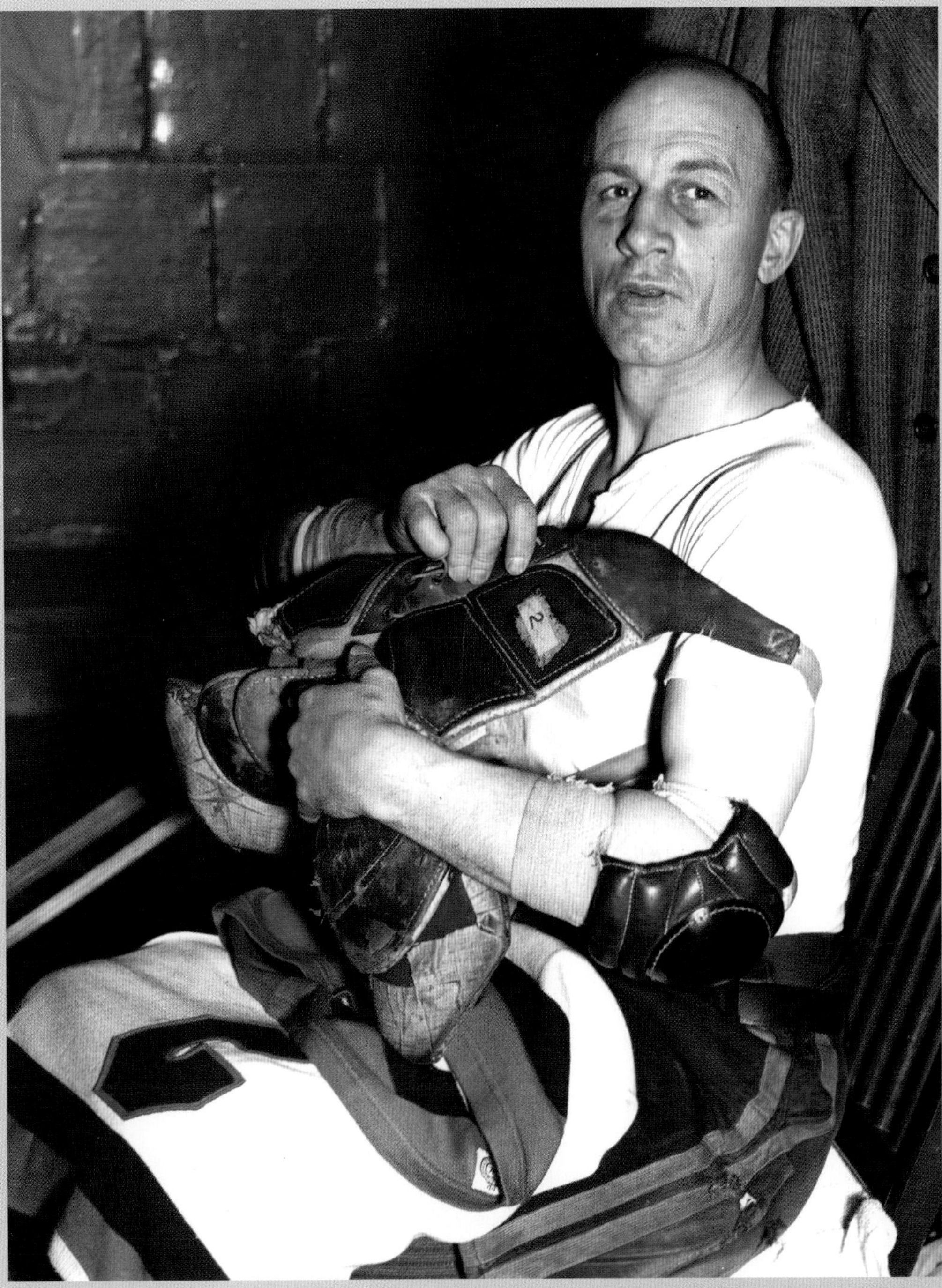

Defenseman Eddie Shore was both the Babe Ruth and Ty Cobb of hockey while serving as the NHL's top drawing card and its most feared competitor. (Photograph by Leslie Jones, courtesy of the Boston Public Library)

The cab roared out of the city and headed north toward Quebec. Shore was optimistic he could make it on time but hadn't factored in the rain and ice along the way. While Shore attempted to get some rest in the backseat, their progress slowed to a crawl due to the weather. By the time they reached the foot of the White Mountains, Shore knew they were in for trouble. He flagged down a passing truck and bought a snow shovel and ice ax from the driver and ordered the protesting cabbie to continue up the slopes. At an all-night gas station, Shore bought tire chains, but they quickly wore out and the taxi slid into deep snow. Using the shovel to clear the snow and the ax to cut down tree branches and shrubs to put under the tires for traction, Shore had the cab driver gun the engine while he pushed, and they were soon on their way again. Through the frozen windshield, Shore could see the lights of a work camp ahead and there he bought another set of chains. They too quickly wore out. "We wound up in a ditch," Shore recalled. "The cabbie quit right there. I found a farmhouse a mile or two up the road. The farmer hitched up a sleigh and drove me to a connecting train line. I made it to Montreal in 22 hours, and so I was there at 6:00 o'clock the night of the game."

Sparked by the appearance of Shore, the Bruins prevailed that night (with Shore scoring the only goal of the game) and continued to prevail for the rest of the regular season with Shore playing his usual 60 minutes (including time spent in the box) per game. As entertaining as ever, Shore was now using his amazing skating ability to outwit opponents instead of running over them, his shot had become trickier, and perhaps most important, he was now passing to his teammates and giving them a chance to shine.

In the playoffs, a sweep of the Canadiens in the semifinals won the Bruins the right to face the New York Rangers in the Final. The Bruins bested their rival two games to none to win the first Stanley Cup in franchise history.

It was rumored that Shore had held out for $17,500 before the start of the 1929–30 season, which would have made him the best-paid player in the league. And if true, it was an investment that paid dividends not only at Boston Garden, where every game was sold out, but also in other NHL venues whenever the Bruins visited. "What makes Eddie Shore the greatest drawing card in hockey," Kyle Crichton wrote in the *New Yorker*, "is the hope—entertained by spectators in all cities but Boston—that he will some night be severely killed." And he was almost killed during his first visit to the Montreal Forum that season. Perhaps mindful of what he had done to Nels Stewart three years earlier, the Maroons were ready for Shore, who later remembered little of the game except waking up in a cold shower before being shoved out onto the ice again. Arriving back in Boston with, a reporter noted, "all the appearance of a man who had exploded a charge of dynamite with a hammer," Shore had missing and broken teeth, two black eyes, a fractured jaw, and a cut and swollen face. Adams complained bitterly to the NHL that during the game Shore had been knocked cold four times, and when the league did nothing to punish the Maroons, Adams gave Shore $500 for his valor. (Shore shared the money with the rest of his teammates, who had also had a rough going-over at the Forum.)

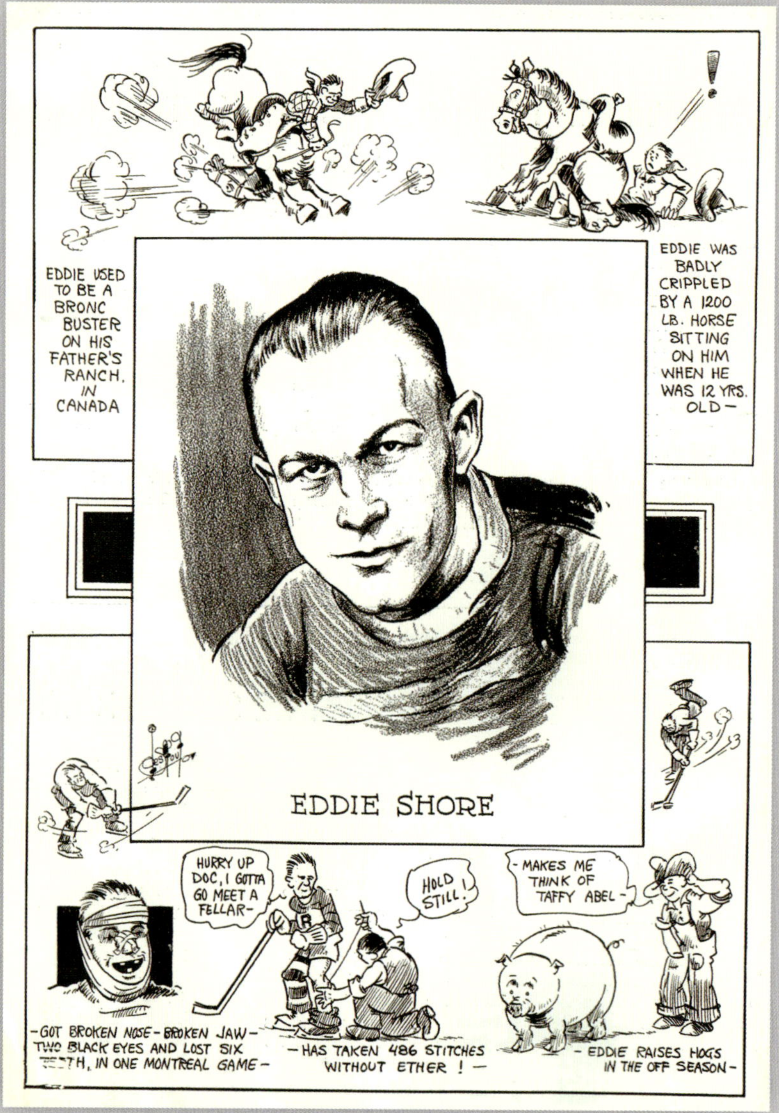

By rights, the 1929–30 Bruins, with an astounding record of 38-5-1 by playoff time, should have brought the Cup back to Boston. It didn't happen. Instead, they were robbed in the Stanley Cup Final by the Canadiens, who won the first two games in the three-game series. Shore had crops to plant, and from Montreal, where the series ended, he took the next train to Edmonton with his wife, who was visibly pregnant. He had met Kate Macrae in Edmonton back when she was an amateur basketball star and he was with the WHL Cougars, but postponed proposing because he had no money. Now that he was a man of means, they had married, and over that summer Eddie Jr. was born.

Although the Bruins again failed to win the Cup that next season, it wasn't due to Shore's not trying. In fact, at age 28, he was at the apex of his NHL career. "If there is any man in hockey harder to get the puck away from before he decides to shoot or pass," the *Boston Evening Transcript*'s A. Linde Fowler observed, "I don't know who it can be." Shore was of course hugely popular in Boston, and before each game at the Garden the band struck up "Hail to the Chief" when he first stepped out onto the ice. And while perhaps not popular outside of Boston, Shore's hockey talent was undeniable. He won the Hart Trophy four times—in 1933, 1935, 1936, and 1938. If not for the Ace Bailey incident, he most likely would have won it in 1934, too.

Cartoonist Les Stout paid tribute to Eddie Shore's legendary toughness and off-season occupation as a farmer. (Les Stout illustration, Collection of The Sports Museum)

The Bailey incident occurred at the Garden on Tuesday, December 12, 1933. With six minutes left in the second period of a rough-and-dirty game with the Maple Leafs, Shore was rushing deep into Leafs territory with a good chance to score when tripped by Red Horner. The officiating had been erratic all evening, and no penalty was called. With Shore down, King Clancy gained possession and took the play to the Bruins' end. Picking himself up and in a dazed rage, Shore bent down and charged at the nearest target available, which was Irving Wallace "Ace" Bailey. The Leaf had dropped back to take Clancy's place on the blue line and was watching the play on the other end of the rink when from behind Shore's shoulder slammed hard into his midsection. Bailey shot up in the air and then went down, his head making a sickening thud as it hit the ice. Instantly, Horner skated over to Shore and sucker punched him. Now two bodies lay unconscious on the ice, but Bailey, who had gone into convulsions, looked to be far worse off.

An on-ice riot ensued between the Bruins and the Leafs until cooler heads managed to restore order. Bailey was carried to the dressing room and regained consciousness. A revived Shore, with seven new stitches in his head walked in and, leaning over Bailey, said, "I'm awfully sorry, I didn't mean it." Bailey replied, "It's all in the game, Eddie." Although still dazed from Horner's punch, Shore was well enough to drive home with Kate.

News came the next day that Bailey was in the hospital and the situation dire. He had slipped into a coma and emergency brain surgery had failed. Bailey's wife Gladys, with their young daughter, had rushed from Toronto when she heard of the injury, and now with Gladys by his side in Boston, radio stations from all across Canada were announcing the death of the Ace at age 31. Fortunately, the announcement was premature and Bailey hung on. Still, the Canadian press continued to excoriate Shore, and even Boston papers predicted that Shore's popularity in the city "was passing." But it wasn't passing because in Boston Eddie could do no wrong. In the days ahead, Bailey made a miraculous recovery, although he would never again play professional hockey. An NHL investigation determined Shore hadn't acted deliberately but still suspended him for 16 games. Later that season, Shore played in an all-star benefit game for Bailey, and the two became and remained good friends until Shore's death in 1985. (Bailey passed away seven years later at the age of 88.)

Shore helped the Bruins win the Cup in 1939 but by the middle of the next season the always contentious relationship between Shore and Ross had become too much. As a result, Shore was traded to the New York Americans. He retired from the NHL at the end of the season.

In 1947, Ross blocked Shore's induction into the Hockey Hall of Fame, and there was outrage in Boston. Adams quickly countermanded Ross and not only was Shore inducted but his number was retired. And so on the evening of April 1, 1947, in a pregame ceremony at Boston Garden prior to the fourth game of their Stanley Cup Semifinals series with the Canadiens, the Bruins announced the retirement of his No. 2 and presented him with a scroll marking his induction into the International Hockey Hall of Fame.

C. Michael Hiam, PhD, is the author of the biography *Eddie Shore* and *That Old Time Hockey*.

BOSTON BRUINS (1930–1939)

Season	W	L	T	PTS	PTS%	Finish	Playoffs	Coach	Division
1929–30	38	5	1	77	.875	1st of 5	Lost Stanley Cup Final	Art Ross	American
1930–31	28	10	6	62	.705	1st of 5	Lost NHL Semifinals	Art Ross	American
1931–32	15	21	12	42	.438	4th of 4		Art Ross	American
1932–33	25	15	8	58	.604	1st of 4	Lost NHL Semifinals	Art Ross	American
1933–34	18	25	5	41	.427	4th of 4		Art Ross	American
1934–35	26	16	6	58	.604	1st of 4	Lost NHL Semifinals	Frank Patrick	American
1935–36	22	20	6	50	.521	2nd of 4	Lost NHL Quarterfinals	Frank Patrick	American
1936–37	23	18	7	53	.552	2nd of 4	Lost NHL Quarterfinals	Art Ross	American
1937–38	30	11	7	67	.698	1st of 4	Lost NHL Semifinals	Art Ross	American
1938–39	**36**	**10**	**2**	**74**	**.771**	**1st of 7**	**Won Stanley Cup Final**	**Art Ross**	

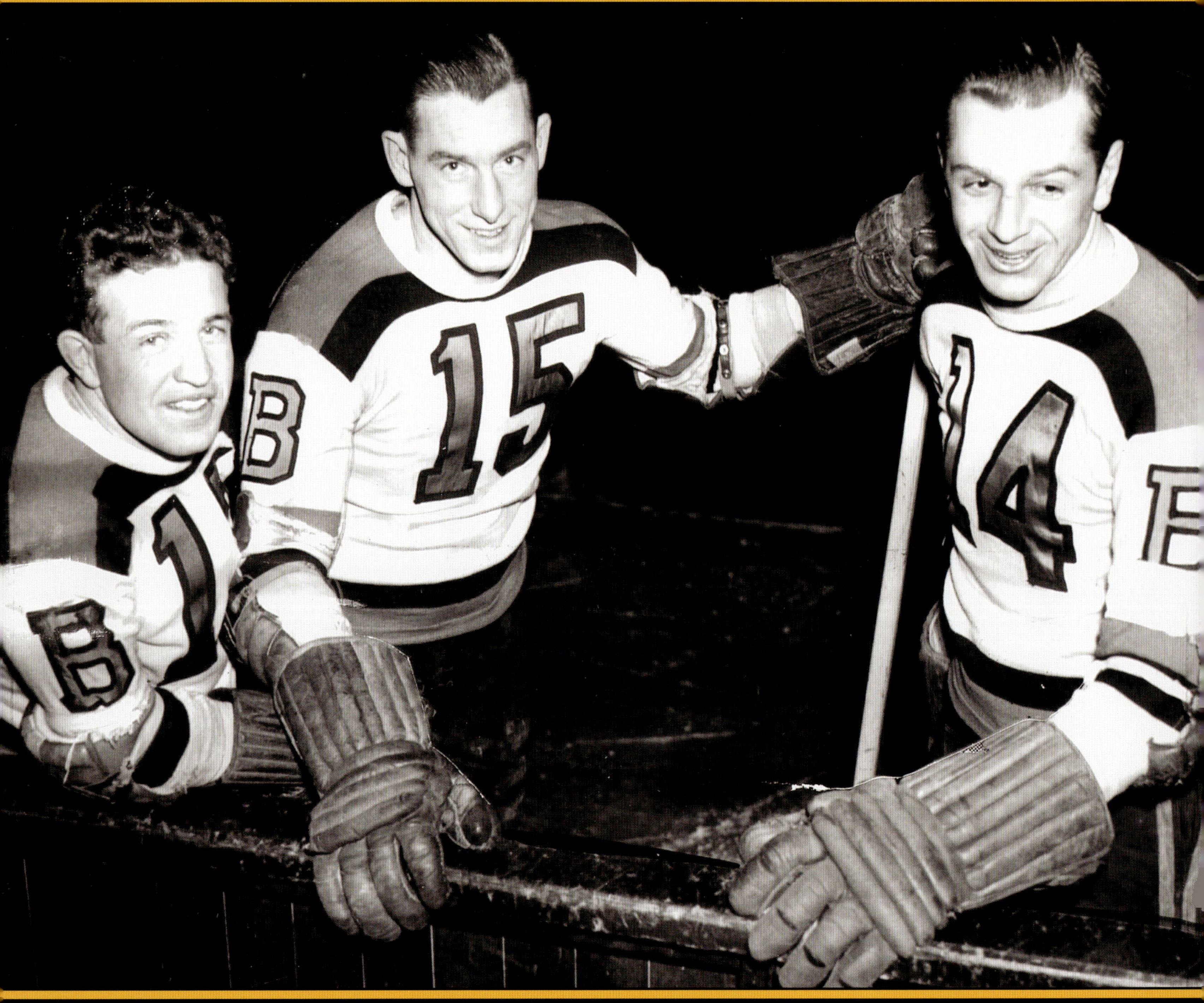

The Kraut Line of (from left to right) Bobby Bauer, Milt Schmidt, and Woody Dumart are shown just prior to their departure for service in the Royal Canadian Air Force in World War II. In their last game prior to entering the service on February 10, 1942, the line collected three goals and eight assists in the Bruins 8–1 victory over the Canadiens. They were carried off the ice by members of both teams. (Collection of The Sports Museum)

1940s

DYNASTY DASHED

You just get established in a business, like hockey, and you have to give it all up. The Japanese bomb Pearl Harbor and a damned war comes along.

—Frank Brimsek, Bruins goaltender

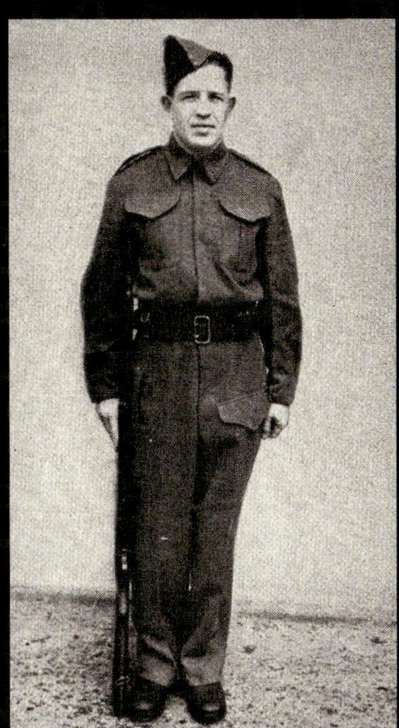
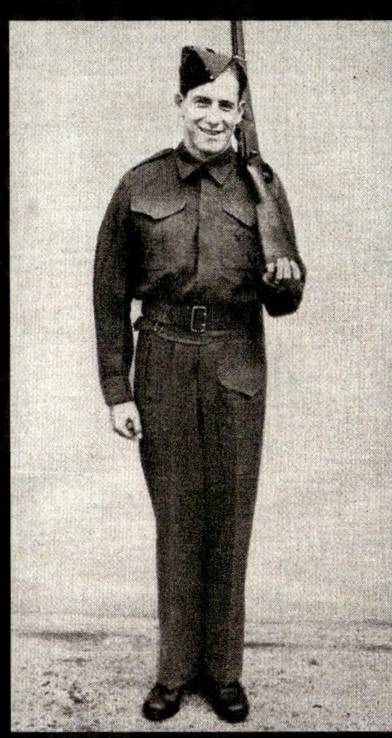
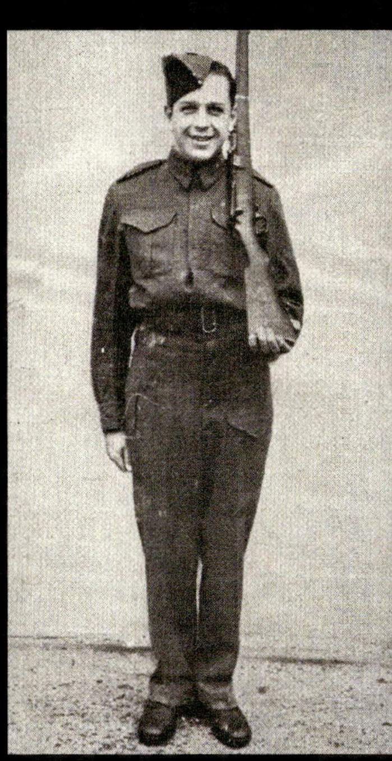

Bobby Bauer, Milt Schmidt, and Woody Dumart in uniform, early 1940s
(Collection of The Sports Museum)

The 1940s began as a golden era for the Bruins. Despite the departure of the legendary Eddie Shore and the retirement of head coach Art Ross, the defending Stanley Cup champions entered the 1939–40 season totally rejuvenated by a group of young stars, led by goaltending sensation Frank Brimsek and linemates Milt Schmidt, Woody Dumart, and Bobby Bauer (all hailing from Kitchener, Ontario, and all from German descent, thus earning them the nickname "the Kraut Line"). All signs pointed to the team reaching dynastic status for the balance of the decade. Alas, global affairs would soon intervene.

In 1940, however, the focus was still squarely on the action on the ice. And the Bruins didn't disappoint, winning their third consecutive Prince of Wales Trophy. Their lineup included the top four scorers in the league, led by Schmidt, Dumart, and Bauer in a league first of linemates securing the top three places in NHL scoring. The season ended in frustration, though, with the New York Rangers spoiling Boston's bid for back-to-back Stanley Cup victories. The tipping point for the Rangers in their 4–2 playoff series win over the Bruins was the superb play of Vezina Trophy winner Dave Kerr, who shut out the Bruins in three games.

The following season, 1940–41, the Bruins regained the upper hand over the Rangers while running up a 23-game unbeaten streak, led by league scoring champ and Hart Trophy winner Bill Cowley. After capturing their fourth straight Prince of Wales Trophy, they successfully battled through an opening playoff series with Toronto that went the distance, concluding with a dramatic 2–1 victory in Game 7 at Boston Garden, courtesy of Mel Hill's winning goal.

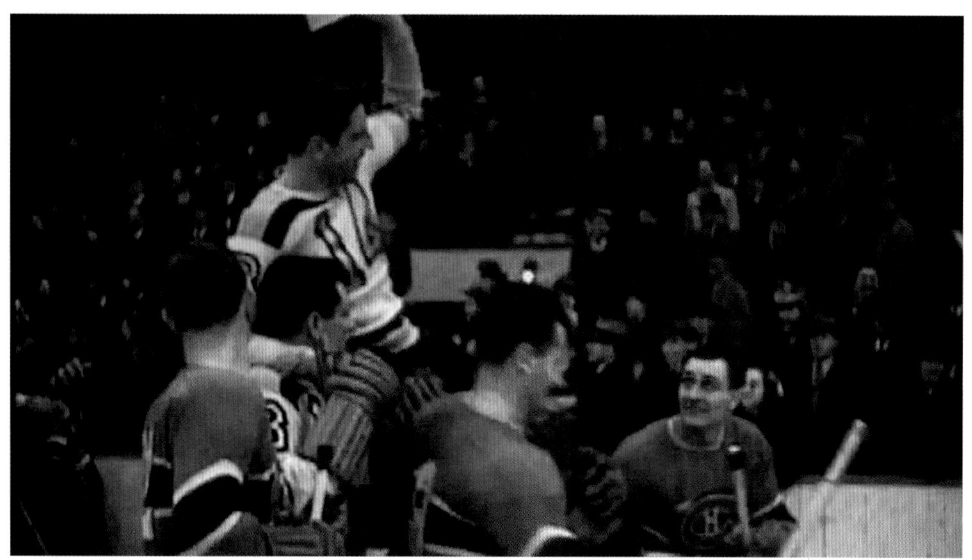

Woody Dumart is carried off the Boston Garden ice by members of both the Boston Bruins and the Montreal Canadiens on the evening of February 10, 1942. At that very same moment on other parts of the Garden ice, Dumart's linemates Milt Schmidt and Bobby Bauer were receiving the same hero's treatment. The occasion was the Kraut Line's last NHL game before leaving for service in the Royal Canadian Air Force. (Photograph from newsreel film in US National Archives)

In the Stanley Cup Final that followed versus the Detroit Red Wings, the Bruins made history by becoming the first team to complete a four-game sweep. It was their second Cup in three years. Surely more championships beckoned.

However, in the 1941–42 season, the Bruins and the entire NHL were utterly changed by the Allies' entry into World War II and the induction of many players to military service for Canada. The Rangers alone lost the services of 19 players. The Bruins nearly matched them, with 17 players heading off to war, including almost all of their stars.

At least the fans sent them off in style. Most notably, on the night of February 10, 1942, in a spontaneous ceremony at Boston Garden that symbolized the solidarity of the war effort, players from both the Bruins and the Canadiens carried all three members of the Kraut Line from the ice on their shoulders at the conclusion of the trio's final game prior to their joining the Royal Canadian Air Force.

For the next few years, the Bruins, despite all of their wartime losses, hung tough, even reaching the Stanley Cup Final in 1942–43 led by Cowley, winner of the Hart Trophy for the second time in three years. Also showcased was the so-called Sprout Line comprised of teenagers Bep Guidolin, Don Gallinger, and Jack Schmidt. It wasn't enough to overcome Detroit in the Final, however, as the Red Wings returned the favor from two years earlier and swept the Bruins in four games.

After missing out on the playoffs altogether in 1943–44 and finishing with a losing record the next season, the Bruins returned to the Stanley Cup Final in 1946 under new coach Dit Clapper (who had inherited the reins from Art Ross). Their 4–1 loss to Montreal represented the last gasp of the powerhouse that had been assembled in the late 1930s and early 1940s by Ross.

For the remainder of the decade, the Bruins were essentially a .500 team and a "one and done" entry in the playoffs. The combination of age and lack of playing time had taken their toll on a group that should have, were it not for the war, won at least two more Stanley Cups during the decade. It remains one of the most pronounced "What Might Have Beens?" in the history of the Boston Bruins.

Frank Brimsek receives his U.S. Coast Guard discharge papers in 1945 after serving for two years during World War II. He resumed his Bruins career in December 1945, and was named a Second Team NHL All-Star in each of the ensuing three seasons. (U.S. Coast Guard photograph, Collection of The Sports Museum)

FRANK BRIMSEK

THE ODDS AGAINST goalie Frank Brimsek were formidable. A native of northern Minnesota, he arrived in Boston in November 1938 as the rare American player in a league comprised almost entirely of Canadians. In addition, he was replacing a franchise legend in Tiny Thompson, whose trade to the Red Wings was considered by Boston sportswriters to be as egregious a transaction as the Red Sox' sale of Babe Ruth to the Yankees nearly 20 years earlier. To make matters worse, Brimsek angered many fans by inheriting Thompson's No. 1 jersey while also insisting on wearing the red pants he had worn as a minor leaguer in Providence.

However, Brimsek quickly answered all the doubts and quelled all the anger. After dropping his first game by a score of 2–0 to Montreal, Brimsek proceeded to earn six shutouts over the next seven games. By season's end, he had achieved the unprecedented feat of being named a First Team NHL All-Star as well as capturing both the Calder Trophy (top rookie) and the Vezina Trophy (top goaltender).

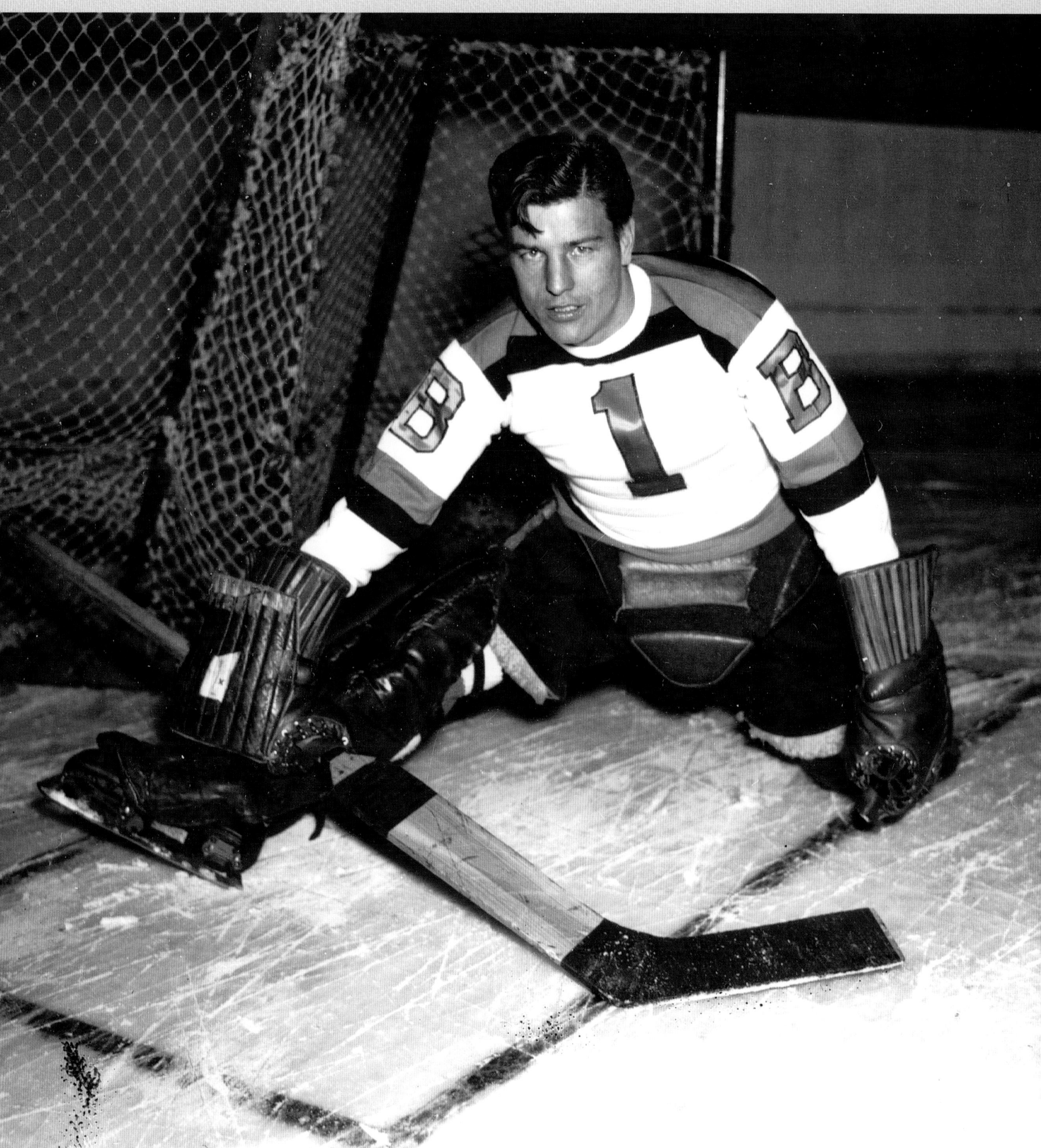

Frank Brimsek was the main man in net for the 1941 Bruins, backstopping the team to their second Stanley Cup in three years. Brimsek would remain a standout for the remainder of the 1940s, finishing top five in voting for the Hart Trophy as NHL MVP in three seasons (1942, 1943, and 1948). (Photograph by Leslie Jones, courtesy of the Boston Public Library)

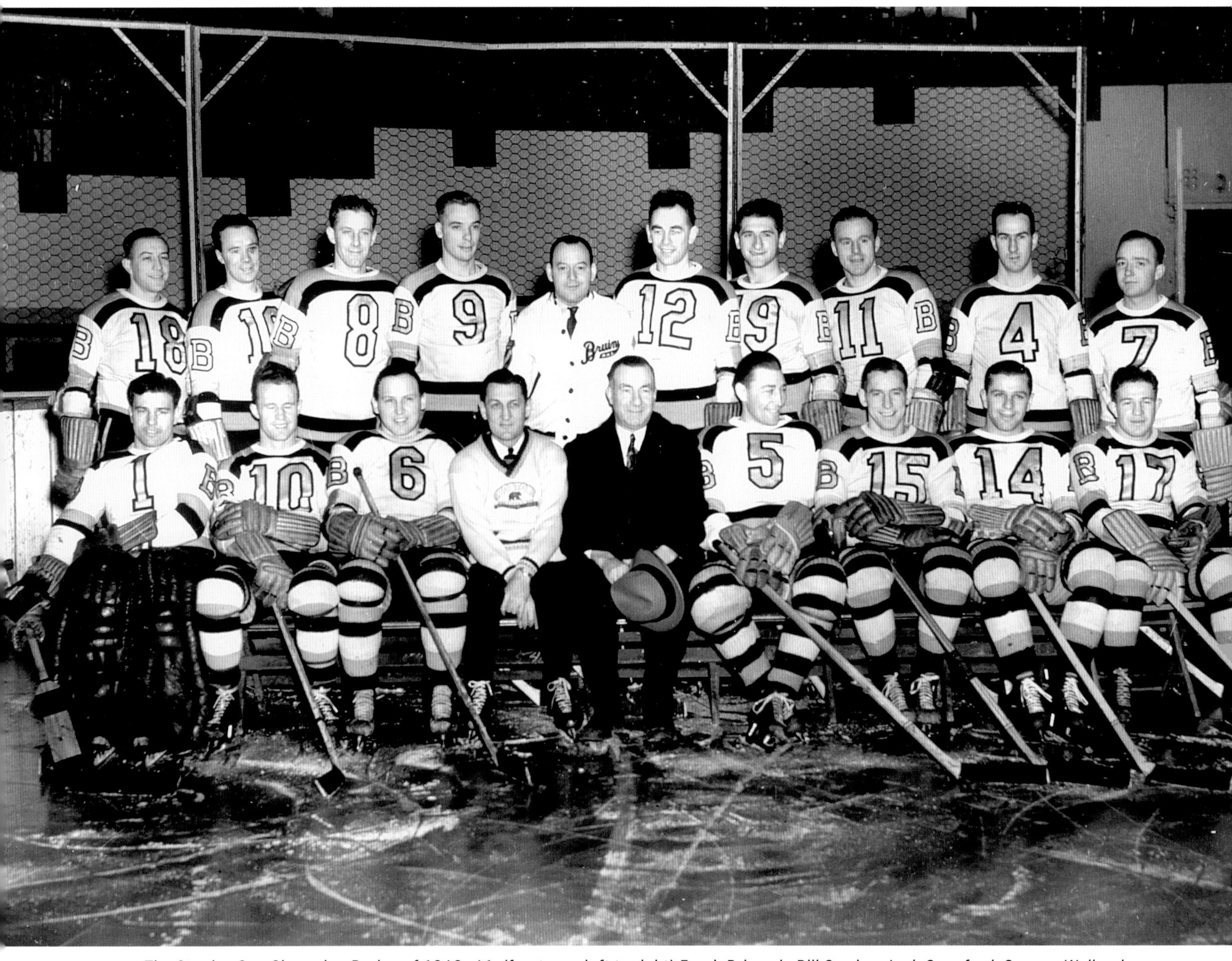

The Stanley Cup Champion Bruins of 1940–41: (front row, left to right) Frank Brimsek, Bill Cowley, Jack Crawford, Cooney Weiland (head coach), Art Ross (general manager), Dit Clapper, Milt Schmidt, Woody Dumart, and Bobby Bauer; (back row, left to right) Art Jackson, Mel Hill, Des Smith, Roy Conacher, Win Green (trainer), Flash Hollett, Jack Shewchuk, Red Hamill, Herb Cain, and Eddie Wiseman. (Photograph by Leslie Jones, courtesy of the Boston Public Library)

He also helped lead the Bruins to their second Stanley Cup, sporting a sparkling 1.50 goals against average in 12 playoff games against New York and Toronto.

Known by the nicknames of "Mister Zero" and "Frigid Frankie" (for his cool demeanor), Brimsek would be named an NHL All-Star for eight of his 10 NHL seasons and capture an additional Vezina Trophy in 1942. He did it with a style that was all his own. "He stood up and often kicked it," teammate Ed Sandford said. "He was unique as a goaltender. An acrobatic kind of a guy."

In 1987, Boston Mayor Ray Flynn was in northern Minnesota canvassing for presidential candidate Michael Dukakis when he walked into a convenience store and introduced himself to the attendant behind the counter, only to learn he was being served by a gentleman who most hockey historians consider to be the best goaltender in Bruins history.

Boston Post | April 13, 1941

BRUINS TAKE STANLEY CUP FINAL, 3 TO 1

Make It Four Straight Victories Over Detroit Red Wings to Set New Series Record

ROSSMEN SCORE THREE GOALS IN WILD SECOND PERIOD TO SEW UP DECISIVE TROPHY GAME

by J.W. Mooney

DETROIT, APRIL 12—The rampaging Boston Bruins tonight set a new Stanley Cup playoff record by turning back the Detroit Red Wings, 3 to 1, to win the highest trophy of the sport in four straight games, a feat that is unprecedented in national hockey history. Outstanding for the Bruins cause tonight was goaltender Frankie Brimsek, who gave a magnificent demonstration of net-minding.

The Bruins had to come from behind and overtake the Wings to bring the series record to Boston. Liscombe fired the goal, halfway through the game and for a time it looked as if that marker might decide the contest, but Flash Hollett drilled the disc past Goalie Mowers of Detroit in the eighth minute of the second period, to tie the count.

A minute later, little Bobby Bauer took a pass from Dutch Schmidt, to put the Boston skaters in front for the first time, and Eddie Wiseman took the strain off the Bruins players by banking the disc into the strings, a few seconds before the second period ended.

One of the smallest crowds in NHL playoff history, 8,125 people attended the windup of the series. The occasion marked the second time in three years the Bruins have won the trophy, and was the first time that a four-out-of-seven final series has been run off in four games.

Right after the game, the Bruins left for Boston by train and are scheduled to arrive home at 8:30 Sunday night.

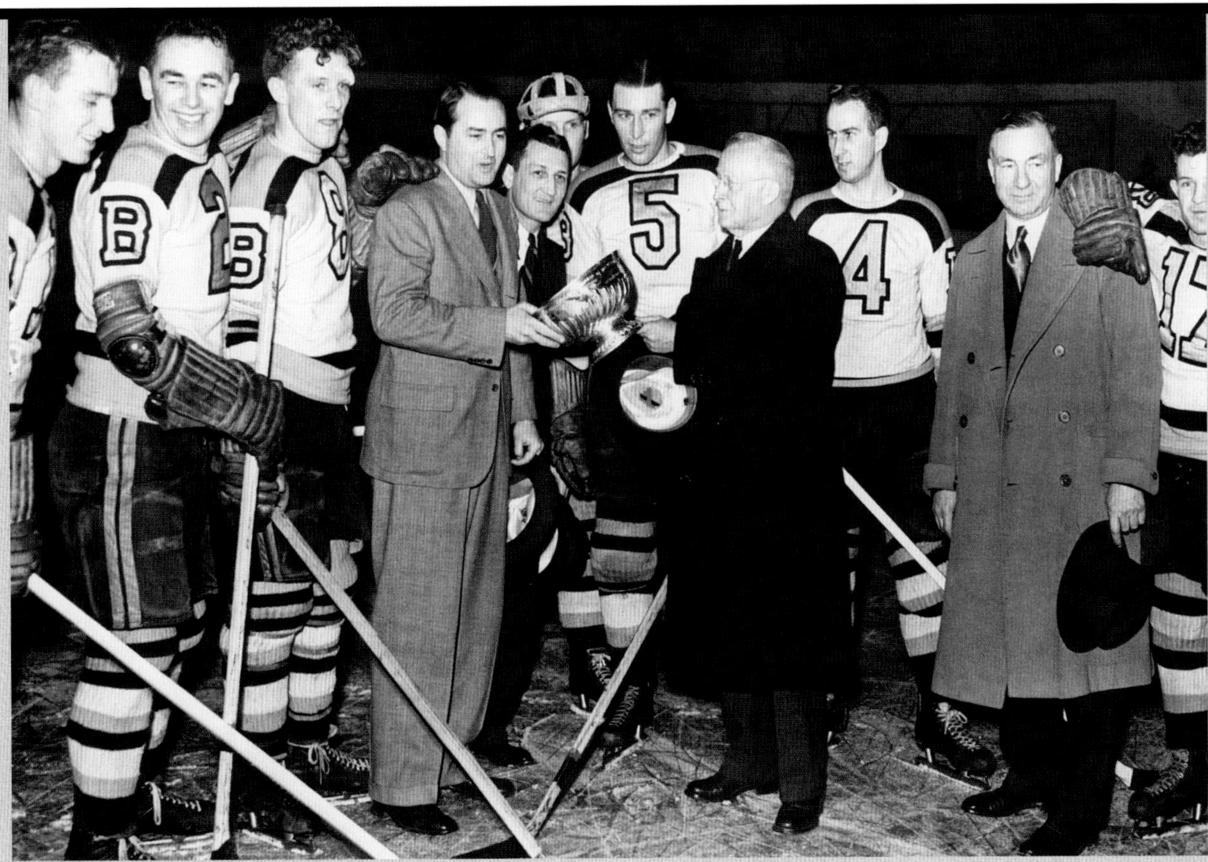

The victorious Boston Bruins are presented the Stanley Cup after sweeping the Detroit Red Wings in the 1941 Stanley Cup Final. The happy group includes (left to right) Milt Schmidt, Flash Hollett (2), Des Smith (8), Bruins president Weston Adams Sr., coach Cooney Weiland, Jack Crawford (obscured in helmet), Dit Clapper (5), NHL president Frank Calder, Herb Cain (4), general manager Art Ross, and Bobby Bauer (17). (Photograph by Bettman/Getty Images)

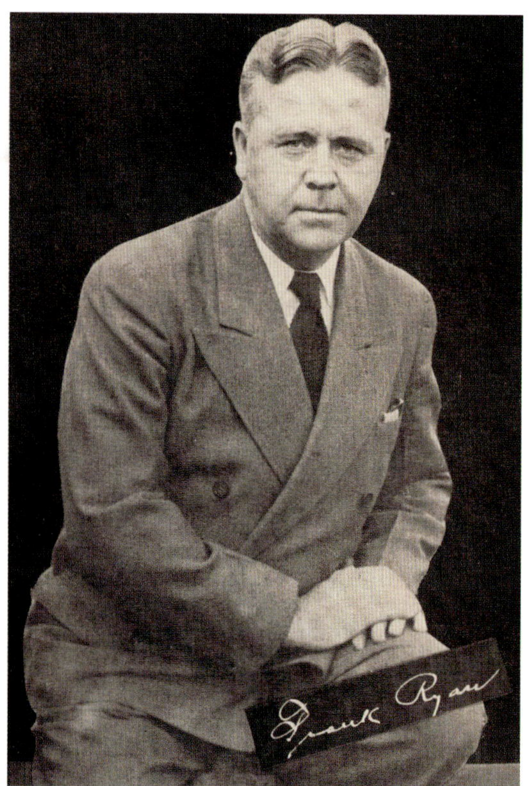

Frank Ryan (above) was the Bruins' first radio broadcaster, starting in the franchise's first year of 1924. He initially called all of the team's home games while recreating road action from telegraph accounts. During intermissions, his brother-in-law provided updates in French for the team's many French-Canadian fans. Ryan was succeeded by Fred Cusick in 1951. (Collection of The Sports Museum)

Your Public Safety Department is taking precautions for your protection in case of

an AIR RAID ALARM

We consider that the safest rule for those attending events in Boston Garden is that in the case of an air raid signal,

THE AUDIENCE REMAIN SEATED

as arrangements have been made for the show or athletic event to continue.

Mass. Committee on Public Safety
J. W. Farley, Executive Director

Following the U.S. entry into World War II in December 1941, the prospect of air raid alarms at Bruins home games was a distinct possibility. (Collection of The Sports Museum)

NOW ON THE AIR
BOSTON BRUINS
ALL HOME GAMES

Bruins broadcast placard, circa 1941. (Collection of The Sports Museum)

BILL COWLEY

IT WAS SAID THAT CENTER Bill Cowley "made more wings than Boeing." Recognized as perhaps the best pure stickhandler of his era, Cowley put up Wayne Gretzky-like numbers in his best season in 1943–44. He averaged 1.97 points per game, a record not broken until 37 years later by Gretzky himself. In fact, the only players in NHL history to average more points per game in a single season are Gretzky and Mario Lemieux. Cowley ranks third. Heady company, indeed, for Mr. Cowley.

Cowley spent much of his career in the shadow of the renowned Kraut Line, but the line he anchored (also featuring right wing Mel Hill) was also instrumental in Boston's Stanley Cup victories in 1939 and 1941. In addition, Cowley captured two Hart Trophies as league MVP in 1941 and 1943.

"He would stick-handle down the ice and zero in on an opposing defenseman," teammate Flash Hollett said in Brian McFarlane's superb history of the Bruins. "He wasn't fast on his feet, but that puck was glued to his stick. Somehow, he seemed to freeze the defenseman in one spot while he cut across into the center. His two wingers—often it was Hill on one side and Roy Conacher on the other—would dart behind the defensemen, who were worried about Cowley. What was he going to do? Well, he knew what he was going to do. He'd feather a pass in between them, right onto the stick of one of his wingers. And they'd be home free. Nobody passed any better than Cowley. He was a pleasure to watch when he made those beautiful passes."

HERB CAIN

IN MANY WAYS, left wing Herb Cain is one of the least appreciated stars in Bruins history. Following a contract dispute with the Canadiens in 1939, he became one of the few players ever traded by the Habs to Boston. Cain fit right in with the defending Stanley Cup champions in Boston, finishing third on the team in goals with 21. The following year, Cain helped the Bruins win their third Stanley Cup. Following the departure of the Kraut Line to active duty in World War II, he and Bill Cowley led the offense, with Cain capturing league scoring honors in 1943–44 while setting an NHL single-season scoring record with 82 points. It would remain a record until the early 1950s, when it was eclipsed by the legendary Gordie Howe.

Despite his scoring prowess, Cain was never a favorite of Art Ross. In later years, it was revealed that Ross had essentially ended Cain's career by refusing to trade him to another NHL team, instead demoting him to Hershey in the American Hockey League.

Of all eligible former players, Cain remains the lone single-season NHL scoring champion not to gain admission to the Hockey Hall of Fame.

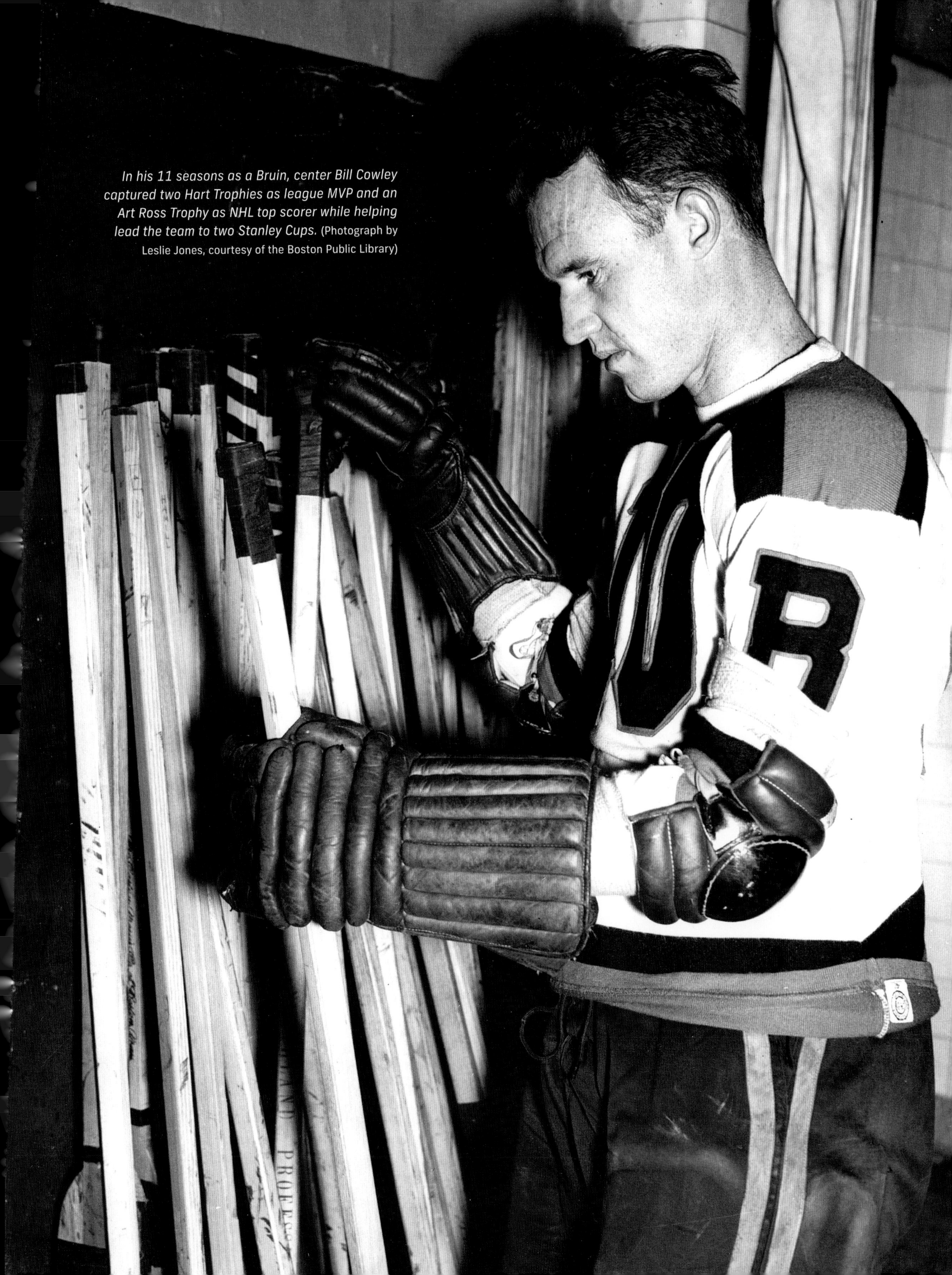

In his 11 seasons as a Bruin, center Bill Cowley captured two Hart Trophies as league MVP and an Art Ross Trophy as NHL top scorer while helping lead the team to two Stanley Cups. (Photograph by Leslie Jones, courtesy of the Boston Public Library)

Boston Post | February 11, 1942

KRAUTS SHINE AS BRUINS WIN, 8-1

Go on Scoring Spree in Last Game— Given Great Ovation by Royal Garden Fans

by J.W. Mooney

The famous Kitchener line known as the Kraut trio wound up their brilliant careers as one of the most noted lines ever in hockey, last night at the Boston Garden, playing their last game for the duration as Bruins members and taking the major part of the 8 to 1 lacing handed Les Canadiens, which was the largest score here of the year and helped keep the Bruins in second position in the National league race.

Steal the Show

Out of the 21 points divided in the point feast for the Bruins, the Krauts split 11 of them to truly make it a night of nights for themselves.

Immediately following the final whistle the teams lined up while the Kitcheners were given their final send-off. The crowd roared its applause for the popular trio soon to see active service with the Canadian Royal Air Force.

Each one of them, Woody Dumart, Milt Schmidt, and Bobby Bauer were presented their pay checks for the remainder of the season and a bonus besides, one they might have received if they had remained around for the series.

Handed "Dog Tags"

Acting Captain Jack Crawford presented his pals with gold identification tags known to the troops as "Dog Tags." Young Art Ross Jr., flight officer of the Royal Air Force, and his younger brother, John, then presented each with a gold chronograph wrist watch used by those in the air service while flying.

Frank Ryan read speeches of appreciation of the Bruin club and Manager Art Ross and in a highly complimentary way, praising all three for their fine sportsmanship and they had the best wishes of all.

It was an impressive scene as both Bruins and Canadiens alike hoisted the popular soldiers on their shoulders for their last exit from the ice where they had so often in their five years with the Boston team entertained so royally to the delight of their thousands of admirers.

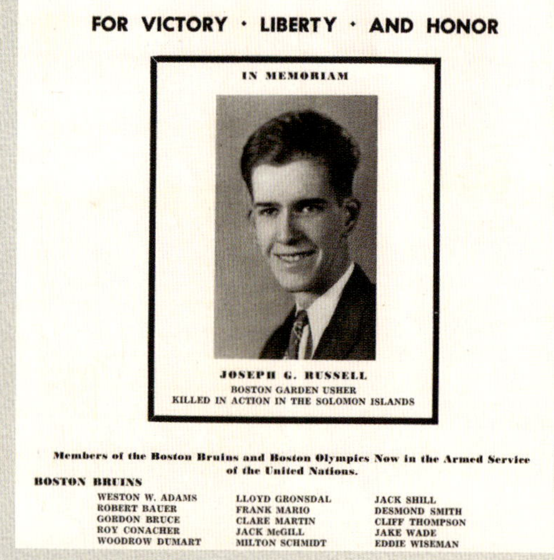

FOR VICTORY · LIBERTY · AND HONOR

IN MEMORIAM

JOSEPH G. RUSSELL
BOSTON GARDEN USHER
KILLED IN ACTION IN THE SOLOMON ISLANDS

Members of the Boston Bruins and Boston Olympics Now in the Armed Service of the United Nations.

BOSTON BRUINS

WESTON W. ADAMS	LLOYD GRONSDAL	JACK SHILL
ROBERT BAUER	FRANK MARIO	DESMOND SMITH
GORDON BRUCE	CLARE MARTIN	CLIFF THOMPSON
ROY CONACHER	JACK McGILL	JAKE WADE
WOODROW DUMART	MILTON SCHMIDT	EDDIE WISEMAN

No NHL team did more to support the war effort than the Bruins, as general manager Art Ross scheduled several games for military affiliated charities. In this notice from a 1943 program, the team listed its personnel in uniform while also paying tribute to Boston Garden usher Joseph Russell, who was killed in action. (Collection of The Sports Museum)

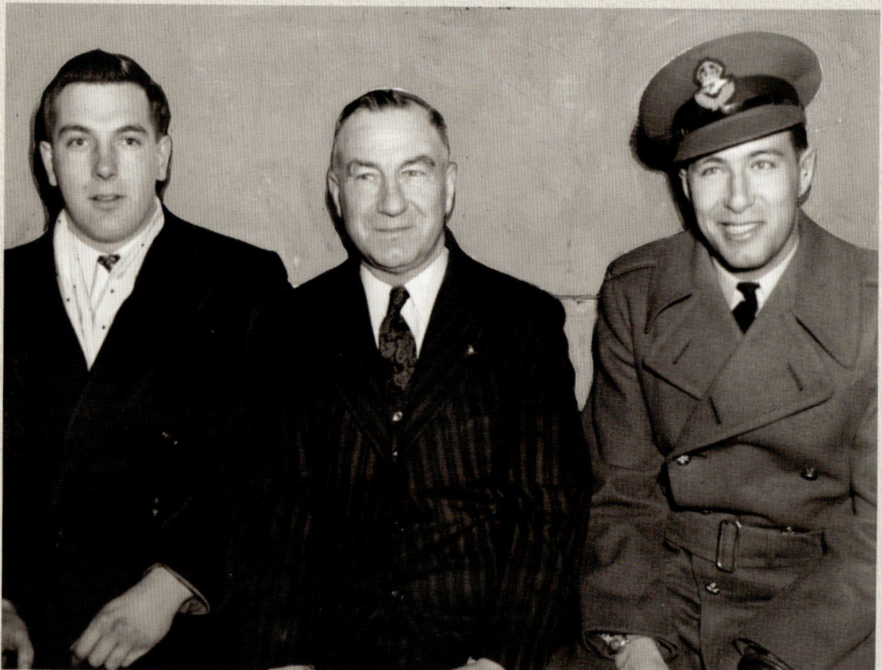

Art Ross poses with sons John and Art Jr. in 1942. Art Jr. had just received his wings from the Royal Canadian Air Force while his brother was still in training to be a pilot. (Collection of The Sports Museum)

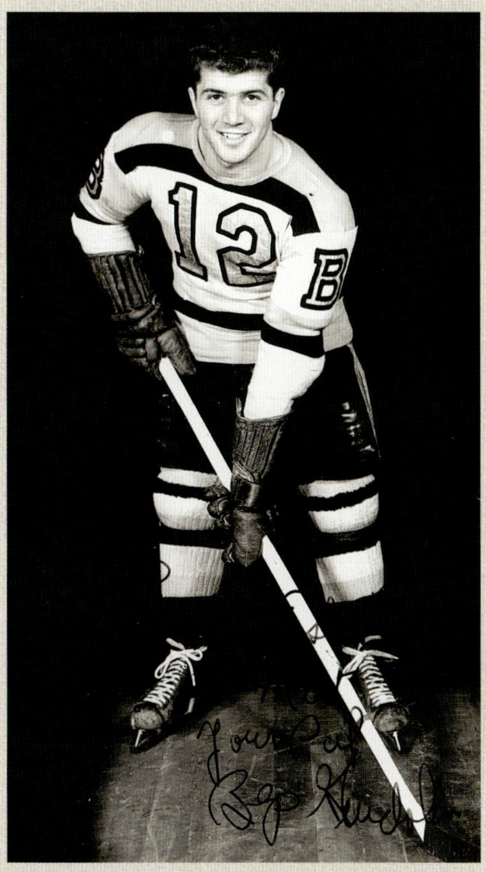

In November 1942, Bep Guidolin became the youngest player in NHL history at the age of 16 years, 11 months. Guidolin was one of a cast of teenagers, older players, and career minor leaguers called up to the big time because of a talent shortage due to World War II. He later coached the Bruins for a season and a half in the early 1970s. (Courtesy of J. Harvey McKenney)

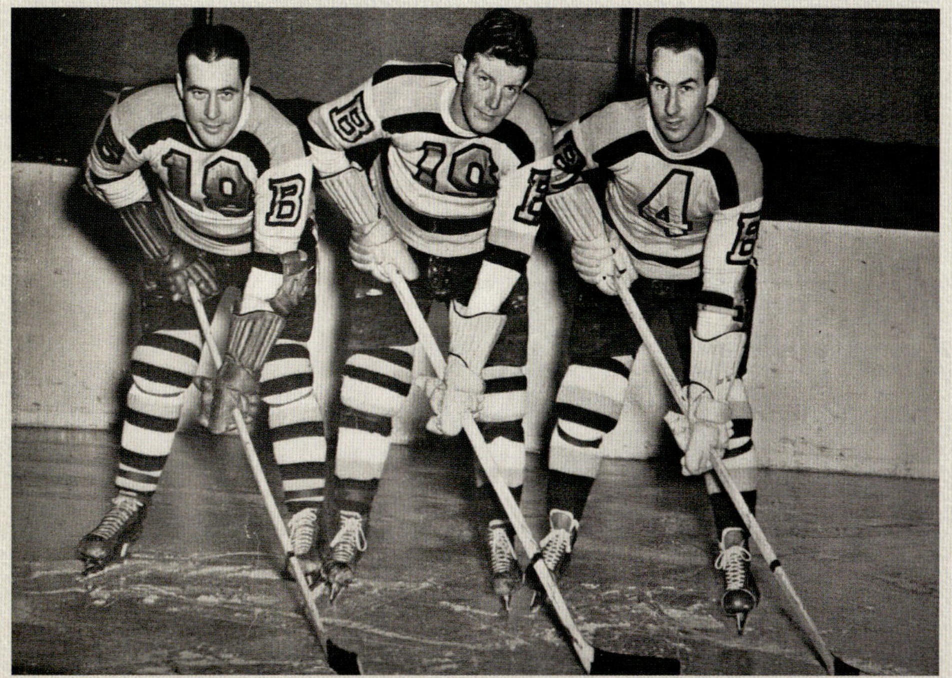

Left wing Herb Cain (No. 4) is shown with linemates Busher Jackson (18) and Murph Chamberlain (19) in 1942. In 1943–44, Cain had a breakout season, winning the Art Ross Trophy while setting the single-season NHL scoring record with 82 points. (Collection of The Sports Museum)

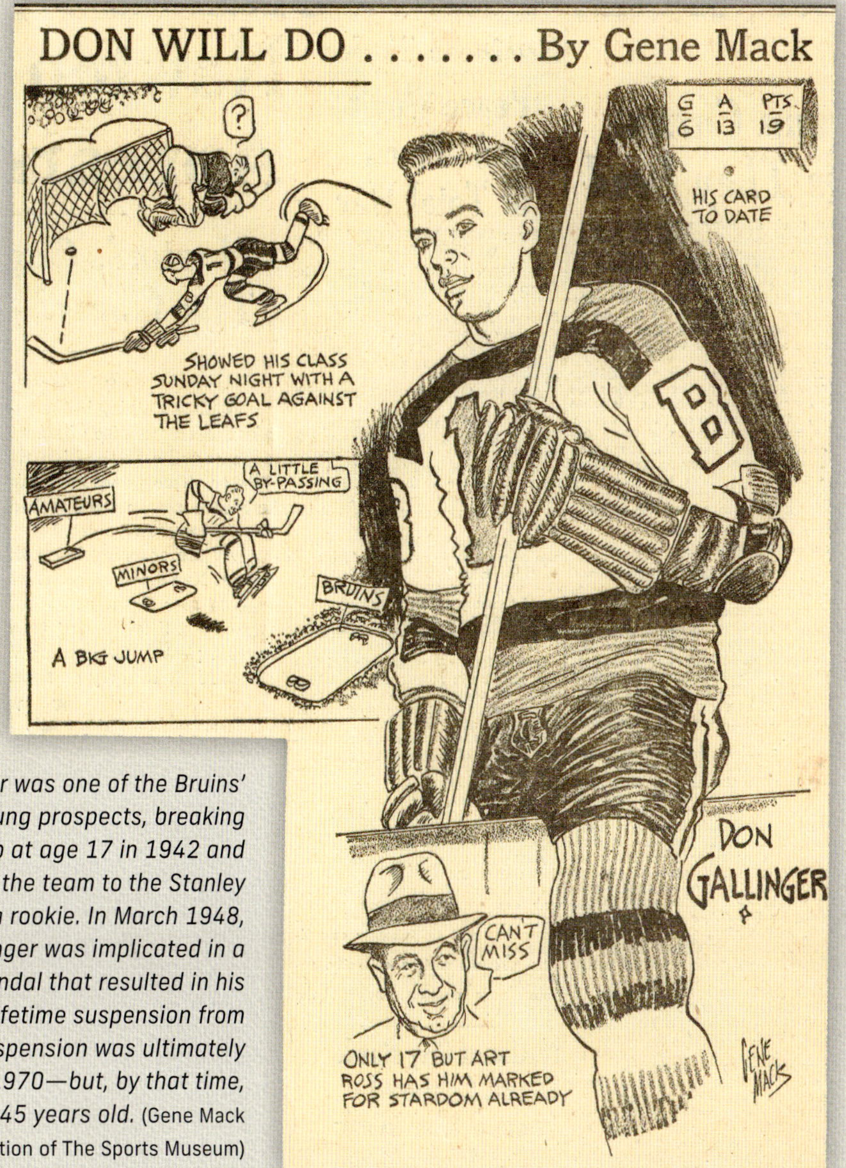

Don Gallinger was one of the Bruins' brightest young prospects, breaking into their lineup at age 17 in 1942 and helping lead the team to the Stanley Cup Final as a rookie. In March 1948, though, Gallinger was implicated in a gambling scandal that resulted in his receiving a lifetime suspension from the NHL. The suspension was ultimately lifted in 1970—but, by that time, Gallinger was 45 years old. (Gene Mack illustration, Collection of The Sports Museum)

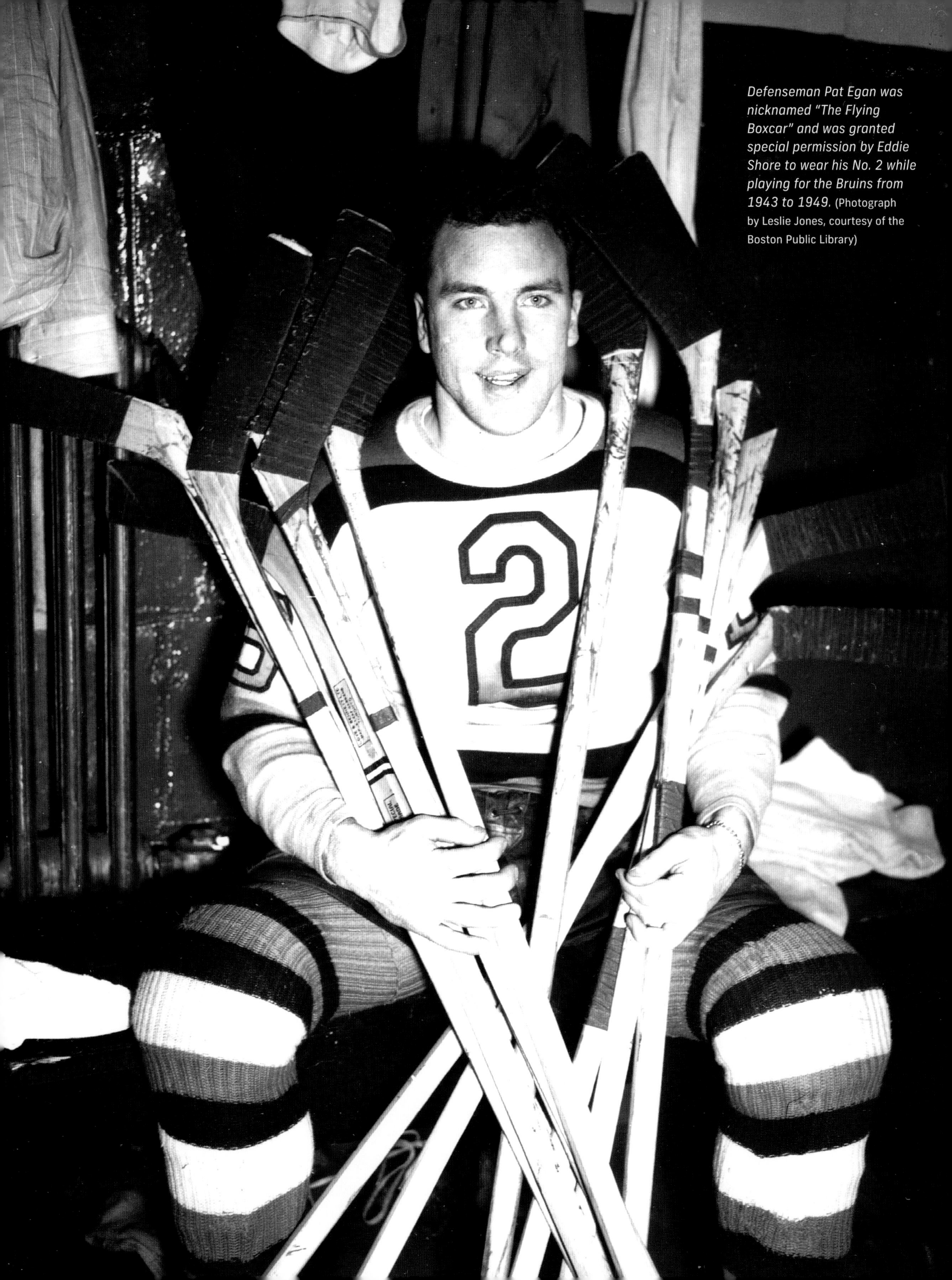

Defenseman Pat Egan was nicknamed "The Flying Boxcar" and was granted special permission by Eddie Shore to wear his No. 2 while playing for the Bruins from 1943 to 1949. (Photograph by Leslie Jones, courtesy of the Boston Public Library)

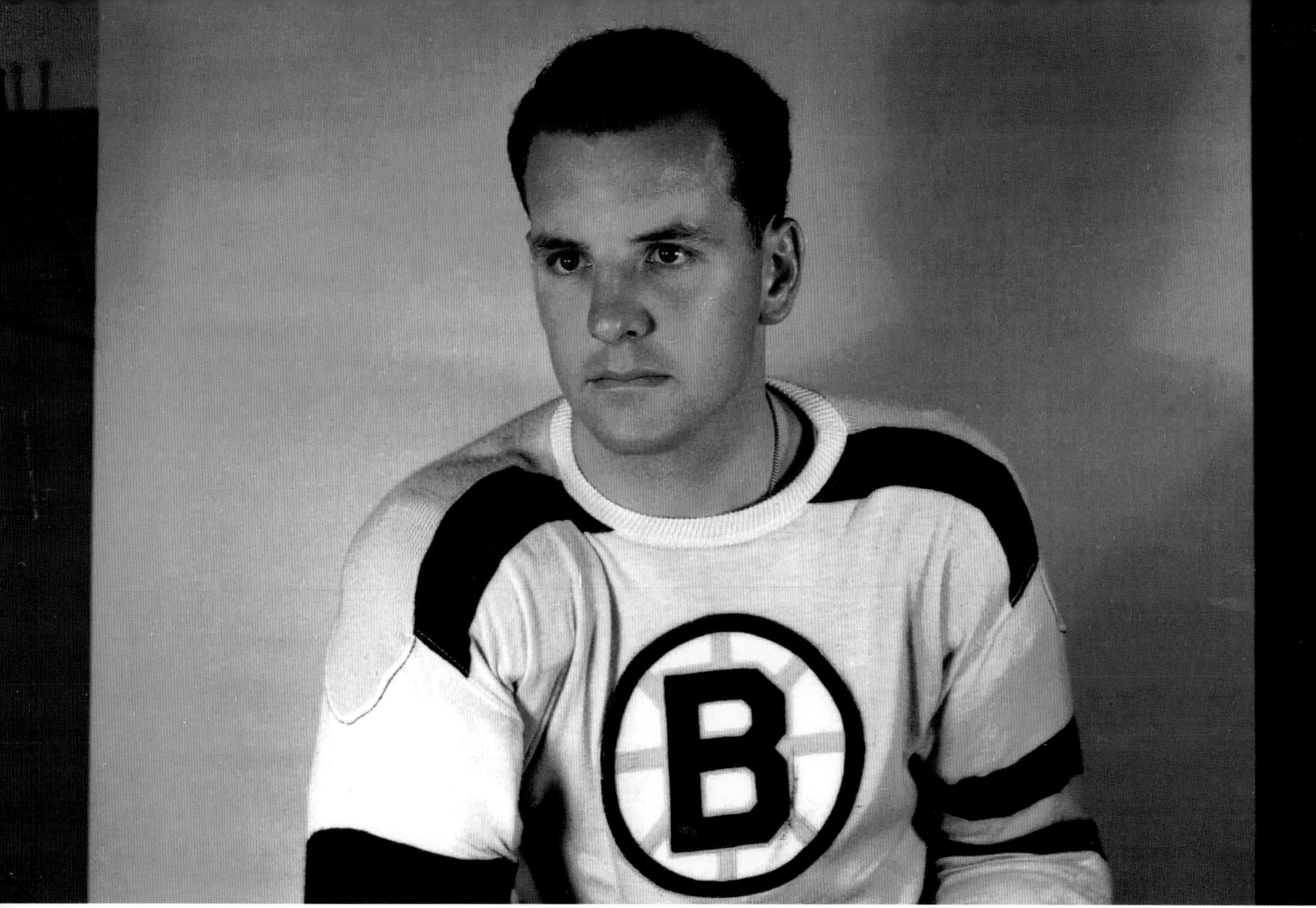

After forward Ed Sandford led his St. Michael's College team to victory in the 1947 Memorial Cup, he was quickly signed by Art Ross. During his eight-year Bruins career, he scored 94 goals. Sandford served as Bruins captain for the 1954–55 season. (Collection of The Sports Museum)

ED SANDFORD

LEFT WING ED SANDFORD joined the Bruins in the autumn of 1947, not long after he had led St. Michael's College to a junior Memorial Cup championship in Canada. "I was very lucky to go from juniors to the pros," said Sandford in a 2022 interview for this book. "Looking back, I probably should have gone to the minors, the American Hockey League, and worked my way up. But, at that time, they were short on people and rebuilding. I was kind of filling in a spot for them."

Over the next eight seasons with the Bruins (1947–48 to 1954–55), Sandford more than just filled a roster spot, becoming one of the team's top scorers and helping lead the Bruins to seven playoff appearances, including a trip to the Stanley Cup Final in 1953.

Sandford's success in the NHL may have brought him attention, even fame—but, as with his contemporaries across the league, that didn't necessarily translate into financial security. "I think most of us did work [non-hockey jobs] in the summertime," said Sandford. "Our salaries weren't that large—at least mine wasn't. But we did what we wanted to do. We wanted to play pro hockey—and that was part of it."

In 1954, Sandford succeeded Milt Schmidt as team captain. Sandford was traded to the Red Wings in 1955 in a nine-player deal that brought Terry Sawchuk to Boston. After his retirement as a player, Sandford was a Boston Garden and then a TD Garden fixture for many years as an off-ice official for the NHL.

"I was always proud to say that I played for the B's," Sandford said. "I was scouted by them and I played for them. I eventually became the captain of the team. It was a place that I grew fond of.... And I still like to see them play and cheer them on. I'm very proud of them and proud to say that I was a member of the club."

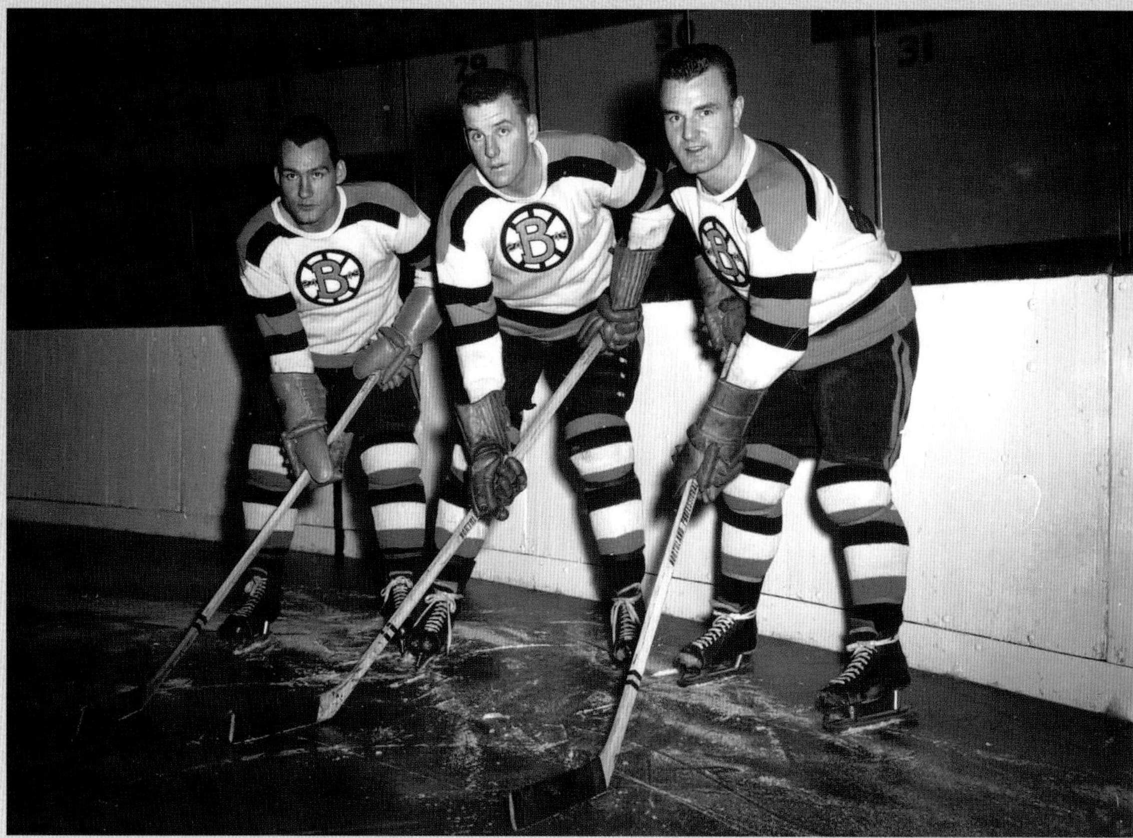

Linemates (left to right) Grant Warwick, Ed Sandford, and Pete Babando at Bruins training camp in September 1948. (Photograph by Leslie Jones, courtesy of the Boston Public Library)

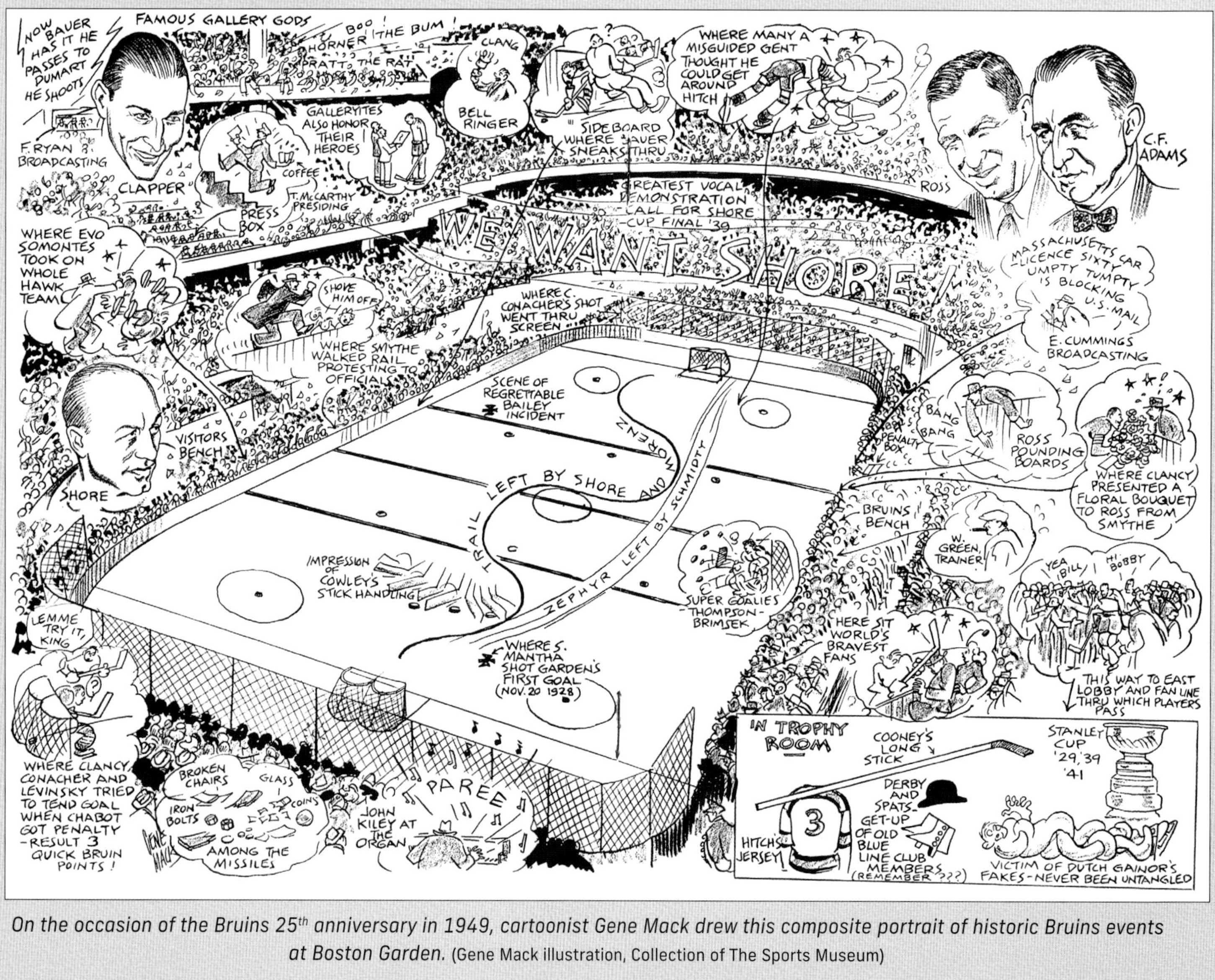

On the occasion of the Bruins 25th anniversary in 1949, cartoonist Gene Mack drew this composite portrait of historic Bruins events at Boston Garden. (Gene Mack illustration, Collection of The Sports Museum)

THE ORIGINAL SIX

THE 1940S MARKED the beginning of the "Original Six" Era, with NHL teams planted in just a half dozen cities: Boston, New York, Chicago, Detroit, Toronto, and Montreal. The era began in 1942 and would last until 1967, when expansion would come at long last to the NHL.

In the heyday of the six-team NHL, the league was nothing less than the single most exclusive athletic club ever assembled in North American sports. As a showcase for the 116 best skaters on the planet, the "Original Six" was an oak-paneled boardroom in which even the lowliest team such as the Rangers could boast of Hall of Famers like Andy Bathgate and Harry Howell. In contrast, Montreal and Detroit routinely had 14 or 15 Hall of Famers on their rosters at any given time. Whole lines and defensive pairings awaited future enshrinement, and nearly every power play was consecrated with the entire ice surface occupied by soon-to-be certified immortals, officials included.

Teams played each other several times a month in a competitive slam dance that doubled as a serial drama, in which hits and high sticks were never forgiven or forgotten by players or fans alike. A slash or spear delivered at the Olympia was reciprocated with a hook or trip at the Garden. No exceptions. Teammates and opponents were literally blood brothers and often recounted their battles over beer and bridge games while sharing a rail car traveling through the northern sections of the United States and southeastern Canada.

Those long train trips invariably helped forge close bonds between teammates. "We played every weekend," Ed Sandford recalled. "We would play at home on Thursday and then travel Friday to Montreal, Detroit, or Toronto, play Saturday night, get the train back home and then play the following night, Sunday, at home. Every weekend was three or four games in those three or four days.... We were together a lot more than players are today."

Time it was, and what a time it was...and the Boston Bruins were right in the thick of it.

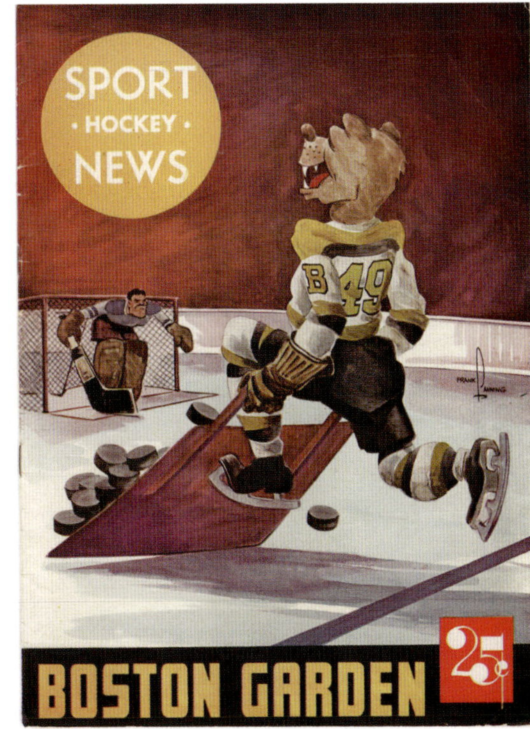

Bruins program from 1948–49 season. (Collection of Richard A. Johnson)

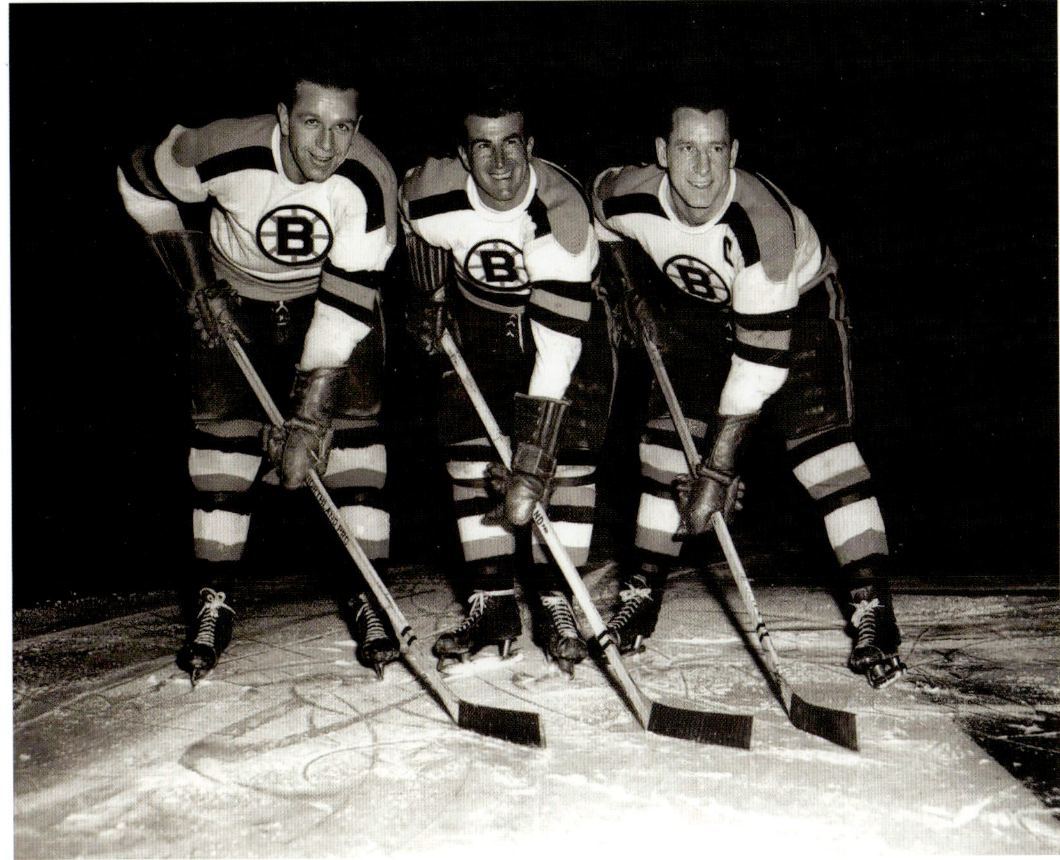

Boston Red Sox shortstop Johnny Pesky poses between Woody Dumart (left) and Milt Schmidt (right) at a Bruins practice in the late 1940s. In his youth, Pesky was a stickboy for the Portland Buckaroos of the Pacific Coast Hockey League. As an adult, he was adept enough to skate with his friends on the Bruins. (Photograph by Leslie Jones, courtesy of the Boston Public Library)

THE BEST OF ENEMIES: THE ART ROSS–CONN SMYTHE FEUD

by Eric Zweig

ART ROSS SERVED the Boston Bruins from the team's inception in 1924 until his retirement in 1954. During those 30 years, Ross worked as the Bruins' coach, general manager, and vice president—often holding all three jobs at the same time. When Charles Adams had announced he would bring an NHL team to Boston on September 30, 1924, he credited Ross as the main reason he got involved.

"I would never have aligned myself so strongly with professional hockey but for the fact that I secured Art Ross to manage the new team," said Adams for a story in the *Boston Globe* the next day. "Ross represents all that is high class in hockey, Boston fans will like Art Ross."

Over the years, Ross was generally beloved by the fans and respected by sportswriters, who dubbed him "Uncle Arthur." But he was a gruff uncle. In a Bruins publication from 1946–47, Ross is described as a man of raw courage and fierce spirit, but also as being "not the most tactful and sympathetic man, even in the NHL." The words most often used to describe him in the press during his years in Boston were "dour" and "sarcastic."

A Hall of Fame player before the formation of the NHL, Ross could be rough on his own men. Many Bruins stars—including Eddie Shore, Cooney Weiland, Bill Cowley, and Herb Cain—ended their time in Boston barely speaking to their boss. But the battles for which Art Ross is best known are part of the feud that existed for years between him and his Toronto rival, Maple Leafs owner Conn Smythe. Stories of their run-ins are legendary...and many of them may even be true!

One story has Ross planting a couple of longshoremen behind Smythe at a game in Boston to try and goad him into a fight. Another has Smythe giving Leafs star King Clancy a bouquet of roses to deliver to Ross (who was suffering from hemorrhoids at the time) with a note written in Latin telling him where he could stick them!

In Smythe's autobiography (*If You Can't Beat 'Em in the Alley*, written with Scott Young and published shortly after Smythe's death in November 1980), he writes with glee about another NHL executive, Red Dutton of the New York Americans, beating up Ross at an NHL governor's meeting in the late 1930s—although there's no proof it actually happened.

Toronto sportswriter Bill Roche, in *The Hockey Book* (1953), quotes longtime Montreal Canadiens owner Leo Dandurand recalling a different incident involving Ross and Smythe at an NHL meeting on September 26, 1936. A few weeks before, a horse that Smythe owned was involved in a doping scandal at Saratoga. Smythe and his trainer would later be exonerated, but the NHL governors didn't know that yet and were all very quiet as they awaited Smythe's late arrival at their meeting. "Smythe finally came in and sat down," remembered Dandurand. "Ross, with a perfectly straight face, spoke up: 'Mr. President, I insist that a saliva test of all those present be taken before proceeding any further with the business at hand!'"

Dandurand said the laughter almost blew down the walls, "and the man who got the biggest bang out of the episode was Smythe."

One has to wonder.

Many would claim the feud between Ross and Smythe was played up to increase ticket sales. It probably did, but the two men definitely had a hate-on. "[W]e detest each other," Smythe told Boston sportswriter George C. Carens in 1933. "The feeling is mutual."

The animosity between Ross and Smythe rarely spilled over onto the ice. The Ace Bailey Incident late in 1933, when Eddie Shore knocked down the Toronto right wing from behind and fractured his skull, ending his career (and nearly his life), is one of the darkest moments in NHL history. With that noted exception, however, there was rarely anything especially heated or sordid between the Bruins and the Maple Leafs on the ice. The strong feelings and grudges were all in the executive suite.

But where did the bad blood come from?

Over the years, Ross said little about the feud in public, but Smythe said plenty. He seemed to think it all began during Boston's first NHL season, when the Bruins were struggling and Smythe mocked the team while he was in town coaching the University of Toronto against Boston College, Dartmouth, and Harvard. Art Ross's son, John Ross, felt the feud started when his father encouraged the New York Rangers to fire Smythe after he had put together the original roster when that team entered the NHL for the 1926–27 season. In the 1933 interview with Carens, Smythe didn't say that Ross was behind his ouster in New York, but did offer that, "When I joined the National Hockey League, Ross told me a college coach would not last in big league company. He said he'd run me out of the league in a year and a half."

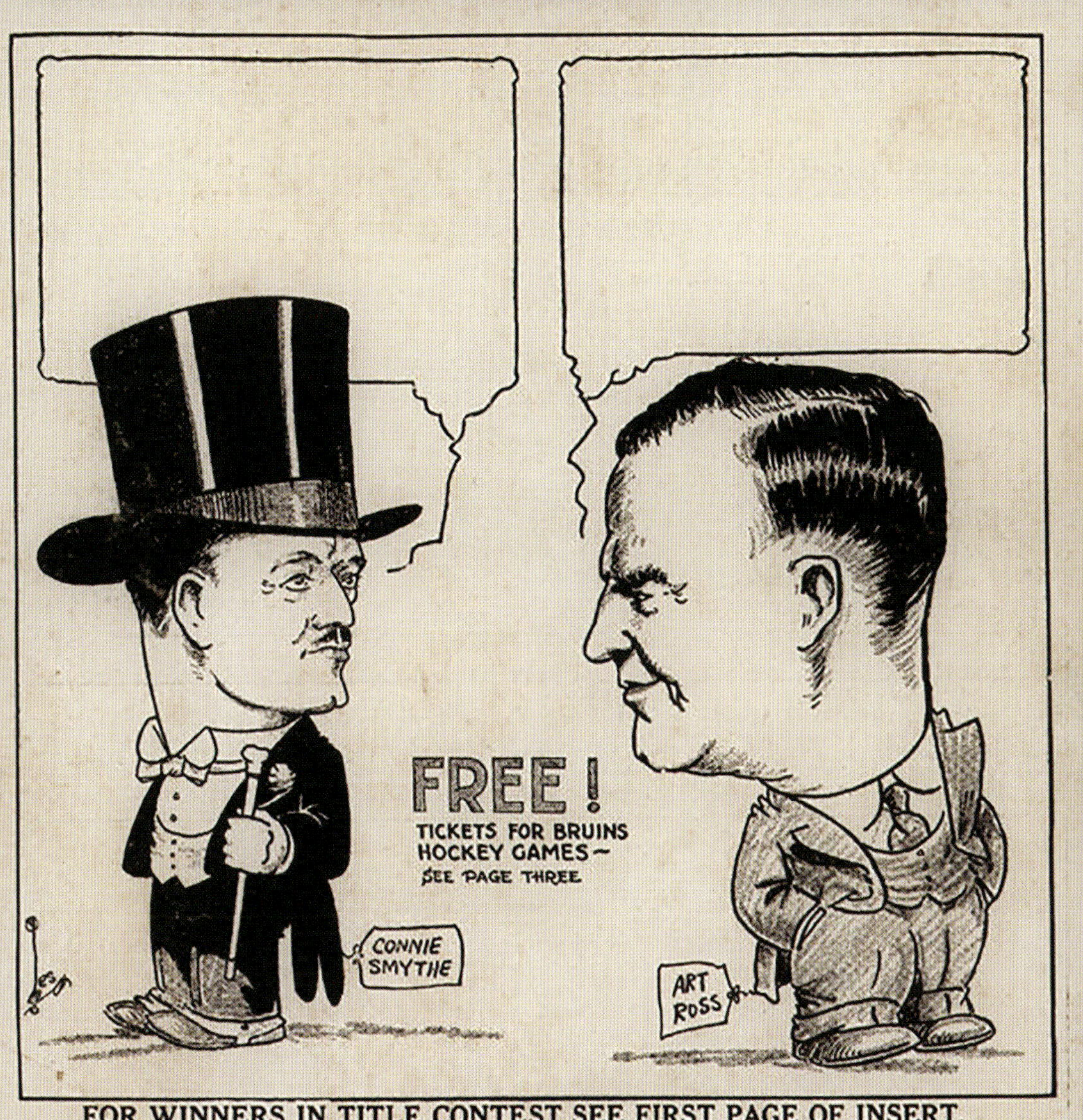

The heated rivalry between Maple Leafs owner Conn Smythe and Bruins general manager Art Ross inspired a contest in which Boston fans were asked to submit cartoon captions for a chance to win tickets. (Collection of The Sports Museum)

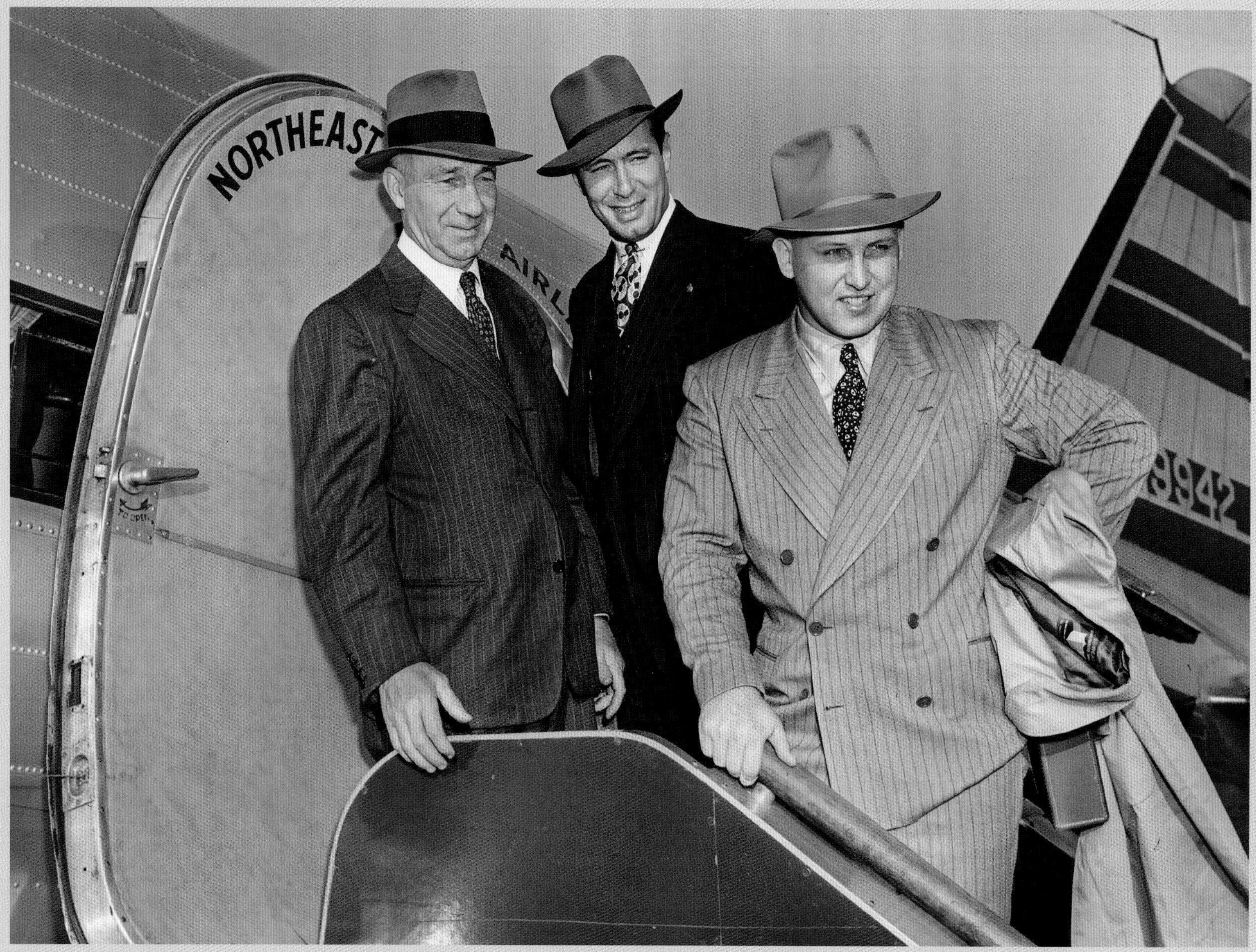

Bruins coach and general manager Art Ross, his son Art Ross Jr., and longtime Boston defenseman Jack Crawford (left to right) board a plane for Montreal in October 1945. The wartime service of Art's two sons—John and especially Art Jr., a pilot who escaped from a German POW camp—helped thaw his icy relationship with Maple Leafs owner Conn Smythe. (Northeast Airlines Photograph, Collection of The Sports Museum)

Other stories claim the feud began when Ross convinced Smythe to purchase a washed-up Sailor Herbert from the Bruins during the 1927–28 season, or the following year when Ross snatched Boston native George Owen from Toronto after the Maple Leafs had convinced him to go pro.

However it started, Smythe was grudgingly willing to admit in his autobiography that Ross, "along with his stubborn, insulting, devious way of dealing with people," did have "unlimited courage." And yet, "every place Ross and I met, we fought."

The last great blowup in the Ross-Smythe feud came in mid-December 1939. The Bruins were coming off a Stanley Cup season, but Smythe was angry at what he perceived to be their defense-first strategy in a 1–1 tie in Toronto on December 14. Arriving in Boston ahead of a Leafs game there on December 19, Smythe descended on the *Boston Globe* office "spouting fire and brimstone." He blasted the Bruins, saying: "They're still the champions, aren't they? Everybody calls them champions? Why can't they play like champions?" He then took out an ad that appeared above his signature in the *Globe* that evening:

ATTENTION, HOCKEY FANS!
If you're tired of seeing the kind of hockey
the Boston Bruins are playing
COME TO THE GARDEN TONIGHT
and see a real hockey club,
The TORONTO MAPLE LEAFS

The Bruins won that night in front of a crowd of 14,107 that was the largest of the season. Even so, Ross demanded that Smythe be fined $1,000 for his unbecoming conduct. Smythe was still worked up about it 11 years later, telling a reporter from *Life* magazine, "Can you imagine that? I put money in their pockets and they want to fine me." Discussion of a fine was dismissed at the next NHL meeting, but a motion was passed censuring both Ross and Smythe for their unseemly bickering over the years.

By this time, the Second World War was under way. The United States wouldn't become involved until after the bombing of Pearl Harbor on December 7, 1941, but Art Ross's sons, Arthur and John, had been born in Montreal. They lived in Boston, but both returned to Canada to enlist in the Royal Canadian Air Force. Smythe, a World War I veteran who would soon reenlist for World War II, was impressed.

"I was a little sorry about having been on [Ross] all the time when his sons came up and joined the RCAF," he'd write. "We weren't so hard on one another after that."

Indeed, when Art Ross died on August 5, 1964, perhaps the most touching tribute was a simple telegram sent to the Boston Garden offices:

SORRY TO HEAR THE OLD BRUIN WARRIOR HAS GONE ALONG. GIVE MY DEEPEST SYMPATHY TO HIS FAMILY. REGARDS. CONN SMYTHE

Eric Zweig is a bestselling Canadian author who has written nearly 50 books about sports and sports history since 1992. He worked from 1996 to 2018 with Dan Diamond & Associates, the official publisher of the NHL.

BOSTON BRUINS (1940–1949)

Season	W	L	T	PTS	PTS%	Finish	Playoffs	Coach
1939–40	31	12	5	67	.698	1st of 7	Lost NHL Semifinals	Cooney Weiland
1940–41	**27**	**8**	**13**	**67**	**.698**	**1st of 7**	**Won Stanley Cup Final**	**Cooney Weiland**
1941–42	25	17	6	56	.583	3rd of 7	Lost NHL Semifinals	Art Ross
1942–43	24	17	9	57	.570	2nd of 6	Lost Stanley Cup Final	Art Ross
1943–44	19	26	5	43	.430	5th of 6		Art Ross
1944–45	16	30	4	36	.360	4th of 6	Lost NHL Semifinals	Art Ross
1945–46	24	18	8	56	.560	2nd of 6	Lost Stanley Cup Final	Dit Clapper
1946–47	26	23	11	63	.525	3rd of 6	Lost NHL Semifinals	Dit Clapper
1947–48	23	24	13	59	.492	3rd of 6	Lost NHL Semifinals	Dit Clapper
1948–49	29	23	8	66	.550	2nd of 6	Lost NHL Semifinals	Dit Clapper

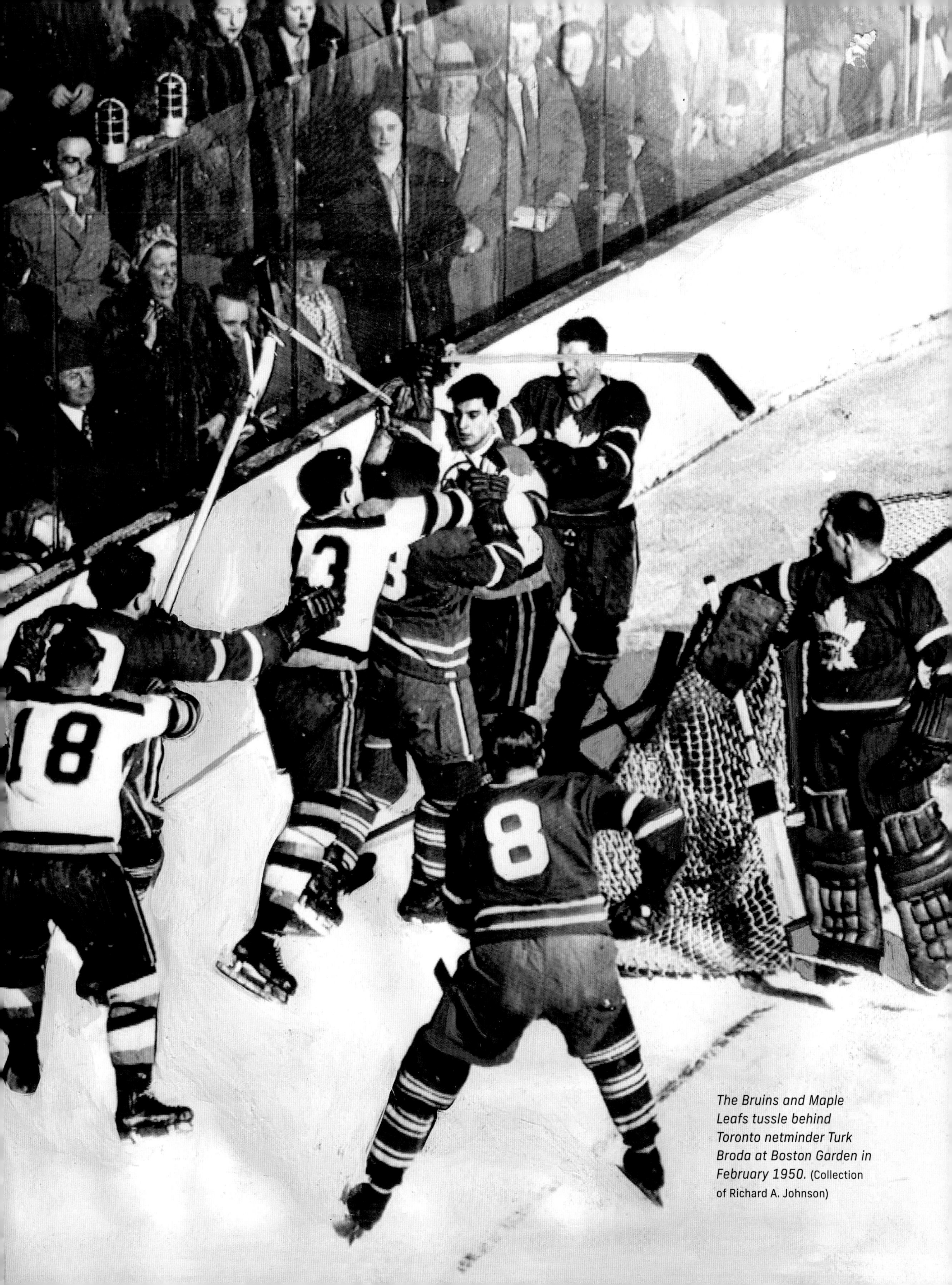

The Bruins and Maple Leafs tussle behind Toronto netminder Turk Broda at Boston Garden in February 1950. (Collection of Richard A. Johnson)

A FLAGSHIP FRANCHISE

Win or lose, Boston fans seem to get more fun out of hockey than fans in any other city. But they like their hockey simple and as tough as possible.

—Peter Gzowski, *Maclean's Magazine*, 1958

People didn't like to come and play in Boston. The style that Boston had was a rough and tumble one. We were very physical.

—Don McKenney, Bruins center (1954–1963)

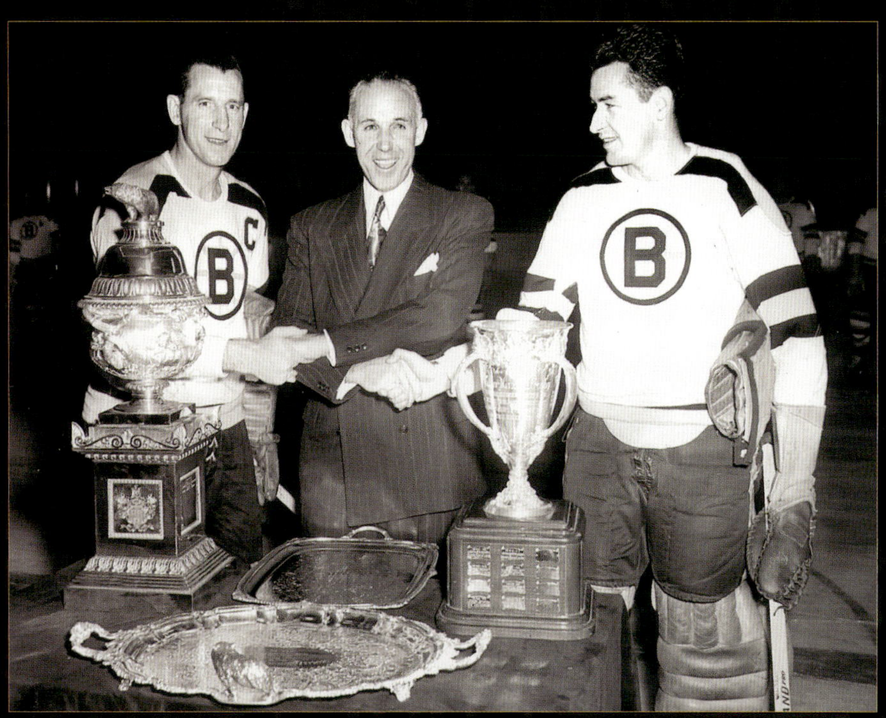

In October 1950, NHL president Clarence Campbell presents the C.F. Adams Memorial Trophy (outstanding Bruins player at home games) to Milt Schmidt (left) and the Calder Trophy (NHL rookie of the year) to Bruins goalie Jack Gelineau (right) at Boston Garden. (Collection of The Sports Museum)

In many ways, the 1950s were the most challenging decade in franchise history. The team entered the decade having only recently bid farewell to such future Hall of Famers as Dit Clapper, Bobby Bauer, Bill Cowley, and Frank Brimsek. The 1950 squad finished out of the playoffs for the first time in six years in the first season of the NHL's new 70-game schedule. In 1951, led by new coach Lynn Patrick and Hart Trophy winner Milt Schmidt, the Bruins made it back to the postseason only to lose to the Maple Leafs in the five-game Stanley Cup Semifinals.

The franchise was also on shaky financial ground, with attendance dropping to an all-time low. The Bruins were averaging only 7,800 fans per home game at the beginning of the 1951–52 season, down from an average of 11,500 in their Stanley Cup season of 1941 (representing a whopping 33 percent decline). In fact, nearly every NHL team experienced an almost identical financial downturn during the early 1950s. The shortfall of competitive balance resulting from the lack of

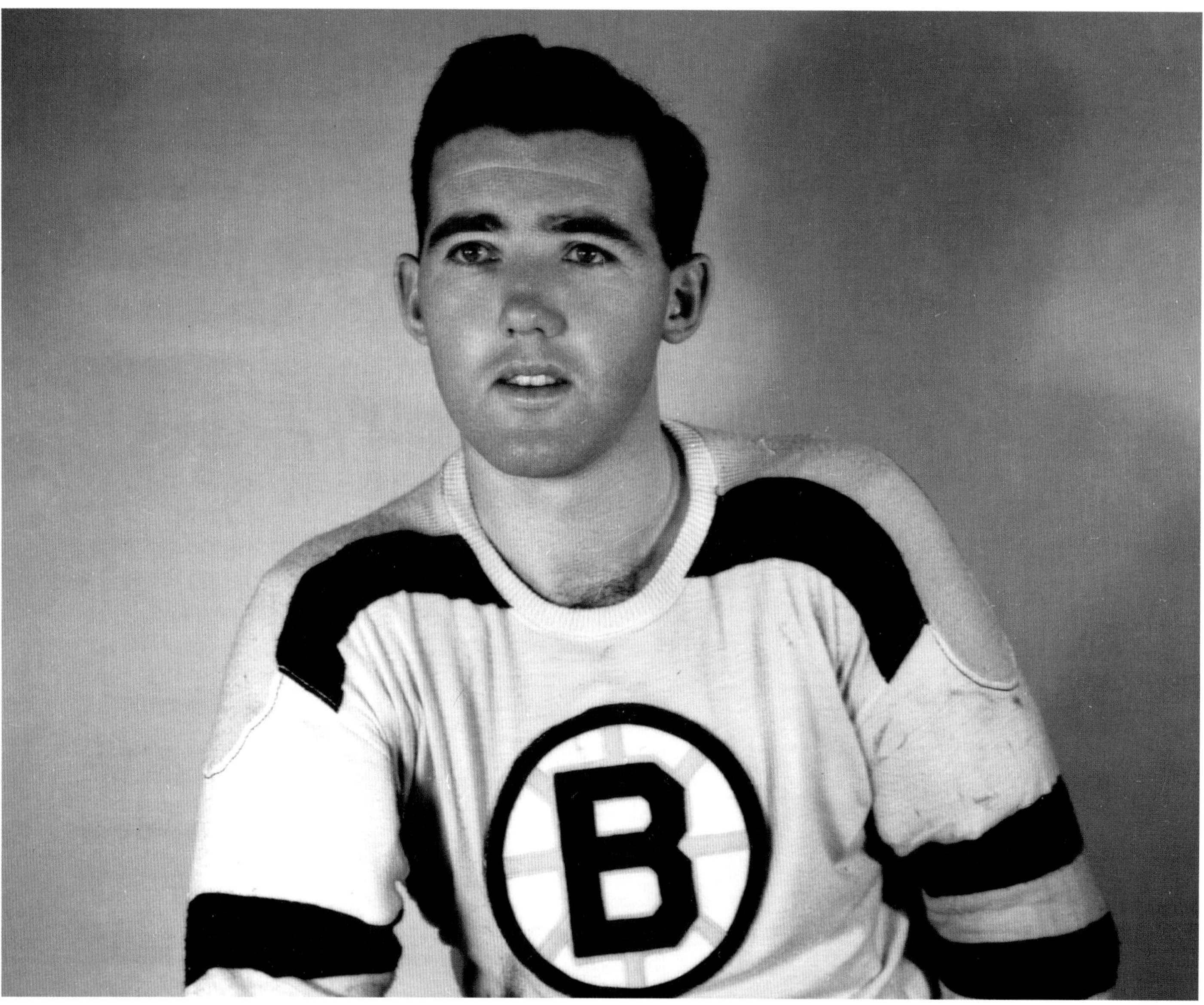

Johnny Peirson was a superb right winger who averaged more than 20 goals per season in the half dozen seasons between 1948 and 1954. He later became known for his expert color commentary during Bruins games broadcast on Channel 38 (WSBK-TV) in the 1970s and 1980s. (Photograph by Al Ruelle, Collection of The Sports Museum)

revenue-sharing with visiting teams (the Bruins led the NHL in road attendance yet never saw a dime) plus the counter-attraction presented by the influx and sudden impact of television proved a major challenge.

The team's renaissance began back on the ice in the spring of 1952, when the Bruins gave the Canadiens all they could handle—and then some—in the Stanley Cup Semifinals. The series captured the spirit of the Bruins in this era in a multitude of ways. First, they surpassed all expectations by bouncing back from consecutive losses in the first two games to lead the series, three games to two. Alas, they would end up falling to the more talented Canadiens, losing in overtime in Game 6 at Boston Garden and then by a score of 3–1 in Game 7 in Montreal.

The heartbreaking defeat in the series finale was the result of one of the most famous goals in NHL history, courtesy of Montreal legend Maurice "Rocket" Richard. Stunned and bleeding from a collision with Bruins forward Leo Labine, Richard emerged from the Canadiens locker room with four minutes left in regulation of a 1–1 game and convinced coach Dick Irvin to allow him one more shift. Seconds later, he made an electrifying rush through the Bruins defense and slipped the puck under Bruins goalie Sugar Jim Henry to give the Habs a 2–1 lead. The roar from the Montreal Forum crowd was reported to be the loudest in the history of the famed arena, and their team never looked back, adding an insurance goal to clinch victory in one of the hardest-fought playoff series in NHL history.

It was the 1953 Bruins team, however, that really turned the fortunes of the franchise around with a dramatic Stanley Cup Semifinals victory over the heavily

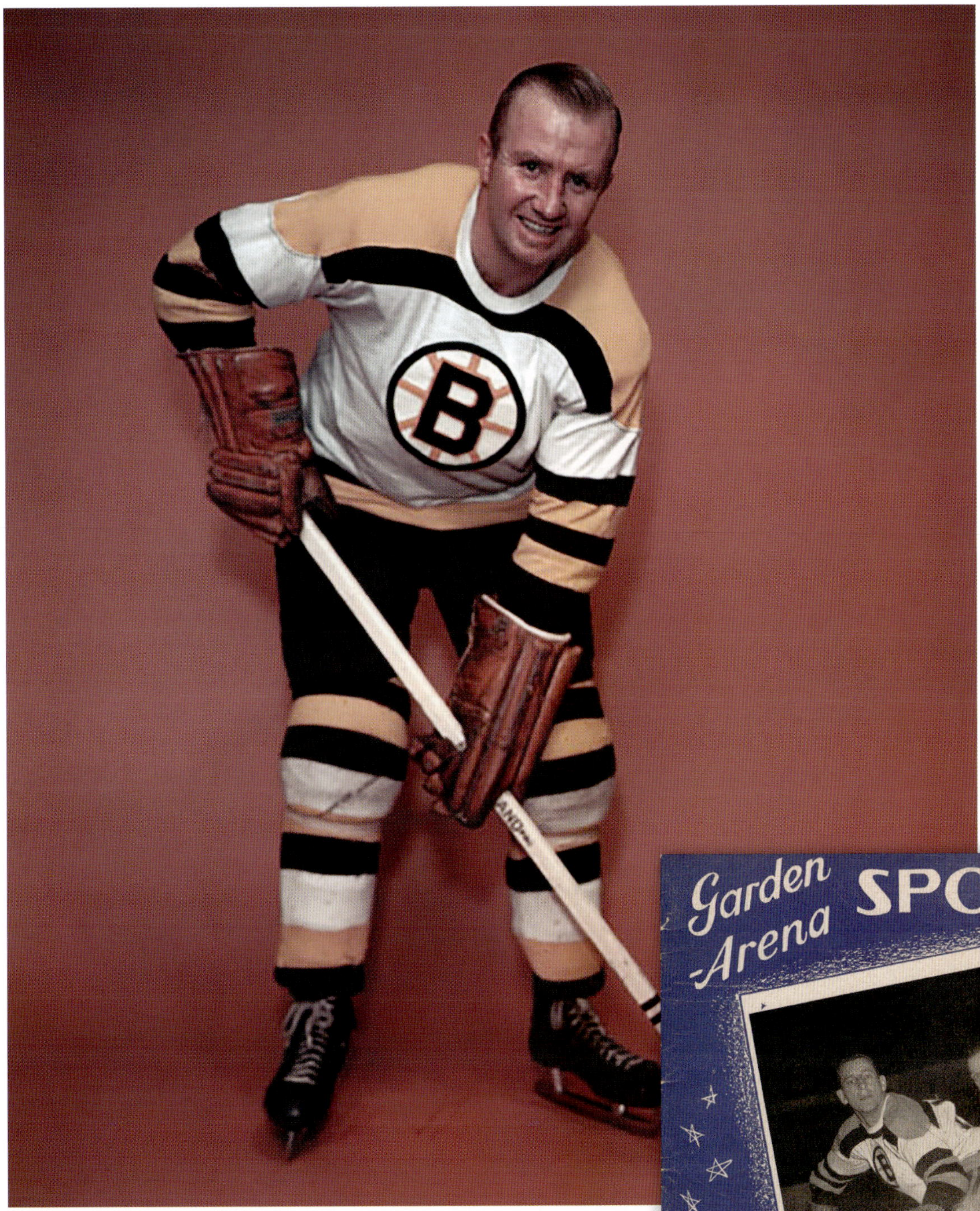

Hall of Famer Bill Quackenbush was one of the NHL's first great offensive defensemen. He also won the Lady Byng Trophy as a Detroit Red Wing in a season where he wasn't called for a single penalty. Quackenbush skated for the Bruins from 1949 to 1956, twice being named an NHL All-Star during his tenure in Boston. (Photograph by Weekend Magazine/Louis Jaques/Library and Archives Canada/e002505701)

On the occasion of Milt Schmidt–Woody Dumart Night on March 18, 1952, the duo's former linemate Bobby Bauer came out of retirement to play in his first NHL game in five years. Bauer returned in style, scoring a goal and assisting on Schmidt's 200th career goal. (Collection of Richard A. Johnson)

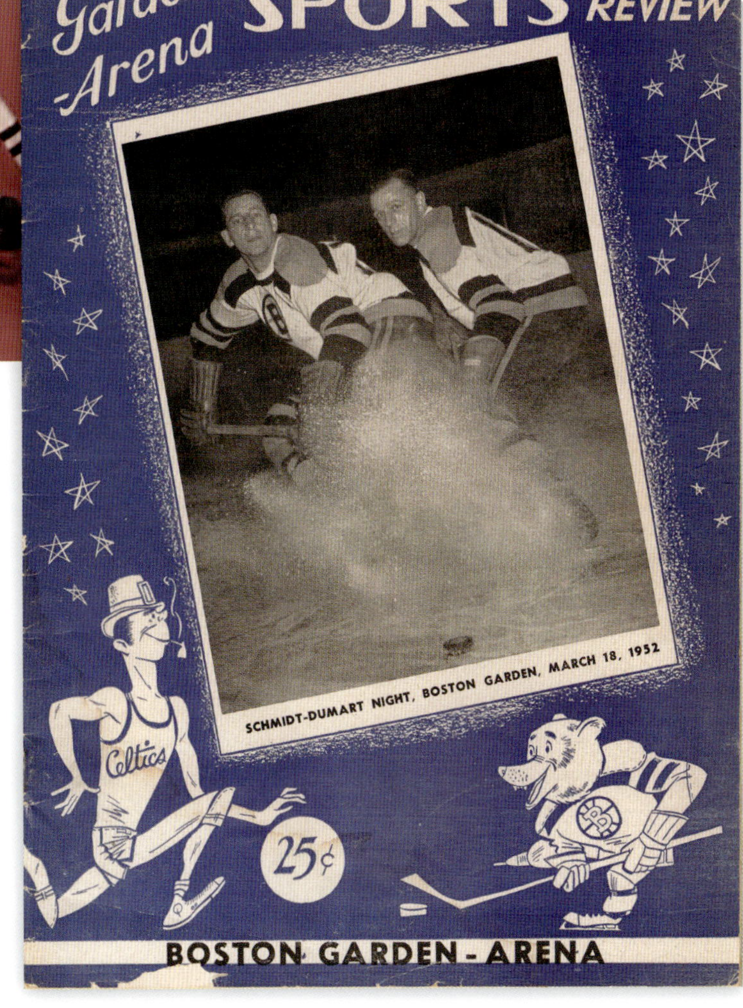

favored Detroit Red Wings. In that series, Boston more than justified its reputation as a hockey hotbed. Prior to the decisive Game 6 at Boston Garden, the only tickets available were 35 single tickets, each with a face value of 80¢—prized ducats that were reportedly later offered by scalpers for $4.00 apiece.

The magic number of 13,909—representing a full house—soon became a regular statistic for nearly every home game for the balance of the decade. The Bruins overachieved while reaching the playoffs for eight of 10 years in the 1950s. That included three trips to the Stanley Cup Final in 1953, 1957, and 1958, each time against the Canadiens.

So close and yet so far for a team with all the heart of the teams of Shore and Clapper but none of their luck. Brighter days lay ahead for a team that had restored its preeminence in Boston through sheer will—and, along the way, cemented its status as one of the flagship franchises in the NHL.

WALTER BROWN

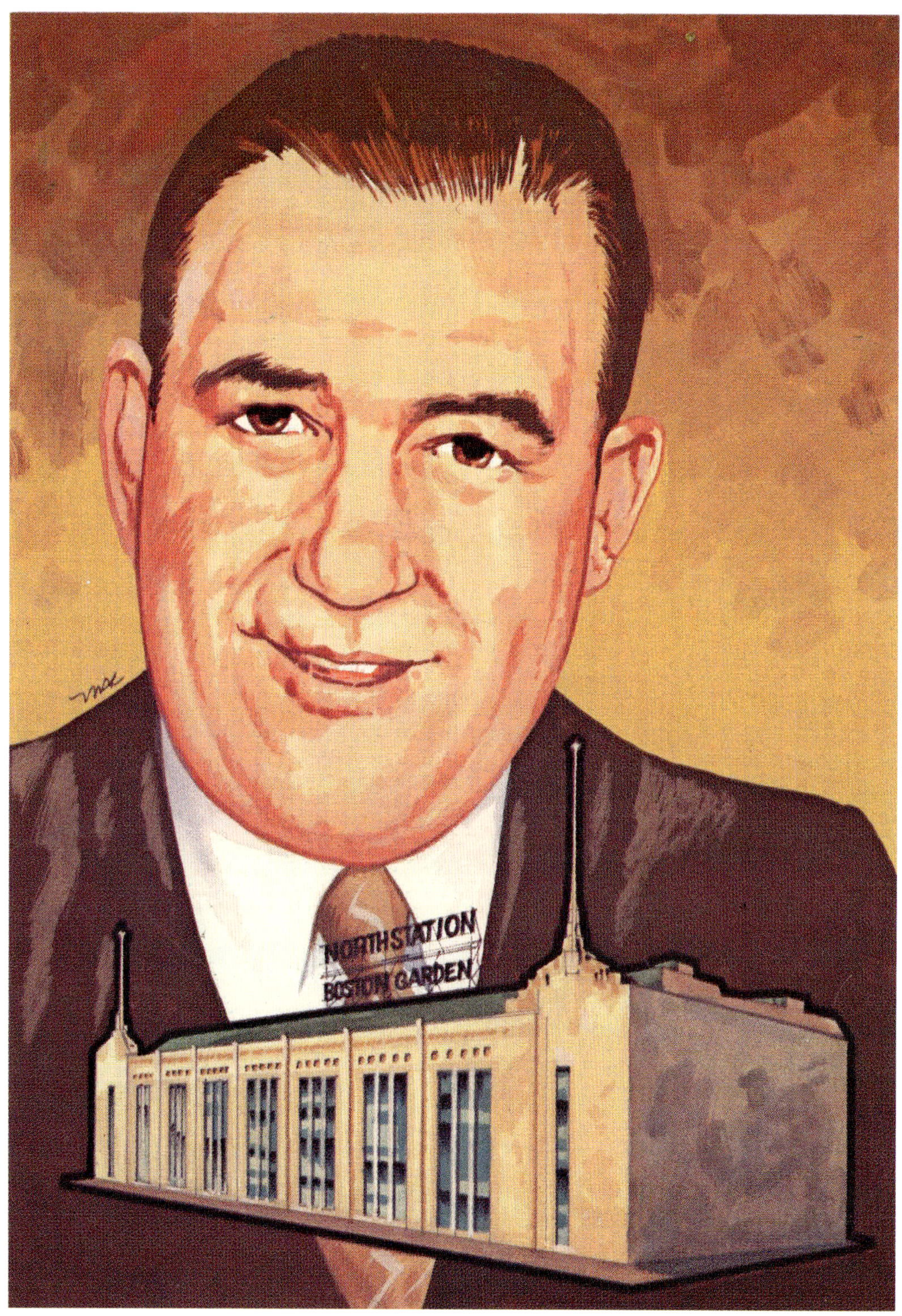

Over his multifaceted, five-decade career, Walter Brown served as president of Boston Garden, owner and president of the Boston Celtics, president of the International Ice Hockey Federation, and president of the Boston Bruins from 1951 to his death in 1964. Boston has known no finer sportsman. (Carlton McDiarmid illustration, Collection of The Sports Museum)

Long recognized as one of the greatest owners in the history of professional sports for his founding and stewardship of the NBA's Boston Celtics, Walter Brown also served as president of the Bruins for 14 years (1951–1964). It was a tenure that saw the franchise battle back from near bankruptcy to enjoy a full-blown financial and competitive resurgence. He remains one of the most underrated figures in team history.

As the son of Boston Arena and Boston Garden executive George V. Brown, Walter literally grew up in the business before succeeding his father as manager of Boston Garden. Though principally known for his success in basketball, hockey was Walter's first sporting love. He coached the minor league Boston Olympics to five Eastern League championships and also helped guide the United States to a gold medal in the 1933 Ice Hockey World Championships.

In September 1951, in his role as head of Boston Garden, Brown arranged for a loan to cover the training camp expenses for the financially strapped Bruins. Weeks later, the Garden-Arena Corporation purchased a controlling 60 percent share of the Bruins for $179,520 and installed Brown as president of the franchise. At the time, Bruins general manager Art Ross proclaimed, "I'm most pleased with the change which has been made. I've been advocating it for years. I'm sure under Walter Brown's rule the Bruins will regain their prestige."

In short time, the Bruins went from fifth-place irrelevance to garnering annual playoff appearances that included three trips to the Stanley Cup Final against Montreal. Brown laid the groundwork for the return of the Adams family as principal owners in the mid-1960s and the glories that followed with Bobby Orr and the Big Bad Bruins. Brown remains the only person ever elected to both the Hockey Hall of Fame and Naismith Memorial Basketball Hall of Fame.

Upon his death in September 1964, Montreal Canadiens general manager Frank Selke said of Brown, "If you could model your friends, Walter Brown would be the ideal."

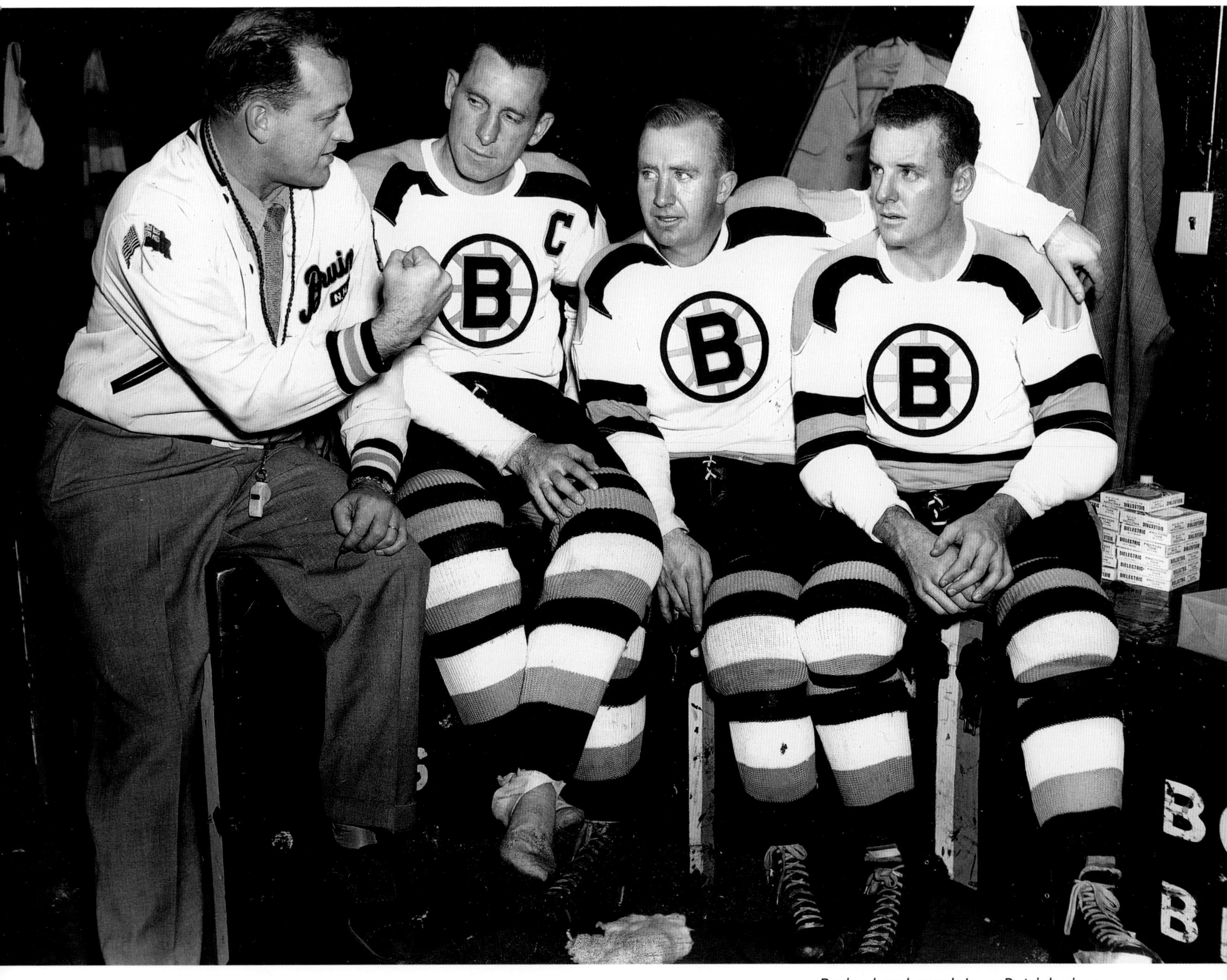

Bruins head coach Lynn Patrick gives a pep talk to (from left to right) Milt Schmidt, Bill Quackenbush, and Ed Sandford during the 1950–51 season. At season's end, Schmidt would win the Hart Trophy as NHL MVP, and Quackenbush would be named a First Team NHL All-Star. (Collection of The Sports Museum)

THE PLAYOFF SERIES THAT SPARKED A REVIVAL

THE BACKDROP for the 1953 Stanley Cup Semifinals series between Boston and Detroit could not possibly have been more foreboding for the Bruins, as they had lost 10 of the 13 regular season games they had played against the Red Wings that season, earning just one win and two ties. They were outscored by an aggregate total of 61–15 in those games, which included two separate games at Boston Garden where the Red Wings fired 10 pucks past Bruins goalie Jim Henry.

Led by the league's leading scorer, Gordie Howe, and Vezina Trophy goalie Terry Sawchuk, the Red Wings had finished 21 points ahead of Boston and were prohibitive favorites to win the 1953 Stanley Cup. Their odds looked all the better after they demolished the Bruins 7–0 in the opening game.

Despite the defeat, Bruins Head Coach Lynn Patrick called on his team to back his strategy of countering Detroit's famed "Production Line" of Howe, Ted Lindsay, and Alex Delvecchio with a checking line of Milt Schmidt, Woody Dumart,

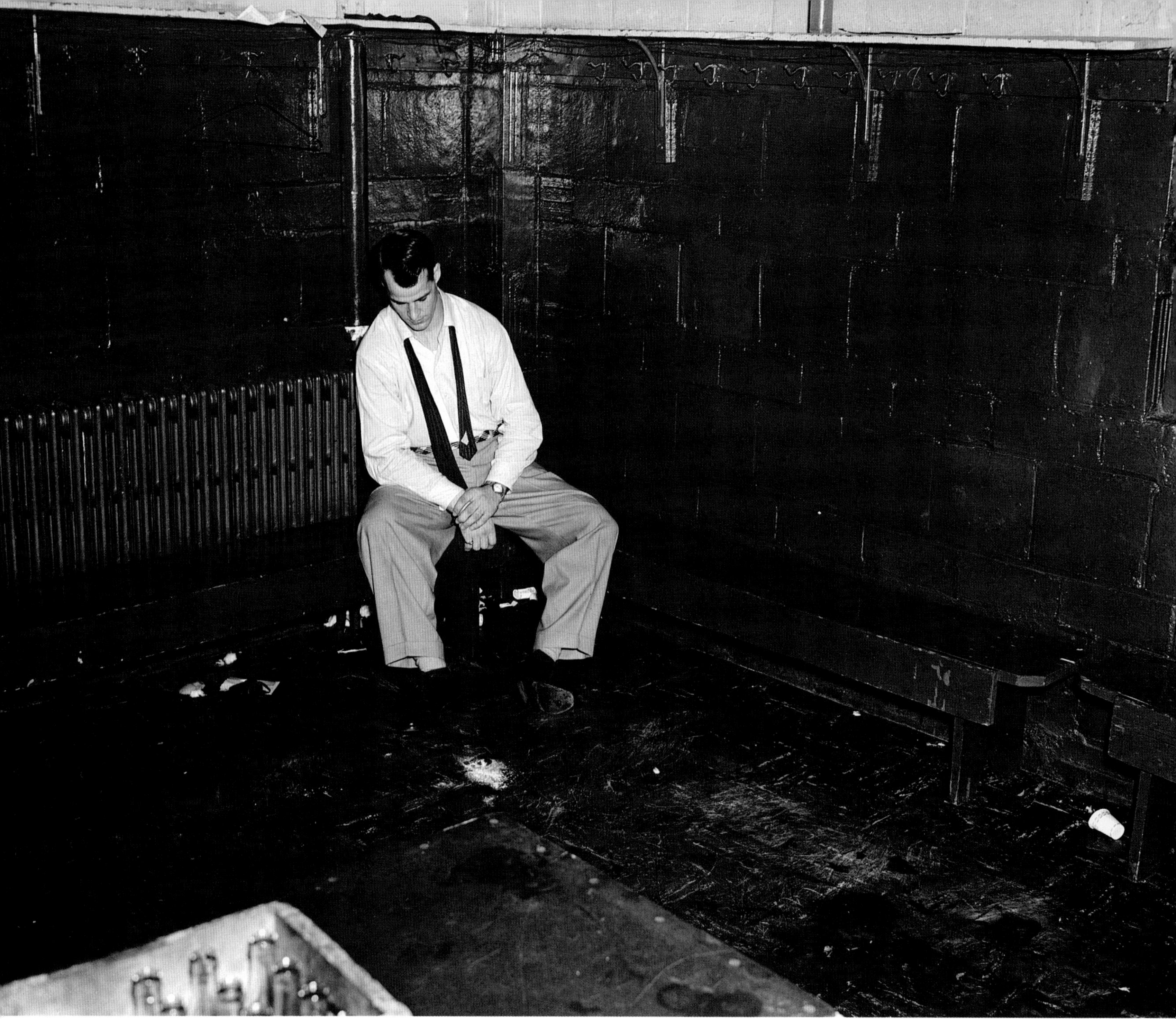

To upset the Red Wings in the 1953 Stanley Cup Semifinals, the Bruins had to beat the best—namely, Gordie Howe, the famed "Mr. Hockey," shown here in the locker room of Boston Garden after the decisive Game 6. (Photograph by Bettman/ Getty Images)

and Joe Klukay. Dubbed the Blanket Line, the trio was ordered by Patrick to "shadow them wherever they go. If Lindsay or Howe go to the bathroom, go with them." The scheme worked perfectly in Game 2, as the Bruins won by a score of 5–3 in Detroit.

Returning to Boston, the Bruins achieved a seminal victory in Game 3 when winger Jack McIntyre scored the overtime winner at 12:29 of sudden-death overtime. The next day's headlines proclaimed the goal to be worth an additional $30,000 in revenues for the Bruins. Hockey historian Stan Fischler would later cite this Game 3 victory as the benchmark for the revitalization of the franchise.

In Game 4, a capacity crowd of 13,909 at the Garden roared their approval as the home team dominated in a 6–2 victory, with one sportswriter describing the Bruins as "running the red shirts off the Depot pond."

Following a 6–4 loss in Game 5 at The Olympia, the Bruins returned to a deluge of fan support in Boston. Anticipating the biggest upset in franchise history, fans stormed the box office, prompting the Bruins to announce the following message over North Station's loudspeakers: "There are no tickets available for this game. There have been none on sale since early in the afternoon. If you have no tickets, please clear the lobby."

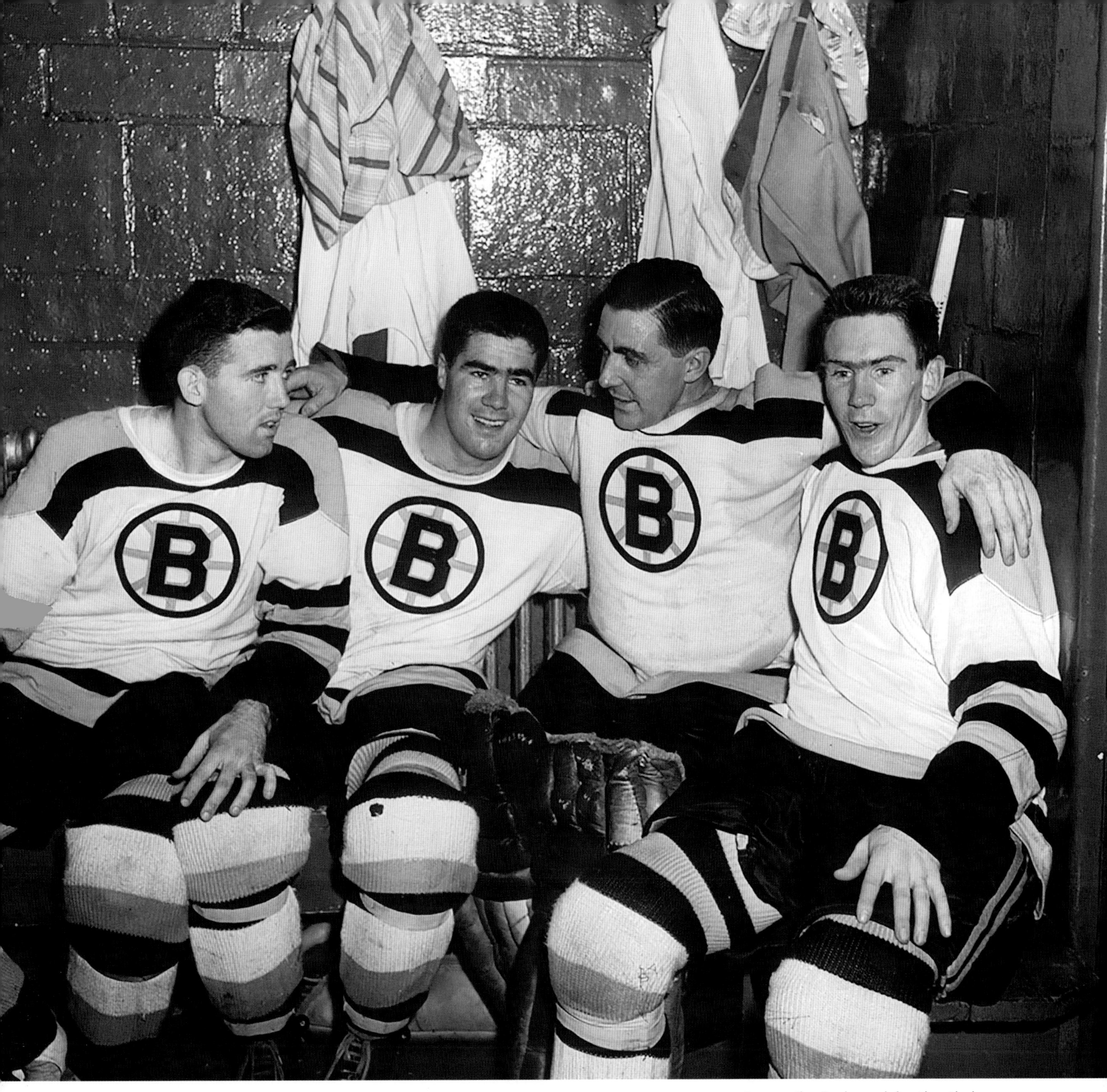

Among the Bruins celebrating their monumental upset playoff win over Detroit in the 1953 playoffs are (from left to right) Johnny Peirson, Fleming MacKell, Jim Henry, and Leo Labine. (Collection of The Sports Museum)

Soon afterward, the Bruins capped the most unexpected playoff victory in their history with a 4–2 win that was largely made possible by goalie Jim Henry's 42 saves and the relentless defensive pressure supplied by the Blanket Line. Following the game, Patrick revealed that he had promised revenge against the Red Wings after their 10–1 rout of his team at Boston Garden on December 11. In an exchange with Red Wings trainer Lefty Wilson, he remarked, "We'll get even for that humiliation someday, and when we do, we'll really make you fellows feel it. We'll knock you out of the playoffs."

In a distant corner of the victorious locker room, Woody Dumart had the line of the night after reflecting on how close he had come to Gordie Howe while shadowing him. When informed the Red Wing star had just announced his upcoming wedding, Dumart quipped, "Here I've been so close to Howe all during the past two weeks, and he didn't even tell me about it."

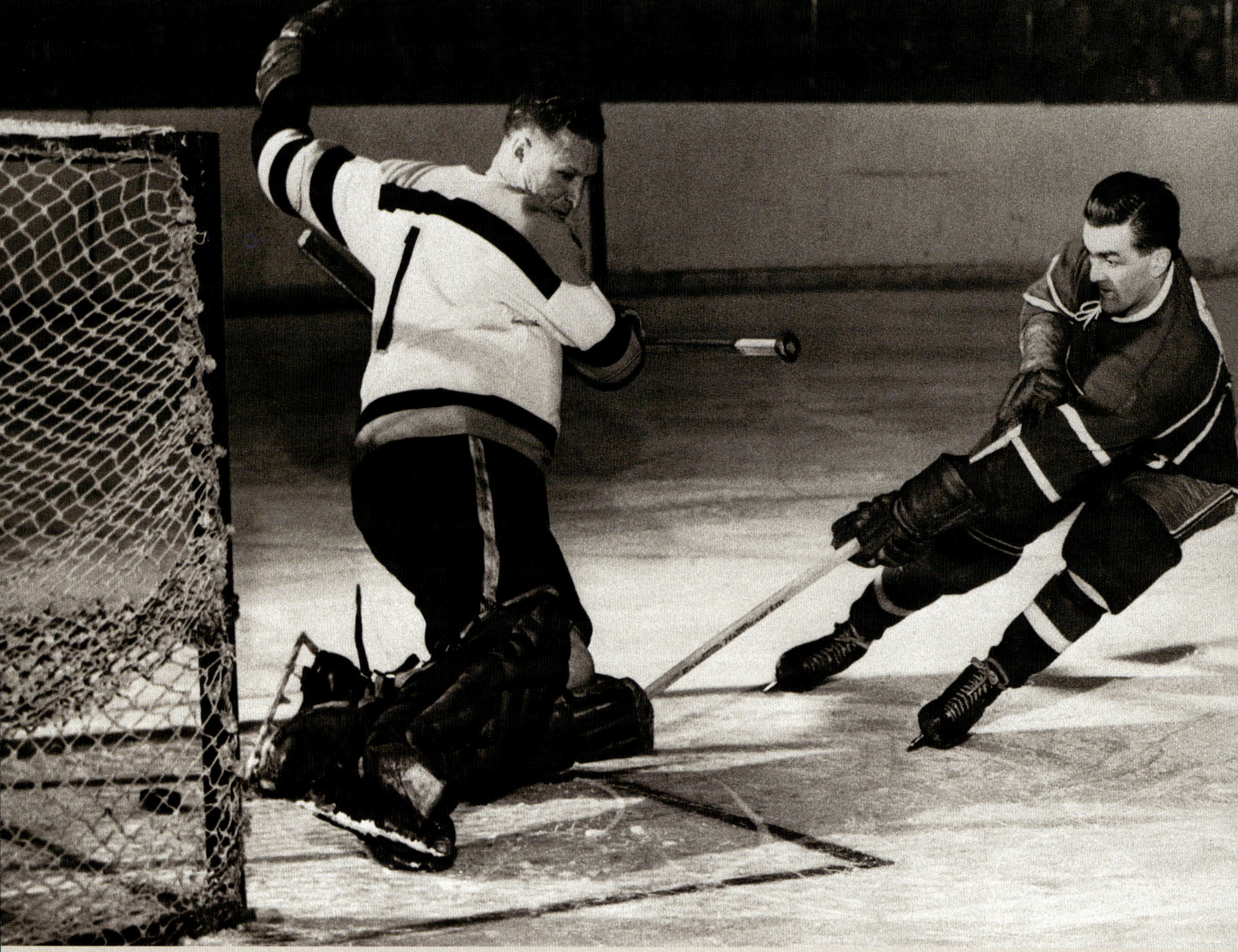

Maurice Richard scores on Boston goaltender Gord "Red" Henry in the first period of Montreal's 7–3 victory in Game 4 of the 1953 Stanley Cup Final. (Photograph by Bettman/Getty Images)

Boston Herald | April 17, 1953

CANADIENS WIN STANLEY CUP ON LACH OVERTIME GOAL, 1–0

by Henry McKenna

MONTREAL, April 16—Elmer Lach, 35-year-old center who has worn the Montreal Canadiens' colors for 13 seasons, fired the only goal of tonight's game in the Forum to win the Stanley Cup series from the Bruins, four games to one.

Elmer's 25-footer from the right face-off spot at 1:22 of the first "sudden death" overtime period gave Canadiens a 1–0 triumph over as battling a Bruins team as ever skated the ice lands of the National Hockey League. "I'll ever be grateful for this bunch of kids for what they did for hockey in Boston," said President Walter Brown of the Bruins as President Clarence Campbell was presenting the coveted trophy to the cheering Canadiens and an equally daffy crowd of 14,450 partisans.

This was Canadiens' sixth Stanley Cup triumph and it was a personal achievement for Coach Dick Irvin, who was hoisted on the shoulders of his players as he waved his hat in recognition of this fourth Cup coaching performance.

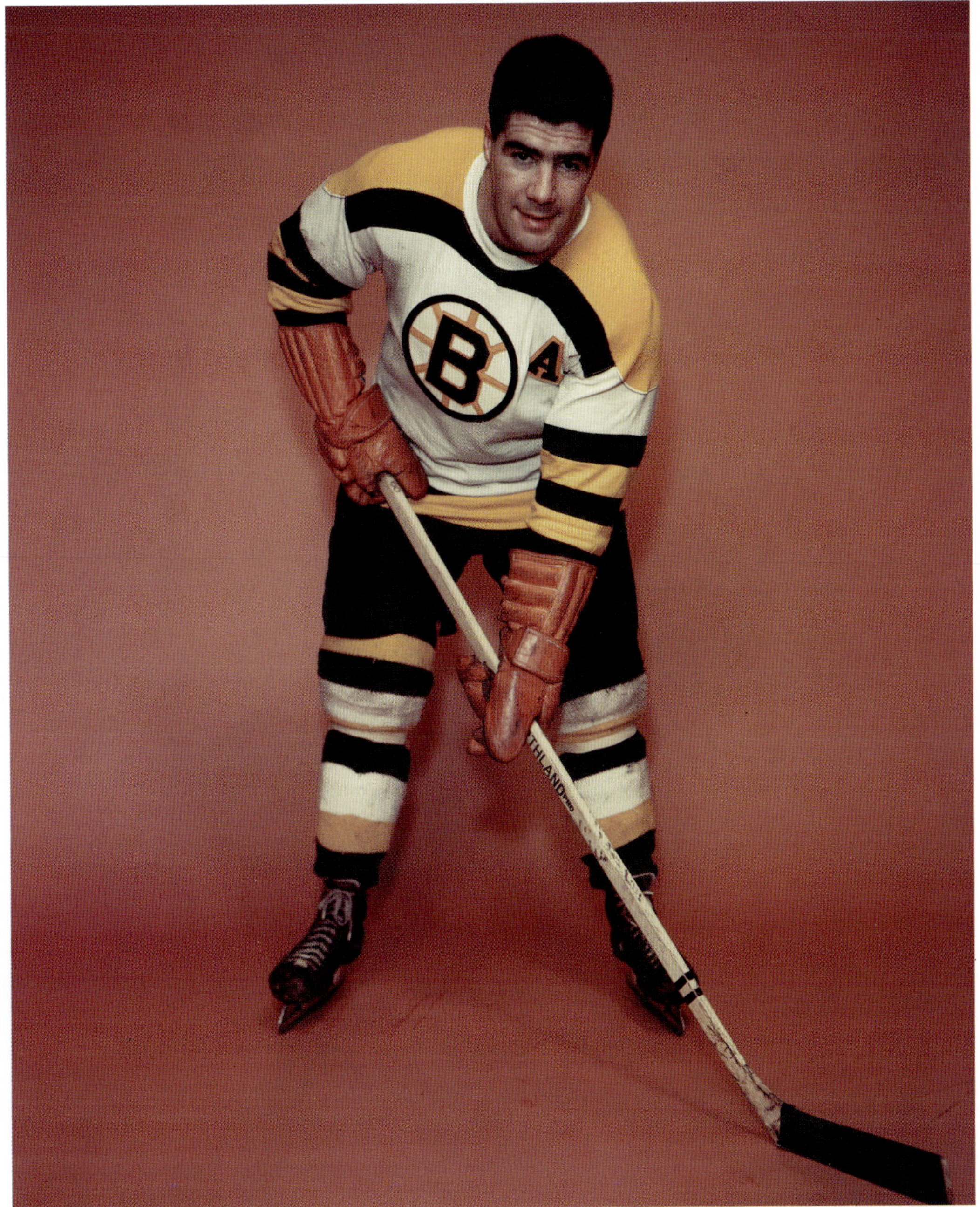

"Flaming" Fleming MacKell was a fan favorite, known for his scoring skill and buzz-saw skating style. In his first full season with the Bruins, 1952–53, he was named a First Team NHL All-Star. Five years later, he would lead all scorers in the 1958 Stanley Cup playoffs. (Photograph by Weekend Magazine/Louis Jaques/Library and Archives Canada/ e002505700)

FLEMING MACKELL

CONSIDERED ONE OF the best penalty killers of his era, center Fleming MacKell was a nimble skater whose choppy strides inspired sportswriters to refer to his "busy" or "crazy" legs. He was also among the Bruins leaders in penalty minutes during his nine seasons with the Bruins, despite the ironic fact that he was literally an altar boy, serving in that capacity on occasion at St. Paul's Church in Hingham, Massachusetts.

MacKell was also a top-flight scorer who captured First Team NHL All-Star honors in 1953. Winger Jerry Toppazzini said of his linemate, "He can put you in there. He lays the puck right on your stick, and he'll deke a man or two before he gives it to you. You can't help but get goals playing with a center like him. He's a real pro."

Always a great playoff performer, MacKell scored four of the Bruins' six goals in their five-game loss to Montreal in the 1957 Stanley Cup Final. The following year, he set an NHL record for playoff assists with 14 and led all playoff scorers with 19 points as the Bruins fell to the Canadiens in the 1958 Stanley Cup Final in a hard-fought six game series.

FERNIE FLAMAN

SOMETIMES A PHOTOGRAPH perfectly captures the competitive essence of an athlete.

Some perfect examples are the freeze frames of Willie Mays making his impossible catch of Vic Wertz's wallop in the 1954 World Series, Muhammad Ali standing over a semi-conscious Sonny Liston in their 1965 title bout, and Roger Bannister crossing the finish line to complete history's first-ever four-minute mile. Such photographs endure as visible and comprehensible encapsulations of character, personality, and accomplishment.

One of the more underappreciated photographs of this vintage is a shot of Bruins All-Star defenseman Fernie Flaman grinning as he bowls over Maurice Richard, launching the famous Rocket airborne. It was not an unusual occurrence. Indeed, Flaman, despite being just 5′10″ and less than 200 pounds, delivered body checks with both frequency and ferocity, making him an Original Six legend. He was also the player Gordie Howe claimed was his toughest opponent. It's hard to imagine a higher accolade bestowed upon any hockey player.

In action at the Montreal Forum in 1955, defenseman Fernie Flaman delivers a hit to Maurice Richard. Flaman led the league in penalties that season while also being named a Second Team NHL All-Star. (Photograph by David Bier, Collection of The Sports Museum)

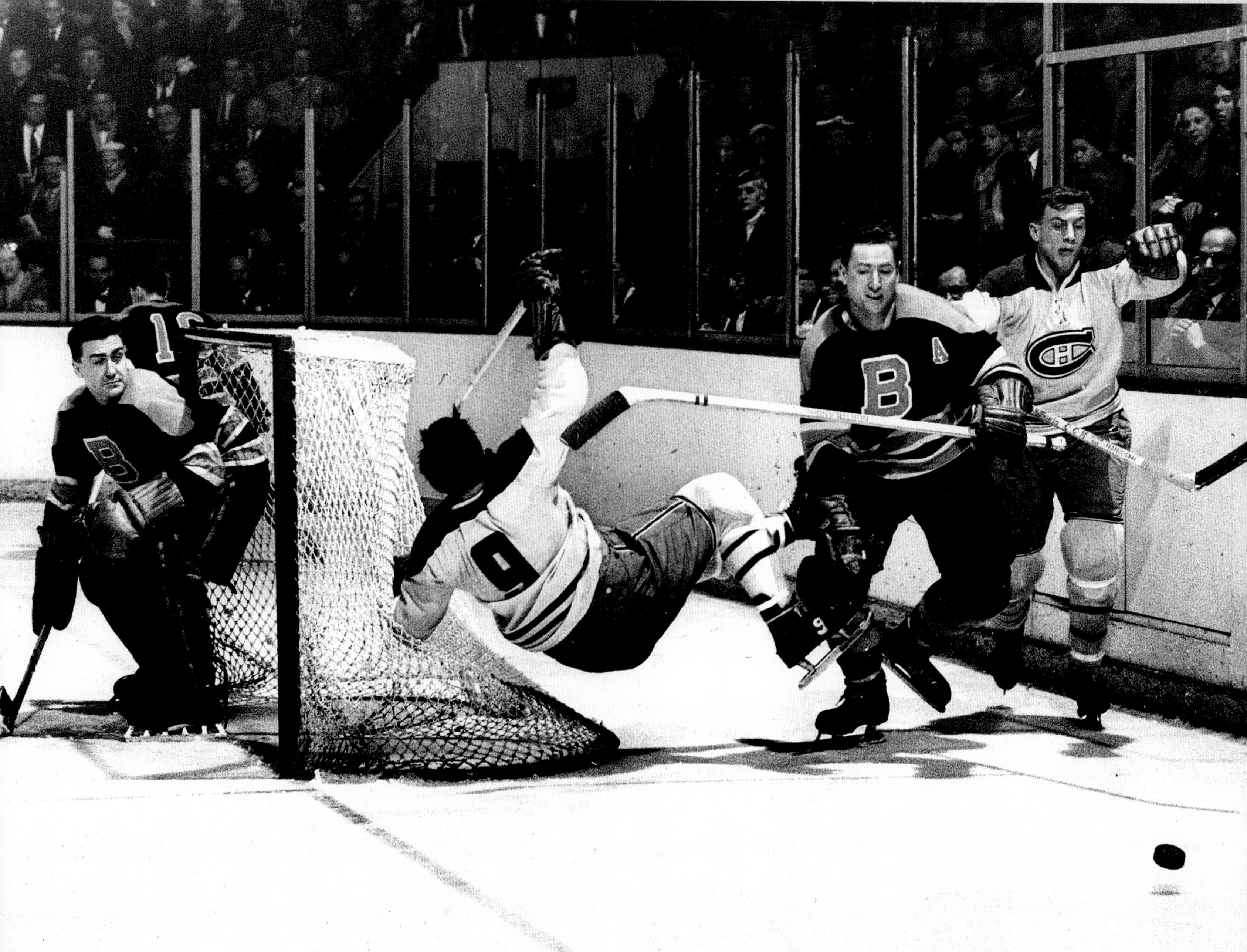

Flaman signed with the Bruins at age 16 and played for the minor league Olympics at Boston Garden before being traded to Toronto. While with the Leafs, Flaman won a Stanley Cup in 1951 as part of the famed club that felled the mighty Canadiens on defenseman Bill Barilko's celebrated overtime goal.

Flaman then returned to Boston for seven seasons (1954–1961) in which he led the team to two improbable Stanley Cup Final appearances in 1957 and 1958 while also playing in five NHL All-Star Games. In 1960, the Bruins captain was fêted with a night in his honor at Boston Garden, where he received a framed portrait and a silver tea set, among other gifts.

Following his retirement from the NHL in 1961, Flaman served as a player, coach, and general manager for the Rhode Island Reds and then coached in the Western and Central Hockey Leagues. In 1970, he became the head coach at Northeastern University. Over the course of 19 seasons on Huntington Avenue, Flaman led the Huskies to four Beanpot titles (including their first ever in 1980) and a Hockey East championship in 1988. In later years, Flaman scouted for the New Jersey Devils and was once again a regular on Causeway Street in that capacity.

Boston Traveler | March 14, 1955

RICHARD LIKE EDDIE SHORE IN REACTIONS

by Arthur Siegel

Only an inch or two kept Maurice "Rocket" Richard's stick-swinging attack on Hal Laycoe from being another Eddie Shore–Ace Bailey tragedy. Yet those who saw the blind fury of the Rocket's red-eyed glare went back two decades in their minds. They recalled that while the incidents were not parallels, the two great players were so similar in their primitive temperaments. Shore and Richard are hockey legends because of their brilliance in performance. The Shore of Boston stardom was great because of his intense emotional build-up. So, too, is Richard great for the same reason. Without that quality, they might never have become part of hockey's colorful history. Bruins coach Milt Schmidt observed, "In my 19 years of hockey, I've never seen anything so savage."

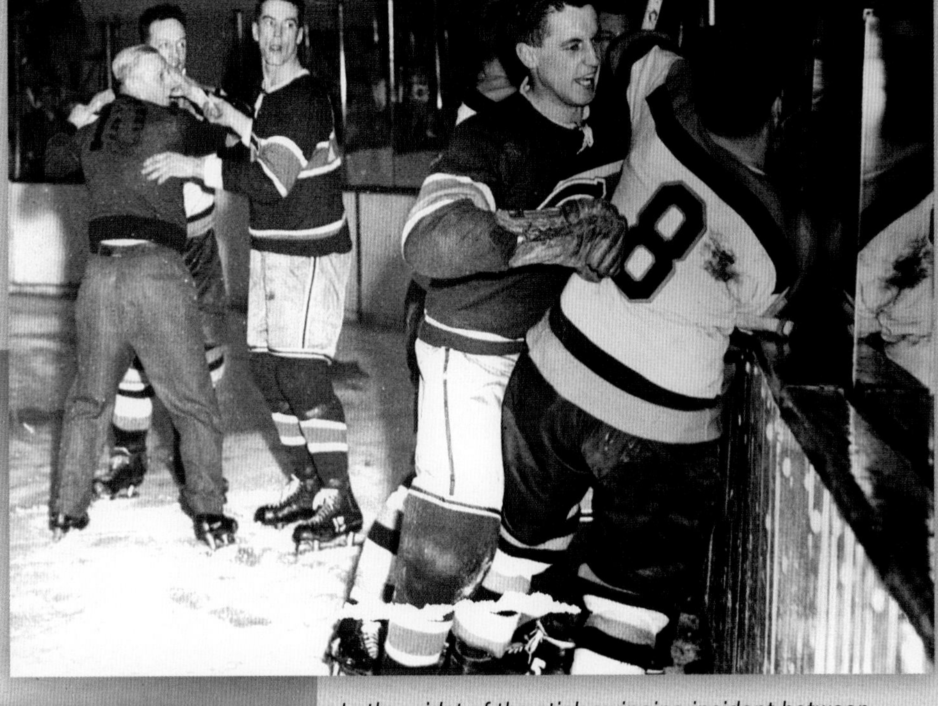

In the midst of the stick swinging incident between Boston's Hal Laycoe and Montreal's Maurice Richard, linesman Sam Babcock holds back Laycoe at far left as Jean Beliveau checks Boston's Fleming MacKell. Concealed from view is Richard, who is being restrained behind Beliveau. (Photograph by Bettman/Getty Images)

Bruins defenseman Hal Laycoe (left) is shown without his trademark eyeglasses in this portrait. Known as one of the NHL's toughest competitors, it was Laycoe's stick swinging duel with Maurice Richard on March 13, 1955 that resulted in the controversial suspension of the Canadiens star for the remainder of the regular season and the playoffs. (Collection of The Sports Museum)

In 1954–55, the line of Leo Labine, Don McKenney, and Real Chevrefils led the Bruins with 42, 42, and 40 points respectively, inviting comparisons with the famed Kraut Line. (Collection of Richard A. Johnson)

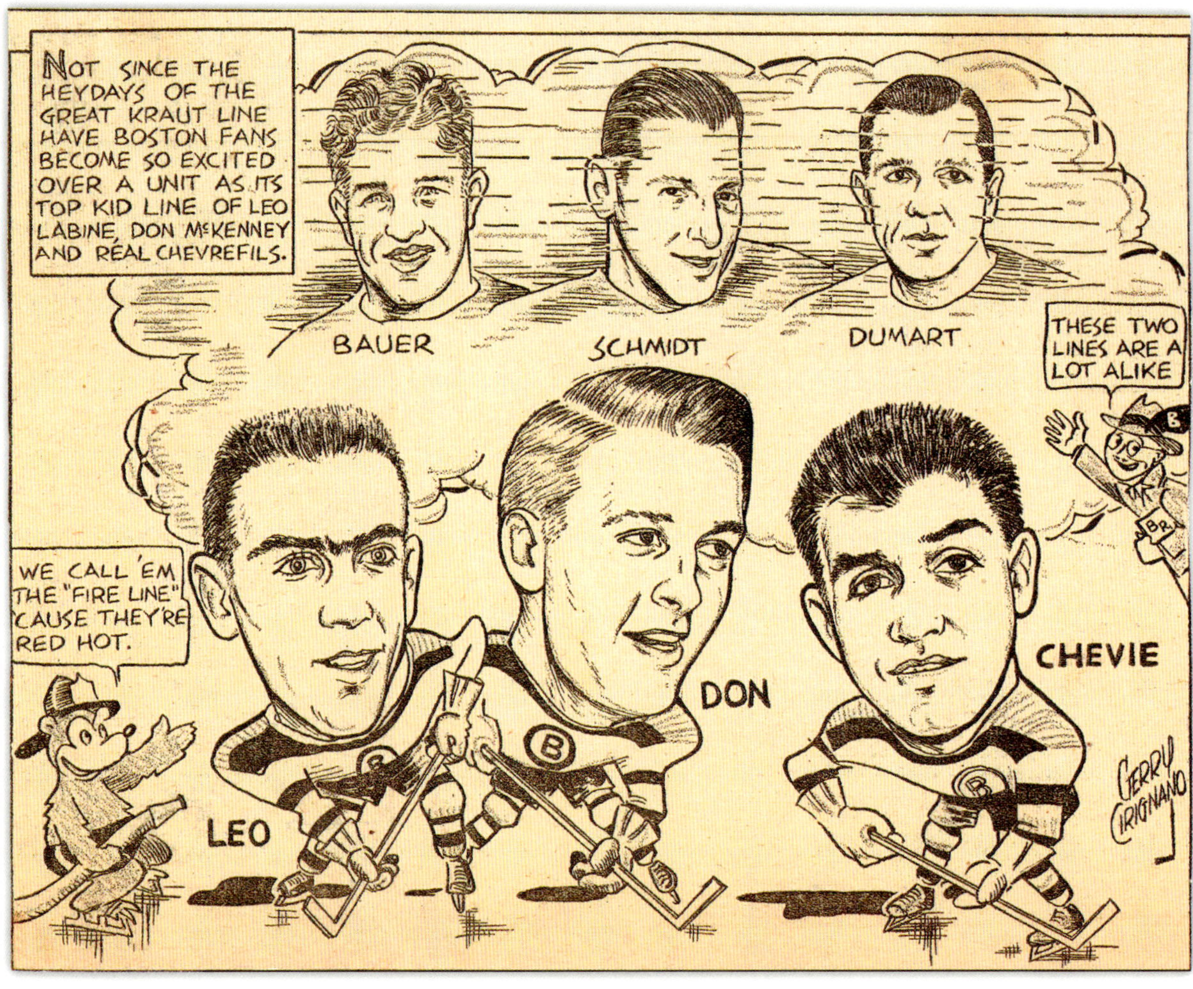

LEO LABINE

Leo Labine was a ferocious body checker known for his sharp tongue and equally sharp elbows. He was named one of the NHL's five toughest players by a panel of GMs in 1958. (Collection of Richard A. Johnson)

KNOWN AS THE "Haileybury Hurricane," right wing Leo Labine was described by hockey historian Stan Fischler as "Derek Sanderson before Derek Sanderson." Colorful, brash, irreverent, and hard-hitting, he was the perfect fit for a Bruins team that overachieved for most of the 1950s.

"Leo Labine was a tough little kid, not afraid to step into guys," teammate Ed Sandford said in a 2022 interview. "He could play hockey and was rough when he needed to be. A good all-around player."

Labine's on-ice confrontations with Rocket Richard were the stuff of legend and were partially fueled by the Rocket's reference to his rival as a "bad Frenchman" in the column he penned for a Montreal newspaper. Apparently, Richard was unaware of the fact that, despite Labine's French surname, he was raised in northern Ontario by parents who didn't speak a word of French. Their son didn't speak French, either. Still, Richard was convinced Labine was holding out on the language front just to aggravate him.

Soon after, in a memorable on-ice exchange in Montreal, Labine, having been coached by Bruins teammate Real Chevrefils, skated past Richard and remarked, *"Comment ça va, mon vieux? Prenez guard se soir"*—which translates as, "How's it going, old man? Watch yourself tonight."

In 1956, Bruins General Manager Lynn Patrick said of Labine, "I wouldn't trade him for the Rocket. He's the most colorful player to come into the league in 10 years, the most colorful since Wild Bill Ezinicki, and now he's the second-best player in the world. The only player I'd consider trading him for is Jean Beliveau, and well, I'd have to think a while about that."

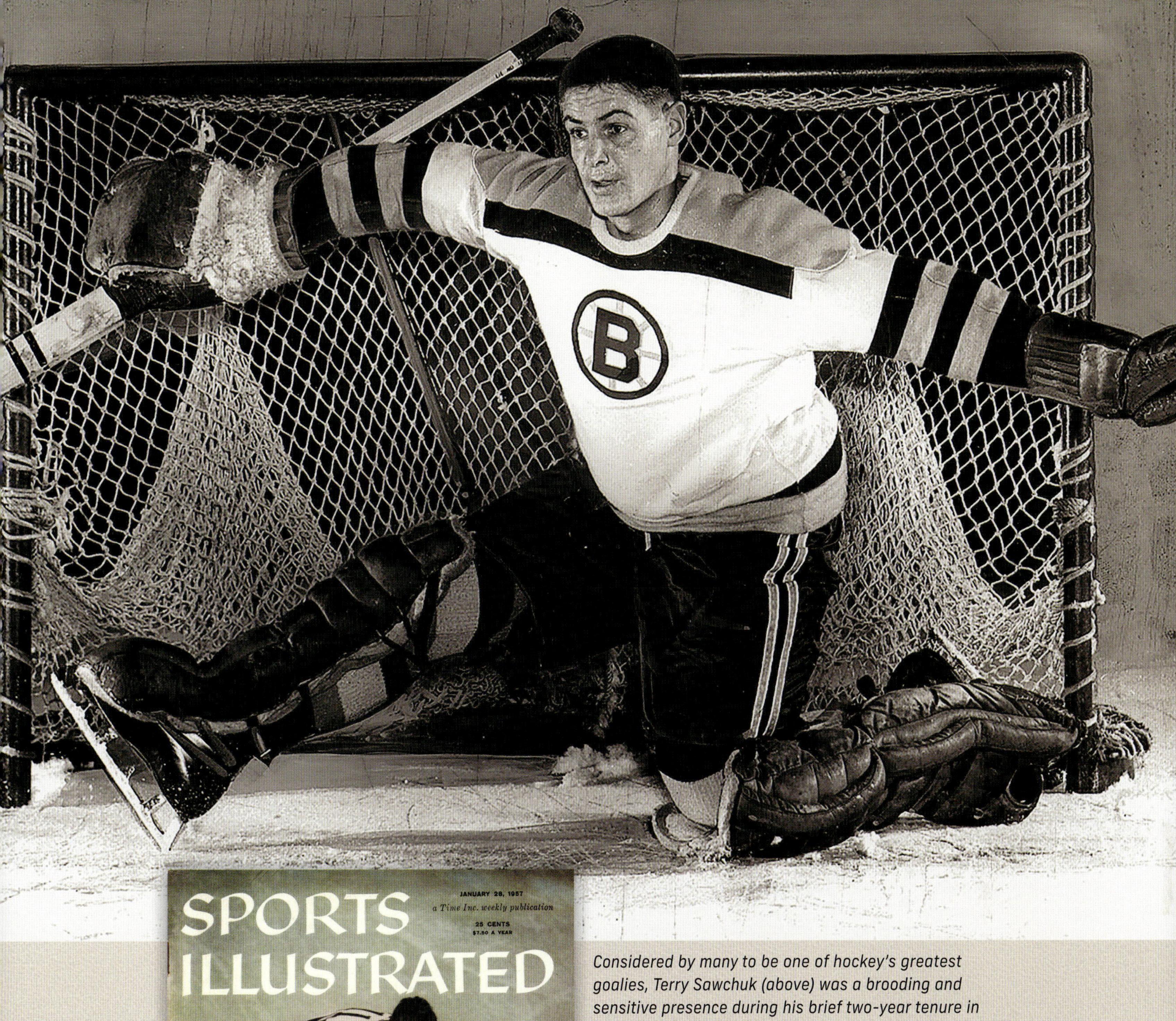

SPORTS ILLUSTRATED

JANUARY 28, 1957
a Time Inc. weekly publication
25 CENTS
$7.50 A YEAR

MEXICO
THE CITY
THE BULLS
THE SPORTING LOOK
plus
SAN DIEGO TO ACAPULCO
A YACHTSMAN'S GUIDE

THE BOSTON BRUINS
HOCKEY'S SURPRISE TEAM

Considered by many to be one of hockey's greatest goalies, Terry Sawchuk (above) was a brooding and sensitive presence during his brief two-year tenure in Boston. In June 1957, the Bruins traded him back to Detroit for Johnny Bucyk, a player who would prove to have more staying power in Boston. (Collection of The Sports Museum)

The 1956–57 Bruins attracted national press coverage (left) on their way to their appearance in the Stanley Cup Final against the Canadiens. (Courtesy of Sports Illustrated)

DON MCKENNEY

ON THE LIST OF underrated Bruins, center Don McKenney ranks near the top. In an era when scoring 20 goals or more in a season was a benchmark for excellence, McKenney topped the mark in seven of his nine seasons in Boston.

As a rookie in 1954–55, McKenney made an immediate impact, leading the team in scoring. "I was very fortunate," McKenney said in a 2022 interview shortly before his passing at the age of 88. "I played with a couple of older guys who were pretty good players. Milt Schmidt was one of them. They were a big help to me."

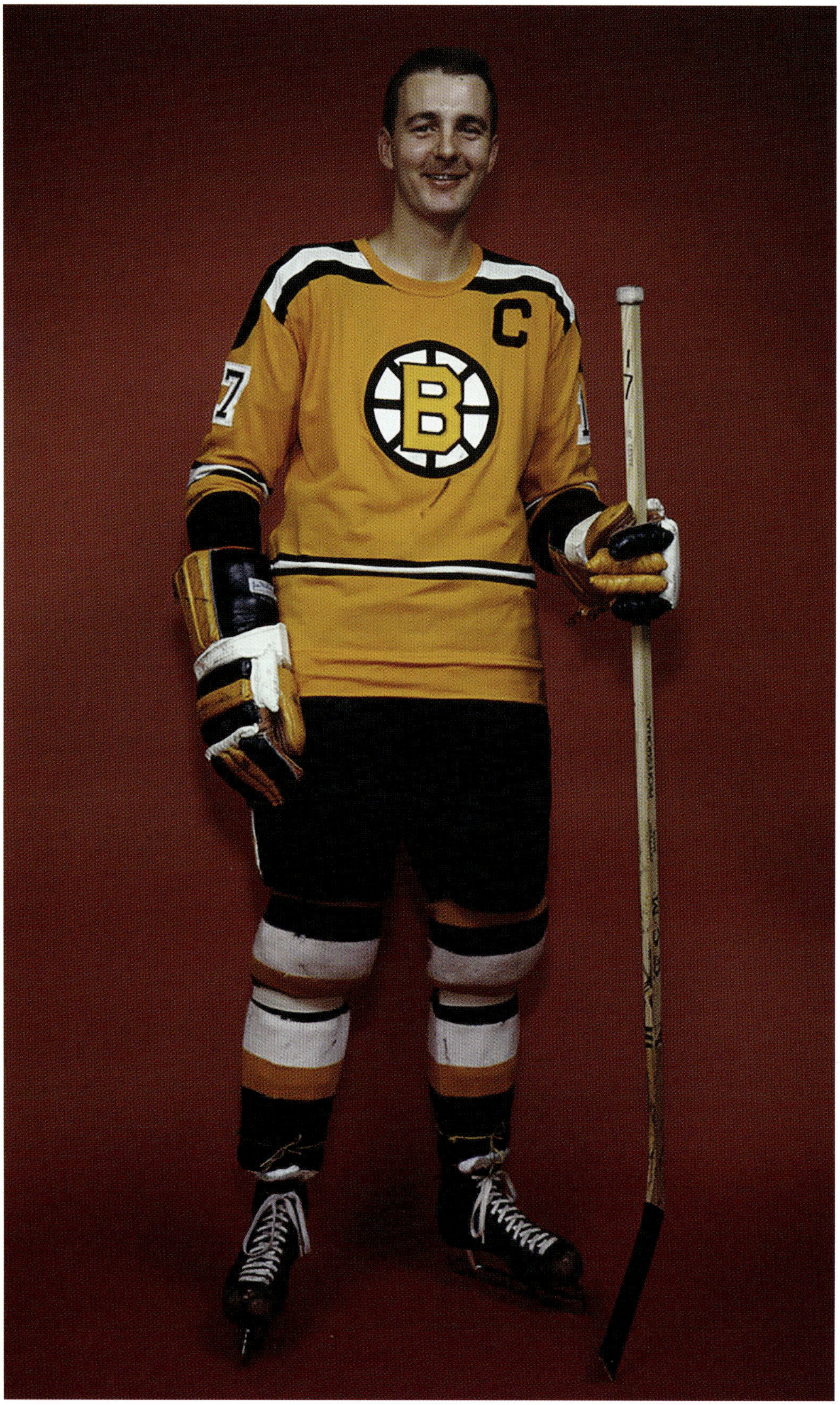

Always a smooth skater, McKenney represented Boston in the NHL All-Star Game in six straight seasons (1957–1962). In the 1959–60 season, he captured the Lady Byng Trophy while also leading the league with 49 assists. Along the way, McKenney established himself as a clutch performer while helping lead Boston to consecutive Stanley Cup Final appearances in 1957 and 1958.

"I think when I played, we played the game the way it was meant to be played," said McKenney. "And skill was very important. As far as the physical guys, they sort of played by themselves. They stayed away from guys that just wanted to play, which made it easy for guys like me."

In February 1963, Boston traded McKenney to New York, which traded him a year later to Toronto, where he won a Stanley Cup in 1964. After retiring as a player, he worked as assistant coach for the Northeastern University men's hockey team under former teammate Fernie Flaman and later served as head coach of the Huskies from 1989 to 1991.

Center Don McKenney was the scoring ace for overachieving Bruins teams that reached the Stanley Cup Final in 1957 and 1958. Over a seven-year period, McKenney led the team in scoring three times. (Photograph by Jaques, Louis/Library and Archives Canada/ e002343745)

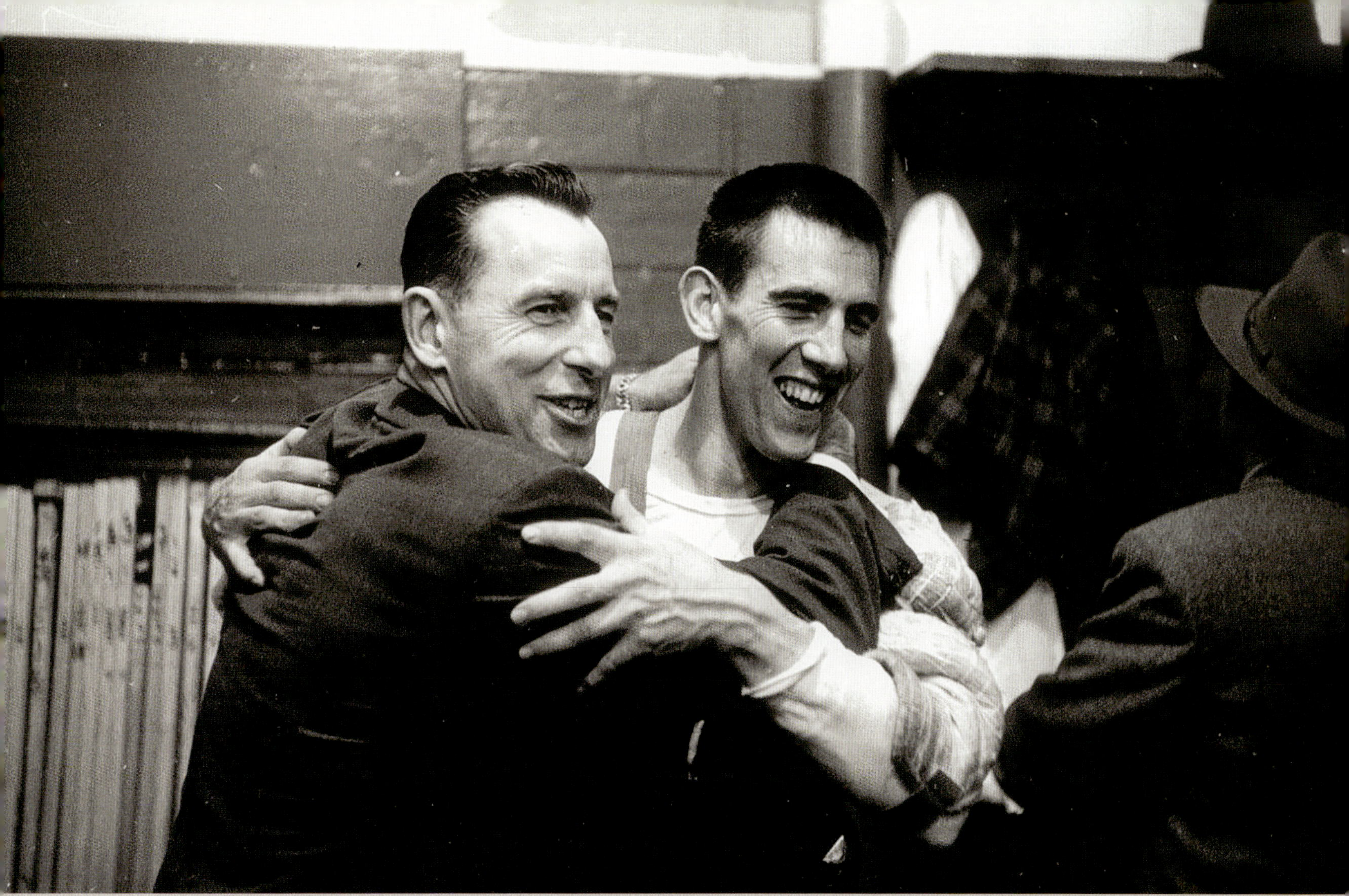

Head coach Milt Schmidt embraces goalie Don Simmons (above) following the Bruins' series-clinching 4–3 win at The Olympia in Detroit to claim a place in the 1957 Stanley Cup Final.
(Courtesy of J. Harvey McKenney)

Milt Schmidt scatters towels (below) in celebration of his team's five-game series upset of the Red Wings.
(Collection of Richard A. Johnson)

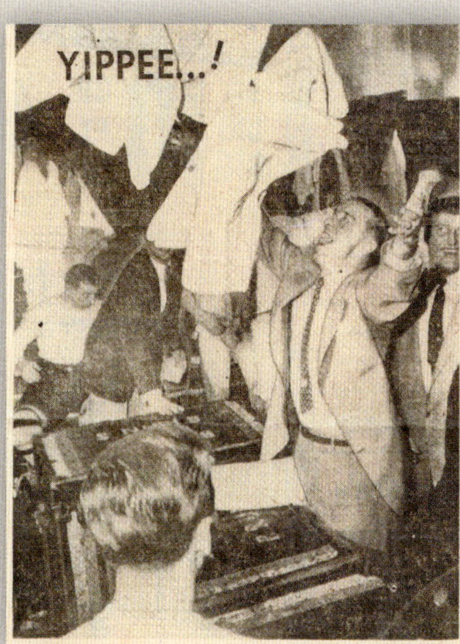

Boston Traveler | April 16, 1957

B'S GAVE THEIR ALL; IT WASN'T ENOUGH

MONTREAL—The Bruins gave all they had, but it wasn't nearly enough to win the Stanley Cup from Les Canadiens.

The never-quit Bruins will leave here tonight for Boston after being defeated last night, 5–1, in what became the final game of the Stanley Cup series.

Only minutes after Montreal had wrapped up its second straight hockey championship, Schmidt talked to bitter Bruins. There were tears in the eyes of many of the players.

"I want to give you my sincere thanks," Schmidt said in low halting fashion. "You gave me everything you had and I'm proud of you. Every one of you."

With that touching speech, Schmidt then made the rounds of the dressing room and shook hands with each player. Most of the players only mumbled their appreciation.

"We have nothing to be ashamed of," Schmidt said to a host of invading sportswriters. "We lost to a great hockey club in the Canadiens."

"We had our chances, but we just couldn't score. Once Real Chevrefils was in all alone and if he had scored then, it might have been different."

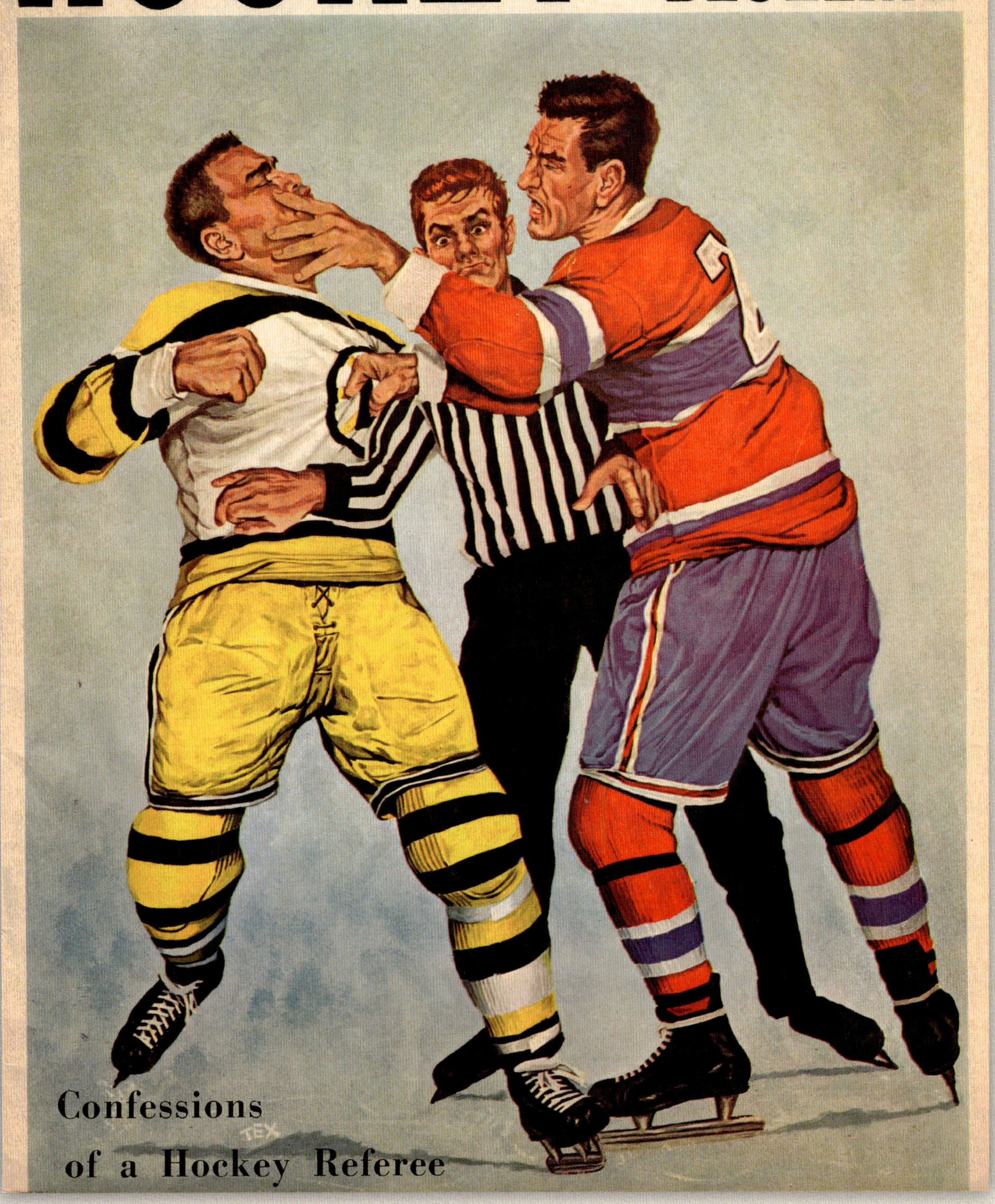

The Bruins' rivalry with the Montreal Canadiens is captured on the cover of Hockey Blueline *by artist Tex Coulter, a former lineman for the NFL's New York Giants.* (Collection of Richard A. Johnson)

THE 1959 EUROPEAN EXCURSION

Atop the list of episodes from franchise history that would surely be the basis for a first-rate movie is the 23-game exhibition tour of Europe that the Bruins made with the New York Rangers in the spring of 1959 following the Bruins' playoff loss to Toronto. Think *Slap Shot* meets *National Lampoon's European Vacation*.

Organized by Swiss businessman Othmar Delnon and sponsored in part by Italian vermouth distiller Cinzano, the tour made stops in London, Geneva, Paris, Antwerp, Zurich, Dortmund, Essen, Krefeld, West Berlin, and Vienna. Players received $1,000 in cash, engraved watches, and luggage for playing the equivalent of a third of an NHL season while also enjoying an all-expenses paid tour of Western Europe.

One can only imagine the pleasure derived by a group of young men on their first-ever overseas trip. Among the traveling party, only Bruins executives Milt Schmidt and Lynn Patrick and Rangers general manager Muzz Patrick had been to Europe previously. According to several players, there were few or no curfews and players fully availed themselves of the delights of the bright lights in cities large and small along the way.

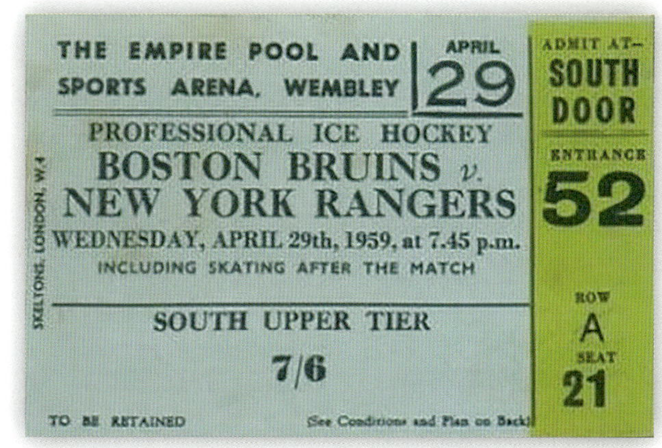

Ticket stub (above) from the European Tour made by the Bruins and Rangers in spring 1959. (Courtesy of J. Harvey McKenney)

Vic Stasiuk, Bronco Horvath, and Johnny Bucyk (left to right) comprised the famed Uke Line from 1957 to 1961. It was one of the most celebrated trios in Bruins history. The line's nickname reflected their shared Ukrainian descent. (Collection of The Sports Museum)

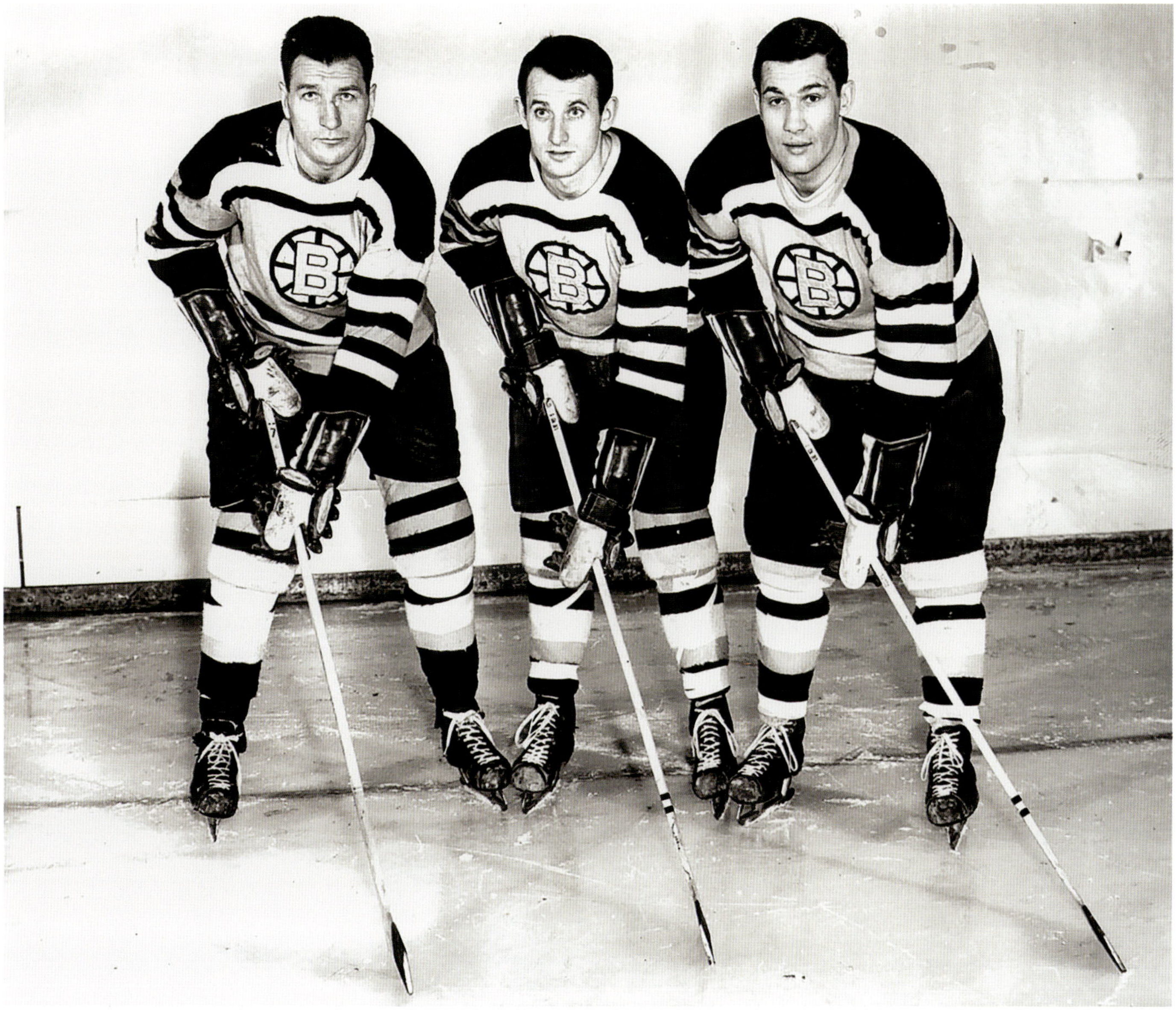

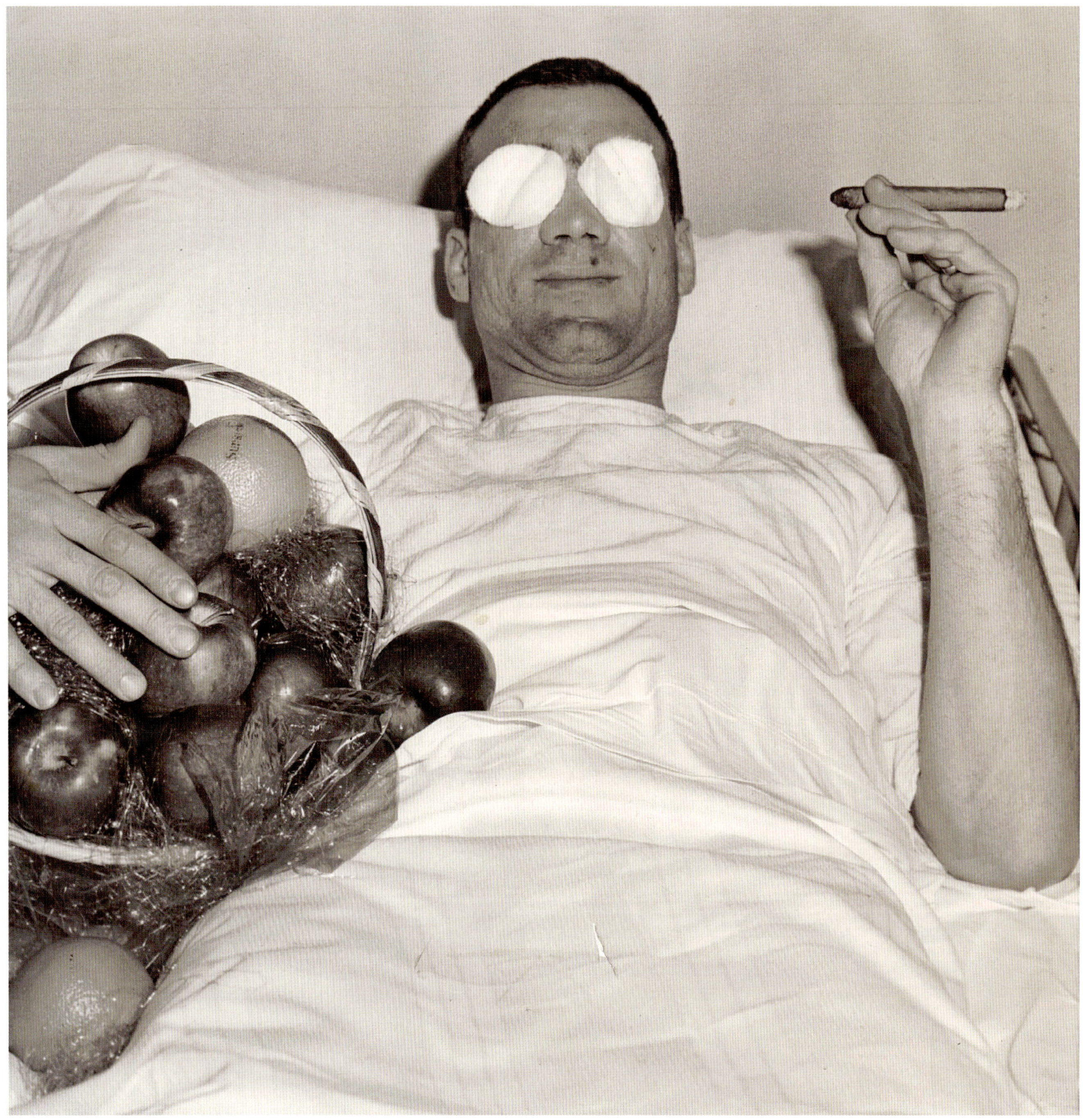

Right wing Jerry "Topper" Toppazzini was the Bruins' class clown as well as a top-flight scorer in his two stints with the Bruins (1952–1954, 1955–1964). Here he keeps things loose from his hospital bed while recovering from an eye injury suffered in March 1958. The Topper returned just in time for the playoffs and delivered in a big way, scoring nine goals (tying for the team lead with Don McKenney) as the Bruins advanced to the Stanley Cup Final against the Canadiens. (Collection of Richard A. Johnson)

Included on the New York roster were Ed Litzenberger and Bobby Hull of the Chicago Black Hawks, since several Rangers, including star forward Andy Bathgate, were unavailable to travel. Hull ended up scoring 14 goals on the tour. Years later, he credited the experience as the turning point in his career, noting, "Playing with so many veterans gave me confidence. When I came to training camp the following fall, I felt that I could accomplish a lot in the NHL."

By all accounts, the tour was a competitive success, with the Rangers edging Boston with 11 wins, 9 losses, and 3 ties. However, on the business side, the tour was a mixed bag with a total attendance of 73,000, which included consecutive games in Geneva that drew 11,000 and 8,000 fans, respectively, but also games in Paris that attracted only 700 apiece.

Despite talk of making such tours an annual event, the NHL only resumed scheduling games in Europe in 1980 with the sponsored DN-Cup, played in Stockholm as a five-game preseason tournament. The Bruins made their return to the continent in October 2010 with a four-game slate that included their first two regular season games, which they split against the Phoenix Coyotes in Prague.

IN HIS OWN WORDS... WILLIE O'REE

WILLIE O'REE occupies a singular place in the history of the Boston Bruins—and the NHL.

On January 18, 1958, O'Ree broke the color barrier in hockey when he skated for the Bruins in a game against the Canadiens at the Montreal Forum. O'Ree thus became "the Jackie Robinson of Hockey." Like Robinson, he had to endure his share of race-based epithets and indignities along the way. His story remains one of character, class, and courage. And it is a story that resulted in O'Ree's No. 22 being retired by the Bruins and hoisted to the rafters of TD Garden in 2022.

Set forth below are excerpts from an exclusive interview that Brian Codagnone, the associate curator of The Sports Museum and a special contributor to this book, conducted with O'Ree in the fall of 2022.

On choosing hockey over baseball

I made a choice between hockey and baseball in 1956 after I came back from Waycross, Georgia, being down there with the Milwaukee Braves minor league operation. I knew the way that Blacks were treated in the South. When I headed back, I was on the bus five days, traveling from Waycross, Georgia, to my hometown, Fredericton, New Brunswick, and you know, Blacks had to sit in the back of the bus. As the bus was moving up north, I moved closer up in the bus and I was in the center of the bus. And when I got to Bangor, Maine, I was sitting at the front of the bus. When I arrived in Fredericton, I stepped off the bus and I said, "Willie, forget about baseball, concentrate on hockey." And that's when the doors opened for me, and you know the rest.

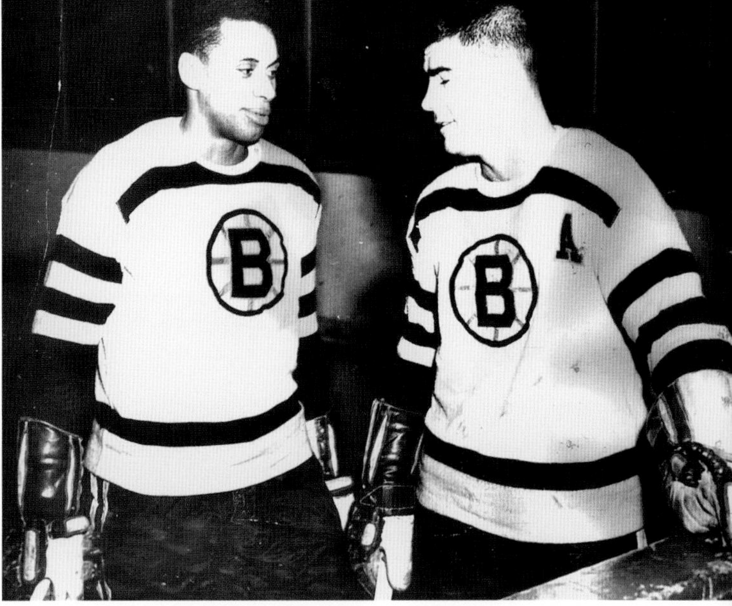

Willie O'Ree and Fleming MacKell talk at the Montreal Forum just prior to O'Ree's historic debut as the NHL's first Black player on January 18, 1958. (Collection of The Sports Museum)

On breaking hockey's color line

The Bruins invited me to their training camp in 1957. I went to their training camp, and then I came back and started again with the Quebec Aces. And then on January 18, 1958, the Bruins called the Quebec Aces and said, "We want O'Ree to meet the Bruins in Montreal to play two games against the Montreal Canadiens." So I had played against the Montreal Canadiens in exhibition games, but when I arrived in Montreal on January 18 and stepped on the ice, I became the first Black player to play in the NHL.

On racial slurs and brotherly advice

You know, there were racial remarks and racial slurs. But I learned from my older brother. He said, "Willie, names will never hurt you unless you let them. You can't change the color of your skin and I don't think you'd want to, even if you could." And he told me, "If people can't accept you for the individual that you are [because I had the skills and ability to play in the league at that time], then that's their problem and not yours. Just go out, stay focused, and work hard. And everything has a way of working out." And, basically. that's what I tried to do all the years I played.

On the Bruins organization

I've been a Bruins fan ever since I went to training camp in 1957. They've got a great organization. The players were all very supportive of me when I played there. And I began to take a great interest in the team and the organization.

WILLIE O'REE—TRAILBLAZER, LIFE-CHANGER, GENTLEMAN

by Gary Bettman

Few are the people who can change the world—at least their corner of it—by their mere presence. Fewer are those who, having affected such change, go on to have second acts that rival, if not eclipse, that signature moment.

And rarest, indeed, are the people who also somehow inspire admiration and affection from everyone they meet.

Willie O'Ree is one of these rarest of individuals. Trailblazer. Life-changer. Gentleman.

On January 18, 1958, O'Ree changed the face of hockey forever by pulling on a Boston Bruins sweater and stepping onto the ice of the Montreal Forum. No Black man had ever appeared in a National Hockey League game before that moment. Our game and our league were doubly blessed that it was this particular man who did.

A great grandson of an escaped slave from the American south, this native of Fredericton, New Brunswick,

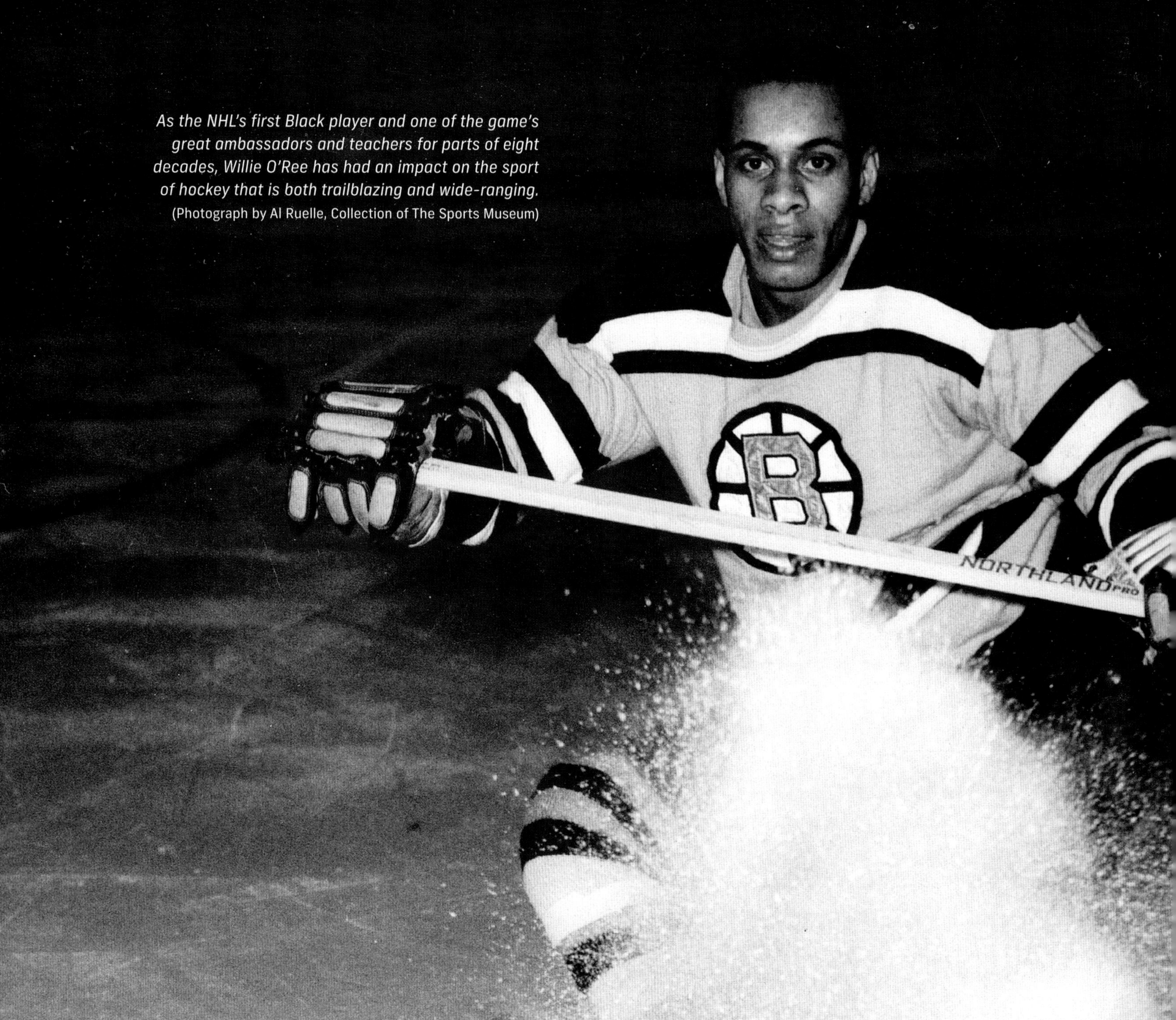

As the NHL's first Black player and one of the game's great ambassadors and teachers for parts of eight decades, Willie O'Ree has had an impact on the sport of hockey that is both trailblazing and wide-ranging.
(Photograph by Al Ruelle, Collection of The Sports Museum)

personified all of the best of hockey, even while showing that there was one thing about the NHL, to that point, that was unacceptable and had to be changed.

He did so not only during an era when racial segregation was the norm and racial stereotyping common in much of North America, but at a time when there were only six franchises in the League and teams dressed only 16 skaters for games—meaning only a few more than 100 roster spots were available.

One more thing: Willie earned his way into the Bruins' lineup by excelling in his ascent from the Canadian Junior leagues to the Quebec Aces of the Quebec Senior League despite being almost blind in his right eye, the result of taking a puck to the face as a teenager. His passion, perseverance, and dedication simply were too strong for him to be denied.

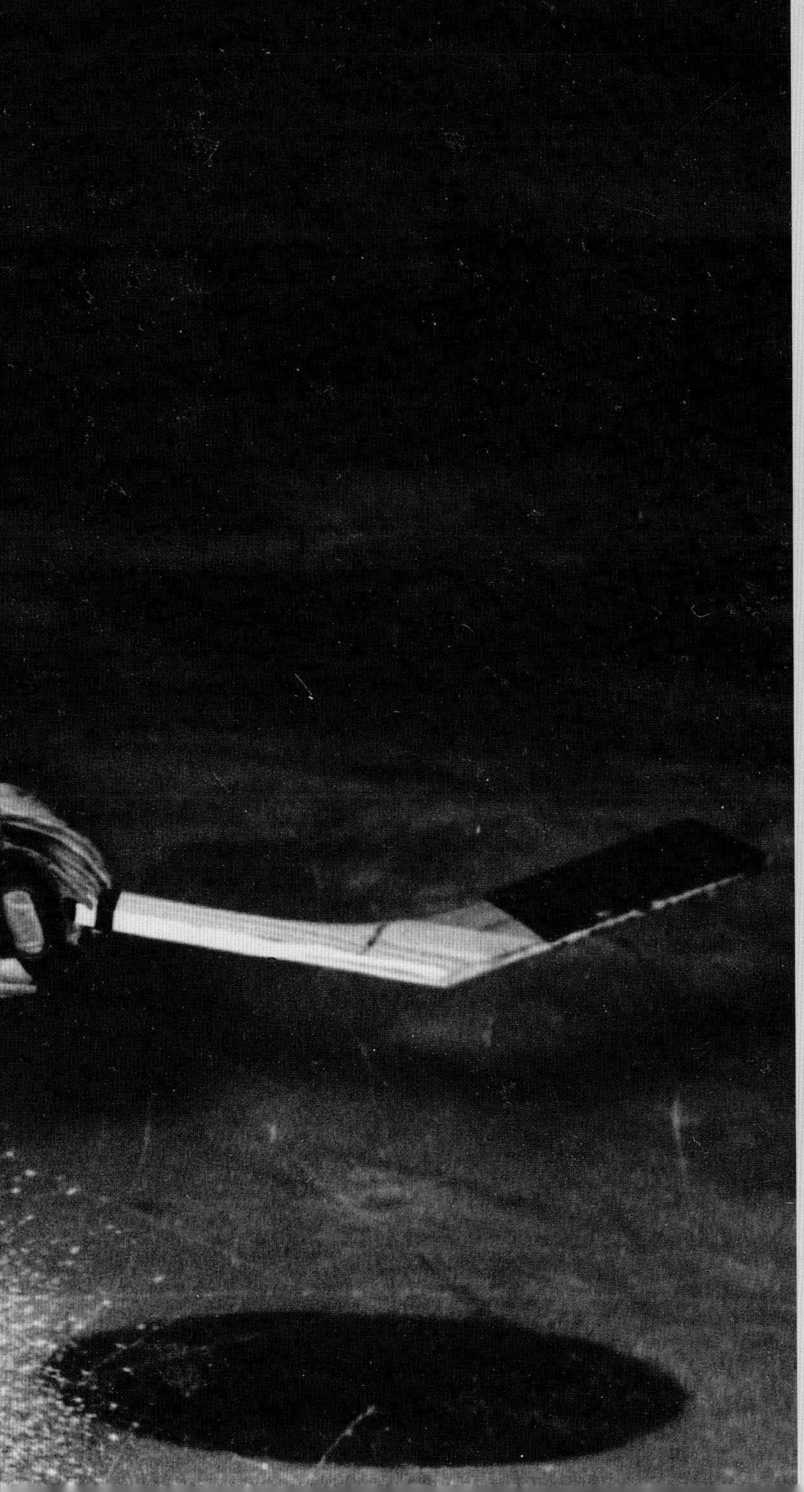

By all accounts, his Bruins teammates welcomed him warmly on that historic night in Montreal and supported him as they would any player wearing their colors. It is reassuring to read quotes like this recollection from fellow Bruins forward Bronco Horvath: "We told him, 'Don't worry, you'll be fine. If anyone hits you, slurs you, or tries to hurt you, there'll be nine guys on him in the blink of an eye.'"

Or this from Bruins Hall of Fame defenseman Fern Flaman: "This was a case of a player deserving an opportunity to have a chance to come up and play in the NHL. Willie was just a hockey player to us."

However, Willie also endured significant abuse—both physical and verbal—from opposing players and fans alike. His stoicism and soft-spoken humility might fool one into believing he was not hurt by any of it. He was. But he refused to show it. And he refused to let it define or derail him, or to douse his passion for the game he adored and his belief that there was so much profoundly good about hockey that needed to be shared, particularly with youngsters.

A speedy forward who could both create scoring opportunities and finish them himself, Willie would play 45 games in the NHL, all with the Bruins—two after that first call-up in 1957–58 and then 43 in 1960–61, when he would score four goals with 10 assists. (I refuse to say he "only" played 45 NHL games because, given the obstacles he had to surmount, it remains remarkable that he played any at all.) He also played in various senior and minor professional leagues during a career that spanned two decades.

Upon his retirement, and for far too long, Willie was neither celebrated by the hockey community, nor sought after to tell his remarkable story. And he was characteristically content.

Fortunately, others were not.

Bryant McBride, a former college hockey player at West Point and Trinity who earned a master's degree from Harvard, was one of my first hires upon becoming NHL commissioner in 1993. Bryant amusingly recalls being upset as a boy in Sault Ste. Marie, Ontario, when he first learned of Willie O'Ree—because Bryant dreamed that *he* would be the first Black player in our league.

Among Bryant's roles as vice president for business development was pursuing the passion we both shared: extending access to our great game to underserved communities. During one of our many conversations on the subject in 1994, Bryant remarked that a mutual friend, longtime USA Hockey coach and executive Lou Vairo, said: "We should find Willie O'Ree." I remember being amazed that such an important figure in hockey history could somehow be "lost" and encouraged Bryant to find Willie.

Through a friend at the FBI, Bryant located Willie. He was working in the security department at the Hotel Del

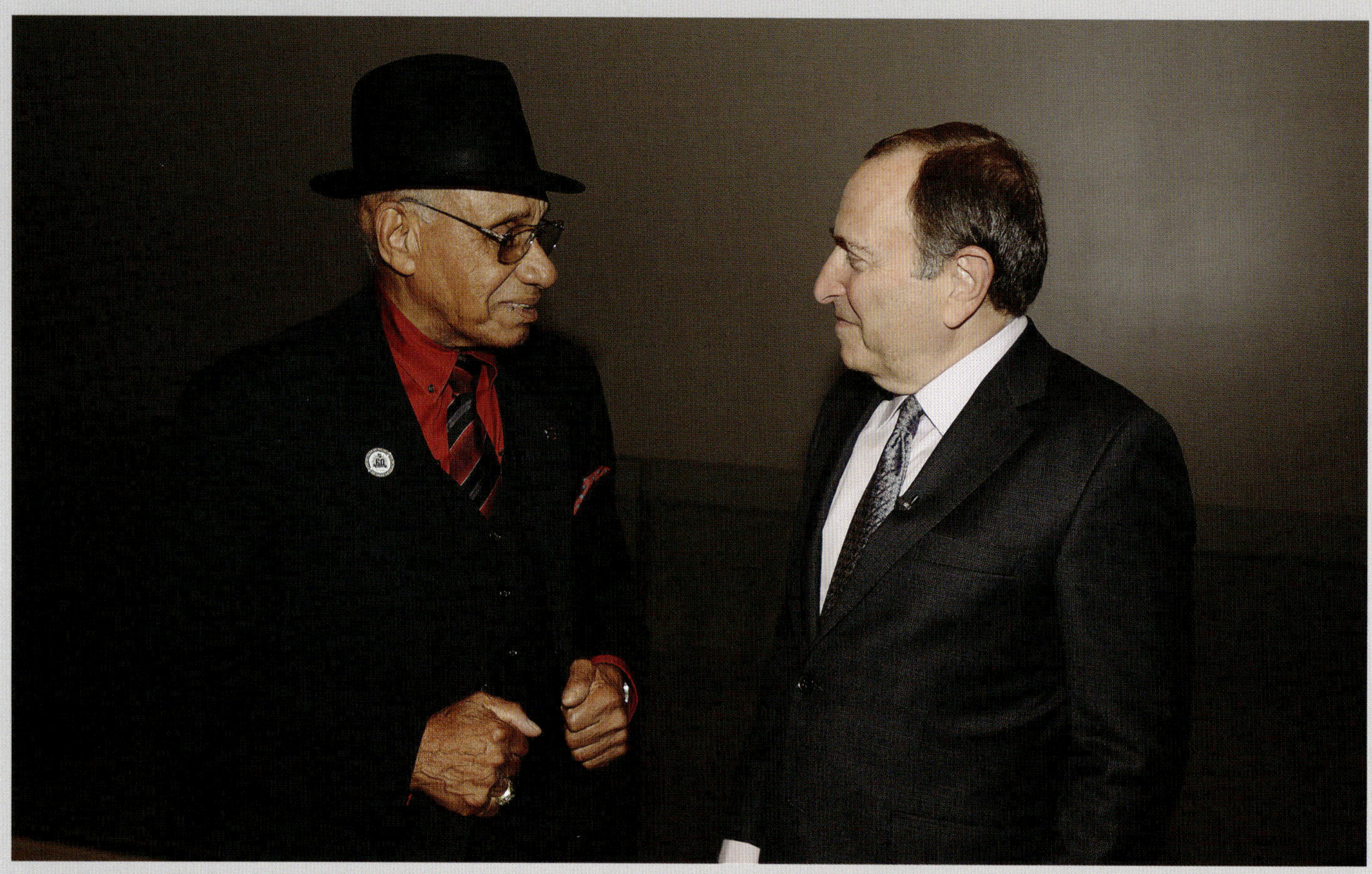

Willie O'Ree and NHL commissioner Gary Bettman tour the Smithsonian Museum of African American History and Culture in 2018. The two have been close friends for decades. (Photograph by Greg Fiume/Getty Images)

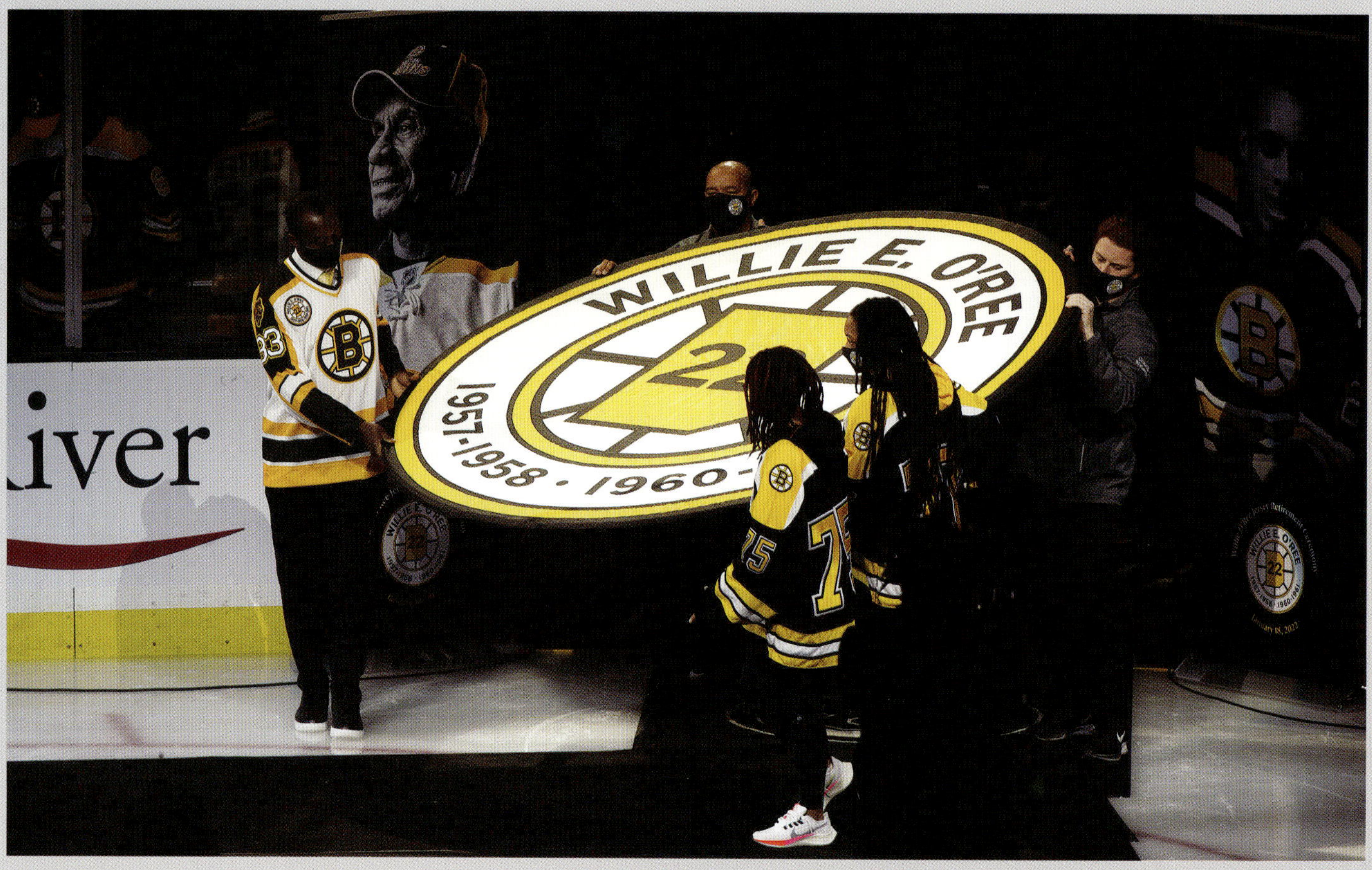

On January 18, 2022, Bruins alumnus Anson Carter leads a contingent carrying Willie O'Ree's retired number banner at TD Garden. O'Ree was just the 12th Bruin to have his number retired. (Photograph by Richard T Gagnon/Getty Images)

Coronado in San Diego. We connected, and soon he joined the league as the NHL's diversity ambassador. Thus began the great second act of Willie's career.

Over the next three decades, Willie would combine his boundless energy, his relentless positivity, his unflinching belief in the power of hockey to transform, and his classy and gentle personal touch to impact the lives of tens of thousands of young people. At hundreds of instructional clinics—including several Willie O'Ree NHL Skills Weekends (the one in Boston in April 2022 cohosted by SCORE Boston comes to mind)—and in countless one-on-one conversations, Willie has imparted hockey values and life lessons concerning personal discipline, teamwork, goal-setting, commitment, and determination.

Had there been no Willie O'Ree to wear that Bruins sweater and step onto the Forum ice on January 18, 1958—or had it been someone who did not possess his rare combination of grit and grace—it is difficult to imagine that there would have been 18 Black players on NHL rosters at the beginning of the 2022–23 season. From Grant Fuhr to Anson Carter to Jarome Iginla to PK Subban to Wayne Simmonds to Seth Jones, many of the finest players in recent NHL history stand on the shoulders of Willie O'Ree.

So many more children over the last three decades owe some measure of their success in life to having met and learned from Willie O'Ree.

That enormous impact at all levels of our game is why Willie earned induction into the Hockey Hall of Fame in 2018 and the Congressional Gold Medal in 2022. And why the Bruins retired his No. 22 to the rafters of TD Garden on January 18, 2022.

As I have been NHL commissioner for some time now, people often ask me what accomplishment makes me most proud. While I usually recoil at such questions, I will say that among the accomplishments that most matter is reuniting Willie O'Ree with the NHL family and helping to share his remarkable story.

The friendship that we have shared over the last nearly 30 years is one of my great joys.

Gary Bettman has served as commissioner of the National Hockey League since 1993.

BOSTON BRUINS (1950–1959)

Season	W	L	T	PTS	PTS%	Finish	Playoffs	Coach
1949–50	22	32	16	60	.429	5th of 6		Georges Boucher
1950–51	22	30	18	62	.443	4th of 6	Lost NHL Semifinals	Lynn Patrick
1951–52	25	29	16	66	.471	4th of 6	Lost NHL Semifinals	Lynn Patrick
1952–53	28	29	13	69	.493	3rd of 6	Lost Stanley Cup Final	Lynn Patrick
1953–54	32	28	10	74	.529	4th of 6	Lost NHL Semifinals	Lynn Patrick
1954–55	23	26	21	67	.479	4th of 6	Lost NHL Semifinals	Lynn Patrick (10–14–6) Milt Schmidt (13–12–15)
1955–56	23	34	13	59	.421	5th of 6		Milt Schmidt
1956–57	34	24	12	80	.571	3rd of 6	Lost Stanley Cup Final	Milt Schmidt
1957–58	27	28	15	69	.493	4th of 6	Lost Stanley Cup Final	Milt Schmidt
1958–59	32	29	9	73	.521	2nd of 6	Lost NHL Semifinals	Milt Schmidt

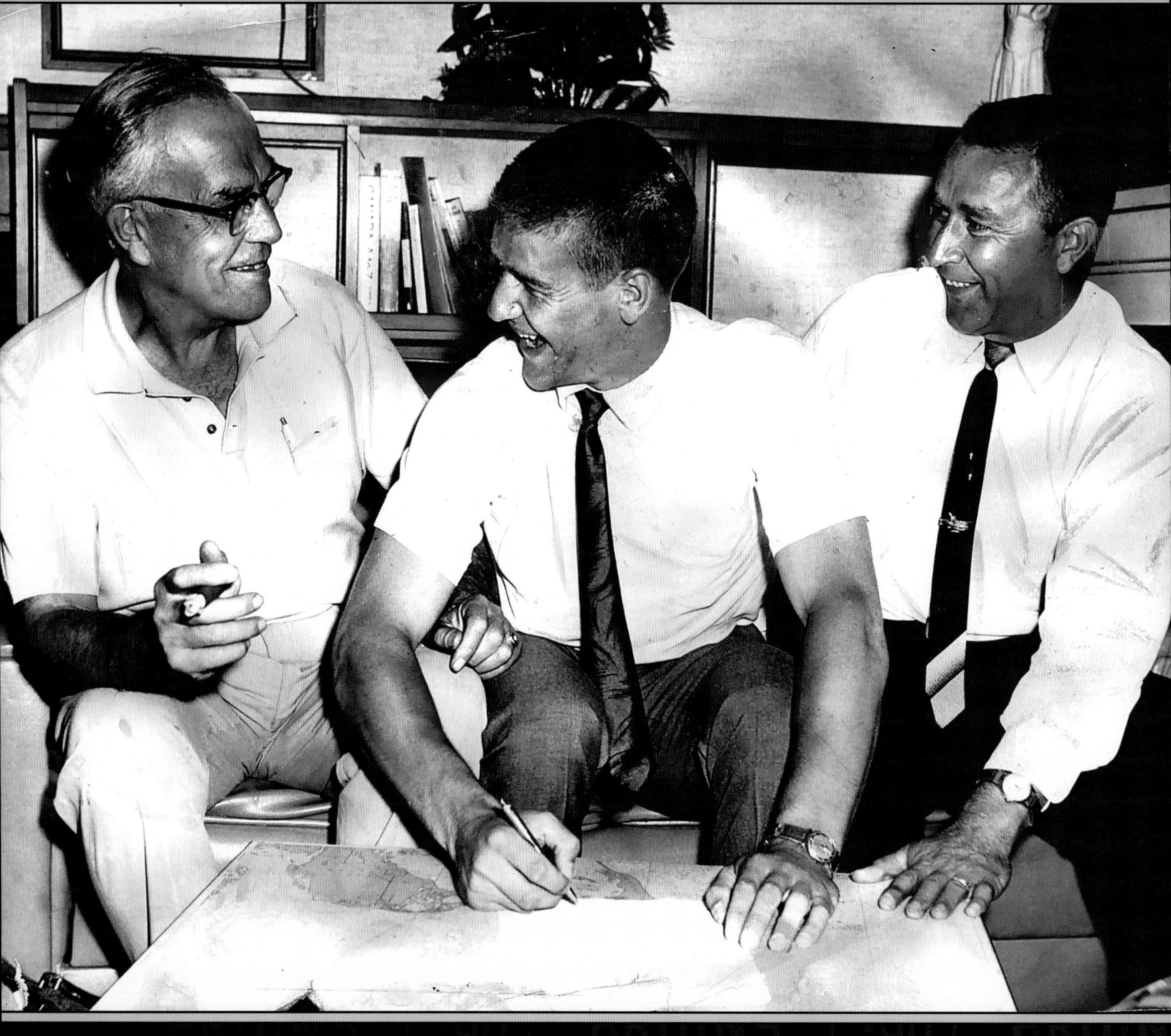

The Bruins and the NHL entered a new era on September 2, 1966, when the teenaged Bobby Orr (center), accompanied by his father, Doug (right), signed his first professional contract aboard Bruins general manager

1960s

THE RISE OF THE BIG BAD BRUINS

I'm not one to go out on a limb. I'd rather be pessimistic and perhaps surprise a few people later on. But in two or three years the Bruins will have a fine hockey team, a winning team. And it'll be a young one, too, a team that'll get better year after year.

—Hap Emms, Bruins general manager, 1966

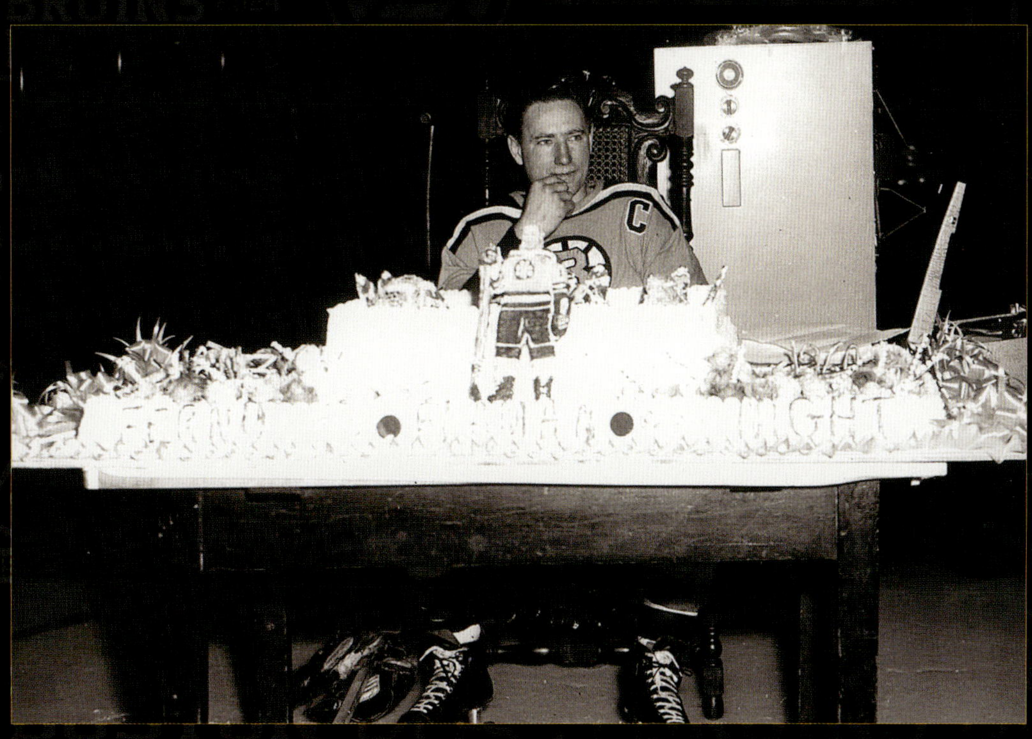

On December 30, 1960, the Bruins held Fernie Flaman Night at Boston Garden. The rugged defenseman served as team captain from 1955 to 1961. (Collection of The Sports Museum)

For most of the 1960s, the Bruins were an oft-dubious work in progress. As the Celtics, their Boston Garden neighbors, were in the midst of winning eight consecutive NBA championships, the Bruins were finishing out of the playoff picture each and every year from 1960 to 1967. The fact that there were only six teams in the entire NHL, and that four of them qualified for the playoffs each season, made the year-over-year performance of Boston's hockey team that much more dispiriting.

Despite their failures in the standings, however, the Bruins were a success at the box office, booking out the 13,909 seats at the Garden on a consistent basis throughout the early and mid-1960s. Boston fans flocked to the Garden to see the many stars residing among the 118 players in the Original Six.

A few players on those early 1960s Bruins teams, however, were destined for long-term tenures in Black and Gold—and would be around when all the losses turned into laurels. There was

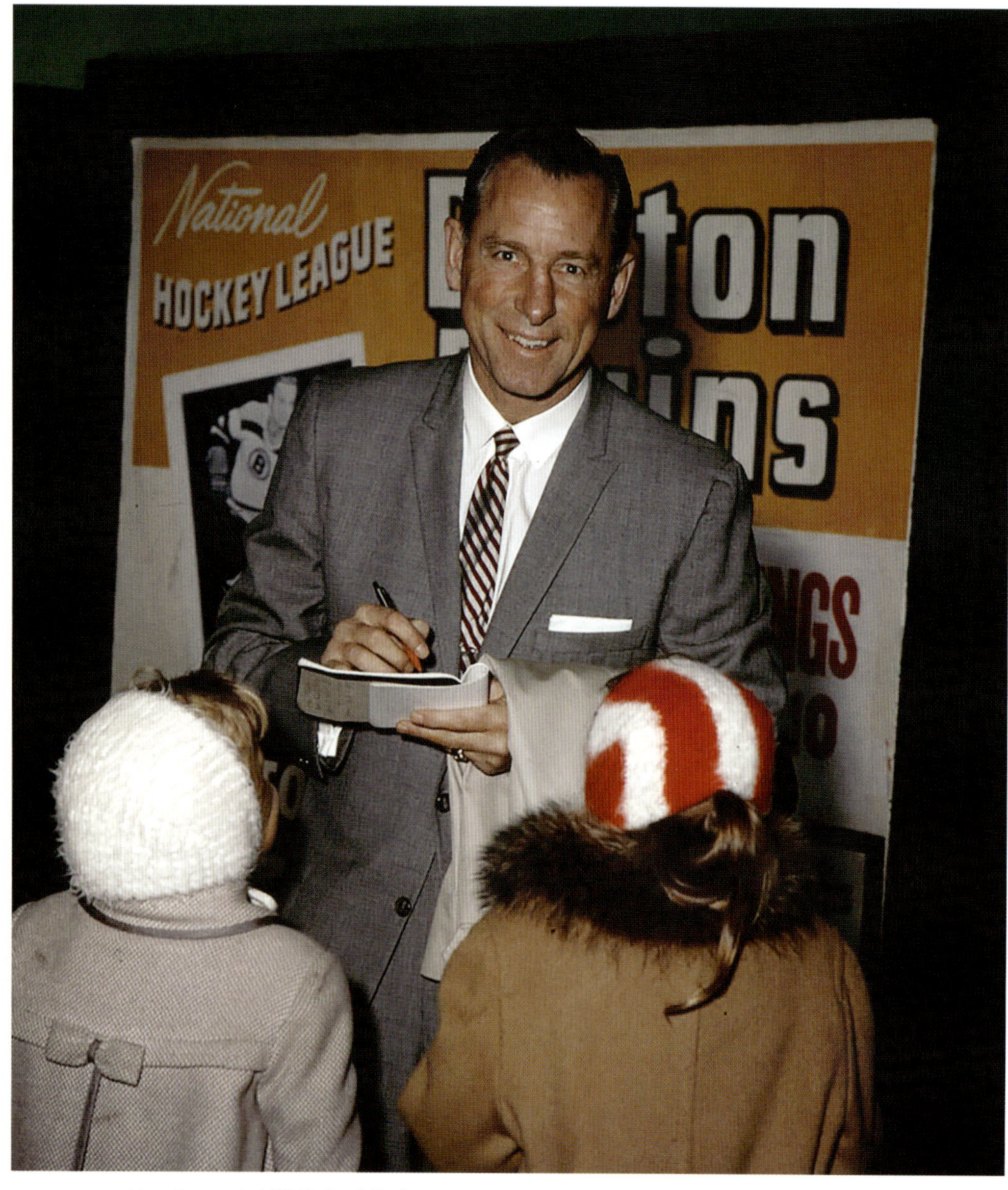

Head coach Milt Schmidt signs autographs at Boston Garden in 1961. Save for the 1961–62 season, the Bruins legend served as head coach from 1954 to 1966, 11 seasons in all. In 1966, he joined the front office as the assistant general manager. Schmidt was promoted to GM the following season. (Photograph by Weekend Magazine / Louis Jaques / Library and Archives Canada / e011166328)

goalie Eddie Johnston, maskless and tireless. There was Eddie Westfall, one of the best defensive forwards in the NHL. There was Ted Green, a tough, fearless defenseman who earned the nickname "Terrible Ted." And, of course, there was resplendent winger Johnny Bucyk.

All the while behind the scenes, the Bruins front office—led by shareholder and future team president Weston Adams Sr., general managers Lynn Patrick and Hap Emms, and head coach Milt Schmidt—scoured Canada for young players to stock their system of junior and minor league teams designed to nurture talent and return the franchise to greatness. These were the days before the NHL entry draft, and the dimensions of talent acquisition were different. And it wasn't easy for the Bruins. "The player supply was tilted pretty good," said Harry Sinden. "New York, Boston, and Chicago…they had trouble getting talent, which mostly went to the two Canadian teams and Detroit."

The Bruins brass managed to overcome the systemic disadvantages and get it done, signing and developing such players as Derek Sanderson, Wayne Cashman, and Don Marcotte (not to mention a certain young defenseman from Parry Sound, Ontario). In the mid-1960s, the young players started to arrive and blend in with the veteran core, supplemented by a few key trade acquisitions. They would all join forces to become the legendary team soon to be known across the sporting world as the "Big Bad Bruins."

It all started to crystallize in 1966 with the concurrent arrival of new head coach Harry Sinden and the aforementioned young defenseman from Parry Sound, Bobby Orr. Soon the Bruins were climbing up the standings and finding their way back into the playoffs. They ended the 1960s on the brink of bringing the Stanley Cup back to Boston for the first time in nearly 30 years.

But it was bigger than that. The arrival of Sinden and Orr marked the start of a golden era of professional hockey in both Boston and the National Hockey League. In the years that followed, the Bruins, with the presence of the supremely talented and charismatic Orr, were primarily responsible for the league tripling in size, player salaries soaring, and the securing of a national TV contract with CBS.

From the deepest depths of the NHL basement to almost regal status in less than a decade.

Never before—or since—has there been an ascendancy in Boston sports annals as rapid or as glorious.

JOHNNY BUCYK

IN THE FALL OF 1957, Johnny Bucyk arrived in Boston. He has never left.

The scope of his tenure with the Bruins is truly remarkable. For nearly seven decades, Bucyk has enjoyed an unbroken affiliation with the Bruins. It is the longest such reign in the history of North American professional sports.

He is known to one and all as "Chief." How did he get the nickname? "The honor goes to Bronco Horvath," said Bucyk in a 2022 interview. "Bronco was my centerman. And when we were playing together back in Edmonton [in the Western Hockey League in the mid-1950s], Bronc used to tell me, 'You know what, you're the Chief in the corners. You get the puck and I will be out in front.'... And whenever the puck went into the corner, I went in after it. I'd get it out of the corner for him and give it to him. Then the name Chief just stuck."

After coming to Boston, Bucyk enjoyed some immediate success on some good Bruins teams in the late 1950s as part of the Uke Line, along with Horvath and Vic Stasiuk (two former teammates from his Edmonton days who were also of Ukrainian descent). And then came the lean years from 1960 to 1967. "Eight years without being in the playoffs," said Bucyk. "And that was tough. I had to get a summer job [with a garage company].... And I did everything from washing cars to serving as the shop foreman. So that was fun. At least I was able to stand on my own ground."

Then, finally, the glory years arrived. As part of a powerhouse line also consisting of Fred Stanfield and Johnny "Pie" McKenzie, Bucyk was a top producer on several of the highest scoring teams in NHL history. He also emerged as a quiet, dependable leader. "Any rookie comes in, Chief would be looking after him," said Bobby Orr. "Chief was the ultimate captain looking after the guys. But Chief would speak up if anyone was stepping out of line."

Bucyk's style of play was tough and physical—but clean. There was some measure of irony that the captain of the Big Bad Bruins in the late 1960s and early 1970s was also a two-time winner of the Lady Byng Trophy awarded to the league's most gentlemanly player.

Following the 1977–78 season, Bucyk retired at age 42 after 21 seasons in Black and Gold. Since then, he has served the Bruins in a variety of capacities, including radio color analyst (frequently alongside legendary play-by-play man Bob Wilson), alumni director, road services coordinator, and goodwill ambassador. Much beloved, his connection to the Bruins mirrors that enjoyed by his Boston pro sports village elders, namely, Tommy Heinsohn of the Celtics, Johnny Pesky of the Red Sox, and Gino Cappelletti of the Patriots.

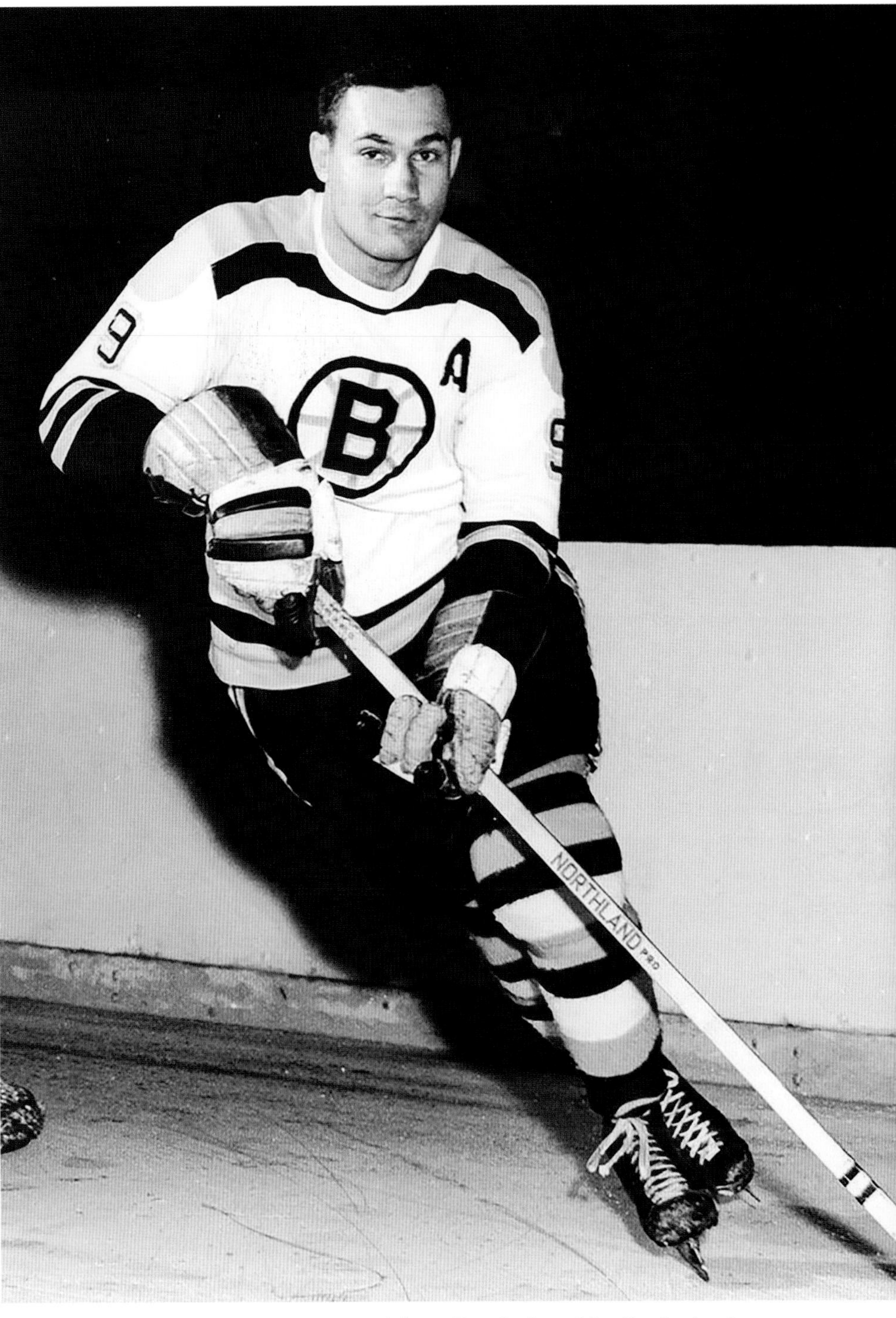

Johnny Bucyk played for the Bruins from 1957 to 1978. He remains the franchise's all-time leader in goals and ranks second in a number of other major categories, including games played, assists, points, and power-play goals. He is the one and only "Chief." (Photograph by Al Ruelle, Collection of The Sports Museum)

"I never ever thought I would do 60-some-odd years with the Boston Bruins organization," Bucyk said. "I am very thankful and happy that Charlie Jacobs and Cam [Neely] kept me on. They made me one of the team ambassadors, which is great. They know that I just love Boston and I love the people and I love the team. The organization has been excellent to me."

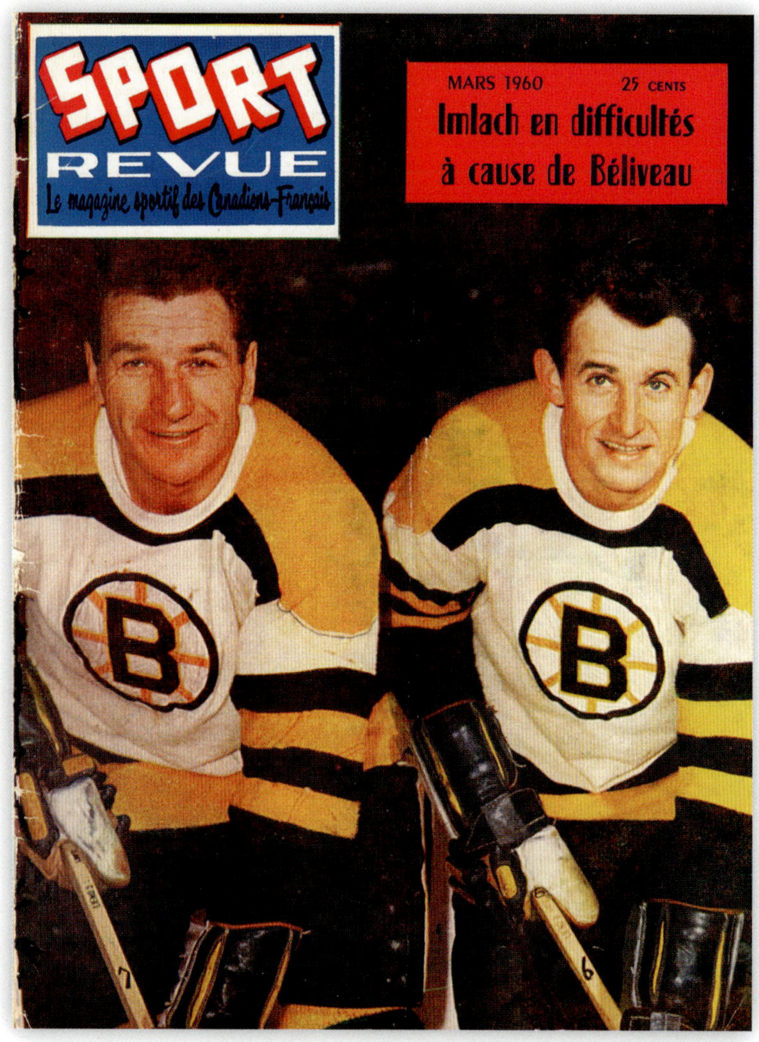

The Bruins tandem of Vic Stasiuk (left) and Bronco Horvath (right) graced the cover of the March 1960 edition of the French-language Sport Revue *magazine. Along with linemate Johnny Bucyk, they comprised the famous Uke Line that skated together for four seasons (1957–1961). During the 1959–60 season, the line was at the peak of its production, with Horvath ranking second in the league with 80 points (trailing only Bobby Hull), Stasiuk recording 68 points, and Bucyk adding 52 points.* (Collection of Richard A. Johnson)

DOUG MOHNS

He broke in as a forward. Then, after several years, he switched to defense. Then it was back to forward. In his 11 seasons with the Bruins (1953–1964), Doug Mohns proved to be the epitome of versatility—and the ultimate team player.

As one of the many players sent to Boston by the Barrie Flyers junior team, Mohns was part of a generation of young players developed by the organization that helped lead the Bruins to consecutive Stanley Cup Final appearances in 1957 and 1958.

In 1959–60, Mohns appeared to have tied former Bruin Flash Hollett's NHL record for goals scored by a defenseman with 20, only to have the record not recognized by the league because he had played seven games at left wing. The fact that he scored all his goals while playing defense unfortunately wasn't taken into account by the league.

Possessed of a distinctively strong skating style that led to his nickname of "Diesel," Mohns also displayed a toughness that endeared him to Boston fans, enduring two broken jaws while skating with the Bruins.

Following the 1964 season, Mohns was traded to Chicago, where he teamed up with Bobby Hull and Stan Mikita, among others, on some powerhouse Black Hawk teams. He retired in 1975 after 22 highly productive, and versatile, NHL campaigns.

LEO BOIVIN

At 5′8″ and 183 pounds, Bruins defenseman Leo Boivin had the perfect build for the body-checking master he became. Checking was an art that he perfected to such a degree that it gained him a Hockey Hall of Fame berth at the conclusion of his 19-year NHL career. As teammate Eddie Westfall relayed to historian Stan Fischler, "Leo's checks were hard, but clean. He was very special and one of the few players for whom it could be said that body-checking became an art form."

Boivin was a symbol of those hard-slogging Bruins teams that missed the playoffs for eight consecutive seasons. His gift for understatement was evident when he told sportswriter Herb Ralby, "I like contact. I don't intentionally try to hurt anybody.... If we win, it means more money to me. If my checking helps our team win, I'll hit everybody I can."

Boivin was named captain of the Bruins in 1963. Shortly thereafter, he willingly switched from defense to left wing despite the fact that he hadn't played forward since his junior days in Port Arthur, Ontario. Answering the call from head coach Milt Schmidt, who was desperate for help up front, Boivin responded, "If it will help the team, I'll do it. I'll play anyplace."

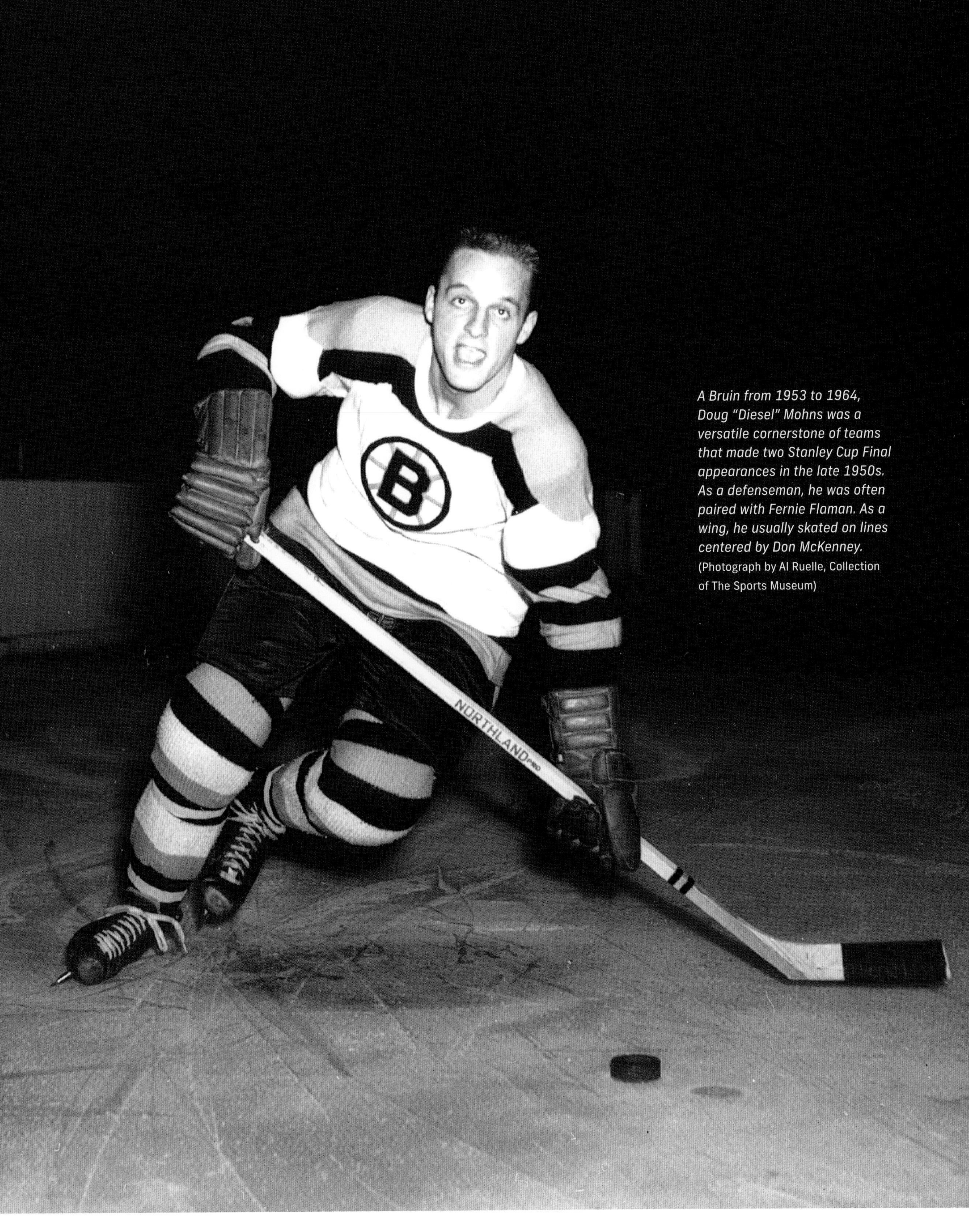

A Bruin from 1953 to 1964, Doug "Diesel" Mohns was a versatile cornerstone of teams that made two Stanley Cup Final appearances in the late 1950s. As a defenseman, he was often paired with Fernie Flaman. As a wing, he usually skated on lines centered by Don McKenney. (Photograph by Al Ruelle, Collection of The Sports Museum)

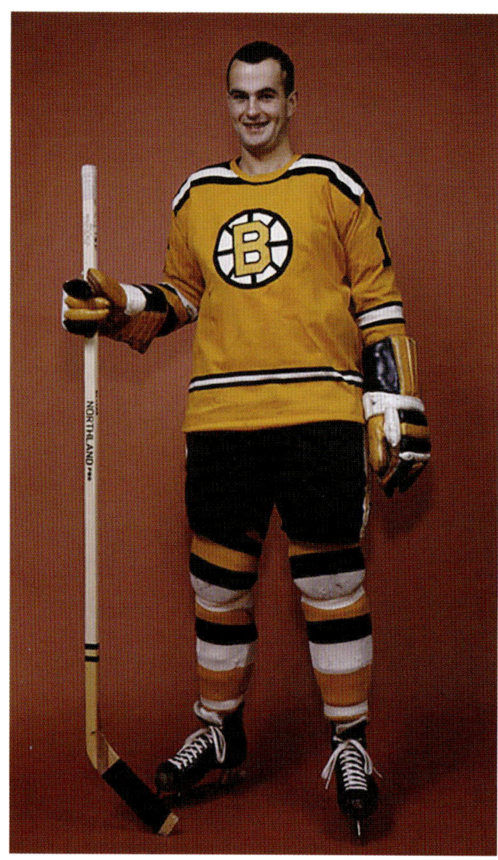

Five-time NHL All-Star center Murray Oliver (right) played seven of 17 NHL seasons for the Bruins. He was one of the team's few bright spots during the first half of the 1960s, averaging 18 goals per season. (Photograph by Weekend Magazine/Louis Jaques/Library and Archives Canada/e002505676)

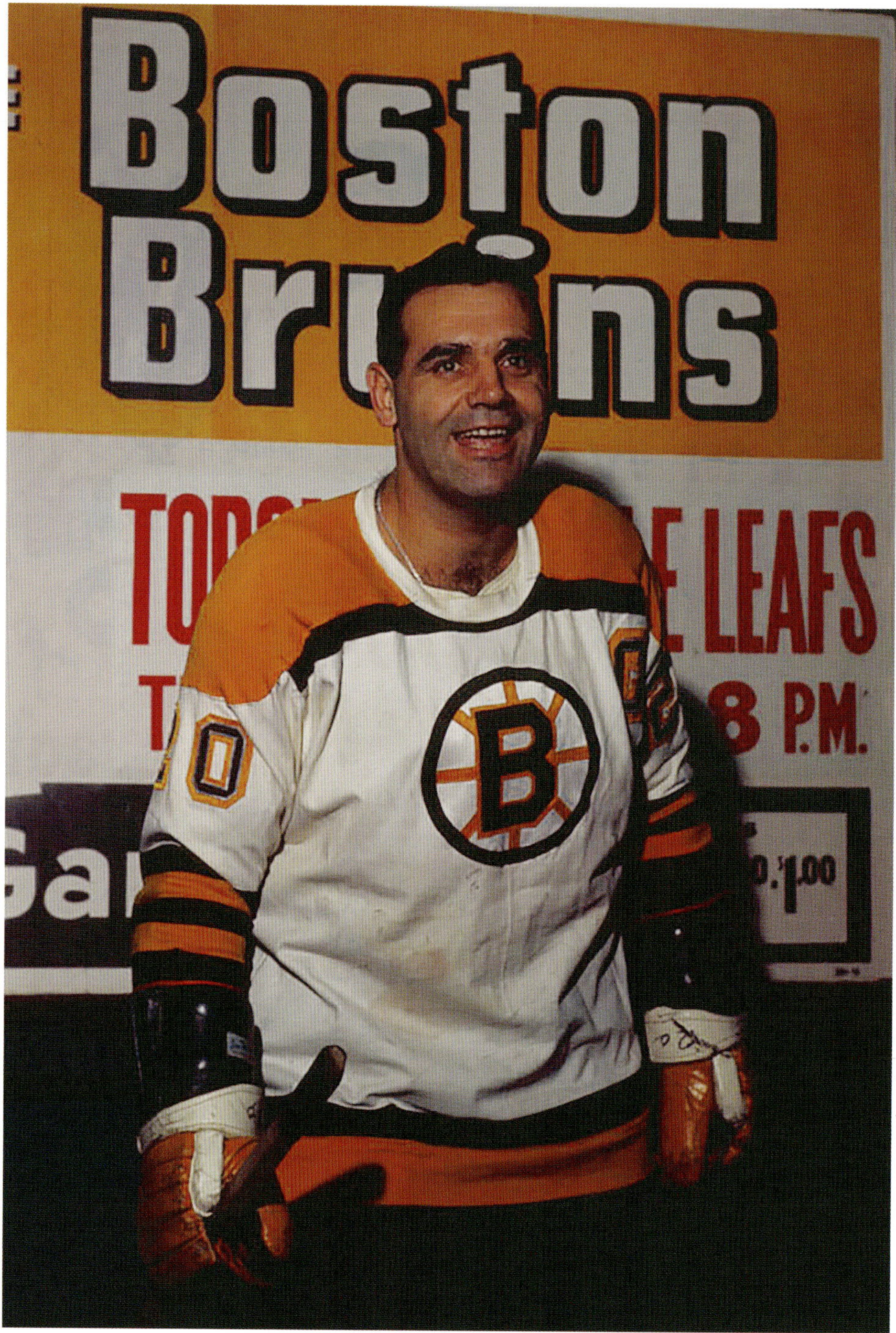

In his dozen seasons as a Bruins defenseman, Leo Boivin was known as one of the most skilled body checkers in the NHL. He later coached the St. Louis Blues for two seasons in the 1970s and was elected to the Hockey Hall of Fame in 1986. (Photograph by Jaques, Louis/Library and Archives Canada/e002343751)

ONE NIGHT IN GANANOQUE: THE DISCOVERY OF BOBBY ORR

On the evening of March 31, 1961, the Bruins sent a group of team executives (including chairman Weston Adams Sr., head coach Milt Schmidt, and scout Wren Blair) to Gananoque, Ontario, to scout two players on the local bantam team, Rick Eaton and Doug Higgins.

Taking their places in different sections of the packed arena, the Bruins executives soon found themselves fixating on the 13-year-old defenseman on the Parry

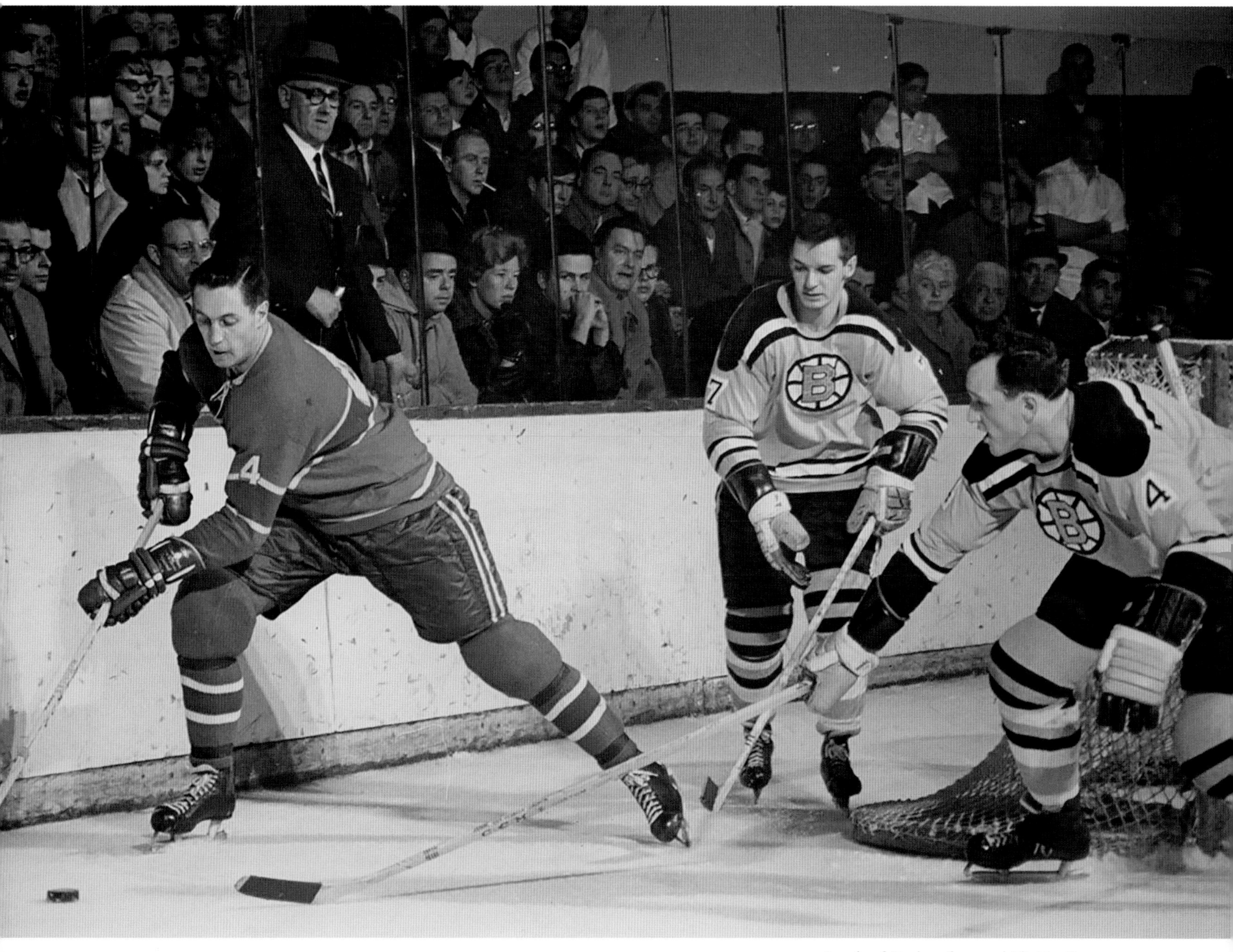

A pair of Bruins, forward Pit Martin (center) and defenseman Al Langlois (right), track Montreal center Jean Beliveau during an exhibition game in 1966. Langlois owns the distinction of being the last Bruin to wear No. 4 prior to Bobby Orr. (Collection of The Sports Museum)

Sound team who was clearly the best player on the ice. "We split up in the rink and decided we would meet up at one end when the game was over," Schmidt recalled in a 2017 interview with *Boston Globe* sportswriter Kevin Paul Dupont. "Well, to make a long story short, we all came out of that game with the same knowledge: forget Eaton and Higgins, we'll take that Orr kid."

The following year, the Bruins signed Bobby Orr at the age of 14 to an NHL C Form. From 1962 to 1966, the teenaged Bobby Orr would continue to grow and develop while playing with the Bruins' amateur affiliate, the Oshawa Generals.

It turned out that the Montreal Canadiens, Detroit Red Wings, and Toronto Maple Leafs had all wanted to sign Orr, too—but the Bruins were the team that got it done.

The key factor was scout Wren Blair and his salesmanship, charm, and persistence. "Wren Blair came and went into Parry Sound until they convinced my mother," said Orr in a 2022 interview. "My dad was all in. My mother needed a little convincing." For that alone, the charismatic scout remains one of the great unsung heroes in Bruins history.

And what about Eaton and Higgins, the original focus of the scouting trip to Gananoque? In due course, the Bruins would sign both prospects. Neither, however, would end up playing in the NHL.

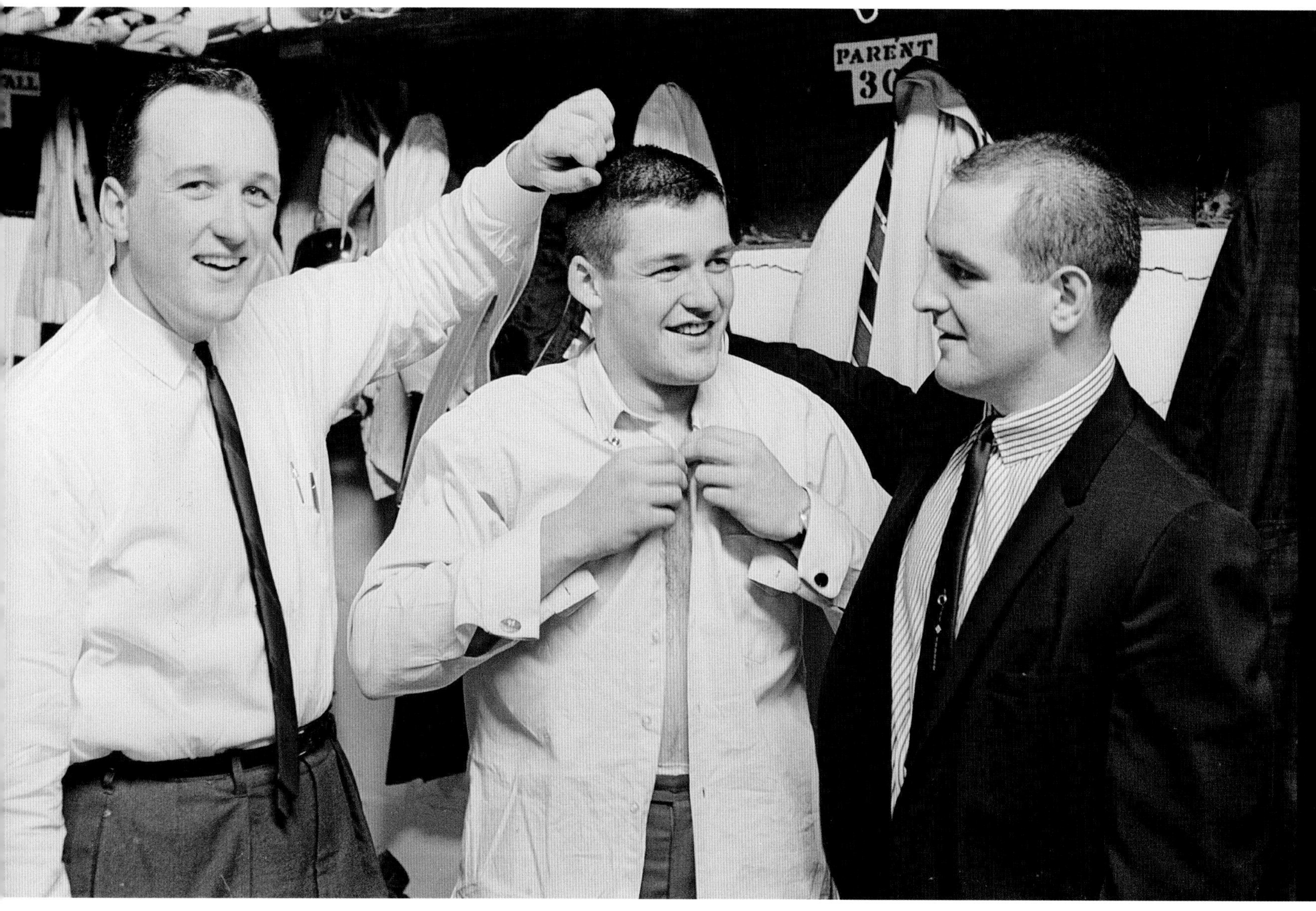

Al Langlois, Bernie Parent, and Forbes Kennedy (from left to right) are shown following a Bruins game at Boston Garden during the 1965–66 season. Langlois was a veteran defenseman in his final NHL season, Parent was a rookie goaltender, and Kennedy, a relentless checker and penalty killer, was wrapping up his four-year stint with the Bruins.
(Photograph from The Brearley Collection, courtesy of the Boston Public Library)

A TALE OF TWO GOALIES

IN AN ODD TWIST OF FATE, two of the goalies who proved to be among the greatest in NHL history and the most formidable opponents of the Big Bad Bruins were either signed or drafted by Boston during the first half of the 1960s.

The first was Bernie Parent, a Montreal native who started to shine on the Bruins' Niagara Falls Flyers junior team in the mid-1960s. Parent was pressed into service with the Bruins during the 1965–66 season, appearing in 39 games. After the next season, which saw him split his time between Boston and the Oklahoma City minor league team, Parent was left unprotected in the 1967 expansion draft. He was promptly poached by the Philadelphia Flyers. In 1974, Parent helped lead the Broad Street Bullies to their first-ever Stanley Cup over a Bruins team that included several of his former teammates.

The other goalie that got away was Ken Dryden. The Bruins selected him with the 14th overall pick in the second NHL Amateur Draft in 1964. Within days, though, they traded Dryden's rights along with minor leaguer Alex Campbell to the Montreal Canadiens for Paul Reid and Guy Allen, neither of whom would ever appear in a game for the Black and Gold. It was only after an outstanding career at Cornell University and then with Montreal that Dryden learned he had once been a Bruins draftee. It seems his agent had led him to believe he had always been a member of the Canadiens organization.

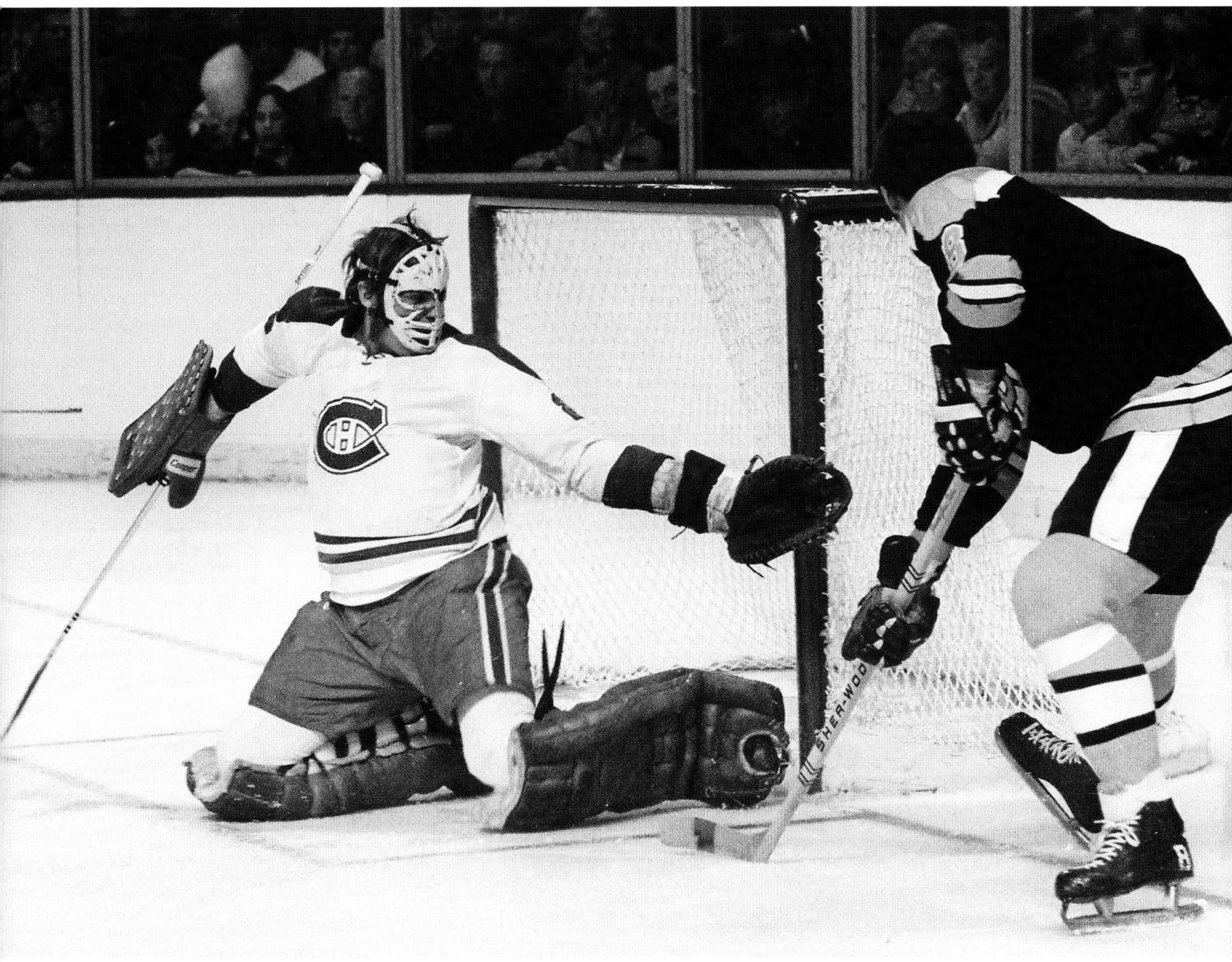

High-scoring Bruins right wing Ken Hodge attempts to put one past Montreal goaltender Ken Dryden in action from the early 1970s. Years earlier, the Bruins had selected Dryden with the 14th overall pick in the 1964 NHL Draft, but quickly traded his rights to Montreal. Had things worked out differently, Hodge and Dryden might have been teammates in Boston. It was not to be. (Photograph by Denis Brodeur/NHLI via Getty Images)

In the decade that followed (the 1970s), only four goaltenders won Stanley Cups—Dryden (6), Parent (2), and the Boston tandem of Gerry Cheevers and Eddie Johnston (2). Somewhat incredibly, all four had roots with the Bruins in the 1960s.

EDDIE JOHNSTON

THE CANADIENS LEFT Montreal native Eddie Johnston unprotected for Boston to draft at the NHL meetings in June 1962. It turned out to be one of the best gifts that the Habs ever bestowed upon the Bruins.

That fall, Johnston was quickly elevated to the position of Boston's No. 1 netminder. The following season (1963–64), Johnston was the last NHL goalie to play every second of the entire season for his team, logging 4,200 minutes and facing a staggering total of 2,454 shots over the course of 70 games for a last-place club that could muster only 18 victories. For his yeoman efforts, he received a salary of $8,500, boosted with a $1,000 bonus.

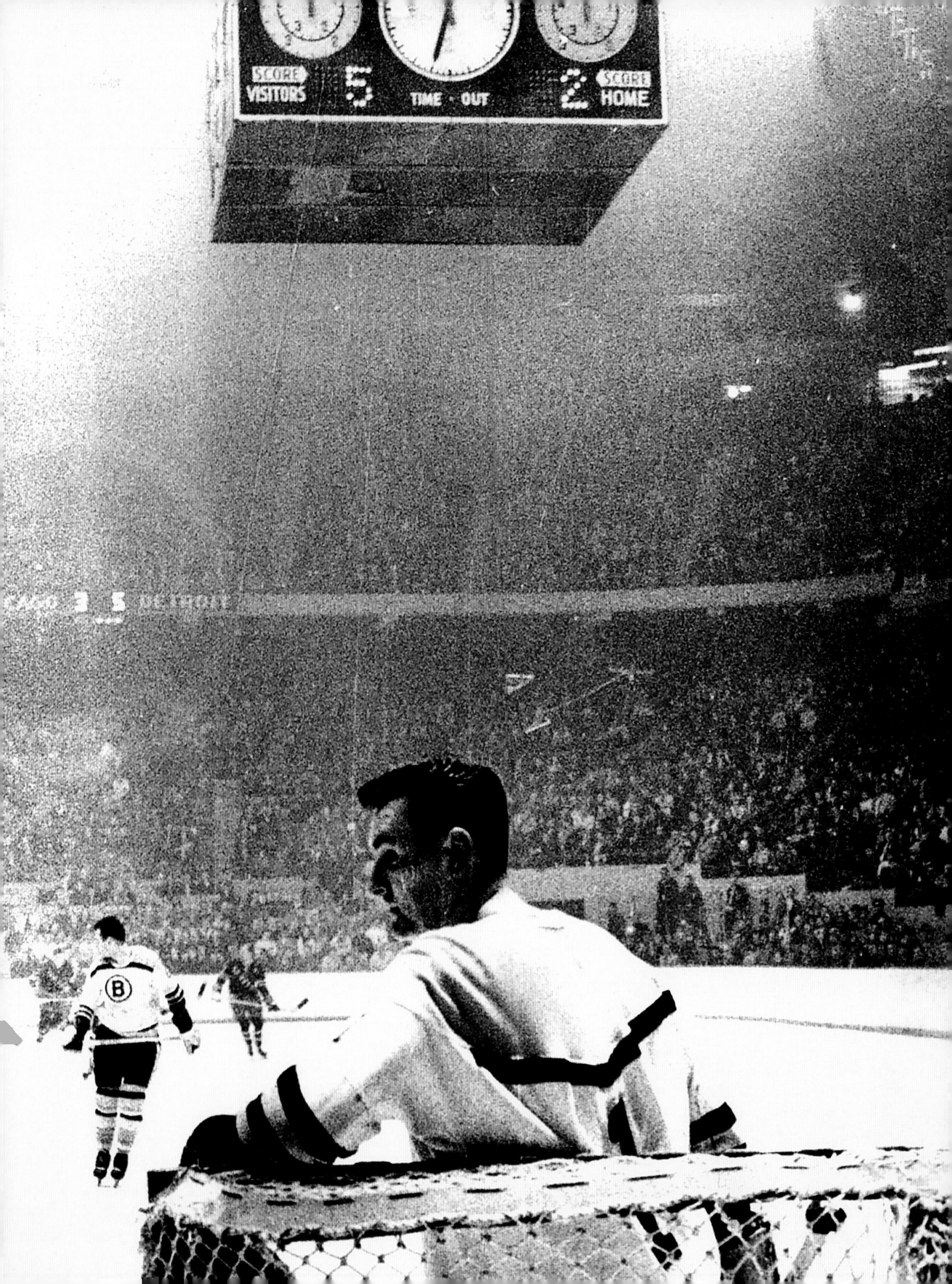

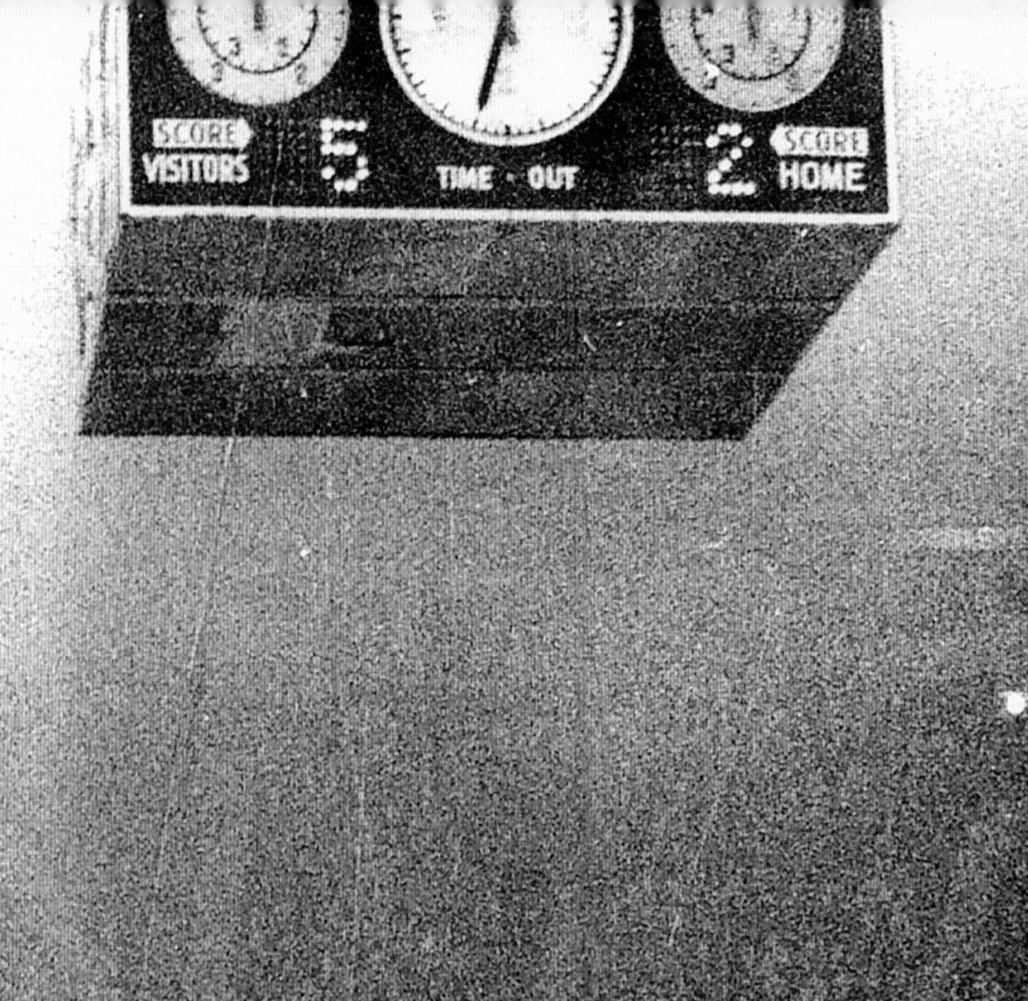
SCORE
VISITORS
5
TIME · OUT
2
SCORE
HOME

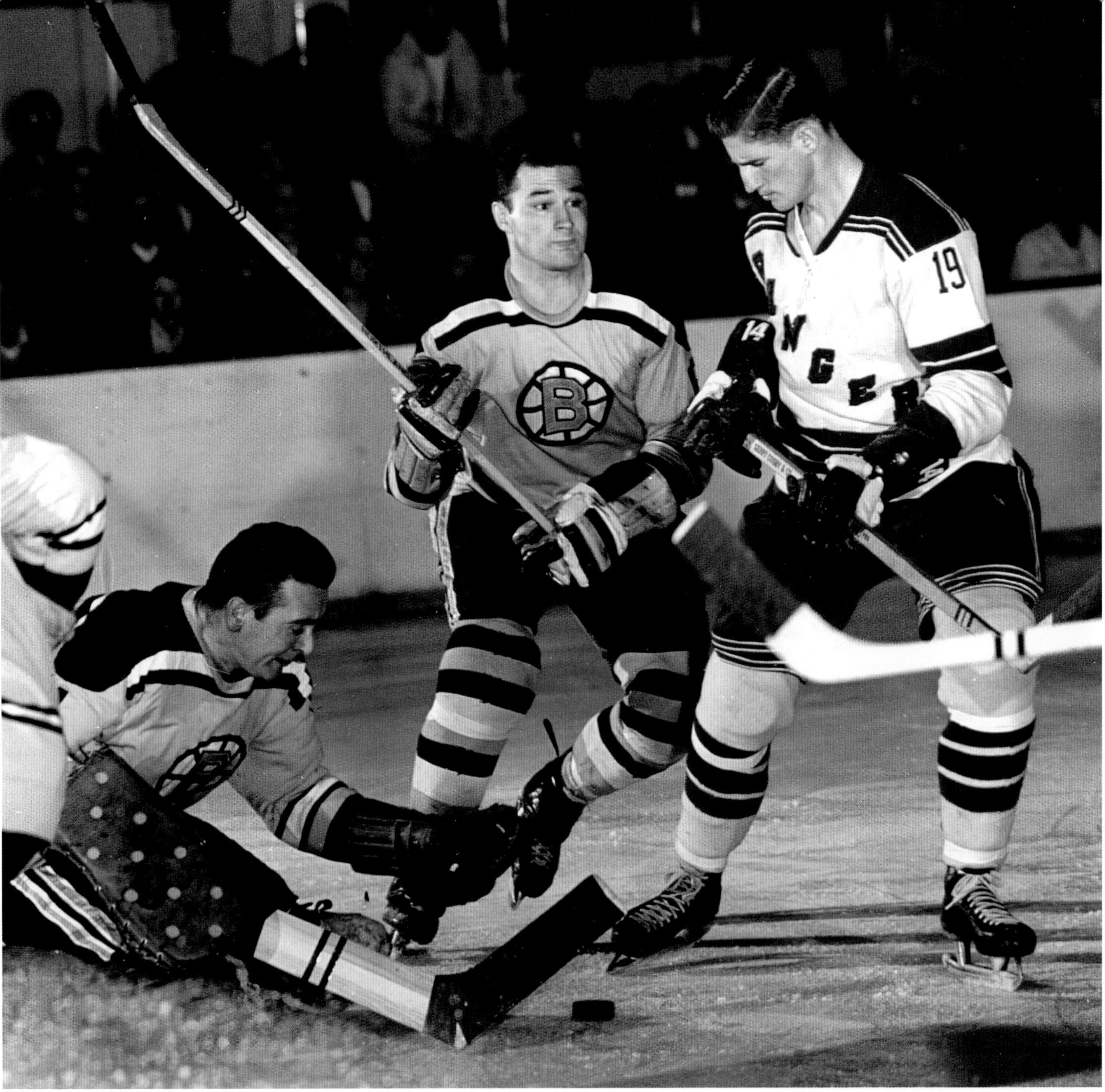

Above: Bruins defenseman Ted Green battles Jean Ratelle of the New York Rangers in front of Eddie Johnston's net during a game at Boston Garden in the mid-1960s. Green racked up 1,029 penalty minutes in 11 seasons with the Bruins. (Photograph by Bruce Bennett Studios via Getty Images Studios/Getty Images)

Opposite page: The struggles of the Bruins in the early 1960s are captured in this photograph of goalie Eddie Johnston leaning dejectedly on his net in the midst of another defeat. Brighter days lay ahead for Johnston, who would join forces with Gerry Cheevers in the late 1960s to form the best goaltending tandem in the league. (Collection of The Sports Museum)

And he did it all without wearing a mask. "Don't forget when I came into the league in 1962, there were only six goalies and we all wore No. 1," said Johnston in a 2022 interview. "And that was our IQ, too."

Teammates respected Johnston for his toughness. The year he played every game, Johnston suffered three broken noses and had the lobe of his ear sliced off. "But with only one goalkeeper, you were afraid to come out of the net," he told broadcaster Dick Irvin. "Somebody would step in and you might be gone."

They also revered him for his leadership, generosity of spirit, and sense of humor. As Bobby Orr recalled, "I used to go down when Eddie Johnston was playing…and I'd pat him on the pad before the game. And he'd look at me and he'd say, 'See you after the game,' thinking I'm gonna be down the ice all night."

Johnston split netminding duties with Gerry Cheevers while helping Boston capture Stanley Cups in 1970 and 1972. Cheevers got more of the playing time, but Johnston (now wearing a mask) saw a lot of action. This was especially true in the Bruins' run to the 1972 Cup, when Johnston started seven playoff games, winning six of them.

After retiring as a player, Johnston became a highly successful executive with the Pittsburgh Penguins. He thus owns the distinction of having played with Bobby Orr and having drafted Mario Lemieux.

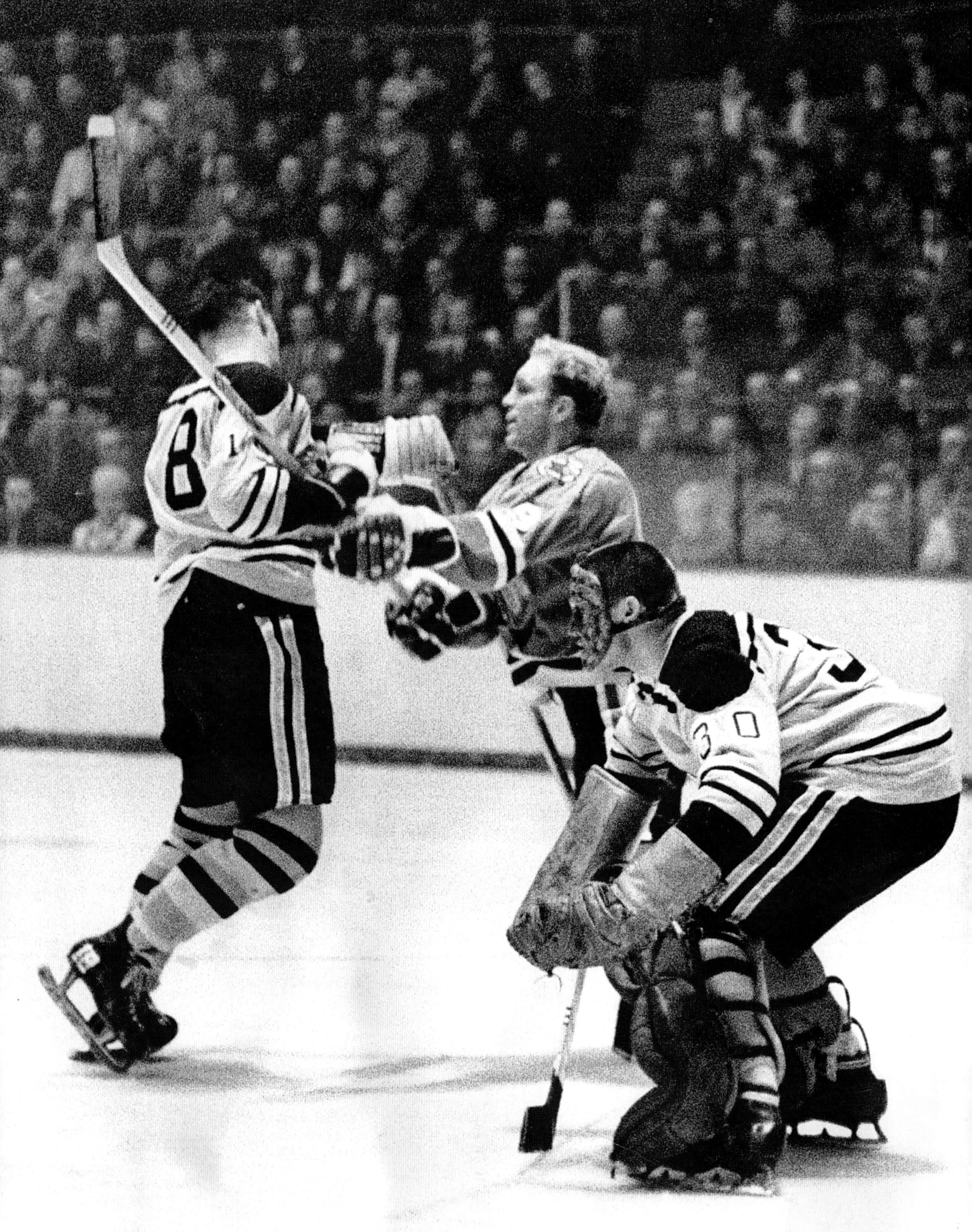

EDDIE WESTFALL

Eddie Westfall exuded character on and off the ice.

He also embodied versatility. In his first five seasons with the Bruins starting in 1961, Westfall played five positions for the team, even joking, "The next move is to get myself some goalie equipment."

He grew up on the blueline. "My four junior years, I was a defenseman," said Westfall in a 2022 interview. "The first two and a half to three years as a Bruin, I played on defense with some wonderful guys—one in particular, Leo Boivin. He was a wonderful help."

In the mid-1960s, Westfall found a permanent home on the right wing, earning the nickname "Steady Eddie." Harry Sinden, for one, thought the nickname was slightly misleading. "When it comes to the word *steady*, they're leaving a great deal unsaid," said Sinden. "There is a tendency to think of the individual things Eddie does well without adding them all together."

Those things included penalty killing, which he usually did in tandem along with a certain colorful linemate. "Eddie Westfall and Derek Sanderson are the two best penalty killers I've ever seen," said Bobby Orr in 2022.

And, individually, Westfall emerged as a premier defensive forward. The image longtime Bruins fans have of No. 18 is of him draped over the likes of opposing wings such as Gordie Howe, Frank Mahovlich, and, especially, Bobby Hull.

After the Cup-winning 1971–72 season, the Bruins lost Westfall to the New York Islanders in the expansion draft. And he will never forget his first game back in Boston Garden as an Islander in October 1972. "The first time I stepped on the ice in a regular game, I got a standing ovation—and I mean that is quite the reception when you come in as a visiting player," said Westfall. "Boy, they certainly made me feel wonderful.... That went on for quite a while too, I kid you not. It was a wonderful feeling to know that you left a nice impression with the people you played in front of for 11 years."

Opposite page: Eddie Westfall (18) became one of the best defensive forwards in NHL history, expertly shadowing the top scorers of the era. Here he jousts with Bobby Hull of the Chicago Black Hawks. Bruins goalie Bernie Parent awaits the outcome of the skirmish. (Collection of The Sports Museum, Donation by Marc Truant)

Boston Globe | December 5, 1964

B'S OSHAWA SIX WHIPS FLYERS

Wayne Cashman tipped in two first-period goals to pace the Oshawa Generals to a 3–1 win over the Niagara Falls Flyers in a Junior Ontario Hockey Association game at the Garden Saturday.

A PREVIEW OF COMING ATTRACTIONS

Boston Garden hosted two amateur games in 1964 and 1965 to give Boston fans a glimpse into their future. They were treated to the sight of nine future Bruins in action—Bobby Orr, Derek Sanderson, Gilles Marotte, Bill Goldsworthy, Jim Lorentz, Don Marcotte, Nick Beverly, Tom Webster, and Wayne Cashman.

Boston Globe | December 27, 1965

OSHAWA TOPS FLYERS AT GARDEN

Future Bruins Star Orr Excels in Rough Clash

Boston hockey fans can believe all those glowing reports they have been hearing about Bobby Orr, the Bruins star of the too-distant future. At least, the well-built 17-year-old defenseman of the Oshawa Generals lived up to the notices in leading his team to a 5 to 3 victory over the Niagara Falls Flyers in their game at the Garden Monday night. A crowd of 5,778 enthusiasts looked in on this demonstration by the two teams which are sponsored by the Bruins in the Junior Ontario Hockey Assn.

Definitely slated for promotion to the Boston varsity next season, Orr scored one of his team's goals, assisted on two others and showed that he can handle his defense chores with considerable skill.

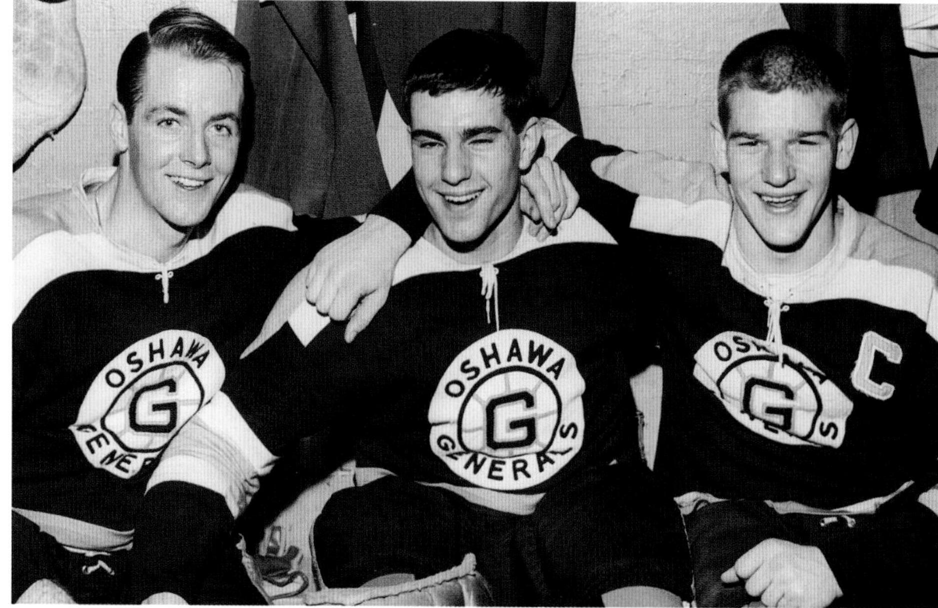

Bobby Orr (right) is shown with two of his teammates on the Oshawa Generals, Danny O'Shea and Ian Young. Orr and his Oshawa mates played two games at Boston Garden in the 1964–1965 time frame. (Photograph by Hulton Archive/ Getty Images)

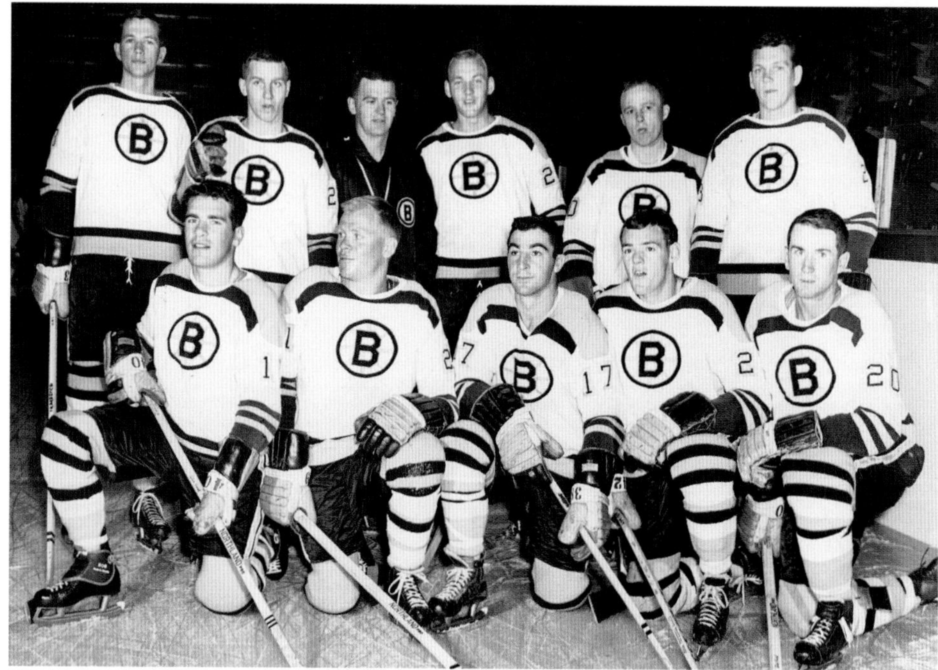

Young Bruins hopefuls at training camp in 1965 with future coach Harry Sinden: (front row, from left) Joe Watson, Glen Sather, J.P. Parise, Keith Wright, and Dallas Smith; (back row, left to right) Ron Buchanan, Skip Krake, Harry Sinden, Bill Goldsworthy, Gerry Cheevers, and Ted Irvine. (Collection of The Sports Museum)

THE ARRIVAL OF BOBBY ORR

IN THE FALL OF 1966, Bobby Orr attended his first training camp with the Bruins. "I can remember like it was yesterday, driving to London, Ontario, where the Bruins trained in those days," said Orr in a 2022 interview. "And I'm driving into the hotel, going and getting my key, walking over to my room. And I open up the door and there's a guy in the second bed. I recognized him. He was sitting. He was over there having a cigar, and I said, 'Hello, Mr. Bucyk.' And he says, 'Oh, no. You don't call me Mr. Bucyk. It's Chief or John.'"

It wasn't a certainty that Orr would make the team, however. He was, after all, only 18 years old—and a year of further seasoning in the minors made a certain amount of sense. Orr himself wasn't sure that he would stick. "When I was invited to my first pro camp, I really didn't think that I'd play on the Bruins that year.... I was living my dream and never really thought about it," he said. "I was having fun. I just couldn't wait to get on the ice, couldn't wait to go to practice, and that's really all I thought about. I wasn't reading newspaper articles or listening to what people were saying. As my dad said one time to me, 'Look, go out and have fun, work hard, be respectful, and we'll see what happens.'"

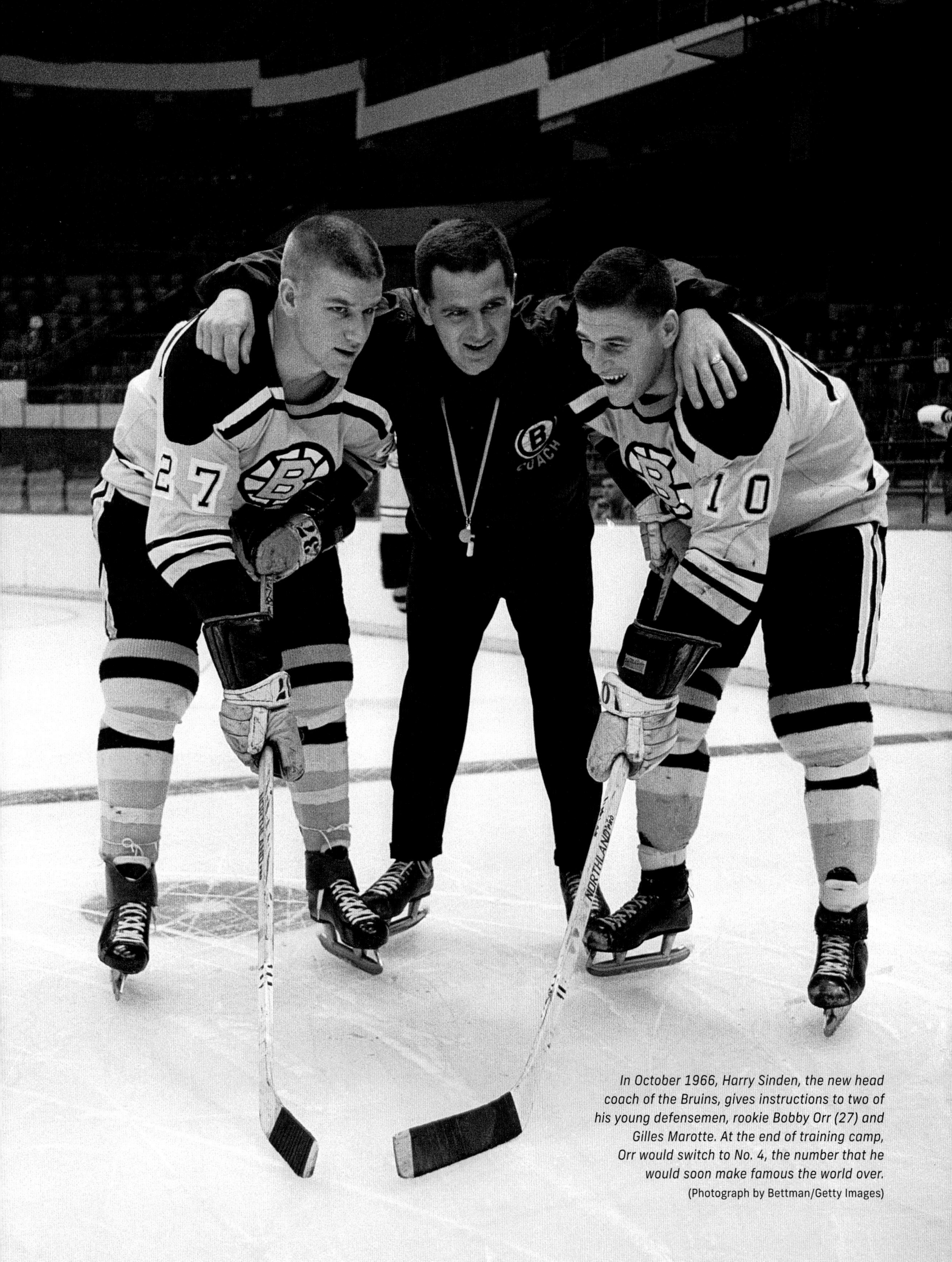

In October 1966, Harry Sinden, the new head coach of the Bruins, gives instructions to two of his young defensemen, rookie Bobby Orr (27) and Gilles Marotte. At the end of training camp, Orr would switch to No. 4, the number that he would soon make famous the world over.
(Photograph by Bettman/Getty Images)

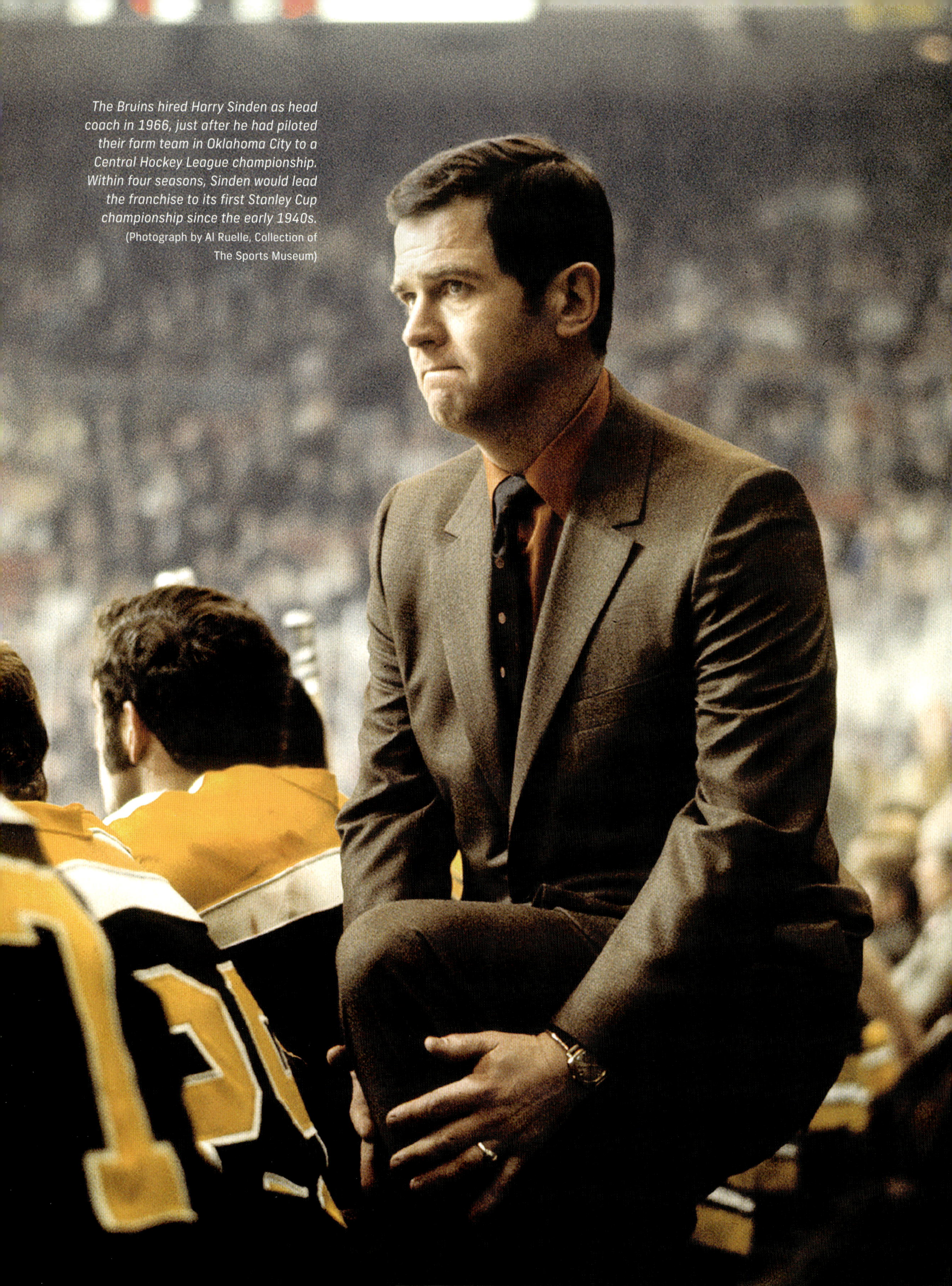

The Bruins hired Harry Sinden as head coach in 1966, just after he had piloted their farm team in Oklahoma City to a Central Hockey League championship. Within four seasons, Sinden would lead the franchise to its first Stanley Cup championship since the early 1940s.
(Photograph by Al Ruelle, Collection of The Sports Museum)

At the end of the day, though, there was no doubt that Orr belonged in the big time. "He came up the same year I did, in '66," remembered Harry Sinden. "I had only seen him play once before as a junior and I was totally impressed then. And things didn't change once he got to the NHL. He was a spectacular player."

Once the NHL season started, Orr quickly began making his mark on the ice. Off the ice, his transition was eased by several supportive veterans, especially Bucyk and Eddie Johnston. As Orr recounted, "They took me under their wings and looked after me, made sure I was going out with the guys, having dinner, talking, and looked after me on the ice.... Right from the first day, they were great."

DEREK SANDERSON

In December 1965, nine months before his first training camp in Boston, Bobby Orr of the Oshawa Generals took part in the "future Bruins" amateur game at the Garden. So did Derek Sanderson of the Niagara Falls Flyers. And young Sanderson went in with a definite plan—courtesy of his father. According to Sanderson, his father told him, "Oh, son, I've been giving this some thought. Bear with me! I don't care how well you play. Nobody is going to remember that. But I'll tell you what. They'll remember Bobby Orr and the one who beats him up."

Sanderson heeded the paternal advice and took on Orr during the contest. "It was a wrestling match," Sanderson said in 2022 interview. "It wasn't much—I jumped him. But that was enough for the press to get all over it and pick it up."

Two years later, Orr and Sanderson were in Boston together for the 1967–68 season, with Sanderson winning the same trophy that Orr had won the year before, the Calder Trophy as top NHL rookie. "Two things that put me in the National Hockey League—my father's love of the game and whistles," said Sanderson. "I never would have made it without a whistle. Laziest person, laziest player—I just was lazy. Blow the whistle and I respond. But that was it. So Harry Sinden sat there blowing the whistle back and forth and you get in shape and you feel great... that whistle."

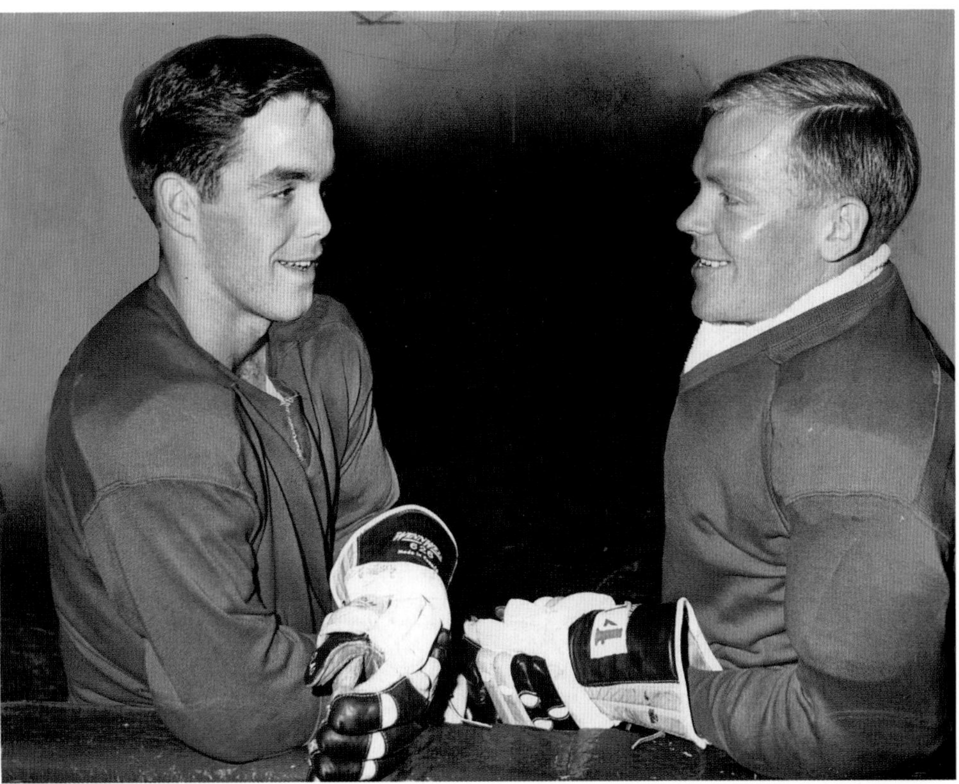

Bruins hopefuls Derek Sanderson (left) and Glen Sather take a break at training camp in 1966. Sanderson would make the Bruins the next season (1967–68), capturing the Calder Trophy as NHL rookie of the year. Sather played for the Bruins from 1966 to 1969. He would later forge his Hall of Fame credentials while coaching the Wayne Gretzky–led Edmonton Oilers to four Stanley Cups in the 1980s. (Collection of The Sports Museum)

Sanderson made noise off the ice, too. It was the hip, fast-moving late 1960s—and "the Turk" was out on the town and in the limelight, earning a reputation as a ladies' man and a playboy. "I never looked at it that way," Sanderson says today. "I was just curious. That's all. You know, everything was new to me. I'm from Niagara Falls. I'm from a small town in Canada. What do I know?"

On the ice, Sanderson was anything but flashy. Instead, he was a pure, fundamentally sound hockey player who did all the little things that help teams win hockey games. That included centering the league's best checking line, winning faceoffs, mastering the poke check, scoring shorthanded goals, and becoming an expert penalty killer. "To tell you the truth, it was Harry Sinden's idea," Sanderson said. "He said to me, 'Do you ever think of it [penalty killing] as an art form? You could be really good at this.'"

Sanderson would leave the Bruins for the World Hockey Association in 1972, signing a big contract that made him the highest-paid athlete in professional sports. Things didn't work out for him in the new league and he would be back the Bruins by early 1973. The Turk's second stint with the team involved two injury-plagued seasons before he left town again, this time for good. After retiring several years later, Sanderson heroically won a battle with sobriety and became a popular color analyst on Bruins television broadcasts alongside legendary play-by-play man Fred Cusick.

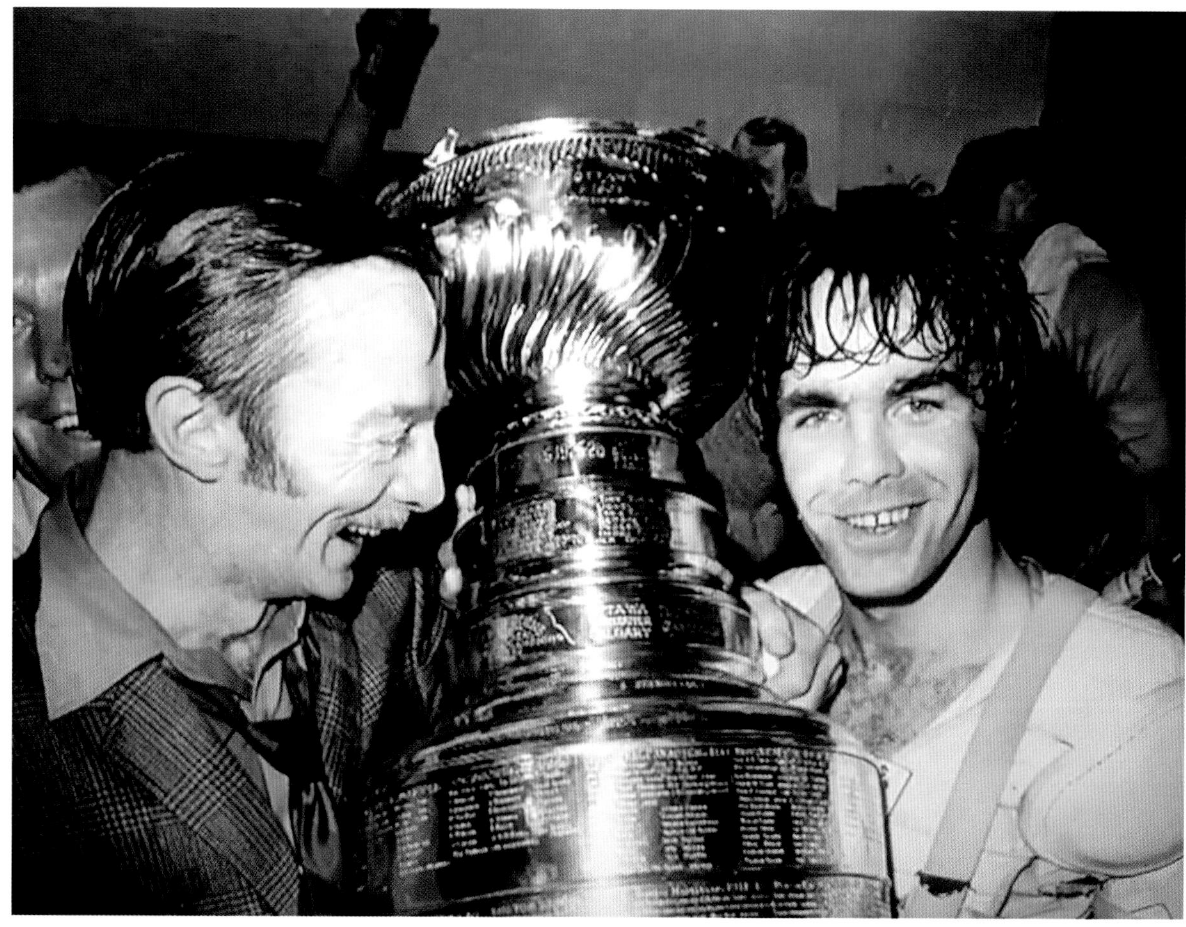

Derek Sanderson is shown here with his father Harold. Upon buying him his first pair of CCM Tacks skates in 1960 for the equivalent of a week's salary, Harold made his son promise to give him his first Stanley Cup ring. In May 1970, Derek would deliver on that promise. (Photograph courtesy of Derek Sanderson)

THE TRADE

On May 15, 1967, with minutes to spare until the trade deadline, Bruins assistant general manager Milt Schmidt completed what is properly considered to be the greatest trade in Bruins history, if not NHL history, sending defenseman Gilles Marotte, forward Pit Martin, and goalie Jack Norris to Chicago for forwards Phil Esposito, Ken Hodge, and Fred Stanfield. Schmidt consummated the trade after several days of negotiating with the Black Hawks as well as many hours lobbying his Boston superiors for permission to make the deal.

That same night, Schmidt acquired forward Eddie Shack from Toronto for Murray Oliver and cash. Schmidt always claimed both trades were significant, as the talented and unpredictably zany Shack helped jell the team, loosening up his mates and matching Bobby Orr stride-for-stride in skating drills.

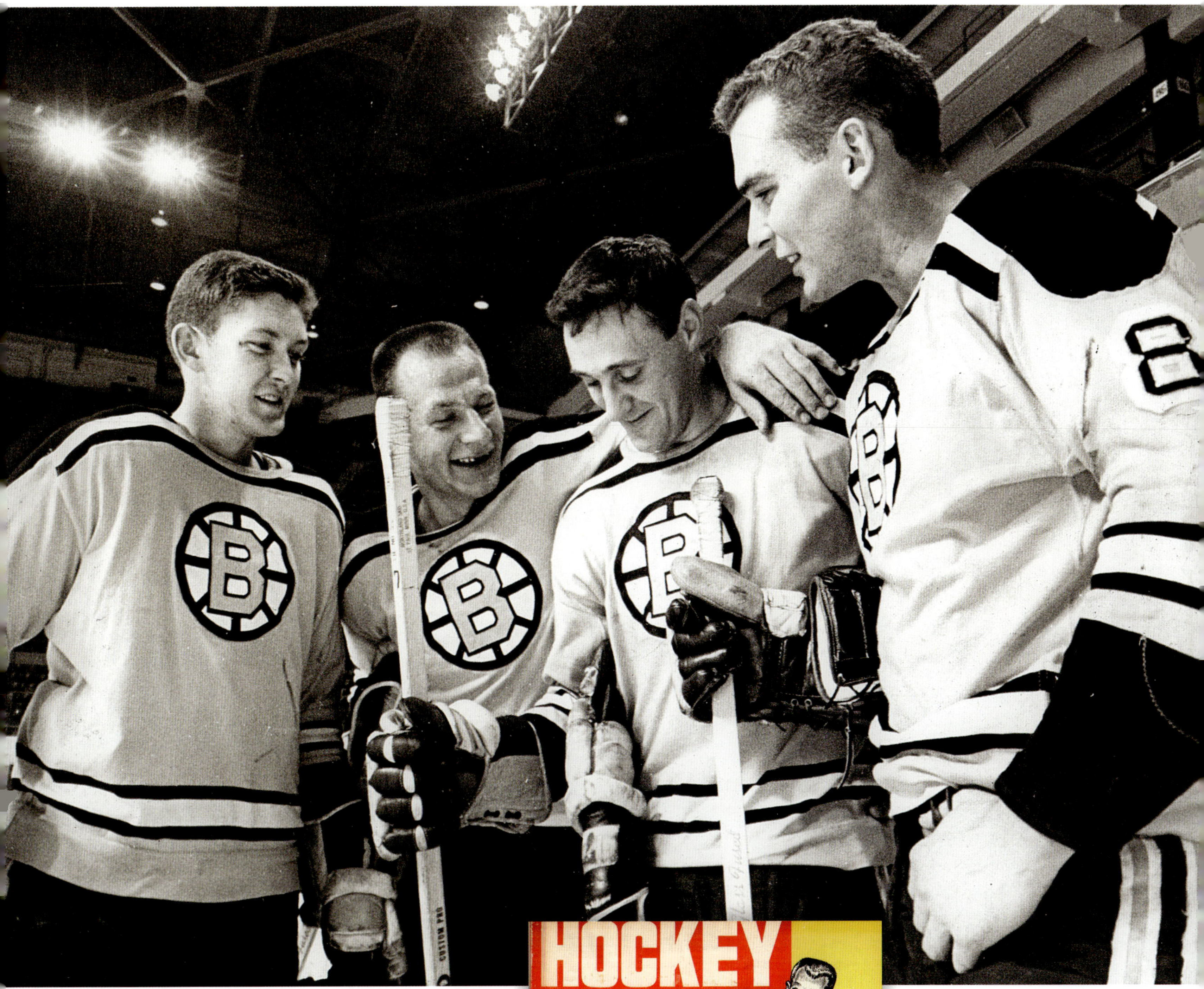

It's hard to beat the haul of Esposito, Hodge, and Stanfield, though. The trade helped transform the Bruins into immediate title contenders and eventual Stanley Cup champions.

That wasn't immediately apparent at the time. And the Chicago trio heading for Boston certainly had some questions about their new team. "I guess [I feared] the unknown," said Hodge in a 2022 interview. "Coming from a team that was in the playoffs, going to a team that wasn't in the playoffs. You know, New York and Boston used to have a playoff to see who would finish fifth out of six."

The avalanche of scoring records and the two Stanley Cups that would follow in the ensuing years would quash any and all doubts in that regard.

Fred Stanfield, Eddie Shack, Phil Esposito, and Ken Hodge (left to right) gather at Boston Garden in October 1967. All four had arrived via trades prior to the season. (Photograph by Tom Landers/The Boston Globe via Getty Images)

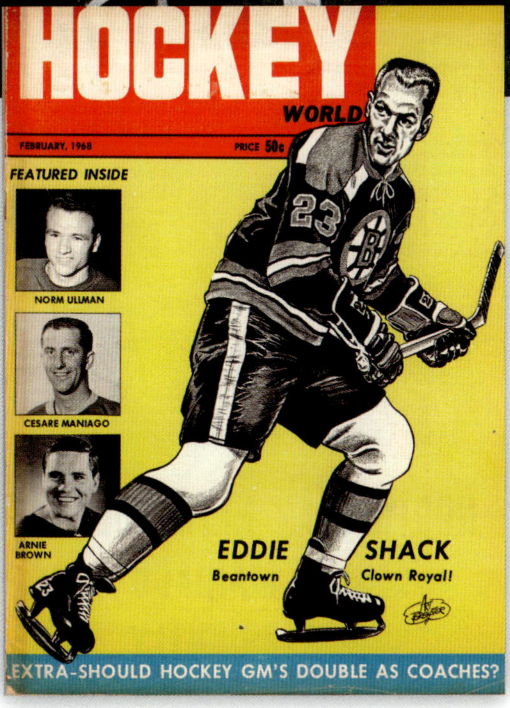

Bruins left wing Eddie Shack on the cover of the February 1968 edition of Hockey World. *Known as "the Entertainer" for his zany antics, Shack won four Stanley Cups with Toronto before arriving in Boston.* (Collection of Richard A. Johnson)

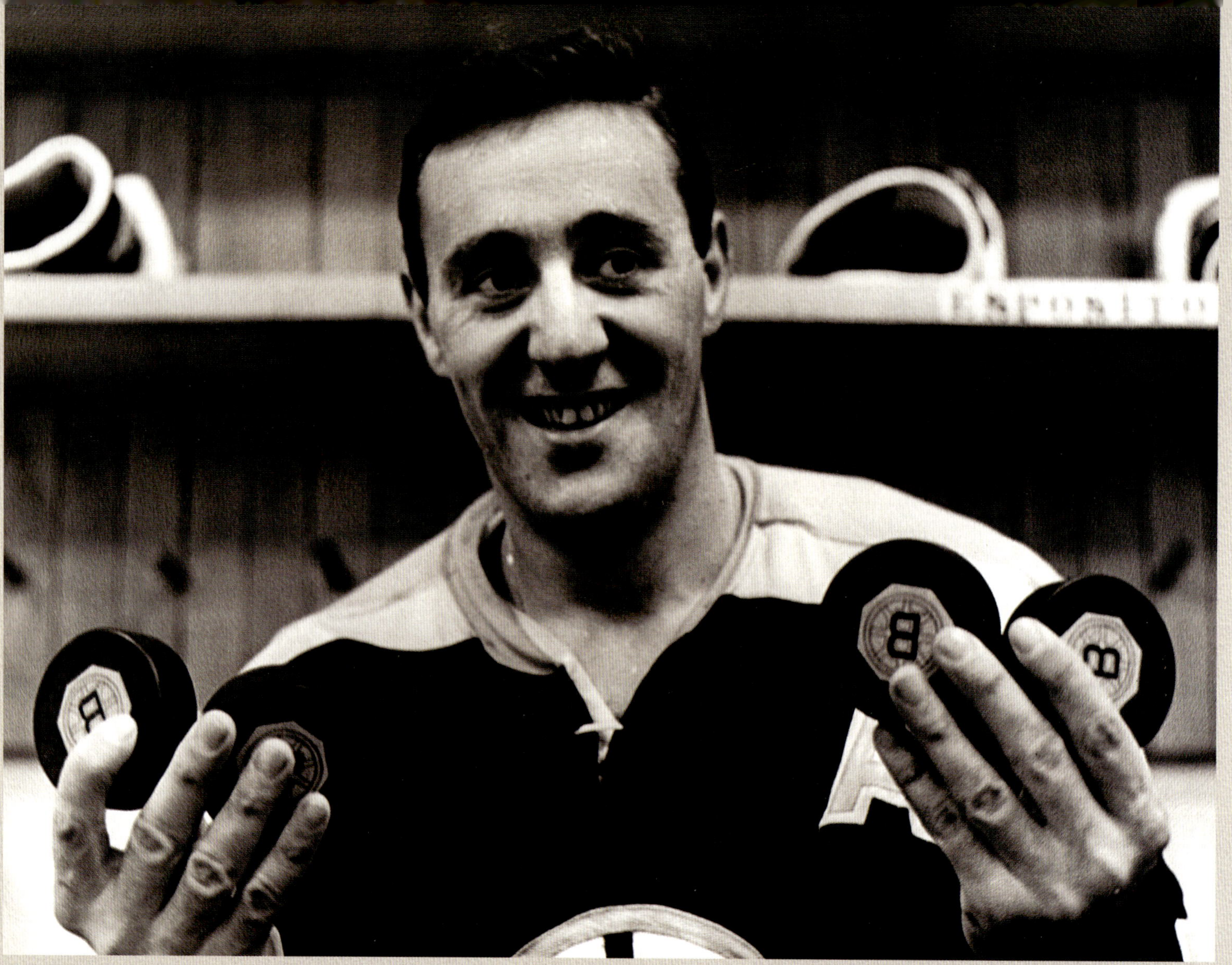

Center Phil Esposito started paying immediate dividends following his trade to Boston. On October 15, 1967, in just the second game of the season, he scored four goals in Boston's 6–2 victory over Montreal. Esposito would finish the season with 84 points, second in the NHL only to Chicago's Stan Mikita (87). (Photograph by Dennis Brearley, Collection of The Sports Museum)

Young center Pit Martin came to Boston in December 1965 and skated for a year-and-a-half with the Black and Gold, displaying considerable promise. He was a crucial part of the blockbuster trade in May 1967 with Chicago that brought Phil Esposito, Ken Hodge, and Fred Stanfield to the Hub. Martin ended up having a long, productive career with the Black Hawks—but there is no question that the Bruins came out way ahead on the trade. (Photograph by Weekend Magazine / Louis Jaques / Library and Archives Canada / e011166348)

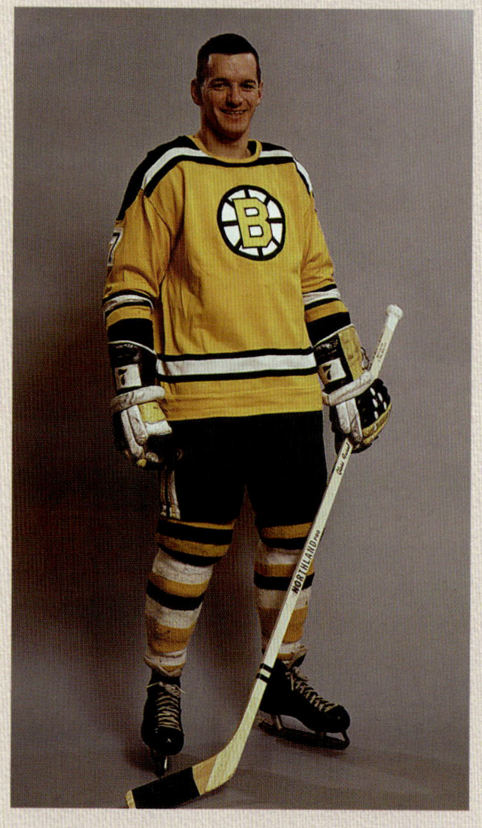

THE TOLL OF THE 1967 EXPANSION DRAFT

THE NHL DECIDED to double in size by adding six expansion teams to form a Western Division in time for the 1967–68 season. An expansion draft took place in June 1967 to stock the new teams.

Even though they were coming off a last-place finish, the Bruins were hit the hardest among the Original Six clubs. Among the 18 Bruins players drafted were future NHL All-Stars Bernie Parent, J.P. Parise, Poul Popiel, Wayne Connelly, Bill Goldsworthy, Gary Dornhoefer, Ron Schock, and Wayne Rivers.

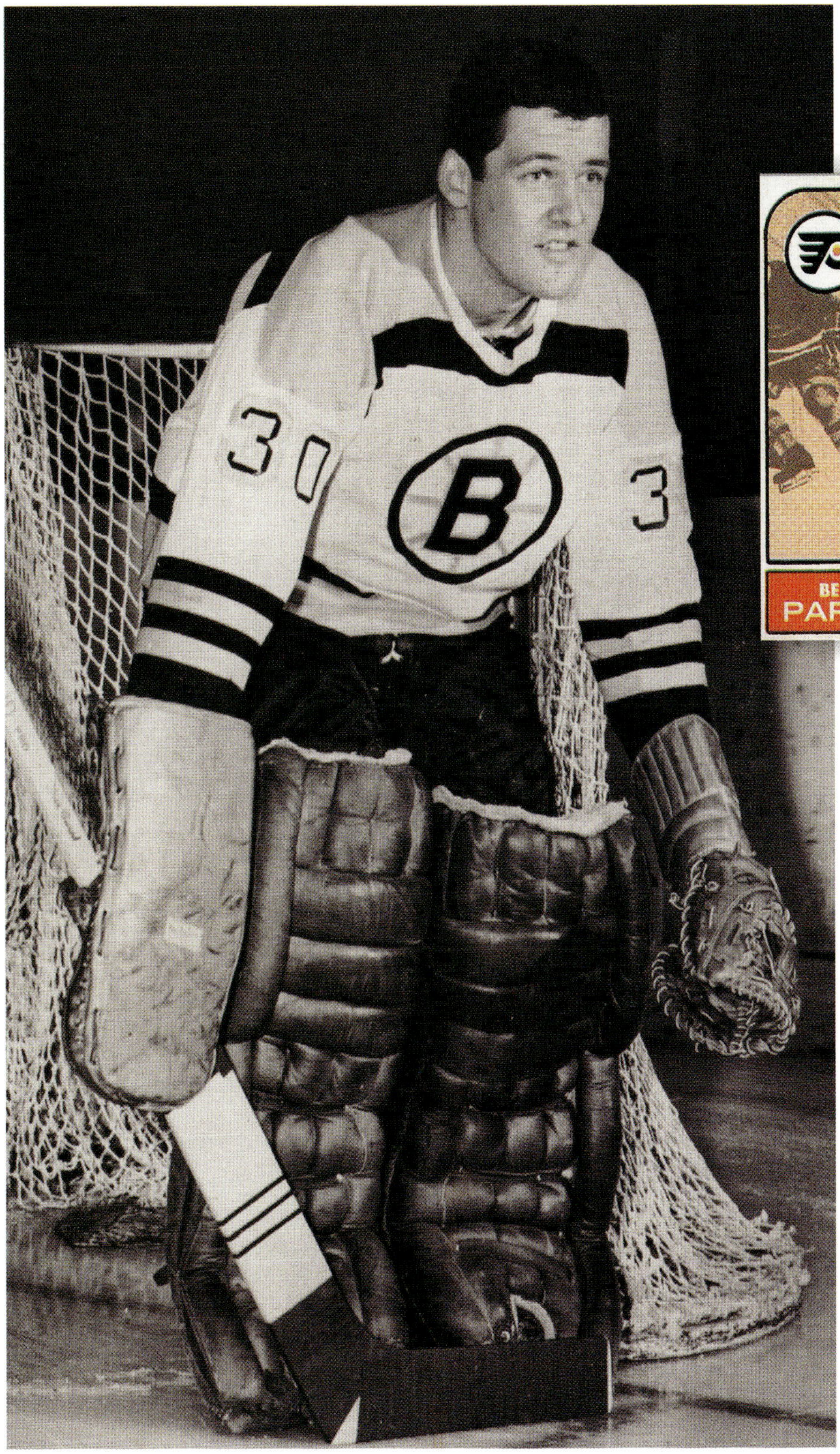

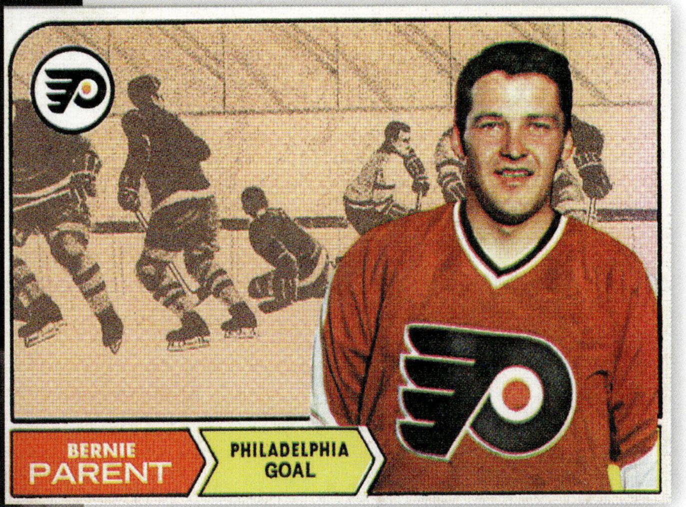

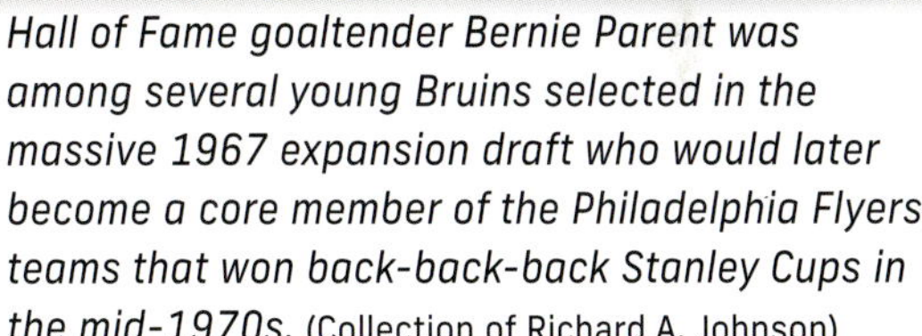

Hall of Fame goaltender Bernie Parent was among several young Bruins selected in the massive 1967 expansion draft who would later become a core member of the Philadelphia Flyers teams that won back-back-back Stanley Cups in the mid-1970s. (Collection of Richard A. Johnson)

It was a heavy price to pay.

"The Bruins were building a dynasty," said Derek Sanderson. "It was Weston Adams Sr. He bought me, he bought Bobby, he bought Cashman, he bought all these guys—and they all came. Everybody was his pick. He would go and beat the bushes. He gave up a seat on the New York Stock Exchange and would just travel Canada, picking players up.... All these guys could play and Weston Adams Sr. picked them. Hand picked them and then—*boom*—he lost two-thirds of his dynasty [in the expansion draft].... He was putting this puzzle together—and he had two-thirds of it taken away from him."

The Bruins would, of course, go on to win two Stanley Cups in the early 1970s. If not for the talent drain from the 1967 expansion draft and a few other key factors (the defections to the World Hockey Association and the injuries to Bobby Orr), how many more would they have won?

THE BLUELINE BRIGADE

PRIOR TO BOBBY ORR, NHL defensemen stayed back, rarely advancing deep into the offensive zone. Orr would establish a new style of play. "I was owned by the Bruins when I was 14 years old and they didn't try to change me," said Orr. "And I thanked them for that.... That was the style I like to play. I don't think I would have enjoyed the game as much if I had to sit back."

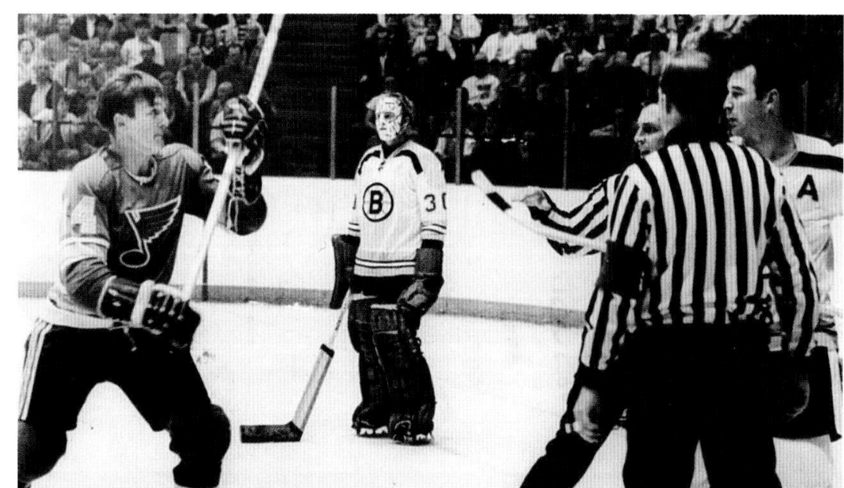

On September 21, 1969, in a preseason game in Ottawa, Wayne Maki of the St. Louis Blues fractured Bruins defenseman Ted Green's skull in a stick swinging incident. Only emergency surgery saved Green's life. "We thought we were going to lose him that night in Ottawa," said Harry Sinden. "The players alternated staying at the hotel that night and the next day with him. Fortunately, he ended up in much better shape than he could have with the type of injuries he had." Green would be out for the year but would return to skate two final seasons with the Bruins in the early 1970s.
(Collection of The Sports Museum)

The fact that Orr could play that type of game with the Bruins was due in part to his compatriots on the blueline, a group of mostly "stay at home" defensemen. They were solid, steady, and superbly complementary to Orr.

Besides veteran Ted Green, their ranks included a quartet of players who established themselves as regulars by the end of the 1960s and would be destined for long careers in Black and Gold—namely, Dallas Smith, Don Awrey, Gary Doak, and Rick Smith.

Dallas Smith went back and forth between the Bruins and the minor leagues from 1960 to 1966 before sticking with the big club for good in 1967. He would remain a fixture in the lineup until 1977, appearing in four NHL All-Star Games and earning the reputation as the strongest man in the league. Like Dallas Smith, Awrey spent several years shuttling between Boston and the minor leagues (Hershey of the AHL) before becoming a Bruins regular in 1967. He was renowned for shot-blocking and his fierce body-checking. And Doak and Rick Smith each had remarkably similar careers, becoming regular contributors for the Bruins in the late 1960s, leaving for other ports of call in the early 1970s, and then returning to the team later in the decade to become card-carrying members of Don Cherry's Lunch Pail Gang.

Collectively, this cadre of capable defensemen would end up playing a big part in the team's success in the late 1960s and well into the next decade.

And no one was more appreciative than Orr. "They sacrificed their bodies," said Orr of his defensive mates. "You didn't want to go to the front of the net with those guys.... They were just hiding those guys, never complained, just did their job, and didn't complain that I was up the ice."

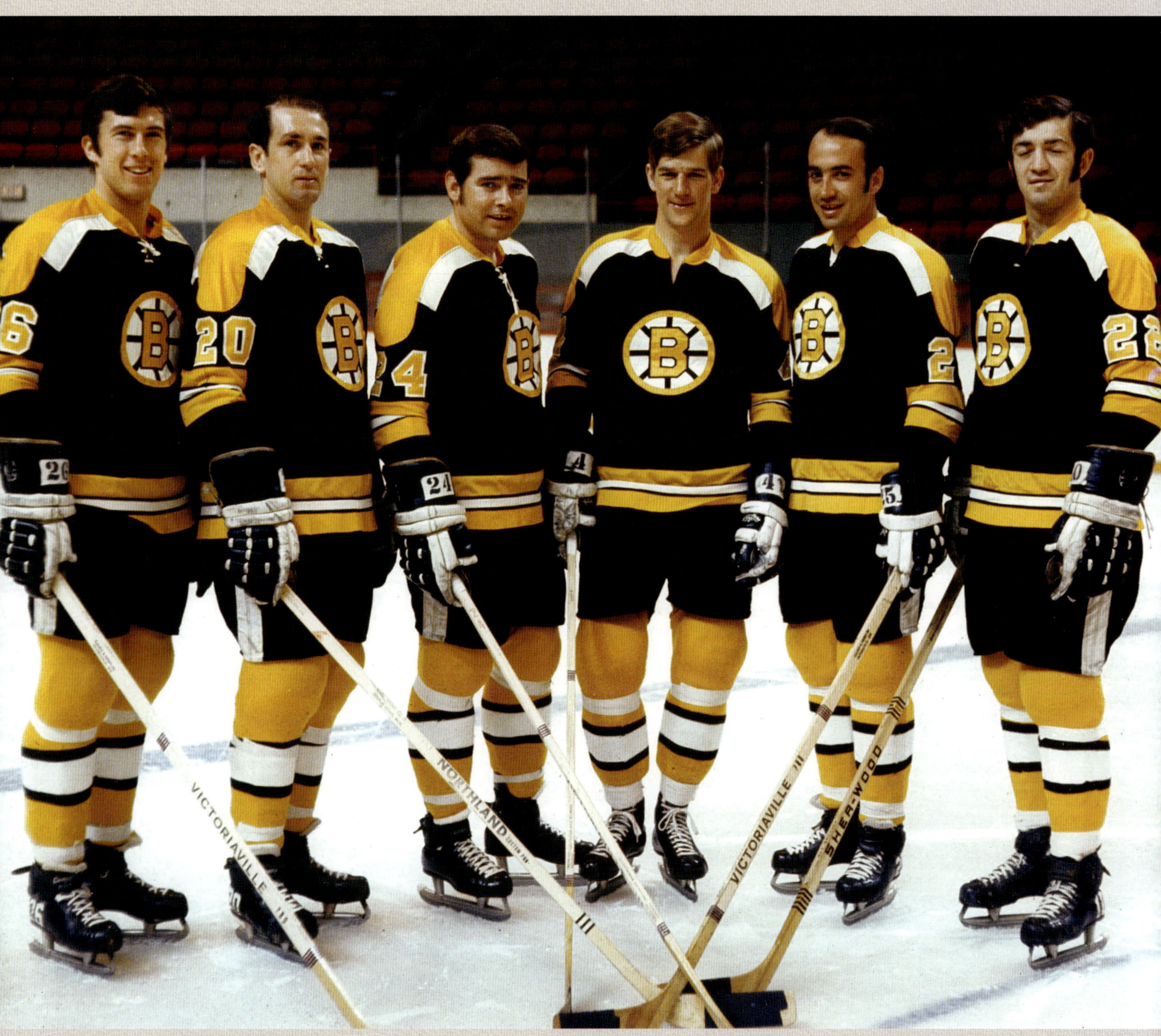

The Bruins corps of defensemen for the 1969–70 season included (left to right) Don Awrey, Dallas Smith, Billy Speer, Bobby Orr, Gary Doak, and Rick Smith. (Photograph by Al Ruelle, Collection of The Sports Museum)

BOBBY ORR & THE MUSIC OF NEAR PERFECTION

by Christopher Lydon

NOBODY'S PERFECT, let's agree. But seriously: have any of us ever seen anybody do anything as well as Bobby Orr played hockey? In sports? In music? In life at large? In hockey, Bobby Orr began with that lights-out combination of supreme speed and crushing power (think: Sugar Ray Robinson). Other players observed from the start that he had "six speeds of fast," some said eight, and maybe more in reserve, flying end to end on a 200-foot sheet of ice, or in zero-to-60 explosive bursts. Skating backward, too. He had split-second timing in his passes and breaks. He had fire in his heart, and also calm and dignity at the Lou Gehrig level. And he revealed each of those qualities, and more, among bigger men, all-time stars like Gordie Howe and Bobby Hull—*as a teenager*! His shot-on-goal may (or may not) have been as hard as Bobby Hull's, but Orr got his off faster. I remember asking Gordie Howe if he could name Orr's "best move" overall. Howe's look said: "Are you kidding?" His words were: "Putting on those bleeping skates. That's all he has to do." And still Bobby Orr was more than all that.

It's one thing to make a stadium cheer, something else to bring crowds to a hush the way Bobby Orr peculiarly did. He was the model of the Apollonian athlete in a Dionysian game. Only to say: he drew the line of order, mastery, elegance in hockey's evident chaos. He brought control to the frenzy of his game. It's a delight to observe that the quiet force of the man is undiminished in the 50 years that the Lydon brothers have watched him studiously. Youngest brother Patrick—the true radical among us in word and life—listed Bobby Orr as a heroic soul from the '60s and a living inspiration.

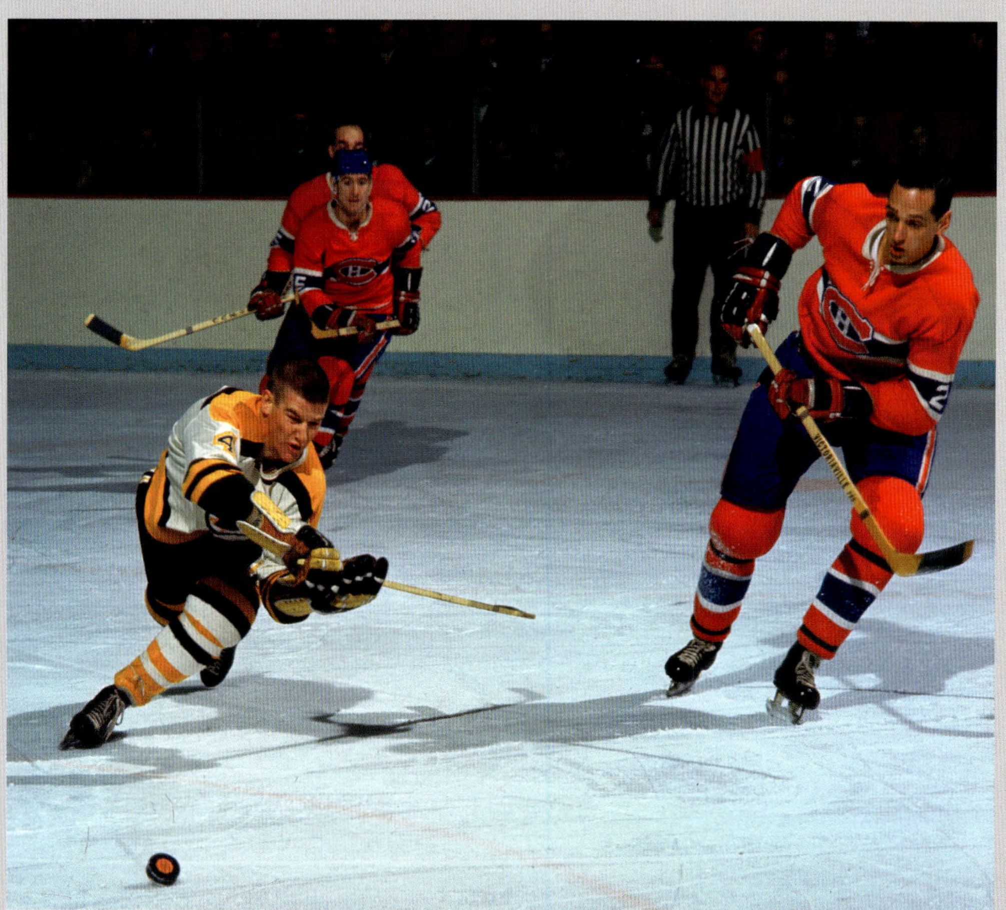

Bobby Orr is shown in his rookie season of 1966–67. The first time he played against Orr, Chicago superstar Bobby Hull saw the rookie score twice in the first period. Hull reportedly then told referee Frank Udvari to toss out two pucks for the start of the second period, "one for Orr and one for the rest of us." (Photograph by Frank Prazak/Hockey Hall of Fame)

In the Bruins' Age of Orr, very early '70s, I was reporting George McGovern's and Richard Nixon's presidential campaigns from the Washington bureau of the *New York Times*, but I held on to my pair of Bruins season tickets—for my sanity and for entrée into pro hockey conversations. Had any player so dominated the imagination of a team sport? Ted Irvine of the New York Rangers was thought to be the fastest skater on his team, but word was that when Irvine got back to the bench after a race with Orr, his teammates told him cheerfully that he seemed to be wearing snowshoes out there. Orr saved a little new magic for every game: rival players never quite got it, and he kept showing them more.

On reflection, Bobby Orr makes a complicated memory. Back in the day, he was the defenseman who scored. At another level he was the artist

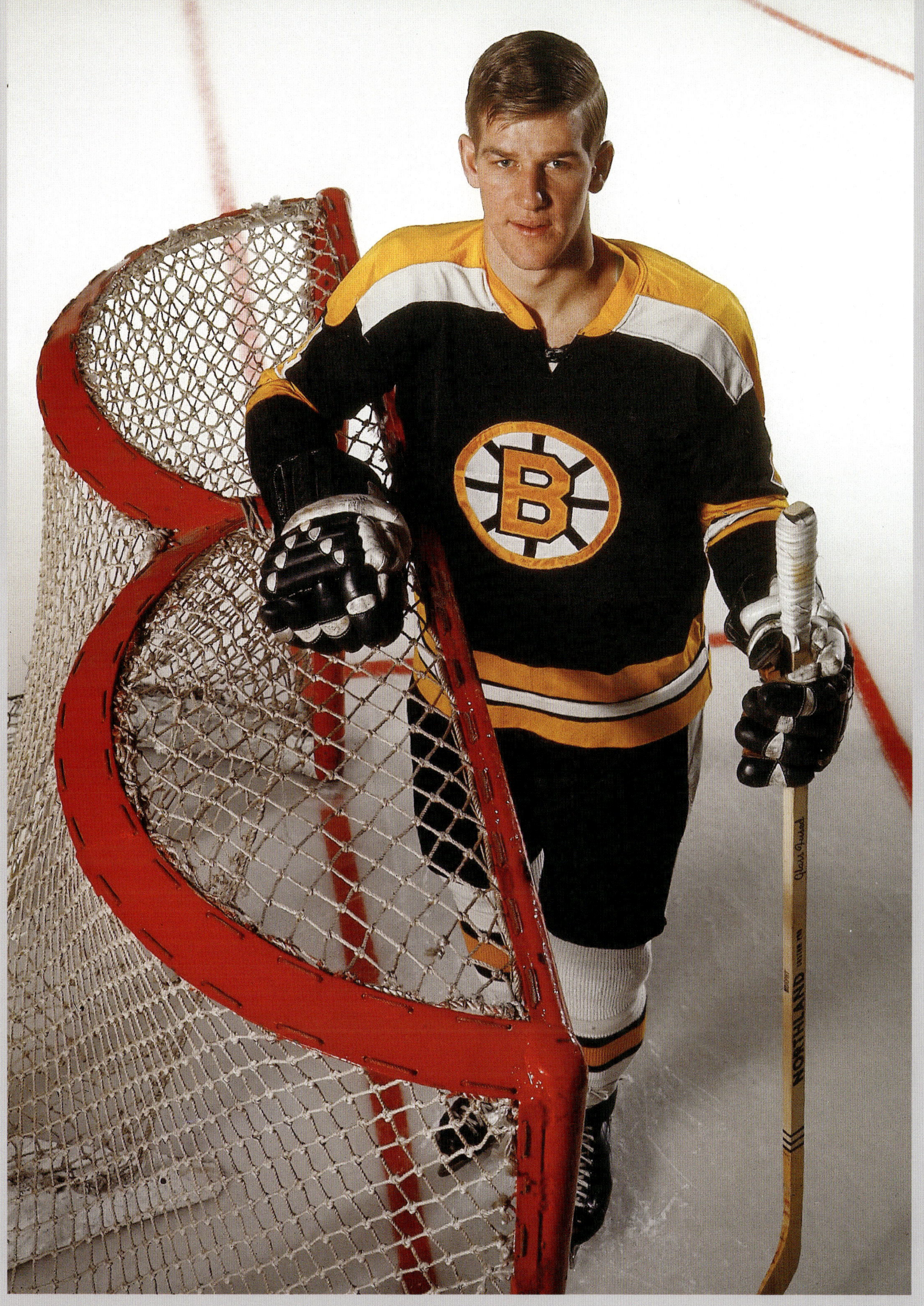

Bobby Orr leans against a net at Boston Garden during the 1968–69 season. It was a year that saw Orr capture his second Norris Trophy as the league's top defenseman while emerging as a full-fledged NHL superstar. He was just 20 years old.
(Photograph by Tony Triolo/Sports Illustrated via Getty Images/Getty Images)

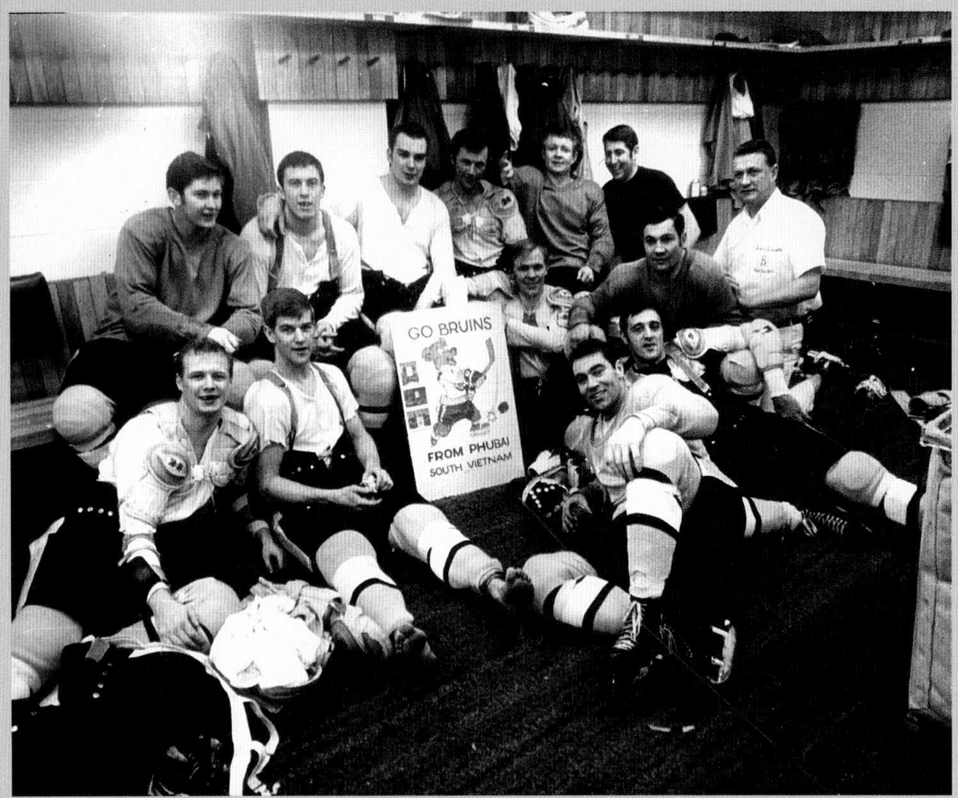

The Bruins accept greetings from Boston fans serving in Phubai, Vietnam, in 1969: (front row, left to right) Wayne Cashman, Bobby Orr, Glen Sather, Eddie Westfall, Phil Esposito, Johnny Bucyk, and trainer Dan Canney; (back row, left to right) Fred Stanfield, Don Awrey, Ken Hodge, Ron Murphy, Johnny McKenzie, and equipment manager Frosty Forristall. (Photograph courtesy of Dennis Brearley)

among brutes. He became the most respected and revered hockey player of all time in just nine-plus professional seasons in Boston (1966–1976) to put the point beyond dispute. As with Sandy Koufax in another short career, we missed what might have been and would have watched through 30 seasons. But we had nothing more to learn about Bobby Orr's mastery. It was never about numbers anyway, nor a feat of mere athletics. For my brother Patrick, who caught Bobby Orr's debut in the fall of 1966, the mark of the man was magnanimity above all, the spirit of generosity in action. He was *non sibi*, in the Latin phrase we came to take seriously—"not for self." He did what was known to be impossible: leading the Bruins' offensive rush *from behind*. He set records on offense with goals and also with assists, typically in telepathic connection with his center Phil Esposito. Search the clippings (and the several books in his name) and what you will not find is Bobby Orr casting himself as the main character on the stage, or the ice.

Fifty years later I am struck by the soul of an artist and an inventive teacher in Bobby Orr—by the mystery in the man's aura as much as the mastery in the hockey player. Legend to legend, Larry Bird is the wonderfully un-shy witness to the tingles that grown men felt about Bobby. Larry volunteered as a young star in the '80s that, when he stared into the Boston Garden rafters during the national anthem, he wasn't looking at anybody's flag; he was looking at Bobby Orr's retired No. 4. Bird had never seen Orr play, "but just being around him gives me a tingling feeling...you're looking up there and you see this number, and all of a sudden you get fired up."

Ken Dryden is an authority on hockey skills and the tingles, too. He was the goaltending hero in five Stanley Cup championships with the Montreal Canadiens in the 1970s—and later a candidate to lead the Liberal Party in Canada's Parliament. I asked Ken Dryden for the essential frame in his memory of Bobby Orr on ice. "It's in that rush, coming my way, probably just before he hits center ice. It's the moment and the jolt that hits me when I recognize that it's Orr. It says: you need to get ready, before you're ready. Something's about to happen..." But even that is not what makes Orr "interesting" to Ken Dryden today, a half century later. "How, in his early teens," Dryden asks himself, "did Bobby Orr fend off the coaches and fans who naturally wanted him forward in the offensive line? How does a man get to be too game-absorbed to be self-absorbed? Bobby Orr's game when he got to the NHL at [age] 18 was skating long shifts and the whole length of the ice, as nobody else did. It was unthinkable in the NHL in the '60s and thought to be undoable. He made it possible by demonstrating he could do it, and in teaching less talented players how to do it. He made it the new norm."

And still there's more to being a game-changer, Dryden observed. "He's interesting. And it's always a good question as to why. And what he meant. Your brother's reaction—that Bobby Orr was the '60s hero who lasted, who came to embody generosity, the passer—is a telling one." The Dryden version: Orr confirmed that hockey is a possession game, against the chronic temptation in the NHL to play "dump and chase," which turns on capturing the puck at mid-ice and belting into the offensive end. "Orr could play the possession game all by himself!" Dryden said. "But he was a passer as well, and he started to make the Bruins better players. Skating up the ice, it's tough to try to beat five opponents before you reach the goalie. No matter how good you are, you'll get slowed down, converged upon, stopped. So Orr started up the ice, forwards ahead of him, and he started moving the puck to them, but the play wasn't over. The forwards all of a sudden are getting a pass and now they had to do something with it. This guy is creating situations where I have to be a better passer, and he needs someone to move with him.... That's what made the Bruins so difficult to play against, because when he was on the ice, you were facing a stampede of five rather than just Orr or Esposito."

Bobby Orr was teaching the home fans as well as players. One night in Orr's rookie season, Bernie Parent in the Bruins goal had been shelled all night and was loudly booed at the final buzzer. Orr jumped from the bench, threw his arm around Parent, and skated off the ice with him. Which gets us back to the mystique.

"If you can take something to levels that very few other people can reach, then what you're doing becomes art." This was basketball's immortal Bill Russell, an authority on character and dignity, in *Sports Illustrated* in 1999, helping me to see Bobby Orr in 2022. Murray Whyte, decorated art critic of the *Boston Globe*, confirms the connection with art, and "hockey's peculiar play of emotion, intuition, and contingency—sheer chance." It doubtless helps that Murray Whyte grew up in Canada and plays unforgiving amateur hockey in mid-life. Yes, Bobby Orr is an artist of a particular and original sort, and the art he's closest to is jazz. "The more I think about it: hockey is jazz, more than any other sport," says Whyte. "It's fast, and structured, but with a prevailing randomness that keeps it on the razor's edge of chaos. Equally thrilling, and equally demanding of gifted players who can change on the fly, to extend the hockey/jazz metaphor. It's all over the place, but it somehow holds together—you could be speaking of jazz or hockey, and it would be equally true."

You could be speaking of musical performance, come to think of it, at the highest levels in many forms. Our friend, the sports historian Richard Johnson, is a searching student of the Orr game who cannot speak of the master without referencing Mozart, which makes perfect sense. When I try to imagine the tribe of Orr, I picture Yo-Yo Ma among the chieftains. He is very much alive to the common ground of sports and music, and we are too when we catch on to the gymnastic miracle he's pulling off: fingering, bowing and seeming to breathe the Bach Cello Suites. I hear and see the physical discipline in Johnny Hodges' unearthly glissando on the alto saxophone—playing with Duke Ellington on Billy Strayhorn's "Passion Flower"—just a man with a reed on a horn doing the impossible, making a sound so beautiful, as Duke said, "It could bring tears to the eyes."

The proximity of hockey and jazz underscores just how and why we remember Bobby Orr. The rarest gift he showed us was an extension of pianist Art Tatum's dictum that, among the great ones, "There is no such thing as a wrong note." Miles Davis embellished the line to say: "It's the note you play afterwards that makes it right or wrong." Bobby Orr invariably came up with the redeeming next note.

Boston-born Christopher Lydon covered city politics for the *Boston Globe* in the 1960s and presidential politics for the *New York Times* in Washington in the 1970s. He anchored *The Ten O'Clock News* on WGBH-TV from 1977 to 1991, and in a switch to radio founded an effervescent call-in talk show, *The Connection*, which he hosted from 1994 to 2001. In June 2003, with Dave Winer, he produced the original podcast, now known as *Open Source*. He was a Bruins season ticket holder through the Age of Orr.

BOSTON BRUINS (1960–1969)

Season	W	L	T	PTS	PTS%	Finish	Playoffs	Coach	Division
1959–60	28	34	8	64	.457	5th of 6		Milt Schmidt	
1960–61	15	42	13	43	.307	6th of 6		Milt Schmidt	
1961–62	15	47	8	38	.271	6th of 6		Phil Watson	
1962–63	14	39	17	45	.321	6th of 6		Phil Watson (1–8–5) Milt Schmidt (13–31–12)	
1963–64	18	40	12	48	.343	6th of 6		Milt Schmidt	
1964–65	21	43	6	48	.343	6th of 6		Milt Schmidt	
1965–66	21	43	6	48	.343	5th of 6		Milt Schmidt	
1966–67	17	43	10	44	.314	6th of 6		Harry Sinden	
1967–68	37	27	10	84	.568	3rd of 6	Lost NHL Quarterfinals	Harry Sinden	East
1968–69	42	18	16	100	.658	2nd of 6	Lost NHL Semifinals	Harry Sinden	East

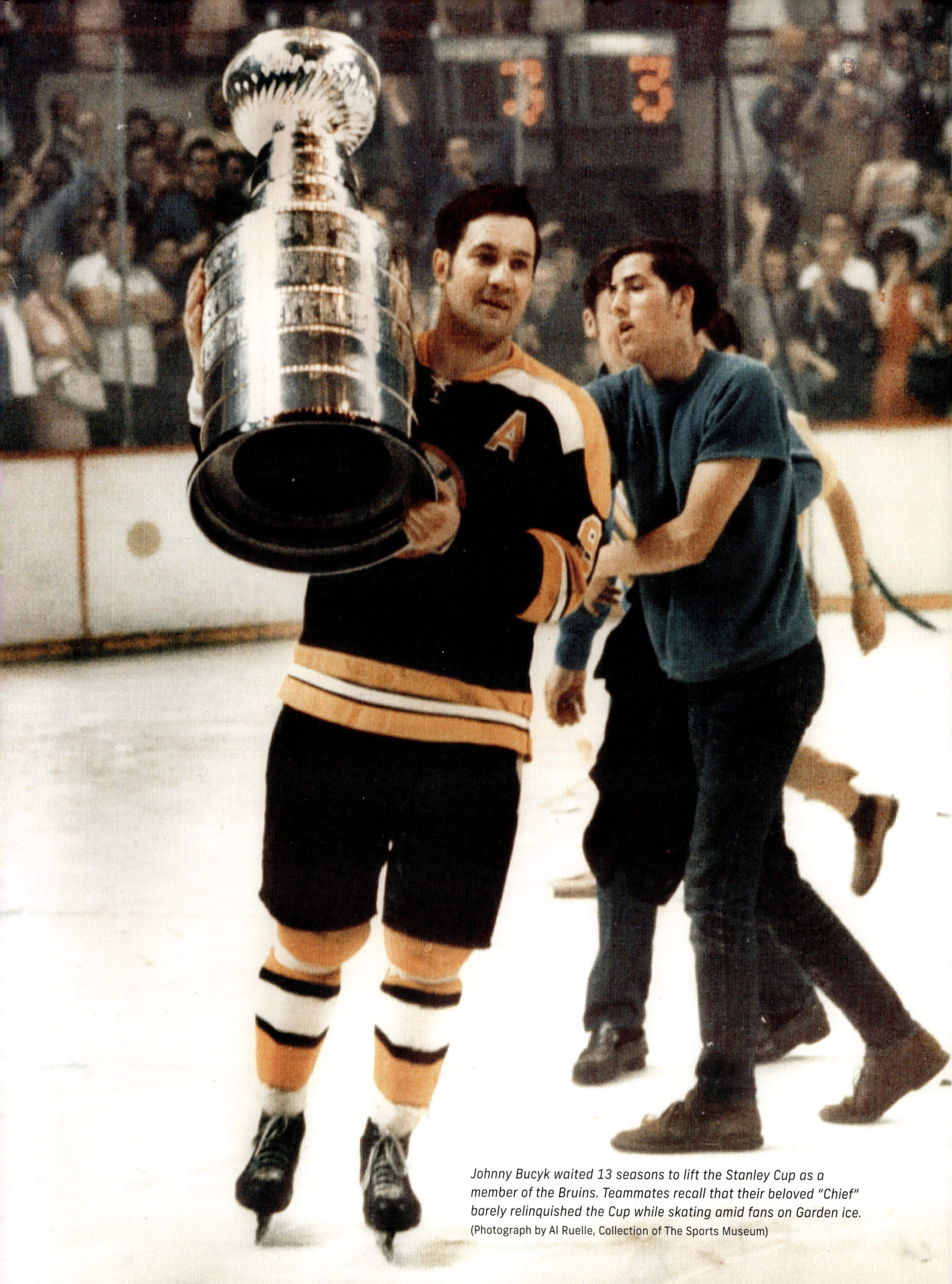

Johnny Bucyk waited 13 seasons to lift the Stanley Cup as a member of the Bruins. Teammates recall that their beloved "Chief" barely relinquished the Cup while skating amid fans on Garden ice.
(Photograph by Al Ruelle, Collection of The Sports Museum)

1970s

CUPS & LUNCH PAILS

Every day was a holiday. It was the Gashouse Gang on skates.
They were Rabelaisian. They didn't beat teams, they engulfed them.
Everything they did reeked of excess. They were rowdy, vulgar, and vain.
But to their adoring legions they could do no wrong.

—Clark Booth, Boston sportscaster, on the Bruins of the early 1970s

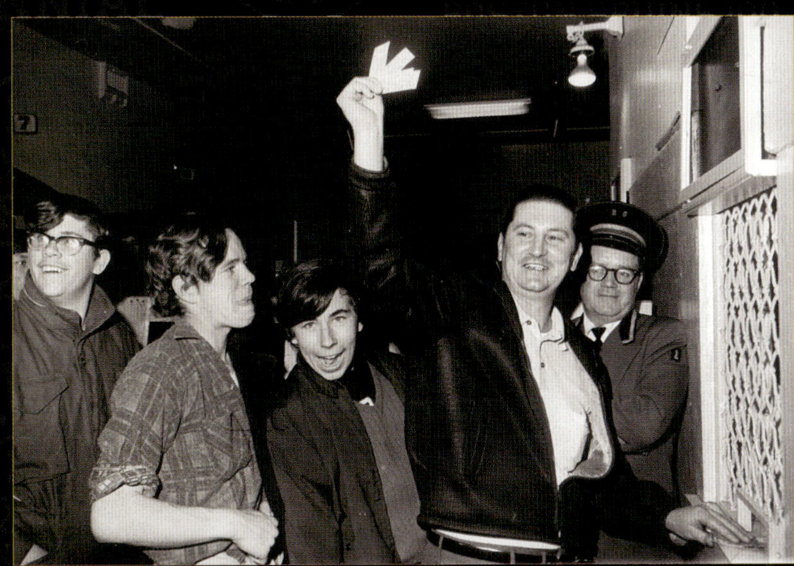

A lucky fan displays the playoff tickets that he waited overnight to purchase at the Boston Garden ticket office. (Courtesy of Sports Temples Collection, Boston Public Library)

The 1970s may have been the most eventful and memorable years in franchise history. It was an era that saw Bobby Orr, Phil Esposito, and the Big Bad Bruins become the most celebrated team in the century-plus annals of Boston professional sports (and win two Stanley Cups, to boot). The latter half of the decade belonged to an equally brash and charismatic group, the beloved Lunch Pail Gang led by Head Coach Don "Grapes" Cherry.

Two bookends stand out as markers for the decade. One bookend involves a date; the other, two defensemen. The first bookend—May 10—represents both one of the most joyful and most painful dates in team history. On May 10, 1970 (Mother's Day), it was all about joy, as Bobby Orr scored "The Goal" and flew into hockey immortality to win the franchise's first Stanley Cup in 29 years.

"It couldn't have been more perfect for our team with Bobby scoring that goal," said Phil Esposito. "Couldn't have been more perfect."

Nine years later, on May 10, 1979, it was all about heartbreak, as the Bruins were called for the fateful "Too Many Men on the Ice" penalty in the waning moments of Game 7 of the Stanley Cup Semifinals against the Canadiens, opening the door for the Habs to tie the game and then win it in overtime. The Montreal playoff jinx would last another nine years, until 1988. But in many ways the 1979 loss was the final crucible for the Bruins and their fans. No loss hurt quite as badly.

The other marker for the decade involves the presence of blueline titans Bobby Orr and Ray Bourque. The former kicked off the decade at the top of his game and the peak of his powers. More than a half century later, there still hasn't been anyone like him. Not even close.

The latter closed out the decade after being tabbed as the greatest draft selection in franchise history in August 1979, just three months after the "Too Many Men on the Ice" game. Hope and renewal beckoned, as did the promise of continued excellence.

In the 1970s, the Bruins won two Stanley Cups (1970, 1972), made the Stanley Cup Final three additional times (1974, 1977, 1978), and packed the Garden to the rafters every single night with their rabid fans. Along the way, they shattered team and NHL records and owned Boston like no other team ever has—before or since.

All in all, it was a momentous and monumental decade for the Black and Gold.

OFFICIAL GUIDE
"THE BEAR FACTS"
1971-1972

Bruins media guide for the 1971–72 season. (Collection of Richard A. Johnson)

PHIL ESPOSITO

PHIL ESPOSITO was the best pure scorer in franchise history.

Even after all these years, the statistics remain eye-popping. In his eight-plus seasons in Boston (1967–1975), Espo piled up 1,012 points (459 goals, 553 assists). He led the NHL in goals for six consecutive seasons (1970–1975) and in scoring for five seasons (1969, 1971–1974). In 1968–69, he shattered the NHL single-season scoring record by ringing up 126 points. Just two years later, he broke his own record by amassing 152 points (76 goals, 76 assists) in a single season. Essentially, he rewrote the NHL record book.

Esposito was nevertheless derided by jealous opponents as a "garbage collector," an immovable object that just stood in front of the net. "I think people were wrong," said Esposito in a 2022 interview. "I didn't get close to the net. Hash marks, hash marks.... You go to hash marks, that puck comes to the hash marks so much, even in today's game.... That's prime location. Prime to shoot, prime for all of it."

Esposito had a special, almost telepathic connection with Bobby Orr. He also worked closely in tandem with longtime linemates Ken Hodge and Wayne Cashman. "Hodgy and I were always together," said Esposito. "And then when Cash was brought up [during the 1967–68 season], it just made our line go. I always called us the Fat Line. They didn't come up with a name for us, so we called ourselves the Fat Line."

"Phil's one of the greatest scorers in the history of our game," said Bobby Orr. "This guy could score. Kenny and Cash were strong, big guys, strong in the corner. They could get the puck. Phil could put it in the net. So it was a heck of a line."

The Bruins teams of the era were loose, fun-loving, and swashbuckling. Much of that emanated from Esposito. "It was always great to play with Phil," Hodge said. "On and off the ice, it was always great to be around him."

One of the more famous stories of the era involves Esposito being laid up at Massachusetts General Hospital recovering from knee surgery while the rest of the team was hanging out at a nearby bar. After a while (and perhaps a few libations), Esposito's teammates hatched a plot to kidnap the patient. "We arranged to get the bed out of the hospital and carried it into the bar," said Bobby Orr. "Phil had some cheese and crackers. It really was funny though. The people in the bar... they're looking down the bar, looking at the hospital bed in the bar. And then I was paged. The doctor said, 'Do you have my patient?' I said, 'Yes, sir.' He said, 'Get him back here!' So we took him back."

Esposito would, suddenly and shockingly, get traded to the New York Rangers in November 1975. After his playing days, he helped found and run the Tampa Bay Lightning. Despite the various NHL allegiances, he retains nothing but fond memories for his time with the Bruins. "I absolutely love Boston," said Esposito. "I just would've stayed there my whole life. Without a doubt."

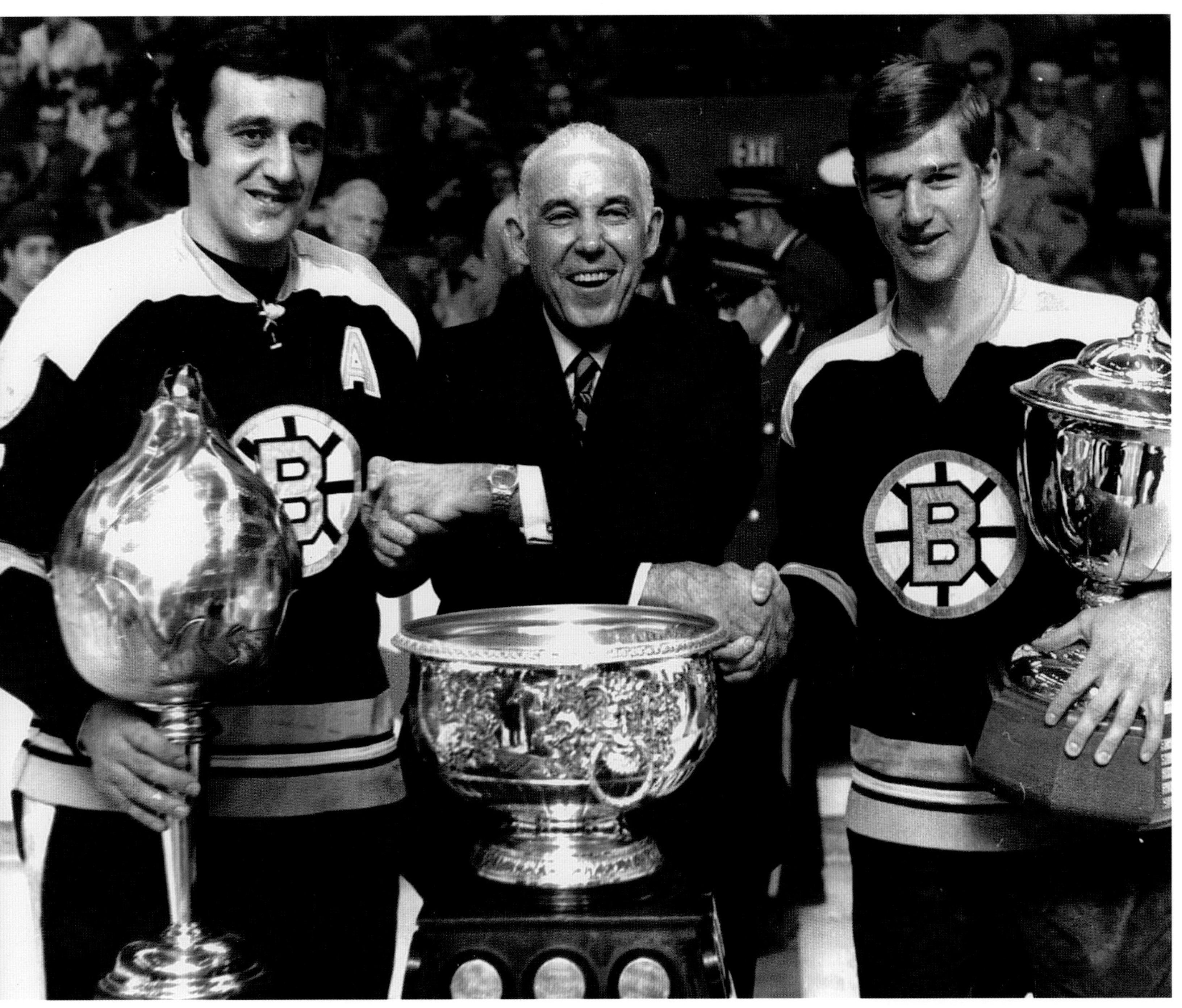

Phil Esposito (left) and Bobby Orr flank NHL president Clarence Campbell as he presents the Hart and the Art Ross Trophies to Esposito and the Norris Trophy to Orr for the 1968–69 season. More hardware would be forthcoming at the end of the 1970 season for the two Bruins stars—as would, of course, the Stanley Cup. (Photograph by Al Ruelle, Collection of The Sports Museum)

KEN HODGE

Known for his immense slap shot and upbeat personality, Ken Hodge was involved in opposite ends of two of the greatest trades in Bruins history. He arrived in Boston in 1967 via the deal with Chicago that also secured centers Phil Esposito and Fred Stanfield and departed in May 1976 in a straight-up deal with the Rangers for Rick Middleton.

In between, in his nine seasons in Boston, the powerful right wing pumped in 289 goals, usually skating on the top line along with Phil Esposito and Wayne

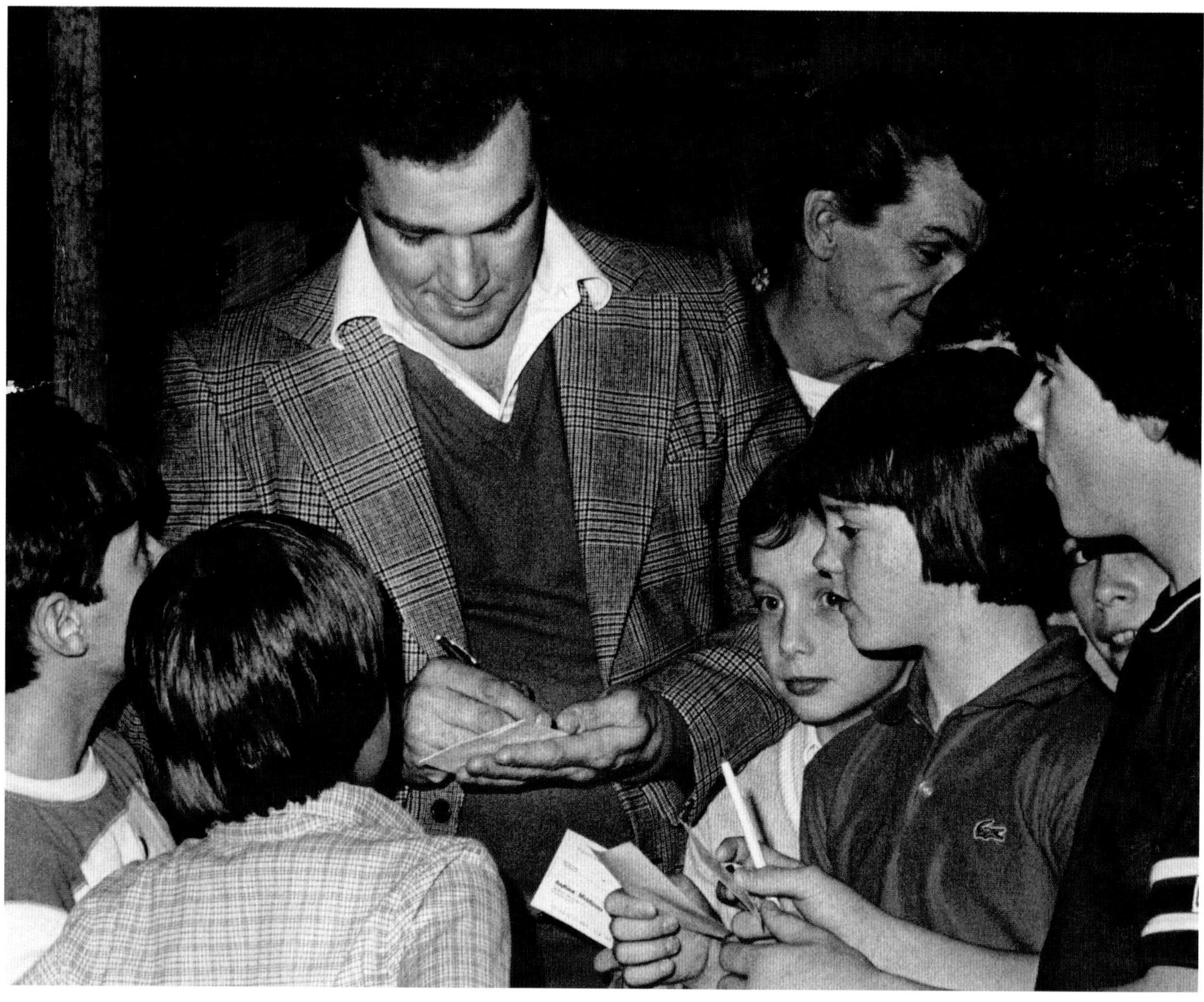

Ken Hodge signs autographs for some young fans. The Bruins of that era were highly accessible, regularly mingling with their adoring fans at charitable events, rink openings, and various restaurants and watering holes throughout the city. (Photograph by Al Ruelle, Collection of The Sports Museum)

Cashman. Hodge scored 50 goals in 1974 and 40 or more goals in two additional seasons (1969 and 1971).

Looking back, he fully recognizes that he played hockey in a different era altogether.

"There was no dietician," said Hodge in a 2022 interview. "There was nobody to tell us what to eat and what not to eat. It was baked potatoes, steak and peas, and ice cream with chocolate sauce [for your pregame meal]. Then you went upstairs to bed to get ready for the game. But everybody was doing the same thing."

By the same token, there was no off-season training regimen. Instead, summer was for golf and family vacations. When training camp started to approach, Hodge remembers, "You grabbed a rubber jacket to lose some weight and that was it. There was no off-ice training that anybody knew about."

Hodge's finest moment as a Bruin may have come in the 1972 playoffs, when he led all playoff scorers with nine goals (including five in the Stanley Cup Final versus the Rangers) to help fuel the Bruins to their second Cup in three years.

GOLDEN SEASONS

THE "BIG BAD BRUINS" broke a 29-year Stanley Cup drought in 1970, beating the St. Louis Blues in a four-game sweep that was punctuated by Bobby Orr's "Flying Goal" in overtime of Game 4. It was a fitting conclusion of a Stanley Cup joyride that saw the Bruins beat the hated Rangers, dominate the talented Black

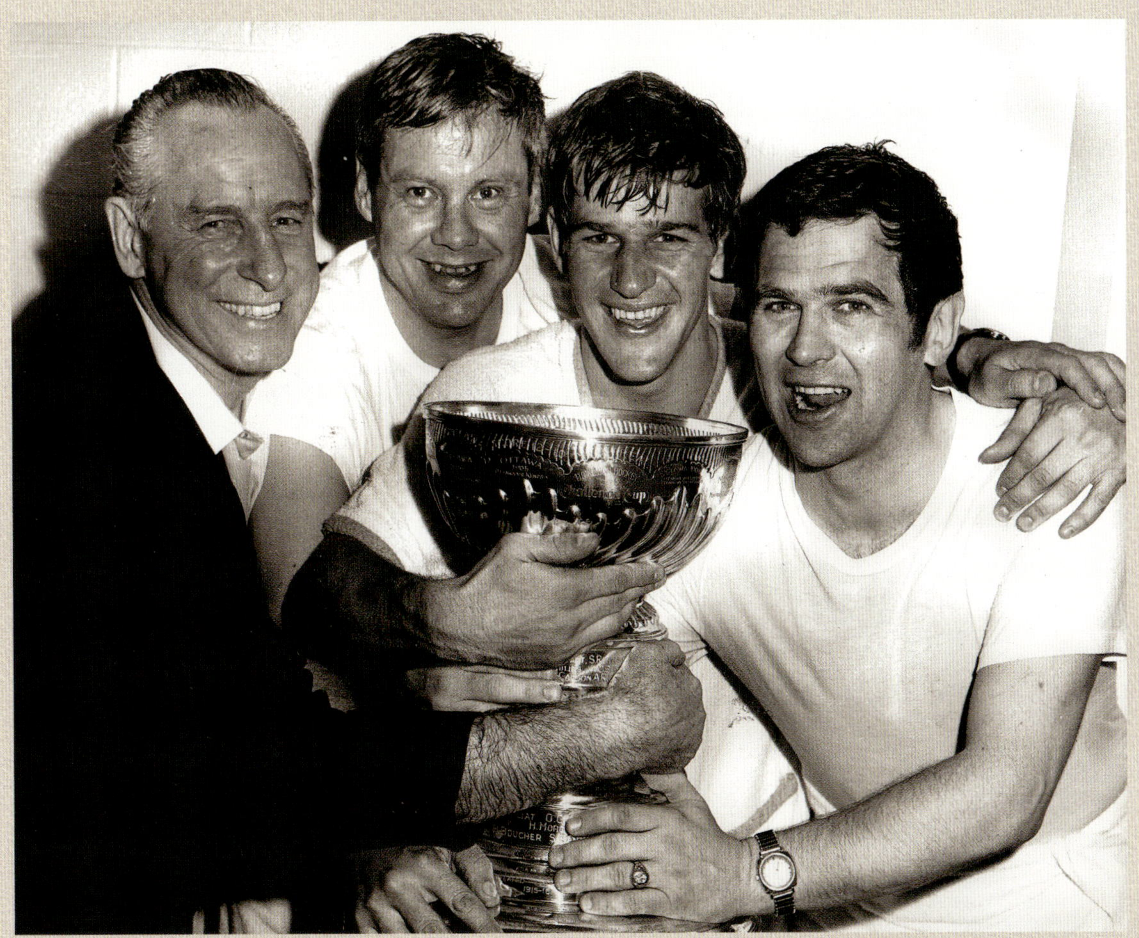

General manager Milt Schmidt, assistant GM Tom Johnson, Bobby Orr, and head coach Harry Sinden (left to right) celebrate the Bruins' first Stanley Cup win in 29 seasons in the jubilant Bruins locker room. (Photograph by Al Ruelle, Collection of The Sports Museum)

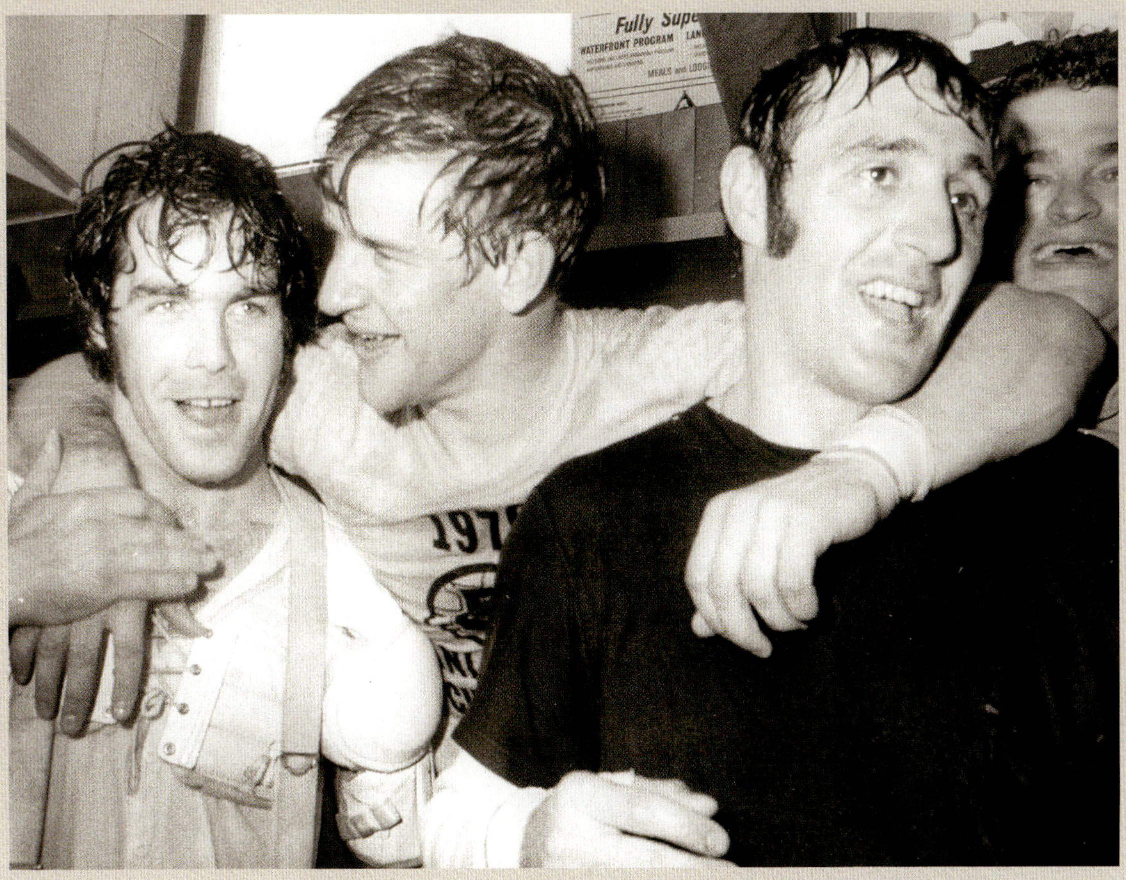

On May 10, 1970, Derek Sanderson, Bobby Orr, and Phil Esposito (left to right) celebrate their Stanley Cup victory over the Blues. (Photograph by Al Ruelle, Collection of The Sports Museum)

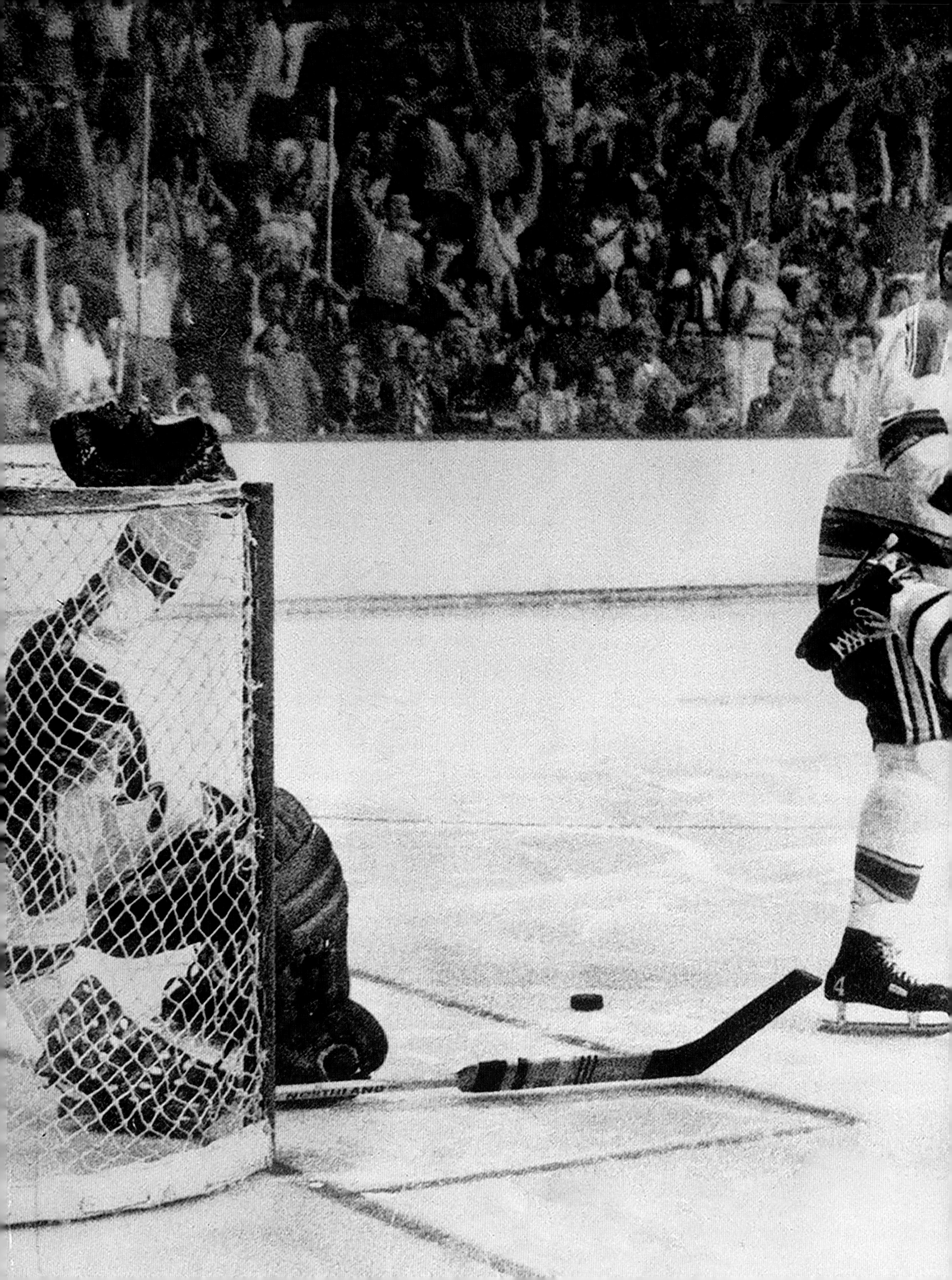
NORTHLAND

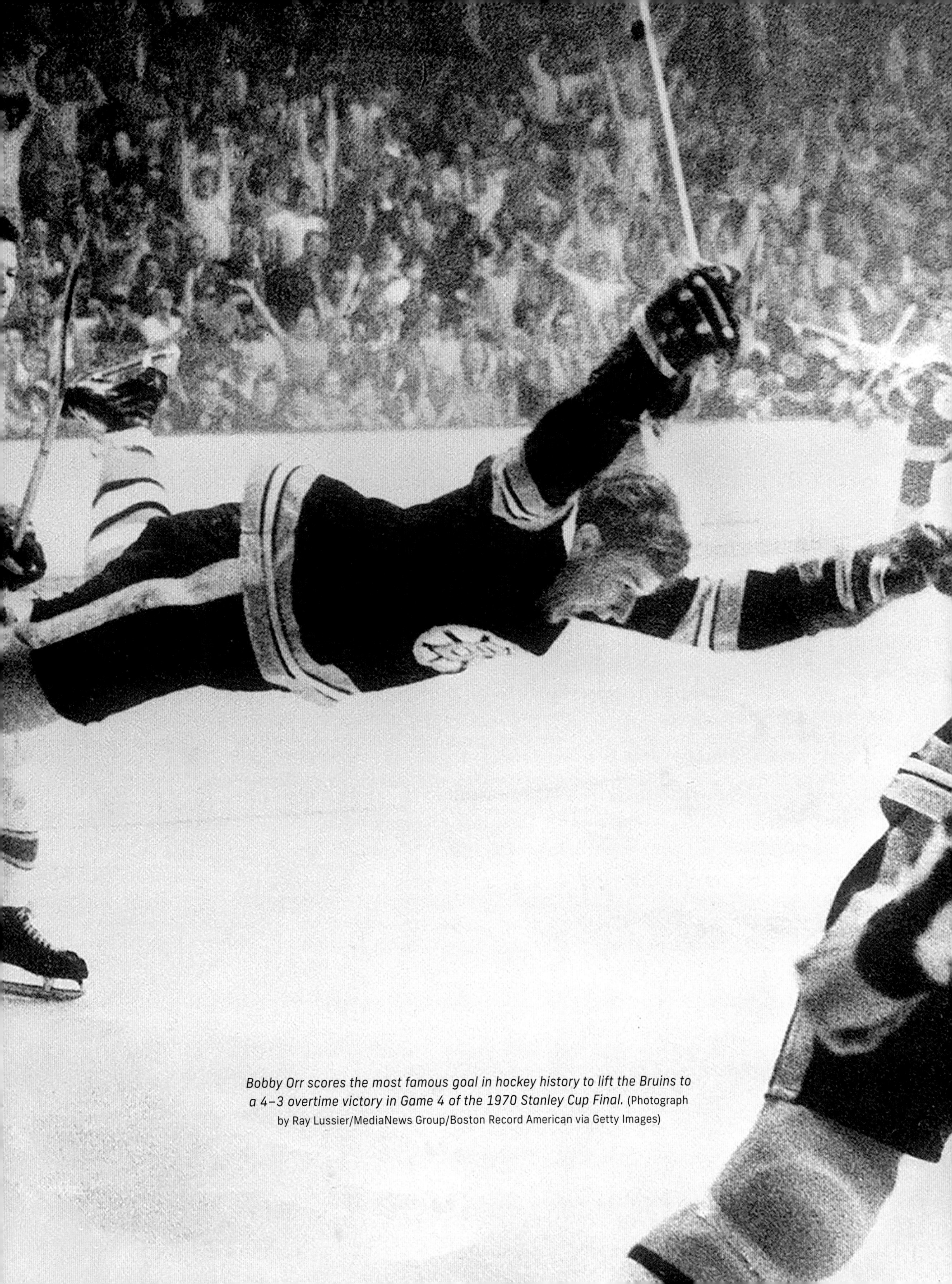

Bobby Orr scores the most famous goal in hockey history to lift the Bruins to a 4–3 overtime victory in Game 4 of the 1970 Stanley Cup Final. (Photograph by Ray Lussier/MediaNews Group/Boston Record American via Getty Images)

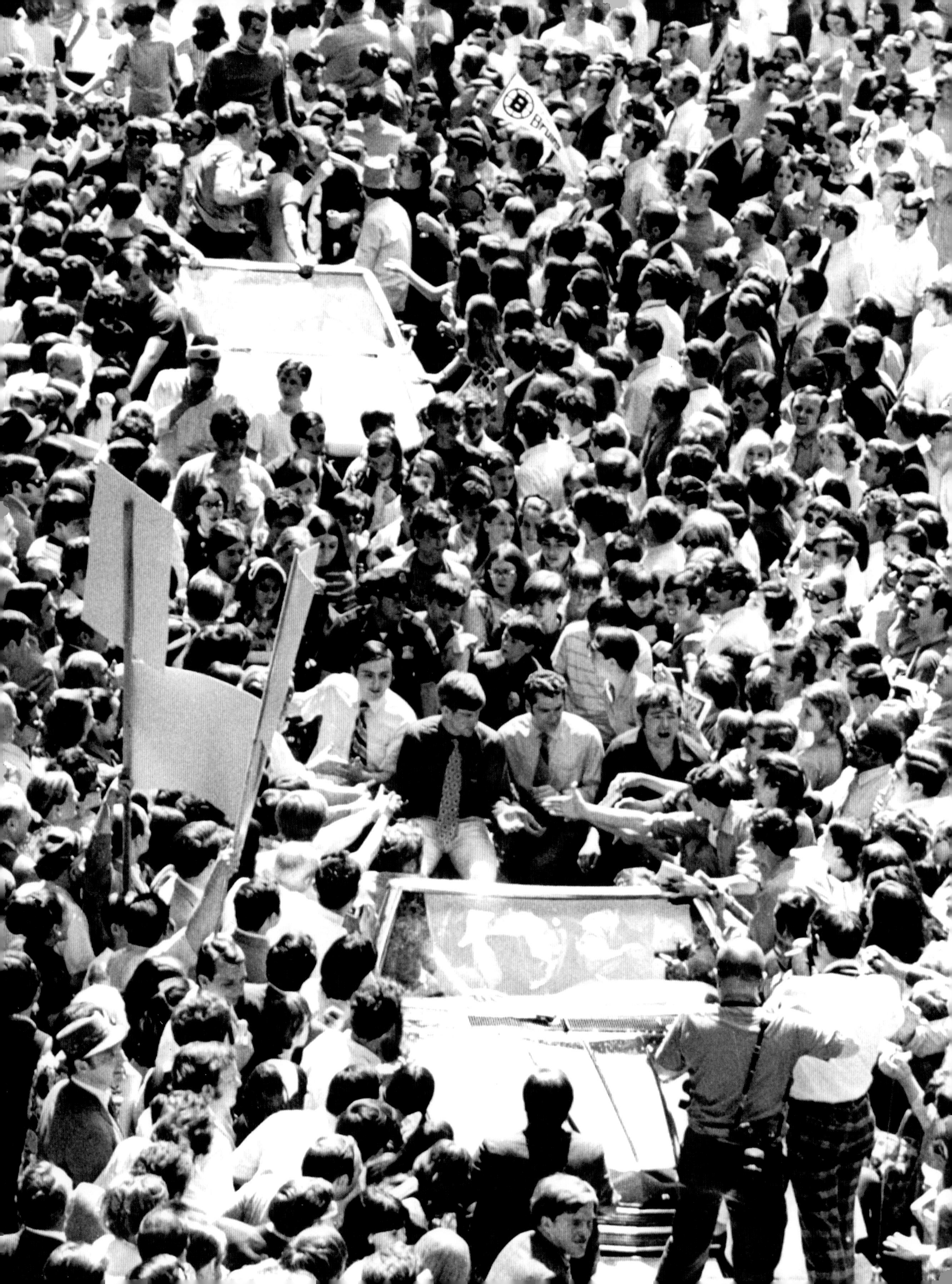
B

Hawks, and then overwhelm the overmatched Blues. They were, unquestionably, the best team in hockey and a worthy winner of the Stanley Cup.

It seemed as though the Bruins would repeat as Cup champions in 1970–71, as they blitzed through the NHL, setting a new scoring record with 399 goals and taking no prisoners along the way. But then, in the playoffs, the Bruins ran into a proud Montreal team led by veteran captain Jean Beliveau and sensational rookie goaltender Ken Dryden. In a tight, tense series, the Canadiens defeated the Bruins in seven games. To this day, more than a half century later, many Bruins fans of Baby Boom vintage still haven't gotten over the shock of the Bruins losing Game 7 at home.

Neither have many of the players. "I don't know what happened," Phil Esposito said. "I mean, I thought about it and thought about it because we were good. But it was really funny, we had trouble with the Canadiens…[they] always seemed to come out ahead. And I don't know why that was." Linemate Ken Hodge cites the men who patrolled the blueline for the Canadiens in 1971. "You try to go through that defense corps," said Hodge. "It was just unbelievable. All Hall of Fame guys."

In 1972, the Bruins continued their regular season dominance, finishing first in the East Division, led by the triple-digit scoring of Orr and Esposito. In the playoffs, they easily got by Toronto and St. Louis to advance to the Stanley Cup Final against their bitter rival, the New York Rangers. They won the series in six games and triumphantly celebrated their second championship in three years on Madison Square Garden ice. And the Stanley Cup returned to where it belonged—Boston.

Opposite page: John Adams, Bobby Orr, Don Marcotte, and Bill Speer (front car center, from left) are mobbed by fans in downtown Boston during a parade celebrating their victory in the Stanley Cup Final the day before. It was Monday, May 11, 1970—and all the world was Black and Gold. (Photograph by Bruce Bennett Studios via Getty Images Studios/Getty Images)

BRUINSMANIA

IN THE EARLY 1970s, the Bruins established themselves as America's Team via a torrent of nationwide press coverage, as well as their frequent Sunday afternoon TV appearances on CBS. Locally, game broadcasts on Channel 38 were appointment television and still prompt fans of a certain age to recount the many ways in which they were forced to manipulate their UHF antennas to receive clear signals. In many households, a family member drawing the proverbial short straw was designated to stand for extended periods of antenna duty, depending on either the significance of the game or the quality of transmission.

A Bruins game at the Garden was the place to be (and to be seen). And tickets were almost impossible to come by. In the best Boston tradition, you had to know somebody. Otherwise, you needed to be willing to literally camp out overnight (or, in some instances, sequester for several days) on the sidewalk adjacent to North Station to get the prized ducats, limited to four per customer.

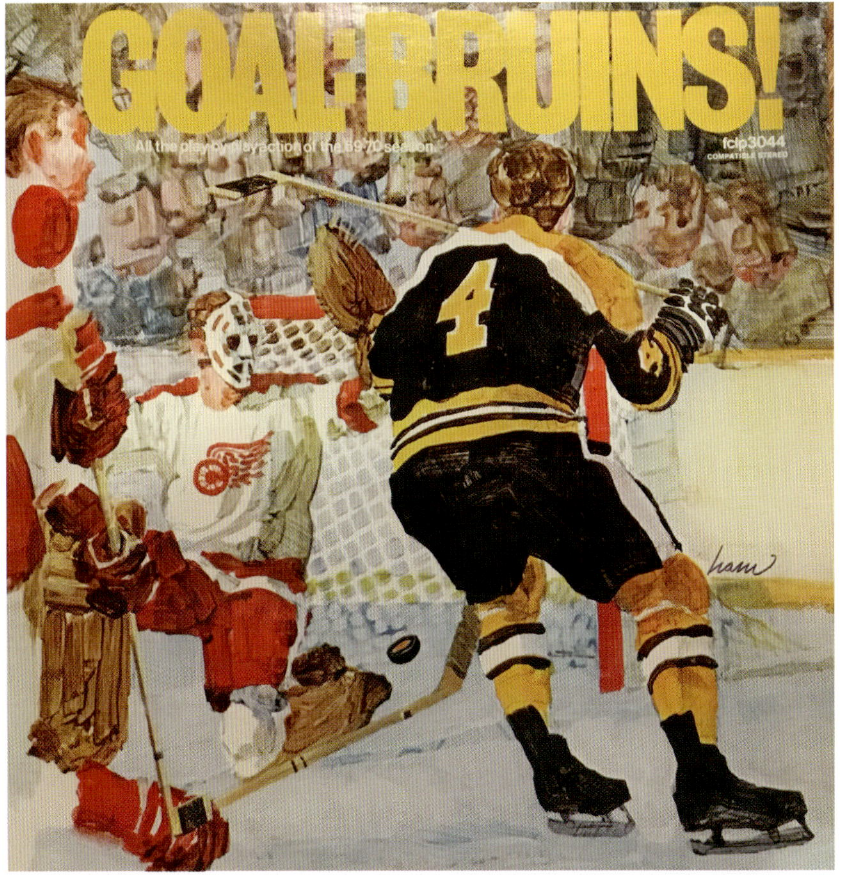

The Bruins' victory in 1970 inspired an array of team-related products, including an album of game highlights, much in the same vein as similar records produced in that era honoring the champion Celtics and the Impossible Dream Red Sox. (Collection of The Sports Museum)

The Bruins of the early 1970s were a team comprised of "characters with character." And they were the inspiration that led to the building of countless rinks in Boston and beyond and helped spawn the next generation of young players, including the local kids (Mike Eruzione, Jim Craig, Dave Silk, and Jack O'Callahan) who would help author the "Miracle on Ice" at the 1980 Winter Olympic

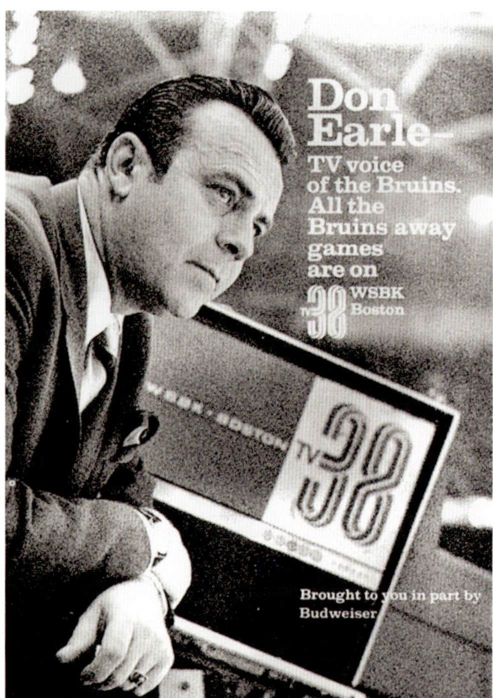

Don Earle was the voice of the Bruins on TV-38 from 1967 to 1971 before departing to take the television job for the Philadelphia Flyers. He was replaced by Fred Cusick, who would masterfully handle the play-by-play duties on TV-38 and NESN for the next quarter-century. (Collection of Richard A. Johnson)

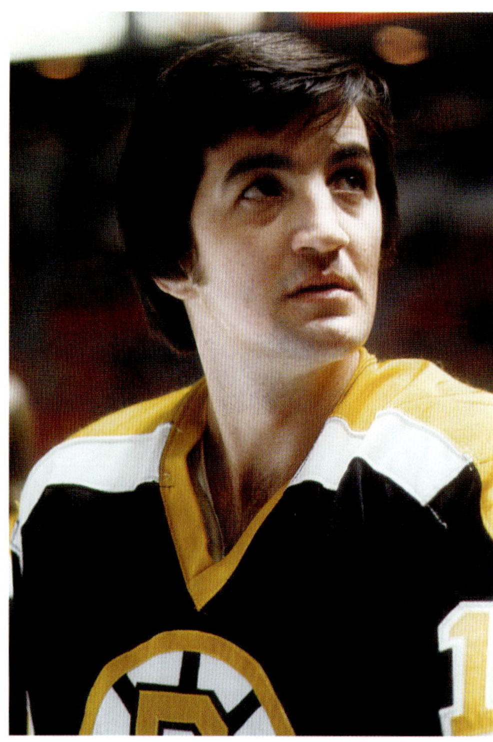

Defenseman Carol Vadnais was acquired via trade from the California Golden Seals in February 1972 and was a vital contributor to the Bruins' successful Stanley Cup run that spring. (Photograph by B Bennett/Getty Images)

Games. "When you have excitement in the community, things are gonna happen," said Bobby Orr. "Rinks are gonna be built—and let's not forget, our players were out there, too. Our players, they didn't hide away. We were in rinks doing clinics. We would do signings. We were a group that was out there."

At the time, the Bruins players realized that they were caught up in something special—and enjoyed every minute of it.

"Everywhere you went, the Bruins were the most exciting topic and the most exciting thing to see," said defenseman Rick Smith, whose first stint with the Bruins took place between 1968 and 1972. "Everywhere you went, you were made to feel very special. People would get excited if they saw you on the street—just anywhere."

Eddie Westfall agrees: "It was a wonderful experience.... We had a real love affair with the fans, I mean it was really something and all the players got swept up into it and enjoyed it and gave back in their neighborhoods. Everywhere we went, it was kind of special."

"The phenomenon of the fans was so much a part of it," echoed Smith. "That magical atmosphere and environment that was provided for us in the '70s, it was the fans that made it. The players were the product, but there were so many people.... They all shared the enjoyment or excitement of being a Bruins fan and being involved with the team."

BIGGER AND BADDER— THE RIVALRY WITH THE RANGERS

In the years prior to World War II, the Bruins and New York Rangers waged a fierce rivalry for NHL supremacy, swapping the Cup back and forth in 1939 (Bruins), 1940 (Rangers), and 1941 (Bruins again). In the late 1960s and early 1970s, both teams emerged from years of doldrums to become leading Cup contenders. And the rivalry was renewed—this time, with even more animosity.

The Rangers of the late 1960s and early 1970s were the team Boston fans loved to hate. Rod Gilbert, Eddie Giacomin, and especially Brad Park all became targets of Boston ire. As with any great rivalry, there were multiple layers of contention, which included the overall bitterness between the two cities, as well as the presence of way too many students from New York at Boston institutions of higher learning. As Rick Smith said in a 2022 interview, "That rivalry was sensational.... For a lot of fans, especially in New York, that rivalry was very, very hot. It was quite a story through the '70s."

But it didn't just involve the fans. The players and coaches felt it, too.

"We might have had some great games with Montreal because they were the best team in the league quite often, but the Rangers were our real rivals," said Harry Sinden. Or, as Derek Sanderson put it more bluntly, "The Rangers were hated."

The passion was on full display in 1970, when the Bruins beat the Rangers in six games in the opening round of the Stanley Cup playoffs. The series was heated—but the Bruins were confident that they would prevail. "We never had any trouble with the Rangers," said Phil Esposito.

The two teams met again in 1972, this time in the Stanley Cup Final, with the Bruins once again emerging victorious, four games to two, to win the championship. Bruins fans will never forget the sight of Johnny Bucyk parading the Cup around the Rangers home ice while dodging the bottles and garbage tossed his way by New York fans. "That was a big rivalry," said Bucyk. "To get the Cup there and skate around Madison Square Garden.... That was a big thrill."

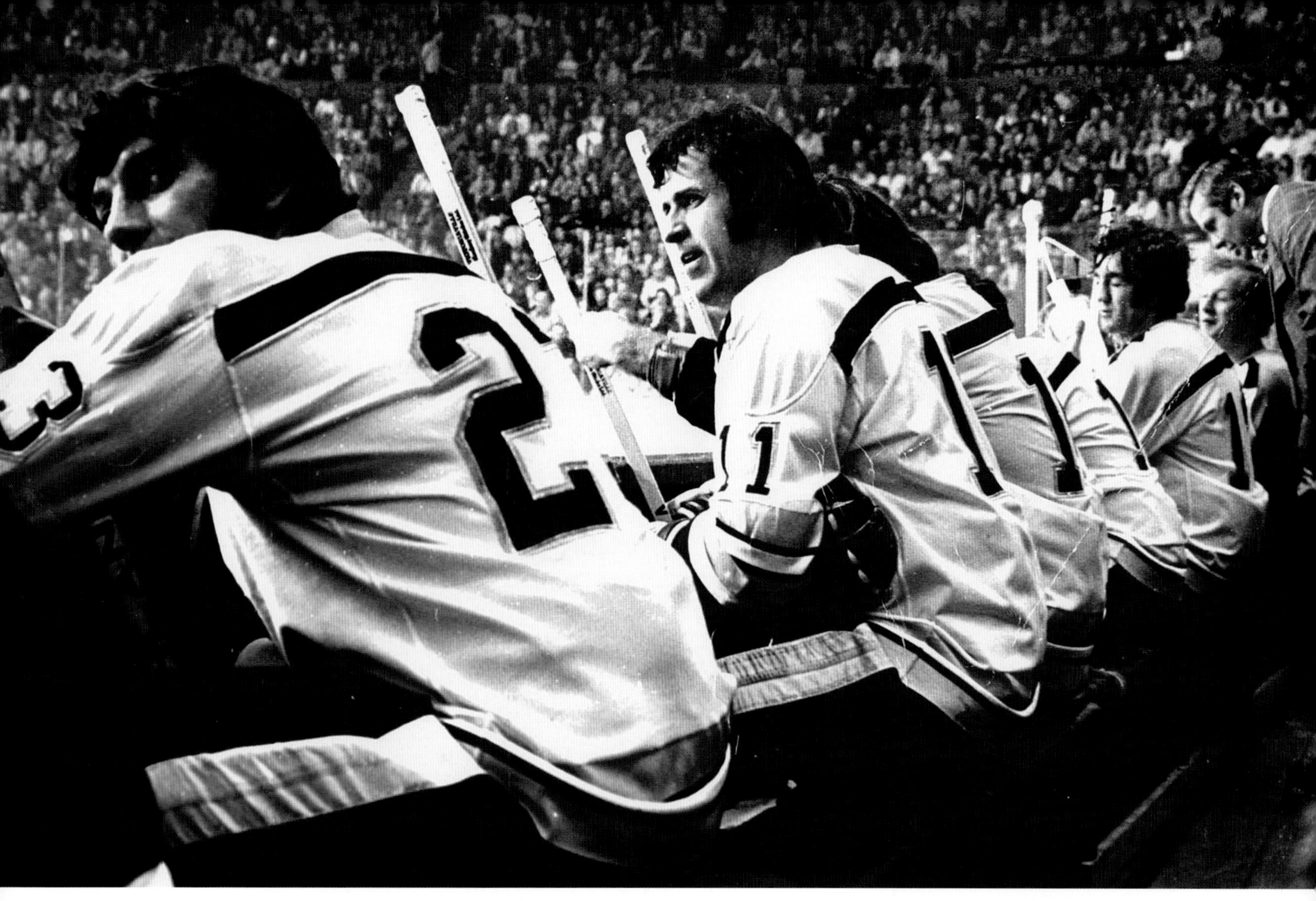

Veteran forward Mike "Shakey" Walton (11) came to Boston in February 1971. He became an integral part of the team that would win the Stanley Cup the next season, scoring 28 goals with 28 assists. Walton is seen here on the bench with defenseman Matt Ravlich (23), who broke in with the Bruins in the early 1960s and returned to the team in late 1971.
(Collection of The Sports Museum)

GERRY CHEEVERS

THE LIST OF NOTEWORTHY athletes identified by a single article of equipment is mighty short. It includes Johnny Unitas's high top cleats, Steph Curry's dangling mouthpiece—and, of course, Bruins goalie Gerry Cheevers's stitch-marked mask.

How did it come into being?

One day at practice, Cheevers was struck in the mask by a wayward puck. Cheevers saw this as a good excuse to miss the rest of practice, so he headed off to the dressing room to recover. Head Coach Harry Sinden wasn't going to let Cheevers off the hook that easy, barging into the locker room and ordering Cheevers back onto the ice. As a joke, Cheevers asked assistant trainer Frosty Forristall to paint a stitch mark on the plain mask where the puck had struck him to prove to Sinden that he had really been injured. Everyone laughed and practice resumed. Cheevers liked the look and had Forristall add stitch marks for every subsequent hit that he took in games and practices. The stitched mask soon became an integral part of his persona.

The man behind the mask was a top-flight goaltender—one of the best of his era. During the 1971–72 season, Cheevers went undefeated in 32 consecutive games, an NHL record that still stands. As the main backstop on two Stanley Cup championship teams, he was celebrated as one of the best "money goaltenders" in the history of the game. "To my mind, [Ken] Dryden was good—but Cheesy was better," said Phil Esposito.

Cheevers also had a big presence in the locker room, frequently leading the team in singing the song "Ob-La-Di, Ob-La-Da" by the Beatles. He even managed

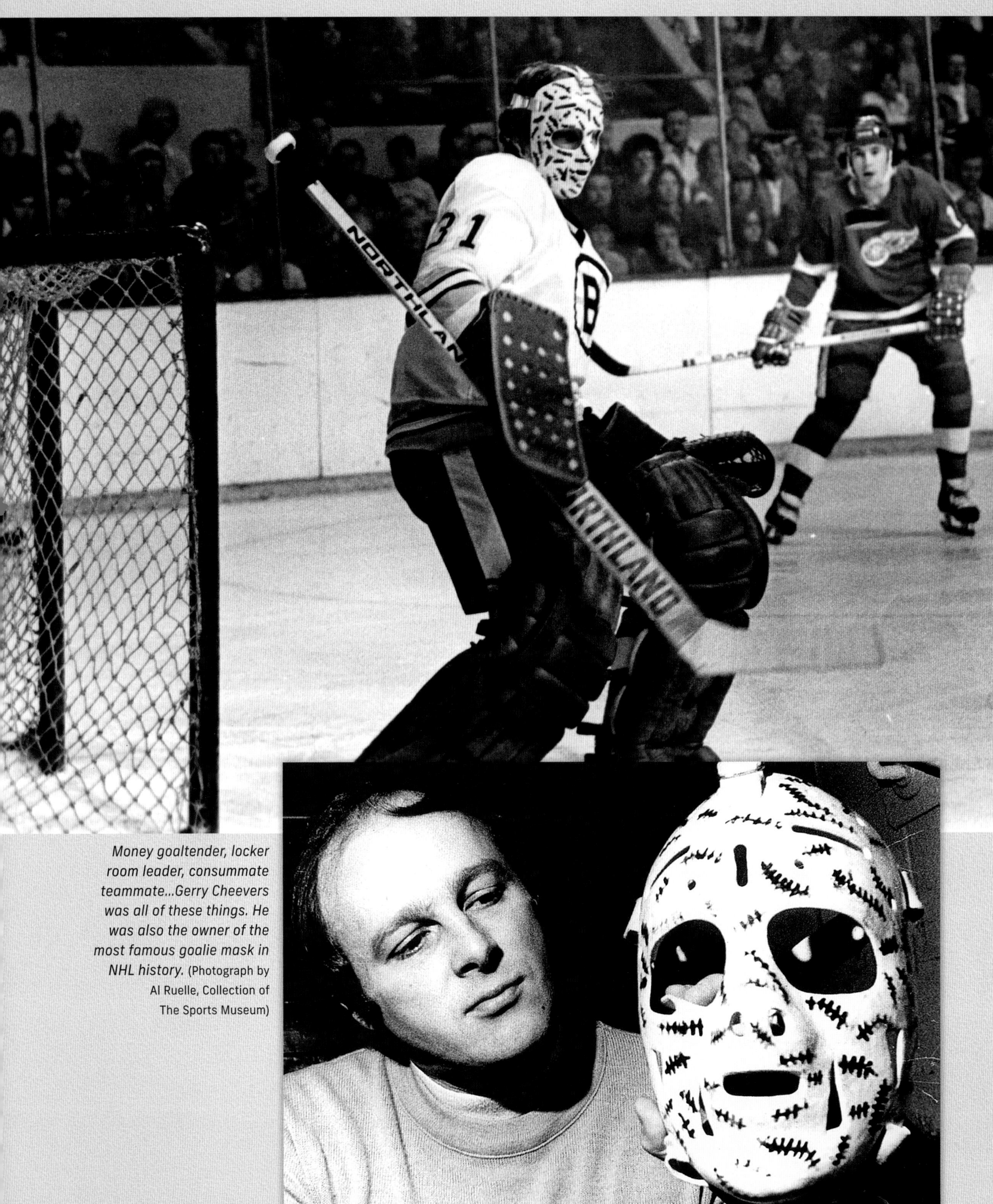

Money goaltender, locker room leader, consummate teammate...Gerry Cheevers was all of these things. He was also the owner of the most famous goalie mask in NHL history. (Photograph by Al Ruelle, Collection of The Sports Museum)

to keep things loose when he was sitting on the bench. "Cheevers, this guy's hilarious," said Bobby Orr. "We're playing the Canadiens one day and [Yvan] Cournoyer was flying. He could skate. Cheevers is not playing. He's on the end of the bench. During the face off by the bench, Gerry says, 'For God's sake, slow down.'"

Cheevers had two stints with the Bruins. The first came from 1965 to 1972 and featured the two Stanley Cup championships. Then, after three and a half seasons with Cleveland of the World Hockey Association, Cheevers returned to Boston in 1976. For the next four and a half seasons, he split the netminding duties with the underrated Gilles Gilbert on the beloved Lunch Pail A.C. teams.

Cheevers later coached the Bruins from 1980 to 1985. He was inducted into the Hockey Hall of Fame in 1985.

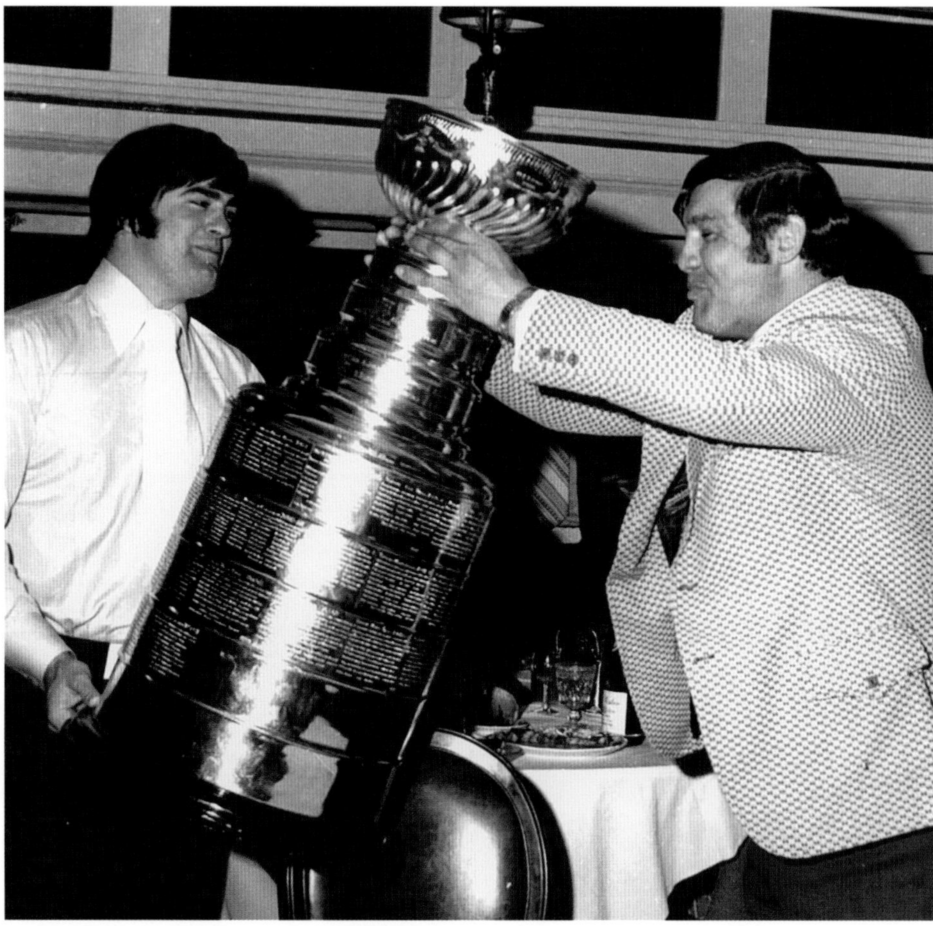

Team president Weston W. Adams Jr. steadies the Stanley Cup while Johnny Bucyk prepares to sip champagne from the trophy at the team banquet following the 1972 Stanley Cup victory over the Rangers. (Photograph by Al Ruelle, Collection of The Sports Museum)

THE IMPACT OF THE WORLD HOCKEY ASSOCIATION

In 1972, another professional hockey league was born: the World Hockey Association (WHA). The new league shocked the hockey world when the Winnipeg Jets signed Black Hawks star Bobby Hull to a 10-year contract worth $2.75 million with a signing bonus of $1 million. And the money started to flow.

Many other NHL players followed Hull's lead and headed for the greener pastures of the WHA prior to the 1972–73 season, including four key players on the Bruins—Gerry Cheevers, Derek Sanderson, Johnny McKenzie, and Ted Green.

Other Bruins considered jumping, as well. "We all explored the WHA," said Ken Hodge. "I don't think there was a player who didn't explore the possibility.... Money is thrown at you." Among the Bruins stars who rejected the overtures and decided to stay with the Bruins included longtime franchise fixture Johnny Bucyk. "Two teams offered me a contract," he said. "One was in Minnesota and one was in

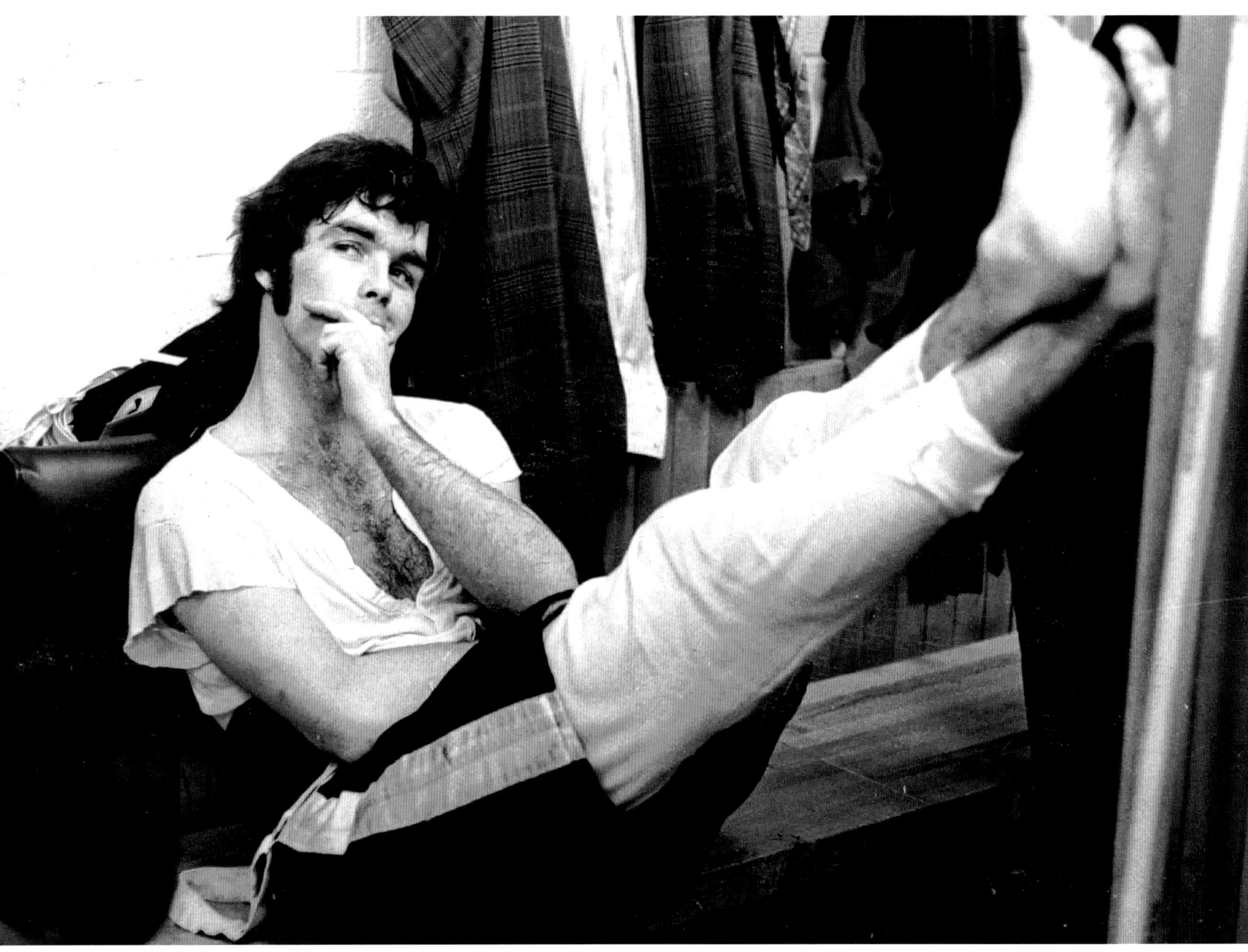

There was no bigger sports celebrity in Boston than Derek Sanderson. He had a big presence on the ice—and an even bigger one off the ice and on the town. Many hearts were broken when he left for the WHA in 1972. (Photograph by Al Ruelle, Collection of The Sports Museum)

Opposite page: Johnny "Pie" McKenzie never shied away from an on-ice confrontation and had a knack for getting under the skin of opposing players. He also had a knack for scoring big goals. On a team of "characters with character," McKenzie may well have been Exhibit A. (Al Ruelle, Collection of The Sports Museum) *Inset: The departure of Sanderson and McKenzie to the WHA was a setback that may have cost the Bruins a dynasty.* (Collection of Richard A. Johnson)

L.A. But I couldn't leave Boston. And it was getting toward the end of my career, and I just said, 'No, I'm not interested.' I didn't want to go. And I'm probably glad I didn't because it didn't last very long."

Still, the four players that the Bruins lost to the WHA (plus Eddie Westfall, who was lost in the NHL expansion draft prior to the 1972–73 season) badly dented the team that had just won a Stanley Cup. "We lost five pretty darn good players," said Harry Sinden. "Very good players. So it was interruptive."

"I hated to see them go, but I could understand why they went," said Bobby Orr. "So we had to get back at it. Changes were made. Some guys were coming. Deals were made, too. So our team, the gang was breaking up. There was no question about that. And it was a difficult period."

Over the next few years, the Bruins would remain one of the best teams in the NHL, coming oh-so-close to winning another Cup in 1974 before falling to the Flyers. By 1976, though, both Orr and Esposito had left town, and the era was over.

Had the WHA never come into existence, and had Orr's glorious career not been curtailed by injuries, how many more Stanley Cups would Boston have won in the 1970s? "We would have had at least another two or three years in a row where we definitely would've won the Cup," maintains goaltender Ed Johnston.

What might have been?

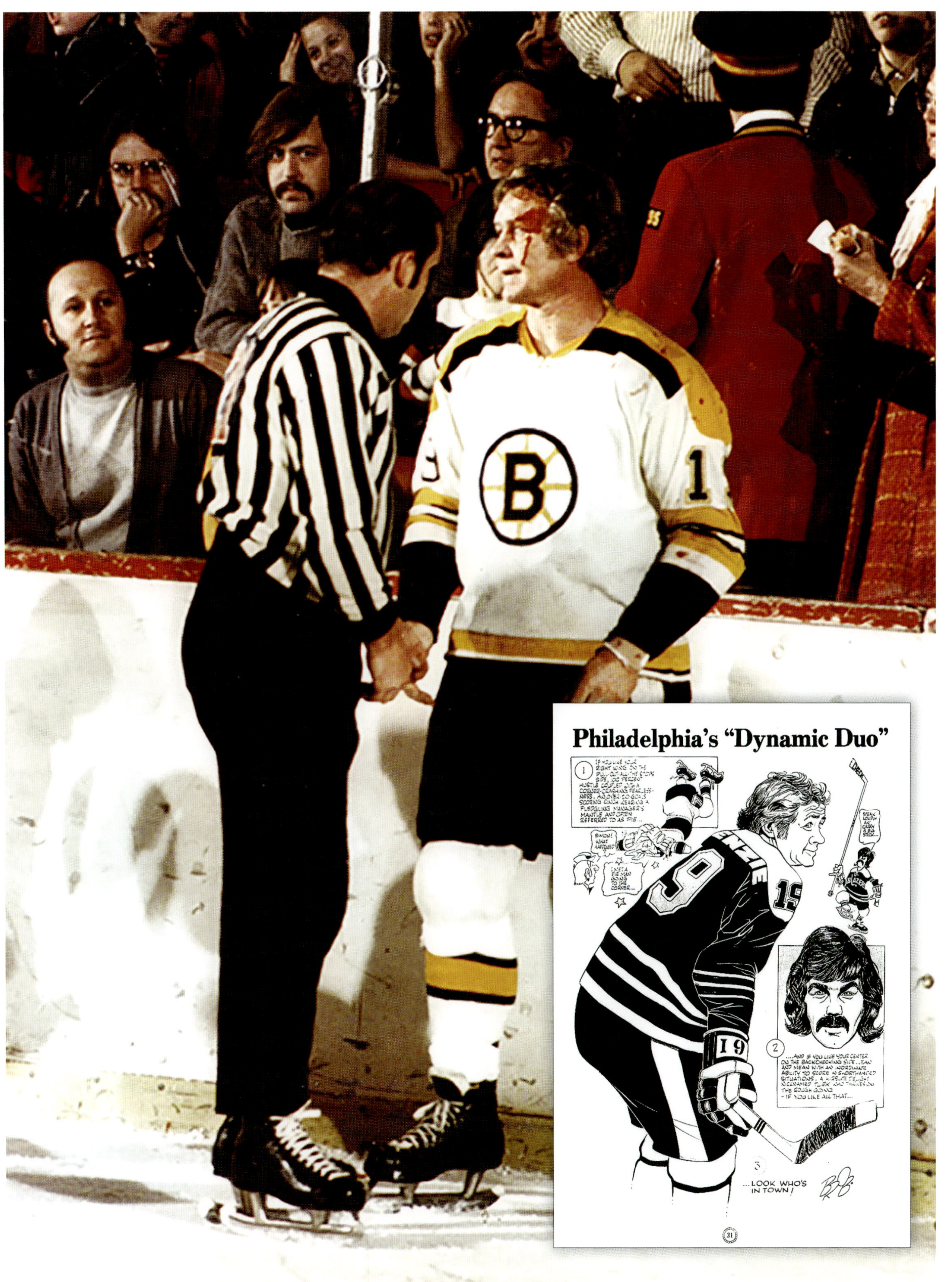

Philadelphia's "Dynamic Duo"

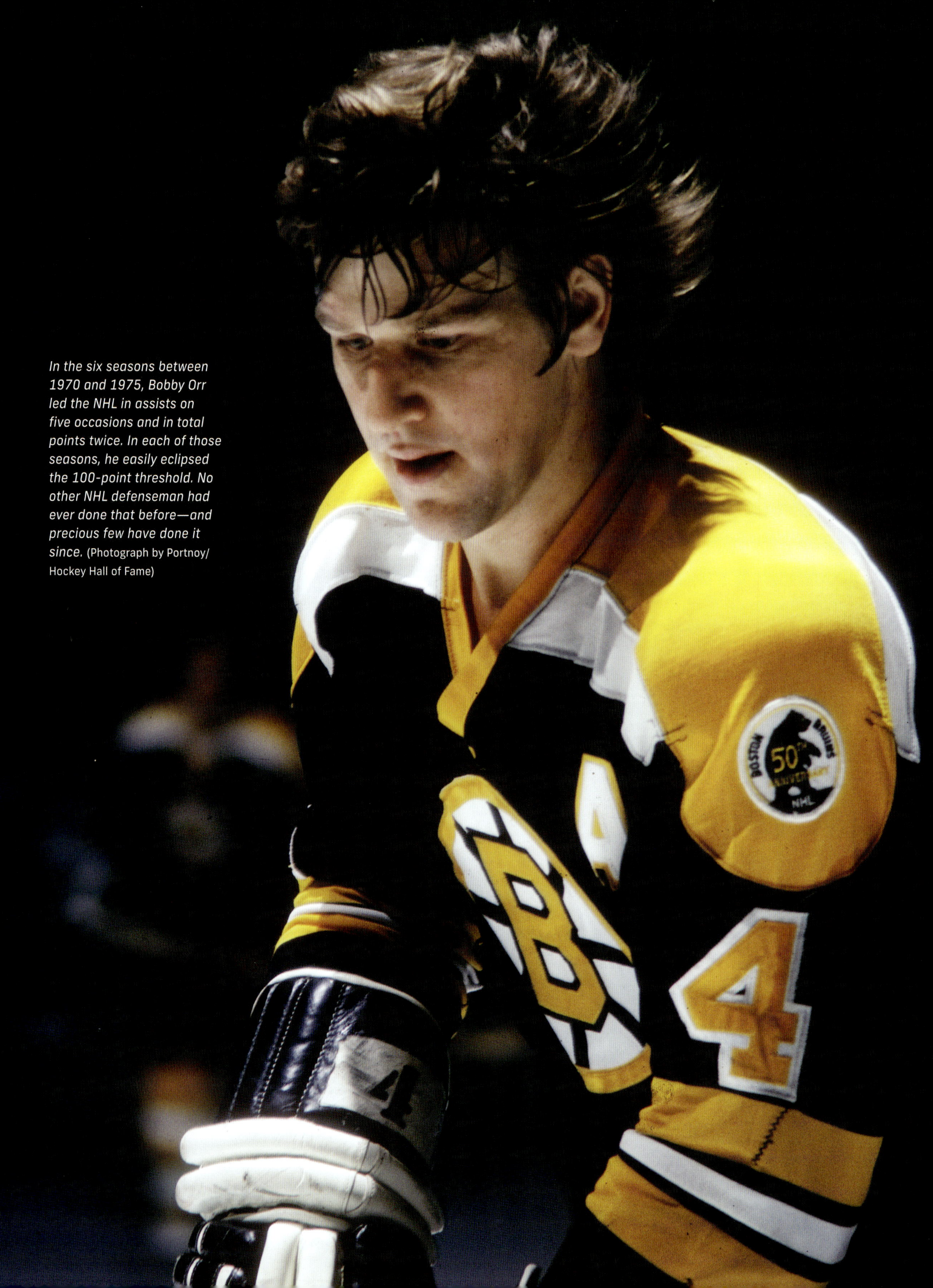

In the six seasons between 1970 and 1975, Bobby Orr led the NHL in assists on five occasions and in total points twice. In each of those seasons, he easily eclipsed the 100-point threshold. No other NHL defenseman had ever done that before—and precious few have done it since. (Photograph by Portnoy/ Hockey Hall of Fame)

NO. 4

Bobby Orr was the best ever and that is going to stand that way.
—Johnny Bucyk, Bruins left wing (1957–1978)

He was the best.... There were games where he would kill the whole penalty by himself. He'd just take it around on one end and then he'd go all the way back down to the other.... He was the only guy ever who could change the tempo of a game. If we were ahead, he would slow it down, and if we were behind, he'd pick it up.
—Ed Johnston, Bruins goaltender (1962–1973)

In hockey there's nothing perfect. Maybe Bobby. Maybe Bobby. That was it.
—Phil Esposito, Bruins center (1967–1975)

Everyone was in Bobby's shadow!
—Brad Park, Bruins defenseman (1975–1984), on being regarded as the NHL's second-best defenseman while Bobby Orr was playing

It was an honor.
—Terry O'Reilly, Bruins right wing (1972–1985), on playing on the same teams as Bobby Orr in the mid-1970s

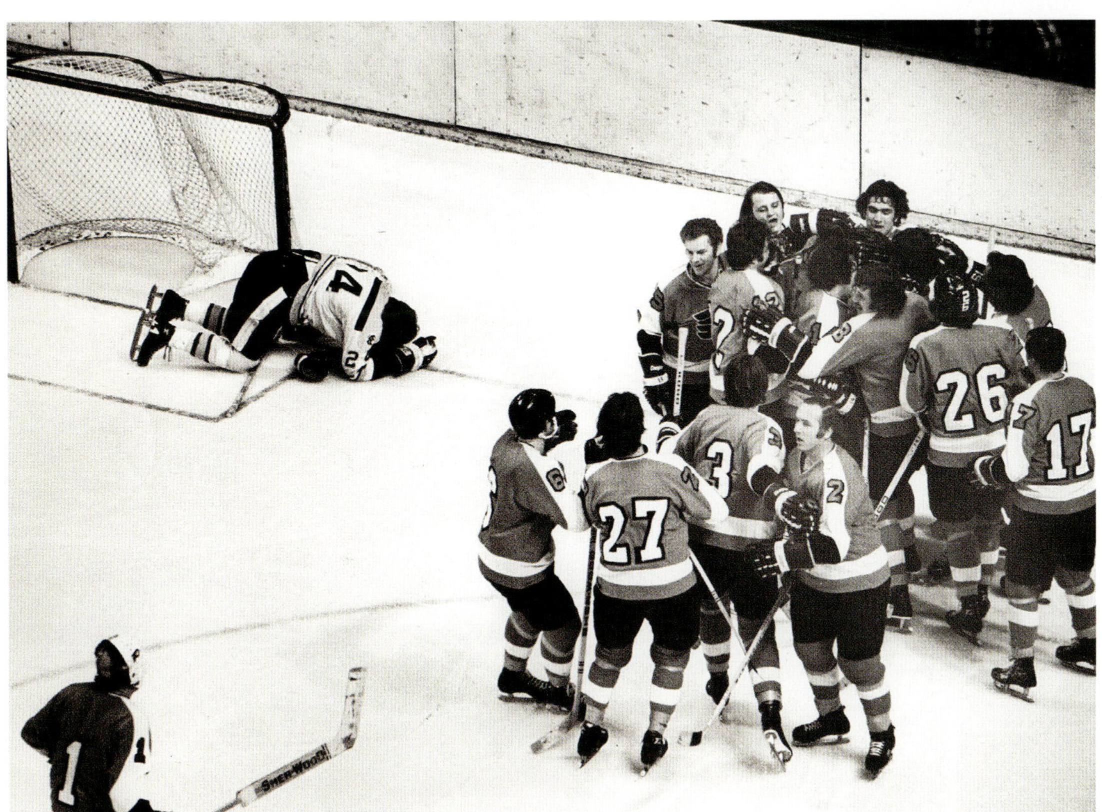

Terry O'Reilly (left) drops to the ice in disbelief after Bobby Clarke (in the middle of a group of happy Philadelphia Flyers) scored the game-winning goal in overtime in Game 2 of the 1974 Stanley Cup Final. The stunning goal gave the upstart Flyers a 3–2 victory and knotted the series at one game apiece. The Flyers would end up prevailing in six games. (Frank O'Brien/The Boston Globe via Getty Images)

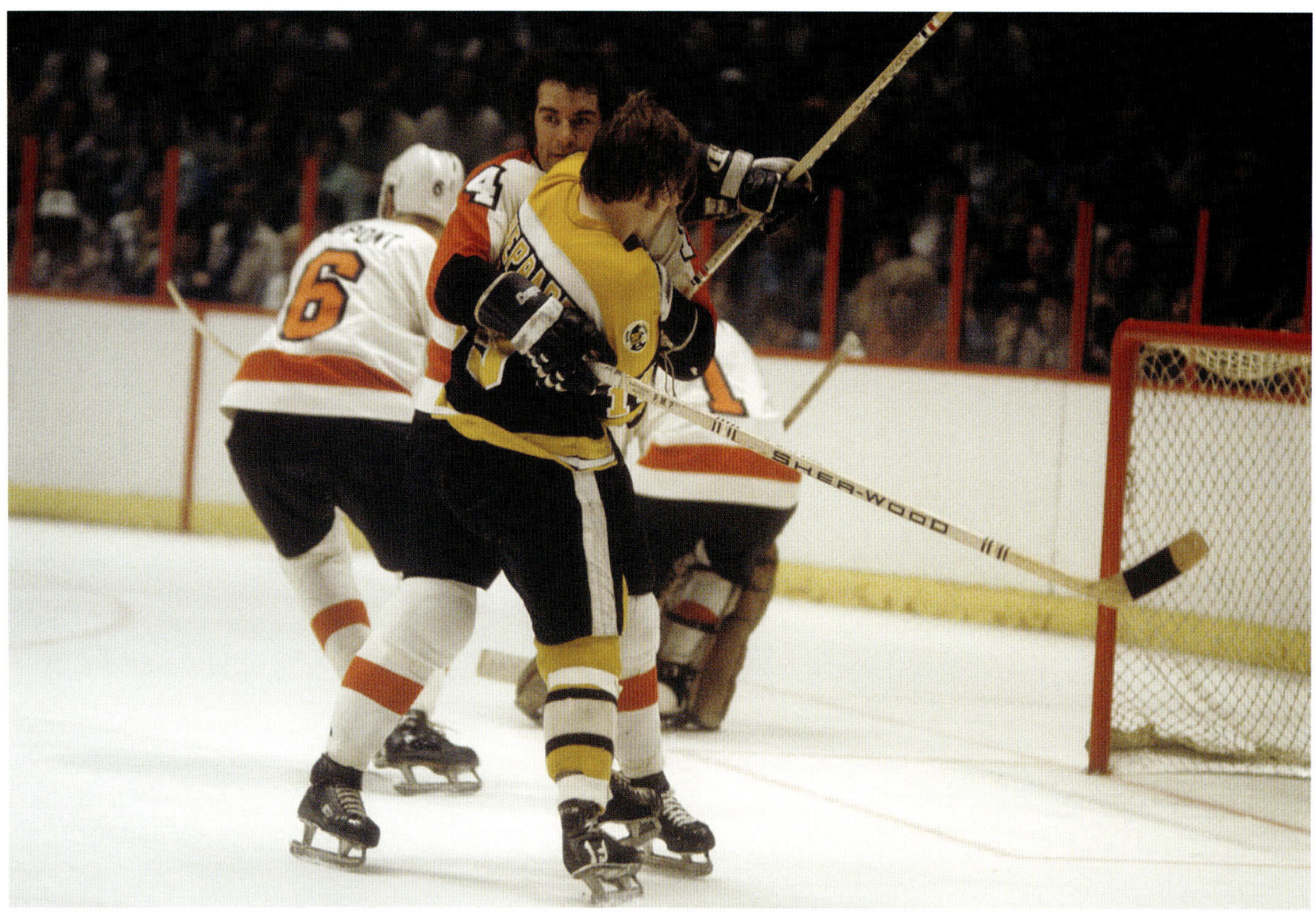

Gregg Sheppard (above) was an undersized and underrated center who scored 155 goals in his six seasons skating for the Black and Gold (1972–1978). Here he is shown battling Joe Watson of the Philadelphia Flyers (4) during the Stanley Cup Final in May 1974. (Photo by B Bennett/Getty Images)

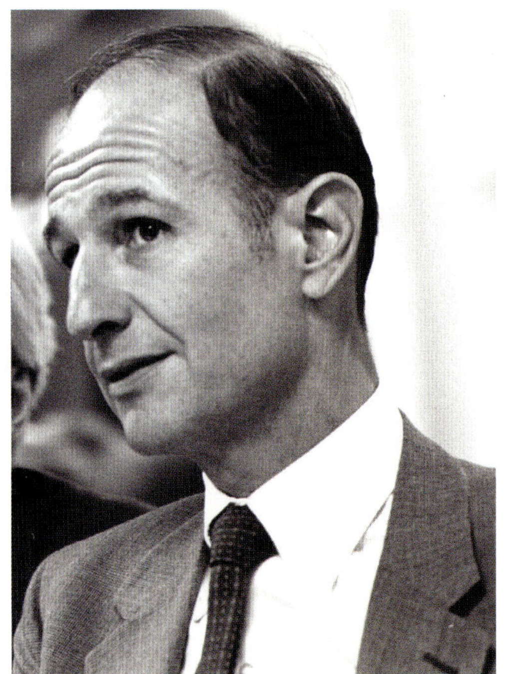

Jeremy Jacobs purchased both the Bruins and Boston Garden from Storer Broadcasting in September 1975. He still owns the team, as well as the distinction of being the longest-serving team owner in the history of Boston sports. (Photograph courtesy of the Boston Bruins)

THE TRADE (1970S STYLE)

ON NOVEMBER 7, 1975, the hockey world was stunned when the Bruins suddenly sent Phil Esposito and Carol Vadnais to the archrival Rangers for star defenseman Brad Park, classy center Jean Ratelle, and journeyman Joe Zanussi.

Bruins fans gasped to see Espo, one of the most popular Bruins and the top scorer in the league, in a blue and red Rangers jersey. Esposito was stunned, too. "I got on a plane that night and played with the Rangers [versus the California Golden Seals in Oakland]," said Esposito. "And I felt so strange. Wow. I felt so strange. Because I loved playing for the Boston Bruins. Loved it. Loved every minute of it. Never wanted to leave there, ever!"

The other principal in the trade, Park, had similar feelings. "Naturally, I was shocked," said Park in a 2022 interview. "I was the captain of the Rangers—and probably at that time, their highest paid player. The shock came through pretty clear."

From the very beginning, though, Park was determined to make the trade pay dividends for the Bruins: "I talked to Ratty as we were flying to Vancouver [to join the Bruins] and said, 'You know, the press is going to see it as the Rangers got the better end of the deal, but we're going to prove that wrong.... I think we're going to make this deal look better for the Bruins as we go along.'"

And that is essentially what happened after Park and Ratelle became Bruins. "That saved us for about seven years," said Harry Sinden, the man who made the deal for Boston. "Brad and Jean Ratelle led this team when they got here."

Indeed, Park would become the stalwart of the Bruins blueline and a team leader into the 1980s. And it turned out that the veteran center Ratelle had a lot

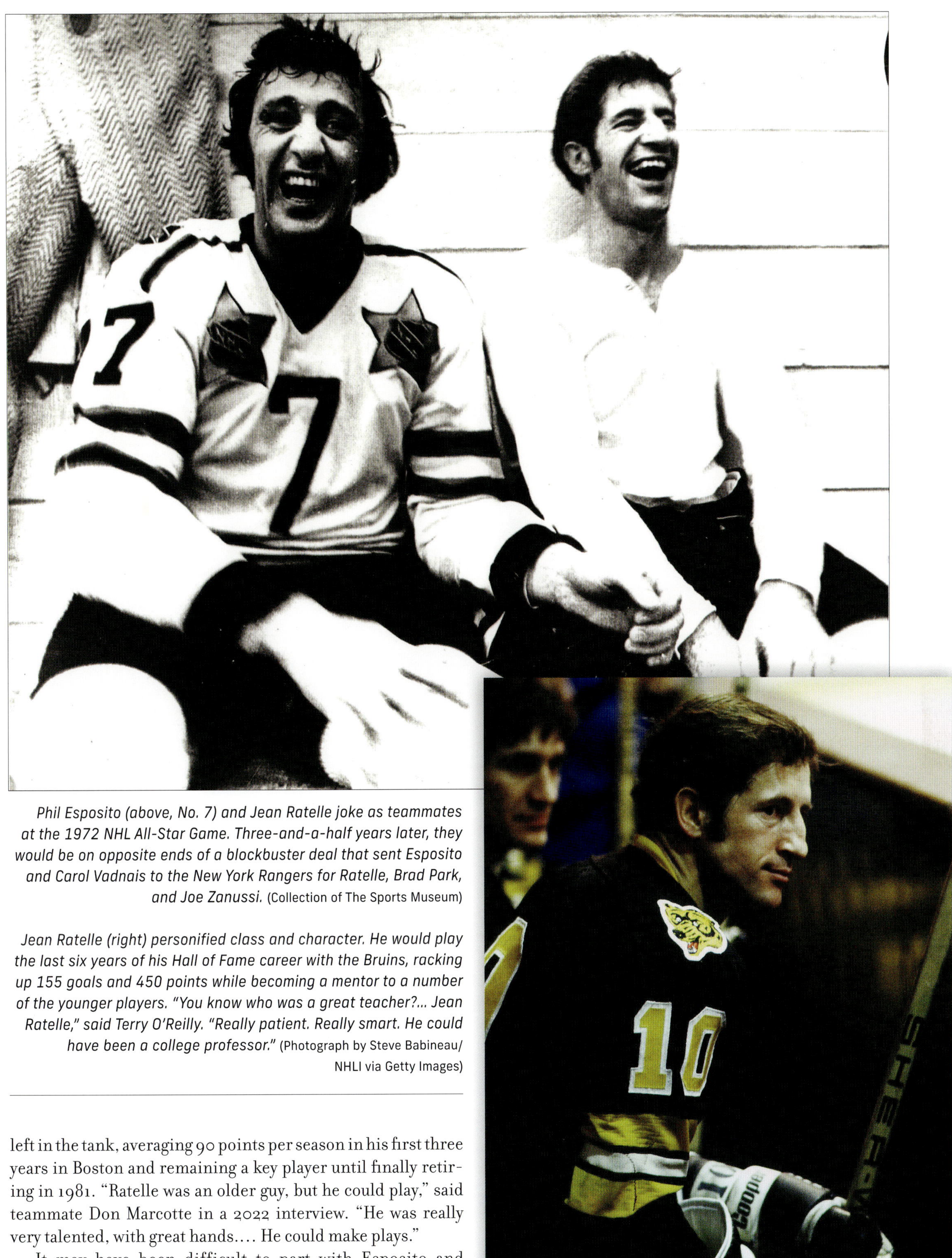

Phil Esposito (above, No. 7) and Jean Ratelle joke as teammates at the 1972 NHL All-Star Game. Three-and-a-half years later, they would be on opposite ends of a blockbuster deal that sent Esposito and Carol Vadnais to the New York Rangers for Ratelle, Brad Park, and Joe Zanussi. (Collection of The Sports Museum)

Jean Ratelle (right) personified class and character. He would play the last six years of his Hall of Fame career with the Bruins, racking up 155 goals and 450 points while becoming a mentor to a number of the younger players. "You know who was a great teacher?... Jean Ratelle," said Terry O'Reilly. "Really patient. Really smart. He could have been a college professor." (Photograph by Steve Babineau/ NHLI via Getty Images)

left in the tank, averaging 90 points per season in his first three years in Boston and remaining a key player until finally retiring in 1981. "Ratelle was an older guy, but he could play," said teammate Don Marcotte in a 2022 interview. "He was really very talented, with great hands.... He could make plays."

It may have been difficult to part with Esposito and Vadnais—but the deal worked out great for Boston.

DON CHERRY

By 1976, BOBBY ORR, Phil Esposito, and the Big Bad Bruins were no more. Fortunately, a new generation of iconic Bruins players were waiting in the wings to join forces with some holdovers from those early 1970s teams to take the team to its next incarnation. They would be known as the Lunch Pail Gang or, alternatively, the Lunch Pail A.C. (Athletic Club). And they would be led by a force of nature named Don Cherry.

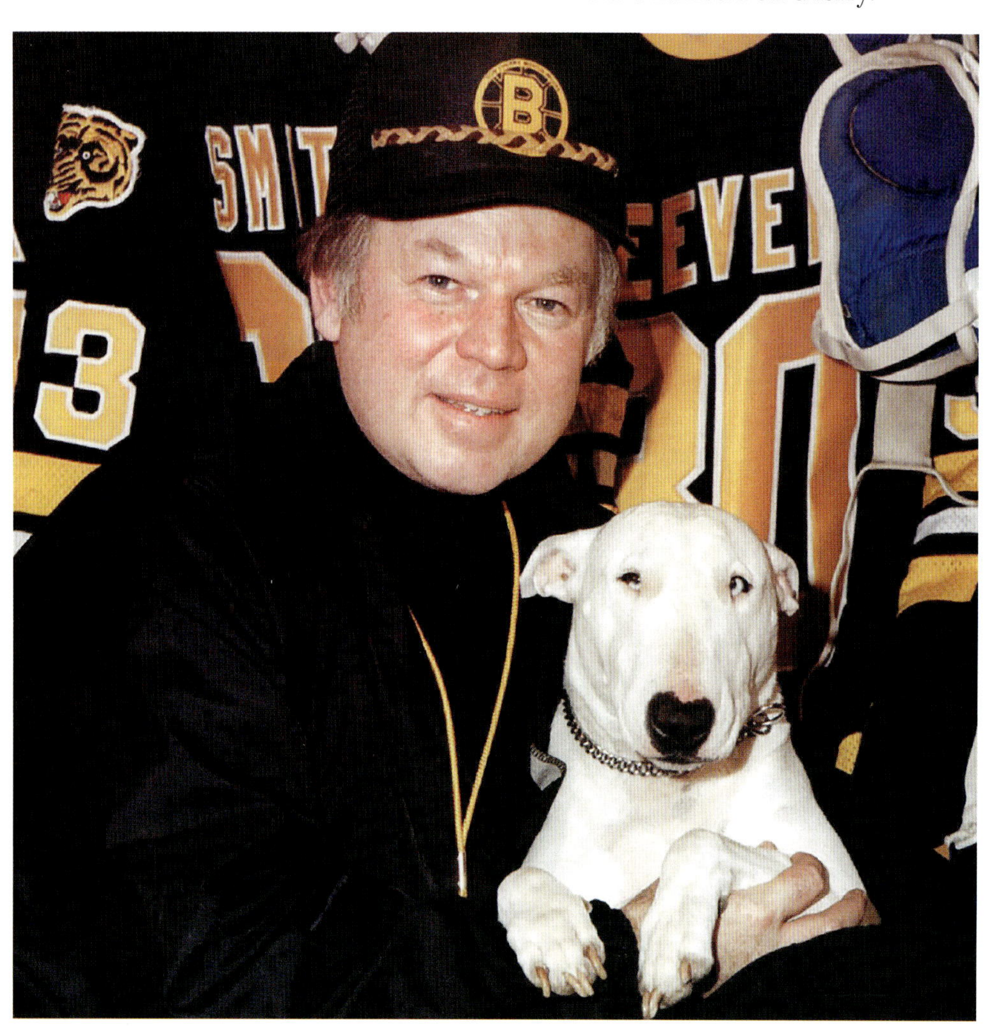

Bruins head coach Don Cherry and his beloved bull terrier Blue became Boston celebrities in the 1970s. The dog often accompanied Cherry to practices and became an essential part of his persona. (Photograph by Al Ruelle, Collection of The Sports Museum)

Much of his coaching persona came as the result of his having played more than 1,000 minor league games. A single-game call-up to the Bruins in the 1955 Stanley Cup Semifinals would represent the entirety of his NHL playing career. "I took a regular shift and we got beat," said Cherry in a 2022 interview. "But I got my picture in the paper. I was getting hit from behind, but I was quite happy."

After a successful three-year stint as head coach of the AHL's Rochester Americans, Cherry was hired to replace Bep Guidolin as head coach of the Bruins for the 1974–75 season. "I turned it down at first and then I phoned Harry the next day and I accepted," said Cherry. "It was an honor to be respected by the Bruins."

He didn't initially feel the love from the fans, though, as the Bruins could only salvage a tie in their 1974 home opener against the Maple Leafs. "My very first game, I recall somebody calling, 'Wake up the coach!'" said Cherry. "I'll never forget that."

Things soon got better, however. Over the course of his five seasons directing the Bruins, his teams overachieved on a grand scale, making a succession of deep playoff runs that included two Stanley Cup Final appearances against Guy Lafleur and the Montreal Canadiens. Along the way, Cherry became the colorful front man, often accompanied by his dog Blue, a feisty bull terrier. "Don was the center of attention," said Rick Smith. "I know he enjoyed that. But he really allowed the players to focus on the game and he took the publicity aspect of it—dealing with the press and everything."

Cherry's Bruins teams became renowned for playing with grit and swagger—and leaving everything on the ice. "There were so many players that came to work and worked in the trenches and slugged away at it," said Smith. "Obviously, with the earlier Bruins, there was so much star power there, it was a juggernaut. Whereas this group, it was toned down a little bit. There was still plenty of talent with Ricky Middleton and Jean Ratelle and guys like that. It was that hard work ethic that was symbolic of the team."

Or as Brad Park put it, "I think Don Cherry's team became the biggest, toughest, meanest sons of bitches in the valley."

Following his coaching career, Cherry became an iconic broadcaster, stirring the pot unapologetically on his "Coach's Corner" slot on *Hockey Night in Canada*.

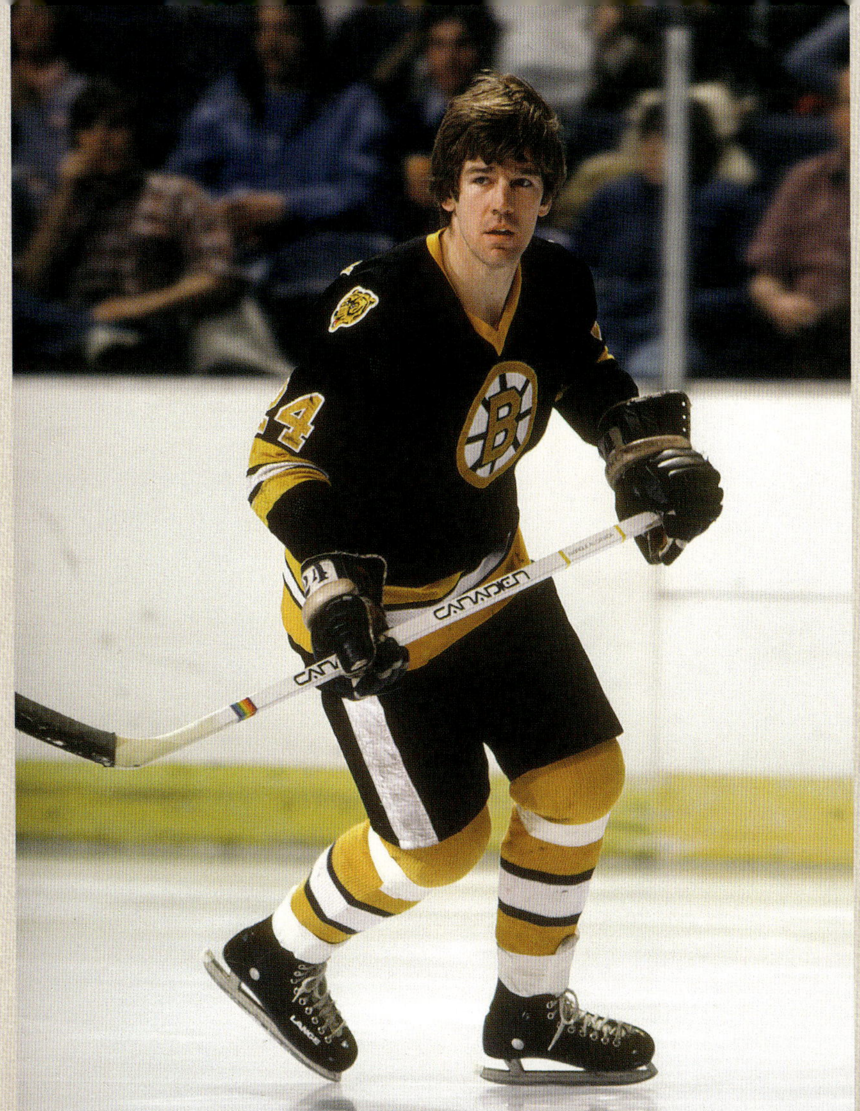

Terry O'Reilly (left) joined the Bruins at the tail end of the franchise's golden era featuring Bobby Orr and Phil Esposito and soon became the face of the franchise for the Lunch Pail Gang teams coached by Don Cherry. (Photograph by Focus on Sports/Getty Images)

Acrobatic goaltender Gilles Gilbert (below) had a successful seven-year run for the Bruins between the pipes (1973–1980). He was Boston's clear No. 1 goaltender for three years (1973–1976), with his best season being 1975–76, when he put up a sterling 33–8–10 record. For the remainder of his tenure, Gilbert split the netminding duties with Gerry Cheevers (back from the WHA for a second stint with the Bruins) on the beloved Lunch Pail Gang teams. (Photograph by Al Ruelle, Collection of The Sports Museum)

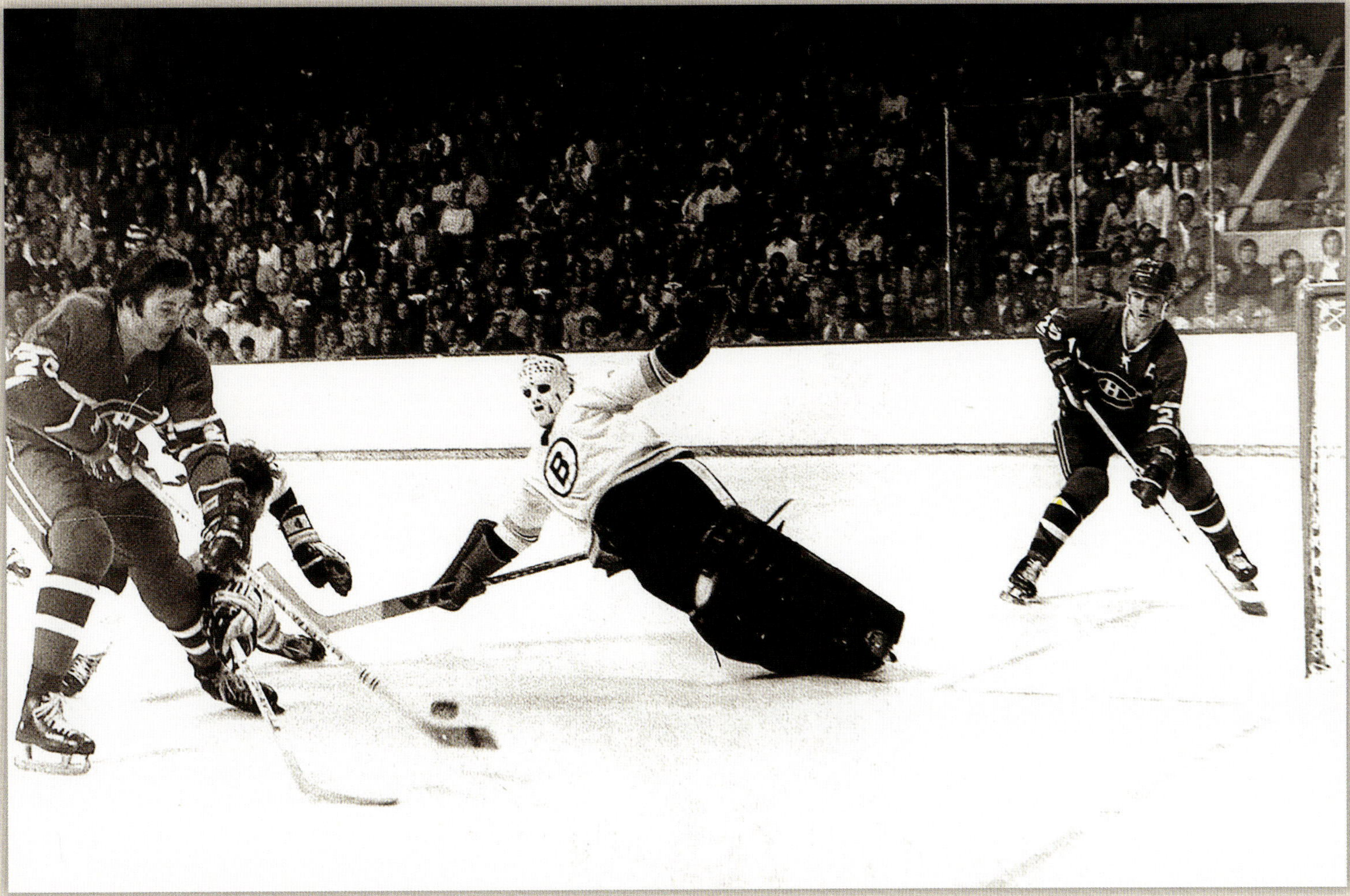

Unlike many of his fiery teammates on the Lunch Pail Gang teams of the late 1970s, Peter McNab had an easygoing temperament. Here, he confers with his coach, Don Cherry, at a Boston Garden practice. (Photograph by Steve Babineau/NHLI via Getty Images)

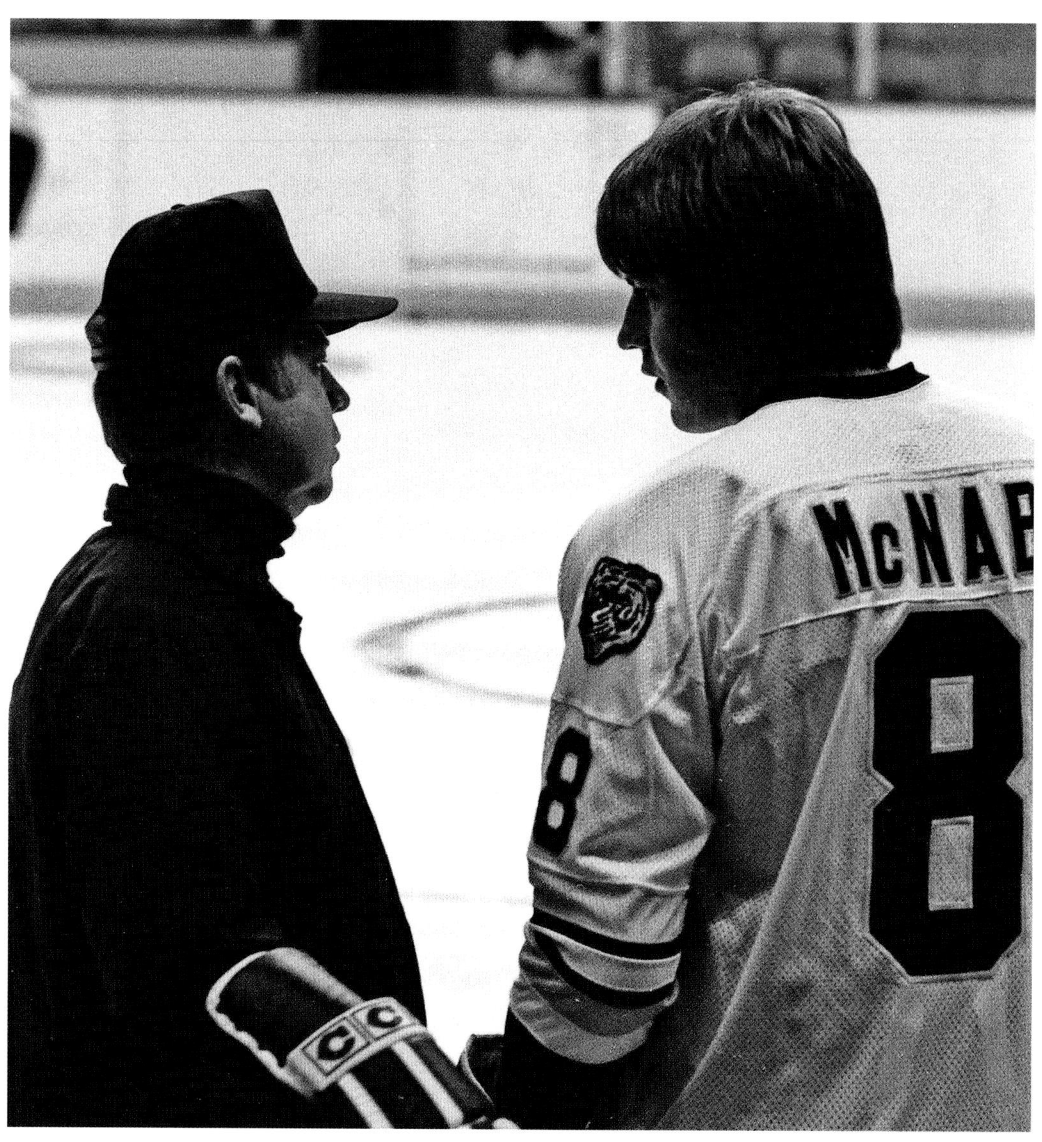

PETER MCNAB

THE SON OF player/coach/GM Max McNab, Peter McNab began his NHL career with Buffalo in the 1973–74 season. After a slow start with the Sabres, he came to Boston for the 1976–77 season. With the Bruins, his career took off.

The burly, 6′3″ center was known for his gentlemanly play (he was usually in the running for the Lady Byng Trophy) as well as being a top scorer for Don Cherry's Lunch Pail Gang. Consistency was his hallmark. In the six seasons between 1977 and 1982, McNab scored between 35 and 41 goals every season.

In 1977–78, McNab led a parade of 11 Bruins who scored 20 goals or more for the campaign, an NHL record that still stands. This "Gang of 11" included McNab (41), Terry O'Reilly (29), Bobby Schmautz (27), Stan Jonathan (27), Rick Middleton (25), Jean Ratelle (25), Wayne Cashman (24), Gregg Sheppard (23), Brad Park (22), Don Marcotte (20), and Bob Miller (20). "They were good teams," said Harry Sinden. "They had a lot of class, they scored a lot of goals, and they were amongst the league leaders in offense all the time."

McNab would tally 263 goals and 324 assists in a Bruins uniform. After leaving Boston in 1984, he finished up his career with Vancouver and New Jersey. He later became a longtime, popular broadcaster for the Colorado Avalanche.

In 2021, McNab was elected to the U.S. Hockey Hall of Fame, one year before he passed away at the age of 70. Upon his death, his former coach, Don Cherry, paid tribute. "I teased Peter that he was my golden Lab on a team of bull terriers," Cherry said. "A great teammate, and one of the best people you could ever meet."

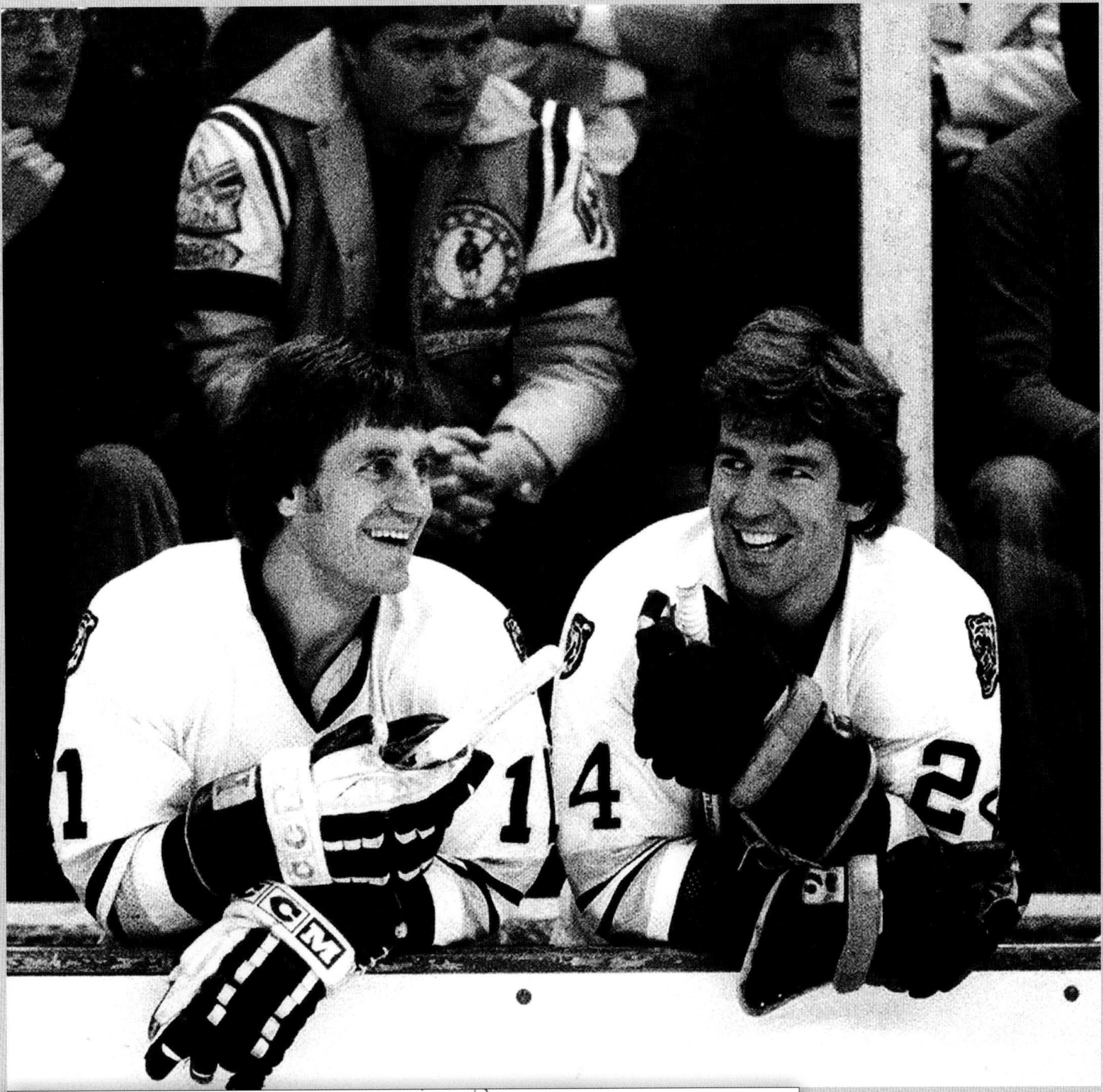

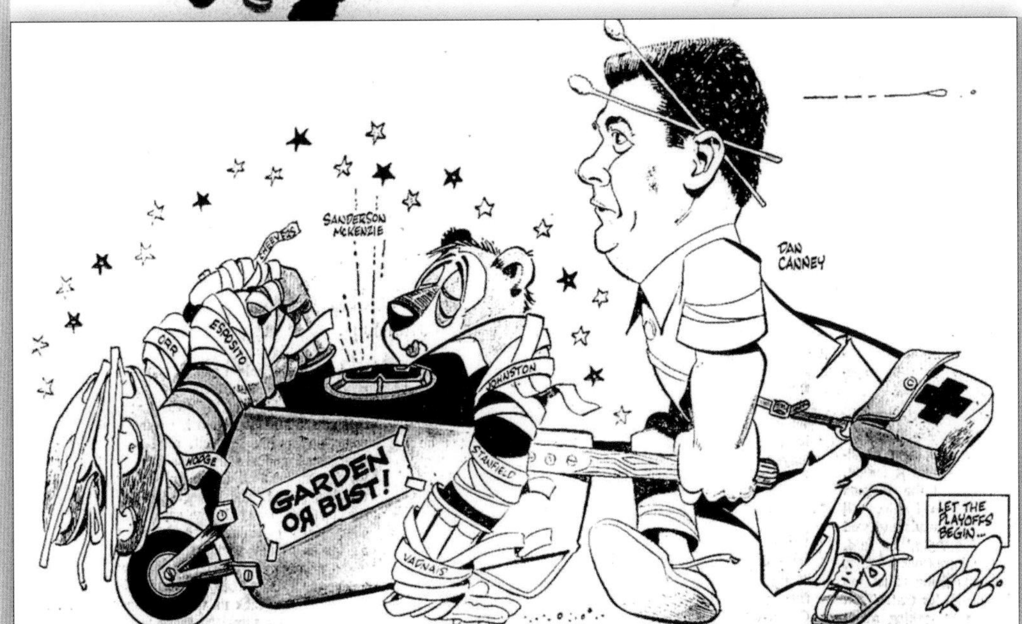

Above: Forwards Bobby Schmautz (11) and Terry O'Reilly (24) were two of the top offensive contributors for Don Cherry's late 1970s teams. "Schmautzie" scored 20 or more goals in five consecutive seasons (1975–1979) while O'Reilly typically ranked among the team's leading scorers. (Photograph by Steve Babineau/ NHLI via Getty Images)

Left: Trainer Dan Canney toiled long hours to keep the Bruins on track. The Charlestown native began working for the team in 1963 and served as head trainer through the 1984–85 season. (Cartoon by Bill Robertson, Collection of Richard A. Johnson)

Don Marcotte's career with the Bruins was in full bloom in the late 1970s and would continue going strong into the 1980s. Several generations of Bruins enjoyed playing with the dependable, selfless left winger. (Photograph by Steve Babineau/NHLI via Getty Images)

DON MARCOTTE

LEFT WING DON MARCOTTE was a lifelong Bruin who played for the team for 15 seasons (1965, 1968–1982) over the course of three decades.

Before arriving in Boston, Marcotte put up some big numbers in juniors and the minors. "I could score," he said in a 2022 interview. "But when I came up with the Bruins, I was a two-way player. So they just said, 'Okay, you can play defensive hockey. You can cover the [best] guys. We have enough guys who can score goals, anyway. So just change your style of game and just play defensive hockey.'"

So that is what Marcotte did, succeeding Eddie Westfall as the Bruin most likely to shadow the opposition's top scorer. Marcotte never complained about his role. "It kept me in the league longer," he admits today.

Along the way, Marcotte emerged as a superb two-way forward and an underrated scorer. With the talent drain to the WHA prior to the 1972–73 season, the Bruins needed players to step up offensively. Marcotte answered the call, scoring 20 or more goals in six of the next seven seasons.

Along with Johnny Bucyk, Wayne Cashman, and a few others, Marcotte served as the bridge between the Big Bad Bruins of the early 1970s and the Lunch Pail Gang later in the decade. Each of those teams were known for its distinct, swashbuckling style—and, in truth, that wasn't Marcotte's personal demeanor. But he fit right in. "We had such a great bunch of guys," said Marcotte. "We were always together."

Those years were marked by heated rivalries between the Bruins and several NHL teams, including the Philadelphia Flyers. "They wanted to build a team just like the Bruins," said Marcotte. "They did a pretty good job of it, too. That's what they went after, with all the tough guys and fighters. It made for some very interesting games between the two of us." After being defeated in the postseason by the Flyers in 1974 and 1976, the Bruins would turn the tables on the Broad Street Bullies, ousting them from the Stanley Cup playoffs in 1977 and 1978 and effectively ending their days as an NHL powerhouse.

Marcotte's teammates appreciated his contributions to their success—and so did his coach. "No one knows the fundamentals of the game better than Don," said Don Cherry. "If you were going to send a hockey player to Mars, it would be Marcotte. They could watch Marcotte play and manufacture perfect players. He skates, checks, and gets his share of goals. That's the perfect hockey player."

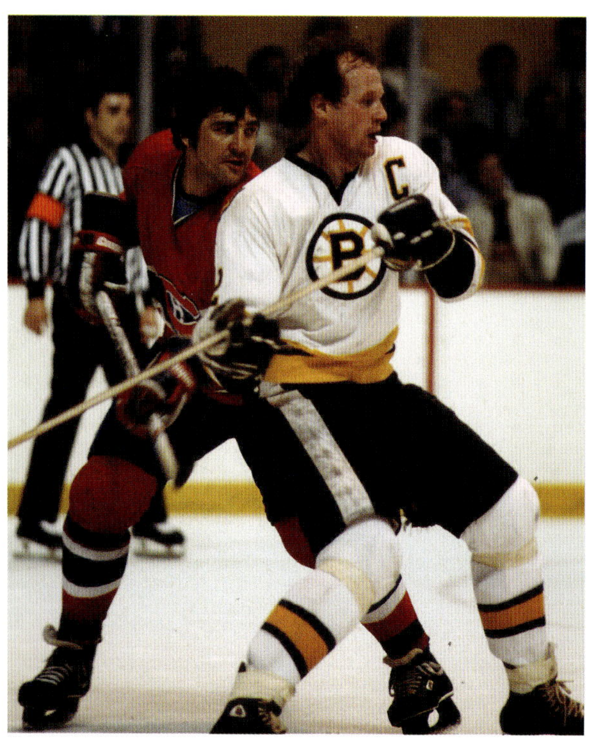

Captain Wayne Cashman jostles with Montreal defenseman Serge Savard at Boston Garden in 1977. (Photograph by Focus on Sport/Getty Images)

WAYNE CASHMAN

TOUGHNESS HAS long been an essential part of the Boston Bruins DNA. And no one was tougher than Wayne Cashman.

"I can't believe there's ever been a player who had a higher pain tolerance than him," said Harry Sinden. "I've seen him lying on the training room floor 20 minutes before a game for his back. He was constantly in pain, but if we had a game, he was still going out to play."

Perhaps it all came from Cashman's upbringing in the small town of Harrowsmith, Ontario. "Cashman's town seems like something out of *Deliverance*," said Don Cherry in a 1977 *Sports Illustrated* article. "A tough town?" said Cashman at the time. "Yeah, I guess so. There were nine Cashman boys in it."

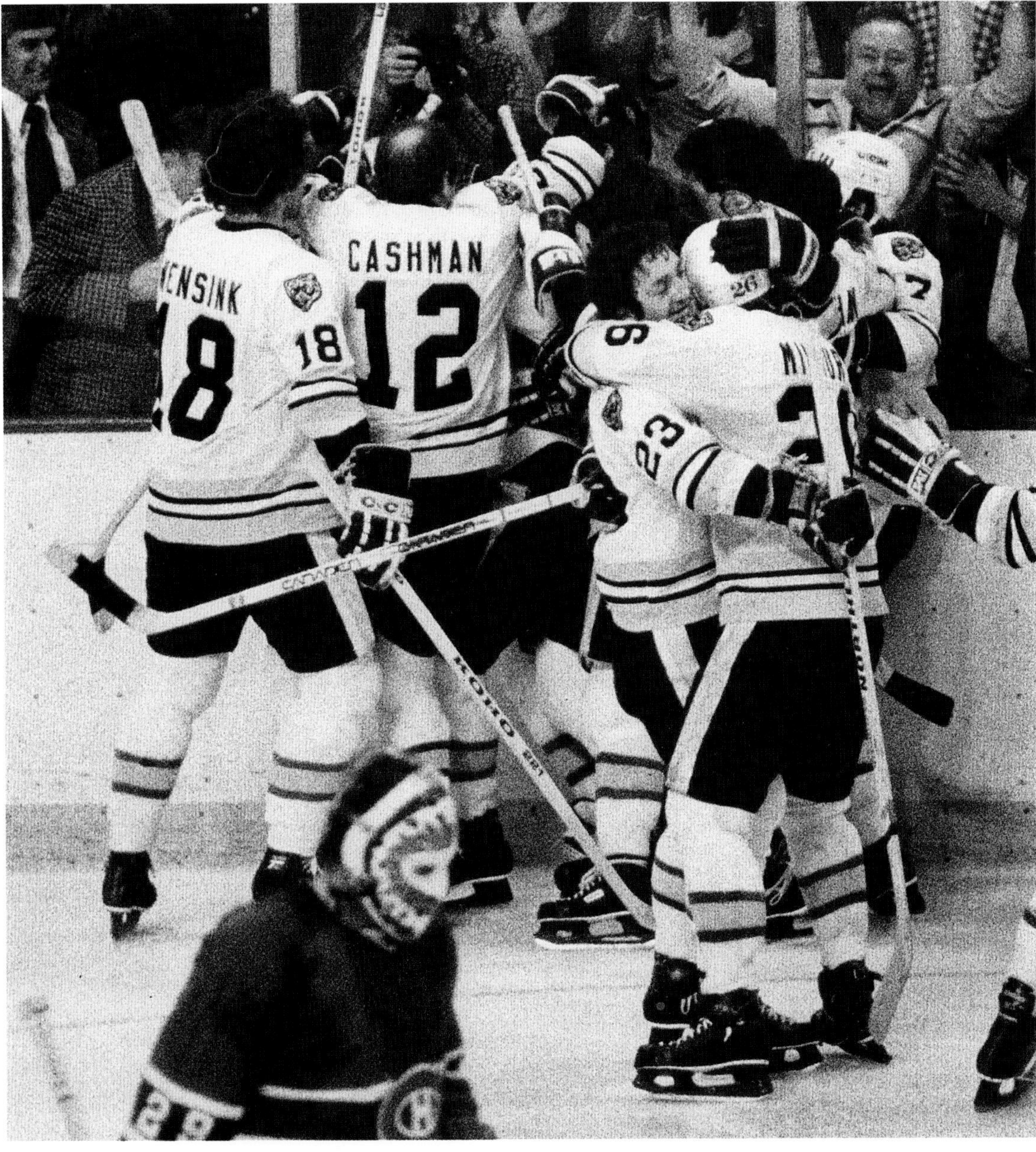

John Wensink (18), Wayne Cashman (12), Rick Smith (23), and Mike Milbury (26) are among a group of happy Bruins who are swarming Jean Ratelle (19) after he scored the overtime goal that won Game 4 of their 1979 Stanley Cup Semifinals series against Montreal, 4–3. The goal was Ratelle's third of the game and tied the series at two games apiece. (Photograph by Frank O'Brien/The Boston Globe via Getty Images)

Cashman's 17-year career with the Bruins (1965, 1968–1983) had two distinct phases. In the first phase, he epitomized the "work hard, play hard" ethos of the team as one of the ringleaders of the off-ice extracurricular activities. On the ice, he played left wing on the team's top line, doing all the dirty work in the corners to get the puck out in front of the net to his high-scoring linemates, Phil Esposito and Ken Hodge. He was also the team's policeman, possessed of a mean left hook. "I knew at an early age I'd never be a 50-goal scorer, so I've spent my career doing what had to be done," said Cashman.

In the second phase of his career, from the mid-1970s on, Cashman continued to do what he had to do. He led. In 1977, he succeeded Johnny Bucyk as team captain—and he flourished in the role. "Cash never used to say a thing," said Gerry Cheevers in the spring of 1977. "Then he became captain, and now he's always talking with the young players—sometimes cheerleading, sometimes being brutally blunt. Cash becoming captain is the most important thing that has happened to this team."

Statistically, Cashman scored 277 goals in his Bruins career, eclipsing the 20-goal mark in eight of his 17 seasons. But mere statistics could never measure the true value of Wayne Cashman.

Fittingly enough, among all the players who played during the rough, tough Original Six era (1942–1967), it was "Cash" who was the last to retire, hanging up his skates for good in 1983.

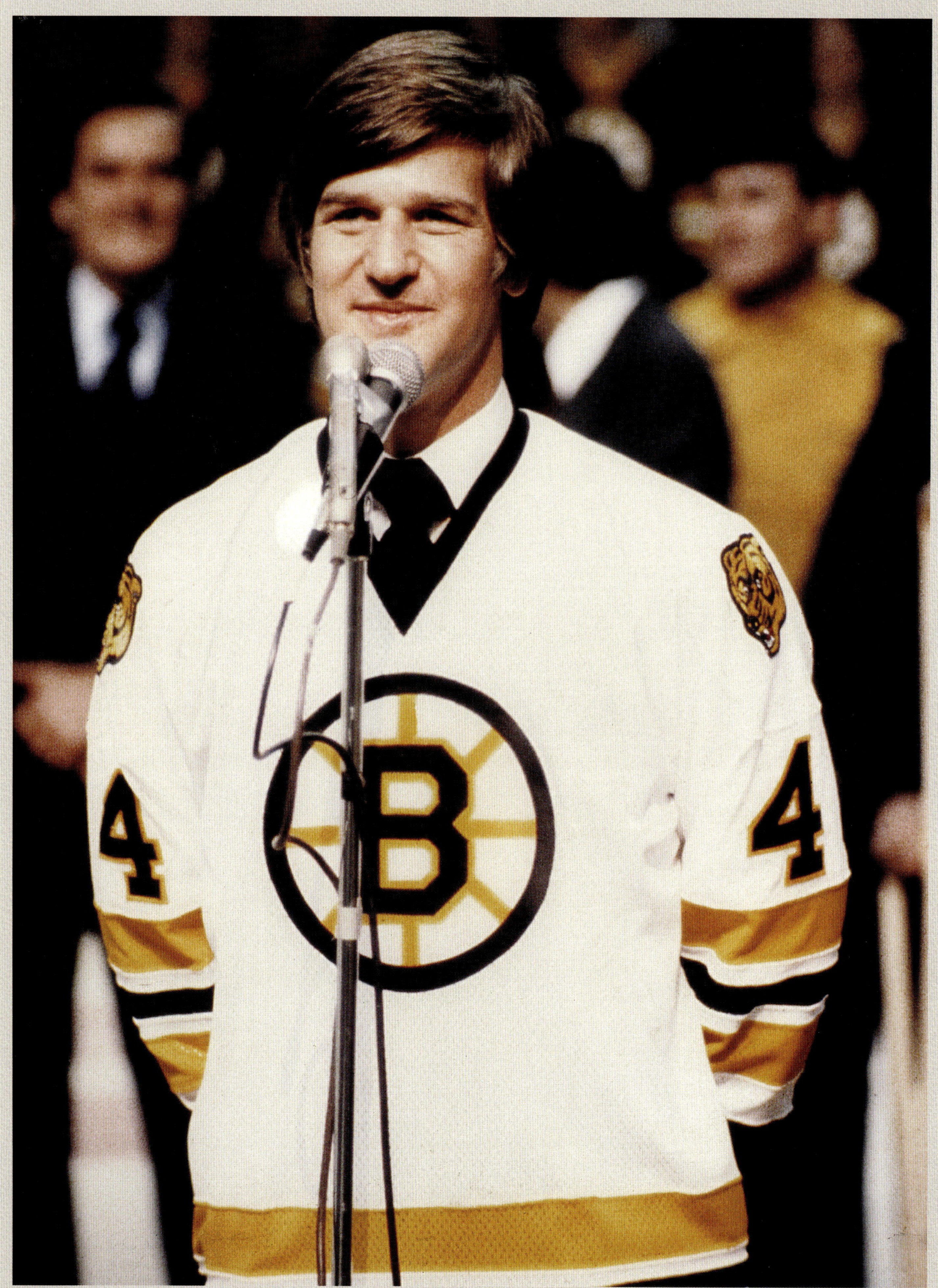

Bobby Orr addresses a packed Boston Garden at his jersey retirement ceremony on January 10, 1979. There wasn't a dry eye in the house. (Photograph by Al Ruelle, Collection of The Sports Museum)

THE LUNCH PAIL A.C.

by Kevin Paul Dupont

They came as advertised, a few of them with helmets but most without, a hard-working, fun-loving bunch who found beauty in a brawl and crafted an enduring legacy around their camaraderie, their triumphs and defeats, their devilish spirit, but mostly their sacrosanct belief that they played for each other.

Because otherwise, those Bruins teams of the late 1970s believed, there would be no damned point in pulling on that sweater. The Lunch Pail A.C. Bruins played as if that Spoked-B crest was stitched through their sweaters and into their hearts.

It was their coach, Don Cherry, a journeyman minor-league defenseman with a loud bark and louder wardrobe, who stamped them as his Lunch Pail Gang. His players called him Grapes, a term of endearment, of course. Cherry, 40 years old upon his arrival in the autumn of 1974, never had it so good in what had been his unremarkable, unheralded playing career. He had a beloved dog, a white bull terrier with oversized goofy ears that he named Blue, that gained near cult status as his ever-present sidekick.

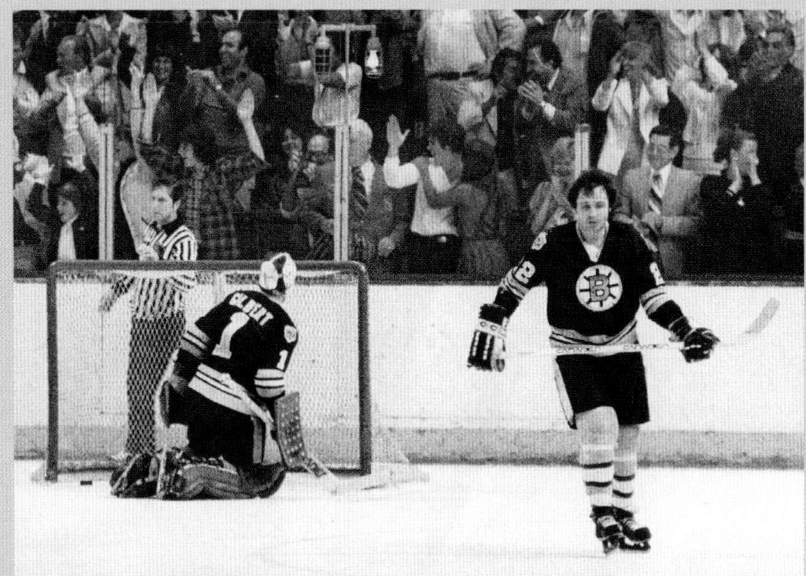

Valiant goaltender Gilles Gilbert and defenseman Brad Park are despondent in the aftermath of Montreal forward Yvon Lambert's overtime goal that defeated Boston in Game 7 of the 1979 Stanley Cup Semifinals. It was the heartbreaking conclusion to the infamous "Too Many Men on the Ice" game at the Montreal Forum. (Photograph by Frank O'Brien/The Boston Globe via Getty Images)

Cherry also had a bench full of players who, like Blue, were trained to his every command, and they faithfully executed a brand of no-frills, high-testosterone hockey that packed the dusty Garden full every night and made the old barn on Causeway Street shake, rattle, and roll.

"My boys, eh?" Cherry would say time and again, as if they were all buddies gathered at his favorite watering hole back home in Kingston, Ontario, after a shift at the nearby auto parts factory. "I'll take my boys over anybody out there, I'll tell ya."

His boys were Taz (Terry O'Reilly), Ratty (Jean Ratelle), Nifty (Rick Middleton), Parkie (Brad Park), Wire (John Wensink), Schmautzie (Bobby Schmautz), Maxie (Peter McNab), Chief (John Bucyk), Cheesy (Gerry Cheevers), Doakie (Gary Doak), and on and on and on....

Snow White had her beloved Seven Dwarfs—Dopey, Happy, Sneezy, and all the rest—but her troop of mostly merry little men had nothing on Cherry's stick-carrying brothers in Black and Gold, be it nicknames or the ability to conjure up enduring memories. Though not all of the memories were as sweet as the nicknames.

The Lunch Pail Gang ultimately defined a transitional era for the franchise in the wake of its heralded Bobby Orr and the Big Bad Bruins days.

Led by the sublime, transformational Orr, the prolific, record-shattering Phil Esposito, and the scar-masked Cheevers in goal, the Bruins of that one generation earlier won the Stanley Cup twice (1970, 1972) and easily could have won more. If only they had not been guilty of some, shall we say, off-ice overindulgences, as well as some dalliances with the World Hockey Association's economic seductions.

The Lunch Pail bunch couldn't score like their immediate predecessors—no one could—and ultimately the city was left to watch Orr depart as a free agent to Chicago in the summer of 1976. The great No. 4 played only briefly under Cherry, 90 games in total, and only 10 of those were with Park, the heralded former Ranger also on the roster courtesy of a blockbuster November 1975 trade that sent Phil Esposito to New York.

It was after Orr's departure, in what were Cherry's last three years as their coach, when the Lunch Pail Gang had their finest, most memorable, and most soul-crushing moments. They included back-to-back losses in the Stanley Cup Final to the Canadiens in 1977 and 1978, followed by yet a third consecutive ouster at the hands of the Habs in 1979—the infamous "Too Many Men on the Ice" Game 7 of the Stanley Cup Semifinals.

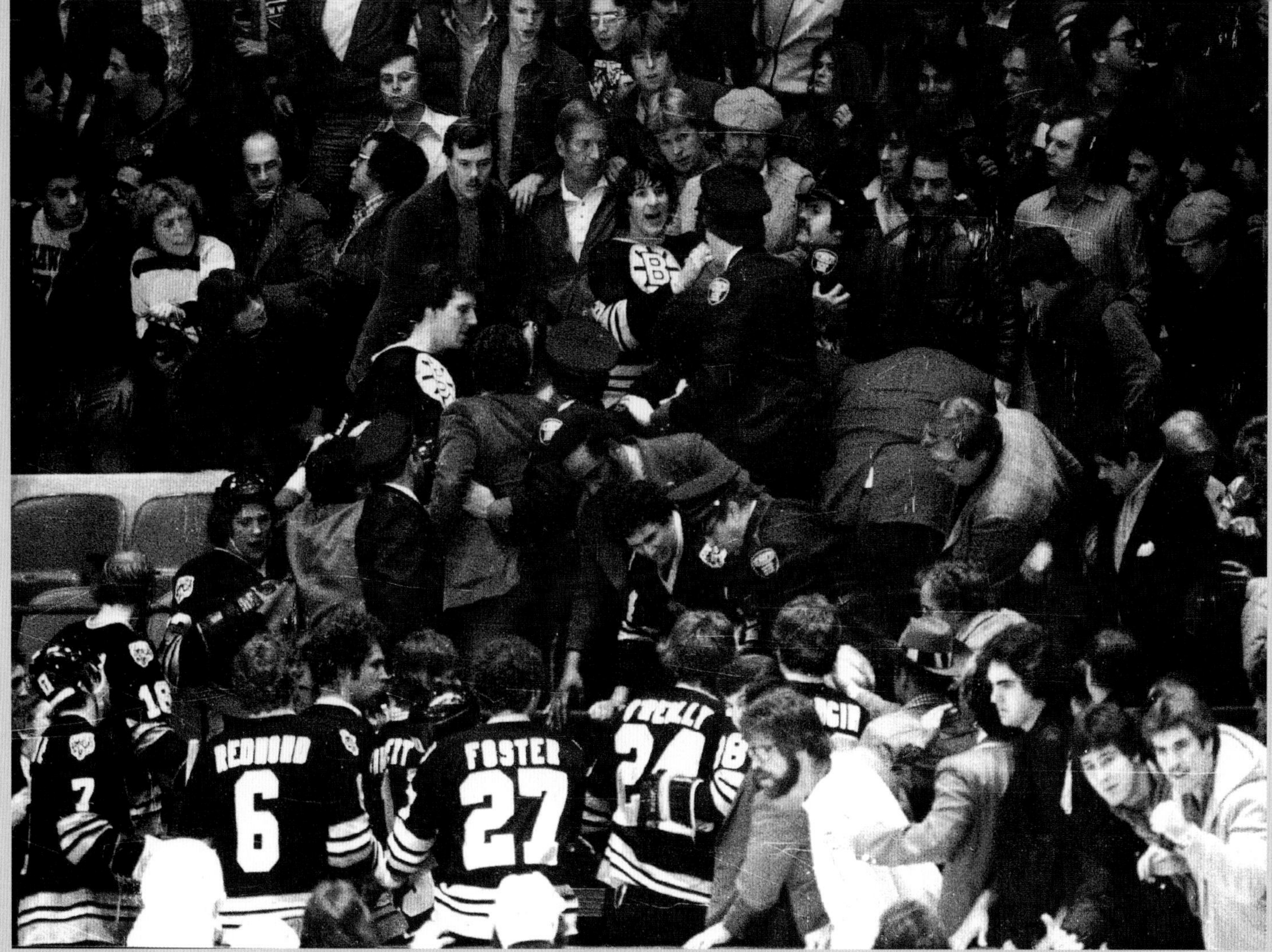

One of the seminal moments of the Lunch Pail Gang era was the incident that took place at Madison Square Garden on December 23, 1979 where numerous Bruins clambered into the stands to defend several teammates. For those Bruins teams, it was all for one and one for all. (Photograph by B Bennett/Getty Images)

As it turned out, that late 1970s era proved to be a sort of capstone for both the Habs and the Bruins.

The Canadiens won four consecutive Cups from 1976 to 1979, a dazzling run backed by Ken Dryden in net. It has stood for decades as the franchise's last dynasty. Approaching a half-century later, they have won but two more titles (1986 and 1993), a drought of unimaginable proportions for Les Glorieux, a franchise accustomed to stamping out Cups like so many croissants at a Rue Sainte-Catherine patisserie.

Following that mind-numbing loss to the Habs in 1979, which included Guy Lafleur's rocket slapper to tie it (4–4) with 74 seconds to go in regulation, the Bruins didn't reach the Cup Final again until 1988. As the franchise's 100th anniversary draws near, the Bruins have not made back-to-back appearances in the Cup Final since those losses to the Habs in 1977 and 1978.

The Bruins had been oh-so-close to reaching the Cup Final again on that night of May 10, 1979, exactly nine years to the day that Orr clinched the Cup in 1970 with his famed "Flying Bobby" goal against the Blues on a steamy Mother's Day at the Garden.

In the Forum on that spring evening, the Bruins held a 4–3 lead when they were caught with an extra man on the ice with 2:34 to go in regulation. The bench had been overzealous, or confused, in trying to keep Lafleur from stealing their dreams.

Cherry took the blame. Maybe it had truly been the fault of Don Marcotte, or perhaps Stan Jonathan. But the coach has charge of the bench, and Cherry, in what would be his final game back as Boston bench boss, pinned it on his broad lapel. "My fault," said Cherry, noting amid the clatter that he had to restrain two other forwards from jumping into the play, saying, "Otherwise we might have had nine guys out there."

All of 1:20 into the power play, Lafleur hammered home the equalizer off of Jacques Lemaire's velvety back-hand feed. The end was inevitable. Yvon Lambert provided the dagger in OT.

Two other episodes sandwiched around that Game 7 loss to the Habs in 1979 also helped define the Lunch Pail era.

Just a year earlier, in Game 4 of the 1978 Cup Final, a pause for an offside call set the stage at the Garden for a legendary tussle between an undersized Stan Jonathan and Pierre Bouchard. It did not end well for the 6′2″ Habs defenseman. Punching up in class by some six inches and 30 pounds, the fiery Jonathan turned Bouchard's face into a bloody mess.

"Oh...look at this heavyweight battle!" exhorted Fred Cusick, Channel 38's legendary play-by-play announcer, as the fight erupted. Blood streamed from Bouchard's mashed visage, much of it spilling on to the face of John D'Amico, the beleaguered linesman charged to untangle the two.

The sellout crowd was in a frenzy. The Bruins would go on to square the series, two games apiece, with a 4-3 win, but the outcome that night wasn't nearly as memorable as the bloodletting. The Bruins hadn't won a playoff series versus the Habs since 1943—a drought that would not end until 1988—and each of Jonathan's jackhammer punches to the staggered Bouchard served as cathartic relief to the masses.

Amid it all, Wensink—who earlier in his career had skated to the front of the Minnesota North Stars bench and invited the entire roster to fight him—wrestled on the ice with towering Habs defenseman Gilles Lupien. "Wire" won that bout, too, lifting both arms triumphantly toward the rafters as he made his way to the penalty box.

On December 23, 1979, the bitter Game 7 loss to the Habs barely seven months behind them, the Bruins turned Madison Square Garden upside down, along with all semblance of decorum and sensibility.

With five seconds to go, Cheevers thwarted a break-in attempt by Esposito, his longtime Boston pal from glory days now in his fifth season as a member of the Rangers. A 4-3 win was in the books as a frustrated Esposito stomped off the ice after smashing his stick and made his way to the Blueshirts dressing room.

Then came the fireworks. While a frustrated John Davidson, the Rangers netminder, yapped away with Wensink, a fan reached over the sideboards and filched Jonathan's stick right out of his hands.

Game on!

Terry O'Reilly, the personification of that "we play for each other" spirit, grabbed the top of the glass, scaled the boards and bounded into the stands to wrestle back Jonathan's stick.

Many of his teammates soon followed, including, most notably, Mike Milbury and Peter McNab, who hopscotched their way some seven and eight rows up into the loge seats. Milbury, the 26-year-old defenseman who later became the club's coach and assistant general manager, had just returned to the ice from the dressing room upon hearing a beef was stewing on the ice. At one point during the fracas, Milbury took hold of a patron's shoe and began smacking him with it, asking him while doing so, "How much did you pay for your ticket? I hope you enjoyed the show!" After which he lobbed the man's shoe onto the ice.

Just over a month later, the night before a game in Pittsburgh, Bruins coach Fred Creighton called the main miscreants into his suite to inform them of word just handed down from NHL headquarters. The list of suspended included O'Reilly (eight games), Milbury (six games) and McNab (six games).

O'Reilly, silent in a comfortable wing chair in Creighton's room, curled tighter into a fetal ball as a solemn Creighton read the decision. Twenty games for the three of them. A steep price, the cost of doing business in that steadfast belief of playing for, and sticking up for, each other.

Those three games, all in a span of only some 18 months, stand as the Lunch Pail A.C. holy trinity. An era unlike any other, the vestiges of an NHL never to return.

Kevin Paul Dupont has covered hockey for the *Boston Herald*, *New York Times*, and *Boston Globe*. In 2002, he was honored by the Hockey Hall of Fame with the Elmer Ferguson Award.

BOSTON BRUINS (1970–1979)

Season	W	L	T	PTS	PTS%	Finish	Playoffs	Coach	Division	Conference
1969–70	**40**	**17**	**19**	**99**	**.651**	**2nd of 6**	**Won Stanley Cup Final**	**Harry Sinden**	**East**	
1970–71	57	14	7	121	.776	1st of 7	Lost NHL Quarterfinals	Tom Johnson	East	
1971–72	**54**	**13**	**11**	**119**	**.763**	**1st of 7**	**Won Stanley Cup Final**	**Tom Johnson**	**East**	
1972–73	51	22	5	107	.686	2nd of 8	Lost NHL Quarterfinals	Tom Johnson (31–16–5) Bep Guidolin (20–6–0)	East	
1973–74	52	17	9	113	.724	1st of 8	Lost Stanley Cup Final	Bep Guidolin	East	
1974–75	40	26	14	94	.588	2nd of 4	Lost NHL Preliminary Round	Don Cherry	Adams	Prince of Wales
1975–76	48	15	17	113	.706	1st of 4	Lost NHL Semifinals	Don Cherry	Adams	Prince of Wales
1976–77	49	23	8	106	.663	1st of 4	Lost Stanley Cup Final	Don Cherry	Adams	Prince of Wales
1977–78	51	18	11	113	.706	1st of 4	Lost Stanley Cup Final	Don Cherry	Adams	Prince of Wales
1978–79	43	23	14	100	.625	1st of 4	Lost NHL Semifinals	Don Cherry	Adams	Prince of Wales

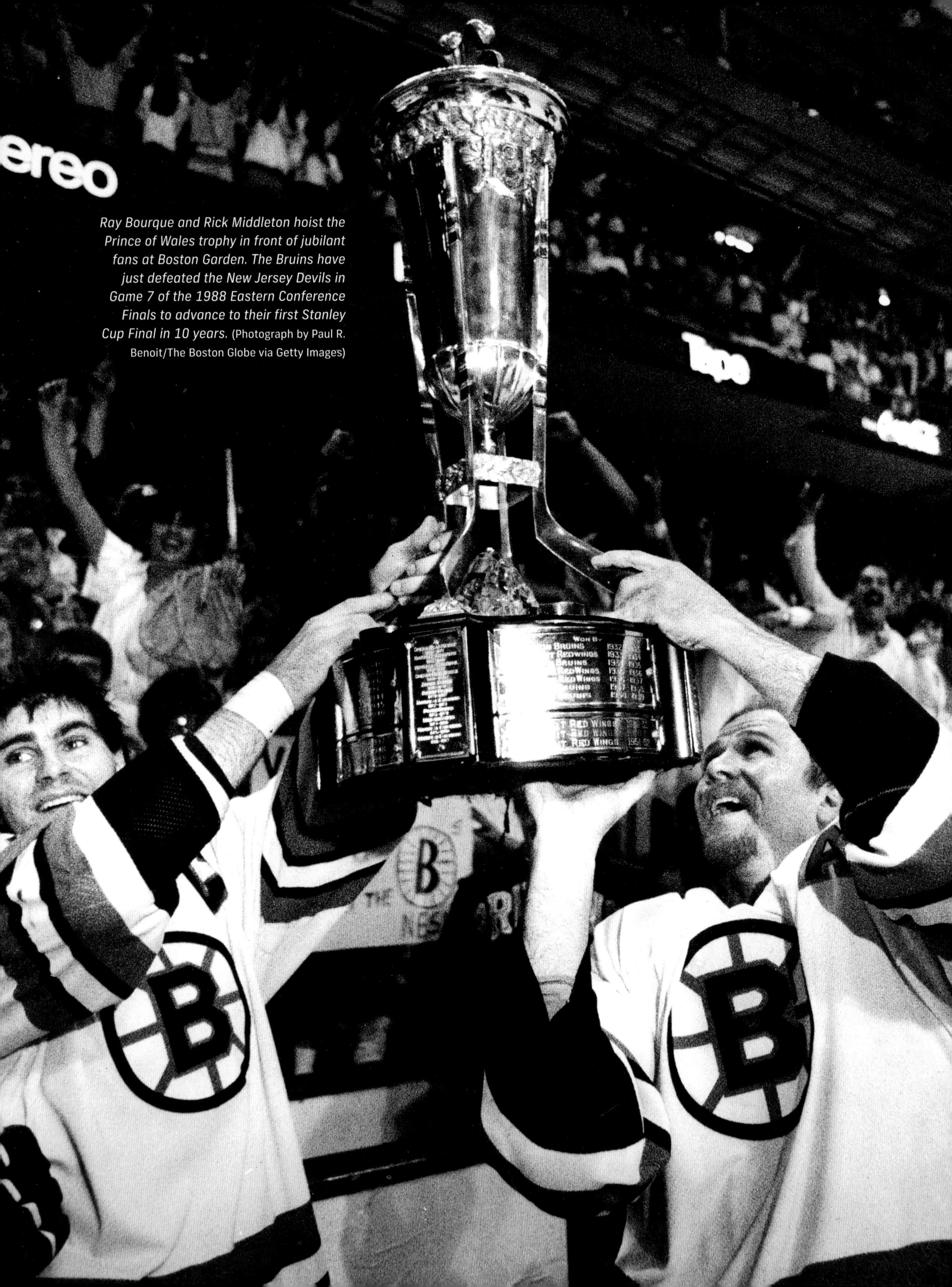

Ray Bourque and Rick Middleton hoist the Prince of Wales trophy in front of jubilant fans at Boston Garden. The Bruins have just defeated the New Jersey Devils in Game 7 of the 1988 Eastern Conference Finals to advance to their first Stanley Cup Final in 10 years. (Photograph by Paul R. Benoit/The Boston Globe via Getty Images)

STANDARDS OF EXCELLENCE

Au revoir, le jinx.

—Kevin Paul Dupont, *Boston Globe* sportswriter, on the night in 1988 when the Bruins beat the Canadiens in the Montreal Forum to end the "Montreal Jinx" and years of playoff frustration

Done, dead, kaput. What jinx?

—Keith Crowder, Bruins right wing, on that same night

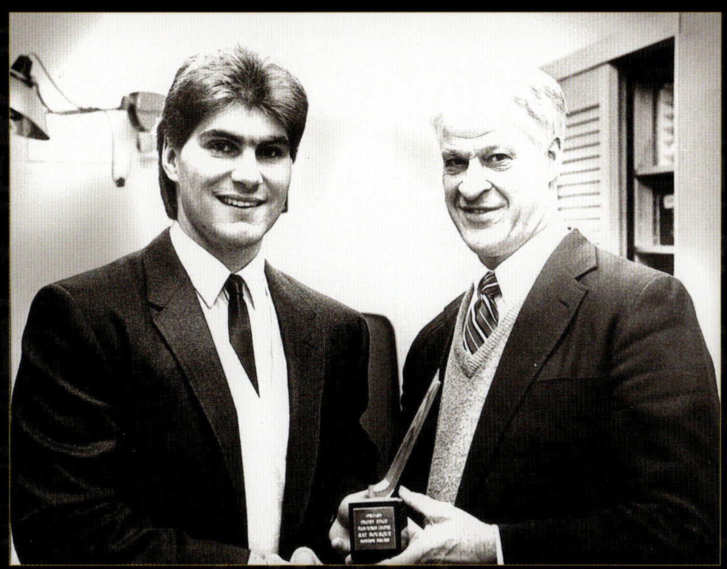

Ray Bourque (left) receives an award from Gordie Howe in 1983. Fifteen years later, in a game vs. Howe's Red Wings, Bourque would pass Mr. Hockey on the all-time list for career assists. (Collection of The Sports Museum)

The history of all great sports franchises often resembles that of a decades-long relay race, with one generational star passing the baton to another. In Boston, the image of Ted Williams being followed by Carl Yastrzemski being followed by Jim Rice—just three players in Fenway's left field over a 50-year span—immediately comes to mind. For the Bruins, the equivalent was most evident on their blueline, as their prized 1979 first-round draft choice, defenseman Ray Bourque, was greeted with a level of anticipation not seen since Bobby Orr's arrival from the Oshawa Generals in the autumn of 1966. The fact that the three-year gap between Orr's departure and Bourque's arrival was more than filled with another Hall of Fame defenseman, Brad Park, makes this Black and Gold line of succession that much more powerful.

During the 1980s, Bourque would prove to be a worthy successor to Orr, securing the Calder Trophy as the NHL's top rookie in 1980, a pair of Norris Trophies as the NHL's best defenseman in 1987 and 1988, and six First Team NHL All-Star selections. He was the key figure in yet another winning decade for the franchise.

The success occurred amid swirling rumors regarding the future of the team in Boston and its home at the antiquated Boston Garden. Ideas and proposals were floated for a massive renovation of the beloved arena, as well as for a completely new building to be constructed on land just behind the Garden. There was even speculation of the Bruins bolting town and moving to Southern New Hampshire.

On the ice, there was far more clarity. In the 1980s, for the second consecutive decade, the team never missed a postseason while assembling rugged teams that would have brought a gleam to the eyes of Art Ross and Eddie Shore. Fans delighted in the grit of Terry O'Reilly, the toughness of Cam Neely, the playmaking genius of Rick Middleton, the scoring touch of Barry Pederson, the leadership of Brad Park, and the overall brilliance of Ray Bourque. A succession of popular, respected former players piloted the team from behind the bench, including Gerry Cheevers (1980–1985), Terry O'Reilly (1986–1989), and Mike Milbury (1989–1991).

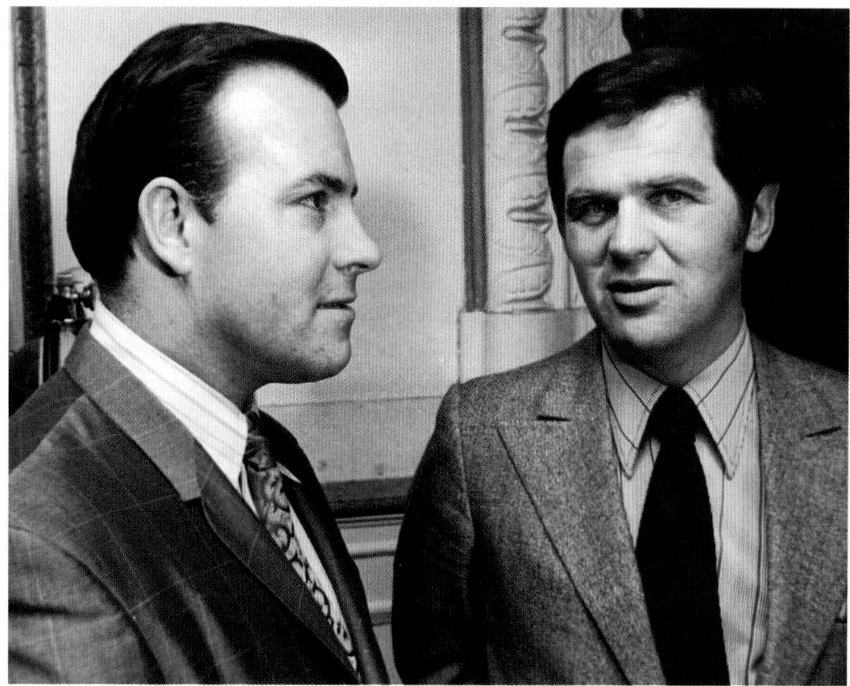

Harry Sinden (above, right), a hockey man through and through, talks shop with someone of the same ilk, the longtime coach of the Montreal Canadiens, Scotty Bowman. (Photo by Bruce Bennett Studios via Getty Images Studios/Getty Images)

The deepest playoff runs of the decade came in 1983 and 1988. The 1983 squad, sparked by the sensational goaltending of Pete Peeters, compiled the best record in the league during the regular season. In the playoffs, the Bruins beat the Quebec Nordiques and then the Buffalo Sabres in dramatic fashion before falling to the eventual champion New York Islanders in the Eastern Conference Finals. It remains one of the most overlooked great Bruins seasons in franchise history.

Then, in 1988, the Bruins broke their 45-year-old Montreal playoff jinx with a decisive five-game win over the Canadiens on their way to the Stanley Cup Final versus the Edmonton Oilers. It proved to be a fitting culmination of another successful stretch where the Bruins continued to live up to their standards of excellence.

HARRY SINDEN

IN THE SPRING OF 1980, Harry Sinden completed his 18th year of service with the Boston Bruins.

It turns out that he was just getting started.

Following a decorated career as one of Canada's top amateur players, Sinden came to the Bruins in 1960. He has been associated with the Bruins organization ever since then (save for a two-year stretch in the early 1970s). He was first a player and coach with several of the team's minor league affiliates (1960–1966), then the head coach for the Bruins (1966–1970), and finally a front office executive with various titles, including general manager (1972–2000), president (1988–2006), and senior advisor to owner Jeremy Jacobs (2006–present).

Sinden initially made his mark behind the bench. Hired as head coach prior to Bobby Orr's rookie season in 1966, Sinden molded a squad of returning veterans, key trade acquisitions, and young players into Stanley Cup champions in just four seasons. "Harry was, in my mind, one of the great coaches," said Orr. "We had characters on our team, and although the players did a lot in keeping everybody in line, Harry was great. Harry did what he had to do, and the guys all had great respect for him."

Just days after the Bruins won the Cup in May 1970, however, Sinden stunned the sports world by stepping down from the bench—and stepping away from

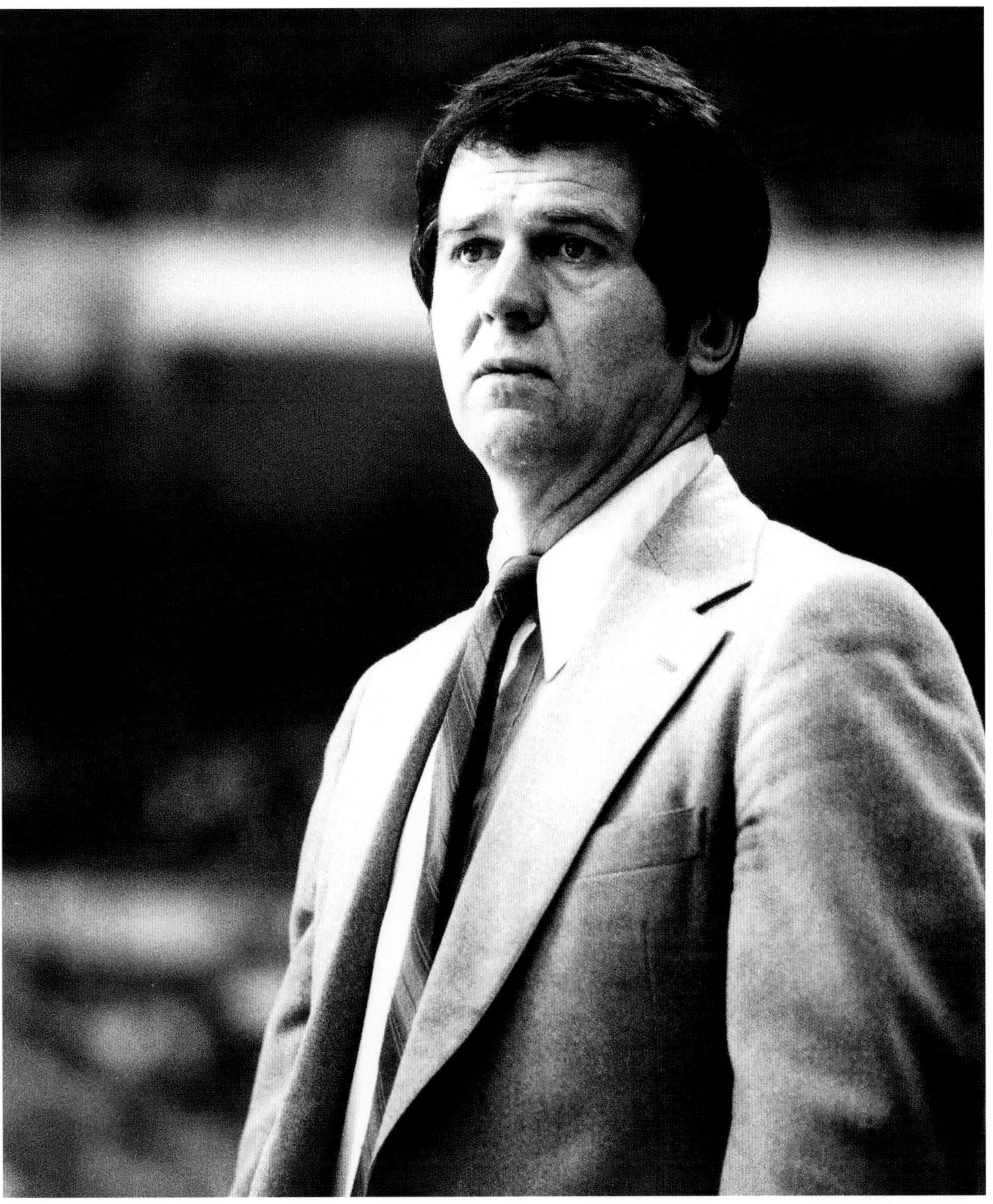

Harry Sinden was primarily a front office executive from 1972 onward. For two brief stretches at the end of the 1980 and 1985 seasons, however, he went back behind the bench to coach the Bruins on an interim basis. He compiled a winning record on each occasion. (Photograph by Steve Babineau/NHLI via Getty Images)

hockey altogether. "I had a very young family and a friend of mine had started up a huge business in Rochester, New York, and had offered me a position there," said Sinden in a 2022 interview. "That was difficult to turn down."

But hockey was in his blood. After coaching Team Canada to a dramatic and historic victory over the Soviet Union in the 1972 Summit Series, Sinden returned to the Bruins—this time as general manager, and this time for good.

With Sinden as "the Architect," the Bruins just kept reloading—and just kept on winning. The final years of the Orr/Esposito teams were followed in succession by the Lunch Pail Gang of the late 1970s, the fine teams of the early 1980s, and the powerhouse Ray Bourque/Cam Neely teams of the late 1980s and early 1990s. All told, the Bruins made the playoffs each and every year for 29 consecutive years (1968–1996). It remains the longest such streak in the history of professional sports.

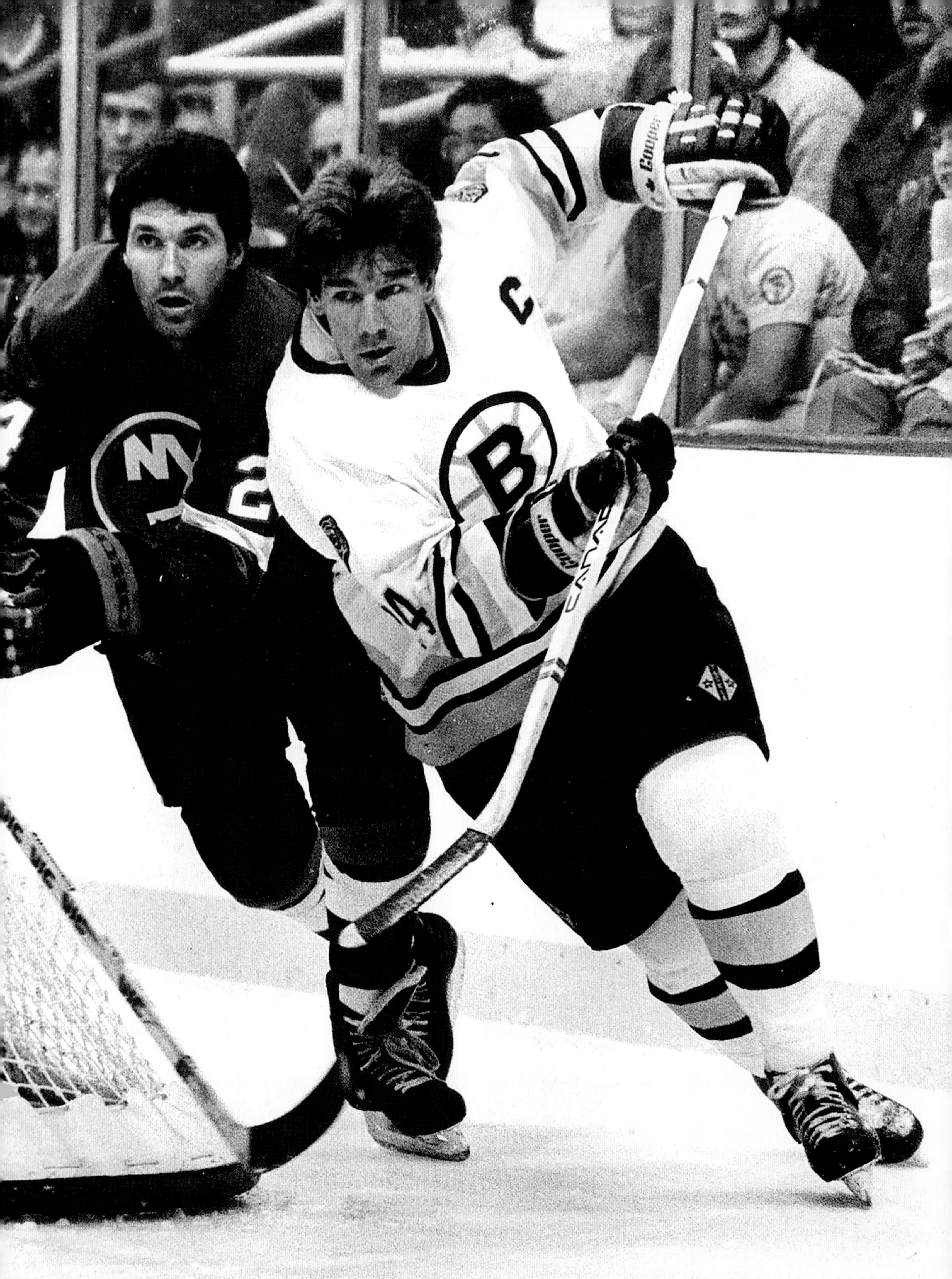
Cooper

Along the way, Sinden made a number of blockbuster deals that brought the likes of Brad Park, Jean Ratelle, Peter McNab, and Adam Oates to the Hub. What was his best deal? "I think the trade of [Ken] Hodge for Ricky Middleton was the best," said Sinden. "And [Barry] Pederson for Neely. Those two..." In each instance, Sinden had the gumption (and the thick skin) to trade an established, high-scoring, and exceedingly popular player for someone who was unproven and relatively unknown. Not many hockey executives would have had the courage, or the confidence, to make that type of deal.

Sinden very much remains involved with the Bruins to this day. "Harry still loves to talk hockey and talk about the team," said Neely, now team president. "He likes to know what is going on and loves to share his opinion, which is great."

Along with Bruins founding president Art Ross, Harry Sinden stands as one of the two most important builders in the history of the franchise.

Opposite page: During the course of his 13 NHL seasons—all with the Bruins—nobody worked harder to improve his skills than Terry O'Reilly. His hard-nosed style of play endeared him to Bruins fans everywhere—and forever. (Photograph by Al Ruelle, Collection of The Sports Museum)

TERRY O'REILLY

WHO IS THE quintessential Boston Bruin? One could make a strong case for Terry O'Reilly.

"Long after Terry is gone, his name will stand for the way they play hockey in Boston," said Joe Fitzgerald of the *Boston Herald.* "It's violent, passionate, emotional hockey, played with heart, and what it comes down to is giving a damn, and no one gives more than O'Reilly."

The Bruins selected O'Reilly with the 14th overall pick in the 1971 NHL Draft. He made his debut at the tail end of the 1971–72 season, playing the last game of the regular season against Toronto and recording his first NHL goal. The next season (1972–73), he became a regular member of the team.

And he soon acquired a nickname: "Taz." It happened during training camp when everyone was sitting on the boards and the dasher on a water break. "I stayed out a little longer and hit a puck," said O'Reilly in a 2022 interview. "Then I did some figure 8s, then I went over to the boards, then I went flying over to the bench. I came in with the brakes on and there was Phil [Esposito]. And he was laughing, 'You don't stop! You know what you look like? The Tasmanian Devil. That's what I'm going to call you! Taz!'"

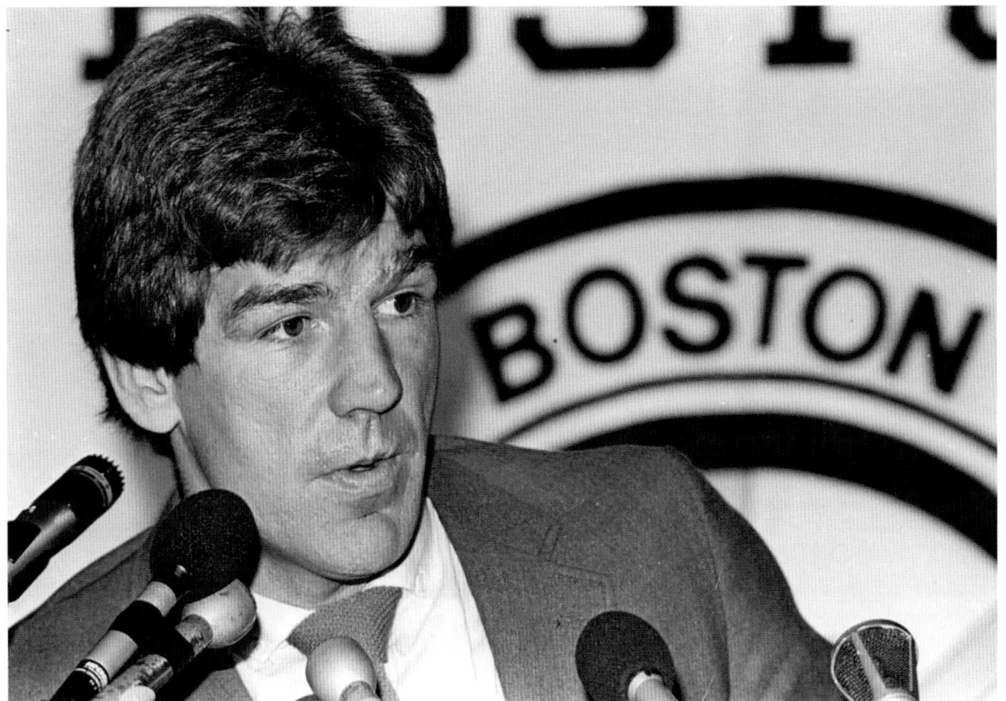

Terry O'Reilly took over as the team's head coach in November 1986, bringing the same passion that characterized his play to his new role behind the bench. In 1988, his team broke the dreaded "Montreal Jinx" on their way to a Stanley Cup Final versus Edmonton. (Photograph by Al Ruelle, Collection of The Sports Museum)

In the early years of his career, O'Reilly was known primarily for his rough-and-tumble play. Often, that resulted in donnybrooks with various members of the Philadelphia Flyers. "I hated playing Philadelphia," said O'Reilly. "I couldn't sleep the night before. During my afternoon nap I got the sweats." O'Reilly knew that, if he played his game, his body checks would lead to fights with the likes of Dave Schultz and Andre Dupont. "And it happened just about every time in Philadelphia," he said.

O'Reilly was also known for giving maximum effort each and every shift. He credits two guys named Don (Marcotte and Cherry) for allowing him to thrive.

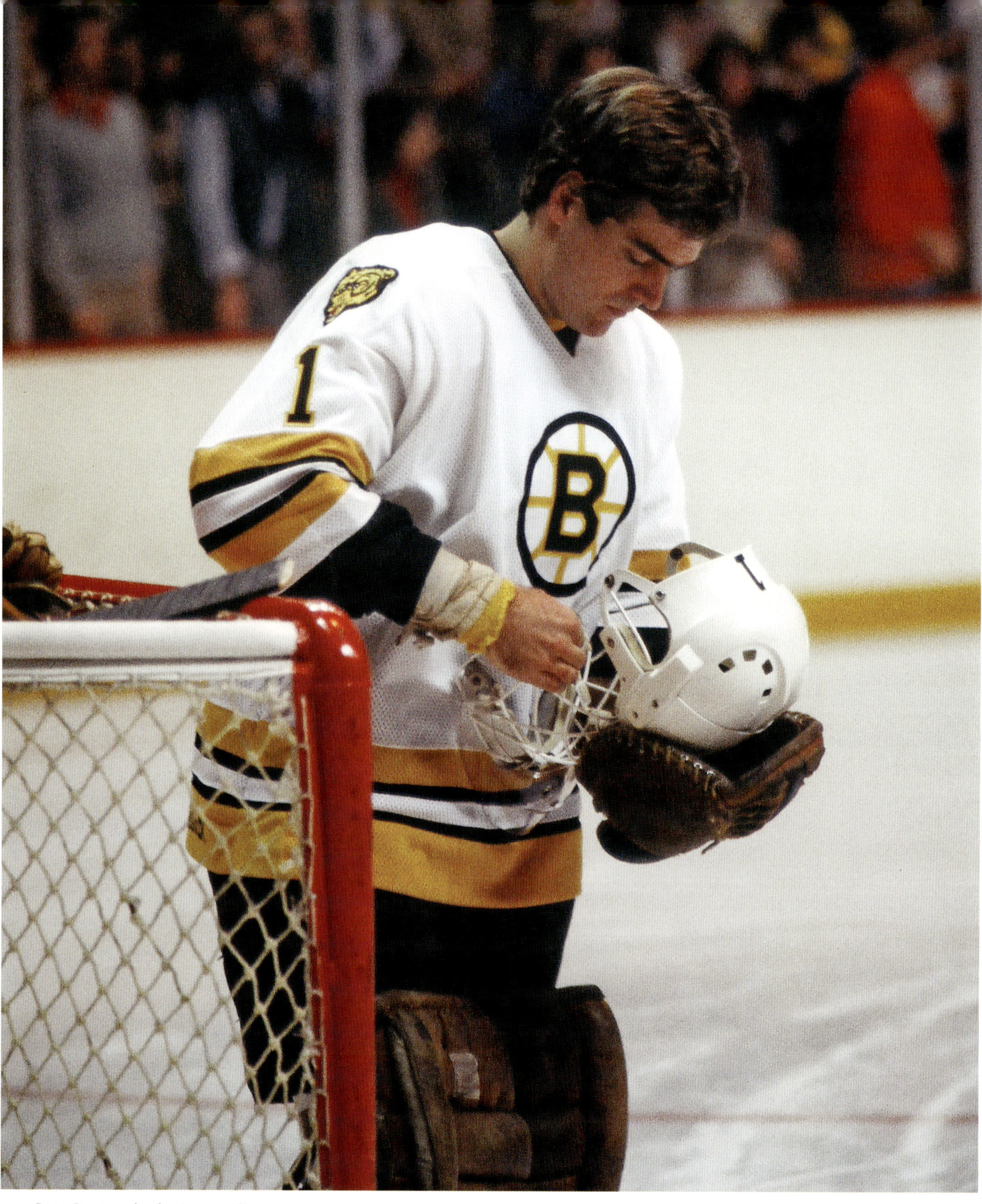

Pete Peeters had a tremendous season between the pipes for the 1982–83 Bruins, posting 40 wins, earning a First Team NHL All-Star spot, and capturing the Vezina Trophy (the first Bruin to win it since Frank Brimsek in 1942). Peeters played in Boston until 1985 but never managed to recapture the magic of that singular season. (Photograph by Steve Babineau, NHLI via Getty Images)

"Donny Marcotte was assigned to play on my left side," said O'Reilly. "He basically said, 'I just go where Terry doesn't go.' Because, I would go off my wing and he would read that.... If the puck gets thrown over there, I'm—*zoom*—over there. He cuts over there to cover this wing. So I always sort of had a green light by Don Cherry to just go be a greyhound chasing the rabbit."

In the late 1970s and into the 1980s, O'Reilly emerged as one of the best defensive forwards in the league, one of the top scorers on the Bruins, and an unquestioned team leader. It surprised absolutely no one when he assumed the captaincy upon the retirement of Wayne Cashman in 1983.

Shortly after retiring as a player in 1985, O'Reilly became head coach of the Bruins, leading them to a Stanley Cup Final in 1988. His No. 24 was retired to the rafters of the TD Garden in 2002.

BRAD PARK

BRAD PARK HAD a huge impact on the Bruins franchise for 15 years.

For his first seven NHL seasons (1968–1975), as the best player for their most bitter rival, the young Rangers defenseman wearing No. 2 was the man that Boston fans loved to hate. It didn't help that Park took several shots at the Bruins in his 1972 autobiography *Play the Man*. "That book made me public enemy No. 1 in Boston," said Park in a 2022 interview.

Three years later, Park suddenly found himself on the other side of the rivalry when he was traded to the Bruins along with Jean Ratelle in the blockbuster deal that sent Phil Esposito to New York. Park now had a new uniform—and a new number, too. "They said, 'No. 2 is retired to Eddie Shore, and we're going to go and ask him if it's okay if you use it,'" said Park. "And I said, 'No. I don't want you to.'" Park chose a different number instead. "They went through the different numbers and I said, 'I'll take 22. That will be twice as good.'"

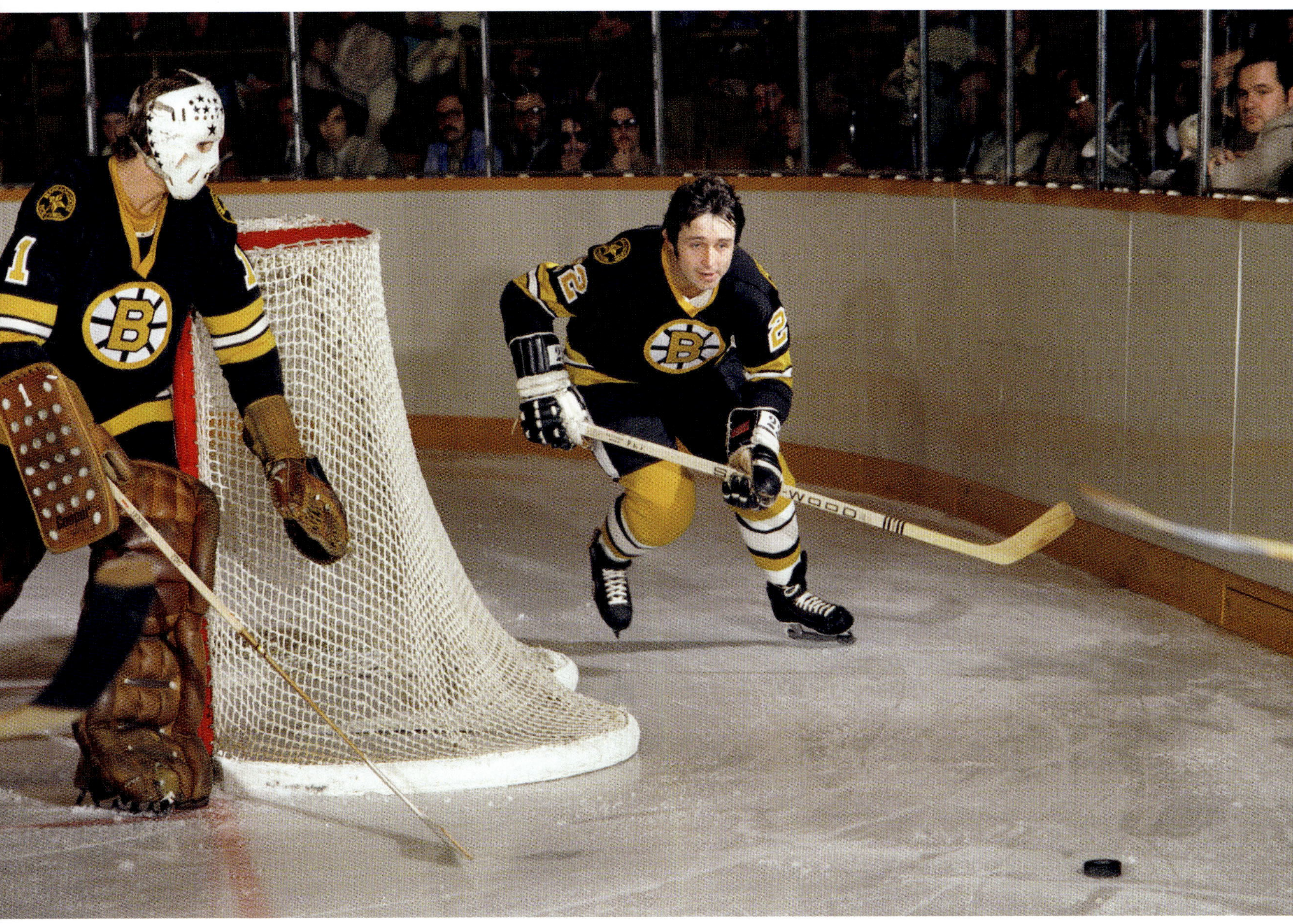

Brad Park was one of the best and most complete defensemen in NHL history. Here, he circles around net while Bruins goaltender Gilles Gilbert stands guard. (Photograph by Graphic Artists/Hockey Hall of Fame)

With Bobby Orr still on the roster, Bruins fans had visions of a dream defensive pairing involving No. 4 and No. 22. Alas, it was not to be, as Orr's career with the Bruins was winding down (and, after a brief stint in Chicago, would soon be over) because of injuries. "It would have been pretty special to play with Brad for a longer period," said Orr. "But we had 10 fun games."

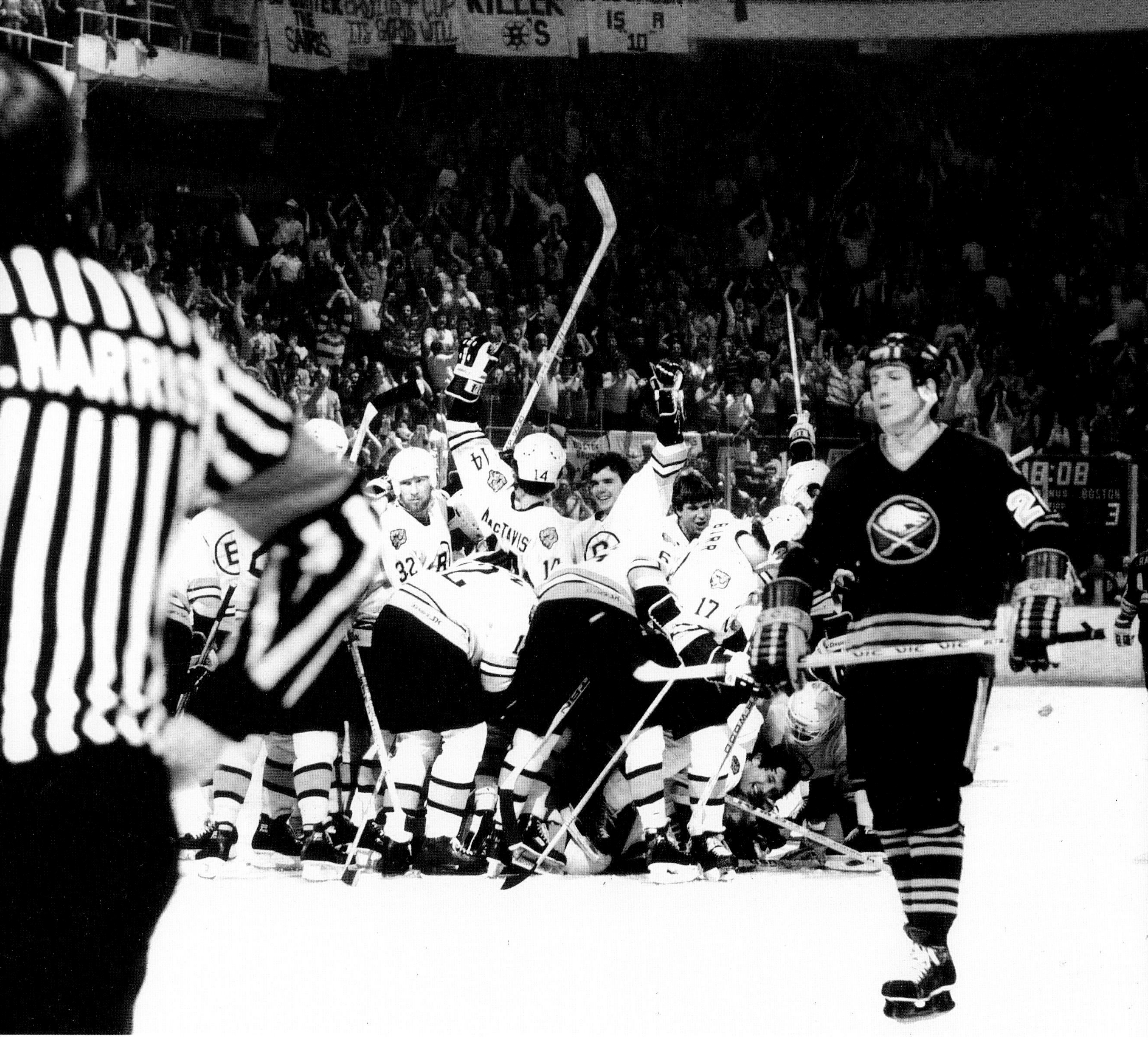

The Bruins celebrate Brad Park's dramatic overtime goal that won Game 7 of the 1983 Adams Division Finals against the Buffalo Sabres. The electricity in Boston Garden that night evoked memories of the Orr-Esposito glory years. (Photograph by Dick Raphael, Collection of The Sports Museum)

With the retirement of Orr, said Harry Sinden, "Brad Park in my opinion was the No. 1 defenseman in hockey.... He was such a brilliant playmaker and puck handler and shooter."

Park credits much of his unique skill set to his development as a younger player. "I was a forward for most of my years," said Park. "When I was 15, my Dad, who was the coach, put me back on defense. Instead of being upset, I said, 'Now I get to go out every second time instead of every third time. That's nice, I like that.' So I adjusted.... I went to defenseman as a skilled guy who wasn't afraid of handling the puck because I played forward."

Park was much more than just the blueline bridge between Orr and Bourque. In his eight seasons in Boston, he helped lead the team to five division titles and two conference championships while twice being named a First Team NHL All-Star. He retired after the 1984–85 season, and in 1988, his first year of eligibility, he was inducted into the Hockey Hall of Fame.

Rick Middleton calls Park "one of the best defensemen in the history of the game." Whether hailing from Boston or New York, few would disagree.

MIKE MILBURY

MIKE MILBURY, a native of Walpole, Massachusetts, was used to bucking the odds, emerging from a somewhat obscure career at Colgate University and a two-year apprenticeship in the minor leagues before finally making it to the NHL. "If ever a man made the National Hockey League through hard work, it's Mike Milbury," said head coach Don Cherry. "He and Terry O'Reilly are cut from the same cloth."

Milbury had a baptism by fire. After having played in just three regular season games for the Bruins, Milbury was pressed into service during the 1976 Stanley Cup playoffs, appearing in 11 playoff games. "The thing about Mike, he was gung-ho, and what worked in college wasn't necessarily going to work in the NHL," said Brad Park in a 2021 interview with hockey journalist Mick Colageo. "We spent time talking, and he was very receptive, to the point where he became more than capable."

Milbury went on to enjoy a 12-year NHL career, spent entirely with the Bruins and marked by his crowd-pleasing, rambunctious playing style. Along the way, Milbury became a team leader. As Harry Sinden told Colageo, "He wasn't the captain, but he was the kind of guy who, if he saw something he didn't like, he would go and find somebody to talk to."

Those leadership traits came to the forefront when Milbury coached the Bruins for two highly successful seasons (1989–1991), with both of his teams amassing more than 100 points and then making deep runs in the Stanley Cup playoffs. After stepping down as coach, Milbury briefly worked in Boston's front office. His hockey life, which continues to this day, has also involved a tenure with the New York Islanders as a coach and executive, as well as extensive work in the broadcast booth on the national level as both a studio and color analyst.

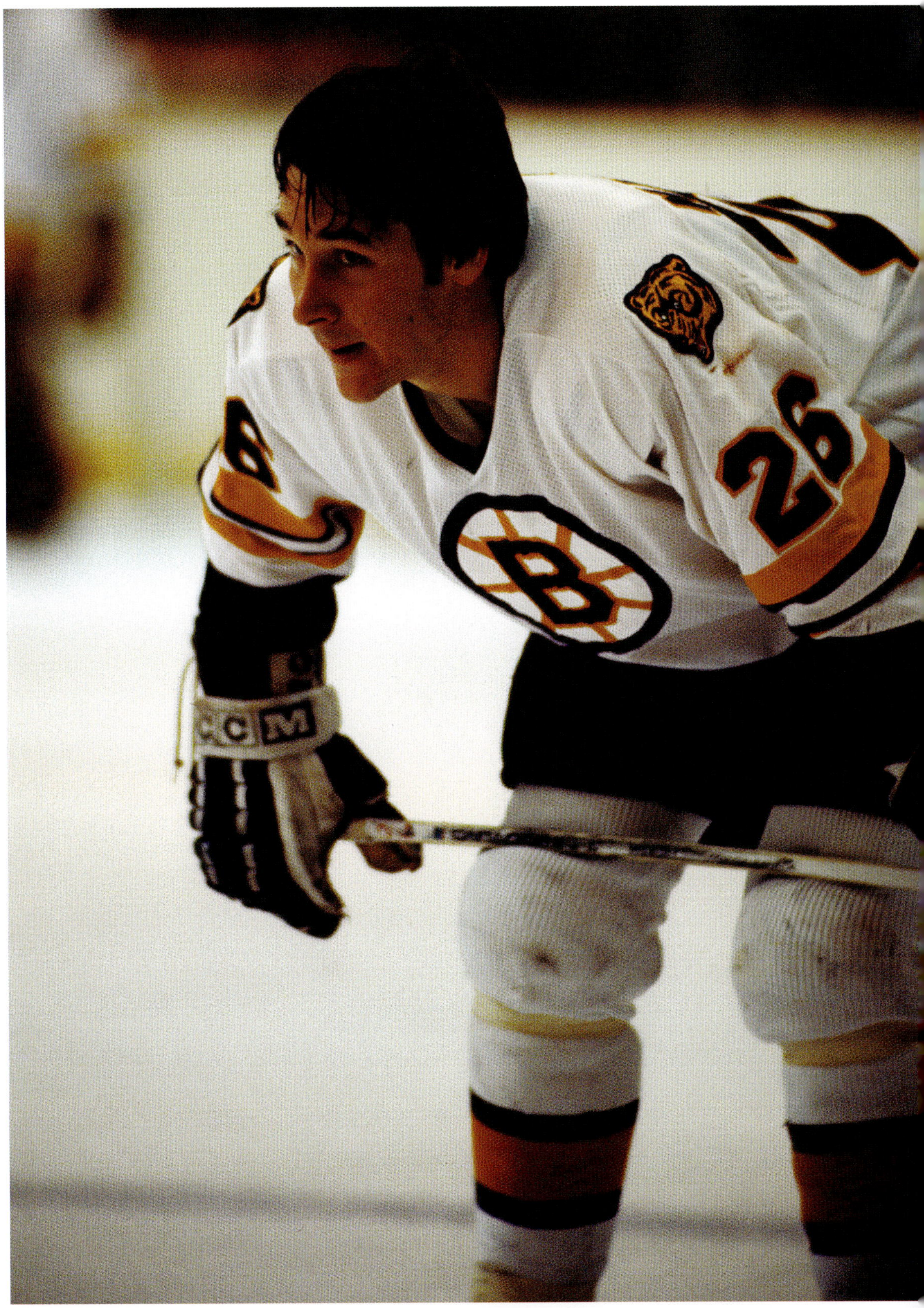

There were just a handful of Americans playing in the NHL when Walpole, Massachusetts, native Mike Milbury made his Boston debut in 1976. The rugged defenseman would play for his hometown Bruins until 1987. (Photograph by Steve Babineau/Boston Bruins)

RICK MIDDLETON

Mere words or statistics cannot do justice to Rick Middleton's legacy. Watch his highlight reels on YouTube, and you will find yourself marveling at his stickhandling, dekes, fakes, feints, and goal-scoring brilliance. The man had moves. His nickname says it all: "Nifty."

A highly touted prospect, Middleton's career began with the Rangers in 1974. And it didn't exactly get off to a roaring start. As Middleton admitted in a 2022 interview, "I was a little bit undisciplined.... Off the ice I was maybe having too much fun in New York."

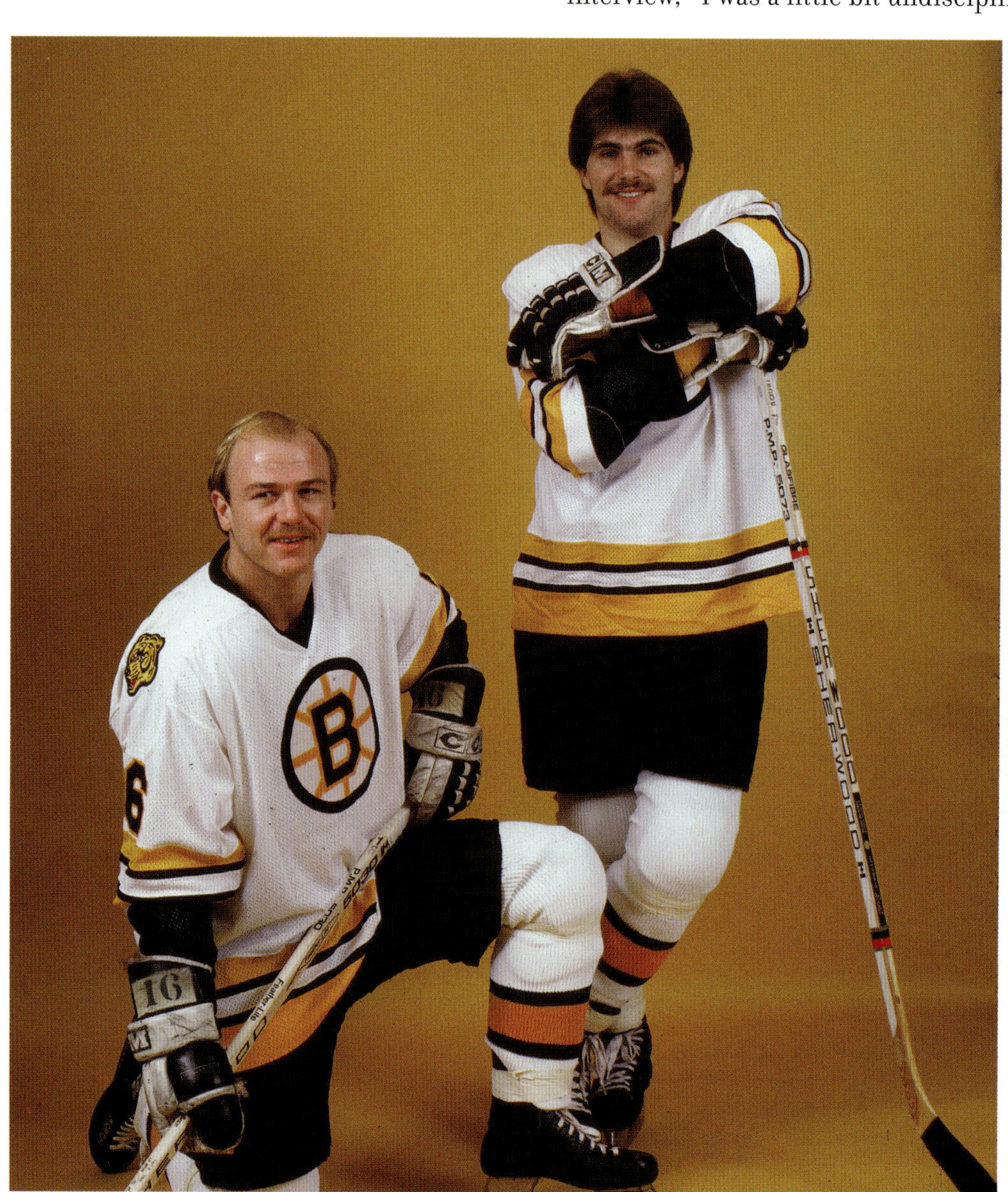

The Bruins careers of Rick Middleton (left) and Ray Bourque overlapped for nine seasons and included deep playoff runs in 1983 and 1988, Middleton's final season. (Photograph by Bruce Bennett Studios via Getty Images/ Getty Images)

Harry Sinden took a chance on Middleton, acquiring him in 1976 in exchange for popular longtime Bruin, the high-scoring Ken Hodge. Middleton quickly endeared himself to fans by scoring a hat trick in his first-ever game for Boston on opening night that October. "Don Cherry played me during my first game as a Bruin, and who did he put me on a line with?" said Middleton. "Jean Ratelle and Johnny Bucyk. It was a dream come true."

Middleton would have to earn his playing time in Boston, though, with Cherry demanding that he become a two-way forward with more focus on the defensive end. "He drilled it through my head by attrition of ice time that year," said Middleton. "And he finally got through this thick skull with what he wanted me to do."

Within a few years, Middleton had become one of the top players on the team. Then, in the early 1980s, Middleton exploded and became one of the best players in the entire NHL, pumping in 40 or more goals for five consecutive seasons (1980–1984). In all, he would score more than 400 goals in his 12-year career with the Bruins.

In 1985, Middleton was named co-captain of the team along with Ray Bourque. "I didn't want to put that all on Ray's shoulders so early in his career," explained outgoing captain Terry O'Reilly. "And I also wanted to acknowledge the leadership of Rick Middleton. I called them in and said, 'I'd like the two of you to be co-captains. Nifty, you're probably looking at one or two more years in the league, and during that time you can show Ray how things work. And then when you retire, Ray will slide into that captaincy.'" Middleton would later call being named co-captain his "greatest thrill as a player."

In 2018, Middleton received an even greater thrill when the Bruins retired his No. 16. As Middleton recalled, "Cam [Neely] called me in July of all times.... After a little small-talk, he just said, 'We decided to retire your No. 16.' And he caught me right off guard. I was like, '*What??*' I didn't think I heard him right. Then my wife came home, and I was emotional, and she thought somebody had died. I said, 'No, no.'" That November, Middleton's number went up to the rafters.

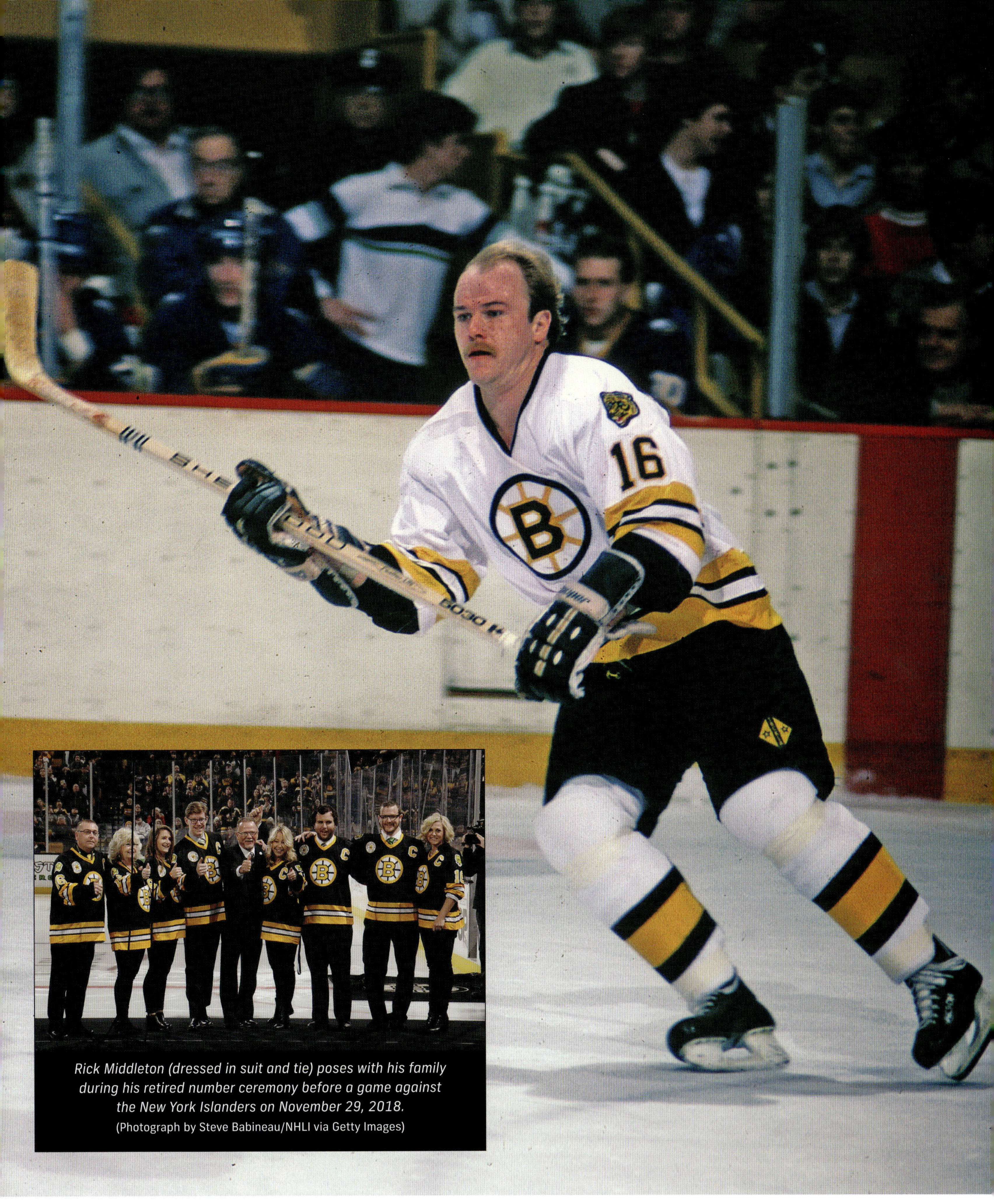

Rick Middleton (dressed in suit and tie) poses with his family during his retired number ceremony before a game against the New York Islanders on November 29, 2018. (Photograph by Steve Babineau/NHLI via Getty Images)

Nicknamed "Nifty," right wing Rick Middleton scored 402 goals for the Bruins in a dozen seasons. Only Johnny Bucyk, Phil Esposito, and Patrice Bergeron have scored more in team history. (Photograph by Steve Babineau, Collection of The Sports Museum)

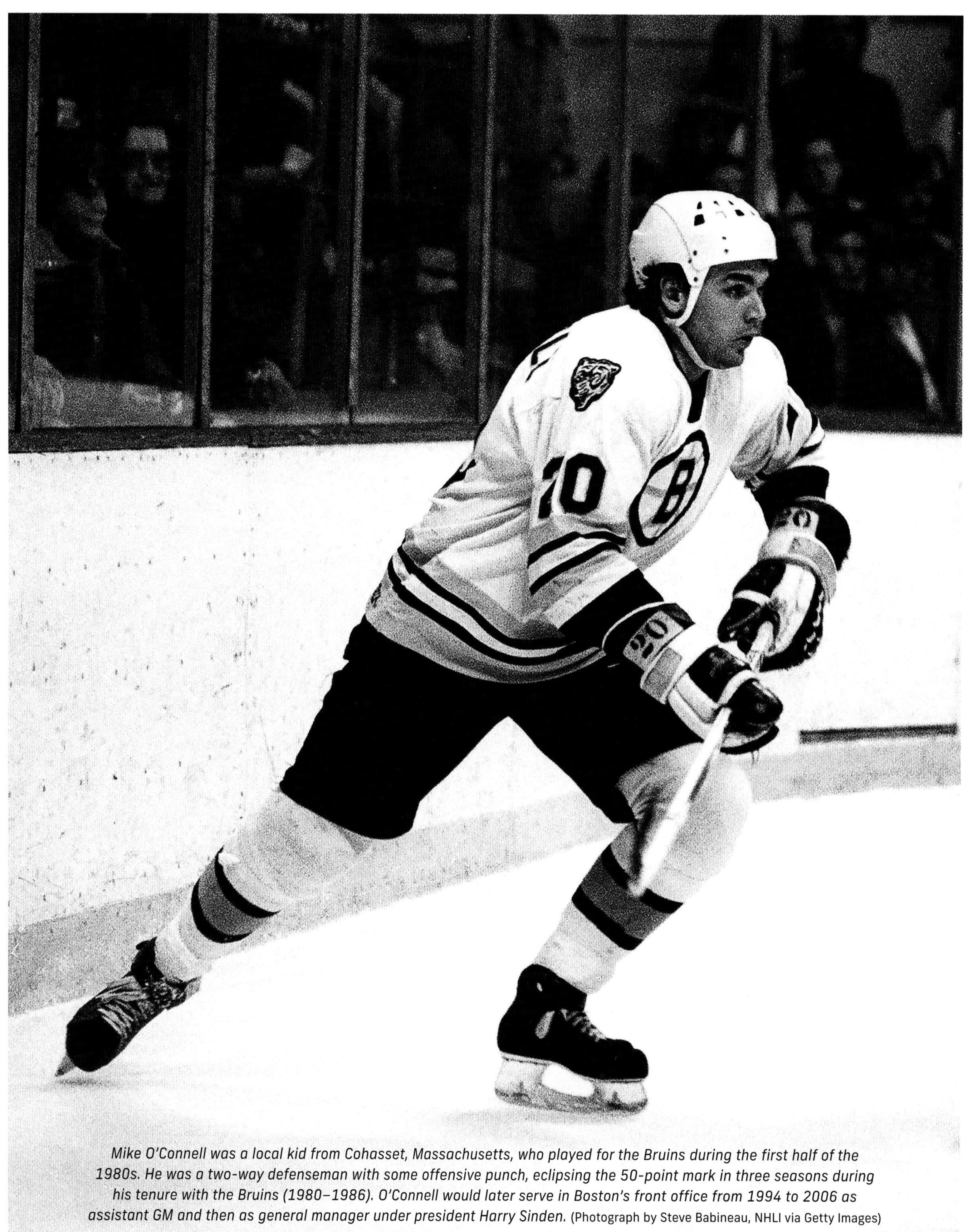

Mike O'Connell was a local kid from Cohasset, Massachusetts, who played for the Bruins during the first half of the 1980s. He was a two-way defenseman with some offensive punch, eclipsing the 50-point mark in three seasons during his tenure with the Bruins (1980–1986). O'Connell would later serve in Boston's front office from 1994 to 2006 as assistant GM and then as general manager under president Harry Sinden. (Photograph by Steve Babineau, NHLI via Getty Images)

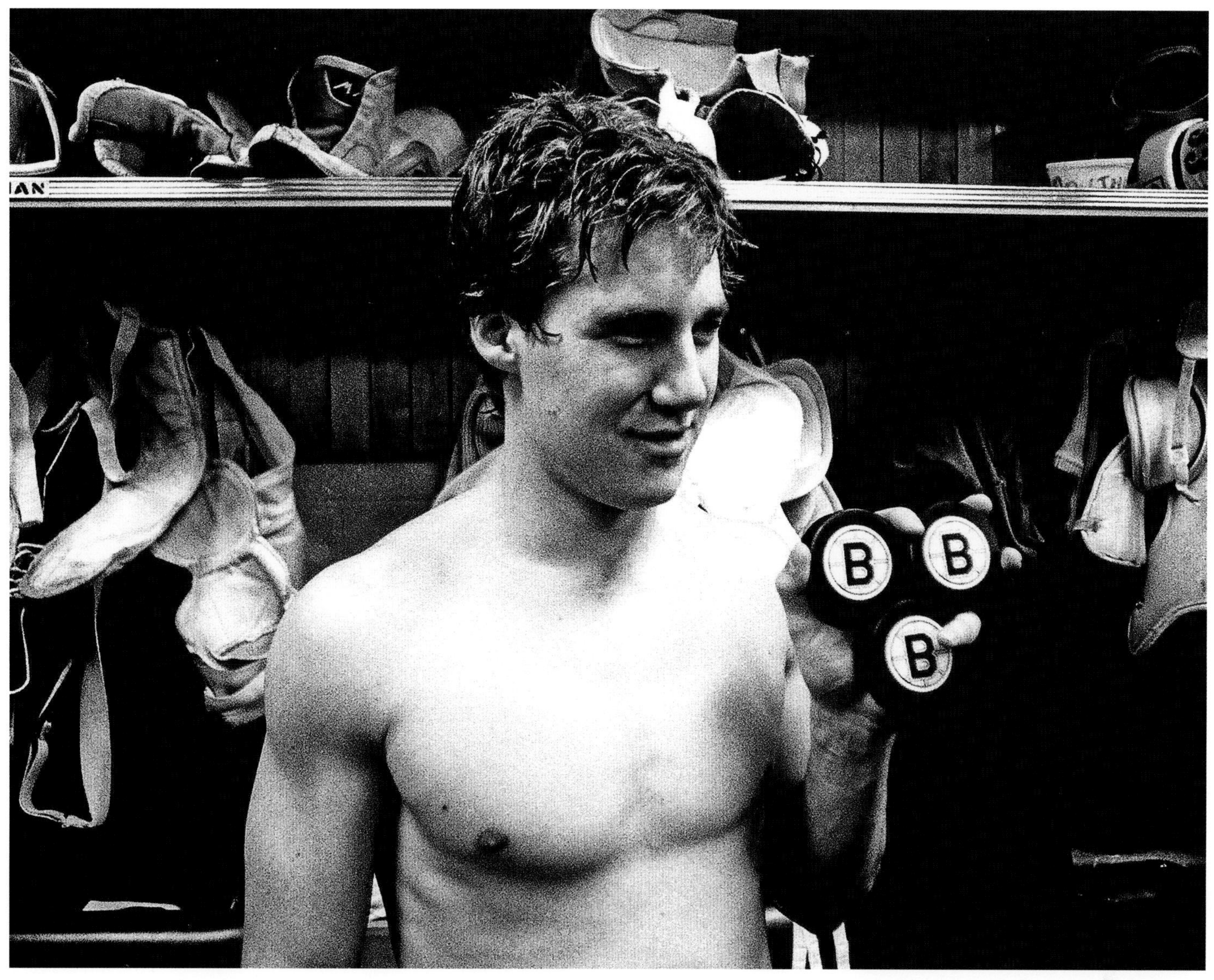

Barry Pederson poses in front of his Boston Garden locker after scoring his first career hat trick, against the Hartford Whalers on April 4, 1982. (Photograph by Steve Babineau/NHLI via Getty Images)

BARRY PEDERSON

BARRY PEDERSON'S first three years with the Bruins were nothing short of spectacular. In 1981–82, Pederson set franchise rookie records for both goals (44) and points (92). He followed that up with back-to-back 100-point seasons in 1983 and 1984.

Along the way, Pederson developed extraordinary chemistry with linemate Rick Middleton. "If he was doing something in the offensive zone, I would know where to go, so that he could get me the puck and I'd have the best chance of scoring," said Middleton. "It wasn't a laid-out play like, 'You go here and I'll go there.' We never went on the blackboard or anything like that. We just read each other so well."

Then, in the summer of 1984, with NHL stardom and a Hall of Fame career beckoning, Pederson suffered a setback when he was diagnosed with a benign shoulder tumor. Following an operation, he was limited to only 22 games for the 1984–85 season. After enduring a second operation, he gamely recovered to score 76 points in 1985–86. At the end of that season, however, the Bruins traded him to Vancouver for Cam Neely and its 1987 first-round draft choice (which Boston eventually used to select defenseman Glen Wesley).

For the next several years, Pederson bounced around the league, from Vancouver to Pittsburgh (where he won a Stanley Cup) to Hartford and, finally, back to Boston for one final season, in 1991–92. After his playing days were over,

Pederson and his family moved back to the Greater Boston Area, where he has enjoyed a highly successful career in the financial services industry and as a long-time studio analyst on NESN's broadcasts of Bruins games.

Pederson has no regrets about his first stint with the Bruins in the early 1980s, triumphant but somewhat truncated. "We had great teams in Boston," said Pederson in a 2011 interview. "I was a member of a very good hockey club throughout those years in an area that was extraordinarily passionate about hockey. It was just a lot of fun."

WHAT MIGHT HAVE BEEN?

BARRY PEDERSON was not the only young Boston Bruin in the 1980s whose career was snakebitten by injury. Indeed, the success of the Bruins during that decade was counter-balanced by two great "what ifs?" regarding a pair of other potential NHL superstars, forward Normand Leveille and defenseman Gord Kluzak.

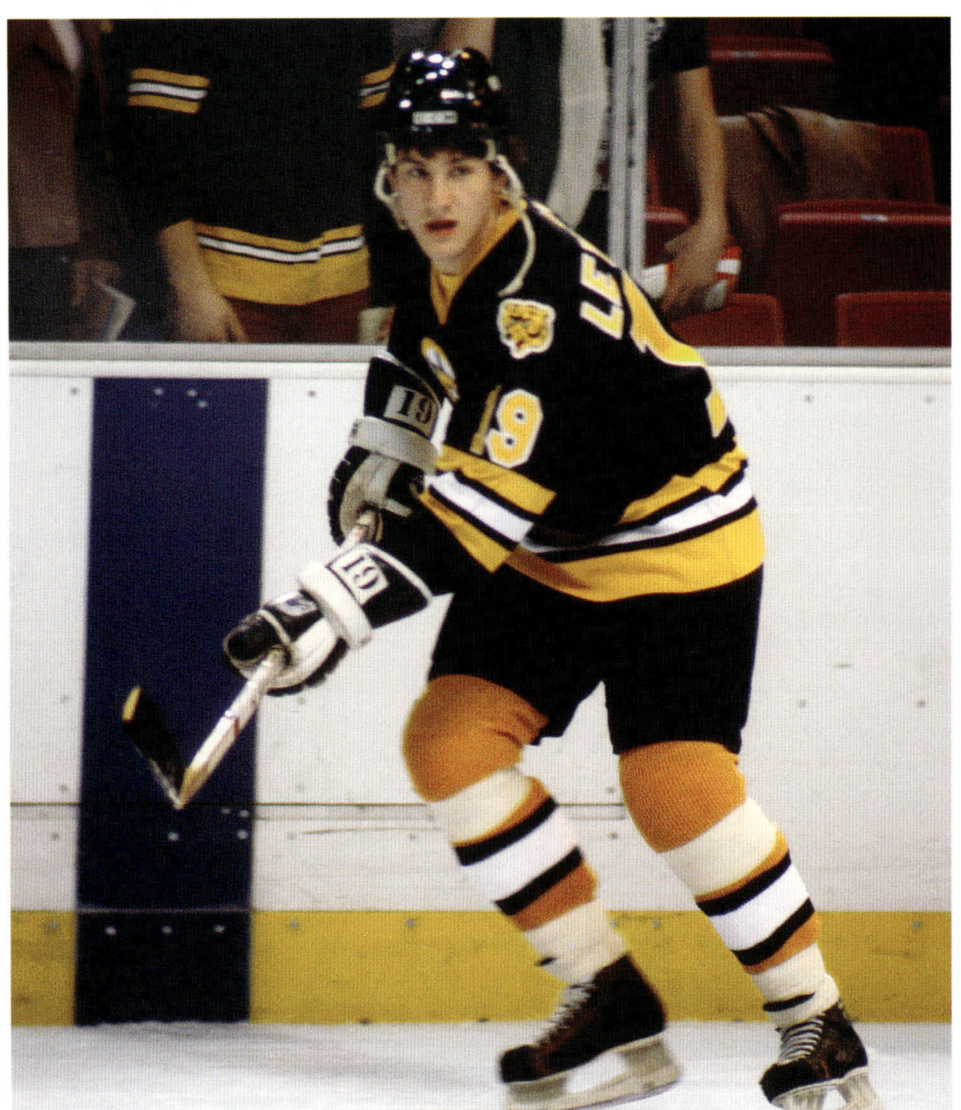

Normand Leveille skates in pregame warmups at the Garden during his rookie season, 1981–82. He flashed enormous potential, leading many to believe he would become one of the best players in hockey. (Photograph by Steve Babineau/NHLI via Getty Images)

Leveille, the 14th overall draft choice in the 1981 NHL Draft, scored 33 points in his rookie season and was on track to be the team's next offensive star. But early in his second season, on October 23, 1982, he suffered a cerebral hemorrhage while playing in Vancouver. Leveille received emergency surgery that saved his life. Eventually he would regain the use of his legs—but, sadly, his hockey career was over. The Leveille tragedy had a profound impact on his teammates for years to come. "It makes you think how frail life is.... It might not change you, but it sure scares you," said Rick Middleton in 1985.

Whereas Leveille's career was completely derailed by tragedy, Kluzak's career was substantially wrecked by injury. The first overall pick in the 1982 NHL Draft, the towering defenseman displayed flashes of brilliance in his first four seasons that saw him being compared with Montreal star Larry Robinson. Unfortunately, Kluzak endured 11 operations during his Bruins tenure and was healthy enough to play a combined total of just 13 games over his final three seasons with the team. "Gordie was on his way to being a star player as well," said Harry Sinden. "Good size, great skater. His career ended in no time.... We tried everything to bring him back, but it wasn't going to happen."

Like his teammate Barry Pederson, Kluzak remained in Boston after his playing career and has enjoyed a successful career in financial services as well as in broadcasting on NESN.

"When we look back on those teams [of the 1980s], you can mention Gord Kluzak and then you can mention Normand Leveille," said Ray Bourque. "What would it have been with those two guys healthy?"

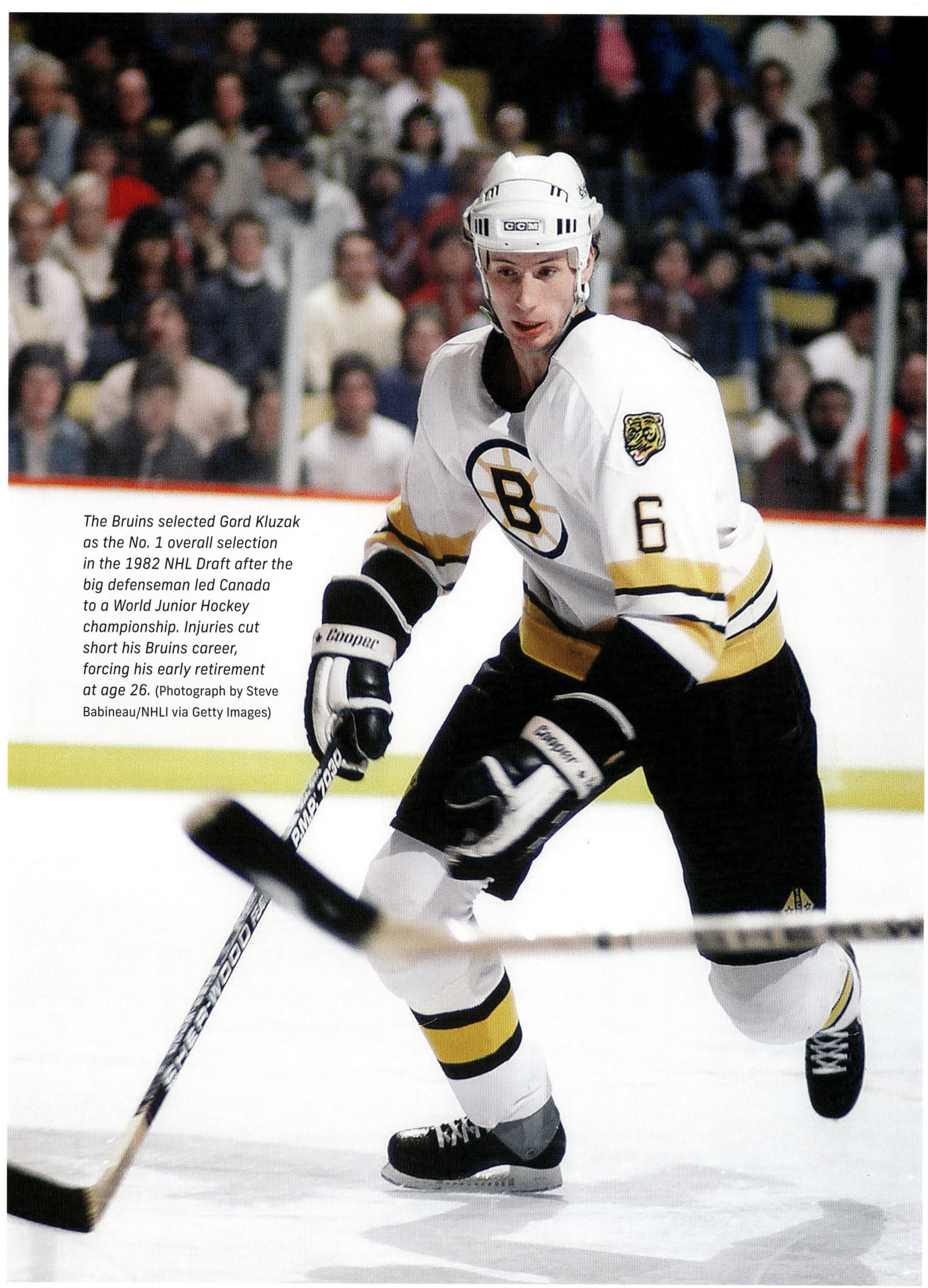

The Bruins selected Gord Kluzak as the No. 1 overall selection in the 1982 NHL Draft after the big defenseman led Canada to a World Junior Hockey championship. Injuries cut short his Bruins career, forcing his early retirement at age 26. (Photograph by Steve Babineau/NHLI via Getty Images)

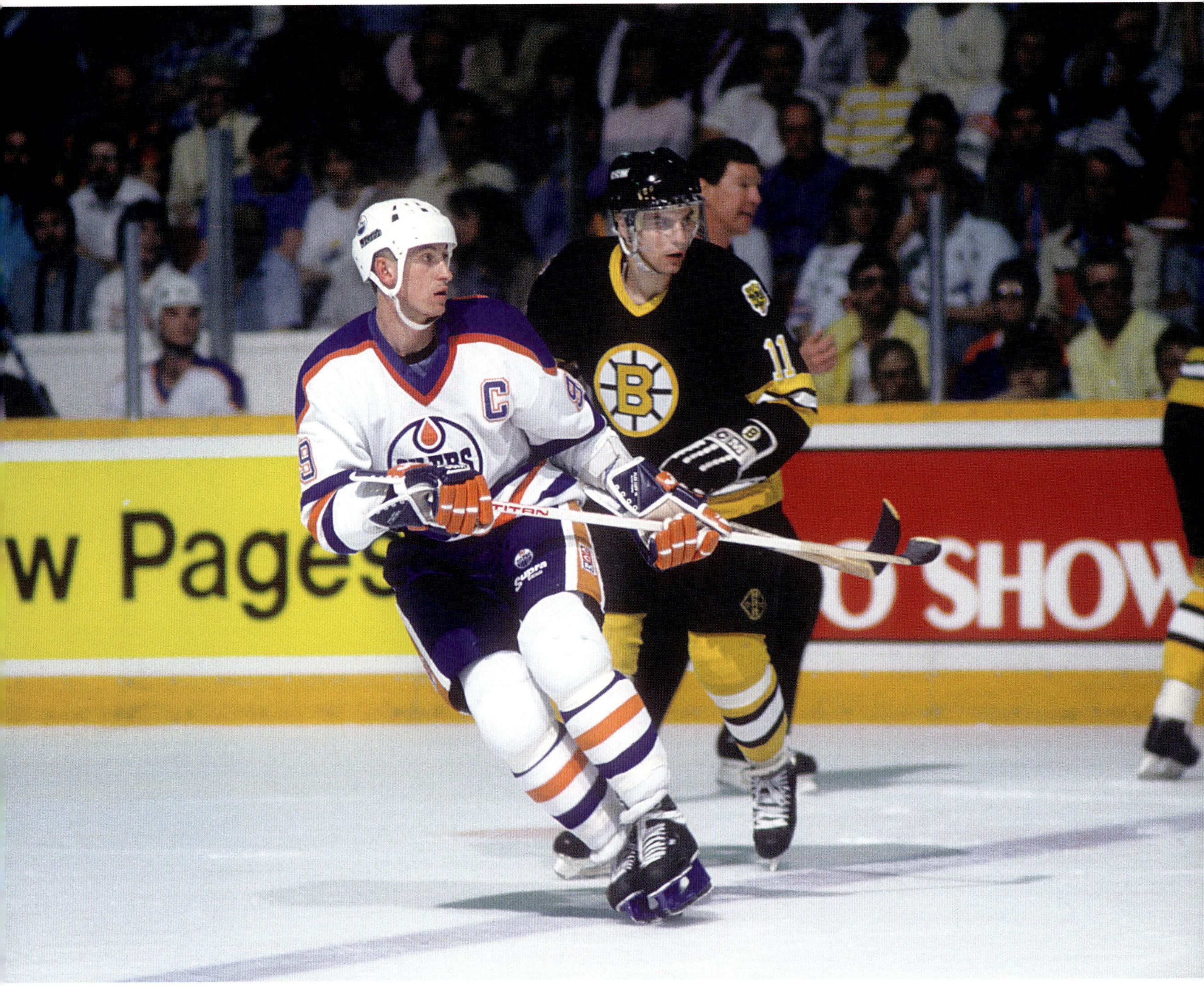

Steve Kasper (11) shadows Wayne Gretzky during the Stanley Cup Final in May 1988 at the Northlands Coliseum in Edmonton. Kasper played for the Bruins from 1980 to 1989 and later coached the team for two seasons during the mid-1990s. (Photograph by B Bennett/Bruce Bennett Studios via Getty Images Studios/ Getty Images)

1980S ROLE PLAYERS

MUCH OF THE SUCCESS of the Bruins through the years has been due to the role players who have toiled in the trenches. In the 1980s, a trio of players stood out especially in that regard:

STEVE KASPER played on the team for the entire decade (1980–1989) and became particularly renowned for being "Wayne Gretzky's Shadow." In that era, no one could completely contain Gretzky—but Kasper came the closest. "The main thing I try to do is keep him on the outside of the ice and nudge him early to get him off his stride, like a bump and run in football," explained Kasper in a 1982 *Sports Illustrated* article. "It's no good trying to line him up for a hard check; he's too mobile. If you start lunging at him, he'll make you look ridiculous." In 1981–82, Kasper won the Selke Trophy as the NHL's best defensive forward. And he could score, too, ringing up 135 goals and 355 points for the Bruins.

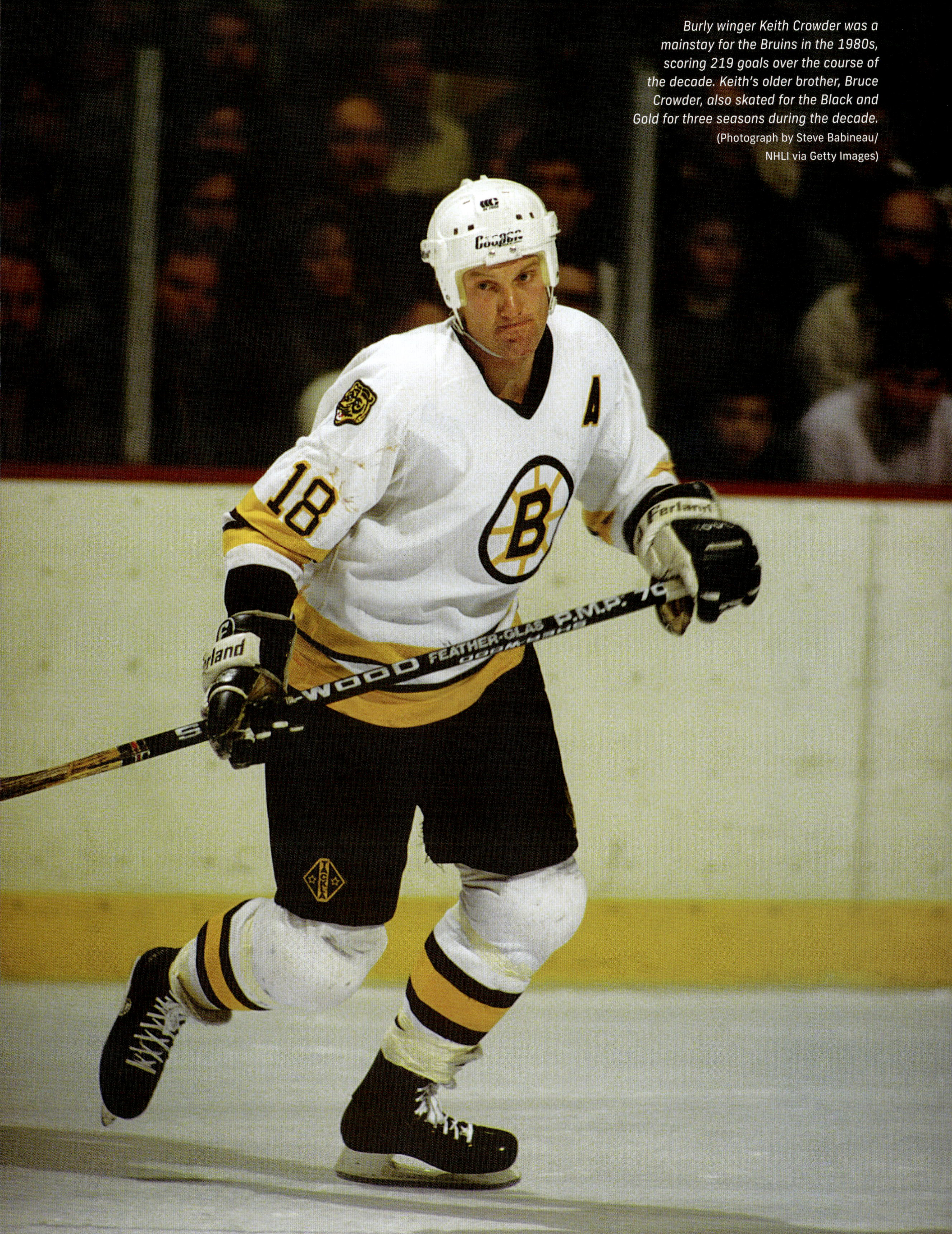

Burly winger Keith Crowder was a mainstay for the Bruins in the 1980s, scoring 219 goals over the course of the decade. Keith's older brother, Bruce Crowder, also skated for the Black and Gold for three seasons during the decade.
(Photograph by Steve Babineau/ NHLI via Getty Images)

KEITH CROWDER, like Kasper, was a fixture in the Bruins lineup for the duration of the decade. He was rough, tough, and physical—in other words, a true Bruin. In many ways, Crowder was a lot like Terry O'Reilly, his teammate and later his coach in the 1980s, racking up plenty of penalty minutes (more than 100 each and every year) but scoring a lot, too. In all, he poured in 219 goals during the decade. Even longtime Bruins fans might be surprised to know that Crowder ranks just outside the top 20 on the list of Bruins all-time scoring leaders.

KEN LINSEMAN was a player who drew the wrath of Bruins fans when he was with Philadelphia and Edmonton in the late 1970s and early 1980s. That all evaporated, overnight, when Linseman joined the Bruins in 1984. Bruins fans instantly fell in love with "the Rat." There has always been a place for a guy who badgered, agitated, and got under the skin of the opposing team—and Linseman fit that role perfectly, much like Johnny McKenzie before him and Brad Marchand in more recent times. And Linseman was talented, too. He could skate, pass, and score, ringing up more than 20 goals and 70 points in all but one of his five full seasons with the Bruins.

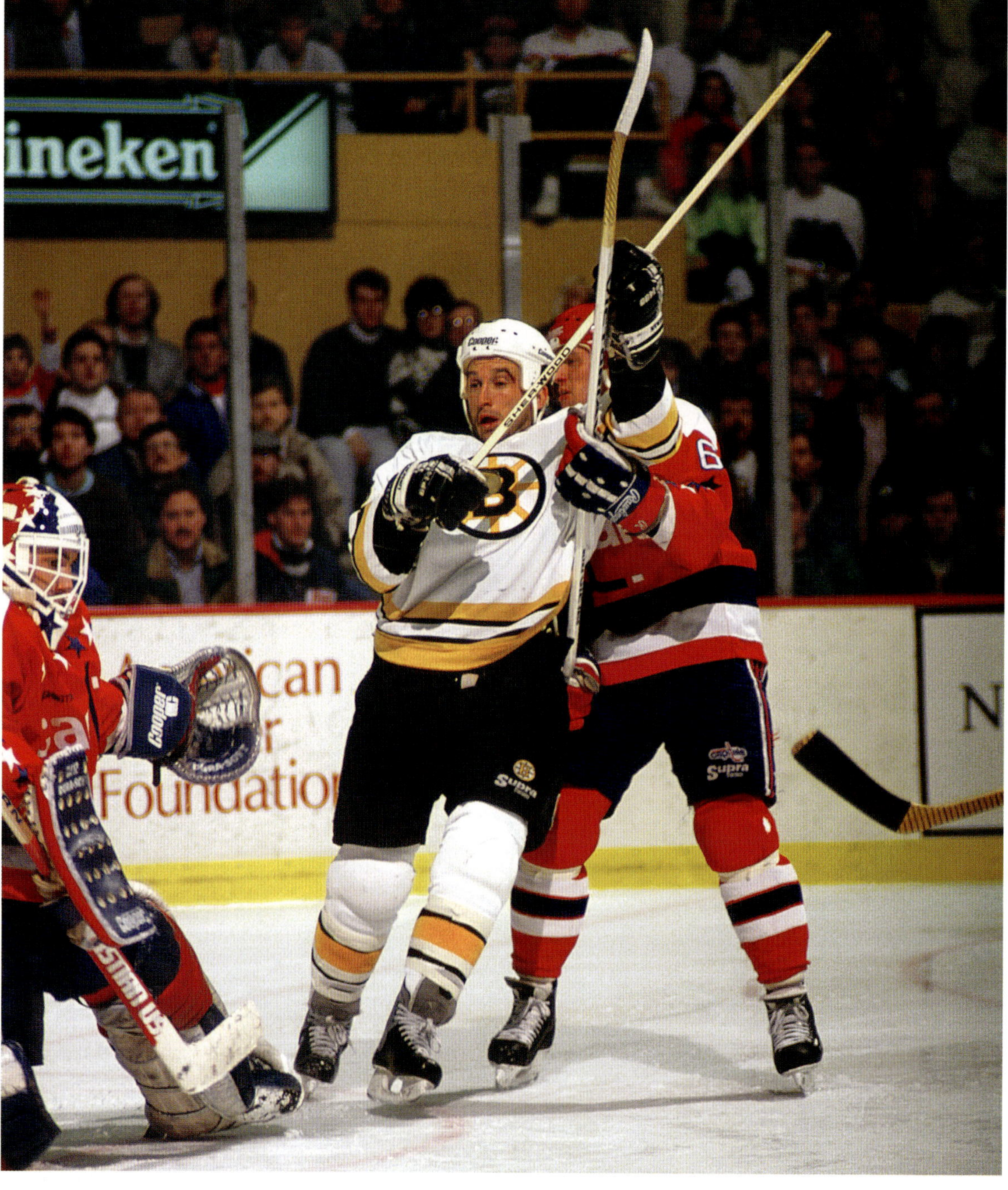

Ken Linseman jousts with Washington defenseman John Barrett in front of the net at Boston Garden. Needless to say, "the Rat" was never hesitant to mix it up. (Photograph by Steve Babineau/NHLI via Getty Images)

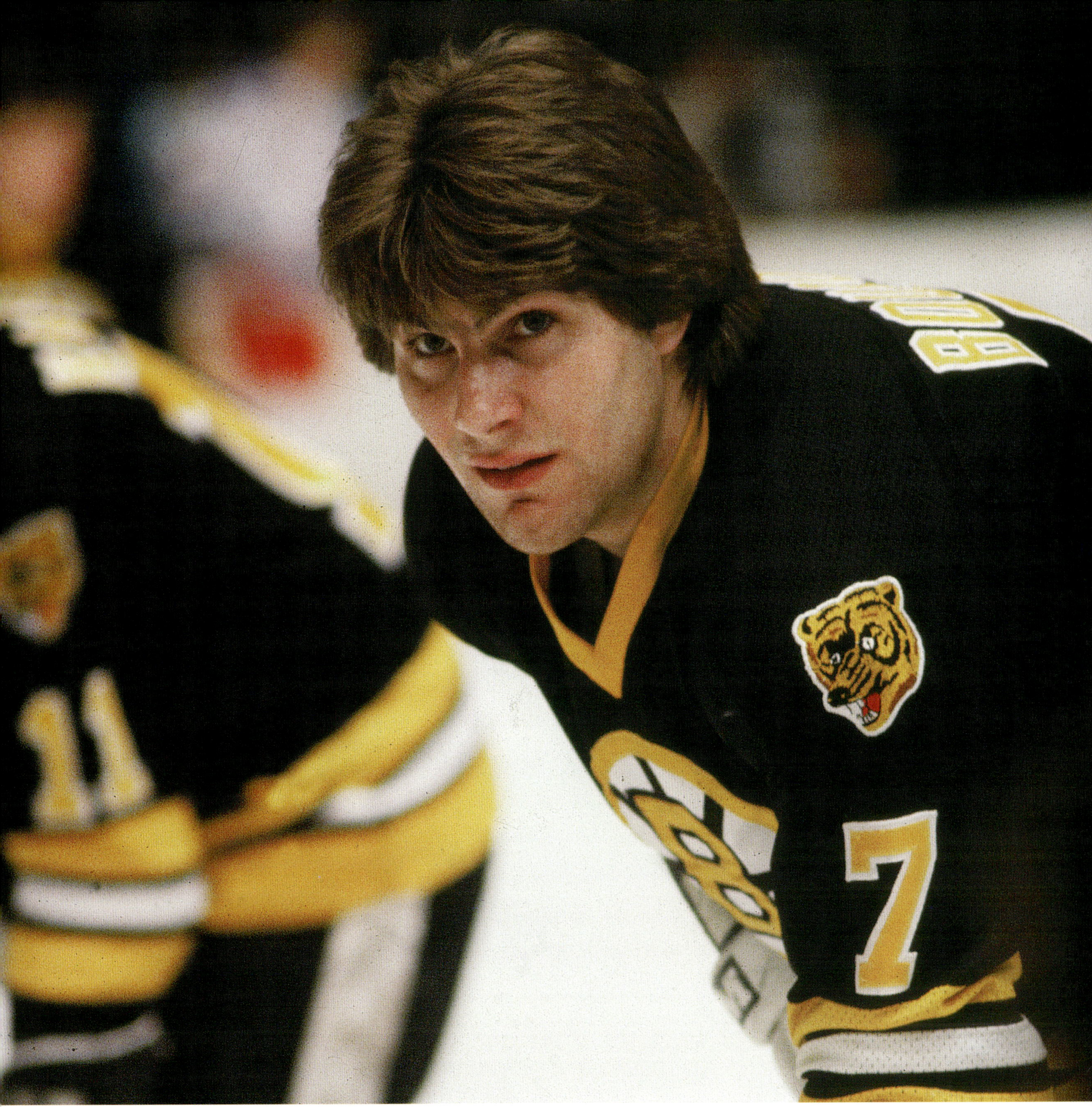

A young Ray Bourque braces for action in a 1981 game. Many NHL awards and honors lay ahead for Bourque, including five Norris Trophies (NHL's top defenseman), a King Clancy Trophy (for leadership and humanitarian contributions), and, in his final season in 2001, a Stanley Cup with the Colorado Avalanche. (Photo by Bruce Bennett Studios via Getty Images Studios/Getty Images)

RAY BOURQUE

RAY BOURQUE was raised in the province of Quebec and grew up a fan of the Montreal Canadiens. "That ended the day I was drafted in 1979," said Bourque in a 2022 interview.

The Bruins may have never had a better draft choice. Selected eighth overall in that 1979 NHL Draft, Bourque delivered immediately (winning the Calder Trophy as rookie of the year in 1979–80) and over the long term (starring for the Bruins for 21 seasons before being traded to Colorado in March 2000). In so doing, he proved himself to be one of the best pure defensemen to ever play the game.

Opposite page: Ray Bourque shakes hands with Phil Esposito after giving up his No. 7 jersey in an emotional pregame ceremony at Boston Garden on December 3, 1987. (Photograph by Steve Babineau/NHLI via Getty Images)

He also learned quickly to shrug off the comparisons to the greatest player who ever skated, Bobby Orr. "It was never an issue or pressure with me to fill Bobby's shoes or skates," said Bourque. "I knew that was impossible. I just went out and tried to be my own player and play my own game."

And Bourque's game clearly began on one side of the ice. "I was a very responsible player," said Bourque. "I always said that defense was the most important thing that I needed to take care of first.... I was a good passer and I saw the ice very well and I had a good shot and could skate well. I just enjoyed playing both ends but knowing that my end came first."

As the 1980s progressed, Bourque gradually assumed a leadership role on the Bruins. "When Ray first got here, he was just a shy French-Canadian kid who only loosened up on the ice," said Mike Milbury in a 1987 interview. "But when he was named co-captain [in 1985], he took the role to heart. He has become a leader who takes young players aside, gives hell to older ones, and never lets the locker room get too tight."

Bourque captained the Bruins from 1985 to 2000—first in tandem with Rick Middleton and then on a solo basis after Middleton retired in 1988. "It is a tremendous honor and responsibility that I took very serious," said Bourque of his captaincy. "I think sharing this with Rick early on allowed me to grow into that role and make sure that I was ready to take it on."

In 19 of his 22 seasons, Ray Bourque was named either First or Second Team NHL All-Star. That means in every year of his 22-season career, save for three, Bourque was viewed as one of the top four defensemen in the league. Which is consistent, excellent—and astounding.

THE BROTHERHOOD OF THE BRUINS

THE BRUINS HAVE always been a brotherhood.

"I will never forget Milt Schmidt, who was our alumni coach when I first took over the alumni [in the late 2000s]," said Bob Sweeney. "He said 'Bob, anyone that played one game for the Bruins is a Bruins alumni.'"

That spirit was never more evident than on December 3, 1987, the evening that the Bruins retired Phil Esposito's No. 7 jersey in a ceremony at Boston Garden. Ray Bourque had worn that same No. 7 since 1979. No one was expecting Bourque to give up the number.

But Bourque did. Willingly. And with Hollywood-like drama.

As Bourque remembers, "What was going to happen with the number wasn't decided until 1:00 PM that afternoon.... Harry [Sinden] called me, and we spoke about what and how we were going to do this that night. And it worked out amazingly well, because no press, no fans, no teammates, nobody knew other than my wife, the trainers, and management of the Bruins.... What we decided to do was that I was going to go out with No. 7 in warmups, come back after warmups, and go in the back room—in the trainer's room—and put No. 77 underneath."

Moments later, during the on-ice ceremony, Bourque dramatically took off his No. 7 jersey to reveal his jersey with his new number No. 77, thereby assuring Esposito's sole possession of No. 7.

"Watching him taking it off, I was thinking, *What the [bleep] are you doing, Ray?*" said Esposito. "It was unbelievable. And he said something to me that will stay with me forever. He said, 'This is yours, big guy. And it always should've been yours. And it never should've been anybody else's.'"

"I did a lot of things in 22 years, but the thing that comes up the most when people meet me is that night," said Bourque. "It was a great, great night just to see

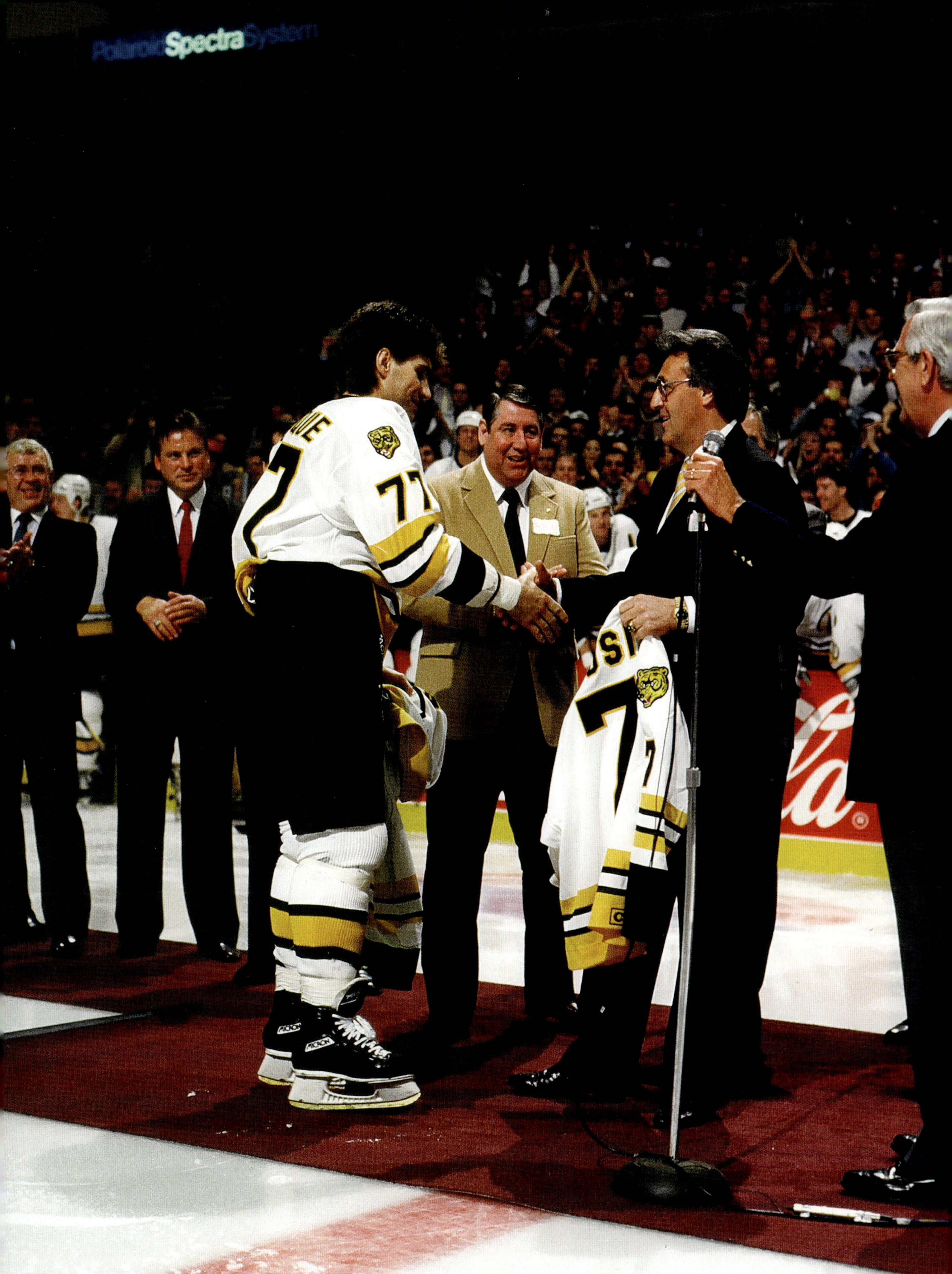
Polaroid Spectra System
77

Phil Esposito's face, his reaction when that happened." Indeed, it is nearly impossible to render Phil Esposito speechless—but, for once in his life, Phil Esposito was speechless.

Other Bruins legends took notice, too. "I thought it was just wonderful," said Bobby Orr. "And that 77 looked pretty good on Raymond, too, didn't it? And he did pretty well with 77."

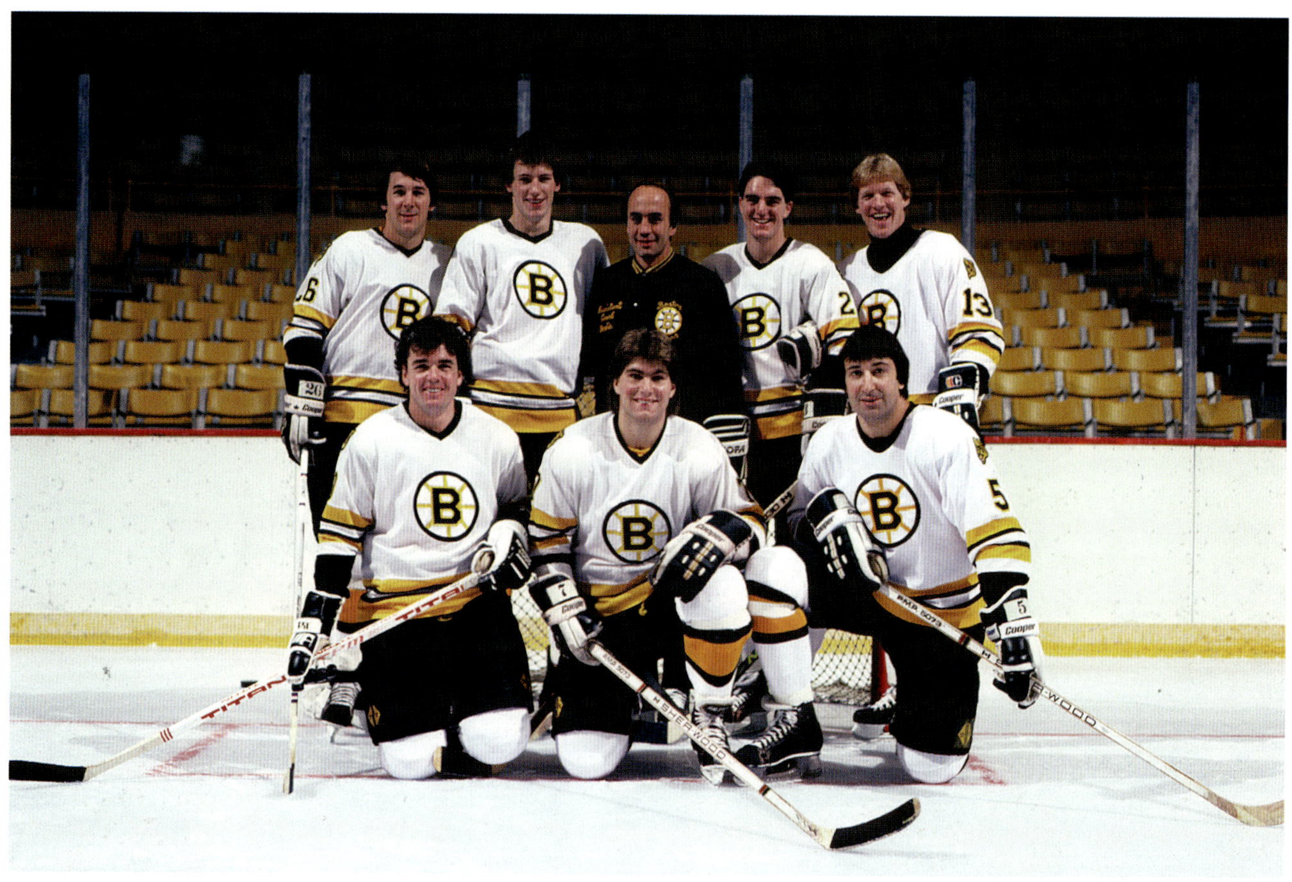

The Bruins defensive corps during the 1984–85 season included: (front row, left to right) Mike O'Connell, Ray Bourque, and Guy Lapointe; (back row, left to right) Mike Milbury, Gord Kluzak, assistant coach Gary Doak, Randy Hillier, and Jim Schoenfeld. (Photo by Steve Babineau/NHLI via Getty Images)

THE END OF THE MONTREAL JINX

Between 1946 and 1987, the Bruins and Canadiens met in the Stanley Cup playoffs 18 times. The Canadiens won all 18 series.

And then came 1988.

The two teams met in the Adams Division Finals that spring. And it looked like the same old story when the Canadiens won the first game 5–2. As Bruins forward Bob Sweeney said, "I remember vividly, the first game, we got smoked.... Someone stood up in the room and said, 'Hey, it is just one game. It is just one game.'"

Indeed it was. The Bruins won the next three games to take a 3–1 series lead. Going back to the Montreal Forum for Game 5, though, the outcome was hardly assured. How many times had the Canadiens stormed back to break the hearts of the Bruins and their fans?

But not this time. On that fateful late April night in the Forum, Cam Neely and Steve Kasper each scored twice and goaltender Reggie Lemelin, as he had all series, stoned the Canadiens to give the Bruins a 4–1, series-clinching victory. And the "Montreal Jinx" was, at long last, over.

The victory had a huge impact. Ray Bourque will never forget "coming back from Montreal after winning that fifth game and having 5,000 people just waiting for us at Logan, where we had to have a state trooper guide us out of the airport because of the fans." Echoed Bob Sweeney, "It was amazing to see the reaction. It was unbelievable at the airport. So many people came out. You would have thought we won the Stanley Cup!"

The Bruins didn't win the Cup that year, of course. After getting past the New Jersey Devils in a seven-game slugfest in the Eastern Conference Finals, they fell to the Edmonton Oilers in the Stanley Cup Final. The Oilers were at the apex of their dynasty, thanks to an all-star lineup that included Mark Messier, Paul Coffey, and, of course, Wayne Gretzky—and while the Bruins competed, they were ultimately overmatched. The series was marked by the bizarre events of Game 4, which saw fog shrouding the ice in the 80-degree Boston Garden, followed by the overloading of a switch that led to a chain of events that knocked out all but the emergency lights late in the second period. The game (which was tied at the time, 3–3) had to be postponed and moved to Edmonton, where the Oilers prevailed to complete the sweep and take the Cup.

But it was a sweet off-season nonetheless.

"I went back to Montreal every summer and had to hear about how we lost to Montreal again in the playoffs," said Bourque. "After '87–88, that summer was the quietest summer I ever had in Montreal. It was awesome."

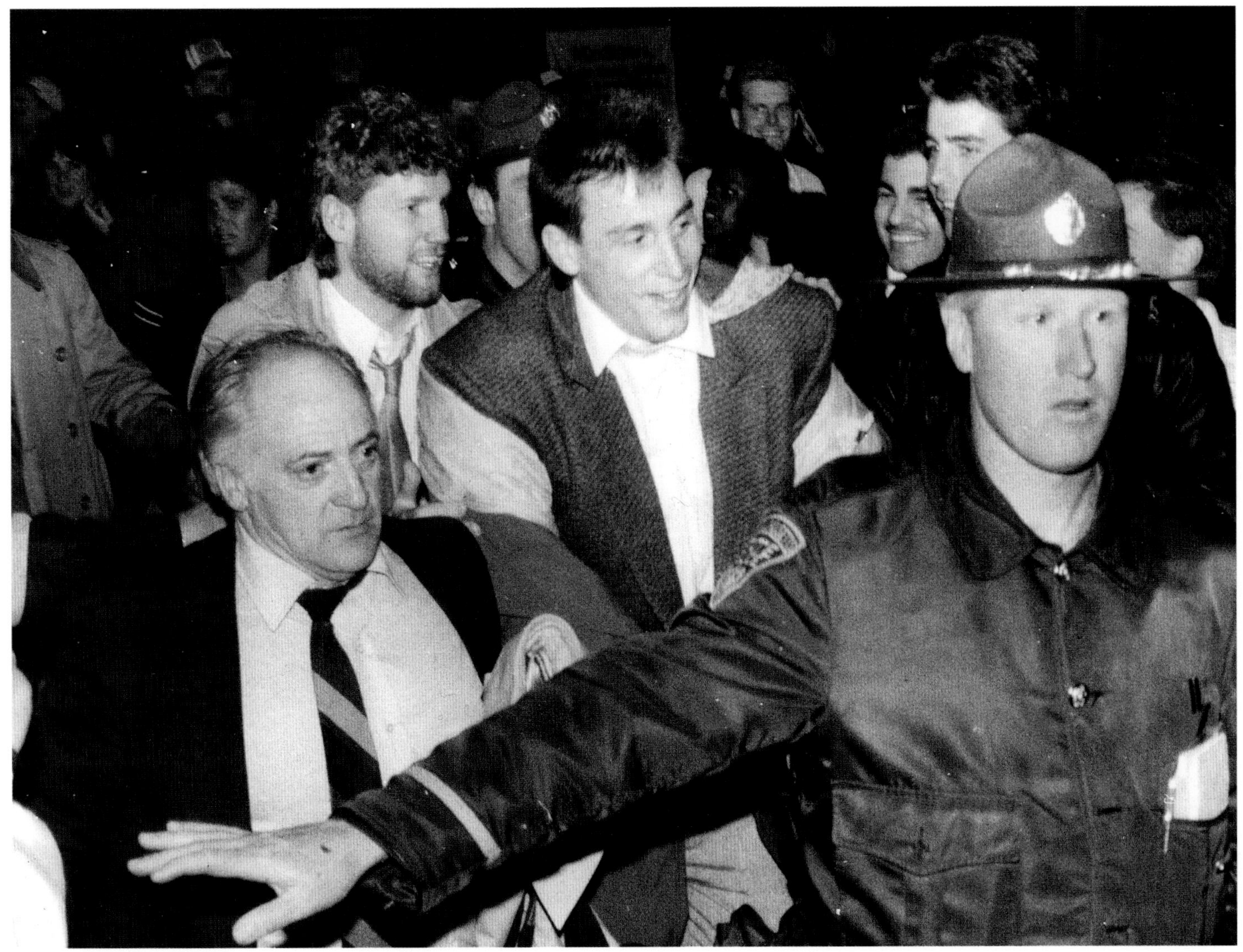

The Massachusetts State Police escort Lyndon Byers (left) and Cam Neely (right) through a crowd of delirious fans at Logan Airport as they return home from Montreal after conquering the Canadiens in the 1988 Stanley Cup playoffs. It was the end of the Montreal Jinx, once and for all. (Photograph by Bob Dean/The Boston Globe via Getty Images)

THE RIVALRY

by Michael Farber

Death, taxes, and the first penalty in the Forum.
—Harry Sinden

We hold these truths to be self-evident...
—Declaration of Independence

THERE IS INDEPENDENCE and there is codependence. Right there is the essence of the nearly century-old, intertwined history of the Boston Bruins and Montreal Canadiens.

They exist separately but are inexorably linked, one animating the other, bringing all the ecstasy and frustration of life—and hockey—to the Original Six soul. They need each other, these heritage franchises, like Federer needed Nadal and the Roadrunner needed Wile E. Coyote. While the Acme anvil kept falling on the Black and Gold for most of the 20th century, New Englanders can take solace in knowing the rivalry expanded the hockey lexicon thanks to a sage observer, Harry Sinden.

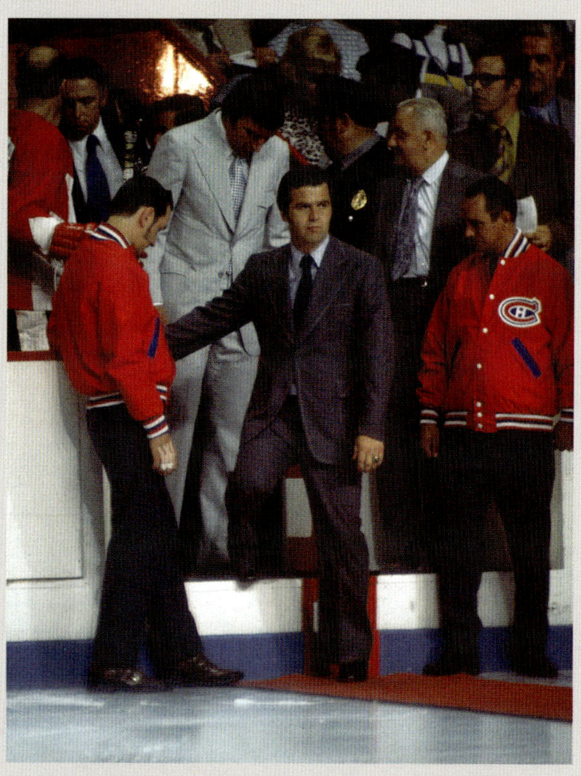

Harry Sinden coined the hockey truism of "Death, taxes, and the first penalty in the Forum" in reference to a visiting team's experiences at the Montreal Forum. (Photograph by Melchior DiGiacomo/Getty Images)

The Bruins coach and later general manager is a colorful figure in Bruins vs. Canadiens history. That color is orange. During a late-1980s playoff game when the broom closet that passed for the visitors' dressing room in the Forum was stuck (or locked) and his players were stranded in the corridor during an intermission, Sinden's apoplectic face zoomed past scarlet to a shade of orange rarely seen outside of undercooked salmon. "The Forum Ghosts Had Keys" might not be a bad title for Harry's memoirs.

As I noted in a 2014 *Sports Illustrated* story that marked the 35th anniversary of the "Too Many Men on the Ice" game in 1979, there are striking similarities between cities separated by some 300 miles, a border, and a language. Not fraternal-twins striking. Maybe more like second-cousins striking. There are the accents, both spoken ("number fawh") and written (like the *aigu* over Béliveau). There are the drivers, all aggressive as Terry O'Reilly. There are notable universities (I have been informed that Harvard is the McGill of the United States).

And religious motifs seep into the core of both teams. A 103-foot cross stands sentry atop Mount Royal, representative of a city and, by extension, a team whose sweaters are sometimes referred to, without a hint of irony, as *La Sainte-Flanelle*. (French 101. The Holy Flannel.) You might even recall a Montreal goaltender who was dubbed St. Patrick. Meanwhile, the Protestant work ethic was the nucleus of Don Cherry's Lunch Pail A.C. and Calvinist predestination is a fixture of Bruins lore (see "Death, taxes, et al.").

You also might have noticed some cross-pollination in the fan bases. Game recognizes game, irrespective of geography. The Canadiens have a significant following in New England, likely fueled by echoes of the Franco-American migration, the sexy Flying Frenchmen of the 1970s, and a front-running fan's natural attraction to a record 24 Stanley Cups. The Bruins also have noisy support in Montreal, a testament to the legacy of Bobby Orr, the Bruins' traditional physical style, and—something that should be recognized more widely—the career of Stan Jonathan, who remains a guiding light to the Indigenous communities around Montreal. Bruins fans travel well. The bars on Crescent Street say hello.

The Bruins and Canadiens have played in more than 900 regular-season games, have contested a record 34 playoff series, and have produced innumerable

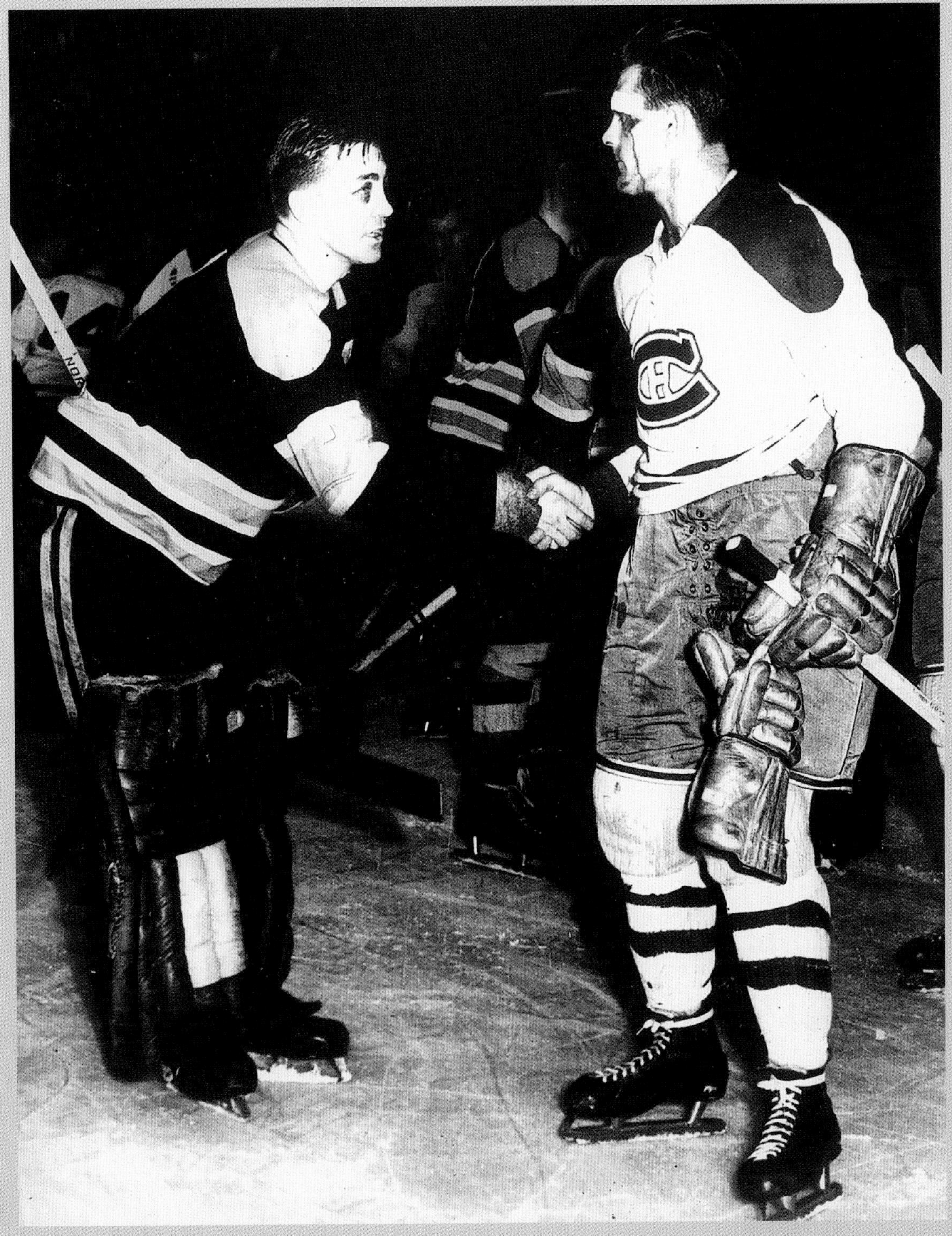

Bruins goalie "Sugar" Jim Henry and Canadiens forward Maurice "Rocket" Richard shake hands after Montreal's 3–1 win over Boston in Game 7 of the 1952 Stanley Cup Semifinals. This iconic image of "the Handshake" reflects both the intensity and the respect that has long marked the Boston-Montreal rivalry. (Courtesy of the John Brooks Collection)

heroes and villains. Their relationship is also the subject of one of the most memorable sports photographs of all. The Rocket. Sugar Jim. Handshake line. You probably know the photo almost as well as Flying Bobby, but maybe not the backstory. Here goes.

Maurice Richard had been knocked unconscious early in Game 7 of the 1952 Stanley Cup Semifinals playoff match. (Quebec author Roch Carrier: "The Rocket collapses onto his back, spread-eagles, arms outstretched. Fans think of the crucified Christ.") He returned late in the third period and scored the winning goal. Later at center ice, the semi-conscious Rocket, blood oozing from his bandages and Bruins goaltender Sugar Jim Henry, whose eyes had blackened after suffering a broken nose the previous game, shook hands. Henry bowed slightly from the waist, almost an act of deference.

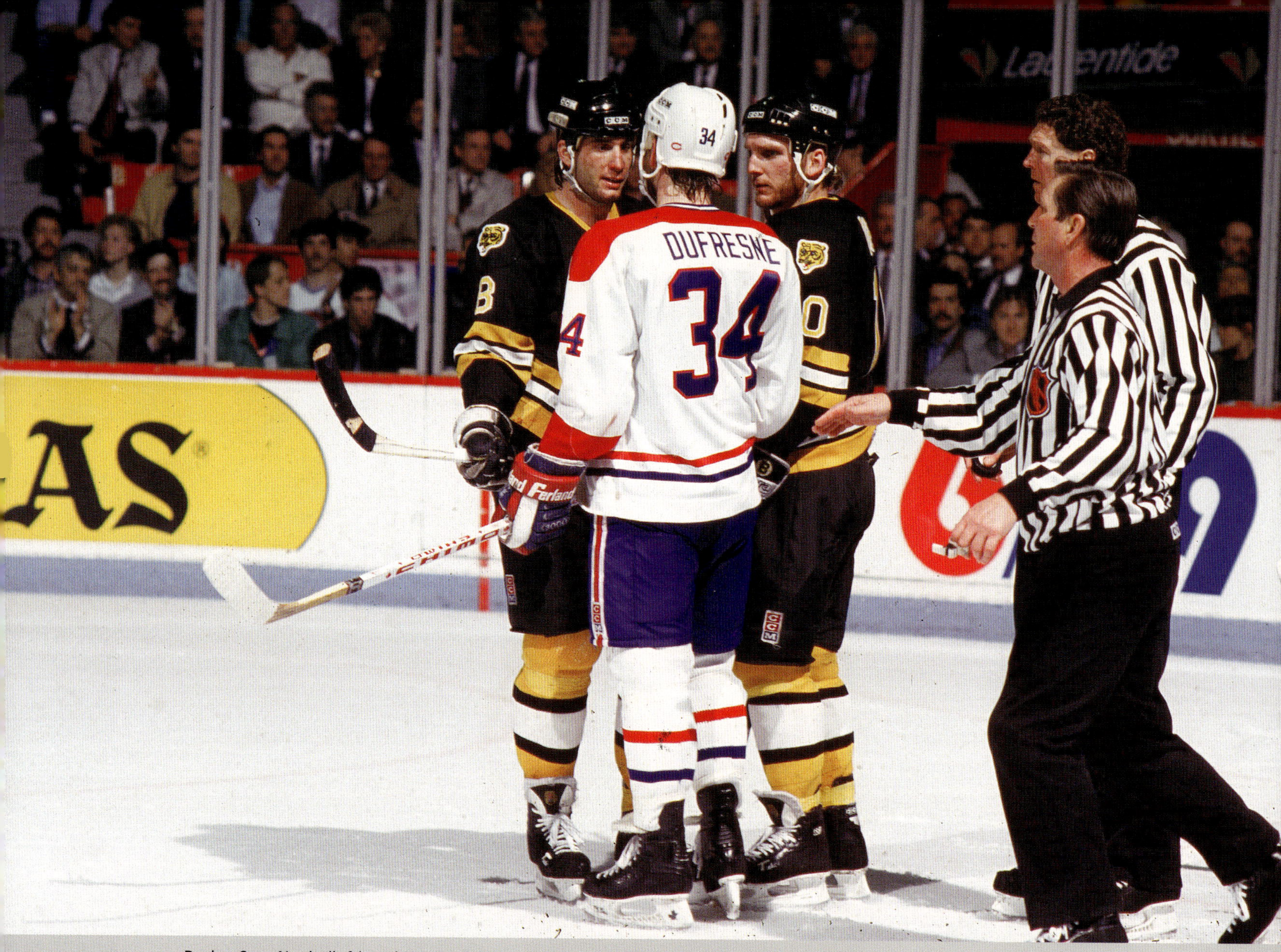

Bruins Cam Neely (left) and Ken Hodge Jr. exchange pleasantries with Donald Dufresne of the Canadiens during a game at the Montreal Forum in 1991. (Photograph by Brian Miller/Getty Images)

There are two things to take away from the indelible tableau:

1. The respect between the players, and, by extension, the franchises.
2. Montreal won Game 7.

The Handshake Game was the first of a record nine Game 7s between the Bruins and Montreal. (The Canadiens have won six.) The next two hurt Boston more than Sugar Jim's disfigured mug that April night.

At the height of their Orr/Espo dominance, the Big Bad Bruins should have claimed full ownership of the early 1970s. Instead, Montreal happened. Nineteen seventy-one. Backstopped by a rookie who had played just six regular-season games, the Canadiens readied for Game 7 at the Garden. Before the match, Montreal GM Sam Pollock, who generally gave players a wide berth, entered the dressing room. "Well, we've come this far. Might as well win it," said Pollock, who spun on his heels and marched out. Montreal 4, Boston 2. The upset derailed what could have been, what should have been, three straight Cups. Phil Esposito labeled the kid goalie "a thieving giraffe." Ken Dryden. In 1964, when Dryden was 16, Boston had drafted him in the third round. Just 17 days later, the Bruins flipped the college-bound Dryden to Montreal.

All bad things seem to come in threes. The Handshake Game. A Thieving Giraffe. Too Many Men on the Ice. In the 1979 Stanley Cup Semifinals, Montreal, exhausted by three long Stanley Cup campaigns, was practically begging to be beaten. And then the Bruins beat themselves. The Game 7 penalty in the dying moments was too obvious to ignore. The ice was jammed with so many Bruins it could have been the Sagamore Bridge on a July weekend. Guy Lafleur beat Gilles Gilbert cleanly with a superb 40-foot power play slapper off the right wing to tie it, Yvon Lambert cashed in during overtime, and Montreal would go on to win a fourth straight Cup on muscle memory.

Some Canadiens, among them Serge Savard, believe there is a genetic flaw in the rough-and-tumble Bruins, something in their DNA that might undermine them at critical moments. This is the height of Montreal arrogance, mythologizing run amok. Or not.

Nineteen eighty-four, 1985, 1986, 1987. The Canadiens ran their winning streak to 18 playoff series against Boston, a span of four-plus decades and a couple of dynasties. Then, 1988. This Adams Division Finals felt different right from Game 1 when, at 8:08 PM, a faulty transmission line in Churchill Falls, Newfoundland, blew, plunging the province of Quebec into darkness. There were no lights anywhere, except in the Forum, where, courtesy of a generator, the game continued in shadows that made the ice look like a film noir. (Curiously, this power outage was in direct contrast to Boston where, weeks later, during Game 4 of the Stanley Cup Final, the only power outage in Massachusetts was at the Garden. With the heat and fog and gloom, the old barn resembled the airport scene in *Casablanca*.) The Canadiens won that powerless night in Montreal, but Boston took the next four, including a spirited Game 3 at home when Montreal coach Jean Perron sent out his hammerheads for a second-period faceoff. Bruins coach Terry O'Reilly countered with Lyndon Byers and Jay Miller. Mayhem ensued. When asked later about the flurry of fights, Taz, failing to suppress a grin, said, "I was just matching lines." That night a banner with Greek lettering hung on the end-arena balcony. When two reporters collared a native speaker to translate, they discovered it read, "Eat shit, Chelios," which prompted *Globe* columnist Leigh Montville to observe, "That's why they call Boston the Athens of America."

Montreal and Boston met in five of the next six springs. The Bruins won four. And so the foofaraw continued, although since the mid-1990s these annual spectacles have occurred sporadically, like reunions of families whose children have grown. In 2004, Montreal rallied from being down three games to one. In 2011, Nathan Horton scored the Game 7 winner, the third Boston overtime victory. Horton's goal capped a tumultuous year for the rivalry. In March of that year, Zdeno Chara had driven Max Pacioretty inadvertently into a padded stanchion in the Bell Centre. The Canadiens winger sustained a broken vertebra in his neck plus a concussion, prompting an eight-month investigation by Montreal police. This was the millennial version of the rivalry. In the 20th century, the only cops summoned were John Ferguson and Chris Nilan and John Kordic and Gilles Lupien and Bruce Shoebottom and Lyndon Byers and Stan Jonathan and Jay Miller...

It's quiet. The playoffs have muddled on without Boston vs. Montreal for coming up on a decade. We can only hope they will visit again soon, allowing us to retrieve musty recollections of Adams Division spring battles tucked away in the footlocker of memory. The old Forum is an entertainment complex now, and the ghosts haven't been in any particular hurry to float a mile east to haunt the Bell Centre. And the Causeway Street vermin—no, not Ken Linseman—are scarce at the TD Garden. The world evolves.

But like the first penalty at the Forum, you sort of hope some things stay the same.

Michael Farber was a *Montreal Gazette* columnist and later a senior writer for *Sports Illustrated*. He and his wife live in the town where Raymond Bourque played Juniors.

BOSTON BRUINS (1980–1989)

Season	W	L	T	PTS	PTS%	Finish	Playoffs	Coach	Division	Conference
1979–80	46	21	13	105	.656	2nd of 5	Lost NHL Quarterfinals	Fred Creighton (40–20–13) Harry Sinden (6–1–0)	Adams	Prince of Wales
1980–81	37	30	13	87	.544	2nd of 5	Lost NHL Preliminary Round	Gerry Cheevers	Adams	Prince of Wales
1981–82	43	27	10	96	.600	2nd of 5	Lost NHL Division Finals	Gerry Cheevers	Adams	Prince of Wales
1982–83	50	20	10	110	.688	1st of 5	Lost NHL Conference Finals	Gerry Cheevers	Adams	Prince of Wales
1983–84	49	25	6	104	.650	1st of 5	Lost NHL Division Semifinals	Gerry Cheevers	Adams	Prince of Wales
1984–85	36	34	10	82	.513	4th of 5	Lost NHL Division Semifinals	Gerry Cheevers (25–24–7) Harry Sinden (11–10–3)	Adams	Prince of Wales
1985–86	37	31	12	86	.538	3rd of 5	Lost NHL Division Semifinals	Butch Goring	Adams	Prince of Wales
1986–87	39	34	7	85	.531	3rd of 5	Lost NHL Division Semifinals	Butch Goring (5–7–1) Terry O'Reilly (34–27–6)	Adams	Prince of Wales
1987–88	44	30	6	94	.588	2nd of 5	Lost Stanley Cup Final	Terry O'Reilly	Adams	Prince of Wales
1988–89	37	29	14	88	.550	2nd of 5	Lost NHL Division Finals	Terry O'Reilly	Adams	Prince of Wales

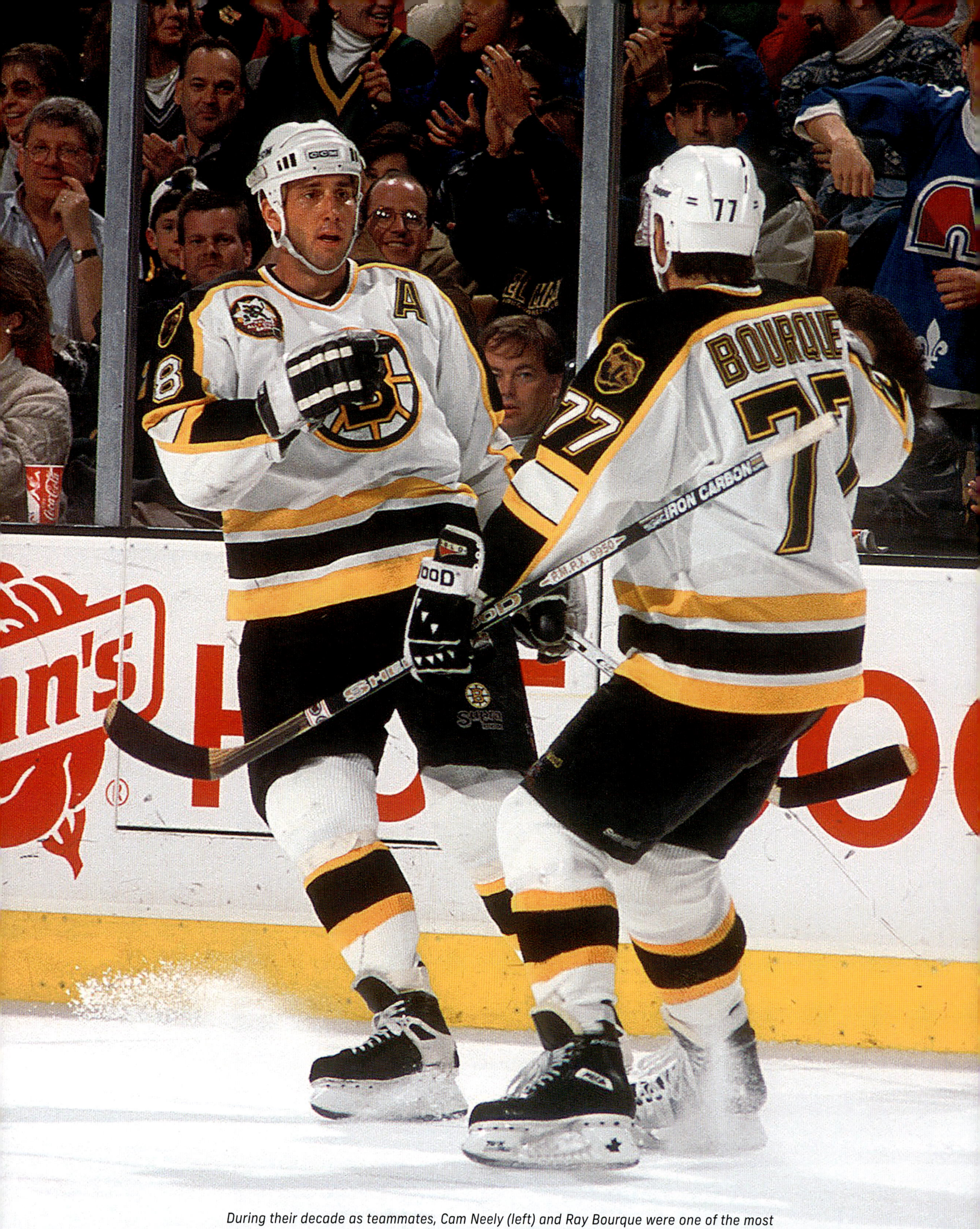

During their decade as teammates, Cam Neely (left) and Ray Bourque were one of the most formidable tandems in team and league history. They were the key players on the Bruins teams that advanced to the Stanley Cup Final in 1988 and 1990. (Photograph by Steve Babineau/NHLI via Getty Images)

1990s

HELLO GOODBYE

First off, right off the top, best place to play…ever.

—Andy Brickley, Bruins right wing and NESN color analyst, on Boston Garden

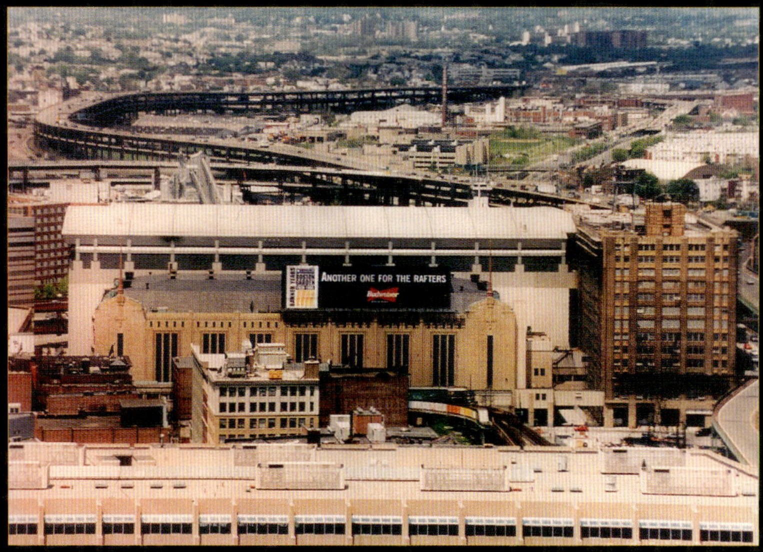

The FleetCenter, which opened in 1995, was the first major sports facility built in Boston since Boston Garden in 1928. (Photograph courtesy of TD Garden)

The 1990s were years of triumphs, trials, and transition for the Boston Bruins. The greatest triumphs occurred in the early 1990s—and especially in the first season of the decade (1989–90), when Mike Milbury led Boston to the Stanley Cup Final against Edmonton in his rookie season as head coach. The playoff run capped a season in which the Bruins were the lone NHL team to reach the 100-point regular season threshold. Over the next several years, the winning ways continued, thanks to the dominance of the NHL's first power forward in Cam Neely, the continued year-over-year excellence of Ray Bourque, and the contributions of a strong supporting cast that included playmaking center Adam Oates and the goaltending tandem of Reggie Lemelin and Andy Moog.

The trials came later in the decade, after the 1995–96 season that saw the Bruins extend their North American pro sports record of consecutive postseason playoff appearances to 29 seasons. In 1996–97, that streak finally came to an end—and the team bottomed out, finishing with the worst record in the NHL. The next two seasons, the Bruins would climb back to respectability under new head coach Pat Burns, but clearly more progress would need to be made for the Bruins to bring the Stanley Cup back to Boston.

The transition involved home ice. In October 1995, the Bruins bid farewell to the old Boston Garden and welcomed a new, state-of-the-art "Boston Garden arena" to town. Everyone agreed that the original Boston Garden had long outlived its shelf life and that the new Garden (initially known as the FleetCenter and now officially known as TD Garden) was sorely needed. Still, saying goodbye to the old building was a huge adjustment for the Bruins and their fans.

As the Bruins closed out the 20th century, they found themselves well-positioned to continue competing at the top ranks of the NHL as one of the league's flagship franchises.

CAM NEELY

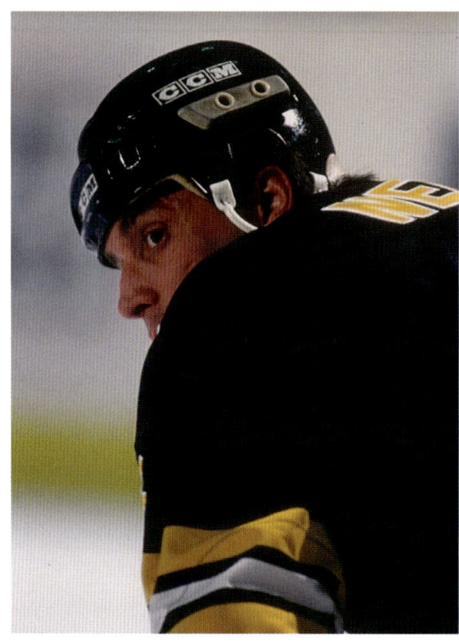

Cam Neely was tough, tenacious, and talented. Add it all up and you had one of the best players of his generation—or any generation, for that matter.
(Photograph by Rick Stewart, courtesy of the Boston Bruins)

The Bruins acquired Cam Neely from Vancouver in 1986 for Barry Pederson. It turned out to be a masterstroke of a deal, with Neely proving to be a perfect match for the team's DNA.

At the time, though, Neely was an unknown quantity. He was just 21 years of age, and his first three seasons in the NHL had been under the radar and unremarkable. Neely himself had his doubts. "When I was struggling to get ice time in Vancouver and then found out I was traded to Boston," he said, "I was like 'Oh, boy, where is my career going? I'm having trouble getting minutes in Vancouver. How am I ever going to get minutes in Boston?' I wasn't really sure where my career was headed at that point.... It was really more about being the best player I could be and staying in the league."

Neely would stay in the league—and then some. In his first season as a Bruin in 1986–87, he immediately made his mark by leading the team in goals with 36. The goals would keep coming (he would end up scoring 344 goals in 525 career games with the Bruins) and a distinctive style of play would emerge. The Neely brand of hockey involved a blend of physicality, toughness, and power, with an overarching relentlessness and a pronounced goal-scorer's mentality. Add it all up, and you had what many regard as the ultimate Boston Bruin.

"Even as a kid, I liked playing physical," said Neely. "I felt that this was a big part of my game. Then at the NHL level, it certainly helped my game, and I think it was one of those situations where I said to myself, 'It's easier to be physical than to score goals in this league.'... That's how I had to play to be successful."

"Everyone who played against Cam had to keep his head up because Cam would crush you and then go in and score a goal," said longtime teammate Ray Bourque.

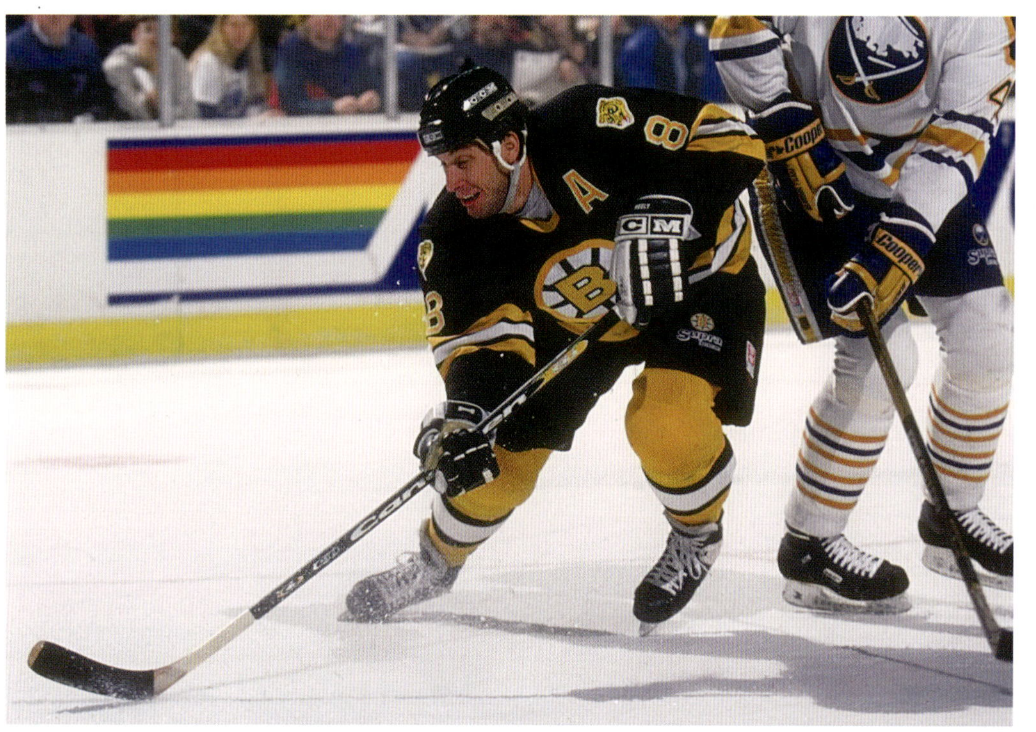

Cam Neely had a nose for the net—and a penchant for finding the back of the net, too. In three seasons (1990, 1991, and 1994), he scored 50 or more goals. Other than Phil Esposito (with five), no one has more such seasons in franchise history.
(Photograph by Rick Stewart, Collection of The Sports Museum)

Neely was one of the best players in the NHL in 1990 and 1991, putting up back-to-back 50-goal seasons. Then, in the 1991 Eastern Conference Finals, he was the target of one of the most flagrant hits in NHL history, delivered by Ulf Samuelsson of the Penguins. The resulting bruise on Neely's left thigh was so severe that it caused Neely's thigh muscles to calcify and led to knee surgery that limited him to 22 games over the next two seasons.

Neely roared back in 1993–94 with one of the greatest individual performances in NHL history. Even though he missed some time to rest his knee and then suffered a season-ending injury in March, Neely still managed to score 50 goals in just 44 games. His magnificent season was a story of power, perseverance, and his mastery as a goal scorer. "People talk about his brute strength," said teammate Adam Oates. "But they forget about his brain. You don't score that many goals without reading the ice."

Neely played two more seasons with the Bruins before injuries forced him into retirement. In 2004, the Bruins retired his No. 8 to the rafters of TD Garden, and in 2005, he was inducted into the Hockey Hall of Fame. The Bruins named him their eighth team president in 2010, the first former Bruins player to hold the position.

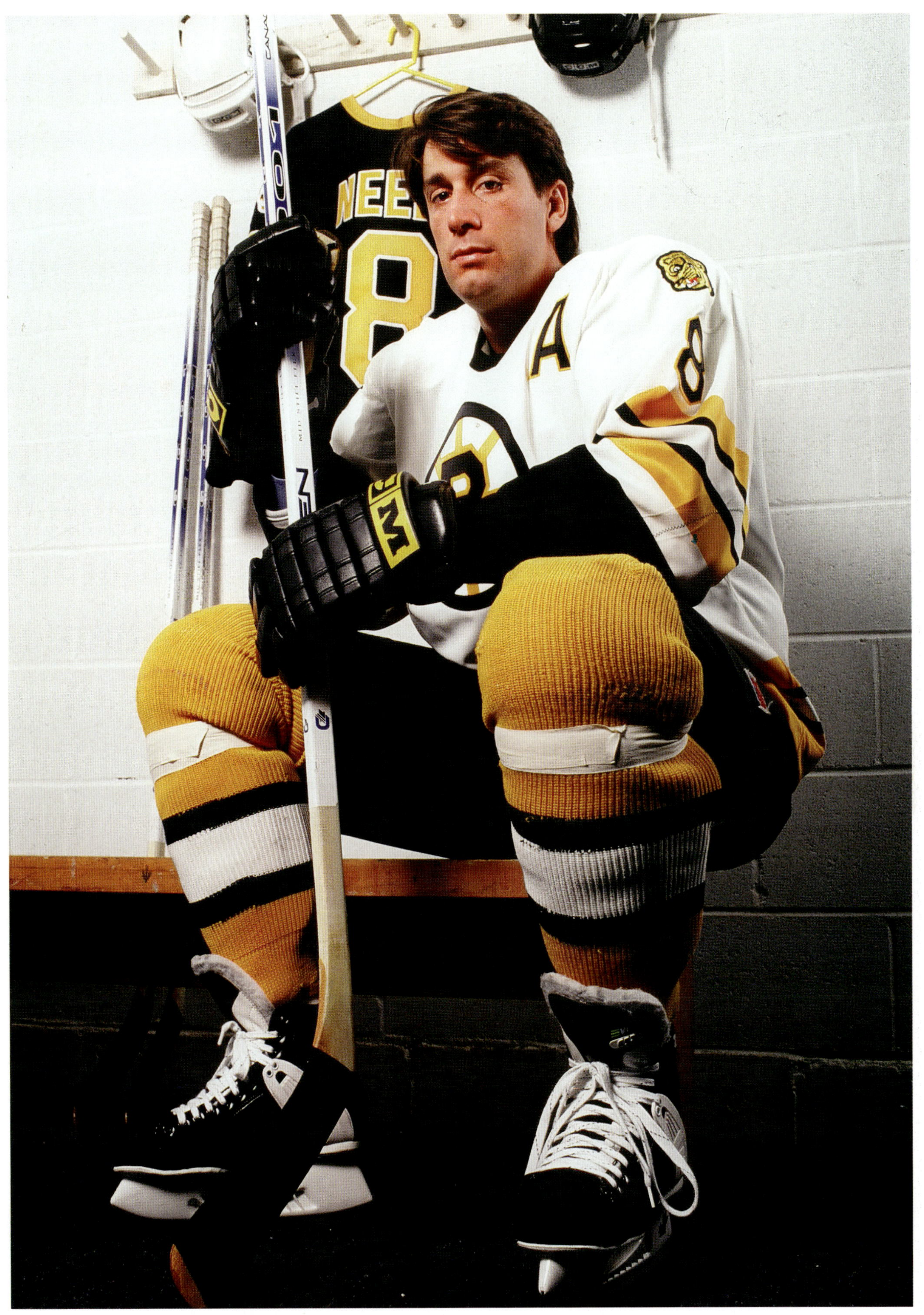

Bruins right wing Cam Neely was focused and intense, a mindset that helped him forge a Hall of Fame career and that made him a Boston sports legend. (Photograph by Steve Babineau/NHLI via Getty Images)

THE 1989–90 TEAM

THE 1989–90 Boston Bruins didn't win the Stanley Cup but may nevertheless have been one of the best teams in franchise history.

"My four years in Boston [1988–1992], we had very good teams," said Andy Brickley. "In '90, we were a great team. We had two unbelievable studs to ride in Bourque and Neely." Then again, there were talented players up and down the roster, including depth at forward (Craig Janney, Bobby Carpenter, Bob Sweeney, Dave Poulin, Randy Burridge, and Brickley himself), a cadre of puck-moving defensemen (Glen Wesley, Don Sweeney, Garry Galley, etc.), and a high-quality goaltending duo of Reggie Lemelin and Andy Moog.

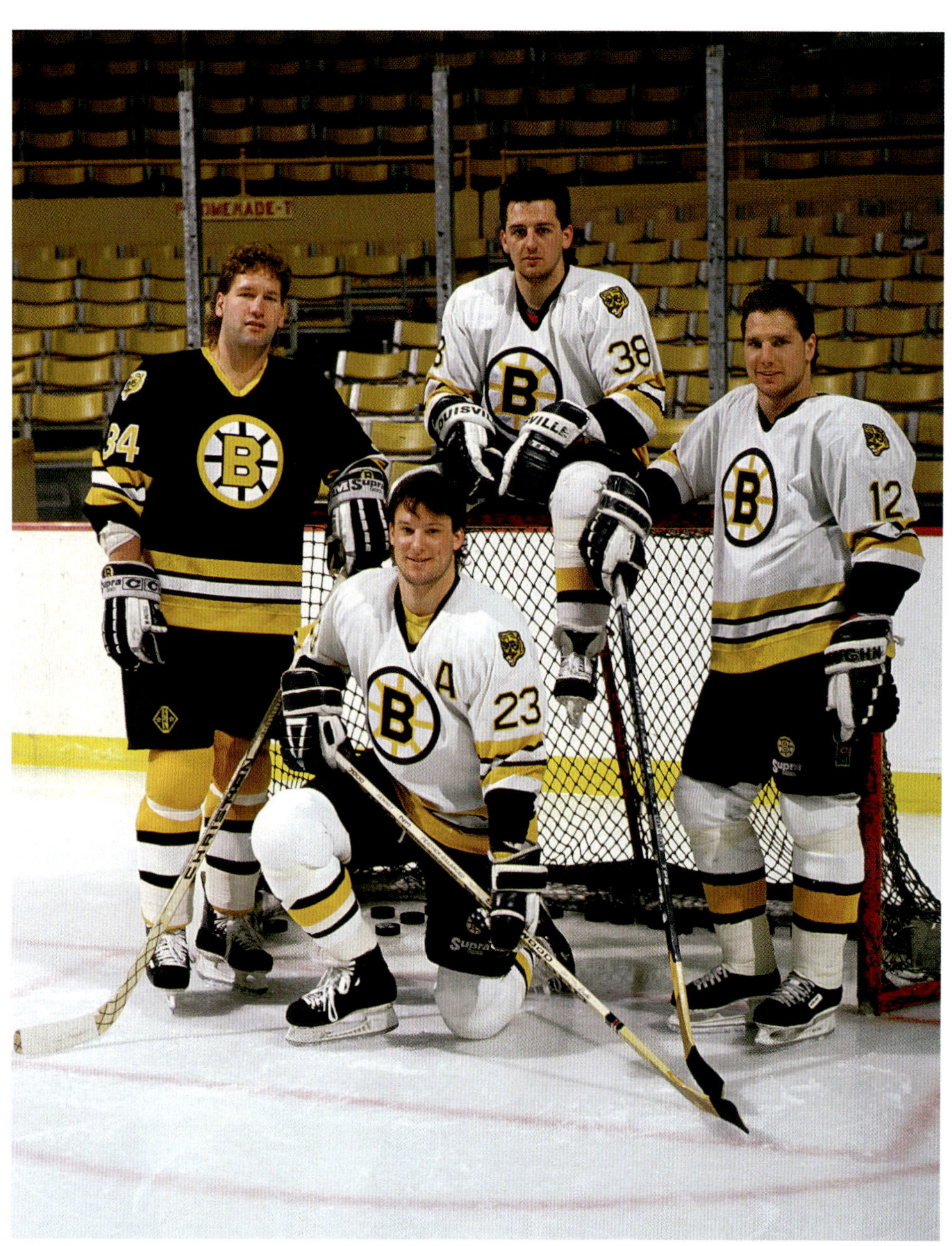

Four valuable contributors to the Bruins in the late 1980s and early 1990s pose at Boston Garden after practice (left to right): physical defenseman Lyndon Byers (34), playmaking center Craig Janney (23), puck-moving blueliner Greg Hawgood (38), and plucky wing Randy Burridge (12). (Photograph by Steve Babineau/NHLI via Getty Images)

"We had great talent," said Brickley. "Really great talent. And we had great leadership and great unity. We had a small locker room...if you look at today's facilities, they are spectacular, but they're spacious. I believe love grows best in small houses, right? We had a small locker room, so we were right on top of each other. I think all that stuff mattered."

The 1989–90 Bruins won the President's Trophy with the best record in the league. In the opening round of the playoffs, they outlasted the Hartford Whalers in seven games, with their victories including a rousing Game 4 comeback to erase a three-goal, third-period deficit. They then steamrolled the Montreal Canadiens (4–1) and swept the Washington Capitals to advance to the Stanley Cup Final. Their opponent would be the Edmonton Oilers, the team that they had met in the Stanley Cup Final just two years earlier in 1988.

"In '90, I thought we matched up way better," said Ray Bourque. "We didn't match up that well in '88, but in '90 I thought we had a real legit shot." The fact that Wayne Gretzky had moved on from Edmonton only increased the optimism among Bruins Nation.

Alas, it was not meant to be. In what remains the longest game in Stanley Cup Final history, the Bruins ended up losing Game 1 at home, a heartbreaking 3–2 loss that ended when Petr Klima connected at 15:13 of the third overtime. The Bruins never really recovered, falling to Edmonton in five games. "I'm not sure we would have won the series had we won Game 1," said Brickley. "But had we won Game 1, I would have liked to play that out, see how that looked. We didn't recover very well in Game 2 after losing the way we lost in Game 1. You don't get down 2–0 on home ice and expect to win a series."

Added Ray Bourque, "It was disappointing that we didn't compete—or make it more of a series than it was." It was, indeed, an anticlimactic end to an inspiring season.

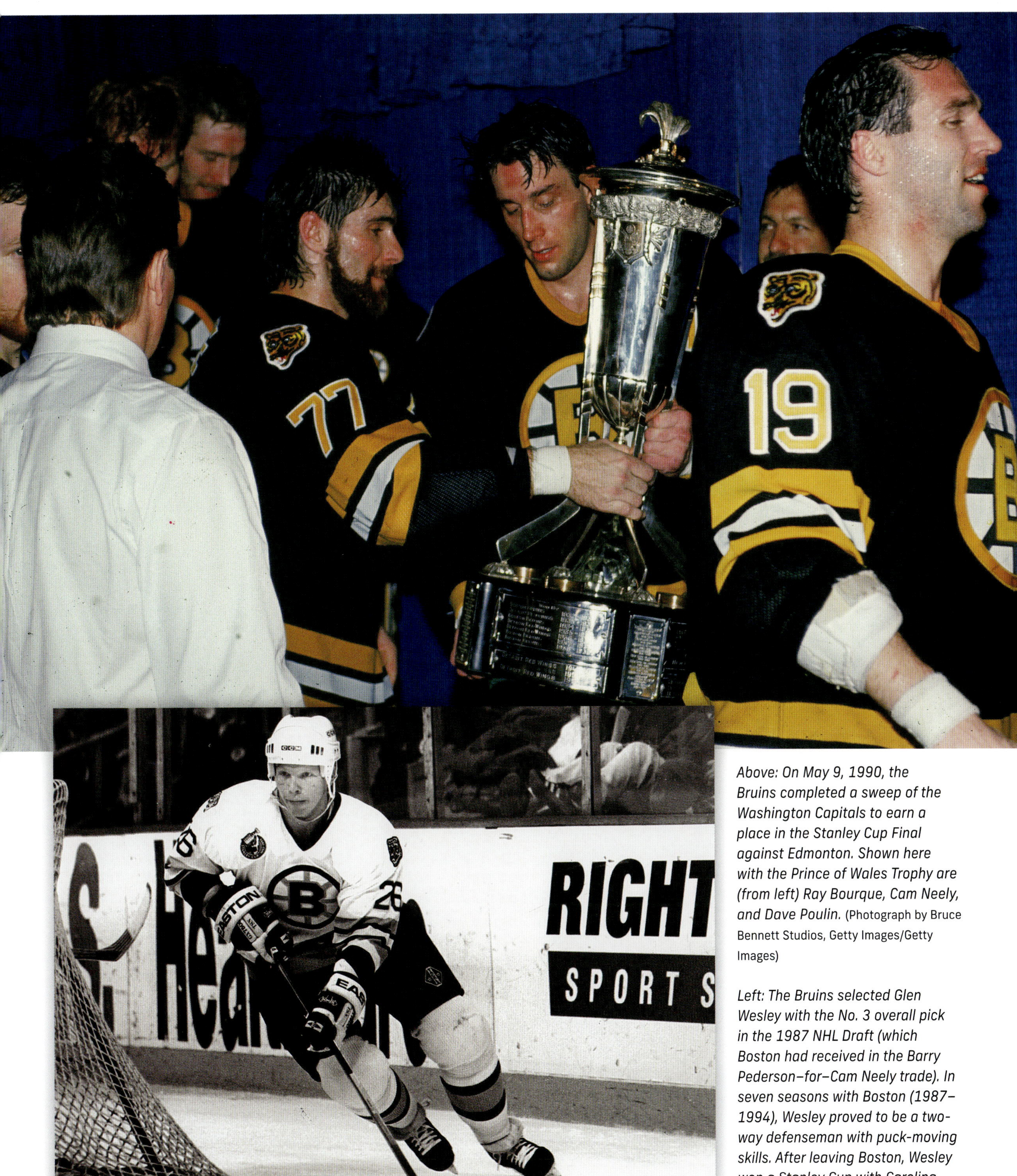

Above: On May 9, 1990, the Bruins completed a sweep of the Washington Capitals to earn a place in the Stanley Cup Final against Edmonton. Shown here with the Prince of Wales Trophy are (from left) Ray Bourque, Cam Neely, and Dave Poulin. (Photograph by Bruce Bennett Studios, Getty Images/Getty Images)

Left: The Bruins selected Glen Wesley with the No. 3 overall pick in the 1987 NHL Draft (which Boston had received in the Barry Pederson–for–Cam Neely trade). In seven seasons with Boston (1987–1994), Wesley proved to be a two-way defenseman with puck-moving skills. After leaving Boston, Wesley won a Stanley Cup with Carolina in 2006. (Photograph by Al Ruelle, Collection of The Sports Museum)

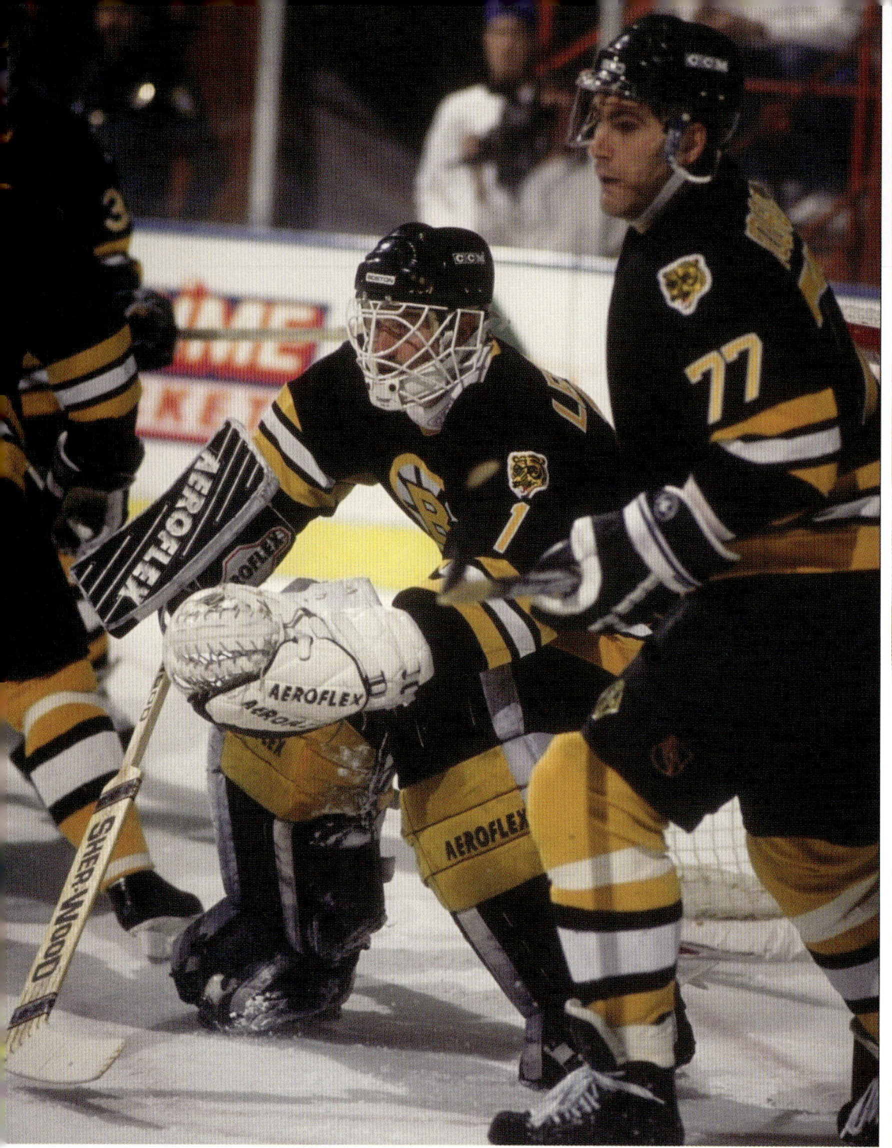

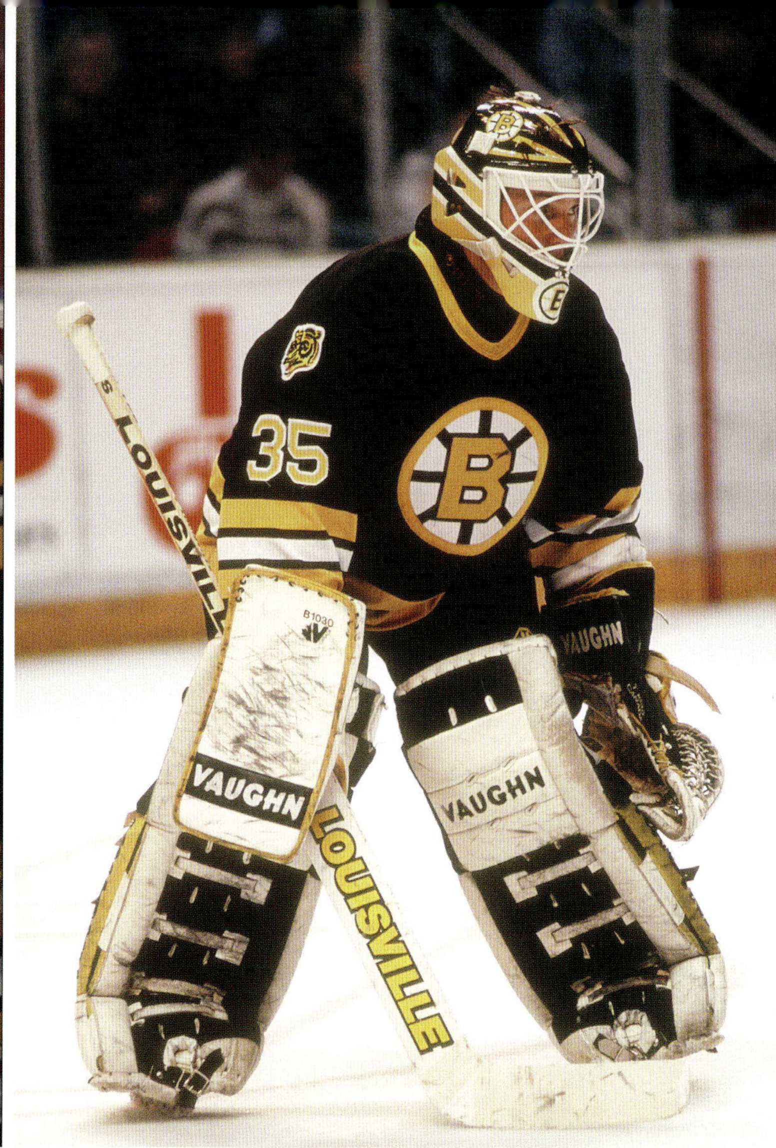

Above, left: Bruins fans will never forget all that Reggie Lemelin did to help bring an end to the "Montreal Jinx" in 1988. For five seasons (1988–1993), he and Andy Moog were one of the best goaltending tandems in Bruins history. (Photograph by Ken Levine/Getty Images)

Above, right: Andy Moog defends his goal against the Hartford Whalers in 1990. Moog was a key playoff performer in 1990 as the Bruins defeated Hartford, Montreal, and Washington on their way to the Stanley Cup Final. (Photograph by Focus on Sport/Getty Images)

REGGIE LEMELIN AND ANDY MOOG

In the late 1960s and early 1970s, the Bruins had a pair of goalies, Gerry Cheevers and Eddie Johnston, who split time and manned the nets. Twenty years later, history repeated itself for the Black and Gold with Reggie Lemelin and Andy Moog.

Lemelin arrived in Boston first, coming to the Bruins as a free agent in 1987 after spending several years backstopping the Calgary Flames. When the Bruins at long last broke the Montreal Jinx in the spring of 1988, Lemelin was one of the heroes. By that time, Moog was on the Bruins roster, too, arriving from Edmonton late in the 1987–88 season. Moog had won three Stanley Cup championships with the Oilers but felt that he was playing in the shadow of goaltender Grant Fuhr.

Together, Lemelin and Moog would win the Jennings Trophy (fewest goals scored against) in the 1989–90 season. More of a tandem than a "starting goalie/backup goalie" arrangement, Moog and Lemelin made for a formidable pair. For the season, Moog went 24-10-7 and Lemelin went 22-15-2 to help propel the Bruins to the top of the NHL.

The two goaltenders took turns between the pipes—and learned from each other, too. "From Reggie I've learned quite a few things about the mind game,' said Moog during the 1990 Stanley Cup playoffs. "Reggie taught me how to be a bit more patient and a little more relaxed. I would get down on myself, and he taught me how to stay relaxed."

After 1990, Moog became more of the No. 1 goalie, with Lemelin serving as the veteran backup. They would each play in Boston until 1993.

REGIONAL RIVALS: BOSTON VS. HARTFORD

A CHARTER MEMBER of the World Hockey Association in 1972, the New England Whalers began playing their games at Boston Garden in the shadow of the Big Bad Bruins. Despite winning the first WHA championship in 1972–73, it was clear that a change of venue was in order for the Whalers, so they moved to Hartford, Connecticut. As part of the NHL-WHA merger in 1979, the NHL absorbed four WHA teams—and the Whalers were one of them.

Re-christened as the Hartford Whalers, they soon emerged as a regional rival of the Boston Bruins. The Bruins had long-standing rivalries with several NHL teams. The Whalers became part of that portfolio.

Things were considerably hotter on the Hartford side of the ledger. "The Bruins, being so close, are the team we've always wanted to beat the most," said Ray Ferraro of the Whalers prior to their 1990 opening-round playoff series versus the Bruins. Boston head coach Mike Milbury sensed the heat. "For the last two months, Hartford has been saying, 'We want Boston,'" said Milbury on the eve of that series. "It's going to be a very big series for them—an emotional series."

Ken Hodge Jr. (10) faces off against Dean Evason of the Hartford Whalers at Boston Garden in the first round of the 1991 playoffs, as Randy Burridge (12) looks on. A product of Boston College, Hodge scored 30 goals that season to make the NHL All-Rookie Team. Meanwhile, the speedy Burridge was a consistent performer for the Bruins for six seasons (1985–1991), earning the nicknames of "Stump" and "Stump Pump" in honor of the fist pump that he did after scoring goals. (Photograph by Focus on Sport via Getty Images)

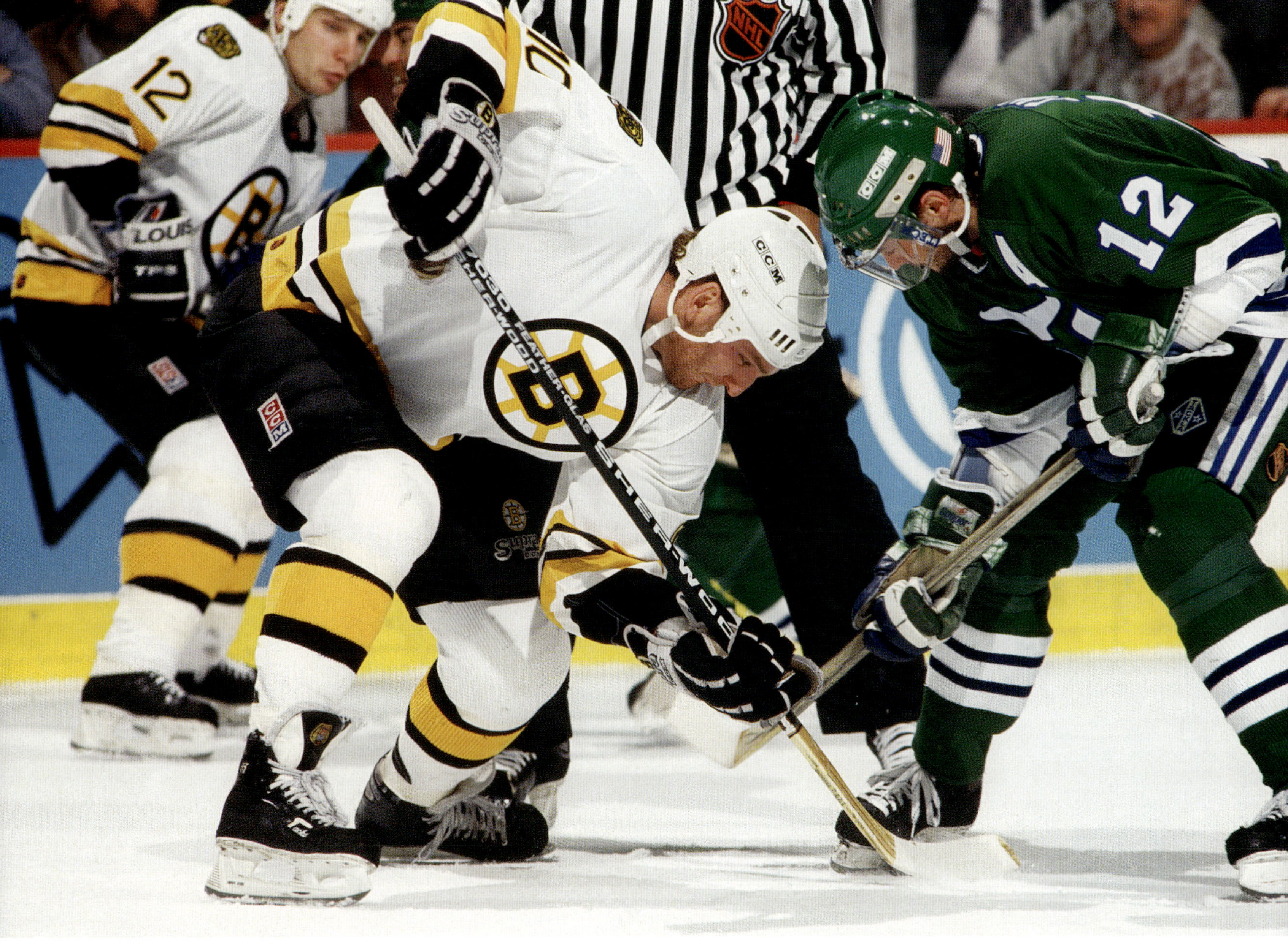

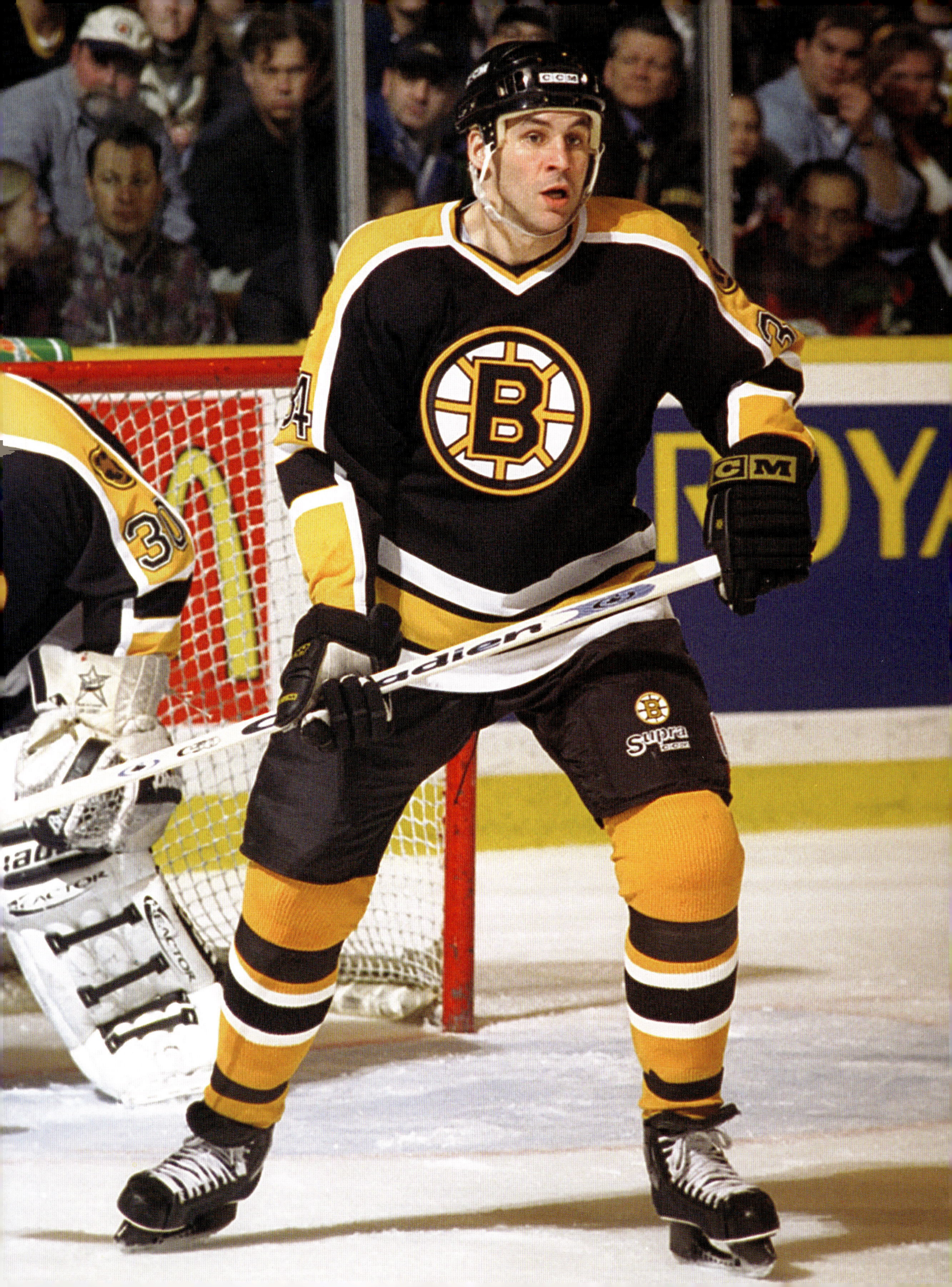
CCM
CCM
Supra
CCM

The Whalers ended up nearly toppling the top-seeded Bruins in that 1990 series. In Game 4 at the Hartford Civic Center, they headed into the third period with a big 5–2 lead. Had they held on, they would have taken a commanding 3–1 series lead. But they didn't hang on. The Bruins mounted a furious third-period comeback, scoring four unanswered goals to prevail 6–5. Boston would go on to win the series on their way to the Stanley Cup Final. The next year, the Bruins would oust the Whalers from the playoffs once again.

In 1997, the Whalers left Hartford and moved to Raleigh, North Carolina, rebranding themselves as the Carolina Hurricanes. And that was the end of the regional rivalry between the Black and Gold and "the Whale."

Opposite page: Defenseman Bob Beers scored a key goal in Boston's epic third-period comeback against Hartford in Game 4 of the opening round of the 1990 Stanley Cup playoffs, helping the Bruins rally from a 5–2 deficit to win 6–5. Beers was a "stay at home" defenseman who skated for the Bruins for four seasons (1989–1992, 1997). Since the late 1990s, he has served as the color analyst on the Bruins radio network, 98.5 The Sports Hub, with his play-by-play partners including Bob Neumeier, Dave Goucher, and, most recently, Judd Sirott. (Photograph by Graig Abel/Getty Images)

HOMETOWN HEROES

IN THE ORIGINAL SIX ERA, very few American-born players found their way into the NHL. The Bruins had a few—star goaltender Frank Brimsek in the 1940s and Olympic hero Tommy Williams in the 1960s, among others—but they were the exception, not the rule.

By the 1990s, the landscape had changed considerably. The league was filled with American players, many of whom played for the Bruins—and many of whom had New England roots. The Bruins players of the 1990s who were either born in New England or who played for local colleges included the likes of Andy Brickley, Bobby Carpenter, John Carter, Ted Donato, Hal Gill, Ken Hodge Jr., Craig Janney, Steve Leach, Shawn McEachern, Chris Nilan, Kevin Stevens, Bob Sweeney, Don Sweeney, and Tim Sweeney. And for all these local players, it was an absolute thrill to play for the Boston Bruins.

Bob Sweeney grew up in Boxborough, Massachusetts, and played at Boston College before enjoying a six-year career with the Bruins that lasted through the 1992 season. "I think any local kid who had the opportunity to be drafted by the Bruins, let alone, play for the Bruins, I think it was a dream come true," he said. "We were all growing up during the era of Bobby Orr, Phil Esposito, Chief, Gerry Cheevers. Obviously no video games then, so everyone played street hockey. We played street hockey almost every day. If you played goal, you were Cheesy. If you were forward, you were Espo. And if you played 'D,' you were Bobby Orr."

"I was eight and 10 when they won the Cups in '70 and '72," said Andy Brickley of Melrose, Massachusetts, and the University of New Hampshire. "Like most kids my age, we all dreamed about not only playing in the National Hockey League but playing for the Boston Bruins and being one of those swashbuckling Boston Bruins players that were so special to all. We loved them, they were our heroes, they were our idols, our champions—and you dreamed about that. And it happened for me.... To play for the Bruins? Are you kidding me? That was the 'be all, end all.'"

Added Bob Sweeney, "If you ask anyone who played and was able to play high school hockey here, then college hockey [here] and then be able to take that next step and eventually put on that Spoked-B, that is something you will never forget. And you're always part of it."

The early 1990s Bruins featured a host of local skaters, including (below, left to right) John Carter (Woburn), Bob Sweeney (Boxborough), head coach Mike Milbury (Walpole), Bobby Carpenter (Peabody), and Andy Brickley (Melrose). For kids who grew up in the Boston area during the Bobby Orr–Phil Esposito era, playing for the Bruins was a dream come true. (Photograph by Steve Babineau/NHLI via Getty Images)

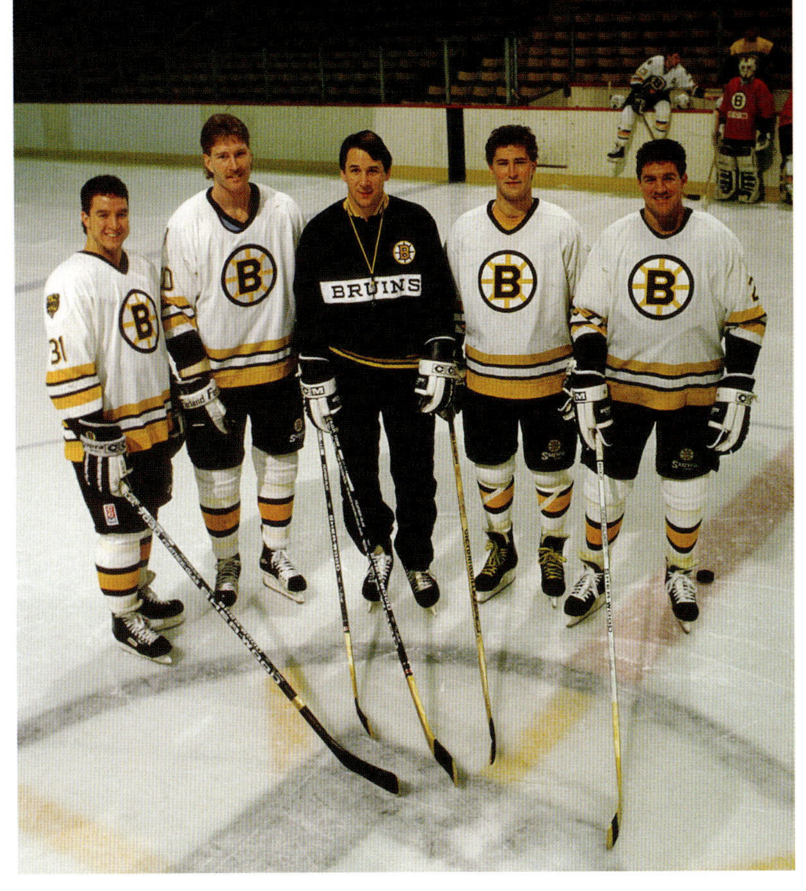

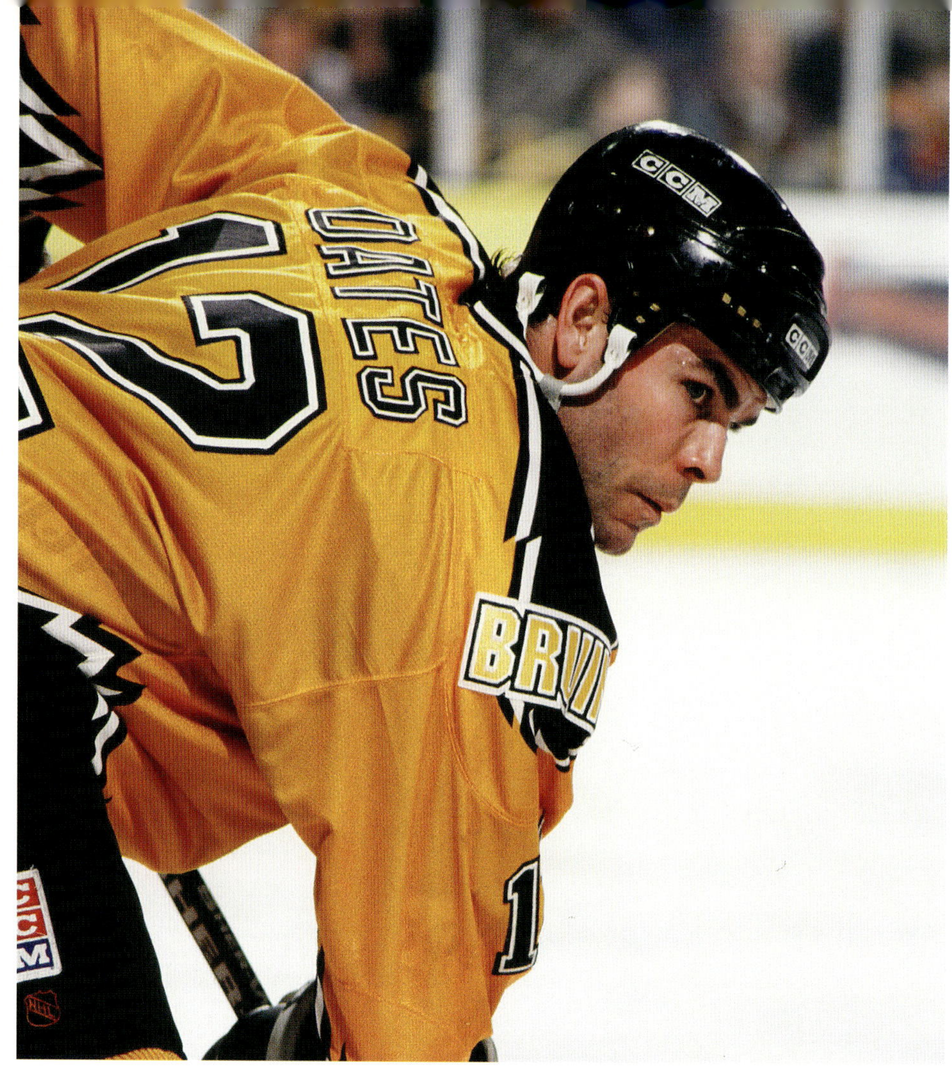

Adam Oates awaits a faceoff at the FleetCenter in 1996. In his first full season in Boston (1992–93), Oates led the team in scoring with 142 points—a total that included 97 assists, the second-highest single-season total in team history behind Bobby Orr's 102 in 1970–71.
(Photograph by Steve Babineau/ NHLI via Getty Images)

ADAM OATES

ADAM OATES could pass the puck. For five and a half years (1992–1997), Bruins fans marveled at his playmaking ability that helped the team stay competitive in the Eastern Conference.

Oates enjoyed an All-American career at Rensselaer Polytechnic Institute in the 1980s but, somewhat incredibly, went undrafted. Perhaps it was because he lacked the traditional skill set of an NHL player. His college coach, Mike Adessa, called Oates "a stumpy, heavy-footed, poor-skating, no-shooting kid." Adessa meant it affectionately—but that is what NHL scouts saw when they sized up Oates.

Oates proved the NHL scouts wrong. After several years with Detroit, Oates blossomed with the St. Louis Blues in the early 1990s, where he put up back-to-back 100-point seasons, feeding the likes of Brett Hull (who, with help from Oates, scored an incredible 86 goals in 1991).

The Bruins acquired Oates for the stretch run in 1992—a season in which the Bruins were rather ordinary during the regular season but made a surprising playoff run that saw them return to the Eastern Conference Finals for the third consecutive year.

The next season (1992–93), Oates had a monster year—one of the best in franchise history. Centering Boston's top line, Oates amassed 45 goals and 97 assists for a total of 142 points. His linemates, the speedy Joe Juneau (102 points) and the sharpshooting Dmitri Kvartalnov (72 points), both rookies, also enjoyed big seasons. Oates' deft hands and supreme passing skills were on full display the next year, when Cam Neely returned from a two-year hiatus and scored 50 goals while riding on the same line as Oates.

Oates would play for Boston until 1997 and then retire in 2004. Over the course of his 19-year NHL career, he would ring up 341 goals and 1,079 assists (1,420 points in all). He was elected to the Hockey Hall of Fame in 2012.

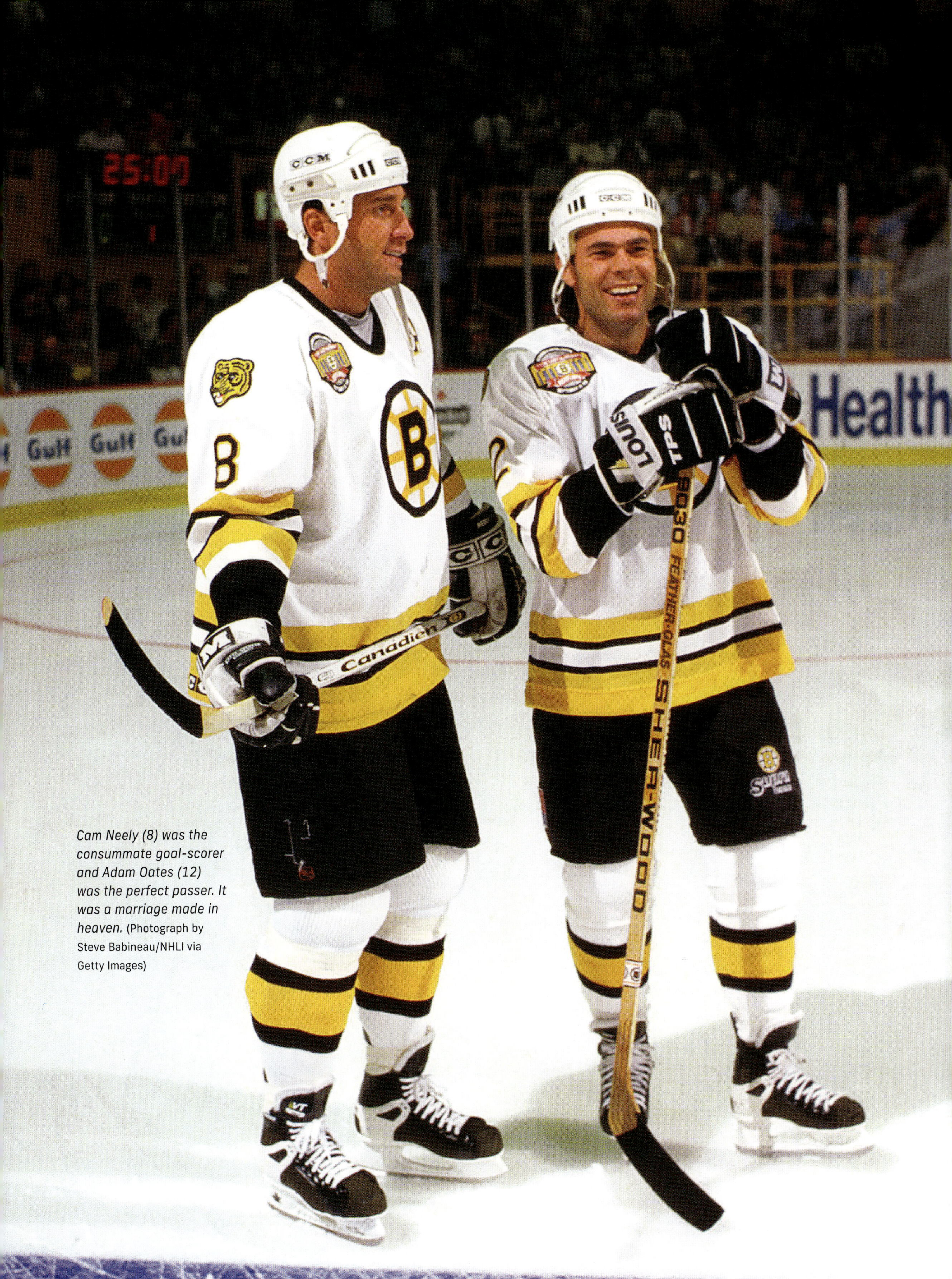

Cam Neely (8) was the consummate goal-scorer and Adam Oates (12) was the perfect passer. It was a marriage made in heaven. (Photograph by Steve Babineau/NHLI via Getty Images)

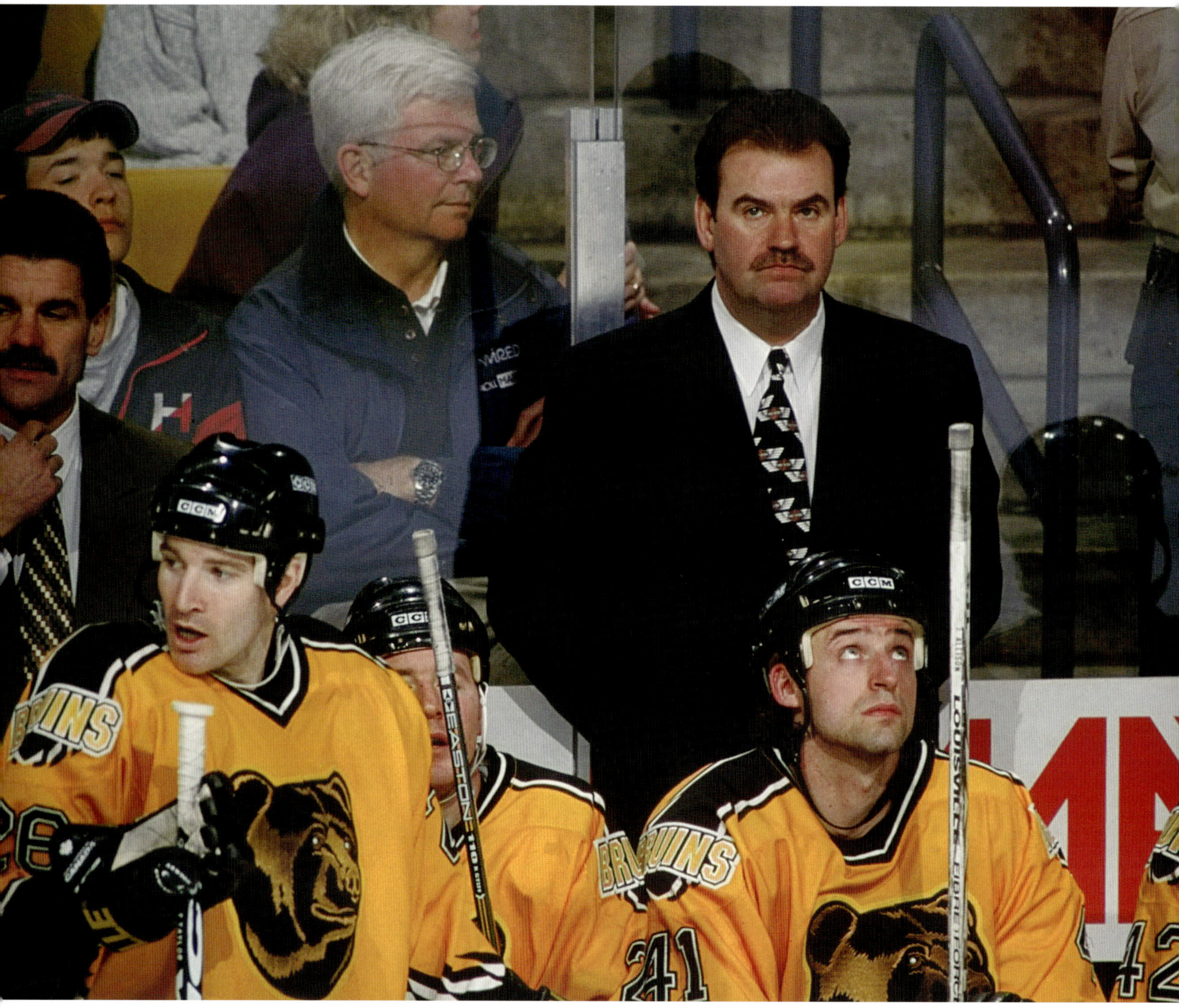

Hard-nosed, blunt, and honest, Pat Burns led the Bruins to the playoffs in two of his three seasons behind the bench in Boston. (Photograph by Steve Babineau/ Allsport, Getty Images)

PAT BURNS

"WE HAD A GOOD RUN there from '87 to the early '90s," said Ray Bourque. "It was fun, we had a nice group—great group, great chemistry. It was a blast winning a lot of hockey games and having some good runs in the playoffs." By 1994, though, the Bruins were starting to decline. It didn't help when Cam Neely retired after the 1995–96 season. Then, in 1996–97, the team tumbled all the way into the basement of the NHL. It was a rough year for everyone.

Harry Sinden responded by hiring Pat Burns, a tough taskmaster of a coach. It proved to be an excellent choice for a team that needed to turn things around.

Burns was a former police officer in Quebec and Ottawa who stumbled into a career coaching hockey. After working his way through the juniors and the minors, Burns coached the Montreal Canadiens for four seasons, leading them

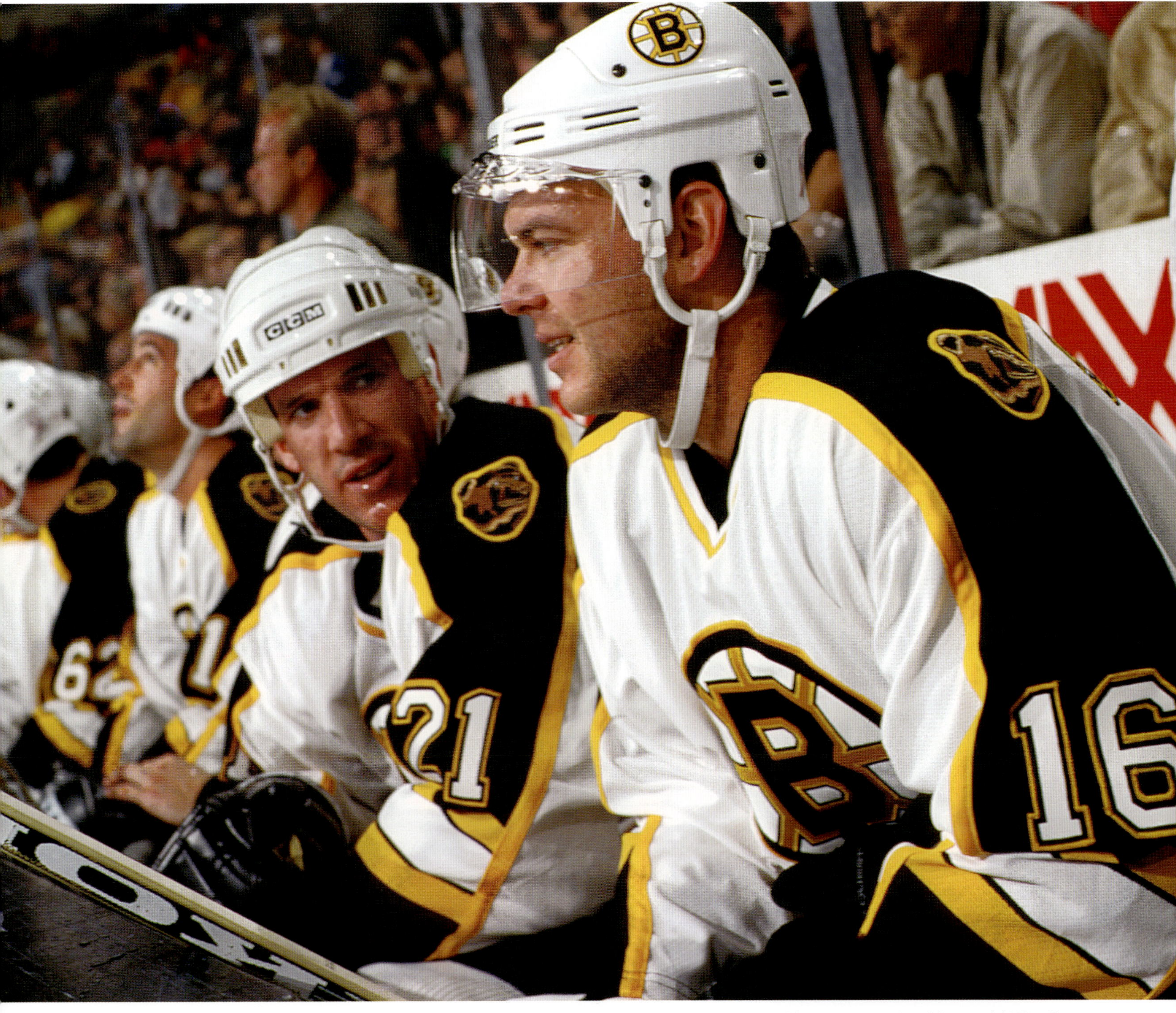

back to the Stanley Cup Final in 1989. He later had a successful four-year tenure with Toronto, further building his reputation as a "Mr. Fix-It" type of head coach.

Burns fixed the Bruins, too, taking them from the cellar back to the playoffs in his first season with the team (1997–98). At the end of that season, Burns won the Jack Adams Award as NHL Coach of the Year. It marked the third time that he had won that award (having captured it at each of his previous NHL stops in Montreal and Toronto), a feat that remains an NHL record. Burns would end up coaching the Bruins until 2000, becoming a fan favorite for his police officer background, Irish wit, and no-nonsense approach.

"There was this mystique with Pat, as a former police officer, the gruff demeanor," said Don Sweeney, a defenseman on those Bruins teams, in a 2014 interview. "But he was a real good-hearted guy. He had a great persona, you could talk to him about anything.... But with hockey, it was black-and-white. You were going to play the way he wanted you to play."

Big centerman Jozef Stumpel (16) talks with longtime teammate Glen Murray (21) during a game. Stumpel had two stints with the Bruins (1991–1997 and 2001–2003), playing eight seasons in all.
(Photograph by Steve Babineau/ NHLI via Getty Images)

Another player from the late 1990s, Ted Donato, compared Burns to another famous coach in a different sport. "In some ways, and I mean this in the most positive way, he handled some situations like Bill Parcells did," said Donato in a 2014 interview. "He handled a lot of the pressure in the media, and behind closed doors, even though he was very tough, his players appreciated that."

After parting ways with the Bruins early in the 2000–01 season, Burns moved on to the New Jersey Devils, where he won a Stanley Cup in 2003. After a six-year battle with colon cancer, he passed away in 2010 at the age of 58. In 2014 he was inducted into the Hockey Hall of Fame as a builder.

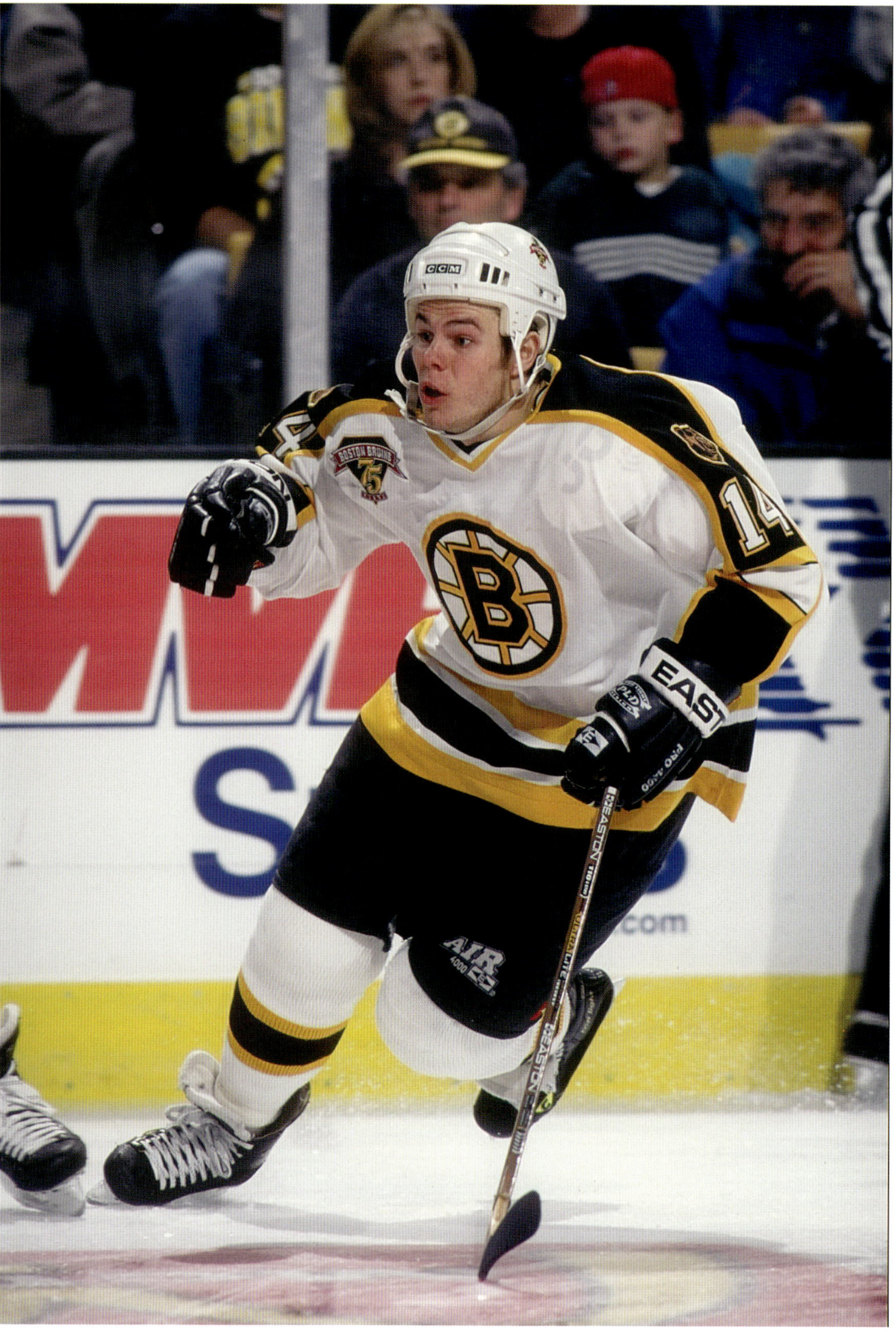

A product of the elite HC CSKA Moscow (also known as the Red Army Team), Sergei Samsonov scored 22 goals with 25 assists in 1997–98 to win the Calder Trophy as NHL rookie of the year. While he never became a superstar, Samsonov was a good player who consistently delivered, scoring 164 goals during his tenure with the Bruins (1997–2006). (Photograph by Steve Babineau/Getty Images)

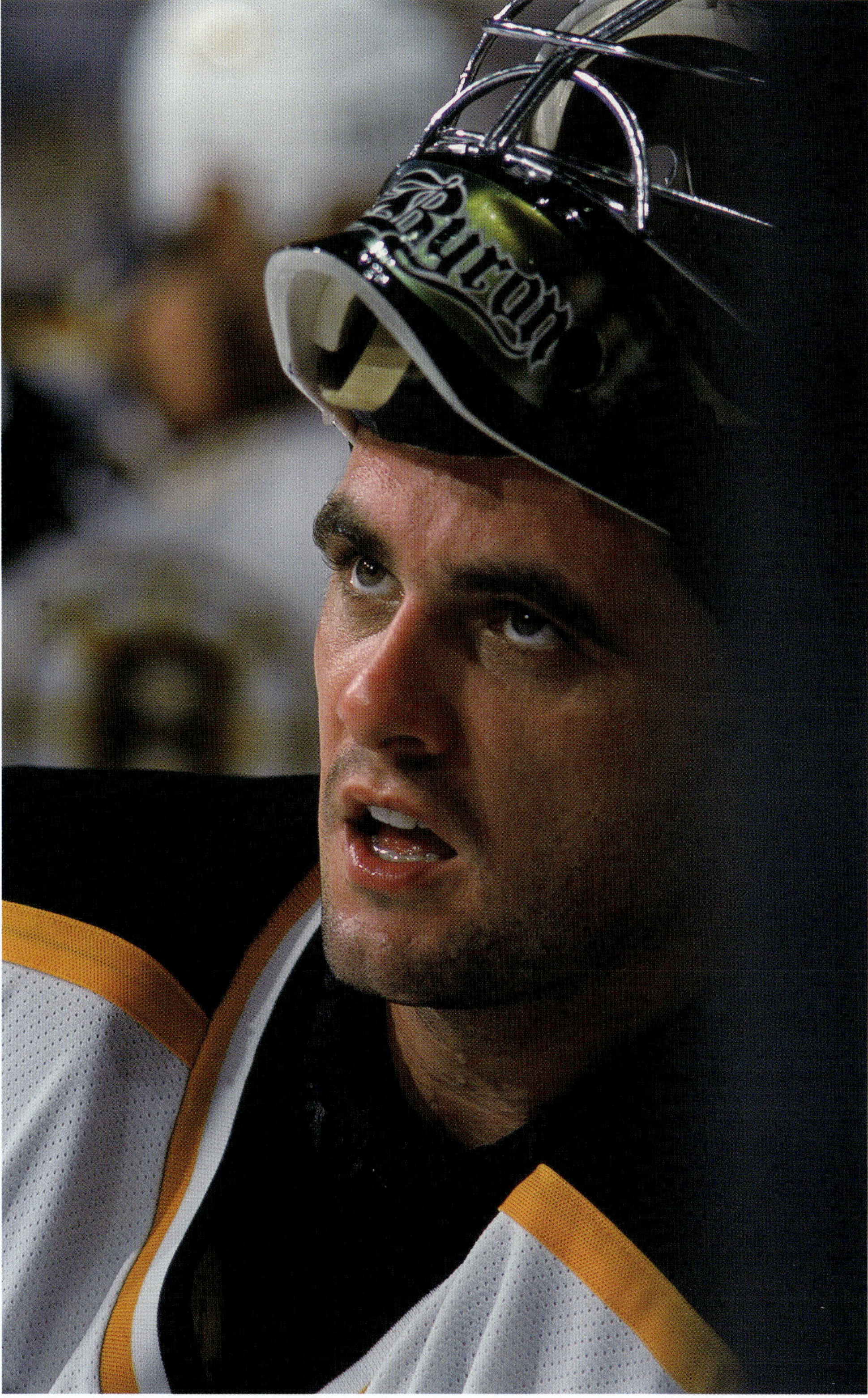

Byron Dafoe, aka "Lord Byron," had three of the greatest goaltending seasons in the history of the Boston Bruins. (Photograph by Steve Babineau/ Allsport, Getty Images)

BYRON DAFOE

LIKE ANOTHER BRUIN of yesteryear (Ken Hodge), Byron Dafoe was born in England. He lived there until his family moved to Canada when he was a teen. It was only then that he started to play hockey. He progressed quickly and eventually made the NHL. After five rather ordinary seasons in Washington and Los Angeles, he arrived in Boston for the 1997–98 season.

Playing for the rebuilding Bruins and head coach Pat Burns, Dafoe emerged as an elite goaltender. In 1997–98, he had a sparkling 2.24 goals against average (GAA) and finished in the top 12 for both the Vezina Trophy (top goaltender)

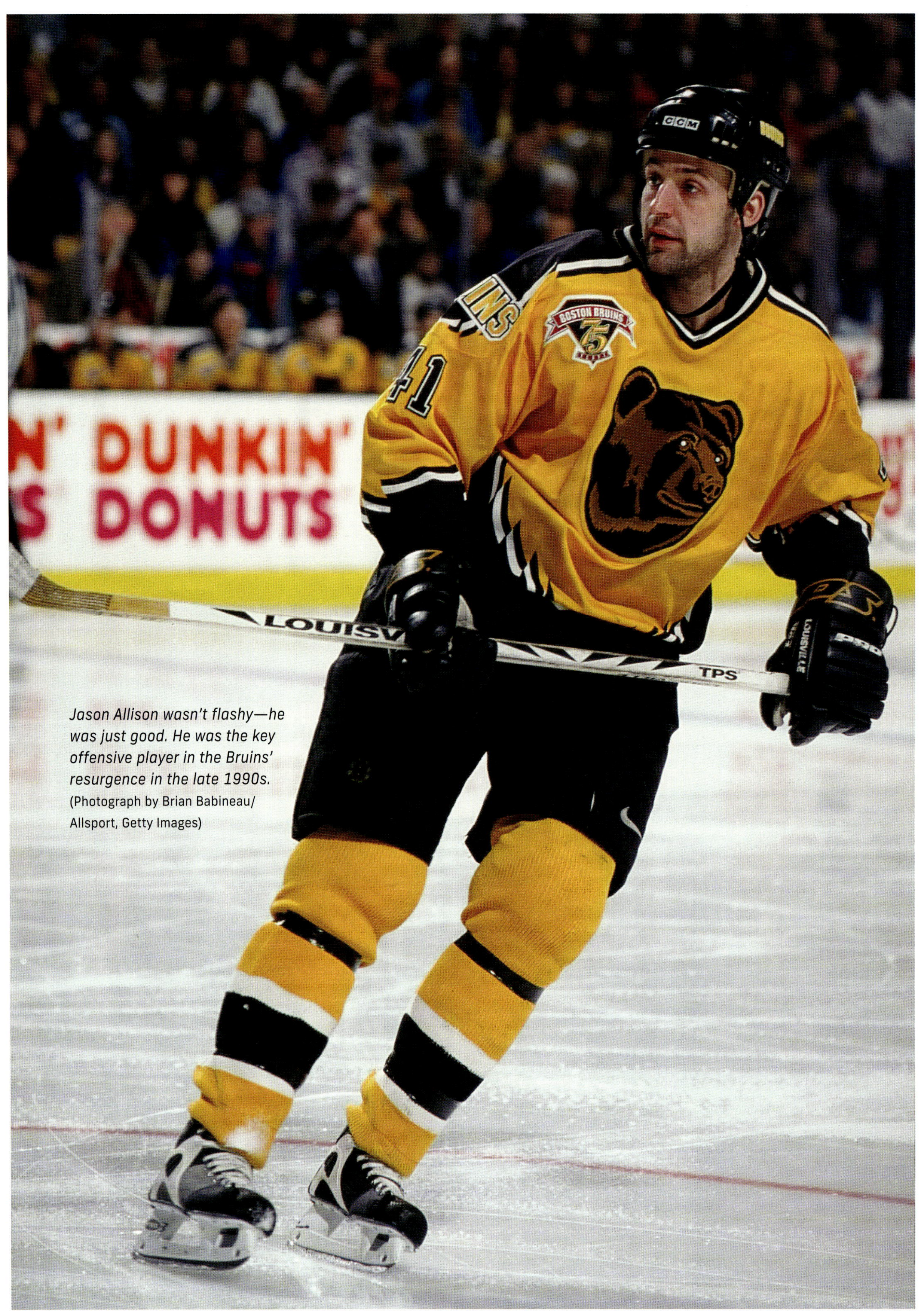

Jason Allison wasn't flashy—he was just good. He was the key offensive player in the Bruins' resurgence in the late 1990s. (Photograph by Brian Babineau/Allsport, Getty Images)

and the Hart Trophy (NHL MVP). The next season, "Lord Byron" was even better with a 2.00 GAA and 10 shutouts, once again finishing near the top in the voting for the Vezina and the Hart and being named Second Team NHL All-Star.

After two injury-plagued seasons, Dafoe would bounce back in a big way in 2001–02, fashioning a career-best 35-26-3 record in what proved to be his final season in Boston.

Dafoe loved playing for Pat Burns and loved playing in Boston. "I just loved the feel of the city," said Dafoe in a 2010 interview. "The fans are just so passionate.... It's a good pressure. If you are going to play in the NHL, you need to perform under pressure. For me, I think it brought another element to my game that I hadn't had in L.A. or Washington. I loved it."

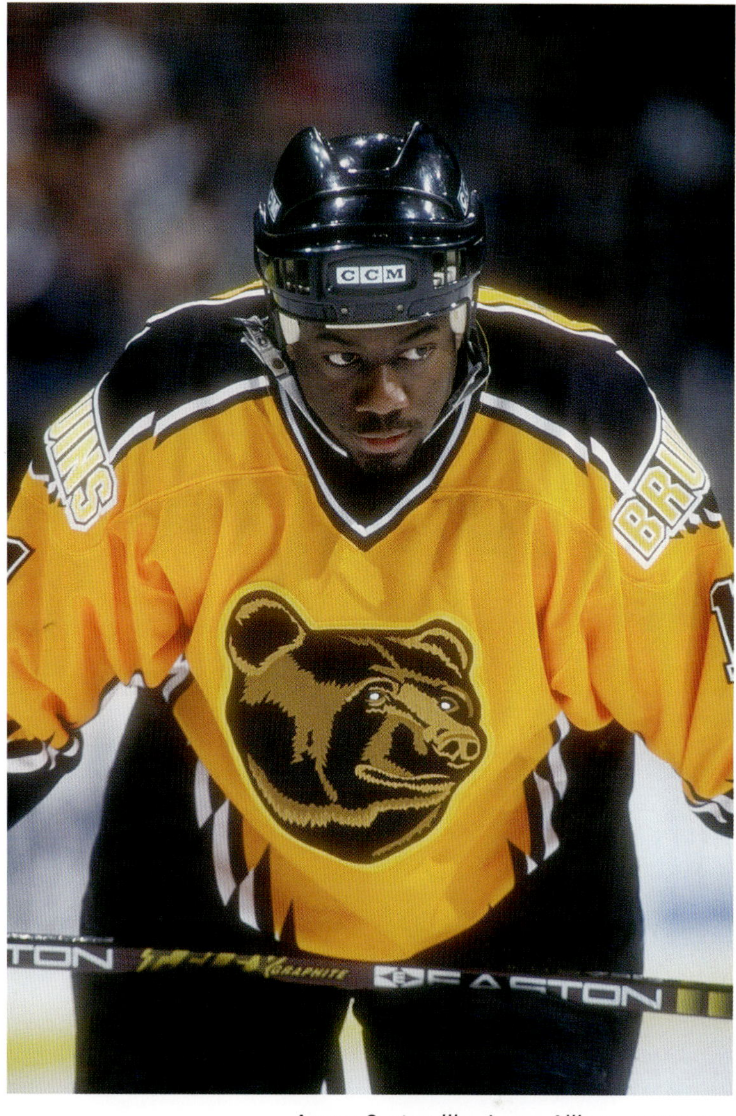

Anson Carter, like Jason Allison, came to the Bruins from the Washington Capitals in the spring of 1997 as part of the Adam Oates trade. A product of Michigan State University, Carter would average more than 20 goals per season in his three full seasons in Boston (1997–2000). (Photograph by Robert Laberge/Allsport, Getty Images)

JASON ALLISON

JASON ALLISON was originally selected in the first round of the 1993 NHL Draft by the Washington Capitals. Things never worked out for Allison with the Caps. So, in March 1997, Harry Sinden, just as he had with Rick Middleton and Cam Neely, traded for a former top prospect with huge upside who had scuffled in his first years in the league.

And just like Middleton and Neely, Allison turned it around once he got to Boston. In his first full season (1997–98), he was an MVP candidate, producing 33 goals and 50 assists while teaming up with another new player, Anson Carter, to give the Bruins an offensive jolt. Allison put up similar numbers the next season as the Bruins continued their resurgence by advancing to the second round of the playoffs.

The knock on Allison was that he was a poor skater. Allison didn't agree, noting, "I'm a lot better skater than people think.... The other thing is, if I was a bad skater, so what? If you're getting it done, you're getting it done."

Allison got it done during the 2000–01 season. That was the year he was named captain of the Bruins, replacing the recently traded Ray Bourque. Allison went on to have a huge year, setting career highs with 36 goals and 59 assists. "I'm not really a flashy guy," said Allison at the conclusion of that season. "I do my damage from playing solid down low and fighting guys off and making other players score goals."

Unfortunately, that was it for Allison in Boston, as he was traded to Los Angeles prior to the next season. But it was good while it lasted.

GOODBYE, BOSTON GARDEN

IN THE FALL OF 1995, the Bruins said goodbye to Boston Garden. It wasn't an easy parting.

The Garden clearly had to go—no one was disputing that. In the late stages of its long arena life, it had become hopelessly outdated in so many different ways. "I will always remember the bench," said Don Cherry. "I didn't like the bench. There were all screws and bolts hanging out. I hate to say it, but it was the worst bench I'd ever seen."

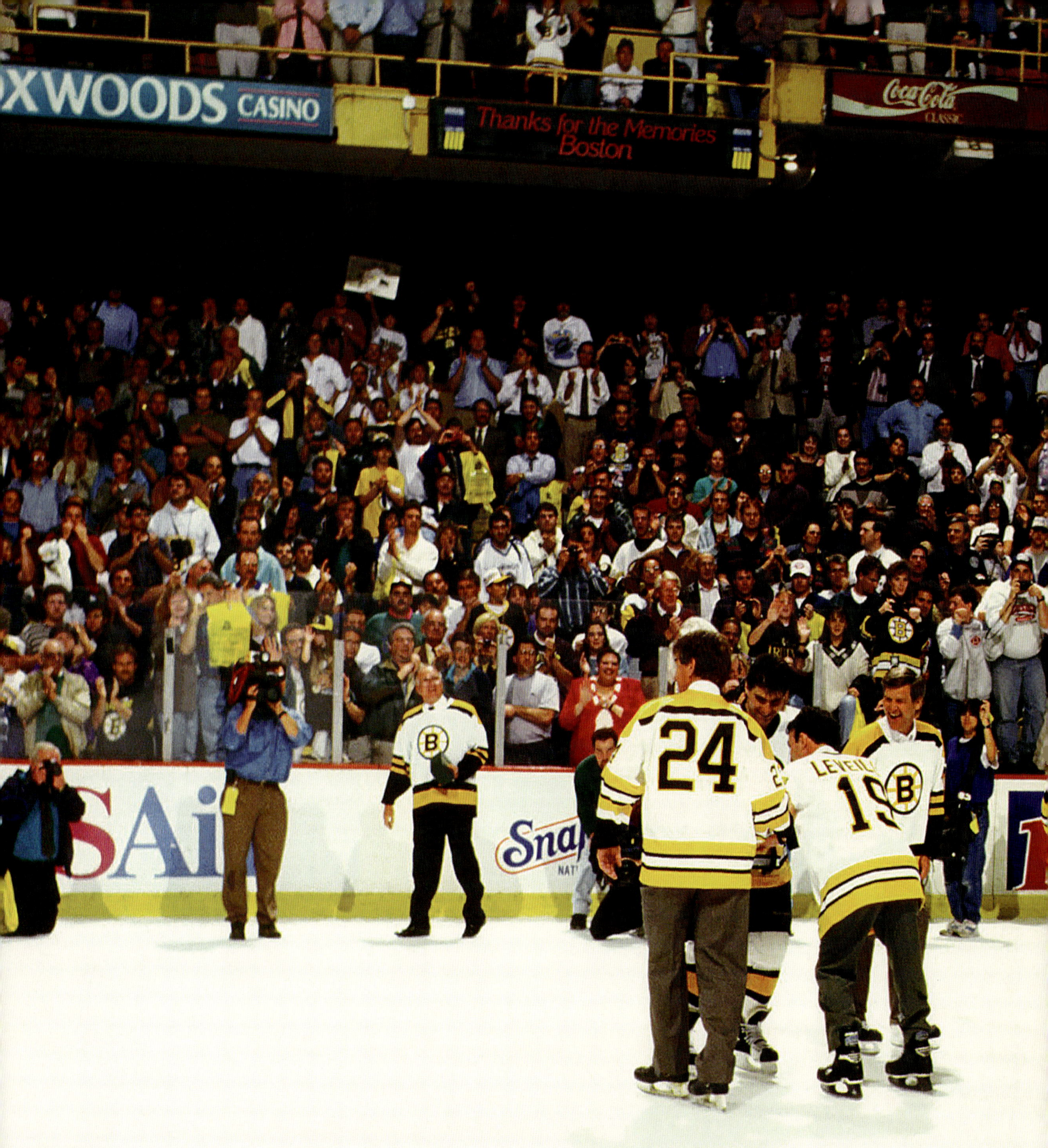

During the "Last Hurrah"—the Bruins' farewell to Boston Garden on September 26, 1995—a contingent of team alumni skated for one last time on their home ice. Included in the group were (left to right) Terry O'Reilly (24), Ray Bourque, Normand Leveille (19), Bobby Orr, Phil Esposito (7), Gary Doak (25), Doug Mohns (19), Fred Stanfield (17), Ed Sandford (7), and Harry Sinden (in white sweater).

(Photograph by Steve Babineau/NHLI via Getty Images)

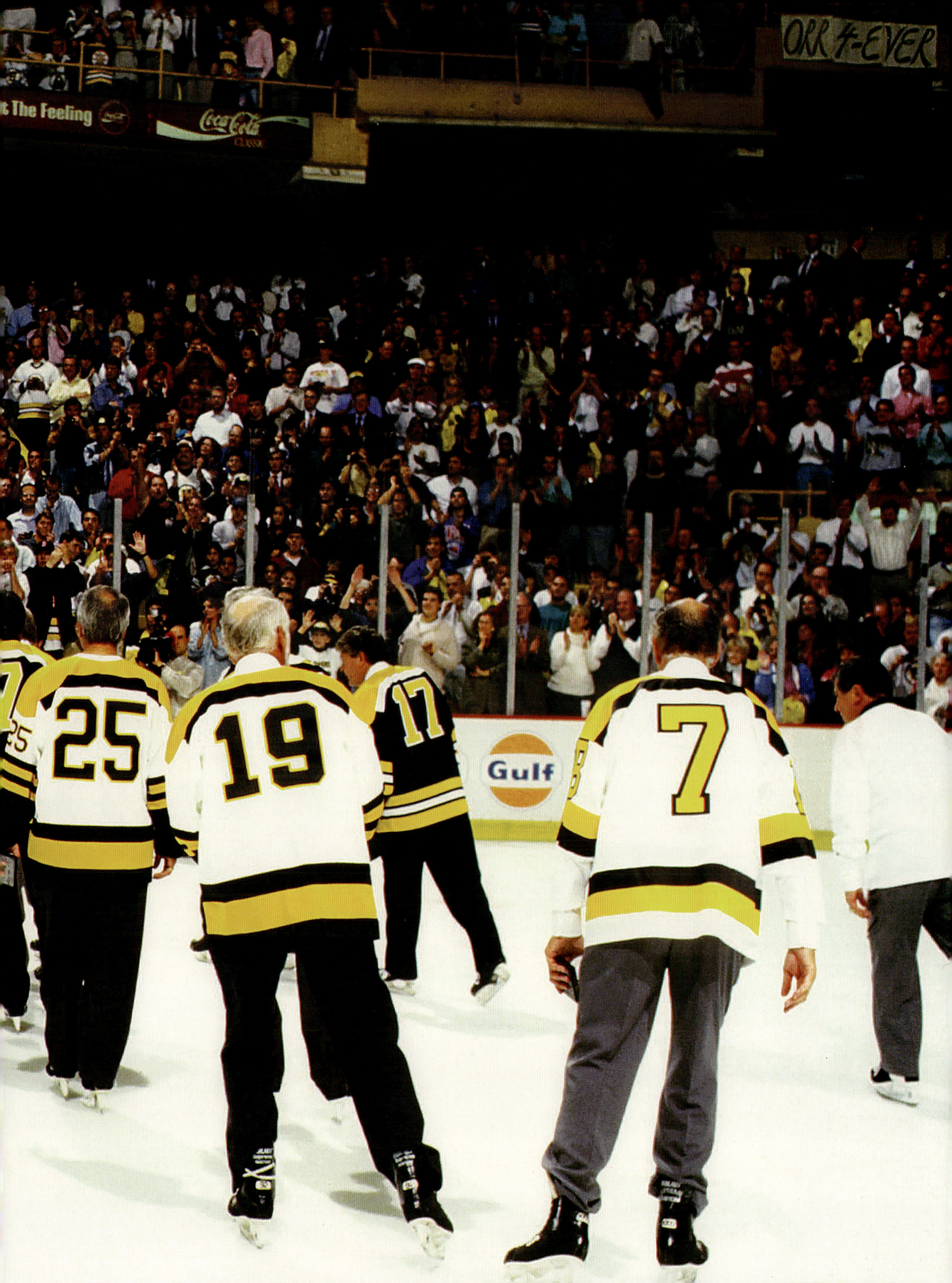
ORR 4-EVER
Coca-Cola
CLASSIC
Gulf
25
19
17
7

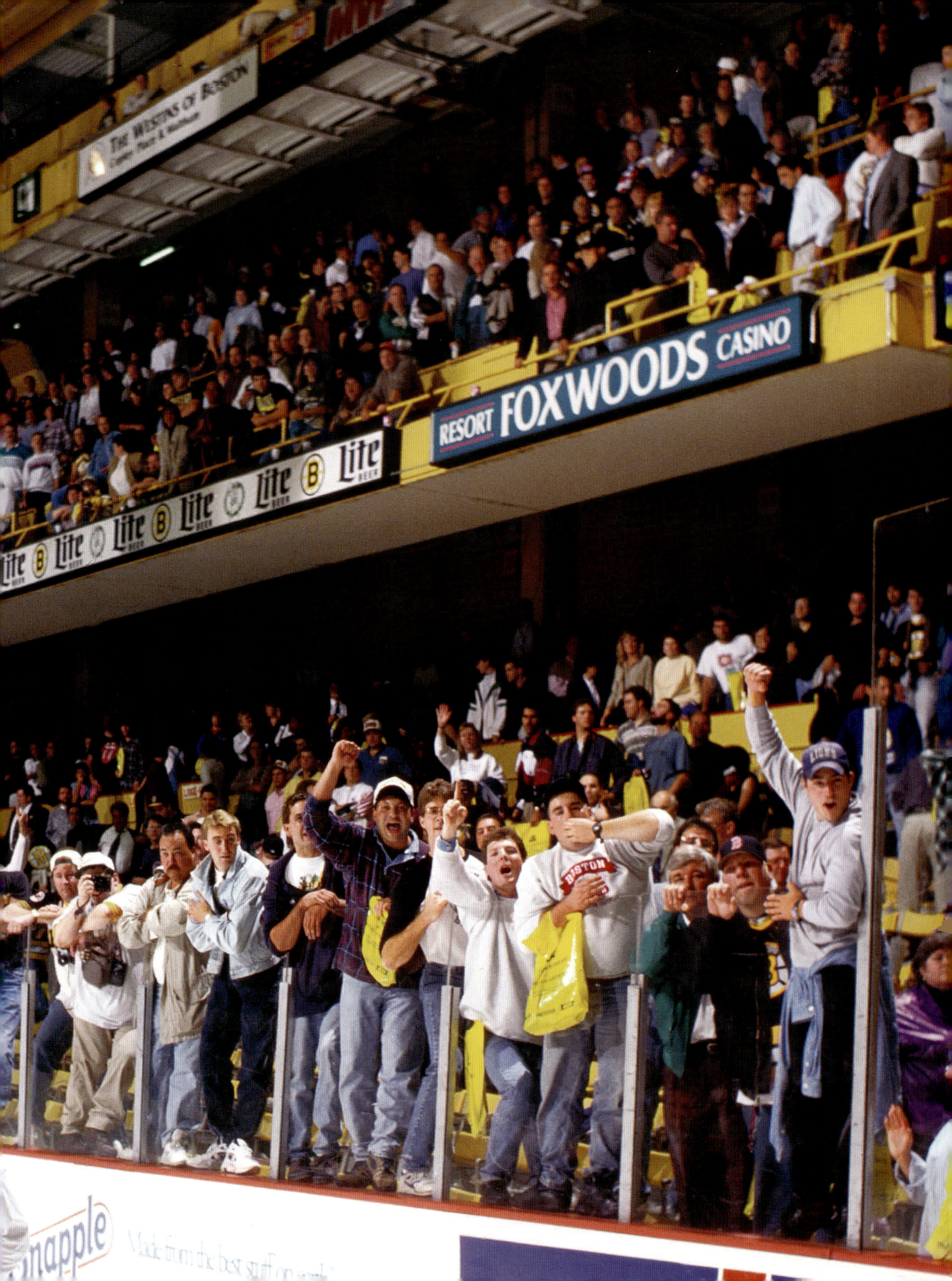
THE WESTIN OF BOSTON
RESORT FOXWOODS CASINO
Lite
Lite
Lite
Lite
Lite
BOSTON
Made from the best stuff on earth

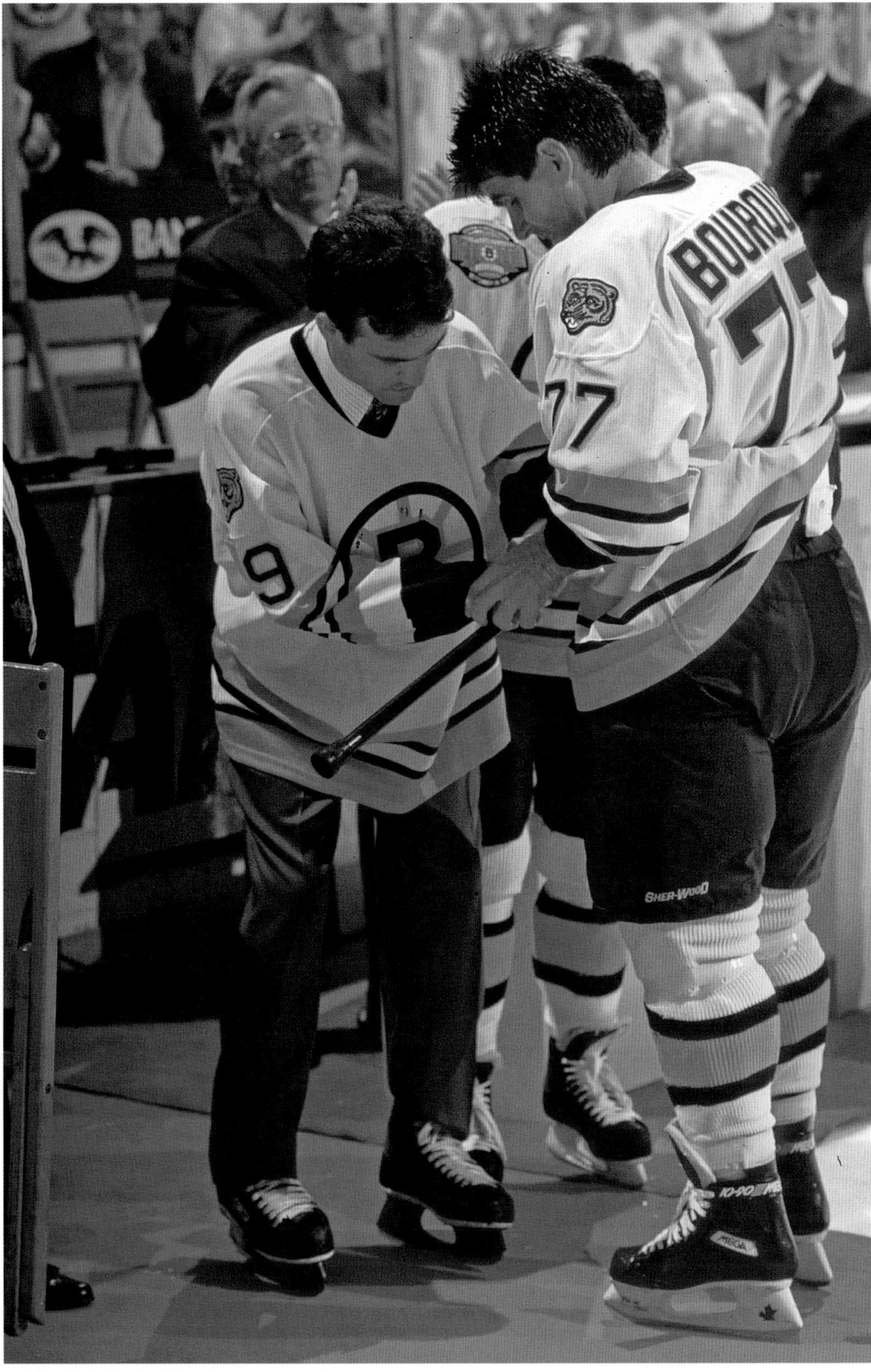

Opposite page: Win, lose, or draw, the crowd at Boston Garden would always bring it. (Photograph by Steve Babineau/NHLI via Getty Images)

Normand Leveille (19) is assisted by former teammate Ray Bourque (77) as he prepares for an emotional last skate at Boston Garden. It was the most memorable moment of the festivities closing the beloved arena in September 1995. (Photograph by Steve Babineau/NHLI via Getty Images)

Then there was the air-conditioning (or lack thereof). As Brad Park remembered, "In the Boston Garden, you would find on a hot day that, with the humidity, 10 minutes into a period, there would be a snow all over the ice. Instead of that staying as like a powder, it would adhere to the ice and make it like sandpaper so the puck would start bouncing. That was from the humidity."

And there were also the small seats...and the obstructed view seats...and the rats....

Even though it was a dump, it was *our* dump. And players simply loved playing there.

For one thing, the Bruins turned the Garden's quirky dimensions into a competitive advantage. As Bob Sweeney noted, the Original Six arenas "had their little

BOSTON GARDEN

I loved playing at Boston Garden. I loved it. You could hear the fans. Oh, there's no doubt about it.... We were good and we knew it. At least I knew we were good, anyway. And the fans knew it.
—Phil Esposito

It was electric! I remember the first time you run up that runway and jump on the ice—the fresh clean ice—and the crowd is into it right off the bat, right from warm-ups! They're hanging over the boards and then the glass, and they're wanting autographs.... It was great.
—Derek Sanderson

It was pretty special in terms of atmosphere...and it gave us an advantage with the ice surface and with how the team was built—and the support we had from the tremendous fans.
—Ray Bourque

It was an unbelievable place to play in as a Bruin. No question. The energy and the atmosphere in that building were pretty special.
—Cam Neely

nooks and crannies." That was certainly true of Boston Garden. For instance, the corners were tight and shallow. "I wasn't the greatest skater in the world," said Rick Smith, "but because there was less room to cover, it helped my game that there weren't any corners for players to go wide on me."

It was a small rink, period—and that, too, played to the Bruins' advantage. "We had a small ice surface, and we had the biggest team...so we were hard to get around on," said Cherry.

And then there was the close proximity of the fans, primarily due to the architecture. "Those buildings were all built straight up and down," said Ken Hodge. "The fans were basically hanging over the balcony in all those old buildings." As Cherry joked, "The crowd was so close, you could give a medical report to the fans."

And this, too, was something that gave the Bruins an advantage. "The people felt like they were sitting right on top of you, so when you got the place rocking, and cheering for you, or when you're playing well, the roof would basically be coming off at times," said Don Sweeney.

If you were an opposing player, it was no fun playing in Boston Garden. Cam Neely admitted that, when he came to the Garden as a Vancouver Canuck, "It was very intimidating because it was loud—it held 14,000, but it was louder than that." Was the Garden an intimidating place to play for opponents? "Yeah, I'm sure it was," said Harry Sinden. "I'm glad it was."

But if you were a Boston Bruin, playing in the Garden was a different story altogether.

Boston Garden...gone, but certainly not forgotten.

HELLO, FLEETCENTER

To get something built in the City of Boston, you often have to move mountains. That was certainly the case back in the 1980s and 1990s when Bruins owner Jeremy Jacobs sought a new arena for the team, the city, and the region. Jacobs faced steep odds and numerous obstacles. He persevered, though, and got it done. It will always be a big part of his enduring legacy.

The FleetCenter was built entirely with private funds and was constructed on a site that placed the new arena just six inches away from the exterior wall of the old Boston Garden. Like its predecessor, the new arena would gain much of its blue-collar identity due to the fact that it was built atop rail and transit hub North Station. As with the old Garden, one could stand in certain parts of the building and feel the barely detectable vibration of the trains entering and departing the station.

The FleetCenter opened for business in October 1995. Because it was replacing a venerable arena that oozed character, the new arena encountered some initial complaints and doubts. It was Boston, after all—a city that embraces the old and is wary of the new.

There was no question, though, that the FleetCenter was needed—and that it was completely state-of-the-art. "The FleetCenter in no way mirrors the building it replaced," wrote Kevin Paul Dupont of the *Boston Globe* at the time. "Is that all bad? Anyone who had the distinct pleasure of buying one of the Garden's horrendous obstructed-view seats, and paid the chiropractor's bill that came with it, will have to embrace the Bruins' new home. The new arena is clean. It is comfortable. It is everything the Baby Boomer generation demands: cushy seats, loads of leg room, a TV monitor at every turn..."

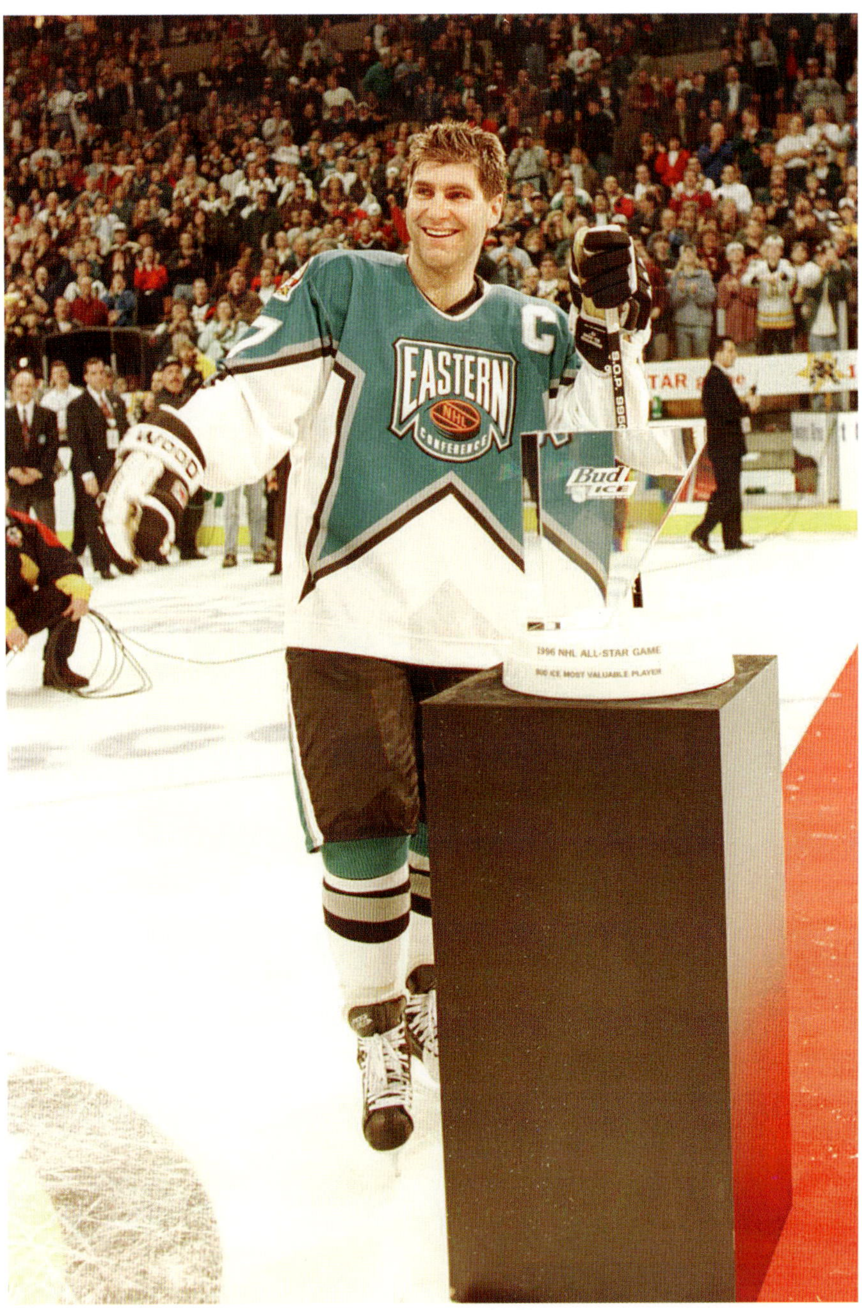

The 1996 NHL All-Star Game was played at the new FleetCenter and, fittingly, hometown hero Ray Bourque was named the game's MVP. Bourque showed no signs of slowing down in the 1990s, being named a First Team NHL All-Star on six occasions while also taking home three more Norris Trophies (1990, 1991, 1994) as the NHL's top defenseman during the decade. (Photograph by Rick Stewart/ Getty Images)

And in virtually no time, the FleetCenter—soon to be known as TD Banknorth Garden and now simply as TD Garden—acquired a character all its own. As Ray Bourque observed, "It was different because we weren't as competitive when that building opened up...[but] once the Bruins and the Celtics started winning again in the new building, there was a crazy atmosphere in the building. I think it all comes with success. With that, ambiance is created in a building."

That ambience started to develop with the 1996 NHL All-Star Game on January 20, 1996, the first major event at the FleetCenter. And it was Bourque who stole the show, scoring the game-winning goal with just 37.3 seconds remaining in regulation time. The building shook as the crowd of 17,565 roared.

It was the first "Great Garden Moment" in the new arena for the Bruins. It would not be the last.

PORTRAIT OF A FAN

by Leigh Montville

Author's Note: *For decades, the number 13,909 stood for the full hockey capacity at the old Boston Garden. With the opening of the FleetCenter in 1995, the new hockey capacity figure became 17,565. And their number is just as loyal, loud, and passionate as their forebears. Indeed, Bruins fandom is a time-honored tradition passed from one generation to the next. The cheers of Bruins Nation have echoed from Shore to Orr to Bourque to Chara to McAvoy, as their sheer numbers and intensity are the envy of their NHL rivals. The essay that follows is a portrait of a fan whose devotion to the Bruins and her favorite player is the perfect representation of a fan culture second to none.*

THE POEM CAME straight from her teenaged heart. Veronica Immaculata Shea, "Vonnie" to everyone at Roslindale High School, wrote an ode to Bruins defenseman Ted Green in the first weeks of the 1970–71 season as he tried to come back from the effects of brain surgery after a stick fight a year earlier.

It was '69 in the middle of September
A tragedy occurred which all Boston will remember
Everyone was wondering in the town of the Baked Bean
Was this the end of the courageous Ted Green?

In further stanzas and verse, iambic syncopation, Shea tried to chronicle the 30-year-old skater's return, back from two operations after "death gave me a little brush on the shoulder" (his words), when the hardest part of the hockey stick of St. Louis Blues winger Wayne Maki, the part where the shaft meets the blade, crushed his skull during an exhibition game in Ottawa. This was a poetic saga, for sure, a classic.

Ms. Shea typed out the finished product and moved to the harder part of her plan: how would she deliver her poem to its subject, now back on the ice with the Bruins?

"How would I get close enough to talk to him?" she wondered. "The players were like rock stars. Bigger than rock stars. They were surrounded by people wherever they went."

Interest in the team had become a civic madness. There never had been anything like this in Boston sports. Never. Not close. Never. The Bruins had won the Stanley Cup in May for the first time in 29 years, precocious defenseman Bobby Orr flying through the air at the end as if he were a cartoon super-hero sent to rescue the inhabitants of the city from decades of disappointment and disgrace. The inhabitants still were gobstruck by the experience.

A song, "Nut Rocker," a rock 'n' roll version of Tchaikovsky's ballet, *The Nutcracker*, by a group of Los Angeles session musicians who called themselves B. Bumble and the Stingers, pounded through every local head. It was the theme song that opened all Bruins telecasts on WSBK TV-38, a station discovered by attaching a weird circular antenna to the back of the family television to receive sometimes-fuzzy UHF interlopers beyond the original 12 choices on the dial. Magic. The voices of play-by-play broadcaster Don Earle and color commentator Johnny Pierson, a former player, arrived to describe the action.

Every game was a sellout, 13,909 fans squeezed, smushed, packed into one another in Boston Garden, while a brisk and expensive secondary ticket market was run by gruff characters on Causeway Street. The games, the players, the front-office plots and intrigues were conversations at the workplace, the dinner table, the library when the librarian wasn't watching. Everyone spoke the same hockey language. Lingua franca. The players were extended hockey family. Bobby (teenaged heartthrob No. 1). Turk (teenaged heartthrob No. 2). Cheesy with the stitches on his goaltender's mask. Hodgie. Pie. Cash, who ordered Chinese food from jail with his one phone call. Jesus Saves, Espo Scores on Rebound! Teddy Green, now playing with a helmet to protect the acrylic plate in his head.

Age didn't matter for any of these conversations. Gender didn't matter. Neighborhood didn't matter. The Bruins were a seven-day, 24-hour fixation.

"I had four brothers, all of them older than me," Vonnie Shea said. "So I tagged along for whatever interested them. I was sort of a tomboy. Everything was hockey. I went right out there and played street hockey. I could tell you the statistics for everyone on the team."

Her father, a man who set out his peanuts and a beer and watched the sometimes-fuzzy action unfold on television on every possible night, gave Vonnie her first ticket to a game. That was enough. If there was a way to get another ticket (standing in line overnight, say, before tickets were released) or to get in without a ticket (a folded-up five dollar bill handed to the right ticket-taker, thank you very much), she was in the Garden again. And again. And again.

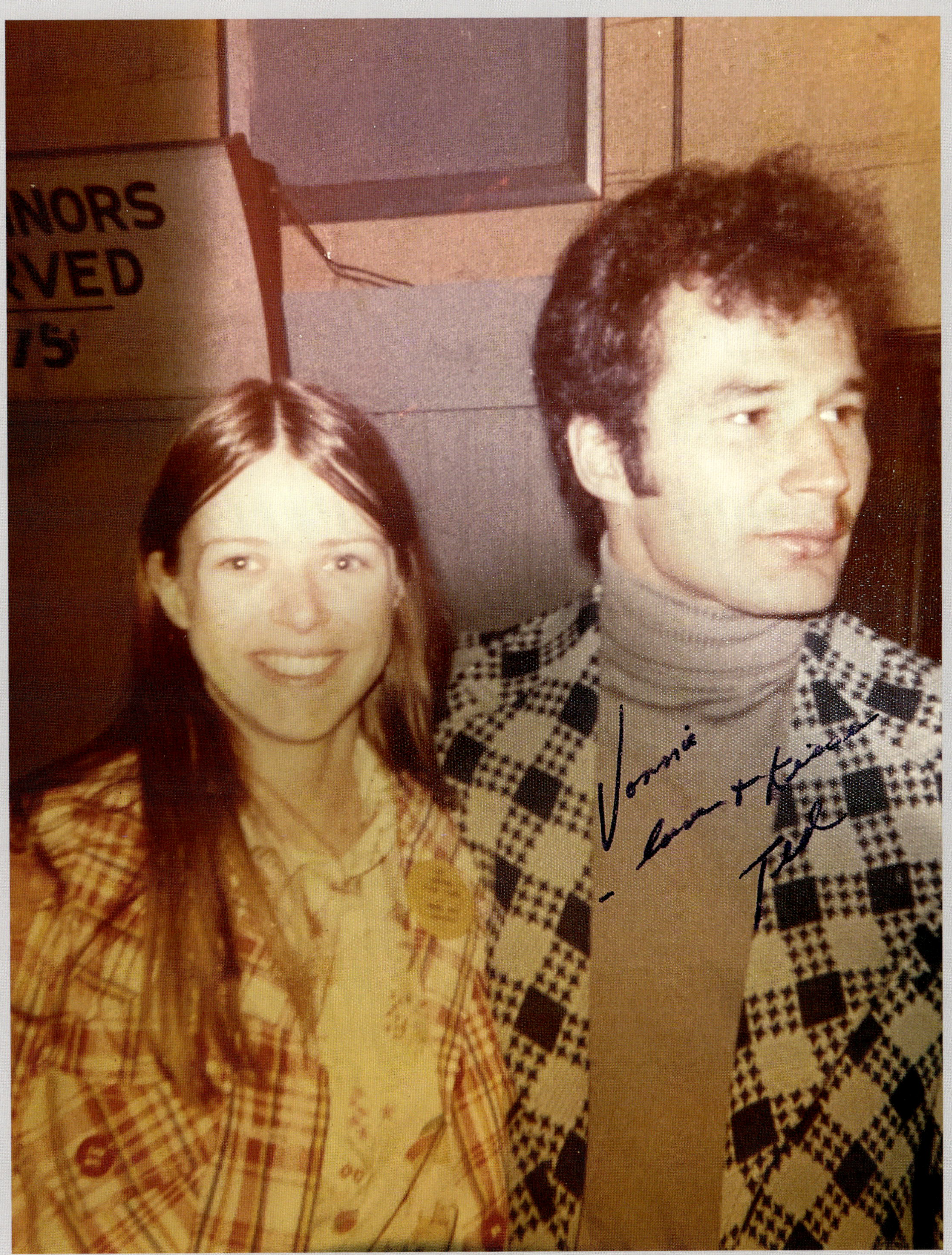

Vonnie Shea of Roslindale, Massachusetts, poses with Ted Green. Shea was president of the Ted Green Fan Club in the early 1970s and embodies the long-standing connection between the Boston Bruins players and their fans. (Photograph Courtesy of Veronica Shea)

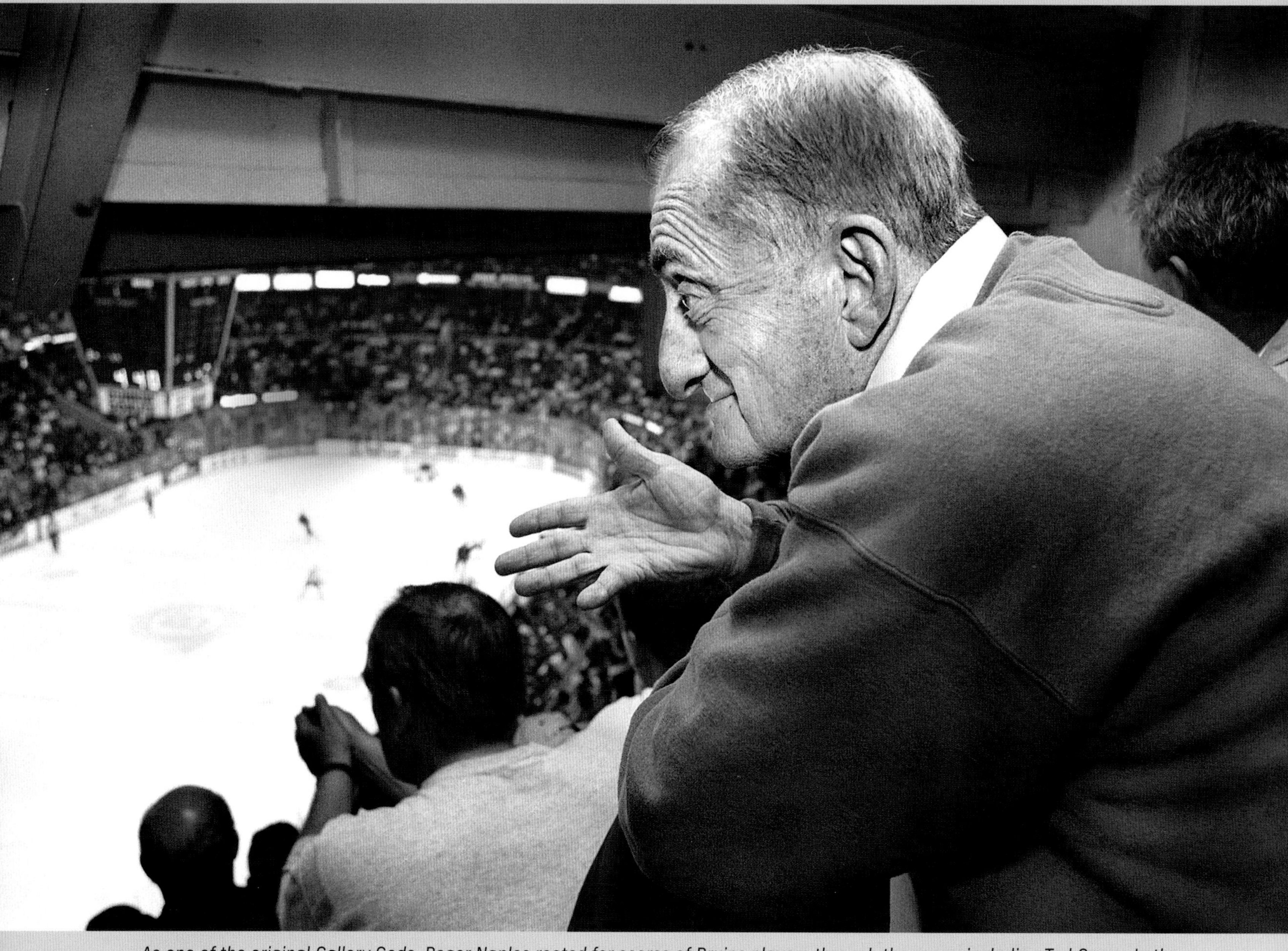

As one of the original Gallery Gods, Roger Naples rooted for scores of Bruins players through the years, including Ted Green. In the early days of the Gallery Gods, during the Great Depression, Bruins general manager Art Ross allowed the "Gods" to pay for their general admission tickets in weekly installments. They remained the team's most loyal and vocal fan contingent for decades and were a key part of the crackling atmosphere of the old Boston Garden. (Photograph by John Tlumacki/The Boston Globe via Getty Images)

She eventually met Ken Davis, a Garden employee who took care of the players' cars, which were parked on a ramp behind the arena. An idea arrived. Could she sorta, kinda wait around on the ramp after a game? Just long enough to deliver a poem to Ted Green? Sure.

"I gave it to Ted," Vonnie Shea said. "He was with his family. He stopped and read it. He liked it. Kept it."

One other thing.

"I asked him if I could be the president of his fan club," she said. "Everybody on the team had a fan club. I knew the president of his fan club had left. The job was open. "

Bingo.

As president, she collected the annual dues, a dollar, which entitled the member to a Ted Green pin, a Christmas card, a birthday card, and a newsletter that appeared periodically. She was in charge of all of this. There were more than 60 members, not nearly as many as the fan clubs for Orr, Esposito, Sanderson, and Cheevers, but a solid number. Nobody asked for a refund.

"Ted Green treated me like his little sister," the president said. "I went to practices. I went to the airport when the team came back from games. The presidents of the fan clubs, we all took a trip to Montreal. It was great."

The craziness continued through a streak of 117 consecutive sellouts and beyond. The *Boston Globe*, in the middle of it all, ran a series called "Our Garden Variety," profiles of different Bruins fans. Martha Ferson, middle-aged, grown kids, talked about how she came to games by herself and bought tickets for friends and family as Christmas gifts. Joe Smith, a social worker from Dorchester, talked about how his quiet personality changed at game time, about how he called Bert Olmstead of the Canadiens "Dirty Bertie" and Jacques Plante, their goaltender, "that pig." Edgar Hill, a blueblood member of the Garden Club, seats in Section 9, talked about the purity of the hockey, the skill involved, but did mention that his biggest memory was the long-ago night when Eddie Shore almost killed Ace Bailey on the ice.

Above all the action, of course, were the Gallery Gods, a group formed in the 1930s, regulars who commanded the first three rows of the third balcony. Hanging over the action, they delivered commentary and judgments, voices heard so often they became familiar to the players on both sides.

"It was all wonderful," Vonnie Shea said. "I had a teacher for sociology at Roslindale High School. He was a big hockey fan. Every day he would begin class by asking me about Ted Green and the Bruins. Every day."

The great ride, the euphoria, did not last. Not the way it was. When the Bruins won the Stanley Cup for a second time in 1972, a rival league, the World Hockey Association, jumped into existence. Substantial money was offered to players who had worked in a league where the average salary was $25,000 a year. Some important Bruins took the offers. Gerry Cheevers left. Derek Sanderson left. Ted Green left. A big part of the magic left. When Bobby Orr left with bad knees four years later, off to Chicago, the Bruins were a hockey team again, still popular, still good, but not the darlings of everyday life.

"It was something when we were going through it," Vonnie Shea says now, a resident of Medfield, years and years later. "It feels good to talk about it all again."

She stayed as president of the fan club for a year or two, Ted Green with the New England Whalers, but that all fell apart. She went on to live a full grown-up life, married, kids, job, the works. Ted Green went on to become an assistant coach in Edmonton with former Bruin Glen "Slats" Sather, then replaced Sather as head coach for a couple of years before he retired.

After a long illness, Green died at the age of 79 on October 8, 2019. Ms. Shea took notice.

"I Googled his obituary," she said. "It was sad, of course. At the bottom, there was a chance to plant a tree in his name."

One tree, it is.

At the Rosehill Cemetery, Edmonton, Alberta.

From the Ted Green Fan Club.

From long, long ago.

Leigh Montville is a former sports columnist at the *Boston Globe* and former senior writer at *Sports Illustrated*. He is the author of 10 books, a member of the National Sports Media Association Hall of Fame, and a recipient of the Red Smith Award, sportswriting's highest honor.

BOSTON BRUINS (1990–1999)

Season	W	L	T	PTS	PTS%	Finish	Playoffs	Coach	Division	Conference
1989–90	46	25	9	101	.631	1st of 5	Lost Stanley Cup Final	Mike Milbury	Adams	Prince of Wales
1990–91	44	24	12	100	.625	1st of 5	Lost NHL Conference Finals	Mike Milbury	Adams	Prince of Wales
1991–92	36	32	12	84	.525	2nd of 5	Lost NHL Conference Finals	Rick Bowness	Adams	Prince of Wales
1992–93	51	26	7	109	.649	1st of 6	Lost NHL Division Semifinals	Brian Sutter	Adams	Prince of Wales
1993–94	42	29	13	97	.577	2nd of 7	Lost NHL Conference Semifinals	Brian Sutter	Northeast	Eastern
1994–95*	27	18	3	57	.594	3rd of 7	Lost NHL Conference Quarterfinals	Brian Sutter	Northeast	Eastern
1995–96	40	31	11	91	.555	2nd of 6	Lost NHL Conference Quarterfinals	Steve Kasper	Northeast	Eastern
1996–97	26	47	9	61	.372	6th of 6		Steve Kasper	Northeast	Eastern
1997–98	39	30	13	91	.555	2nd of 6	Lost NHL Conference Quarterfinals	Pat Burns	Northeast	Eastern
1998–99	39	30	13	91	.555	3rd of 5	Lost NHL Conference Semifinals	Pat Burns	Northeast	Eastern

*1994–95 regular season shortened to 48 games due to NHL labor dispute

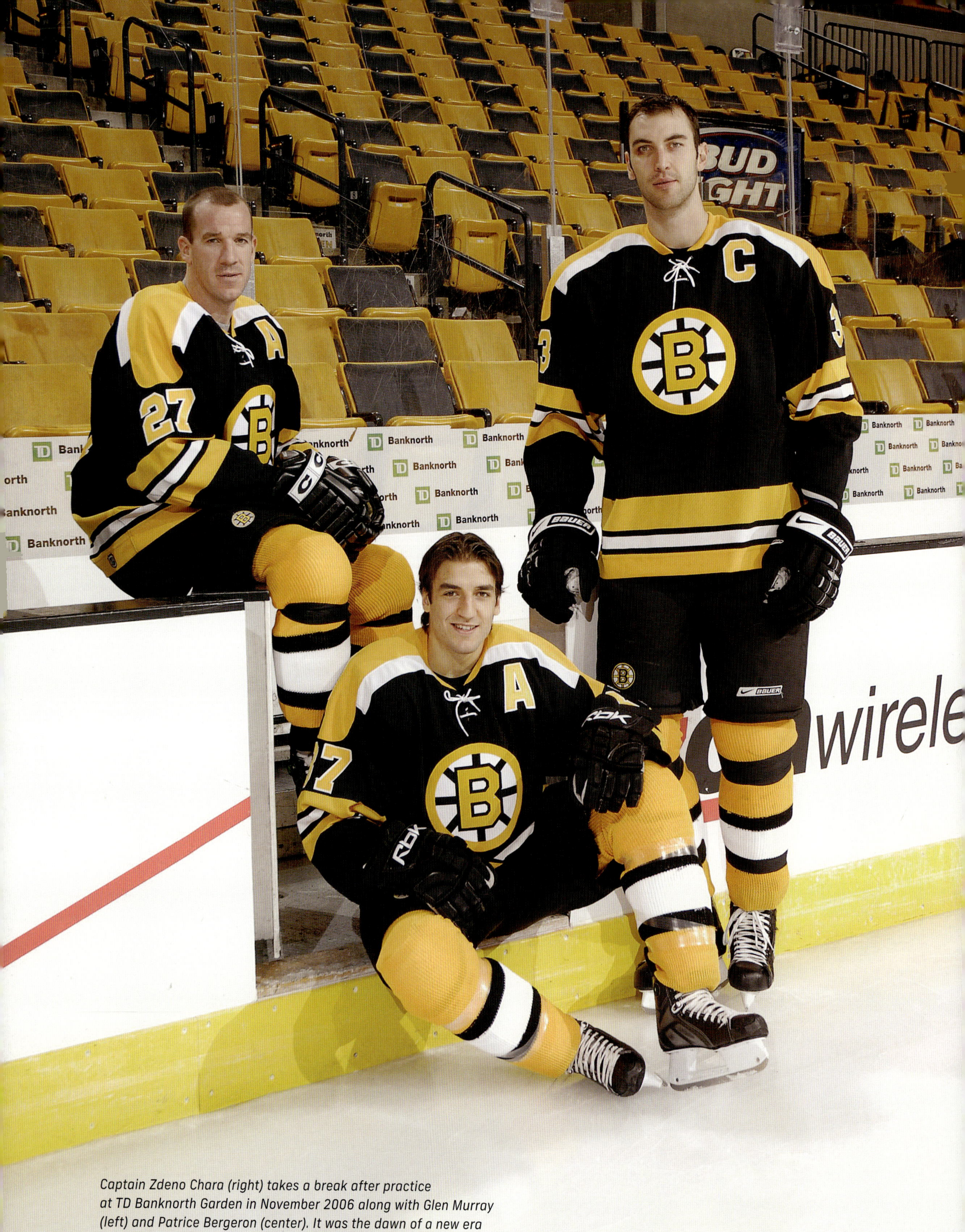

Captain Zdeno Chara (right) takes a break after practice at TD Banknorth Garden in November 2006 along with Glen Murray (left) and Patrice Bergeron (center). It was the dawn of a new era for the Boston Bruins. (Photograph by Steve Babineau/SA/Getty Images)

2000s

BLACK & GOLD REBOOT

Not only are we introducing a new general manager today, but also we are changing our approach. We are creating a culture where players want to come here to play and fans want to watch exciting hockey in one of the best arenas in the world.

—Jeremy Jacobs, Bruins owner, announcing the hiring of Peter Chiarelli, May 2006

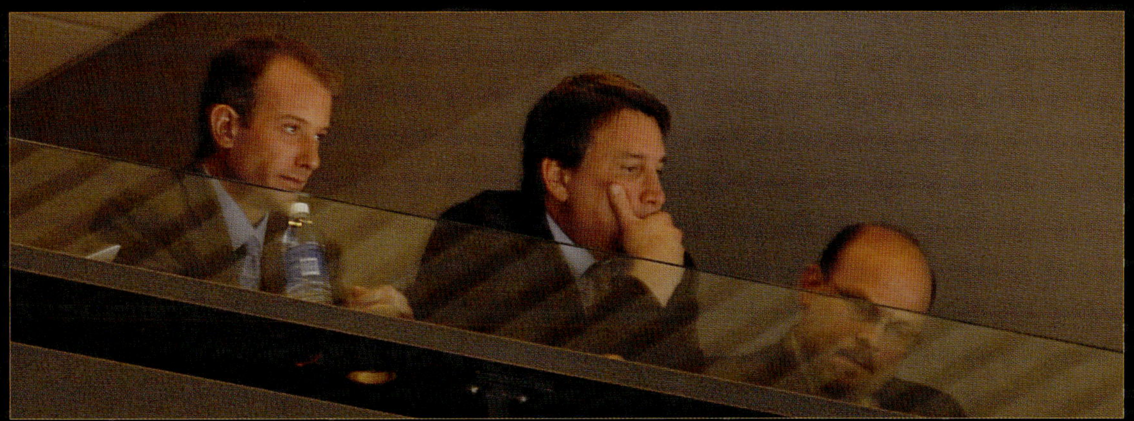

Executive VP Charlie Jacobs, VP Cam Neely, and GM Peter Chiarelli (left to right) survey the action from the rafters of the TD Banknorth Garden in December 2007. Jacobs, Neely, and Chiarelli were key figures in reshaping the Bruins in the mid-2000s. (Photograph by Steve Babineau/NHLI via Getty Images)

The 2000s was a topsy-turvy decade for the Boston Bruins. If the fortunes of the team in that era had been captured in a novel, they would have followed the literary archetype of birth-death-rebirth.

The beginning of the decade was filled with hope and optimism, with the Bruins winning Northeast Division titles in 2002 and 2004. Alas, both of those seasons (as well as the season in between, 2003) ended in frustrating fashion with a first-round playoff loss. Still, with budding superstar Joe Thornton as the centerpiece, and a solid core around him (forwards Glen Murray, Mike Knuble, Brian Rolston, and Sergei Samsonov, star defenseman Sergei Gonchar, and rookie goaltender Andrew Raycroft), the team seemed well-positioned for the future.

Then came the labor dispute and the resulting lockout that first delayed, then disrupted, and ultimately resulted in the cancellation of the entire 2004–05 NHL season. It was painful for all involved.

Coming out of the lockout, the Bruins unexpectedly faced more pain, as a wave of free agent departures (including Rolston, Knuble, and Gonchar) and newfound salary cap considerations left the roster in depleted shape for the 2005–06 season. The team promptly tumbled toward the bottom of the standings. Recognizing the inevitable, the Bruins suddenly traded Thornton in November 2005. Samsonov would be gone by season's end as well. It was time to start over.

Over the next several years, the Bruins would undergo a complete reboot. And it would permeate all levels of the organization. To begin, there was an infusion of new blood in the front office, a process that had actually started prior to the lockout. In 2001, Charlie Jacobs (Jeremy's youngest son) joined the front office to provide a day-to-day Boston presence for the Jacobs Family's ownership of the team. Then, in May 2006, Jeremy Jacobs and Charlie Jacobs joined Harry Sinden at a press conference announcing Peter Chiarelli as the team's new general manager. Shortly thereafter, Chiarelli hired longtime Bruin Don Sweeney as director of player development. One year later, Cam Neely came aboard as vice president.

These additions all proved to have staying power. Chiarelli would have a successful tenure as general manager, which lasted until 2015. And Charlie Jacobs, Neely, and Sweeney all remain in the front office to this day, holding the respective titles of CEO, president, and general manager. And, fittingly, their front office tenures have coincided with the corporate partnership of TD Bank, a company who has been the exclusive naming rights partner of the storied "Boston Garden" arena since the mid-2000s.

The Black and Gold reboot in the mid-2000s also involved a new man behind the bench—former Montreal coach Claude Julien. After the departure of Pat Burns in 2000, the Bruins had a succession of coaches with short-lived tenures, including Mike Keenan, Robbie Ftorek, Mike Sullivan, and Dave Lewis. Julien would bring a new stability to the position.

And, finally, there was an injection of new talent on the ice. Prior to the 2006–07 season, the Bruins signed two high-impact free agents, Zdeno Chara and Marc Savard. They joined forces with a wave of young talent, much of it coming as a result of the Bruins' shrewd selections in the NHL Draft, including Patrice Bergeron (2003), David Krejci (2004), and the trio of Phil Kessel, Milan Lucic, and Brad Marchand (all selected in 2006). Their arrival in Boston in the ensuing years would complete the Black and Gold reboot of the mid-2000s.

And that reboot was a complete success. The Bruins would return to the playoffs in 2007–08 and then ring up 116 points during the 2008–09 regular season, the team's highest point total since the Stanley Cup season of 1971–72. The success of the team in the final season of the decade had Bruins fans dreaming of another Stanley Cup.

They wouldn't have to wait too much longer for those dreams to come true.

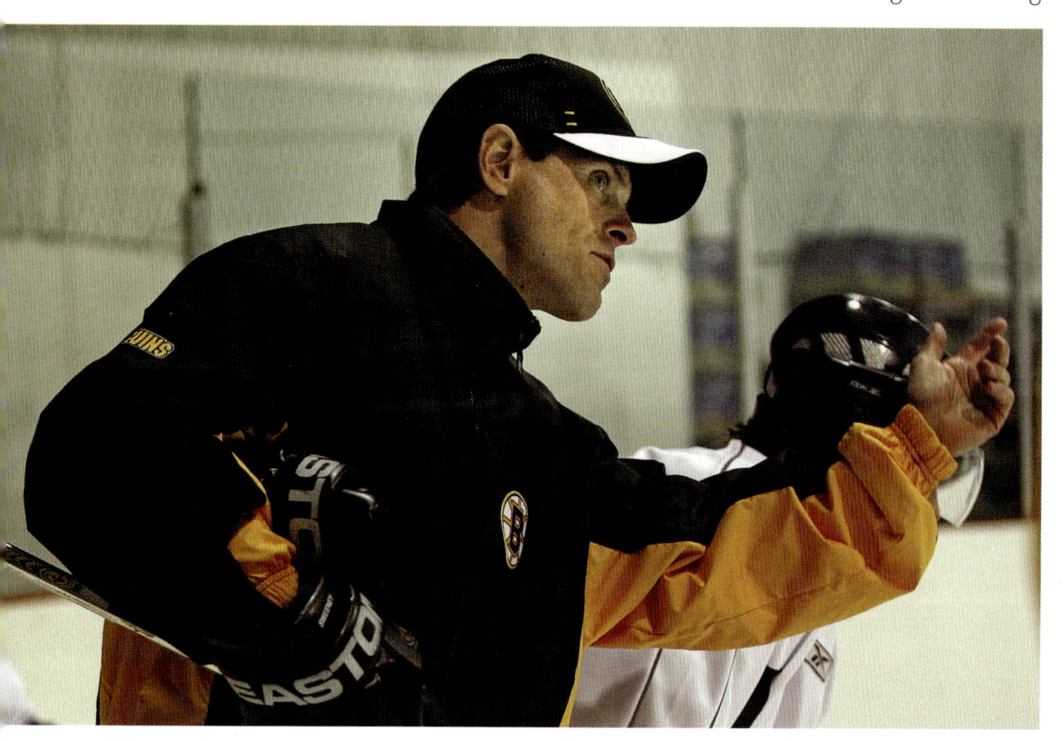

Don Sweeney works on the ice with a young Bruins prospect in July 2007. Sweeney cut his teeth in the Boston front office in player development. It remains a passion of his to this day. (Photograph by Nancy Lane/MediaNews Group/Boston Herald via Getty Images)

DON SWEENEY

For Don Sweeney, the 2000s marked a decade of transformation, one in which he went from playing for the Bruins on the blueline to helping direct the franchise from the front office.

He began the decade by putting the finishing touches on a playing career that saw him skate 15 seasons for the Bruins, from 1988 to 2003. Sweeney was a rock-solid defenseman who provided stability on the blueline—shift after shift, game after game, season after season. This was never needed more than at the beginning of the 2000s, with the departure of longtime franchise icon Ray Bourque to Colorado in March 2000.

When he played for the Bruins, Sweeney had a great reverence for the players who had worn Black and Gold before him. "There was a team toughness and an attitude that permeated to our locker room because of the players in particular that set that standard back in the '70s," said Sweeney in a 2022 interview. "Several of them used to be around quite often, around the locker room and such. I have such great respect for Terry O'Reilly, my first coach in the NHL, and Derek Sanderson and Cheesy. Just a great group of guys to be around and learn from."

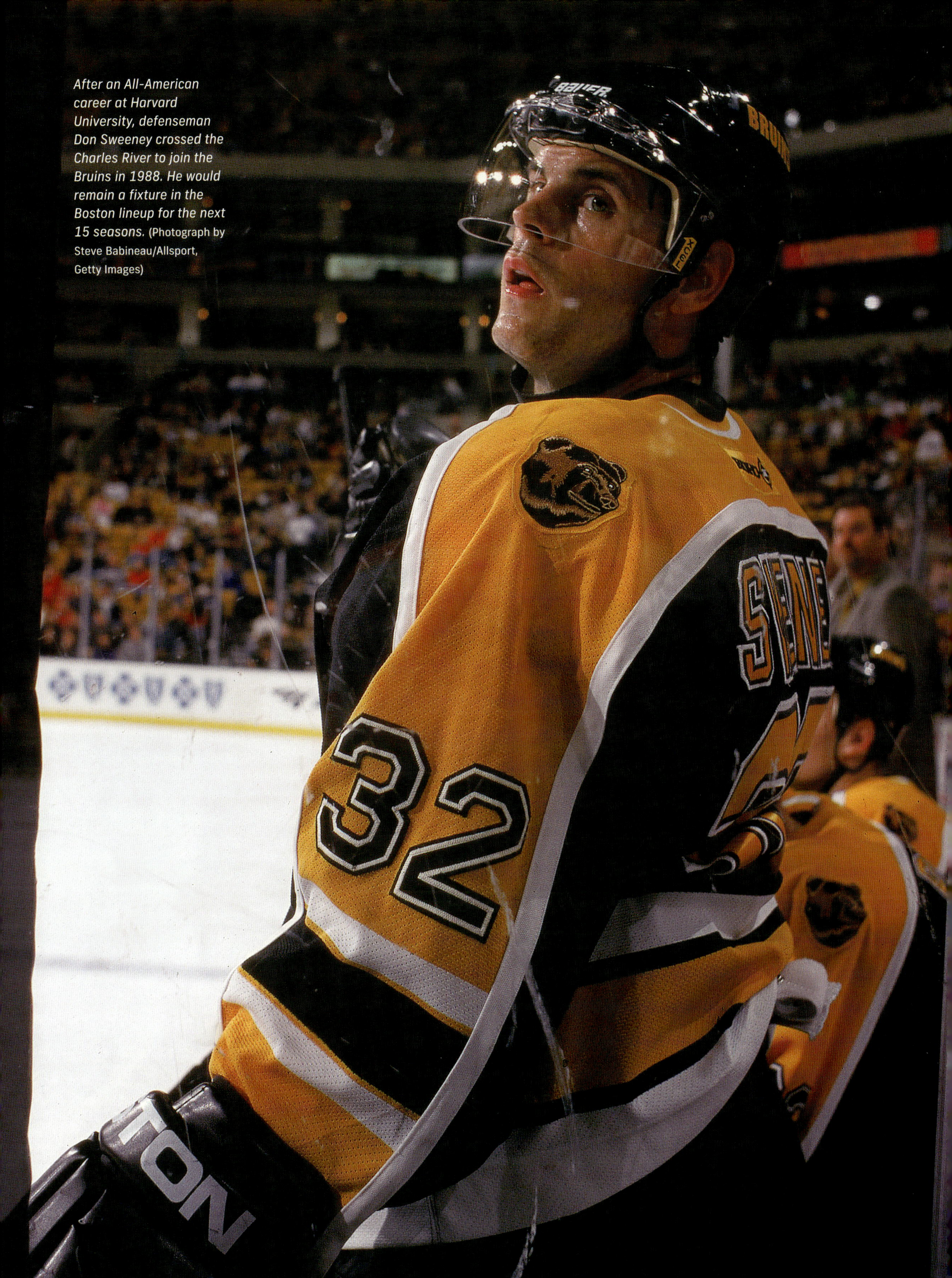

After an All-American career at Harvard University, defenseman Don Sweeney crossed the Charles River to join the Bruins in 1988. He would remain a fixture in the Boston lineup for the next 15 seasons. (Photograph by Steve Babineau/Allsport, Getty Images)

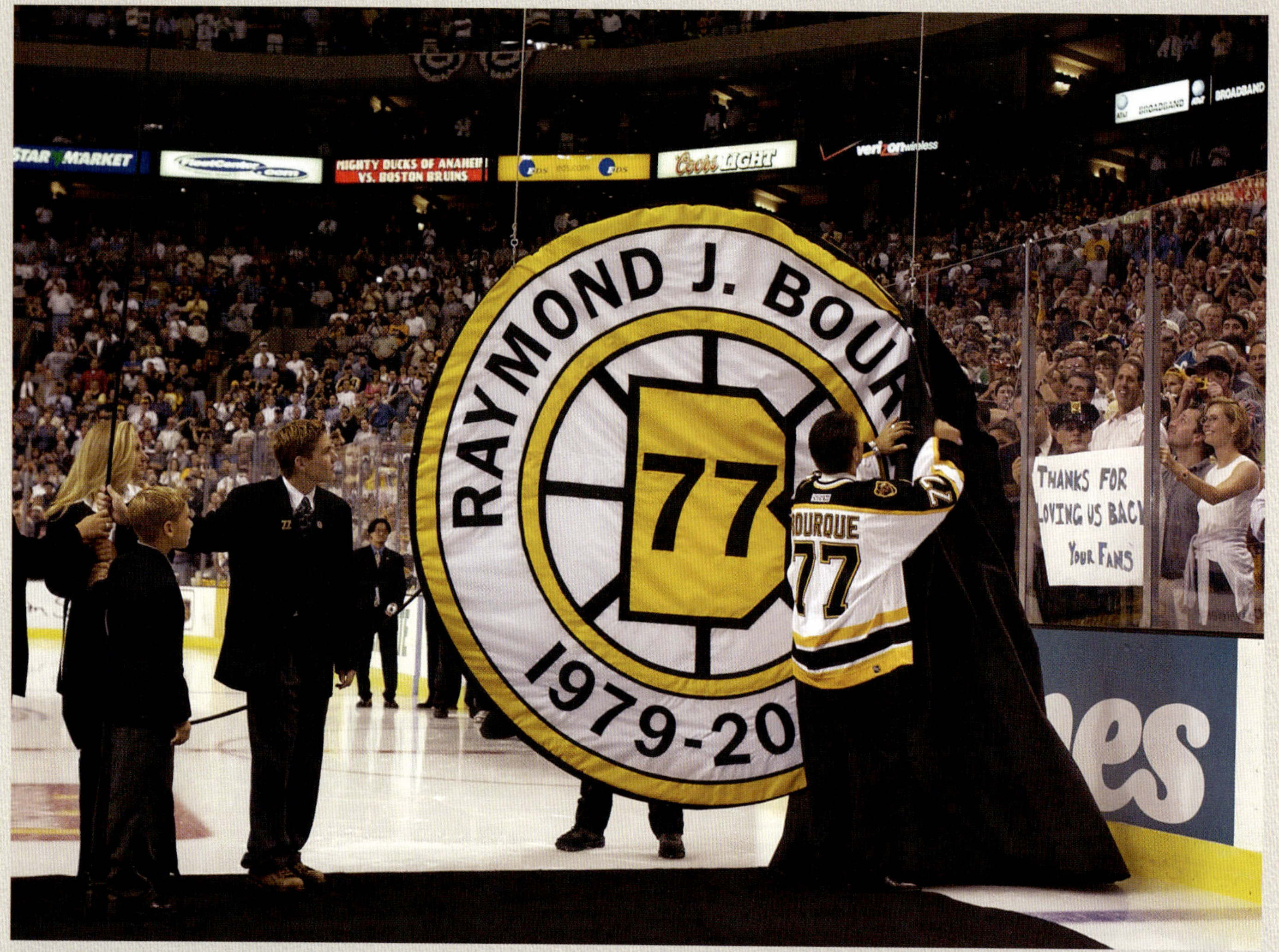

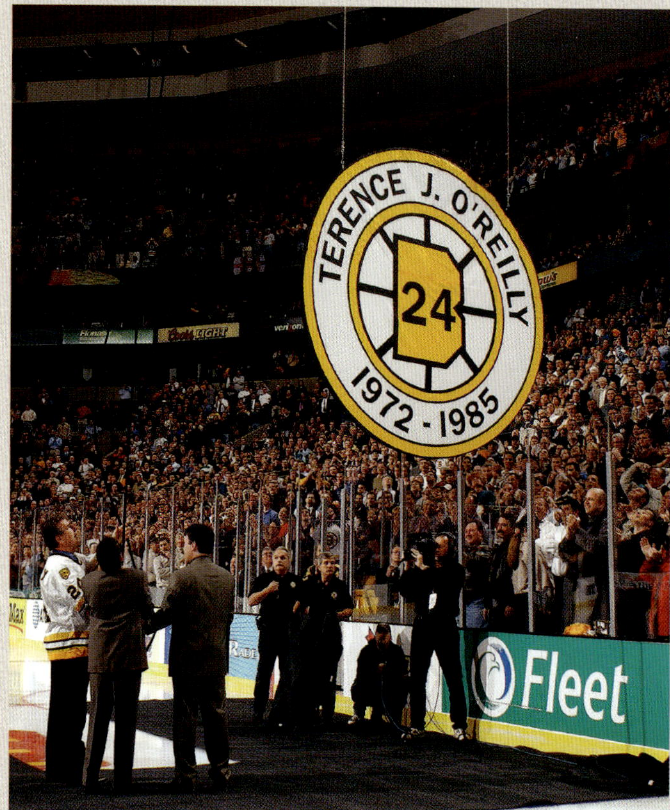

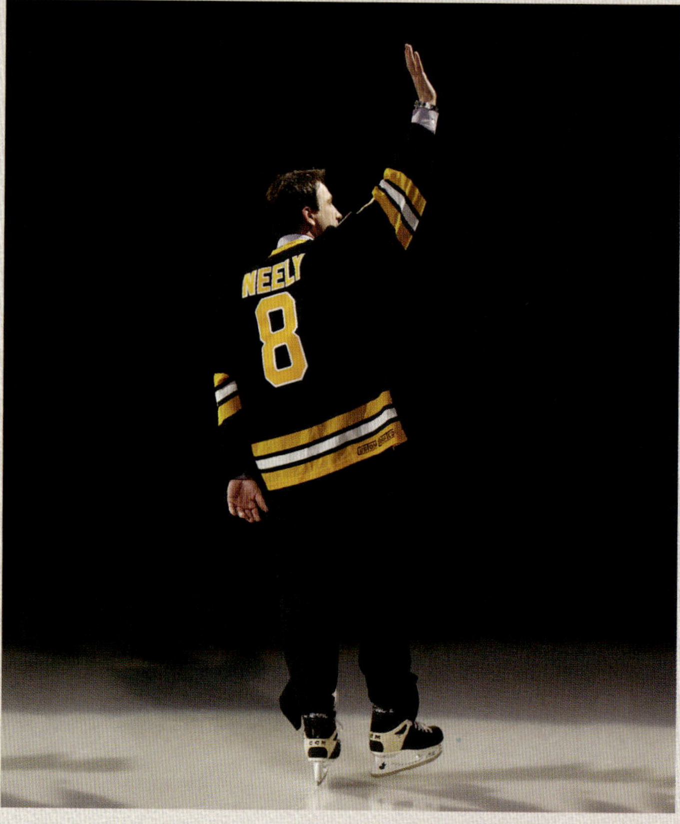

During the first half of the decade, the Bruins raised three numbers to the rafters of the FleetCenter—Ray Bourque's No. 77 in October 2001, Terry O'Reilly's No. 24 in October 2002, and Cam Neely's No. 8 in January 2005. The "retired number club" remains highly exclusive. As of 2023, only 12 men have had their number retired by the Bruins. (Bourque photograph by Ezra Shaw/Allsport, Getty Images; O'Reilly and Neely photographs by Steve Babineau)

There are only seven men in Bruins history who have appeared in more than 1,000 games for the team. Don Sweeney (1,052 games) is one of them.

After leaving Boston at the end of the 2002–03 season, Sweeney played one final year with the Dallas Stars. While he had wanted to finish his career with the Bruins, that final season with Dallas would also prove to be a blessing in disguise—and the beginning of a pathway that would lead Sweeney back to Boston. "It was an older team, and I moved into a bit of a development role while I was playing," said Sweeney. "I connected with some of the younger players down in Dallas.... It just really aligned with what turned out to be the development role that Peter Chiarelli had hired me into two years later. So it kind of jump-started that whole process for me on thinking about what could come after I finished playing."

Sweeney joined the Bruins front office in 2006 as director of player development. One year later, he conceived, organized, and ran the team's first off-season Development Camp for aspiring Bruins. "You realize that these kids are young," said Sweeney. "They [need] a lot of development. Even though they can be star players at such a young age, they have so much more maturing still to do and you try and fill in those gaps."

He rapidly ascended the front office ladder, being promoted to director of hockey operations in 2007 and then to assistant general manager in 2009. Along the way, Sweeney toyed with the idea of coaching ("I think I would have enjoyed it," he said) but decided to stay in hockey operations. "I had a great mentor in Peter Chiarelli that allowed me to do a lot of different things from a cap standpoint, and negotiating contracts standpoint," said Sweeney. "I felt like the challenges associated with the hockey operations were pretty widespread, and it was something that always intrigued me. So I stayed on that path."

That path would eventually result in Sweeney becoming general manager of the Bruins in 2015. Several years later, in 2019, Sweeney was named NHL General Manager of the Year for the job that he had done putting together a resurgent team that made it to the seventh game of the Stanley Cup Final. The various moves he made in the draft, in free agency, and on the trade market also helped fuel the success of the historic 2022–23 season.

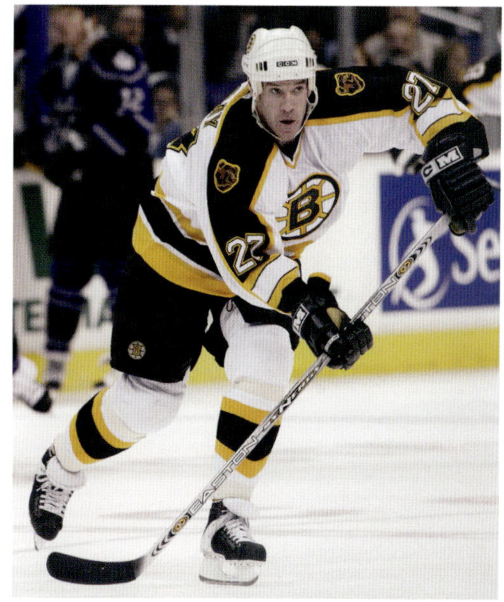

Glen Murray's 16-year NHL career was bookended by two stints in Boston. In the first stint (1991–1995), Murray was a young, developing player. By the time he returned for his second stint (2001–2008), he was a far more polished, productive player, averaging 30 goals per season. (Photograph by Victor Decolongon/Getty Images/NHLI)

JOE THORNTON

JOE THORNTON'S CAREER with the Bruins was marked first by hope, then disappointment, and finally, fulfillment. And then, suddenly, it was over.

Thornton was a big, easygoing kid from St. Thomas, Ontario, who played in juniors with the Sault Ste. Marie Greyhounds (a breeding ground for a number of NHL stars, including Wayne Gretzky). At 6′4″ and 220 pounds, he was a prospect with size, speed, and skills. In 1997, coming off a last-place finish and their first season missing the playoffs in nearly three decades, the Bruins selected Thornton with the No. 1 overall pick in the NHL Draft.

Thornton was seen by many as the savior of the franchise, the latest in the long line of Hall of Fame players who would lead the Bruins back to the top of the NHL.

It didn't happen, at least not right away. It turned out that Thornton was less of a finished product and more of a project who needed plenty of development. The Bruins front office was patient—to a certain degree. "We expected him to be giddy, but we don't expect him to stay giddy forever," said Harry Sinden in a 1998 interview, adding that the Bruins needed Thornton to pick up his intensity.

Bruins fans were not as charitable and initially regarded Thornton as a disappointment, especially when he tallied a grand total of seven points (three goals and four assists) during his rookie year in 1997–98. The fact that the hard-nosed Pat Burns was Thornton's first coach probably suppressed those statistics but also

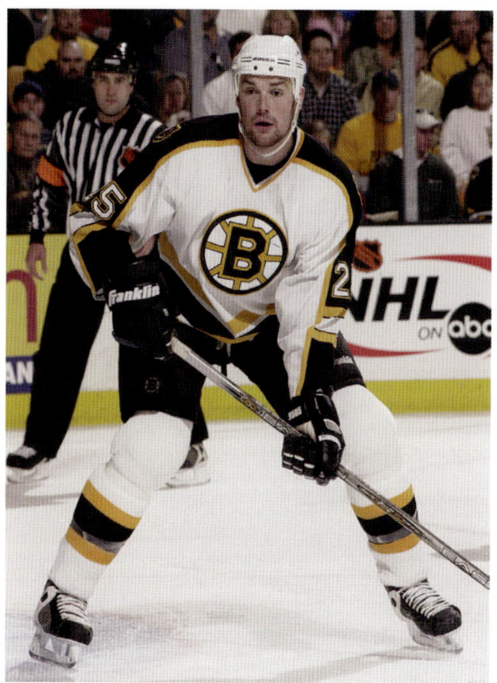

Hal Gill stands guard in front of the Bruins net during a playoff game vs. Montreal in April 2002. A native of Concord, Massachusetts, and a product of Providence College, Gill was a dependable, stay-at-home defenseman with plenty of size (6′7″, 243 pounds). He played the first eight seasons (1997–2006) of his 16-year NHL career with the Bruins. After leaving Boston, Gill won a Stanley Cup while skating with the Pittsburgh Penguins in 2009. (Photograph by Brian Babineau /NHLI via Getty Images)

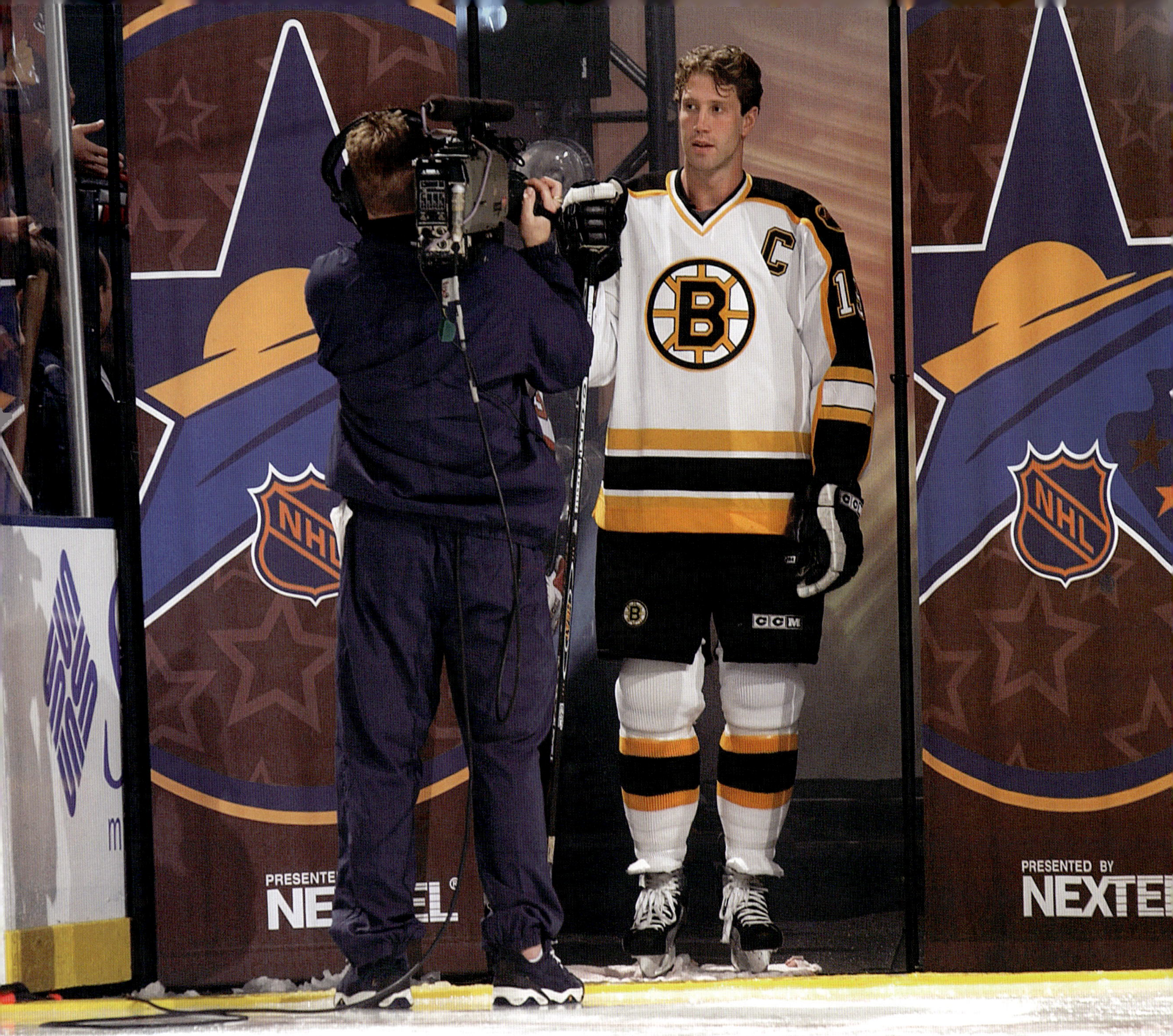

After the Bruins selected Joe Thornton with the No. 1 overall pick of the 1997 NHL Draft, many fans expected him to become an instant All-Star. That didn't happen right away—but Thornton did eventually attain that status. Here, he waits to get introduced during the 2003 NHL All-Star Game in Sunrise, Florida. (Photograph by Dave Sandford/ Getty Images/NHLI)

aided his development in the long run. "He was hard on Joe," Bruins defenseman Hal Gill said of Burns in a 2014 interview. "He made Joe work, he plugged Joe in on the fourth line. He wasn't handed anything."

Over time, Thornton's intensity and production gradually picked up. It all started to blossom for him during the 2002–03 season, when he compiled 101 points (36 goals, 65 assists) while serving as captain of the Bruins, further proof of his growing maturity. For some fans, it still wasn't enough—but the plain fact was that "Jumbo Joe" had emerged as the best player on the team, if not one of the best players in the NHL.

No one knew it at the time, though, but Thornton's time in Boston was about to run out. Early in the 2005–06 season (the first after the lockout), with the roster in flux and the team facing a rebuild, the Bruins took the decisive but drastic step of trading Thornton to the San Jose Sharks. Thornton would go on to have a banner season (winning both the Hart and Art Ross Trophies) and a long and productive career in the NHL, playing 24 seasons in all and amassing 1,539 points. It has been a career that will likely land him in the Hockey Hall of Fame one day.

It just never completely worked out for him in Boston.

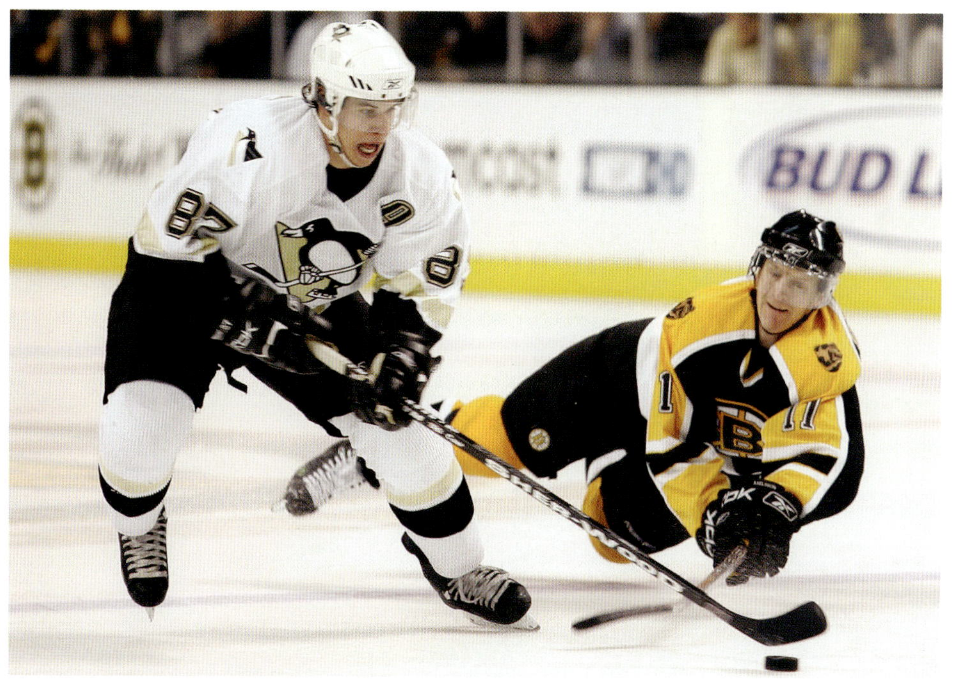

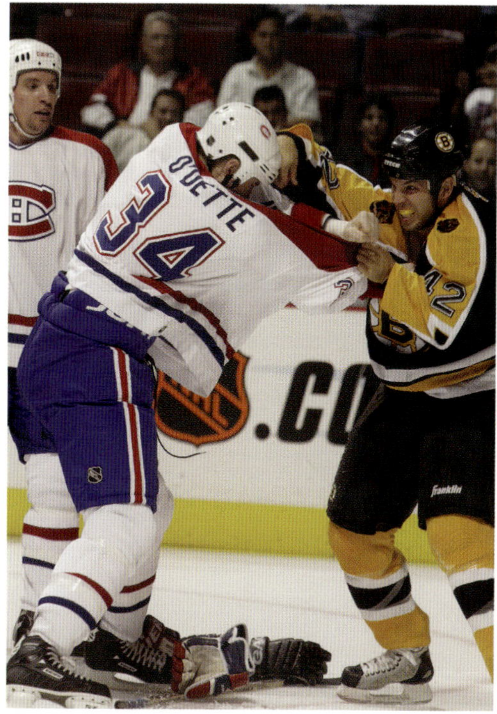

Above left: P.J. Axelsson of the Bruins (right) dives to break up a scoring bid by Sidney Crosby of the Penguins in a January 2007 game at the TD Banknorth Garden. A native of Sweden, Axelsson was a classy, smooth, and defensive-minded left wing. He played all 11 seasons of his NHL career (1997–2009) with Boston.
(Photograph by Elsa/Getty Images)

Above: P.J. Stock played two full seasons for the Bruins (2001–2003), averaging 141 penalty minutes per season. Feisty on the ice, affable and self-deprecating off the ice (he described himself as "a self-proclaimed offensive threat"), Stock became an unabashed fan favorite. Here, he battles Montreal defenseman Matt O'Dette in a preseason game in 2002.
(Photograph by Andre Pichette/Getty Images)

ANDY BRICKLEY

IN THE EARLY 2000S, Andy Brickley was settling into his second act with the Bruins as a broadcaster with NESN.

His first act, as a player, had defied all odds. Consider the fact that Brickley didn't make the varsity team at Melrose High School until his junior year. He wasn't recruited and had to walk on at the University of New Hampshire. And, despite an All-America career at UNH, he wasn't exactly coveted by NHL teams. In fact, the Philadelphia Flyers selected Brickley with the very last pick of the 1980 NHL Draft (210th overall), making him that year's "Mr. Irrelevant."

Brickley looks back on all of this with considerable pride. "All these things are important for young kids to hear," said Brickley. "Because you're not always going to be the best player on the best team, or your own team, and that you can be a late bloomer and still achieve the dream that you dream as a kid. I think that is important, and that is the message I try to deliver because that was my whole life."

Once he entered the professional ranks, Brickley faced an uphill climb to make it to the NHL. But he made that climb. "I had goals, I had aspirations, I had good work habits, and I wanted to play in the NHL," said Brickley. "And then I had the good fortune of playing for Tom McVie. He was my head coach with the Maine Mariners, my first year in the pros. He taught me what it takes to be not only a professional hockey player, but an NHL hockey player, and I am forever indebted to him."

Brickley went on to enjoy an 11-year career in the NHL. The high point came in the four seasons from 1988 to 1992, when the hard-working winger tallied 37 goals and 76 assists playing for his hometown Bruins.

In 1996, two years after he retired from the NHL, "Brick" launched his second career as a Bruins broadcaster—initially on radio, then on Channel 38, and finally, from the early 2000s onward, on NESN. His early play-by-play partners included two media members long associated with the team, Dave Shea and Dale Arnold. Since 2007, his full-time partner on NESN broadcasts has been the current "Voice of the Bruins," Jack Edwards.

As a kid growing up in Melrose, Massachusetts, like everyone else in the Greater Boston Area, Brickley watched scores of Bruins games on television, with Fred Cusick handling the play-by-play and Johnny Pierson and then Derek Sanderson providing the analysis. He expresses admiration for the men who preceded him

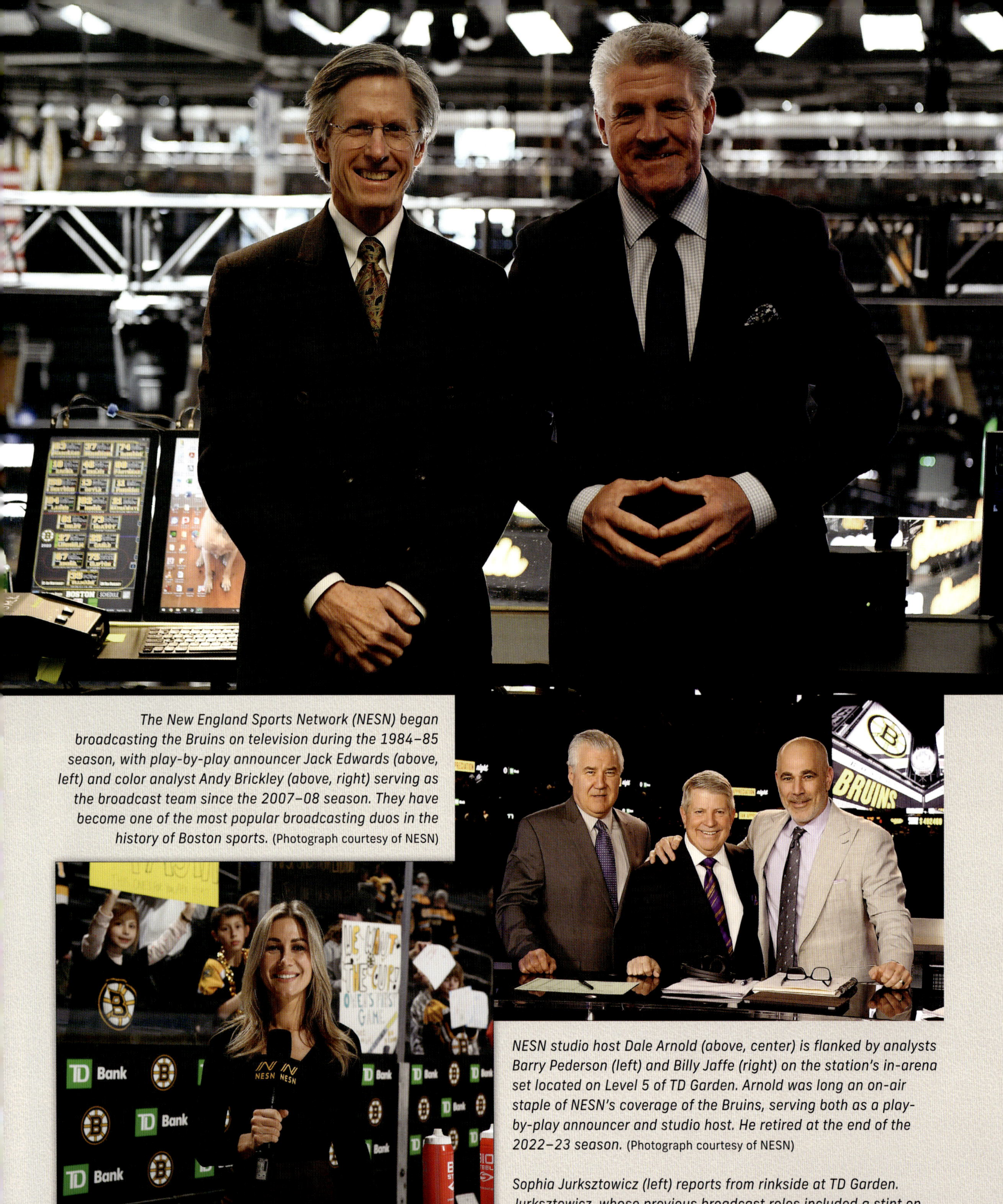

The New England Sports Network (NESN) began broadcasting the Bruins on television during the 1984–85 season, with play-by-play announcer Jack Edwards (above, left) and color analyst Andy Brickley (above, right) serving as the broadcast team since the 2007–08 season. They have become one of the most popular broadcasting duos in the history of Boston sports. (Photograph courtesy of NESN)

NESN studio host Dale Arnold (above, center) is flanked by analysts Barry Pederson (left) and Billy Jaffe (right) on the station's in-arena set located on Level 5 of TD Garden. Arnold was long an on-air staple of NESN's coverage of the Bruins, serving both as a play-by-play announcer and studio host. He retired at the end of the 2022–23 season. (Photograph courtesy of NESN)

Sophia Jurksztowicz (left) reports from rinkside at TD Garden. Jurksztowicz, whose previous broadcast roles included a stint on Hockey Night in Canada, *arrived in Boston in 2019 and has been part of NESN's coverage of the Bruins ever since.* (Photograph courtesy of NESN) in the broadcast booth. "Those guys made the calls so great," said Brickley. "Both the analysts had great insight. And I like to think that through some form of osmosis or something, and that because I paid attention and I was a cerebral person, that I learned a great deal from Johnny Pierson and Derek Sanderson. Both brilliant analysts, both great players. Derek had a great personality. Those guys were phenomenal. We were lucky to have them in Boston."

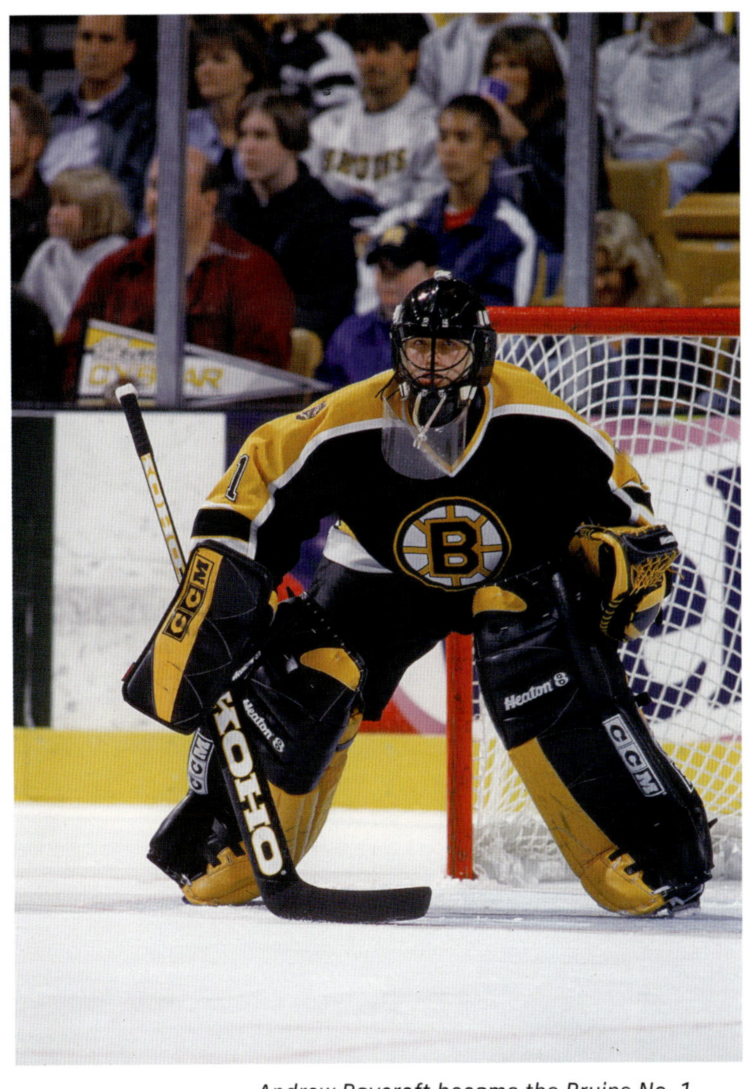

Andrew Raycroft became the Bruins No. 1 goaltender during his rookie season in 2003–04. He responded by winning 29 games with a goals against average of 2.05, a sterling performance that earned him the Calder Trophy as NHL rookie of the year. Raycroft played one more season with the Bruins before being traded to Toronto for the rights to Tuukka Rask. He currently serves as a studio analyst for Bruins games on NESN. (Photograph by Steve Babineau/Allsport, Getty Images)

THE REBIRTH OF THE BRUINS

With the trading of Joe Thornton in 2005, the Bruins essentially admitted that it was time to start over. For Bruins fans, that meant that there would be some rough years ahead.

And things were indeed rough, especially during the 2005–06 and 2006–07 seasons. As Patrice Bergeron remembered, "We were trying to find ourselves as a team and our identity and whatnot.... [There were] a lot of moving parts, guys coming in and coming out. A lot. Kind of a revolving door at that time.... A lot of personnel changes.... It took some time."

Bergeron himself was plainly part of the solution. After getting drafted in 2003, he made the team right away, emerging as a valuable contributor for the 2003–04 Bruins even though he was just 18 years old. In the two seasons after the 2004–05 lockout year, Bergeron scored 73 points and 70 points, respectively. As the franchise moved forward, the young Bergeron was a clear cornerstone.

More help arrived in free agency prior to the 2006–07 season. Marc Savard was a clever, shifty center who promised to help take the Boston offense to the next level. He delivered, scoring 96 points (22 goals, 74 assists) for the season. Savard would remain a top producer for the remainder of the decade.

An even bigger acquisition that season—both literally and figuratively—was defenseman Zdeno Chara. "He was instrumental," said Andy Brickley. "The signing of Zdeno was critical to the revitalization of what the Bruins should always be. They had gotten away from it a little bit as an organization, and then Chara came in and reestablished the culture that should be the Boston Bruins and that is the Boston Bruins."

Despite the additions of Chara and Savard, the Bruins struggled in 2006–07, finishing out of the playoff picture for the second straight season. "The change was right in front of your face, with Zdeno Chara, Marc Savard, and new faces," said Tim Thomas, who had emerged as the team's primary goaltender after the lockout. "But at that point, it's really early. You don't know really where what's being built is going to go. So that was a pretty rough season."

Young talent (David Krejci, Milan Lucic, etc.) was starting to arrive, however, and the team was building a roster—and a culture—that reflected the vision of general manager Peter Chiarelli. "It was being hard to play against, playing hard, being aggressive, and hard workers," said Bergeron. "It was really the main focus from the players that they went out and got—players that would do whatever for the team, unselfish players, very humble.... Of course, Z and what he is and what he does on the ice as well, made us buy in, wanting to put in the effort and the work to keep getting better."

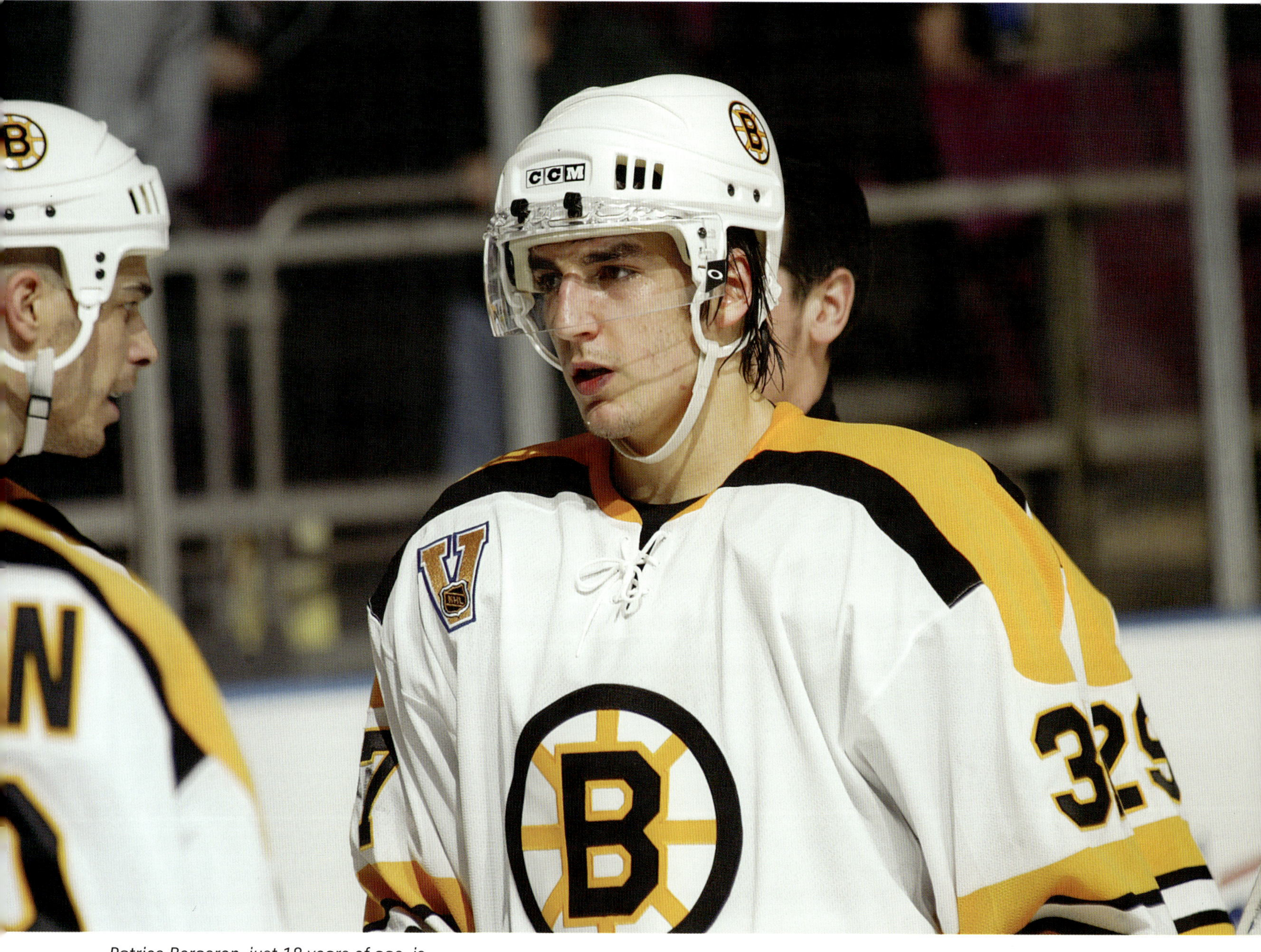

Patrice Bergeron, just 18 years of age, is shown during his rookie season of 2003–04, a campaign where he scored 16 goals with 23 assists. He was talented, hard-working, and mature beyond his years. (Photograph by Bruce Bennett Studios via Getty Images Studios/Getty Images)

The next season (2007–08), the Bruins turned the corner under new head coach Claude Julien. "Chiarelli had put together a team that competed night in and night out, and we ended up squeaking into the playoffs against our rivals, the Montreal Canadiens," said Shawn Thornton, then in his first season with the Bruins. "You could really tell the excitement was starting to build around the team and the franchise again." The playoff performance against the Canadiens was inspirational, as the underdog Bruins battled back from a 3–1 series deficit by winning Game 5 in Montreal and then a dramatic Game 6 back in Boston on a late Marco Sturm goal. Montreal would go on to win the series finale, but the message was clear: the Bruins were back.

Everything came together in 2008–09, as the Bruins became one of the top teams in the NHL with a 53–19–10 record. In the playoffs, they swept the Canadiens in cathartic fashion. They were eliminated by the Carolina Hurricanes in the next round—but even in defeat, there was hope, as the Bruins once again battled back from a 3–1 series deficit before falling in Game 7 on an overtime goal. Individual honors at season's end included a Norris Trophy for Chara as the NHL's top defenseman, a Vezina Trophy for Thomas as the NHL's top goaltender, a Jennings Trophy for goalie tandem Thomas and Manny Fernandez for fewest goals allowed, and a Jack Adams Trophy for Julien as NHL coach of the year. It was a breakthrough season with a promise of more good things to come.

Right: On June 24, 2006, the Boston Bruins selected center Phil Kessel with the No. 5 overall selection of the NHL Draft. Kessel would score 66 goals in his three seasons in Boston, winning the Bill Masterton Memorial Trophy in 2007 in recognition of his successful battle with cancer. After leaving Boston in 2009, Kessel has continued his career with four additional NHL teams. (Photograph by Jeff Vinnick/ Getty Images)

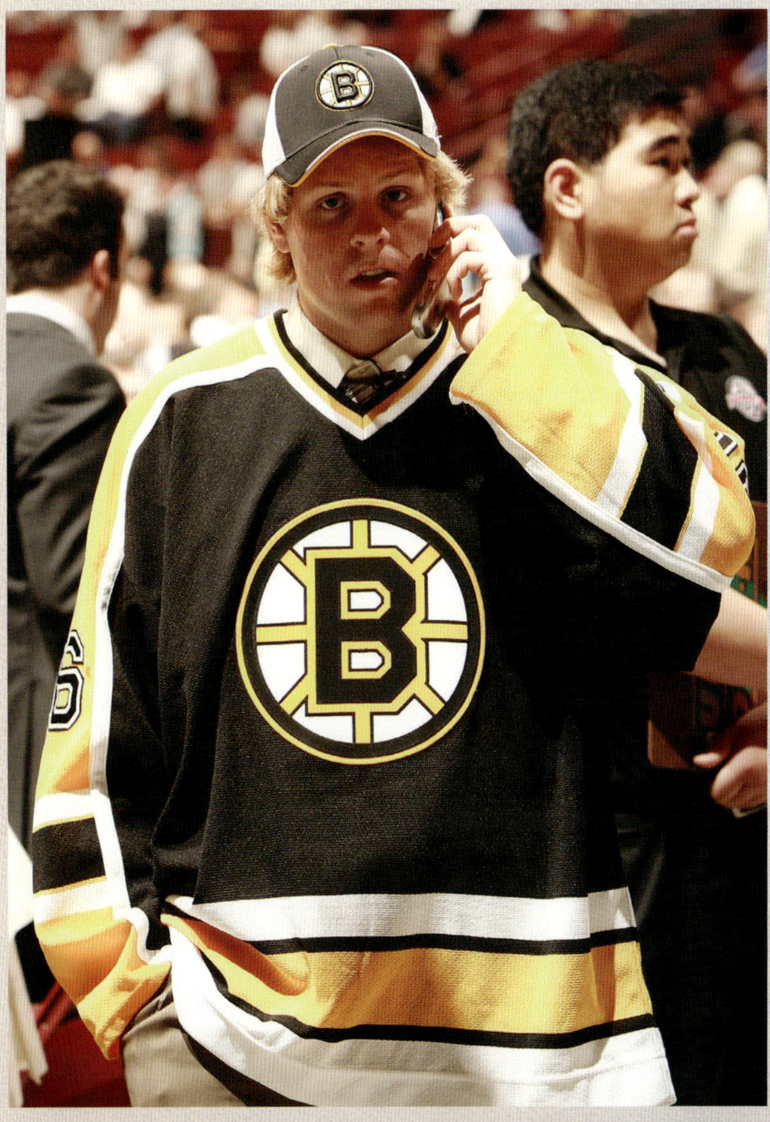

Below: The 2008–09 Bruins cleaned up at the NHL Awards Night at season's end. Hardware recipients included (left to right) Zdeno Chara (Norris Trophy as the best NHL defenseman), Tim Thomas (Vezina Trophy as the best NHL goalie), Manny Fernandez (Jennings Trophy, along with Thomas, for the NHL's lowest team goals against average), and head coach Claude Julien (Jack Adams Award as the NHL coach of the year). (Photograph by Bruce Bennett/ Getty Images for NHL)

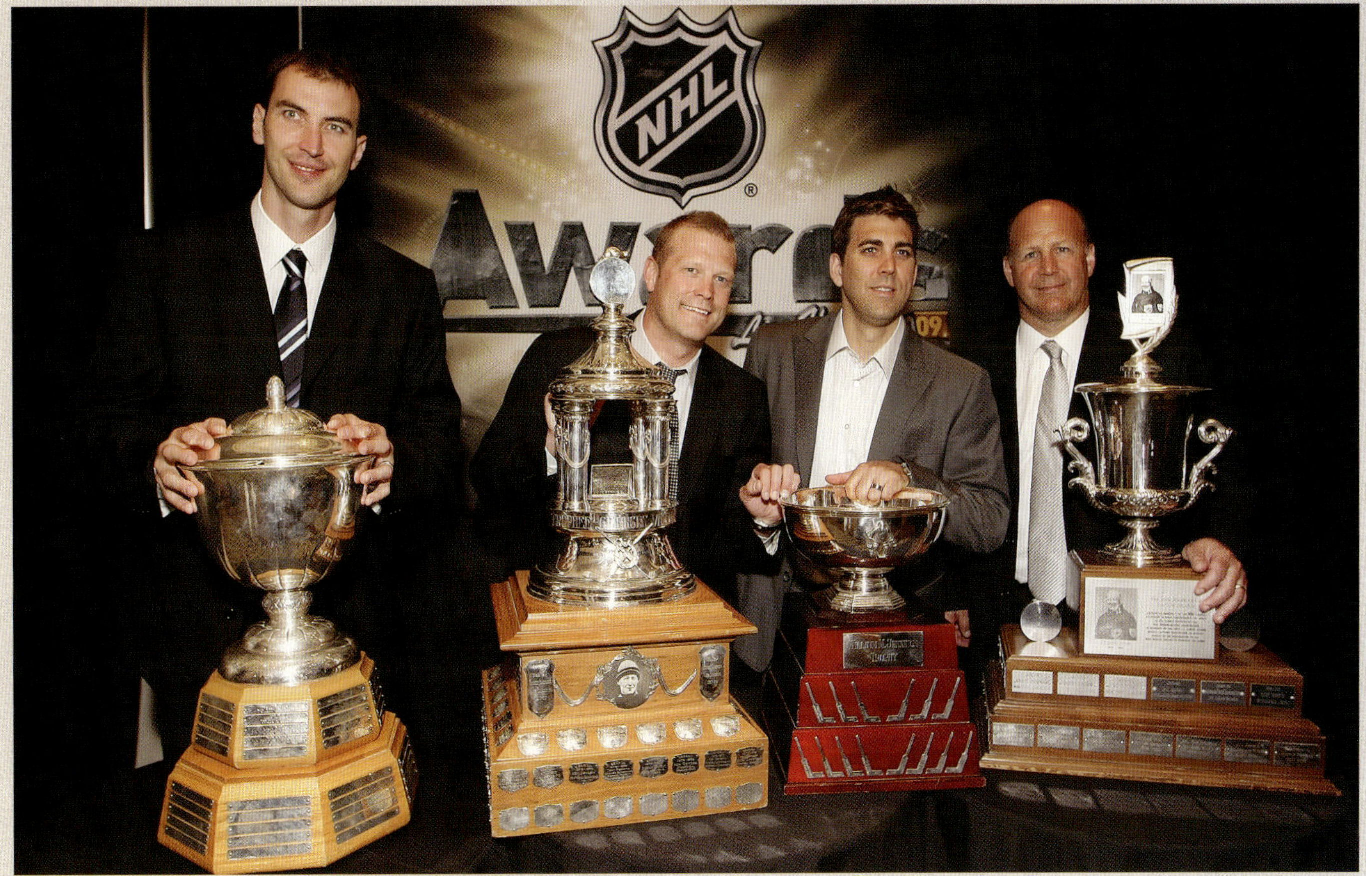

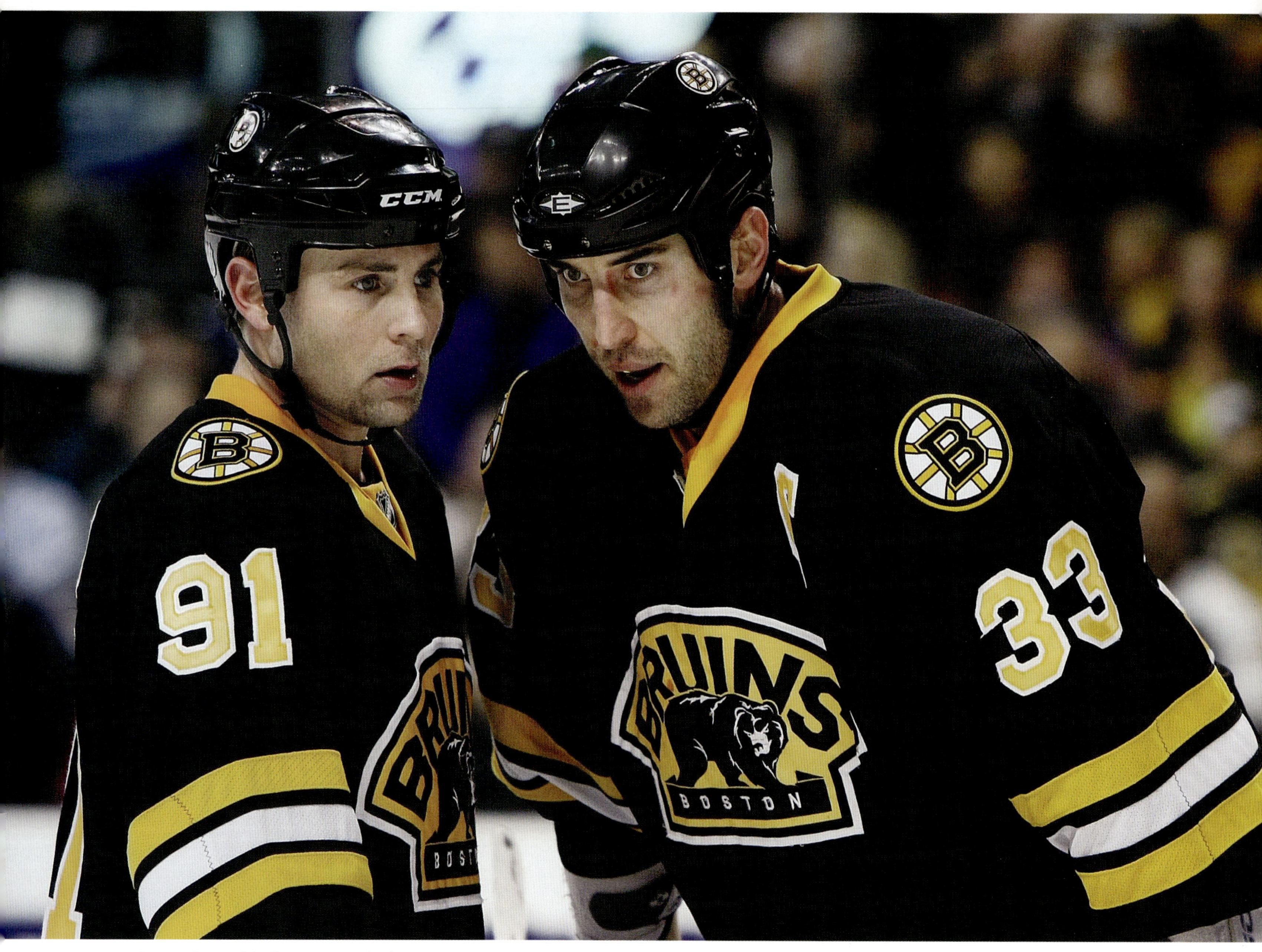

Boston's two big free agent signings prior to the 2006–07 season were center Marc Savard (91) and defenseman Zdeno Chara (33). Savard, a playmaking center in the mold of Adam Oates, put up big numbers for his first three seasons in Boston, averaging 87 points per year. Shortly thereafter, his career was derailed and then altogether curtailed by a series of injuries and concussions. (Photograph by Bruce Bennett/Getty Images)

CLAUDE JULIEN

THE FACT THAT Claude Julien became head coach of the Bruins for the 2007–08 season, and the team began its ascent back to NHL supremacy that very same season, is no mere coincidence.

Julien came to Boston with a track record as a former head coach for both the Montreal Canadiens and New Jersey Devils as well as a reputation for being a defensive chess master. The collapsing box system he perfected in Boston had one defenseman patrolling the slot while his partner was free to engage the puck carrier. It also called for his centers to back-check in support and his wingers to cover the points. Within two seasons, its successful implementation was largely responsible for the Bruins allowing the fewest goals in the NHL, paving the way for goalie Tim Thomas to earn the first of his two Vezina Trophies.

Yet the system didn't take complete hold right away. As Thomas observed, "It wasn't like he came in, and put in a new system in two months, and everybody knew it, and everybody did it.... It was a transition.... It wasn't like, 'Oh, here, we got it. We're going to be good someday.' It was building."

The culture was building, as well—and here again, Julien proved to be a perfect fit for the Bruins. "There's no one true superstar," said Patrice Bergeron of that

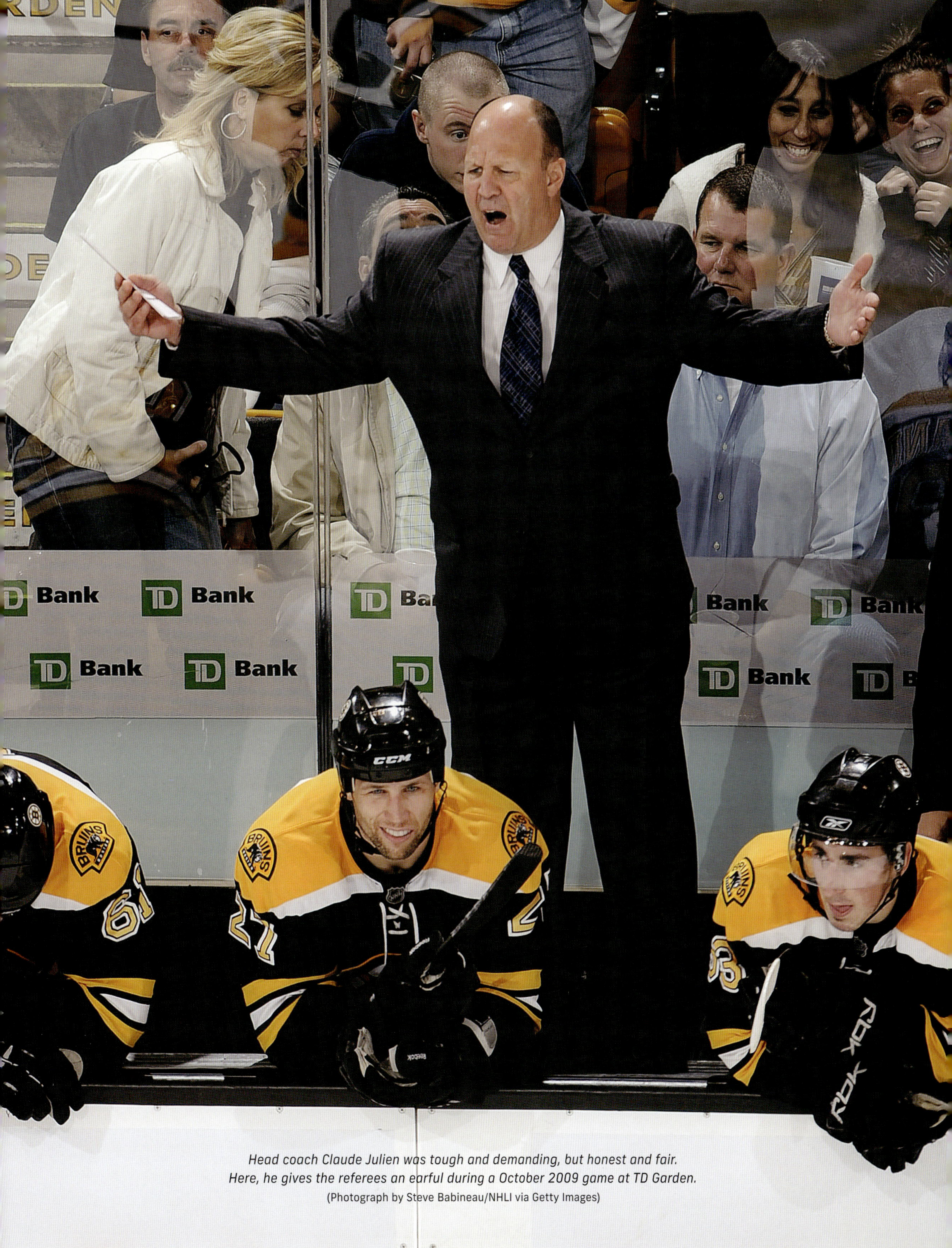

Head coach Claude Julien was tough and demanding, but honest and fair.
Here, he gives the referees an earful during a October 2009 game at TD Garden.
(Photograph by Steve Babineau/NHLI via Getty Images)

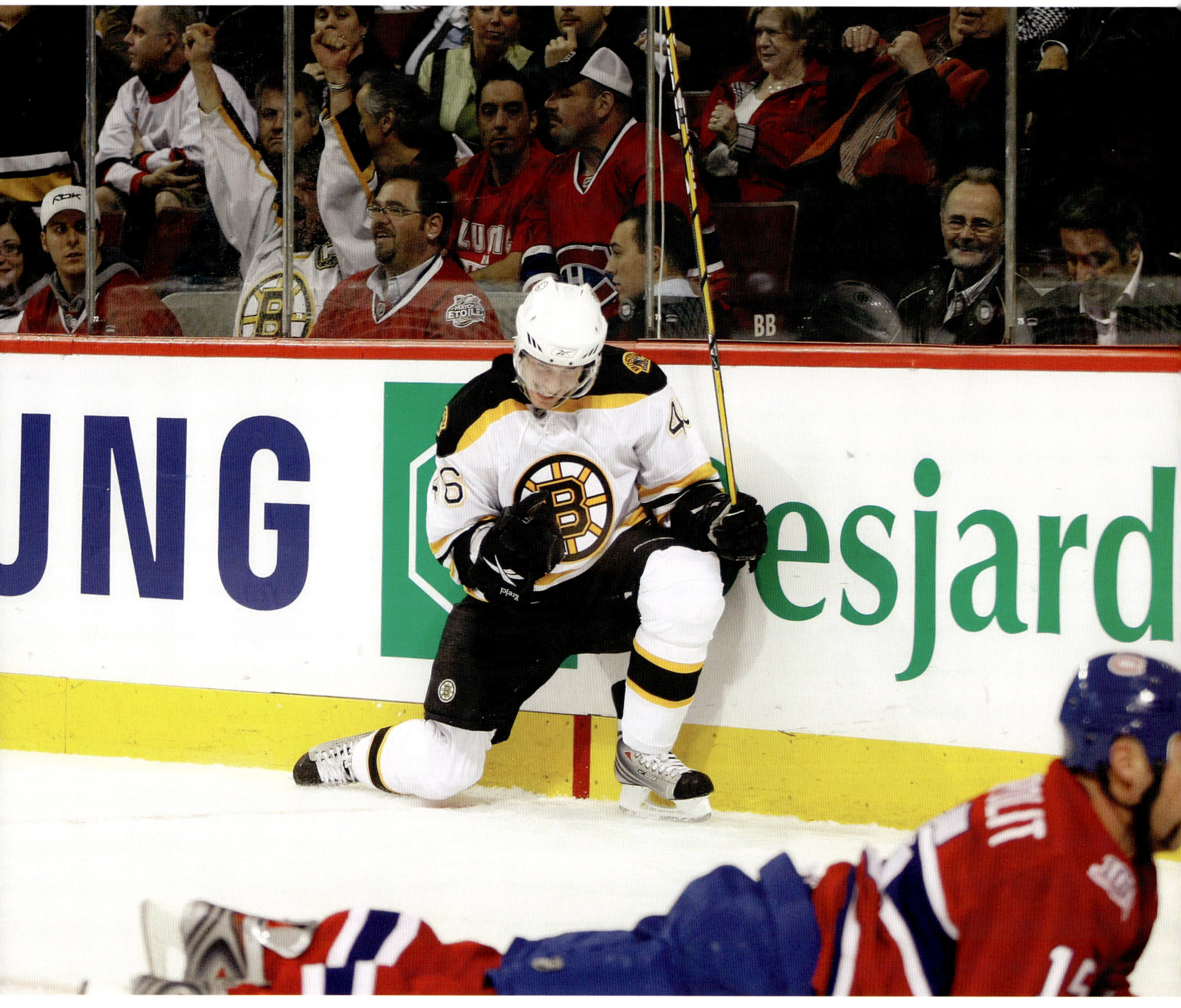

David Krejci has just scored the go-ahead goal in Game 4 of Boston's first-round playoff series against Montreal in April 2009. The Bruins would go on to win the game to complete the sweep. It made the Bruins the talk of the town—which, given the success that the Celtics, Patriots, and Red Sox were all enjoying at the time, was no small feat. (Photograph by Richard Wolowicz/Getty Images)

emerging team culture. "It's about the 20 guys who are working toward the same goal on the ice. I think Claude was really good at that and making sure everyone felt like they had a role. He was fair to everyone, and everyone started buying in at that point."

The man who brought him to Boston, Peter Chiarelli, later proclaimed that hiring Julien was the best move he made as general manager of the Bruins during his tenure, from 2006 to 2015.

During his own tenure in Boston, Julien won the team's first Stanley Cup in 39 years in 2011, led the team back to the Stanley Cup Final in 2013, and coached the team to a President's Trophy (best regular season record) in 2014. He would remain behind the Bruins bench until 2017, departing with franchise records in regular season and playoff victories—419 and 57, respectively. He is the winningest coach in the history of the Boston Bruins.

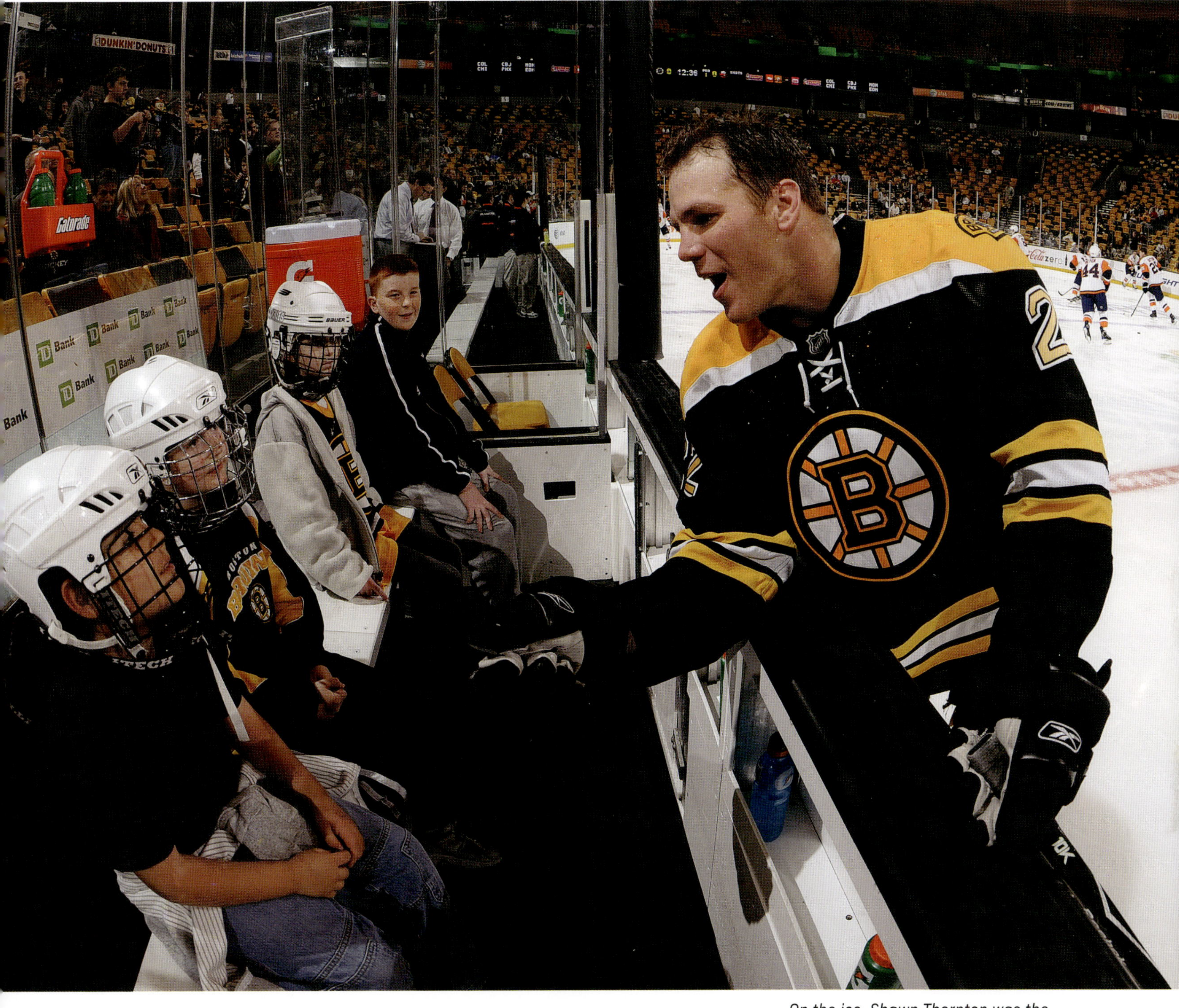

On the ice, Shawn Thornton was the consummate tough guy. Off the ice, he was the ultimate good guy. Here, Thornton says hello to several kids during warm-ups prior to a game at TD Garden in October 2009. (Photograph by Steve Babineau/NHLI via Getty Images)

SHAWN THORNTON

FEW ATHLETES ARRIVE in Boston and immediately plug into the city's history and culture the way Shawn Thornton did when he arrived in July 2007. Living within walking distance of TD Garden, he was the guy you would see outside of Mike's Pastry in the North End posing for selfies with fans. In short, he was one of us.

Much of this was due to his decision to live year-round in Boston. As Thornton remembered in a 2022 interview, "The statement we used was, 'If we're going to put up with the winters, let's enjoy the summers.'"

Thornton completely embraced his new city. "I lived in the community, and people would just run into me," said Thornton. "And I'm fairly approachable. If you're in Charlestown, there is a good chance that you're going to see me and I'll have a beer with you. I come from a small blue-collar town in Canada.... People

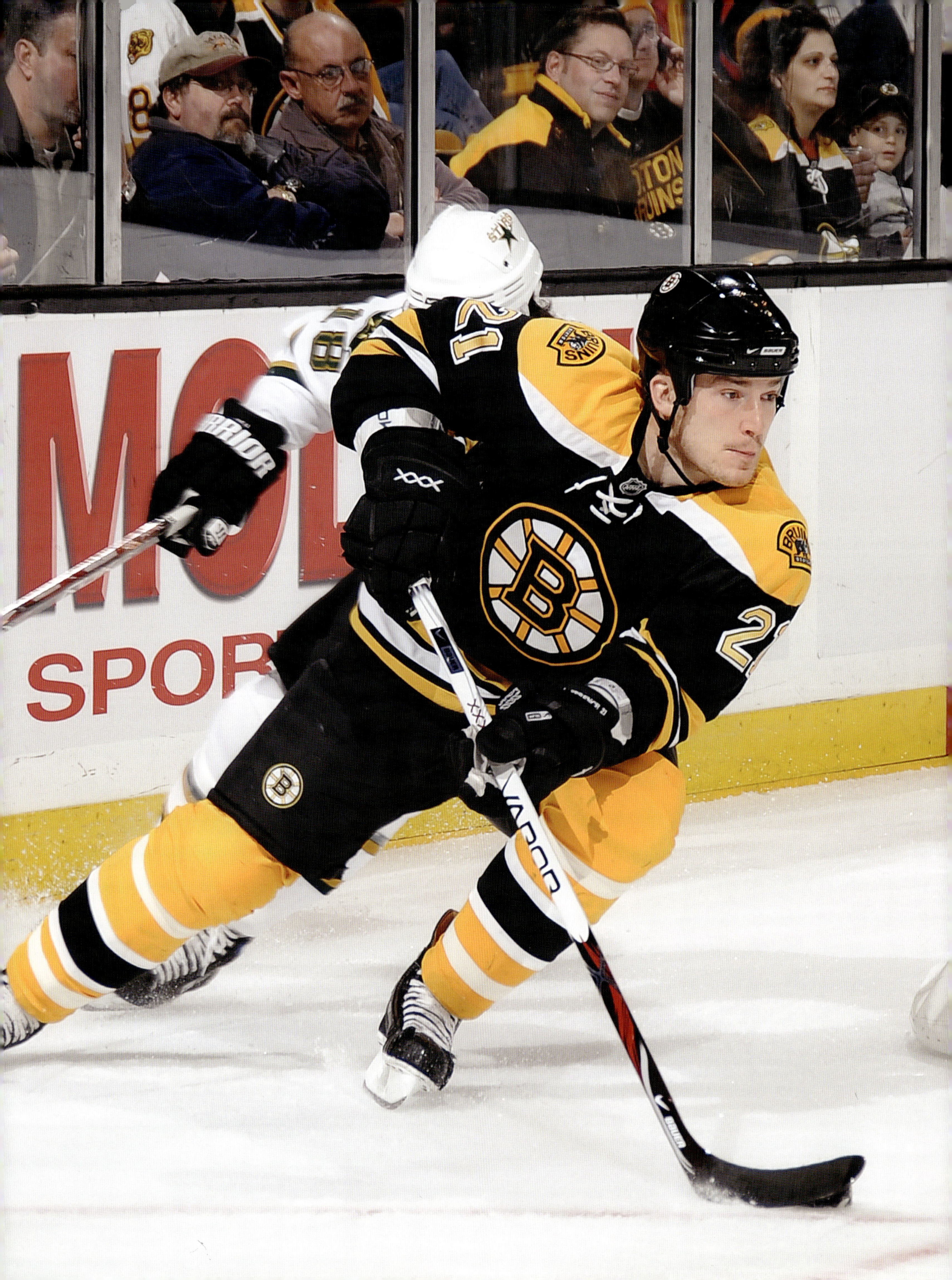

WARRIOR
VAPOR

work day in and day out there as well. It was a great fit.... I really enjoyed the people there [in Boston]. I enjoyed the community. I enjoyed everything about it."

He played for the Bruins for seven seasons (2007–2014). Typically skating on the third or fourth line, his scoring statistics were modest—but, when it came to Shawn Thornton, statistics were beside the point. He was a prototypical Bruin—tough, unselfish, and physical—and the embodiment of Peter Chiarelli's newfound emphasis on "being hard to play against."

He also clearly understood the essence of Boston and Boston fans. "Boston is a sports town, through and through," said Thornton. "All four of the major sports teams have a devout following.... I've seen enough Bostonians with the logo tattooed onto a body part of theirs to know that they are very proud of their sports teams, the Bruins obviously being one of them."

At the conclusion of his 14-year NHL career, Thornton joined the front office of the Florida Panthers, where he currently serves as the chief revenue officer. It is, unsurprisingly, a role that he has completely embraced.

Opposite page: Shortly after his arrival in Boston in 2006, General Manager Peter Chiarelli announced his intention of building a team with players who were "hard to play against." Defenseman Andrew Ference certainly fit that description. Acquired by Chiarelli in February 2007, Ference would be a mainstay on the Bruins blueline and be a key part of the character of the team until 2013. (Photograph by Steve Babineau/NHLI via Getty Images)

MILAN LUCIC

IN SEPTEMBER 2007, Bruins fans were overjoyed at the news that Cam Neely was returning to the organization as a vice president in their front office. "Charlie Jacobs asked if I wanted to get back involved with the team in some capacity," said Neely in 2022 interview. "I said, 'Let's see how a year goes. I want to see if I like it and if you guys like the job I'm doing.'" All the boxes would soon be checked and the NHL's original power forward was back in the fold.

Bruins left wing Milan Lucic (below) was always willing to drop his gloves when necessary or advisable. Here, he goes toe to toe with Mathieu Schneider of the Canadiens in Game 2 of the Eastern Conference Quarterfinals in 2009. (Photograph by Elsa/Getty Images)

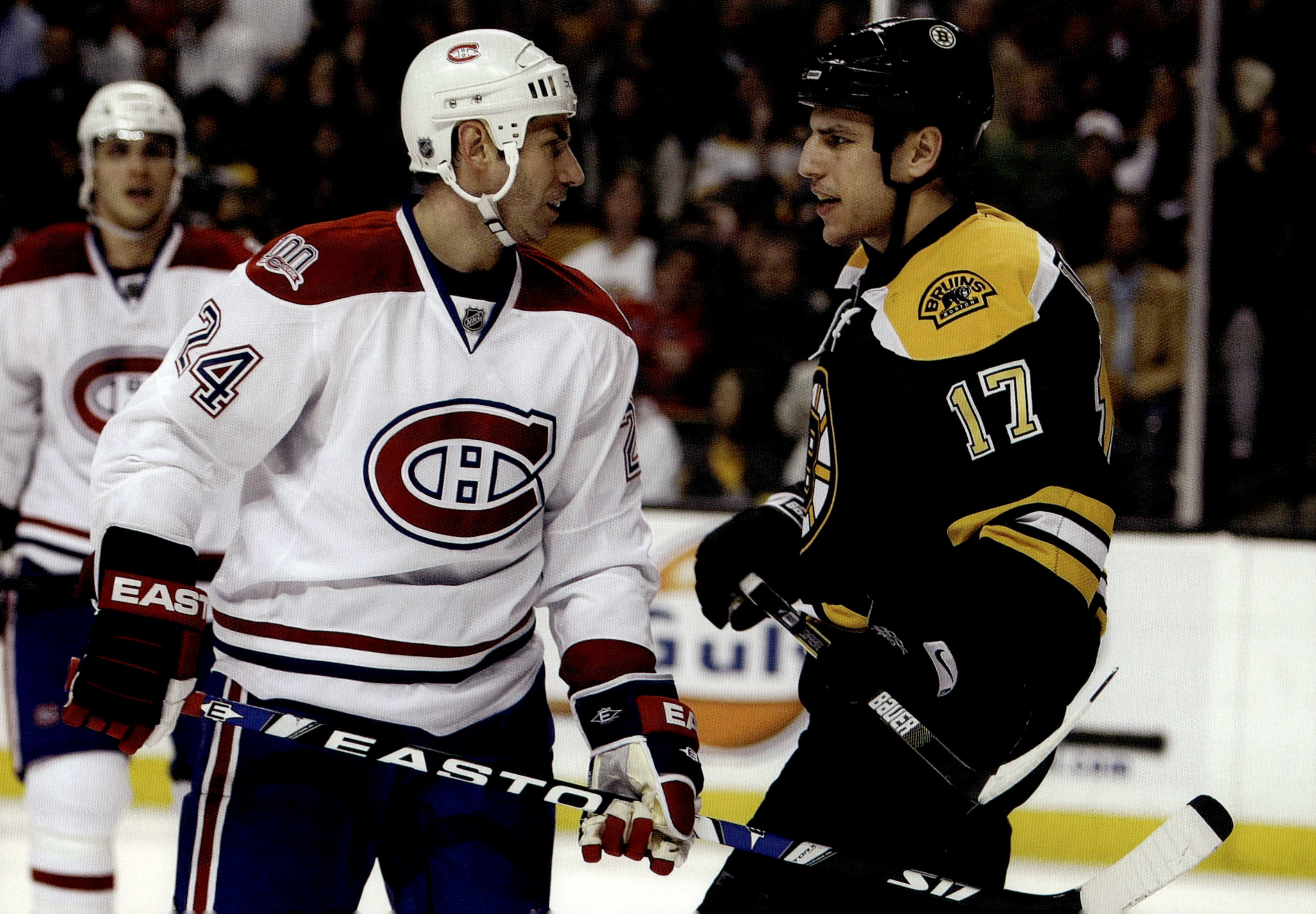

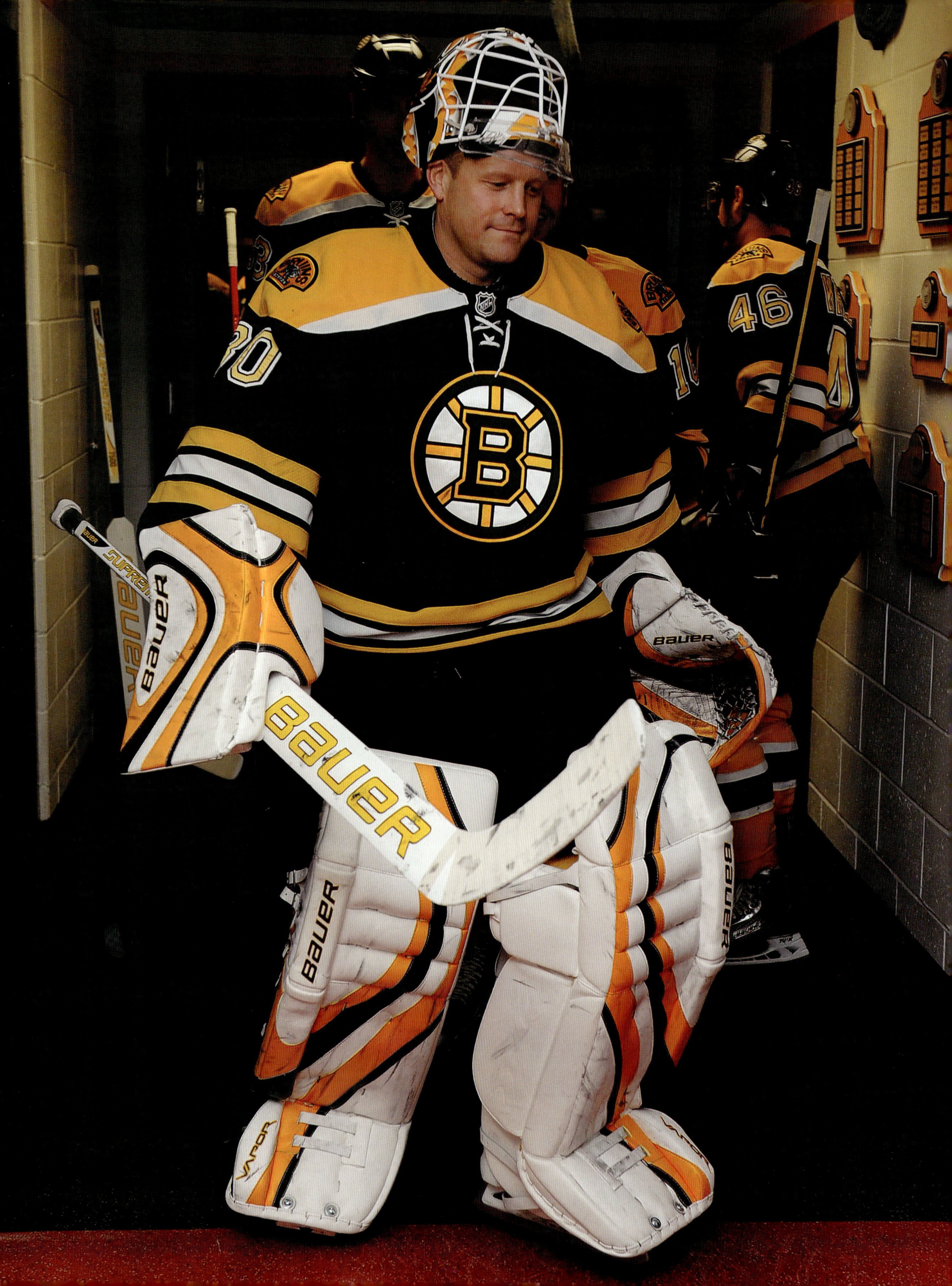
BAUER
SUPREME
BAUER
BAUER
BAUER
VAPOR
46

The Bruins had another power forward on the roster that fall—rookie Milan Lucic, just 19 years of age. And he invited comparisons to none other than...Cam Neely.

Like Neely, Lucic was a native of British Columbia, the son of a Vancouver longshoreman. And like Neely, Lucic was a big, physical forward who was just as likely to change the outcome of a game with a bruising body check as he was with a blistering slap shot. No one actually expected Lucic to become the next Neely—that was an impossible standard—but the fan base was fired up to have someone on the team who played with that style.

Lucic didn't disappoint. By the end of his rookie season, he was skating on one of the Bruins top lines and playing big minutes in the playoffs. His goals for his sophomore season? "If you want to look at it individually, I scored eight goals and 19 assists, and I would like to try and double it in both departments," said Lucic in June 2008. "That is probably a good goal." And then Lucic added with a laugh, "And then have 10-15 fights, maybe even more."

Neely himself, just finishing up his first year in Boston's front office, predicted a bright future for Lucic. "He works hard, he is a great kid, and has great character," said Neely. "He progressed a ton this past season. He has a very physical presence and is the type of player that we expect to see wear this uniform for a long time."

Lucic did end up wearing the Black and Gold for a long time—eight seasons in all between 2007 and 2015. He would reach the peak of his offensive production in 2011 and 2012, when he put up 60+ points in back-to-back seasons. He was, in fact, the leading goal scorer on the 2011 Stanley Cup championship team. And he never lost that physical presence that made him such a fan favorite.

After Lucic left Boston, his NHL career continued with Los Angeles, Edmonton, and Calgary. He looks back fondly on his career with the Bruins, especially playing in the heat of the Boston-Montreal rivalry. "As a competitor and as an athlete, it's why you play," said Lucic in a 2022 interview with The Athletic. "It's in those big moments, those big games, and those big rivalries."

Opposite page: By the time he finally landed in the NHL with the Bruins, Tim Thomas had seen numerous locker room hallways in the minor leagues of North America and overseas in faraway Finland and Sweden. Here, he heads out to the ice before the game against the Tampa Bay Lightning at TD Garden in December 2009. (Photograph by Brian Babineau/NHLI via Getty Images)

TIM THOMAS

THE CAREER OF goaltender Tim Thomas epitomized pluck, passion, and, most of all, perseverance.

Thomas grew up in Michigan idolizing Jim Craig and wanting to be part of a Team USA that won gold at the Olympics. And when your parents care so much about your dreams that they pawn their wedding rings to send you to a hockey tournament, you learn how to persevere.

Following an All-American career at the University of Vermont, Thomas spent six years in the hockey wilderness from 1997 to 2003 trying to make the NHL. His various ports of call in the minor leagues and overseas included Detroit, Houston, Birmingham (Alabama), Hamilton (Ontario), Sweden, and Finland for parts of three seasons.

Why did it take him so long to make the NHL? According to Thomas, it was a matter of optics: "It was because of how I looked stopping the puck, and I had to actually work on that. And I realized I had to look a certain way to make it to the NHL." So Thomas adopted elements of the butterfly style popularized by Patrick Roy and rapidly coming into vogue across the league—"Not so much even because it helped me to save the puck," he recalled, "but because it made me look more normal."

Prior to the 2002–03 season, Thomas got his big break when he was signed by the Bruins. He would finally make his NHL debut that season at the age of 28,

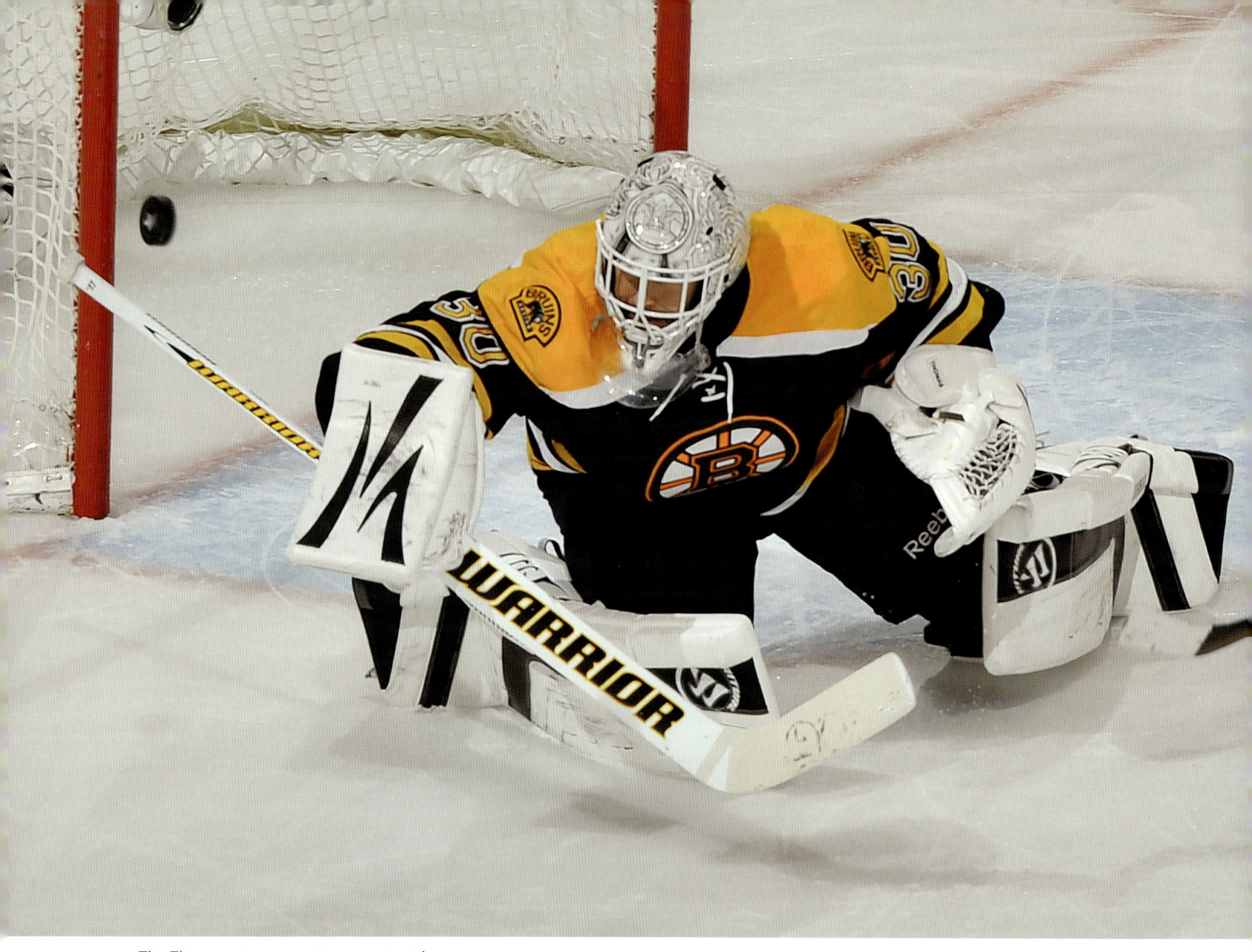

Tim Thomas was never too concerned with style. He just focused on stopping pucks. (Photograph by Steve Babineau/NHLI via Getty Images)

appearing in four games for Boston. Thomas spent most of that season and all of the following season, however, playing with the Bruins' AHL affiliate in Providence before returning to Finland one final time during the 2004–05 lockout season.

The next year, Thomas found himself back in the NHL—and this time for good. Over the next seven seasons (2005–2012), he would be the No. 1 goaltender in Boston. The Bruins occasionally seemed to be trying to bring in someone new, adding veteran Manny Fernandez in 2007 and working the young Tuukka Rask into the mix, but Thomas remained the main man.

"It would have motivated me just to play my best, and, well, to keep the job," said Thomas of the arrival of Fernandez. "And Manny was very supportive of me.... It was a good goaltending partnership. It wasn't like we're competing head-to-head, face-to-face. It wasn't like that with Tuukka either."

During the 2008-09 season, Thomas reached the apex of his career, at least up to that point, compiling a 36–11–7 record with a 2.10 goals against average. The performance brought him, in just his fourth full season in the NHL and at the relatively advanced age of 34, the Vezina Trophy as the top goaltender in the NHL.

Further glories would await Thomas in the next decade, especially in 2011, when he won a second Vezina and then the Conn Smythe Trophy as MVP of the playoffs for a goaltending performance that may well have been the greatest in Stanley Cup history. In achieving all of that, Tim Thomas kept doing what he had been doing all along.

He persevered.

ZDENO CHARA

by Steve Conroy

IF THERE IS A common thread of greatness within Bruins history, it runs along the blueline. The Bruins' star defensemen have come in all shapes, sizes, and breeds, from the take-no-prisoners toughness of Eddie Shore in the organization's infancy, to the revolutionary, shooting-star brilliance of Bobby Orr, to the often overlooked excellence of Brad Park, to the almost perfect combination of offense and defense embodied in Ray Bourque.

But in a grouping of special talents in the club's history, Zdeno Chara might be unique. Standing 6′9″ and weighing 260 pounds, Chara is the largest man to ever play in the National Hockey League. While his intimidating size was a big part of what made him so great, Chara combined that with an athleticism and agility that truly made him stand out.

Another thing that set Chara apart? He was arguably the greatest free agent signing of all time, not just for the Bruins but in NHL history.

In the spring of 2006, the Ottawa Senators had a decision to make. Facing a salary cap crunch, the Senators could sign only one of their top two defensemen, Wade Redden or Chara. Ottawa GM John Muckler chose the Canadian-born Redden.

That was to the great fortune of the Bruins, who had suddenly hit hard times. Several of their top talents signed with other teams just prior to and after the lost lockout season of 2004–05. Then came the shocking trade early in the 2005–06 season of captain Joe Thornton, who would go on to win the Hart Trophy that year with San Jose. The Bruins' famously ardent fan base was disgruntled and the organization needed a shot in the arm.

It came in the summer of 2006, in the form of the towering defenseman from Trencin, Slovakia.

The Bruins' new GM-in-waiting was Peter Chiarelli, who had previously been assistant GM with Ottawa, and

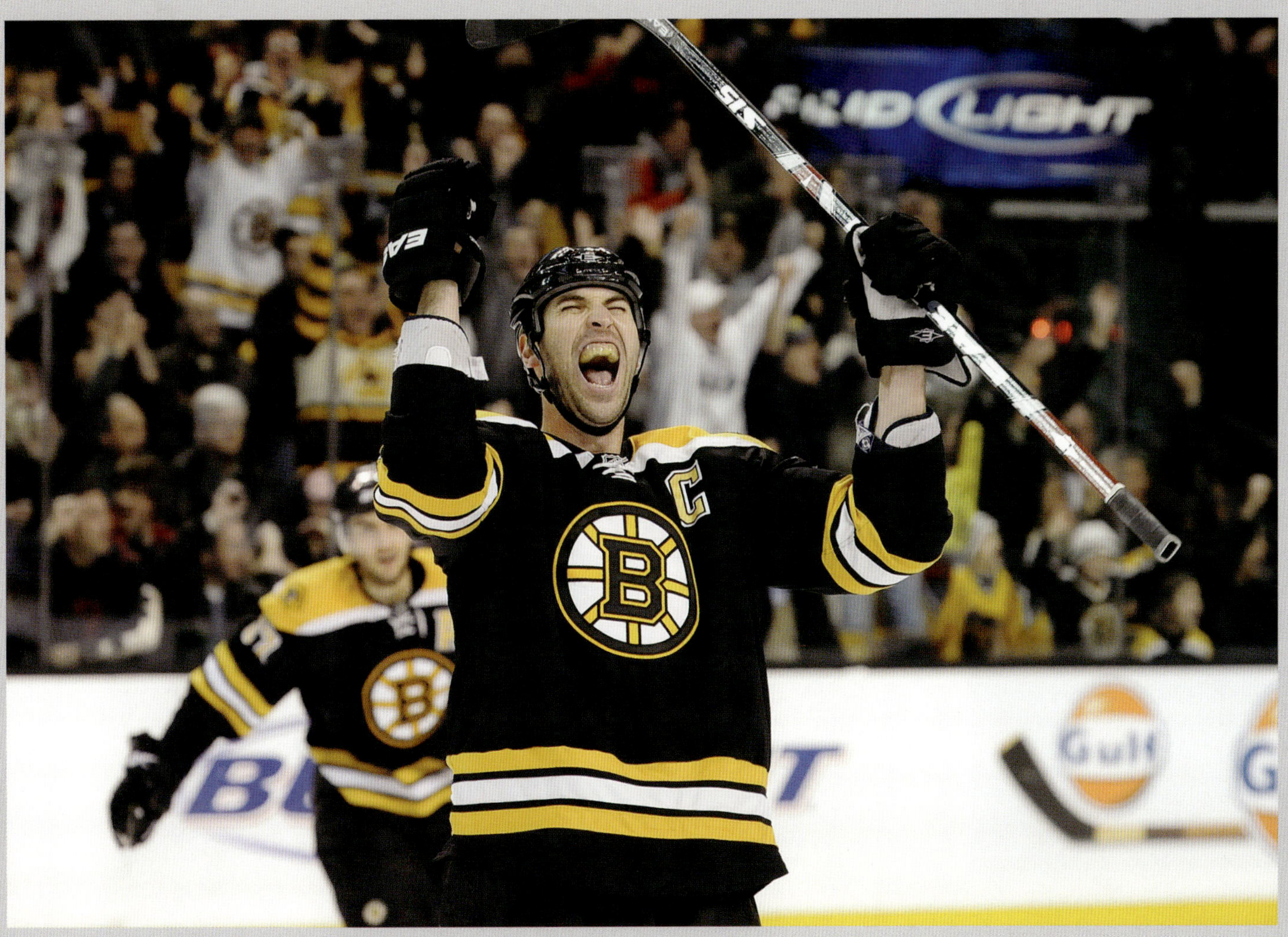

Zdeno Chara celebrates his goal in Boston's victory over the Buffalo Sabres in November 2008.
(Photograph by Brian Babineau/NHLI via Getty Images)

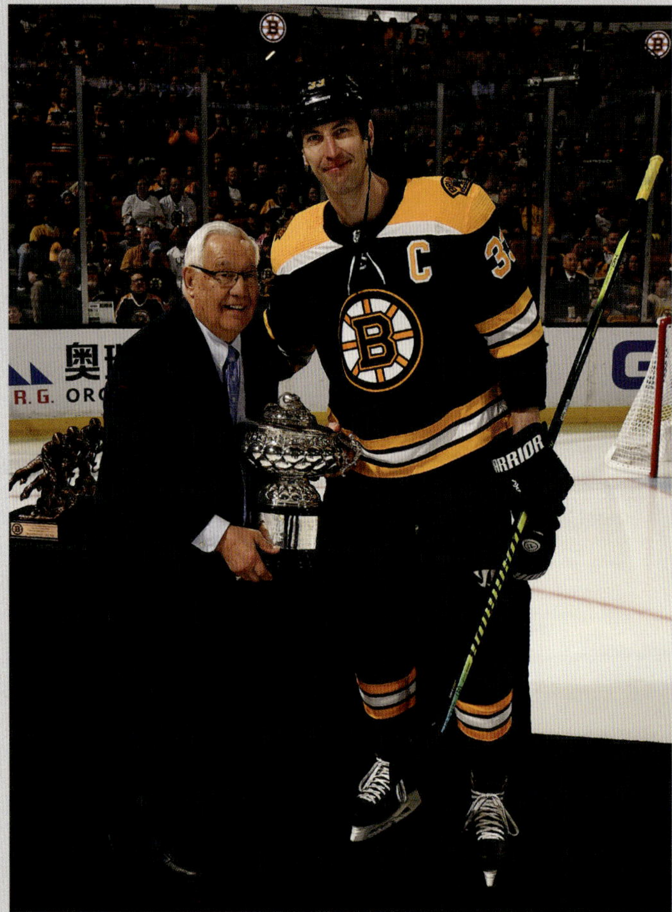

Zdeno Chara appears in a 2019 on-ice ceremony with another long-time Bruins captain, Johnny Bucyk. During his tenure in Boston, Zdeno Chara forged a close friendship with Bucyk. (Photograph by Steve Babineau/NHLI via Getty Images)

in turn enticed free agent centerman Marc Savard to also come to Boston, and the Bruins had successfully reversed course.

Chara, who was to be Boston's first European-born captain, was the rock on which the Bruins' transformation was built. The club returned to the playoffs in Chara's second year with the team, which would regain its identity as the Big Bad Bruins in the coming seasons. Along with his wide wingspan that seemingly covered half the ice, Chara brought a level of intimidation that gave the Bruins an edge before the puck was even dropped.

The Bruins finished in the top three in goals against average in all but one of the six seasons between 2009 and 2014, with Chara averaging over 25 minutes of ice time each season. They were tops in the league in that category in 2008–09 when Chara won his lone Norris Trophy, the voters for once giving him his proper due instead of handing it to the defenseman with a high point total.

Chara helped the Bruins break a 39-year Stanley Cup drought in 2011 in the most dramatic fashion imaginable, with three of their four series wins coming in seven games, en route to a four games–to–three Stanley Cup Final victory over Vancouver.

The first Game 7 victory came against the hated Montreal Canadiens. Then, after a cathartic sweep of the Philadelphia Flyers (who had erased a 3–0 series deficit to beat the Bruins in the playoffs the previous season), the Bruins outlasted the Tampa Bay Lightning in the Eastern Conference Finals, finishing them off in an epic 1–0

that familiarity certainly helped the Bruins' cause. It would also help that the intensely dedicated athlete saw a good fit with the Bruins' blue-collar ethic, for which they had been historically known.

But because of a grievance filed by the Senators, Chiarelli was not allowed to take over the reins until two weeks after the opening of free agency. The interim GM at the time, Jeff Gorton, was charged with sealing the deal.

Gorton did just that—with a five-year, $37.5 million contract—in what has to be the most productive three-month stint of any executive in memory. After drafting Phil Kessel, Milan Lucic, and Brad Marchand in the June draft and also trading for future goaltending stalwart Tuukka Rask in exchange, Gorton beat out a handful of teams for Chara's services. The Chara signing

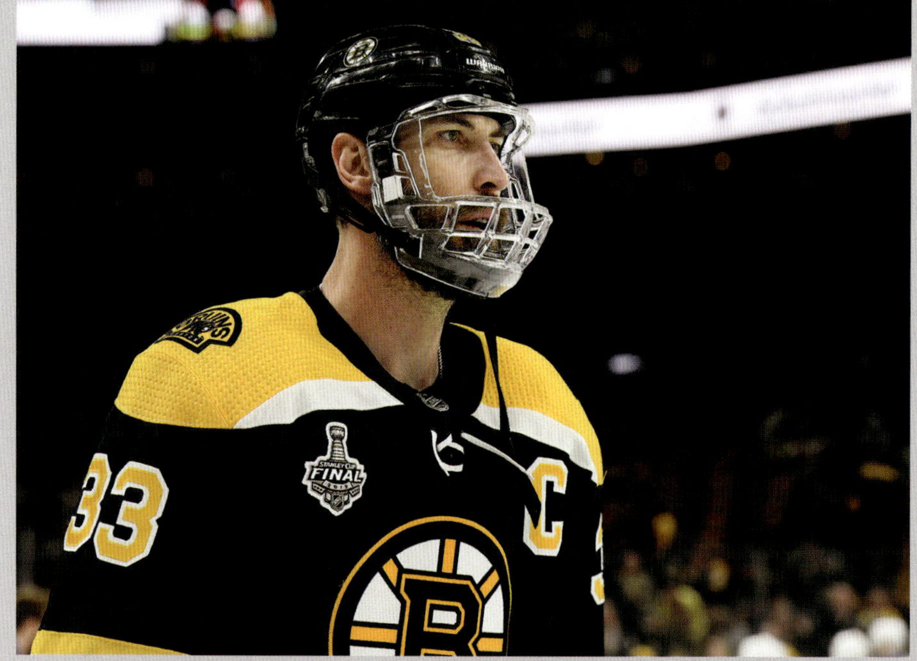

To be a Boston Bruin, you have to be tough and you have to be willing to play through pain. That was never more evident than in the 2019 Stanley Cup Final, when Zdeno Chara suffered a broken jaw in Game 4 but came back to play the final three games of the series with a special facemask. It was the stuff that legends are made of. (Photograph by Brian Babineau/NHLI via Getty Images)

Game 7 victory that many consider a near-perfect defensive effort.

As eventful as the earlier rounds were, the Cup final against the Vancouver Canucks was a classic, the animosity of which could match that of the Boston-Montreal battles. The explosive Canucks were held to eight goals in the seven games. And while Conn Smythe–winning goalie Tim Thomas took center stage following his shutout win in Game 7 in Vancouver, coach Claude Julien's pairing of Chara and Dennis Seidenberg proved a suffocating force.

As fans outside Rogers Arena began to riot after the home team's stunning defeat, Chara accepted the Cup, the first Eastern Bloc–born captain in NHL history to do so. The sight of the massive, bearded Chara lifting the Cup high overhead and releasing his from-the-gut roar is one of the indelible moments in Boston's rich sports history.

Chara was iconoclastic on and off the ice. The son of former Olympic Greco-Roman wrestler Zdenek, Chara's own feats of strength are legendary. His slapshot of 108.8 miles per hour recorded at the 2012 All-Star Game in Ottawa remains the hardest recorded shot in history. Despite his weight and gangly frame, he would almost always win the training camp pull-up competition, much to the amazement of his more compact teammates. A cycling enthusiast, he would unwind in the off-season by riding some of the most challenging stages of the Tour de France through the Alps and Pyrenees.

The constant striving for self-improvement was not limited to the physical. Chara was one of the more intelligent star athletes ever to come through Boston. He spoke seven languages fluently. One year, when he was sidelined for an extended period with a rare injury, he used the free time to obtain his realtor's license.

Chara often showed a stern, stoic face to the media in postgame locker-room situations, especially early in his Bruins career. As a result, it took longer for some Bruins fans to develop an emotional attachment to Chara, as they had done immediately with Orr and Bourque. But their affinity for Chara that evolved and blossomed was clear in the 2019 Stanley Cup Final.

In Game 4 in St. Louis, Chara's jaw was shattered by a puck, requiring surgery to insert screws and plates. Many assumed that the big man was done for the series. But when the starting lineup was announced for Game 5 at TD Garden, Chara—his mouth wired shut—was standing in his familiar spot on the blueline to hear not only his name called but also the spine-tingling ovation from the crowd. It felt like an embrace not just of Chara's heart and courage in that moment, but of all the sweat and dedication that he poured into his job, which he would perform in Boston for 14 years.

It was not Chara's last game as a Bruin, but a more perfect historical coda cannot be found for a player destined for the Hockey Hall of Fame.

Steve Conroy has covered the Bruins for the *Boston Herald* since 2001.

BOSTON BRUINS (2000–2009)

Season	W	L	T	OL	PTS	PTS%	Finish	Playoffs	Coach	Division	Conf.
1999–00	24	33	19	6	73	.445	5th of 5		Pat Burns	Northeast	Eastern
2000–01	36	30	8	8	88	.537	4th of 5		Pat Burns (3–4–1–0) Mike Keenan (33–26–7–8)	Northeast	Eastern
2001–02	43	24	6	9	101	.616	1st of 5	Lost NHL Conference Quarterfinals	Robbie Ftorek	Northeast	Eastern
2002–03	36	31	11	4	87	.530	3rd of 5	Lost NHL Conference Quarterfinals	Robbie Ftorek (33–28–8–4) Mike O'Connell (3–3–3–0)	Northeast	Eastern
2003–04*	41	19	15	7	104	.634	1st of 5	Lost NHL Conference Quarterfinals	Mike Sullivan	Northeast	Eastern
2005–06	29	37		16	74	.451	5th of 5		Mike Sullivan	Northeast	Eastern
2006–07	35	41		6	76	.463	5th of 5		Dave Lewis	Northeast	Eastern
2007–08	41	29		12	94	.573	3rd of 5	Lost NHL Conference Quarterfinals	Claude Julien	Northeast	Eastern
2008–09	53	19		10	116	.707	1st of 5	Lost NHL Conference Semifinals	Claude Julien	Northeast	Eastern

*Ensuing 2004–05 season cancelled due to NHL labor dispute

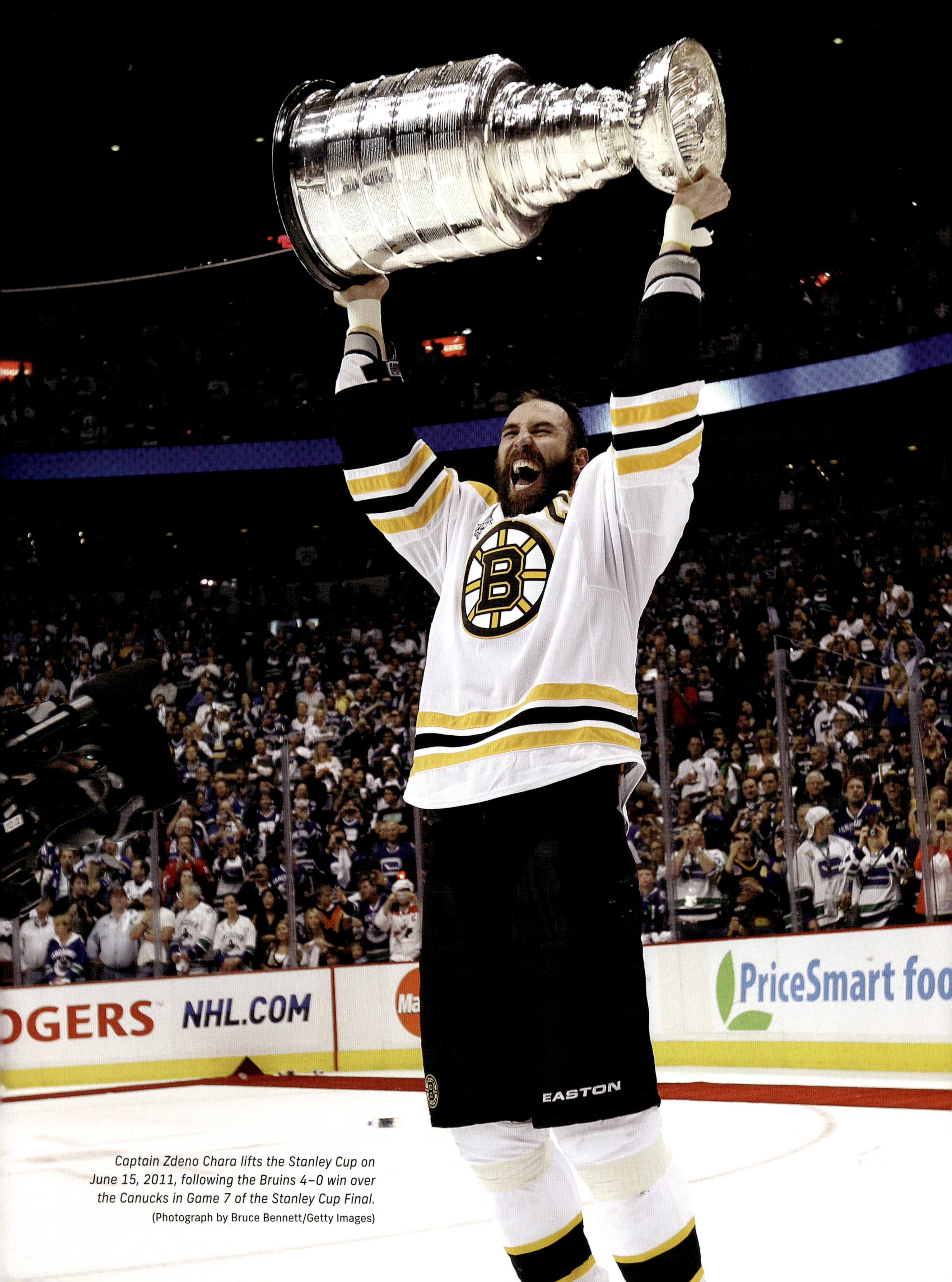

Captain Zdeno Chara lifts the Stanley Cup on June 15, 2011, following the Bruins 4–0 win over the Canucks in Game 7 of the Stanley Cup Final.
(Photograph by Bruce Bennett/Getty Images)

2 0 1 0 s

RETURN TO GLORY

Yaahhhhhhhhh!

—Zdeno Chara, Bruins captain, raising the Stanley Cup, June 15, 2011

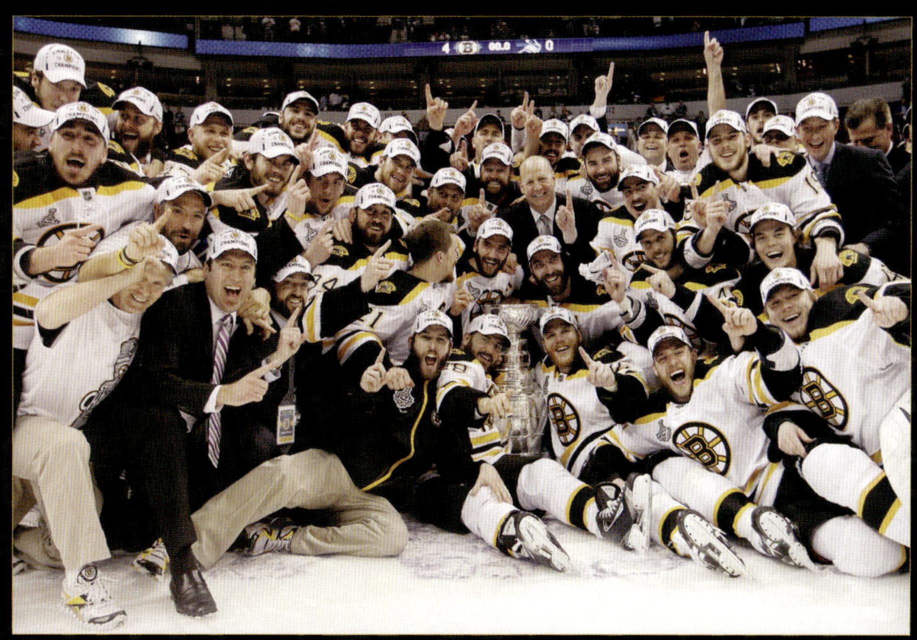

The 2011 Bruins team, coaches, and front office are shown joyously sprawled on the ice at Rogers Arena in Vancouver immediately following their Game 7 Stanley Cup victory.
(Photograph by Bruce Bennett/Getty Images)

The years from 2010 to 2019 were filled with big games and magical moments for the Boston Bruins. And it was like that from the very first day of the decade (January 1, 2010), when the Bruins played an unforgettable Winter Classic at Fenway Park against the Philadelphia Flyers. "Unforgettable" would also describe the spine-tingling rendition of the national anthem at TD Garden just two days after the tragic Boston Marathon bombings in April 2013. The memories continued to pile up after that. A stirring run to the Stanley Cup Final that same spring...a President's Trophy for the best regular season record in 2014...another run to the Stanley Cup Final to end the decade in 2019.

At the end of the day, though, this decade in Boston Bruins history revolves around one very special point in time: 2011.

It had been 39 years since the Bruins had last won a Stanley Cup. Even though the Bruins had been one of the top teams in the NHL in the years following 1972, a sixth Stanley Cup had proven to be elusive. There had been several near misses in the years along the way, most notably, in 1974, 1977, 1978, 1979, 1988, and 1990—but in each instance, the Bruins came up just short. After the team began its rise toward the top of the NHL in 2007, the wait for Lord Stanley to come home to Boston became that much more pronounced for Bruins fans.

In 2011, the wait ended. The Bruins brought the Stanley Cup back to Boston, thrilling the city, the region, and their fans everywhere. And they couldn't have done it in a more dramatic fashion—a 25-game playoff march involving four series, three of which went the full seven games. Their

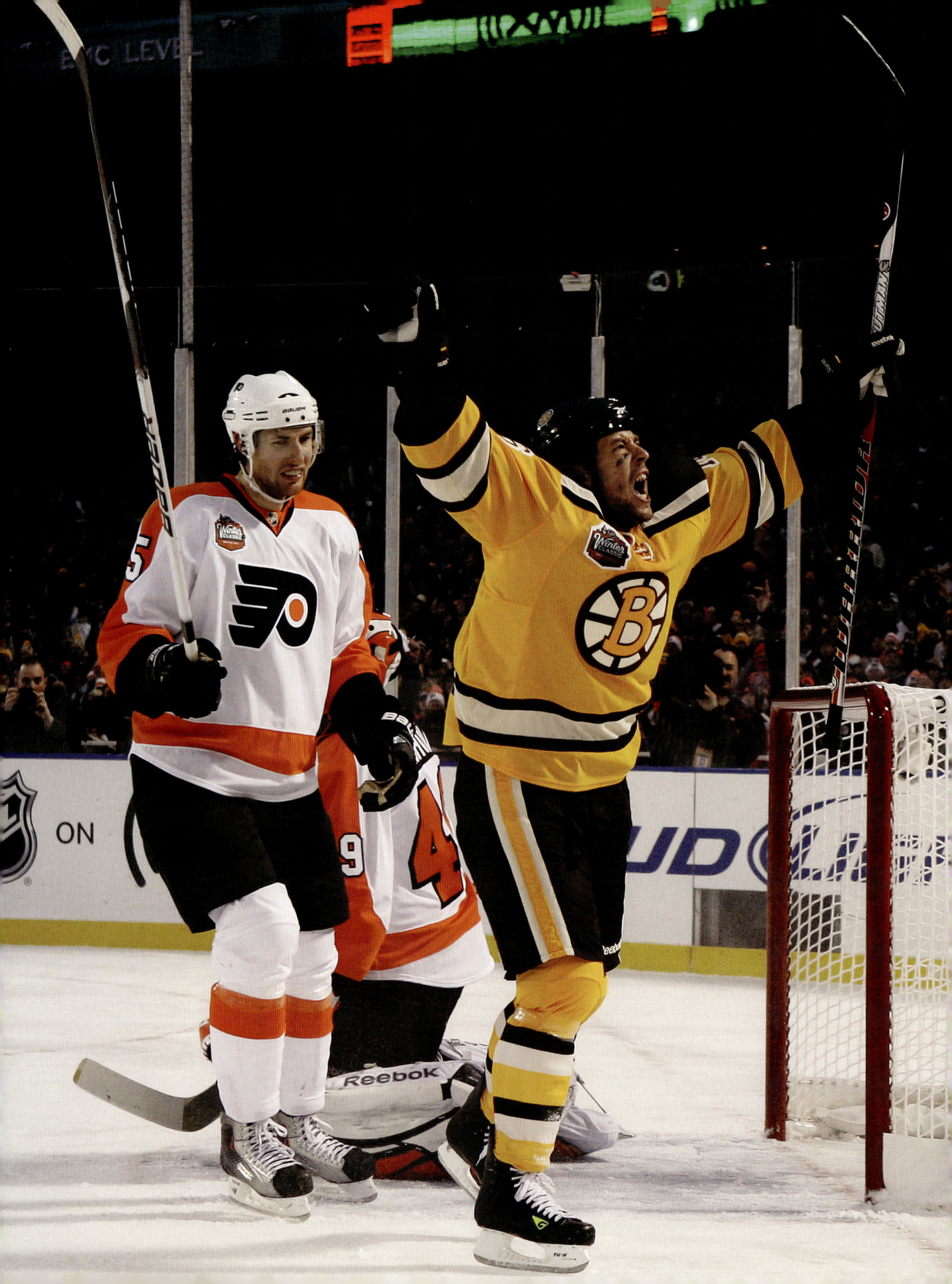

ON
Reebok

raucous opening set with Montreal included an abrupt recovery from a 2–0 series deficit, courtesy of three overtime victories, including a 4–3 nailbiter in Game 7 at TD Garden. Next up was another traditional rival, the Philadelphia Flyers, who had handed the Bruins a devastating playoff defeat the year before. Revenge came swiftly and sweetly in the form of a four-game sweep. The next series, the Eastern Conference Finals against the Tampa Bay Lightning, was capped by a magnificent 1–0 victory in Game 7 that featured tight defense, unbelievable goaltending, mounting tension—and zero penalties. It was a purist's delight.

In the Stanley Cup Final against the Vancouver Canucks, the Bruins came back again and again—winning Games 3 and 4 after losing the first two games of the series, staying alive with a Game 6 victory after being pushed to the brink of elimination with a tough Game 5 loss, and then prevailing 4–0 in Game 7 to capture the Cup in decisive fashion.

The big hero of the 2011 playoff run was goaltender Tim Thomas—but, really, there were too many heroes to count on a team that defined what it truly means to be a team. "That was quite a run," said Bruins president Cam Neely in a 2022 interview. "That team was pretty special. The coaching staff did a great job, and the players were a team. They were a legit team, as far as they played for each other and just a really tight group. It was special to be part of that."

Their victory parade drew more than 1 million fans to downtown Boston on a perfect Saturday morning in June, constituting the largest celebration in the city's history. There was cathartic jubilation everywhere you looked.

The Boston Bruins were back on top of the world.

Opposite page: Marco Sturm celebrates the overtime goal that he has just scored to defeat the Philadelphia Flyers 2–1 in the 2010 Winter Classic at Fenway Park. Sturm scored 20 or more goals in four of the five seasons (2005–1010) in which he skated for the Bruins. None was more memorable than his game-winner that afternoon at Fenway. (Photograph by Jim McIsaac/Getty Images)

THE 2010 WINTER CLASSIC

ONE OF THE MOST memorable games in Bruins history took place on New Year's Day, 2010. The teams were the Bruins and one of their most storied rivals, the Philadelphia Flyers. And the setting was outdoors at iconic Fenway Park. What could be better?

The pregame atmosphere was naturally festive and electric—everyone was thrilled to be there. The Dropkick Murphys performed in center field to get the crowd even more pumped up. Meanwhile, the players had their own form of motivation. "Once we were in the locker room, everyone was getting ready for the game, but we also had time to take some photos for ourselves and with Bobby Orr, Johnny Bucyk, and others who came to say good luck," said Zdeno Chara in an interview with NHL.com's Amalie Benjamin. "That was very kind of them and very humbling."

And then the players took the ice. "Being able to walk out of that dugout, a few people behind Mr. Orr, and really just taking in the whole scene of what it is like to be front and center stage at Fenway, was just an amazing experience," said Bruins forward Shawn Thornton in a 2022 interview.

After the national anthem (which included a flyover) and then a ceremonial puck drop with Bobby Orr and Bobby Clarke of the Flyers, it was finally time to play the game. "The conditions were absolutely perfect," Bruins right wing Mark Recchi told Benjamin. "It's like 32 degrees. It was clouded over.... It was a perfect day to play hockey."

It was a tight, well-played game that saw the Flyers clinging to a 1–0 lead late into the contest. Then the Bruins rallied. "In the third period, it was not about Fenway, it was about how we have to get this job done because it meant so much for all of us, including the city and fans," Bruins left wing Marco Sturm told Benjamin. "That was for me, the biggest thing—it was, no more looking around. It was, let's get the job done here and win this game for all of us."

With just under three minutes to go in regulation, Recchi scored the game-tying goal.

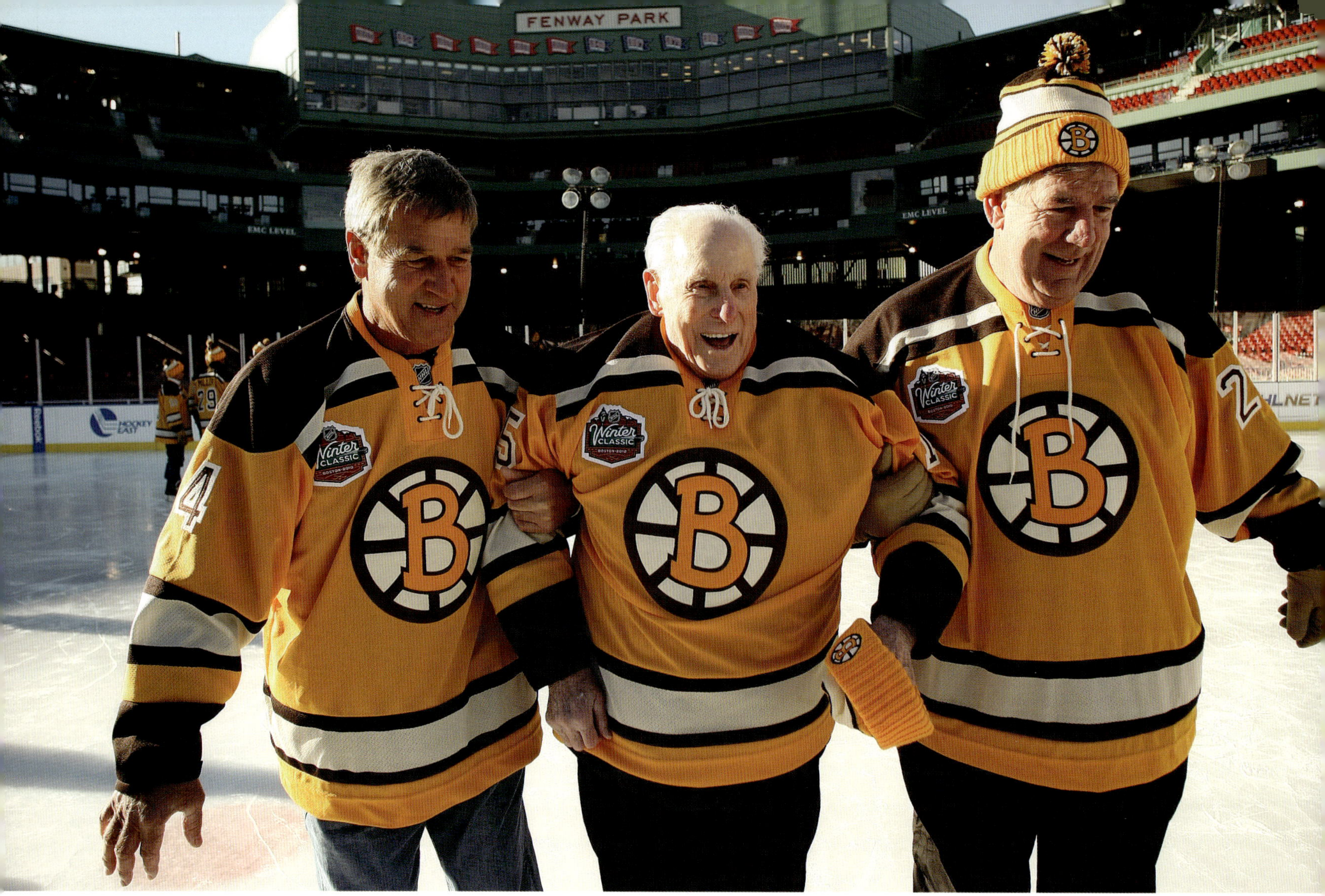

The festive atmosphere in the days leading up to the 2010 Winter Classic included a "first skate" that involved 91-year-old Milt Schmidt (center) taking to the ice at Fenway Park along with Bobby Orr (left) and Terry O'Reilly (right). It was a scene of Black and Gold royalty. (Photograph by John Tlumacki/The Boston Globe via Getty Images)

Sturm was the day's final hero, scoring the walkoff goal two minutes into overtime off a picture-perfect feed from Patrice Bergeron.

"The experience is once-in-a-lifetime," Sturm told SI.com. "Bruins, Flyers, 40,000 fans on a perfect day. You couldn't ask for anything better for the game of hockey."

MARK RECCHI

THE WINTER CLASSIC was not the end of the saga involving the Bruins and Flyers in 2010.

Several months later, the two teams would square off in the second round of the Stanley Cup playoffs. And it would be a painful outcome for the Bruins. Holding a 3–0 series lead, they proceeded to drop four straight games—three of them by just one goal—to lose the series in agonizing fashion. The Bruins had been ascending toward the top of the NHL since 2007. Would the devastating 2010 playoff defeat take things in a different direction?

The fact that it did not was due to a number of factors—including the strong leadership on the team. And much of that came from veteran Mark Recchi.

By the time Recchi landed in Boston in March 2009, he was deep into his 20th NHL season. He had rung up huge scoring totals while skating with the likes of Pittsburgh, Philadelphia, and Montreal and had won two Stanley Cups along the way (with Pittsburgh in 1991 and Carolina in 2006).

Bruins general manager Peter Chiarelli acquired the 41-year-old for the stretch run in 2009. "We had been on the lookout for some veteran presence,"

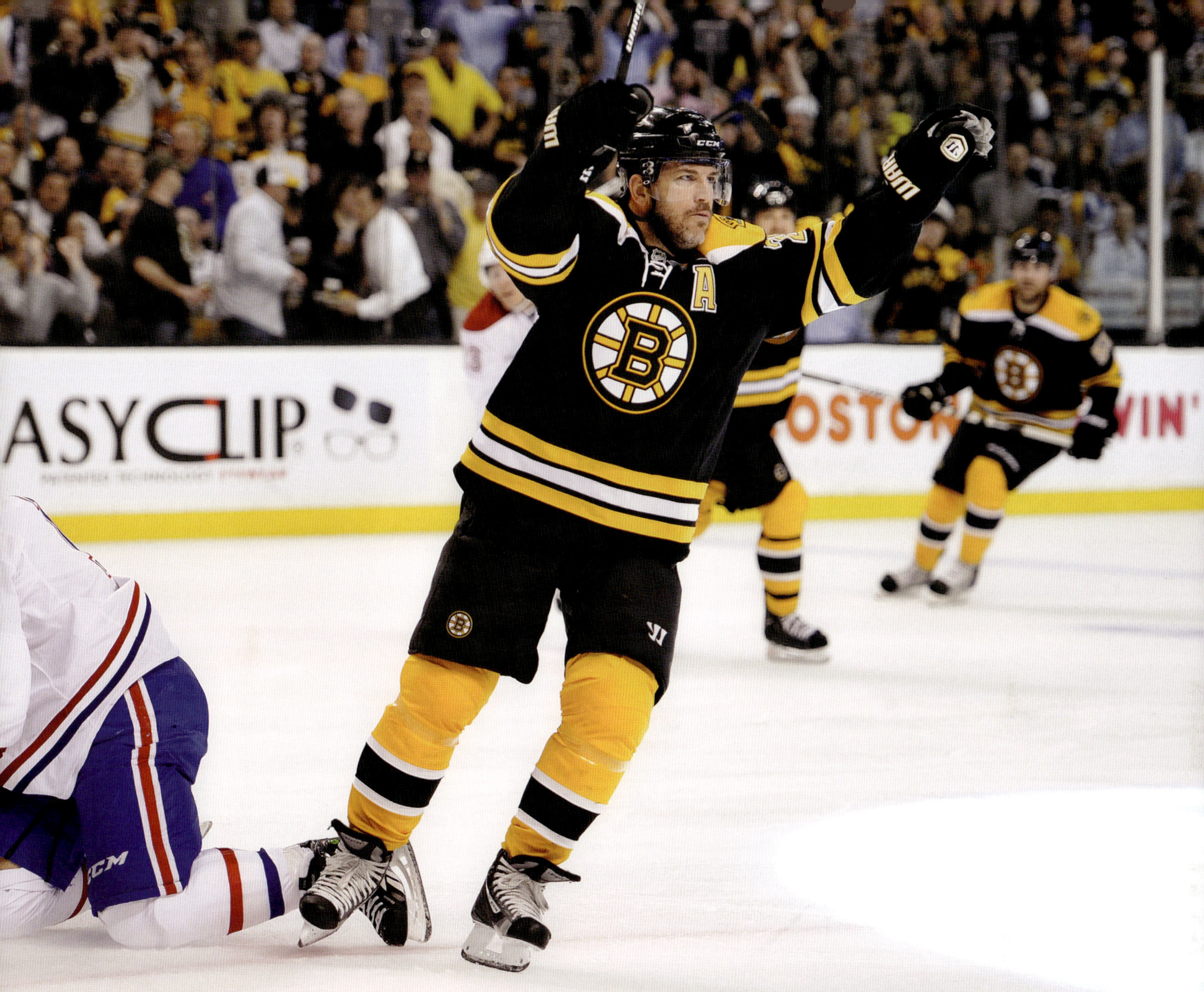

Mark Recchi puts one home in Game 5 of the opening round of the 2011 Stanley Cup playoffs against Montreal. In that postseason, the 43-year-old Recchi proved conclusively that he could still bring it, tallying 14 points across 25 games. He would retire after the Bruins captured the Cup on June 15. (Photograph by Brian Babineau/NHLI via Getty Images)

Chiarelli told hockey journalist Mick Colageo in 2022. "That's hard to find. We got that and a whole lot more."

It turned out that Recchi still had some gas in the tank—enough to be a consistent producer and a top-six forward on the Bruins for the next two-plus seasons. As Chiarelli recalled, "He amazed us a number of times because, at his age, he was slowing down, but he had these reserves.... He had accomplished so much, he was comfortable in his career. He didn't really have to accomplish any more, but he loved the game so much. Z welcomed him into the leadership group, and the young guys loved him."

One of those young guys was Patrice Bergeron. Recchi coming to the Bruins "turned out to be one of the best things to happen to me.... I could ask him questions, and he was so open," Bergeron told Colageo. "He would share his wisdom and share his experience. It was just an amazing experience for me."

Following the Philadelphia flameout in the 2010 Stanley Cup playoffs, Recchi kept the faith. "I saw a group that had all the intangibles to be a championship team," Recchi told Colageo. "They had size, speed, two terrific goalies. That's why I kept hanging around."

The next year (2011) would prove to be Mark Recchi's final season in the NHL. And it would end with another Stanley Cup.

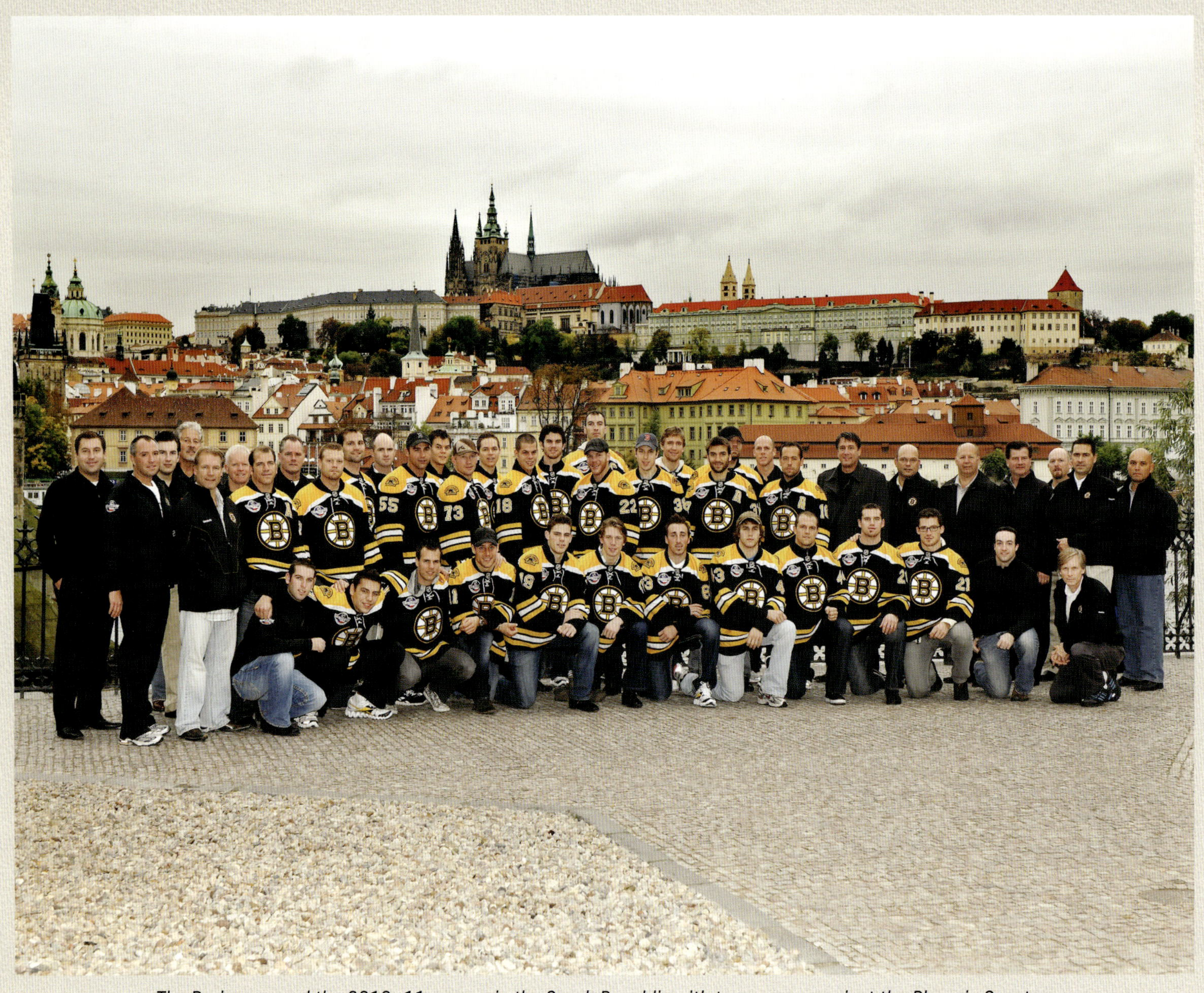

The Bruins opened the 2010–11 season in the Czech Republic with two games against the Phoenix Coyotes. Here the team takes in some sights while overlooking the city of Prague. It proved to be the ultimate team-building exercise.
(Photograph by Brian Babineau)

2011 STANLEY CUP

by Karen Guregian

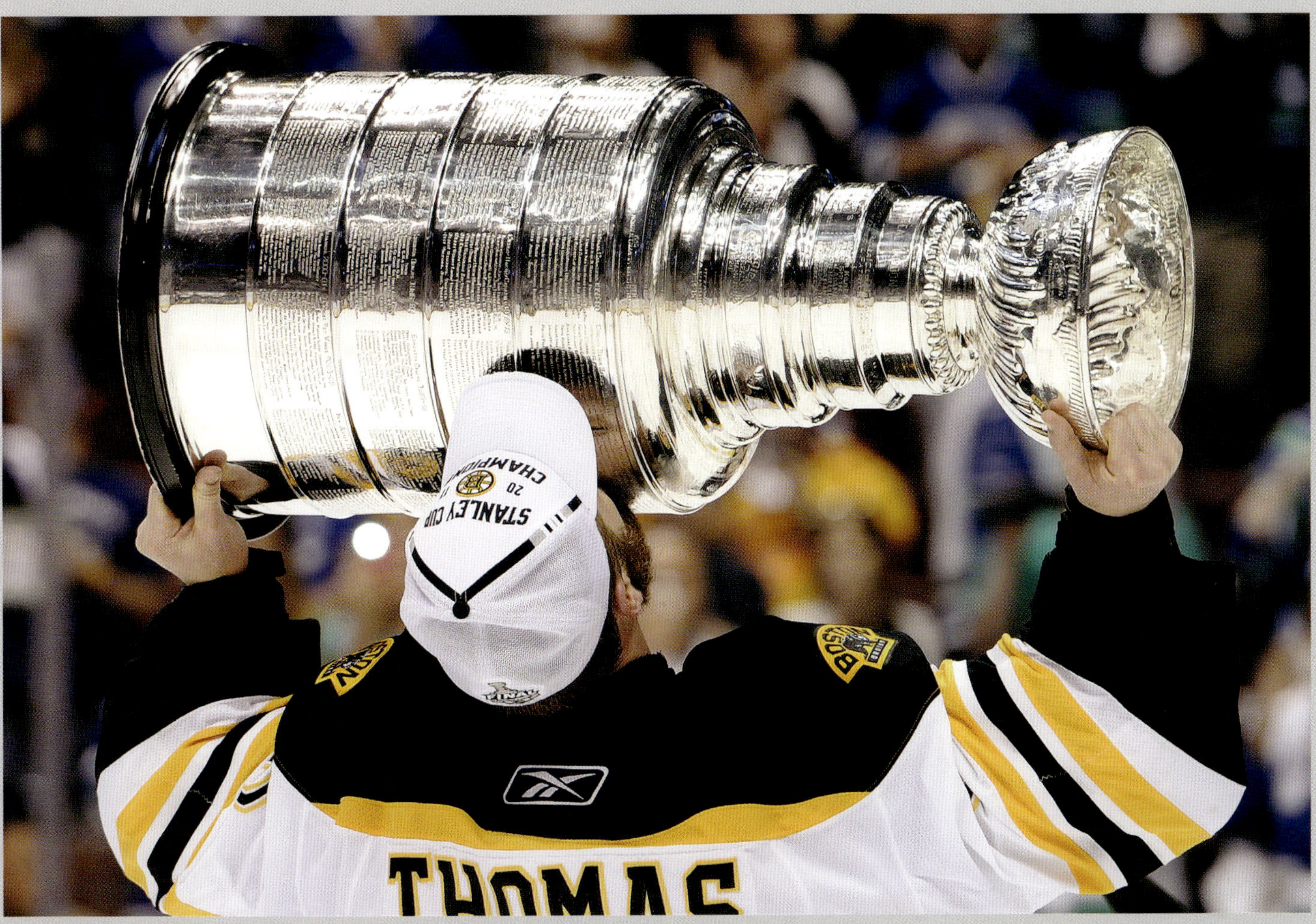

Tim Thomas kisses the Stanley Cup after shutting out the Vancouver Canucks by a score of 4–0 in Game 7 of the Stanley Cup Final. His 2011 playoff performance was one of the best ever by an NHL goalie—if not the best ever. (Photograph by Harry How/Getty Images)

ONE BY ONE, the championships piled up like poker chips on a good night at the casino. First the Patriots in 2001 (followed by two more in 2003 and 2004). Then the Red Sox in 2004 (with another one in 2007). The Celtics followed in 2008. And, finally, the Bruins in 2011.

The Black and Gold finalized the city's big-league sports sweep, cementing Boston as a legitimate City of Champions with all four pro teams earning titles over the course of a decade. In all, the collective has stacked up a dozen titles since the turn of the century. Digging deeper, a common thread can be found between the first championship team for each of the four franchises.

The Patriots, Sox, Celtics, and Bruins were all considered underdogs during their initial championship runs. None of those teams was expected to win but still found a way.

As a prohibitive 14-point underdog, the 2001 Patriots weren't given much of a chance to take down the Greatest Show on Turf in Super Bowl XXXVI. But Bill Belichick's team, behind first-year starter Tom Brady, upset the heavily favored St. Louis Rams.

The 2004 Red Sox? They were a good team, but had little to no chance to make it to the World Series after they went down 3–0 to the New York Yankees in the American League Championship Series. Even before facing that seemingly insurmountable deficit, they were supposed to lose, because that's what they always did. Only the Sox had other ideas. They miraculously came back from that impossible deficit to capture the series and the American League pennant, before sweeping the St. Louis Cardinals in the World Series to claim their first title since 1918.

As for the 2008 Celtics, they were coming off a last-place finish the year before. While they had emerged as one of the top teams in the NBA, they still weren't favored to beat the Lakers in the NBA Finals. And yet, behind Paul Pierce as well as newcomers Kevin Garnett and Ray Allen, they did, taking the series in six games.

Next came the Bruins.

They were the last in line for the Duck Boat parade, but that didn't diminish the excitement and fervor generated during their championship ride. They had long been on the hunt for a Stanley Cup. With the last title coming in 1972 during the Bobby Orr years, the tally was up to 39 years. So fans of the team were more than ready to hoist the next Cup.

And yet, no one saw it coming.

The previous season, the Bruins blew a 3–0 second-round series lead to the Philadelphia Flyers. It was a devastating loss, to say the least, and didn't exactly make anyone believe they would be championship material the following year. Except the Bruins, one of the worst teams in the league only a half dozen years before, were determined to raise another banner.

They figured the best way to deal with that collapse was to hole up in Brattleboro, Vermont, close the doors on the rest of the world, and collectively deal with the aftermath of that loss before embarking on a new season. That's where they figured out how to use that loss as fuel, while moving ahead and planting the seed toward getting on Boston's championship train.

So they left camp, quietly motivated and focused on the big prize. The Bruins began that 2010–11 season in Prague as part of the NHL's Premiere Games, taking on the Phoenix Coyotes. The regular season ended with the team qualifying for the playoffs for the fourth straight season.

Like the 2001 Patriots, 2004 Red Sox, and 2008 Celtics before them, this 2011 Bruins team was identified by its unyielding heart, its steely resolve, and its unwavering resilience. Every time they backed themselves into a corner, every time they dug themselves into a hole, they would respond. Head coach Claude Julien, in his fourth season at the helm, was from the school that taught defense and goaltending win championships. He was unyielding in that belief.

And never was that more apparent than during the Bruins' regular season run, where they tied with the New York Rangers for the most shutout wins (11) en route to winning the Northeast Division. With superb goaltending from Tim Thomas and a stingy defense that was led by Zdeno Chara, the Bruins were a tough team to beat. The No. 1 pairing of Chara and Dennis Seidenberg took on all the top lines, and shut them down. The scoring came from the likes of Milan Lucic, Nathan Horton, David Krejci, Patrice Bergeron, Brad Marchand, and Mark Recchi.

But the championship path was paved by Thomas, who emerged as the team's top netminder after outplaying Tuukka

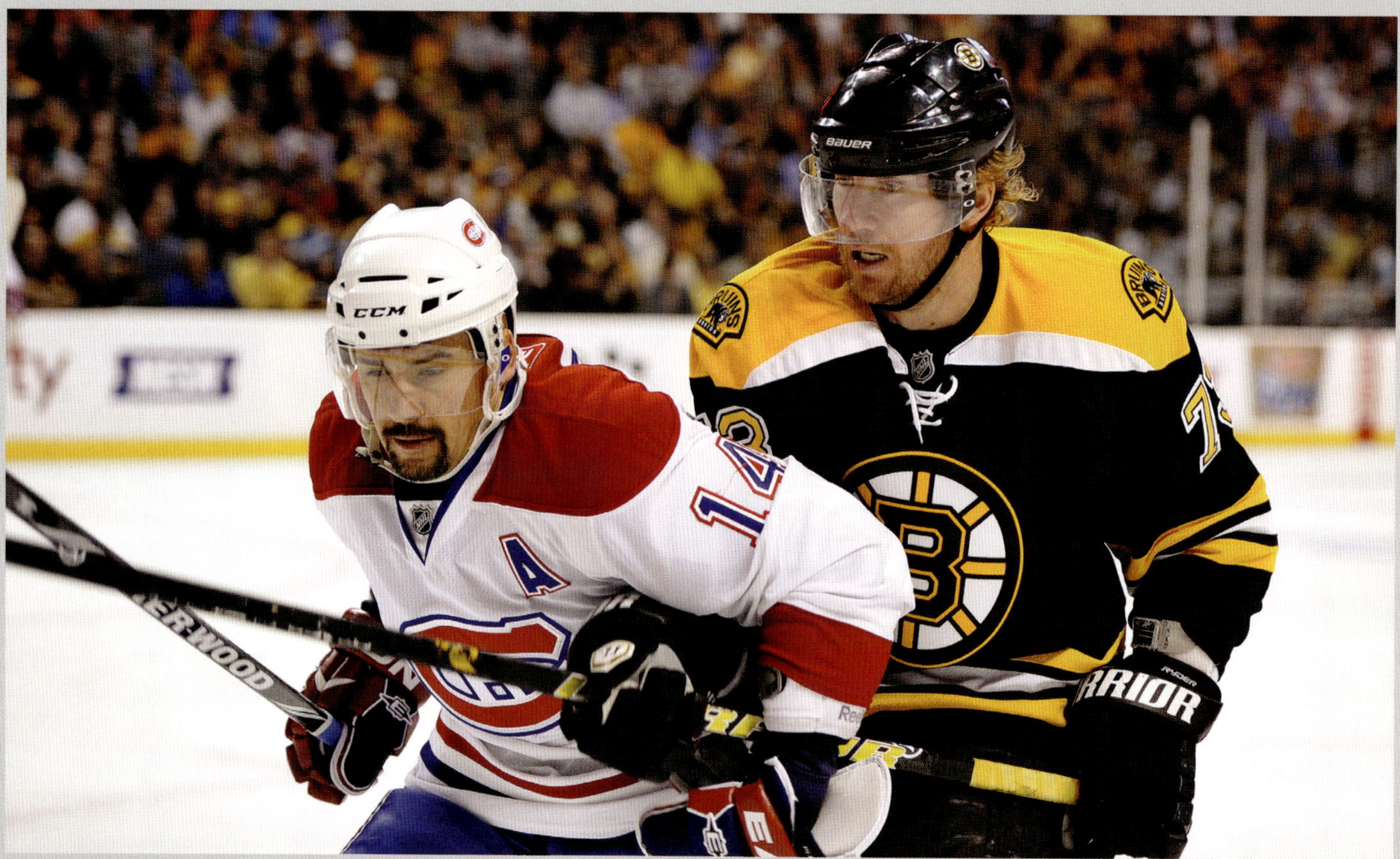

Michael Ryder battles Tomas Plekanec of the Montreal Canadiens in Game 7 of the 2011 Eastern Conference Quarterfinals. Ryder, a former Canadien, skated for the Bruins for three seasons (2008–2011). The speedy right wing was at his best during the 2011 playoffs, scoring 17 points (eight goals, nine assists) to help fuel the Bruins' drive to the Stanley Cup.

(Photograph by Brian Babineau/NHLI via Getty Images)

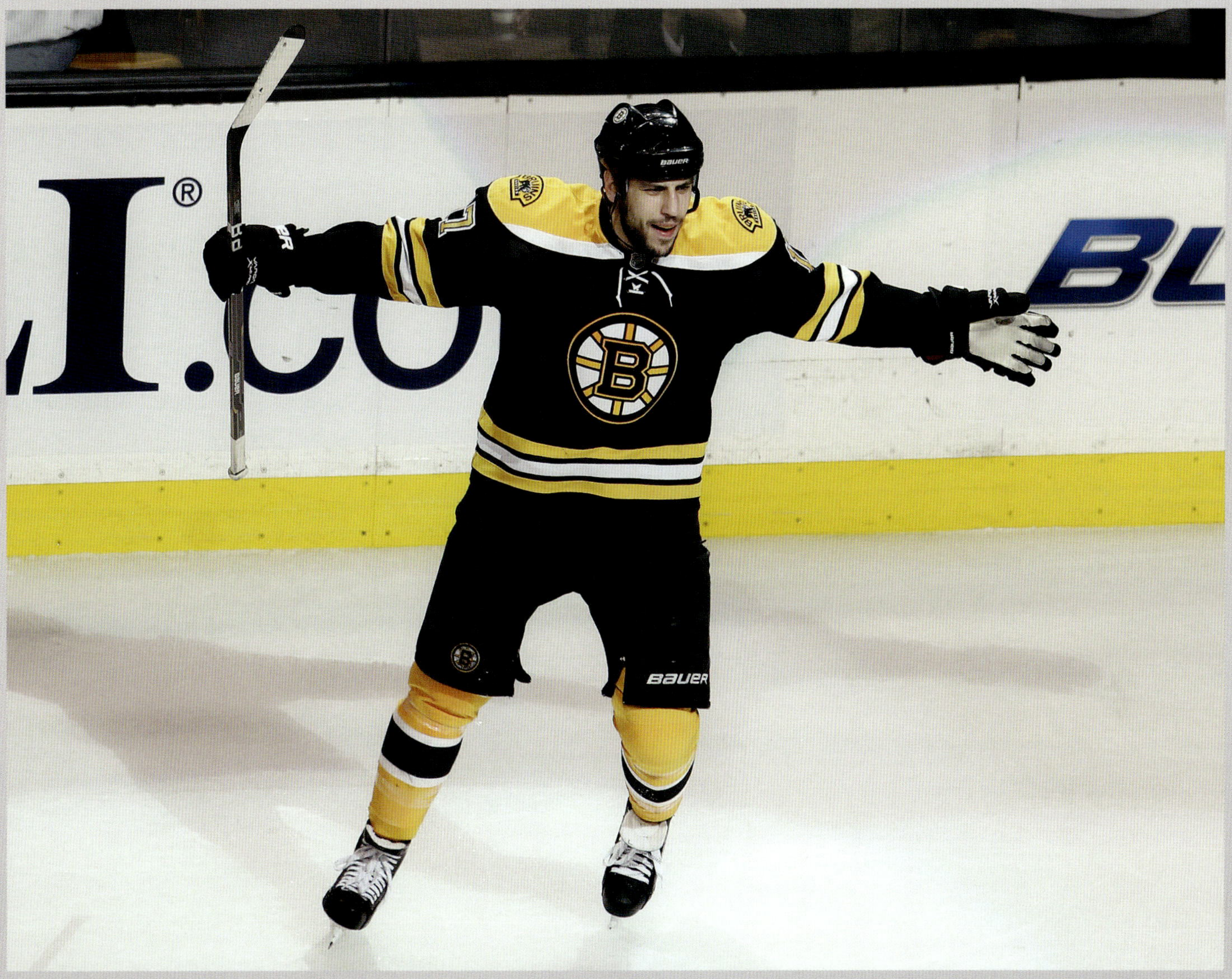

Power forward Milan Lucic celebrates his third-period goal in the Bruins' 5–1 win over the Flyers in the fourth and final game of the 2011 Eastern Conference Semifinals. The victory completed the sweep—and brought the Bruins satisfying retribution against the team that had knocked them out of the playoffs the year before in heartbreaking fashion. (Photograph by Bruce Bennett/Getty Images)

Rask early on. While Thomas's play was great during the regular season, it reached a sublime level during the postseason, where the Bruins topped the Montreal Canadiens, Philadelphia Flyers, and Tampa Bay Lightning before facing the Vancouver Canucks in the Stanley Cup Final. There's being in the zone. Then there's what Thomas brought.

Lightning coach Guy Boucher might have described it best. During the Eastern Conference Finals, he said Thomas was "making miracles" for the Bruins. The notion was apt, given the number of miraculous saves the Bruins goaltender made throughout the 25-game playoff march to the championship. Without Thomas, there would have been no Stanley Cup.

The Bruins would have been bounced from the first round, or any round, without him. The previous postseason, Thomas had watched from the bench, a backup to Rask. But now, he was the man, making stops at every turn. Boston fans won't ever forget what quickly became known as "The Save" in Game 5 against the Lightning. With the series tied at two apiece and the Bruins clinging to a 2–1 lead in the third period, Tampa's Steve Downie looked like he had a sure goal. But Thomas dove from one end of the net to the opposite side, making a stunning, acrobatic stick save on Downie to prevent the game-tying goal, which helped preserve an eventual 3–1 victory.

His performance in the Stanley Cup Final against the top-seeded Canucks wasn't much different. Thomas remained at a superhuman level, willing his team to victories. It came as no surprise that he took home the Conn Smythe Trophy as the postseason's most valuable player.

In addition to the nightly brilliance of Thomas, it seemed like there was a new hero every night, making a huge play or scoring a significant goal. Along the championship ride, the Bruins went the distance in three series, including the Final, winning all three Game 7s.

That was a testament to their drive and determination.

It was also a symbol of how far they had come and the metamorphosis they had undergone after hitting rock bottom during the 2005–2006 season. The Black and Gold only won 29 games that year. They flat-lined. Then Chara arrived, and the hulking 6′9″ defenseman totally changed the culture of the Bruins, reenergizing the fan base in the process.

Slowly, the Bruins crept out of the basement, rose up the ladder, and finally raised the Stanley Cup. But there's more. No story about the Bruins' 2011 championship would be complete without mention of "the MVP Jacket."

That year, the team started a tradition of awarding this not-so-attractive jacket to a player deemed worthy after each game. While a bit hokey, the ritual became emblematic of the team's epic run. The jacket, an old Bruins warmup garment purchased on eBay by defenseman Andrew Ference, served as a kind of team prize, and was handed out after each win to a player whose contributions deserved recognition. Lucic was the first recipient, and soon, everyone wanted to wear the '80s-style Black and Gold jacket following games. It was a fun little exercise that carried on throughout the season and into the playoffs.

During the Stanley Cup Final, however, Canucks defenseman Kevin Bieksa mocked the Bruins' use of the jacket, sarcastically asking: "Don't Peewee teams have that?" The response from Ference was priceless, and in some ways, his words held the key to this particular championship. "You can really only control what your own team does. You talk about Peewee hockey, and my first thoughts when I heard [Bieksa's remarks] was how great Peewee hockey was," Ference said. "You've got the sportsmanship, you've got the camaraderie, and all the good things that go along with youth hockey. And it's a shame if you lose that at this level."

"We've got teenagers on this team, we've got a 43-year-old on this team, we've got different backgrounds, different countries," Ference went on. "And those are the things you play for in minor hockey. Those are the bonds that everyone has in common, and those are the things that make a team. We have a group of guys who embrace the juvenile aspects of the sport. We don't have anyone who thinks they're too awesome for that, which is great. That's been a huge part of our success. And it's a huge part of our sport.... If our sport doesn't have the quality that it had when we were kids, we become a shell of ourselves, really."

Whether it was the 2001 Patriots, the 2004 Red Sox, the 2008 Celtics, or the 2011 Bruins, they all had that kid-like passion to win—and win when few gave them a chance.

MassLive columnist Karen Guregian has been writing about sports in New England for four decades. Her early years with the *Boston Herald* were devoted solely to coverage of the Boston Bruins and the NHL.

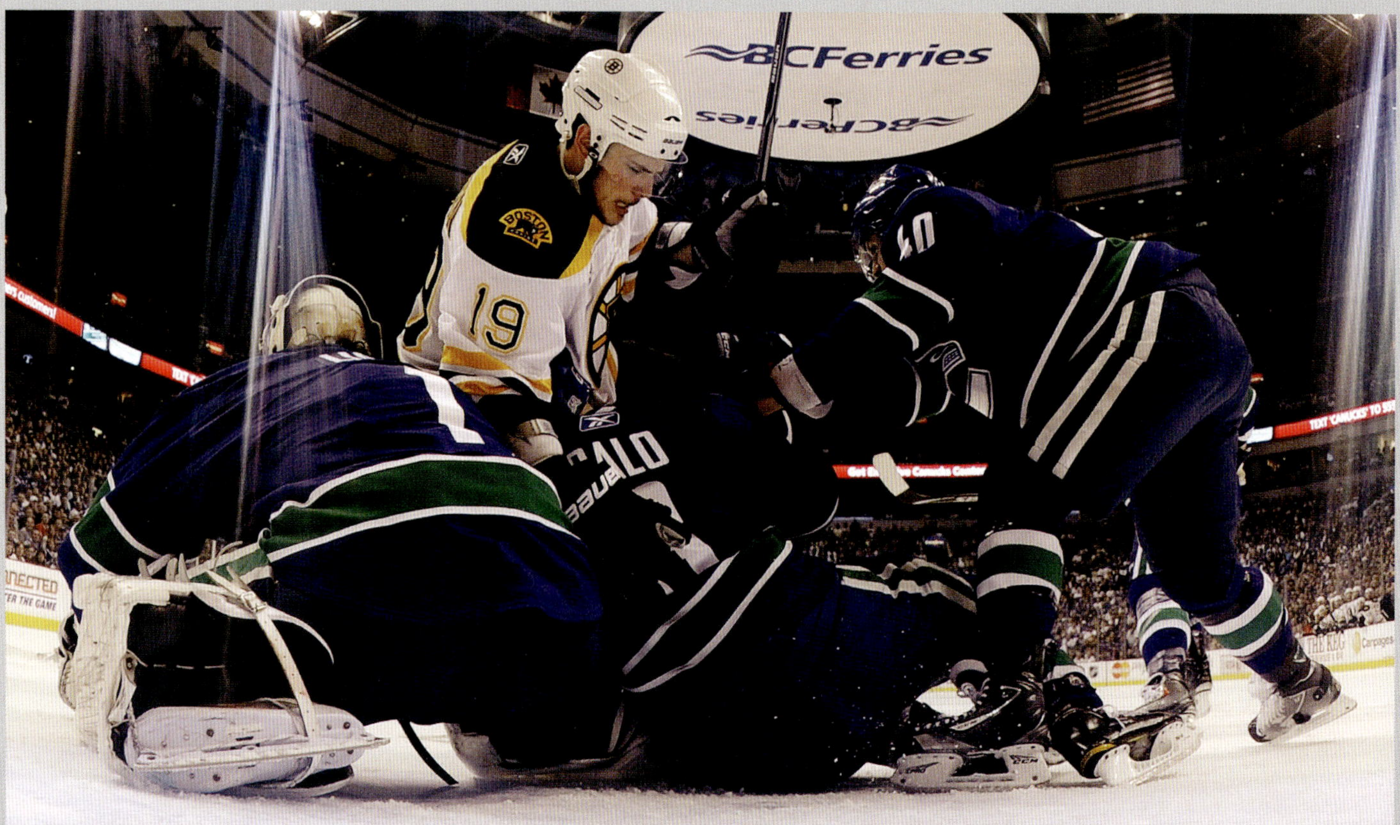

Rookie Tyler Seguin crashes the Vancouver net during Game 5 of the 2011 NHL Stanley Cup Final. The Bruins selected the talented Seguin with the No. 2 overall selection in the 2010 NHL Draft. He would play three seasons in Boston (2010–2013) before being traded to Dallas in the summer of 2013. (Photograph by Bruce Bennett/Getty Images)

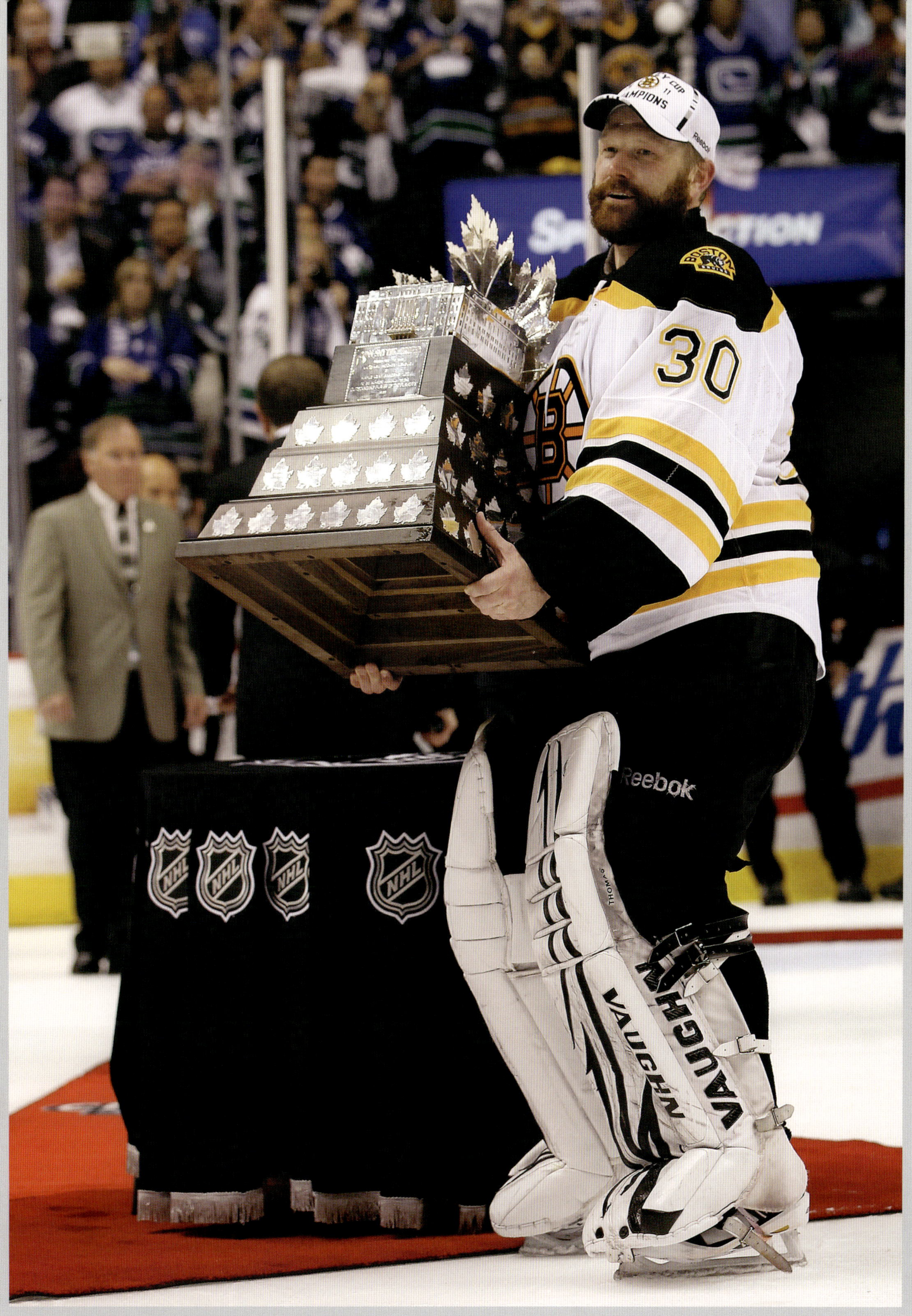

Goalie Tim Thomas became only the second Bruin to receive the Conn Smythe Trophy as Stanley Cup playoff MVP, following the two won by Bobby Orr in 1970 and 1972. (Photograph by Bruce Bennett/Getty Images)

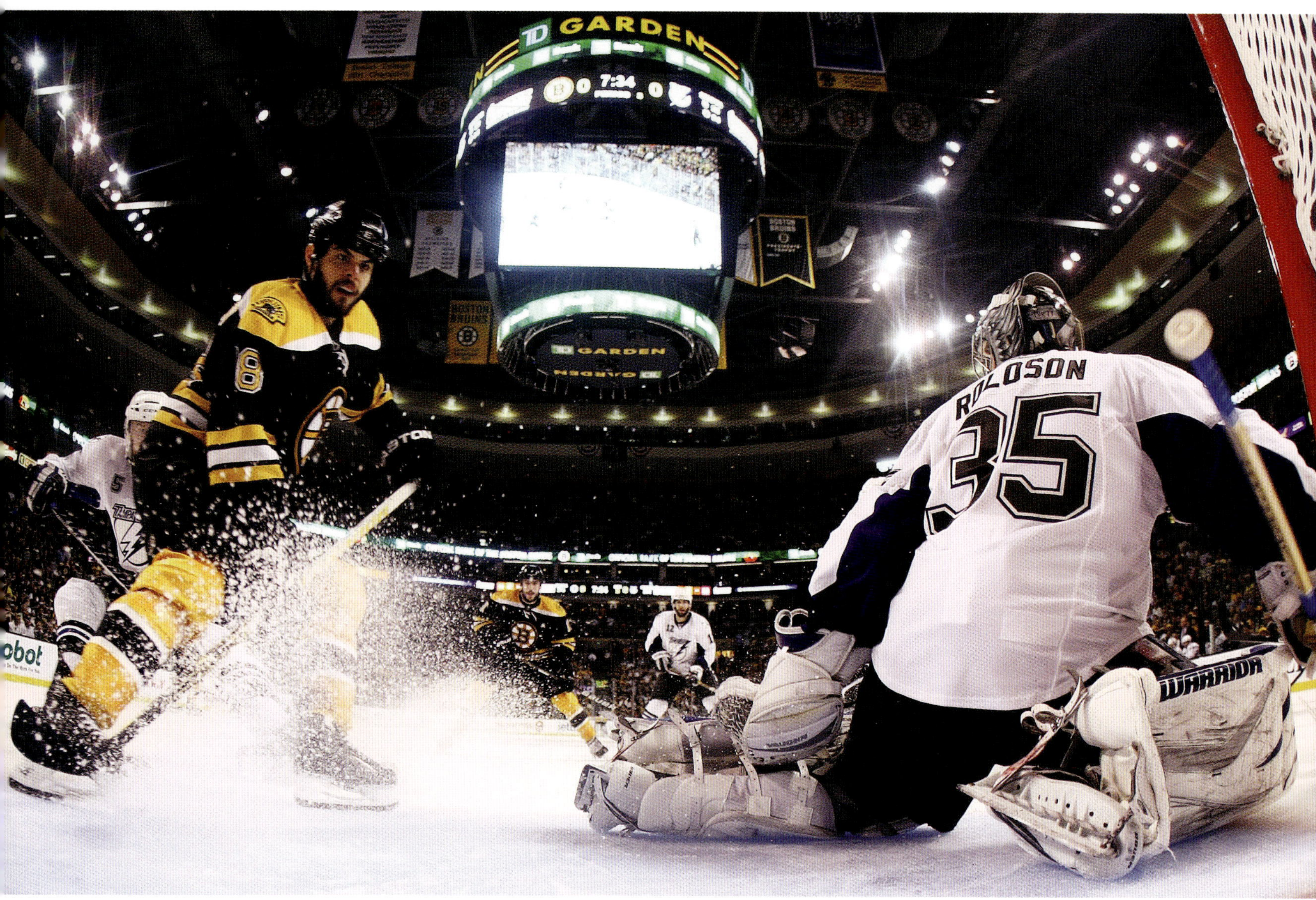

Nathan Horton scores one of the greatest goals in the history of the Boston Bruins to give the Bruins a 1–0 third-period lead over Tampa Bay in Game 7 of the 2011 Eastern Conference Finals. Thanks to late game heroics from goalie Tim Thomas—who else?—the Bruins would hold on to advance to the Stanley Cup Final.
(Photograph by Elsa/Getty Images)

NATHAN HORTON

Ranking high on the long list of Bruins heroes from the 2011 Stanley Cup playoffs is right wing Nathan Horton. It all had to do with three game-winning goals—and, of course, one water bottle.

Horton's heroics began in the first round series versus the Canadiens. The Bruins had fallen into a 2–0 series hole but rallied to win the next two games in Montreal to tie things up. Game 5 at TD Garden went into a second overtime—and it was Horton who won it, putting home a rebound from an Andrew Ference shot to give the Bruins a 3–2 series lead. Horton's heroics won Game 7, too. It was another overtime goal, this one a slap shot off a feed from Milan Lucic that was deflected and found itself past Montreal goalie Carey Price. "He's a clutch player, he's a great player, and I'm just happy to have him on our side," said teammate Patrice Bergeron after the game.

Horton's third and final game-winning goal came in Game 7 of the Eastern Conference Finals versus Tampa Bay. This one came late in the third period of a scoreless, penalty-free game, when Horton beat goalie Dwayne Roloson by deflecting a pass across the slot from David Krejci. It was a thing of beauty.

"He just came up so huge for us, over and over," said Tim Thomas in a 2022 interview.

Finally, there was the water bottle. Horton had been knocked out of the Stanley Cup Final in Game 3, when he was blindsided by a hit from Vancouver's Aaron

Rome. The injury galvanized the Bruins, who steamrolled the Canucks to win Game 3 8–1, to launch their comeback from a 2–0 series deficit. Horton traveled with the team to Vancouver for Game 7, providing his teammates with an emotional lift.

That is where the water bottle came in. A few hours before game time, Horton, accompanied by assistant equipment manager Matt Falconer, wandered out of the Bruins dressing room and poured water from a water bottle onto the Rogers Arena ice in front of the Bruins bench. It was Boston water—melted TD Garden ice that made the trip with the Bruins into Canada. And it was all about the resolve of the Bruins to win Game 7 on Vancouver ice.

It may have been merely symbolic, or even corny—but it worked. Just several hours later, the Bruins were Stanley Cup champions.

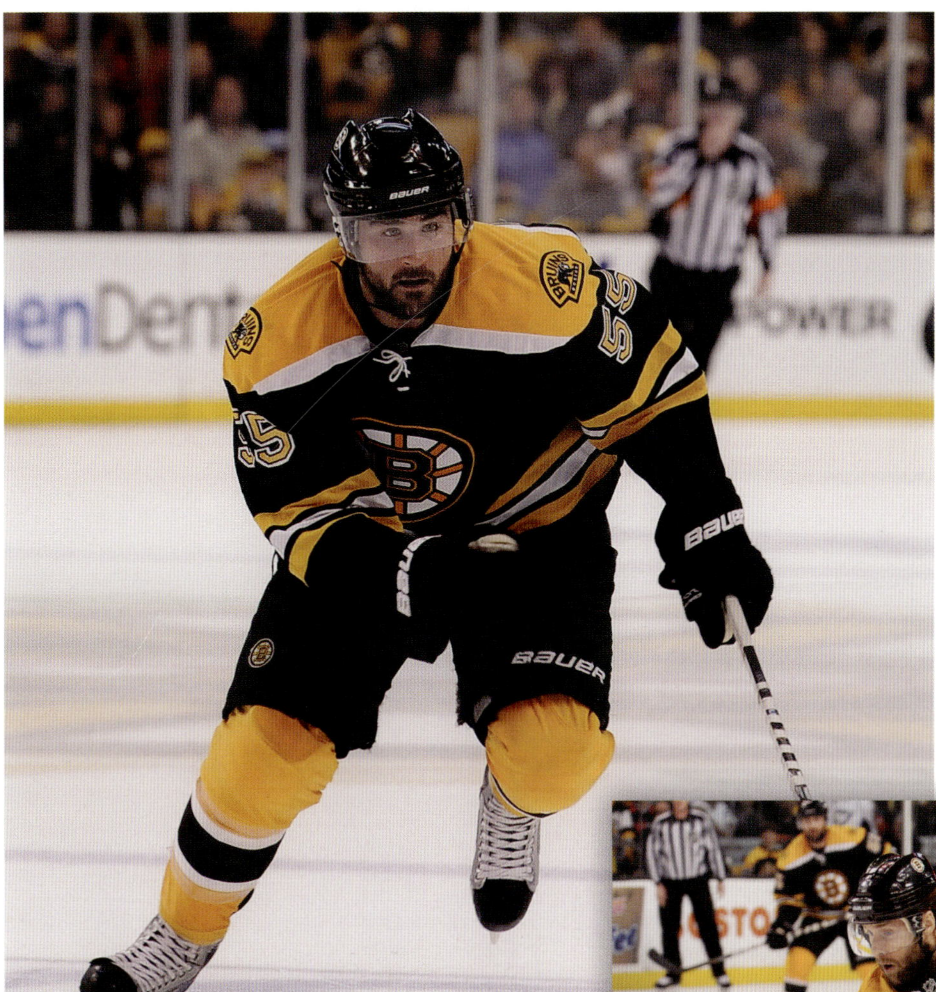

Johnny Boychuk (left) skates against the Tampa Bay Lightning during the 2011 Eastern Conference Finals. Boychuk was a rock-solid, hard-hitting defenseman on the 2011 Stanley Cup championship team who was a key contributor throughout his tenure in Boston (2008–2014). (Photograph by Steve Babineau/NHLI via Getty Images)

Center Rich Peverley (below) heads up ice during the 2011 Eastern Conference Finals versus Tampa Bay. The Bruins had acquired Peverley and center Chris Kelly in separate deals several months earlier. The additions bolstered Boston's forward depth—and proved to be crucial in the team's march toward the Stanley Cup. (Photograph by Brian Babineau/NHLI via Getty Images)

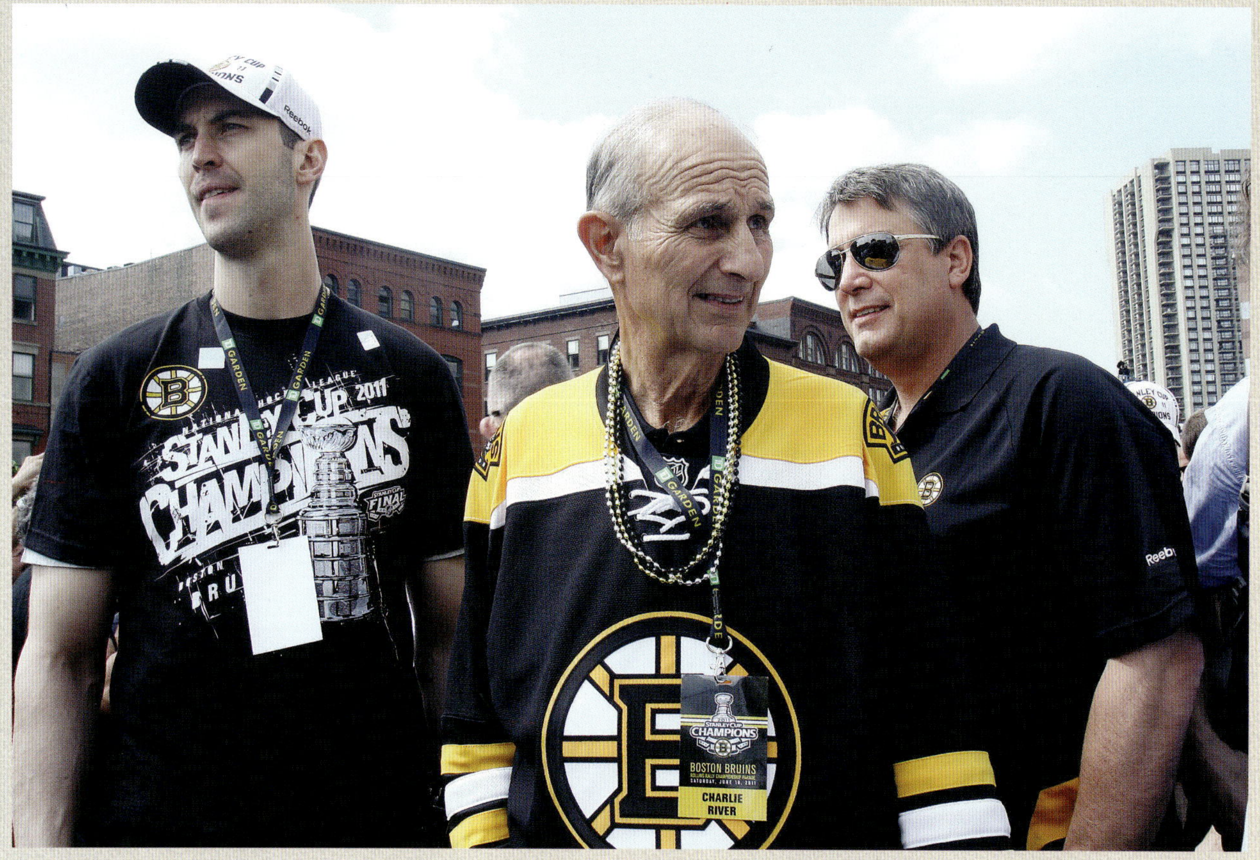

Zdeno Chara, Jeremy Jacobs, and Cam Neely (left to right) get ready to board a Duck Boat for the Bruins victory parade on June 18, 2011. They are three of the most pivotal figures in the history of the Boston Bruins—and they are all savoring the Stanley Cup that the Bruins had just brought back to Boston. (Photograph by Jim Rogash/Getty Images)

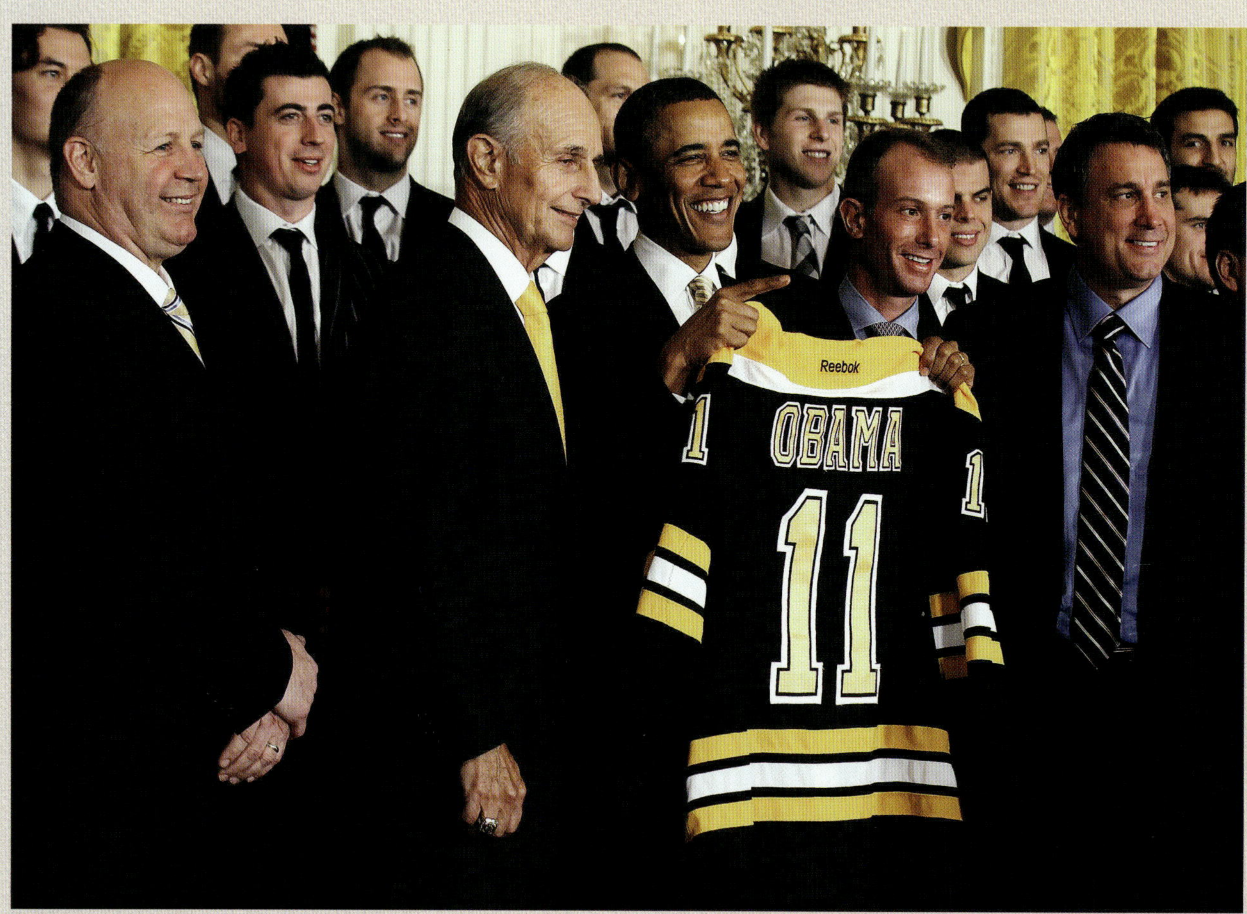

On January 23, 2012, the 2011 Stanley Cup champions visited the White House, where they presented President Barack Obama with a Bruins jersey. While congratulating the Bruins, Obama referred to Brad Marchand by his nickname "Little Ball of Hate," to much laughter. "I guess if the president of the United States gives you a nickname, you have to stick with it," Marchand later said. (Photograph by Alex Wong/Getty Images)

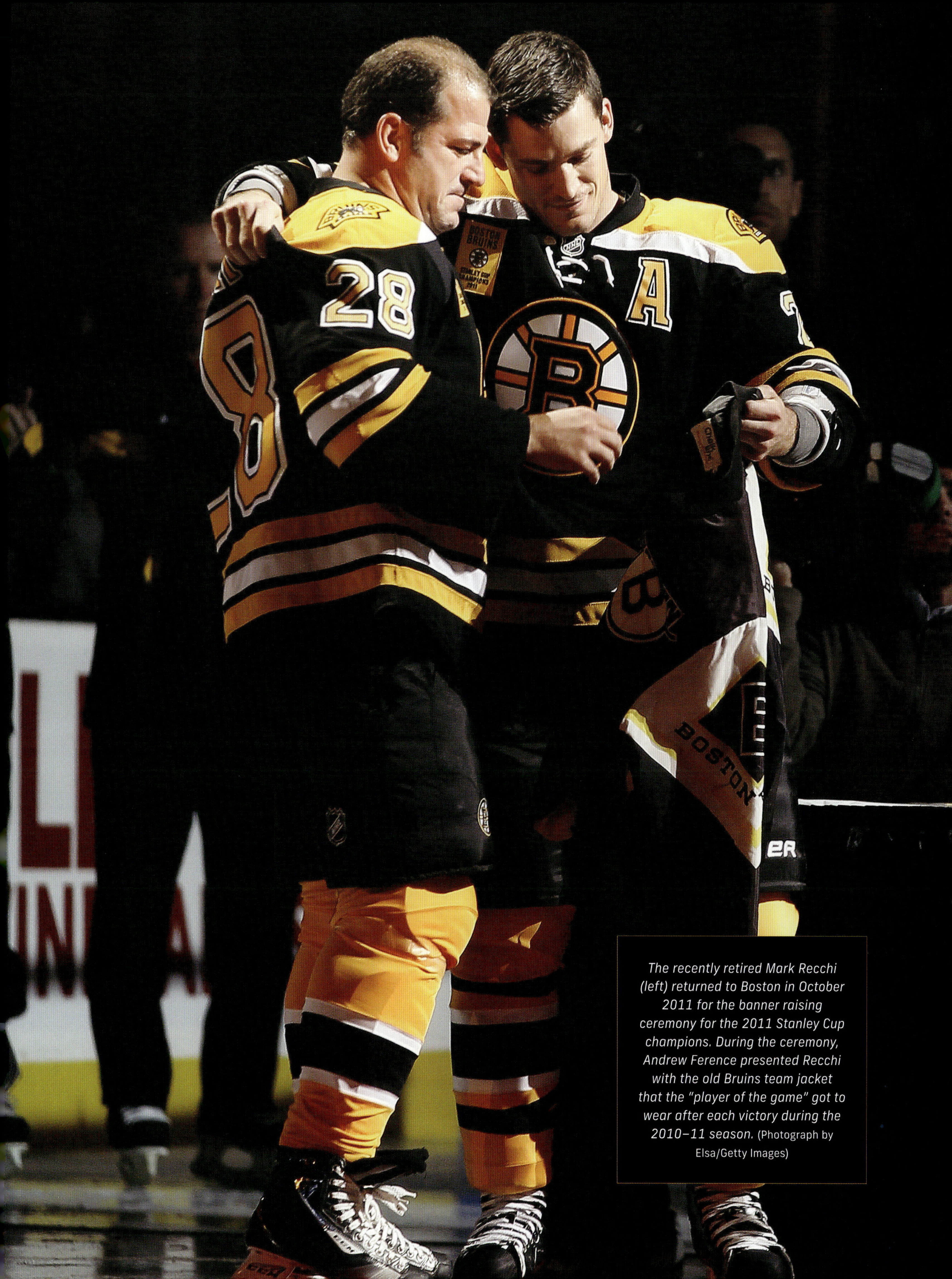

The recently retired Mark Recchi (left) returned to Boston in October 2011 for the banner raising ceremony for the 2011 Stanley Cup champions. During the ceremony, Andrew Ference presented Recchi with the old Bruins team jacket that the "player of the game" got to wear after each victory during the 2010–11 season. (Photograph by Elsa/Getty Images)

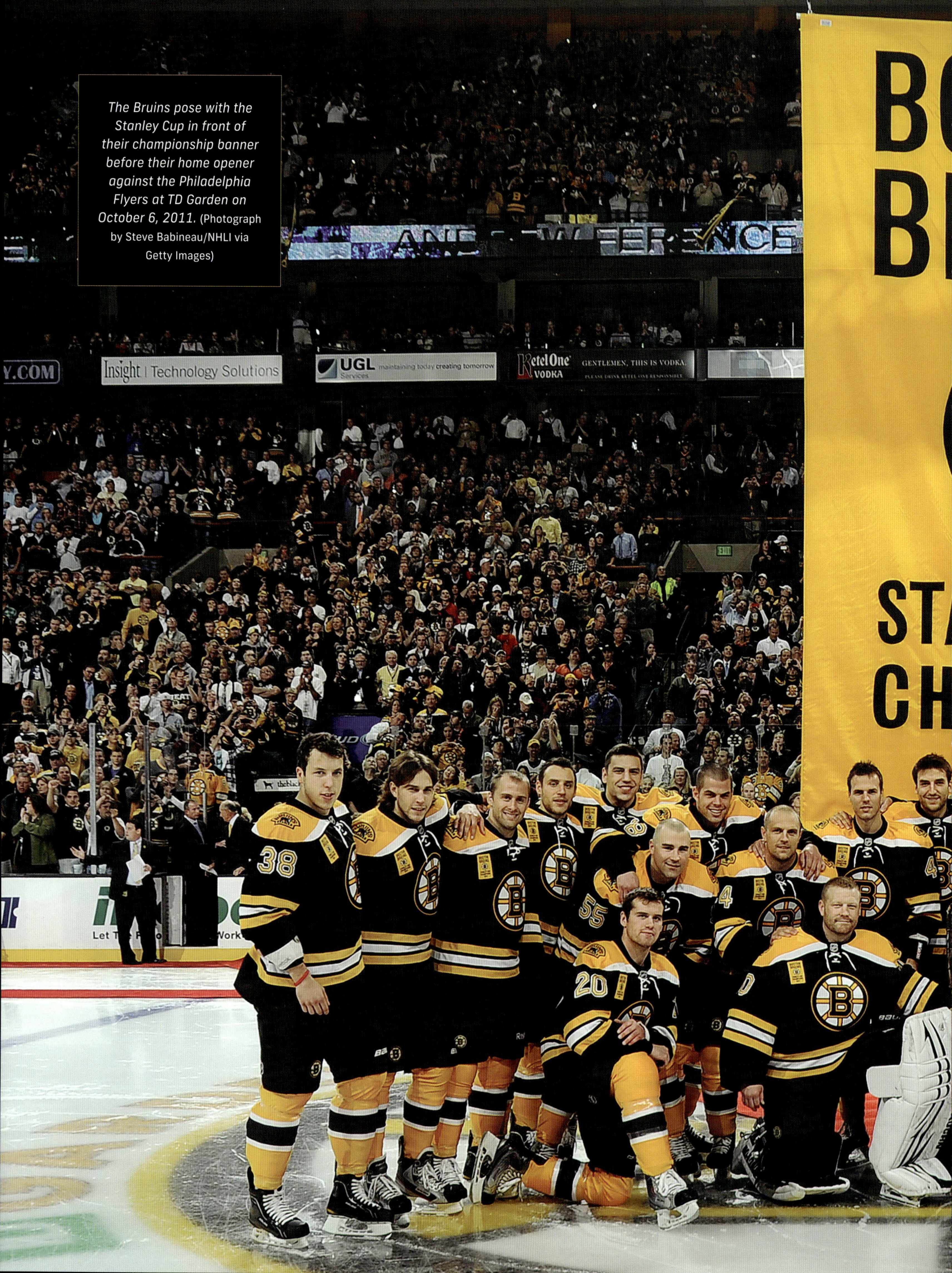

The Bruins pose with the Stanley Cup in front of their championship banner before their home opener against the Philadelphia Flyers at TD Garden on October 6, 2011. (Photograph by Steve Babineau/NHLI via Getty Images)

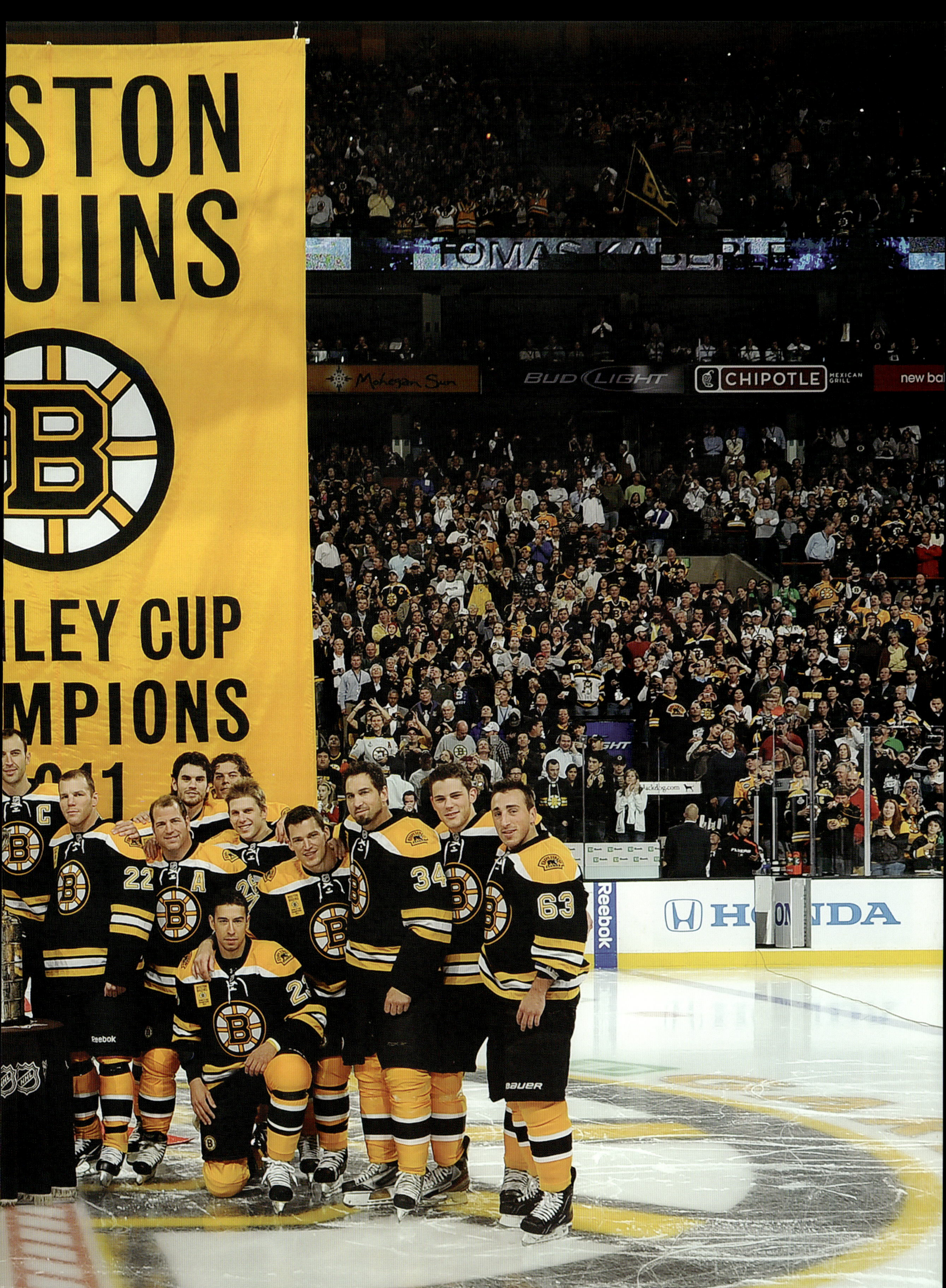

STON
UINS
LEY CUP
MPIONS
BUD LIGHT
CHIPOTLE
MEXICAN GRILL
Reebok

JEREMY JACOBS

According to Jeremy Jacobs, his "greatest accomplishment" came when he went on the ice in Vancouver on June 15, 2011, to join in the celebration as his Bruins won the Stanley Cup, thus fulfilling his dream of bringing an NHL championship to the city of Boston.

It certainly hasn't been the only accomplishment for the longtime owner of the Boston Bruins. In fact, Jacobs stands proudly as the longest-tenured owner in the history of Boston professional sports.

Jacobs is the chairman of Delaware North, one of the world's leading hospitality and food service companies. It is a family-owned company—and one that has deep roots in the sports world, stretching back to the early 1900s, primarily relating to ballpark and stadium concessions. The Jacobs Family also owned several professional teams along the way, including the Buffalo Bisons of the American Hockey League in the early 1940s (coached by Bruins legend Eddie Shore) as well as the Cincinnati Royals of the National Basketball Association in the 1960s.

Jeremy Jacobs, just in his mid-thirties, bought the Bruins in 1975. "It was a heck of a good buy for me," said Jacobs in a 2017 interview with Kevin Paul Dupont of the *Boston Globe*. "We had the building, the team, the concessions, and also the TV rights. The whole deal was put together so well."

For the first two decades of his ownership of the Bruins, Jacobs was very much a behind-the-scenes presence. He was based in Buffalo, raising a young family and building the Delaware North business. The fact that he had Harry Sinden running the club in Boston made all of this possible. And Jacobs doesn't regret the arrangement. "He was a darn good leader," said Jacobs of Sinden in his interview with the *Globe*. "And he taught me a lot about the game."

Jacobs proved to be a quick study—and, in the last quarter century, he has emerged as a major force in NHL circles. Since 2007, he has served as the chairman of the NHL Board of Governors

As Sinden observed in a 2017 interview with NHL.com, "Mr. Jacobs makes a marvelous chairman because he's able to see all sides and corners of the table he sits at, and he has an understanding of all of those things.... He's been very good

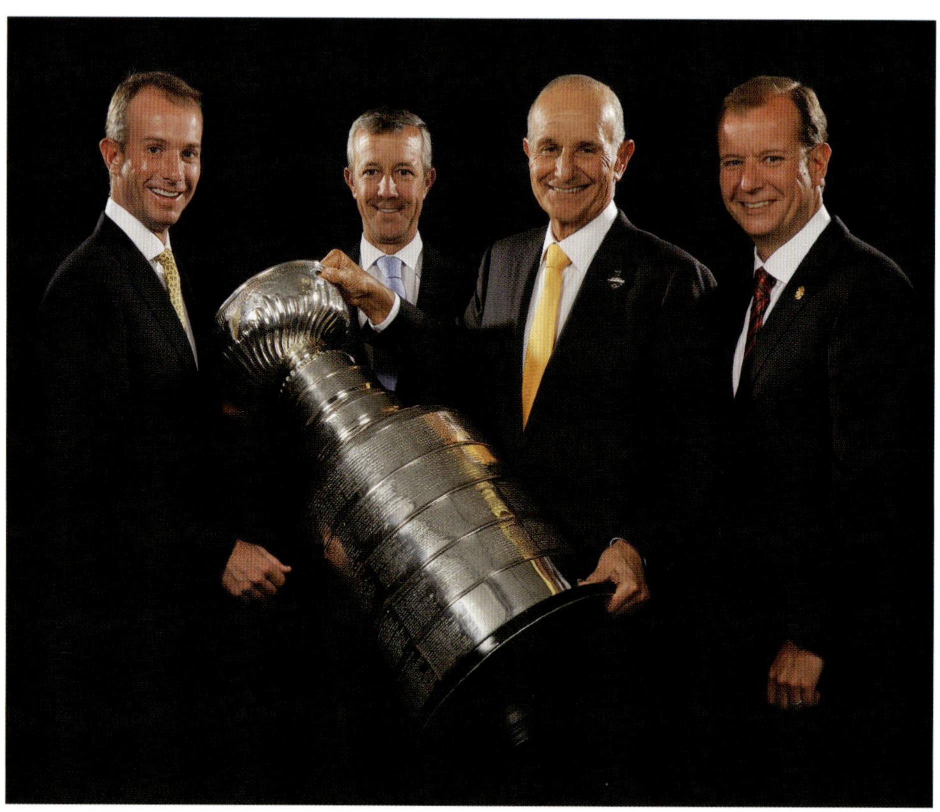

Bruins owner Jeremy Jacobs holds the Stanley Cup joined by sons Charlie, Lou, and Jerry Jr. (left to right) shortly after the team's victory in 2011 over Vancouver. For the Jacobs Family, it was a crowning achievement of their long-term and ongoing ownership of the Boston Bruins. (Photograph courtesy of the Boston Bruins)

at it, and he's earned the position. He's a big part of the growth of this league. He's been a terrific sounding board for Commissioner [Gary] Bettman all these years. He has foresight, and he's able as well as anybody in the league to look at the big picture as it involves expansion or rules or such delicate items as the Olympics, things like that. He's well versed and well aware of every piece of business that goes on in this league."

Along the way, Jacobs led the effort to build TD Garden. Without a new arena in town, where would the Bruins (and even the Celtics, for that matter) be today? The answer is probably not in the city of Boston.

All of this resulted in his induction into the Hockey Hall of Fame in 2017. Jacobs was both appreciative and touched by the honor. "It's humbling in the fact that it's a peer thing," he told the *Globe*'s Dupont at the time. "Peers are bestowing an honor on you that you didn't expect, and it is terribly meaningful to me because I have spent the past 42 years now involved in this sport, and it went from arm's length to something that is very near and dear to me."

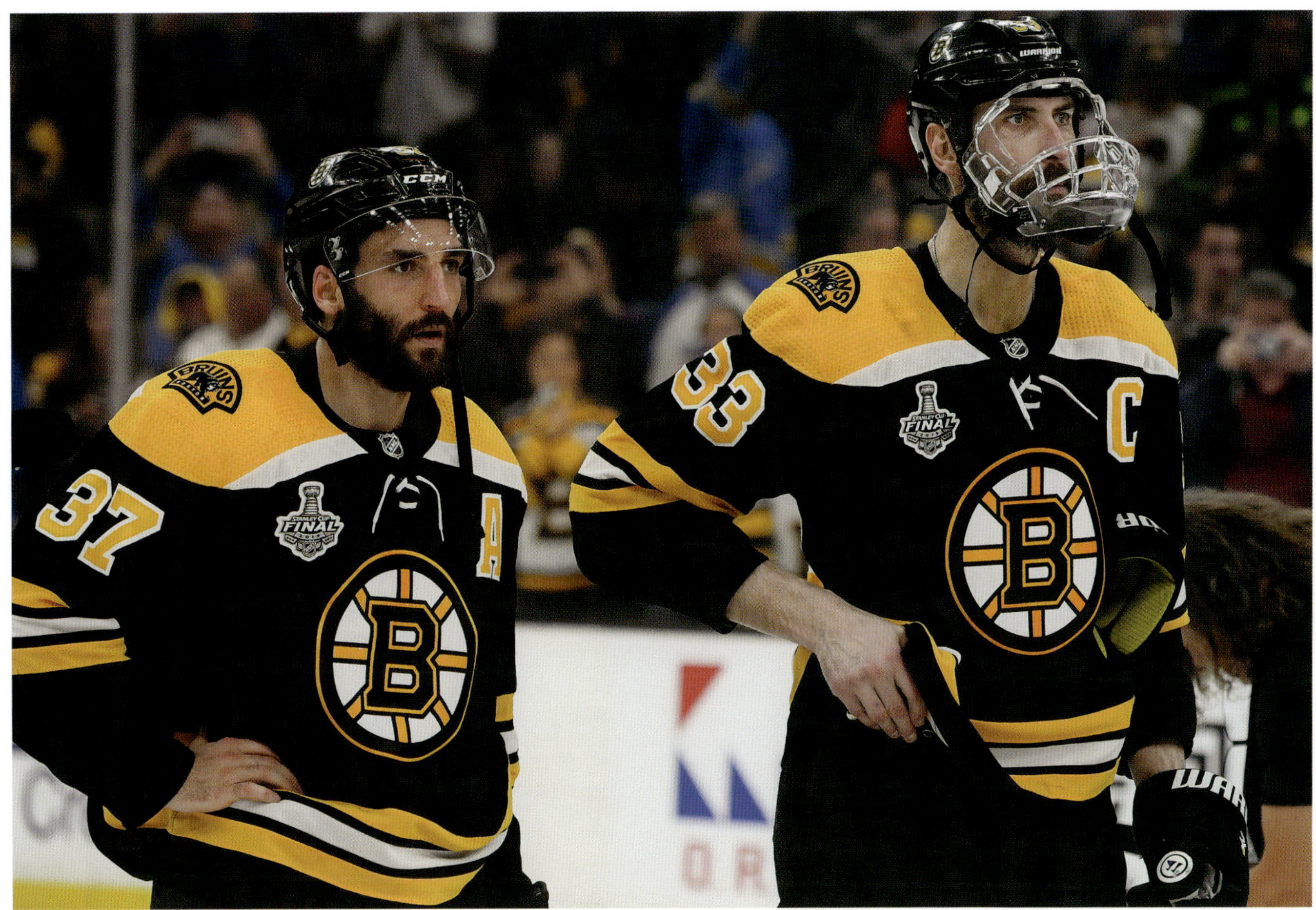

The essence of what it means to be a Bruin was exemplified by the playoff heroics of Patrice Bergeron (37) and Zdeno Chara (33). In 2013, Bergeron played the decisive sixth game of the Stanley Cup Final with a broken rib, punctured lung, broken nose, and separated shoulder. Six years later, Chara played the final three games of the 2019 Stanley Cup Final with a broken jaw. They don't come any tougher. (Photograph by Brian Babineau/NHLI via Getty Images)

THE CHARA-BERGERON ERA

On April 17, 2013, the Bruins met the Buffalo Sabres at TD Garden for the first major event in Boston in the wake of the tragic Boston Marathon bombings just two days earlier. Everyone was on edge and emotions were running high.

The Boston fans at TD Garden that night brought their "A-Game," waving American flags and greeting the first responders who presented the colors with a thunderous ovation. And then came the national anthem. Longtime anthem singer Rene Rancourt sang the first two lines—and then stopped, held his microphone aloft, and let the crowd take over. The 18,000-plus fans belted out the rest of the "Star-Spangled Banner" on their own. It was a rendition that no one would ever forget.

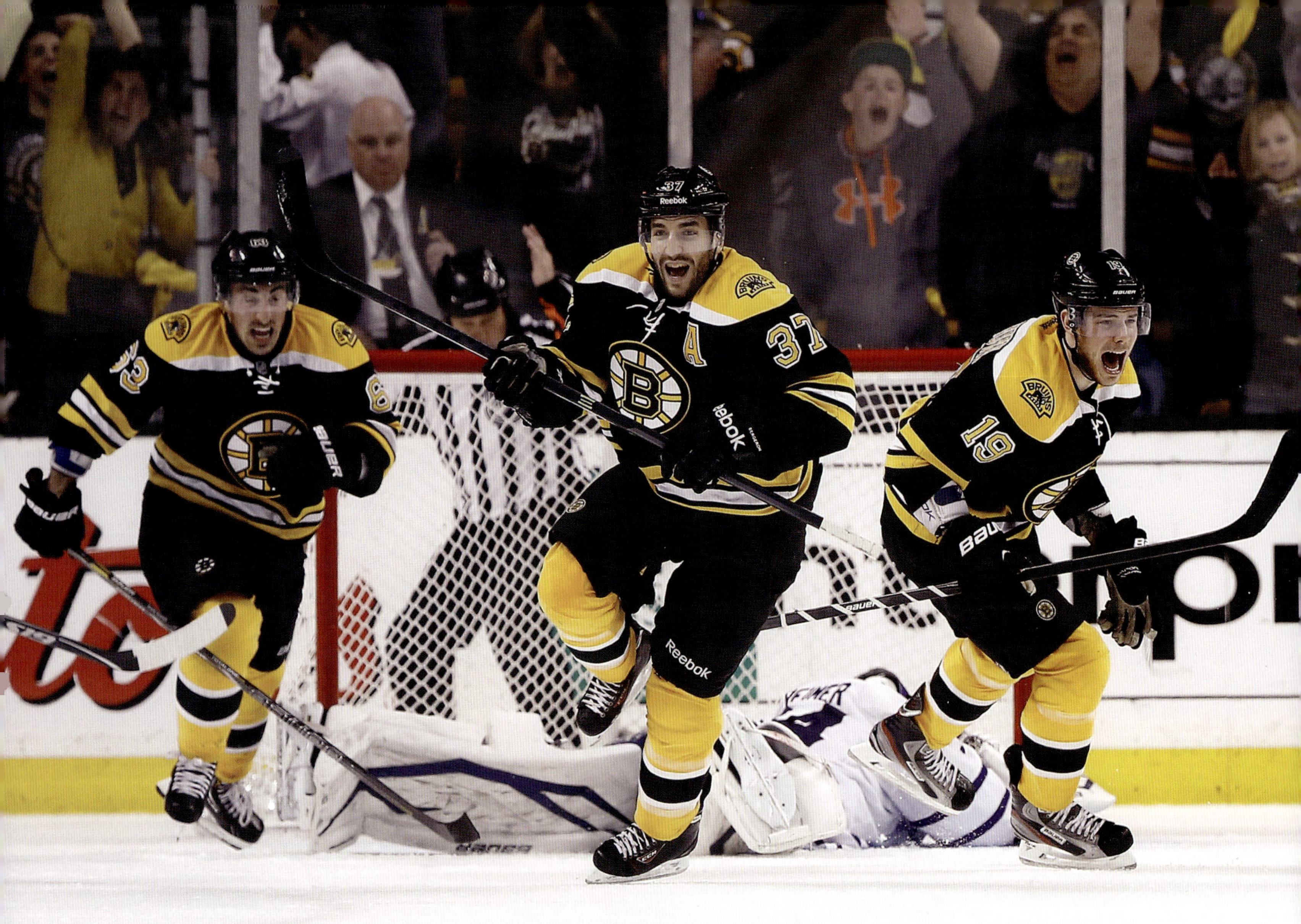

Brad Marchand, Patrice Bergeron, and Tyler Seguin (left to right) celebrate Bergeron's overtime goal that won Game 7 of the 2013 Eastern Conference Quarterfinals against the Toronto Maple Leafs. Boston overcame overwhelming odds in coming back from a 4–1 third-period deficit to win by a final score of 5–4. It stands as one of the greatest comebacks in NHL history. (Photograph by Jared Wickerham/Getty Images)

"I can't remember being more emotional on the ice," said Bruins defenseman Andrew Ference. He was hardly alone.

That evening was one of the first powerful demonstrations of what would become known as "Boston Strong." It was also yet another special moment in a glorious era in Bruins history, which had begun a half dozen years earlier and would soon become known as "the Chara-Bergeron Era" after its two central players, Zdeno Chara and Patrice Bergeron.

The first part of the era involved the special group of players that brought the Bruins back to the playoffs in 2008, won a Stanley Cup together in 2011, and then made another run at a Cup in 2013, advancing to the Final before falling to the Chicago Blackhawks in six games. "Feeling the excitement around the city was amazing," said Shawn Thornton of that 2013 Cup run. "We obviously wanted to win—and it still irks me that we don't have that ring—but we got there, which wasn't easy."

After a stellar 2014 regular season that saw the Bruins claim the President's Cup Trophy with 117 points, the roster started to turn over. Over the next several seasons, the Bruins added a host of young, talented players—David Pastrnak, Charlie McAvoy, and others—as well as a new coach, Bruce Cassidy, who took over behind the bench after the team parted ways with Claude Julien in February 2017.

Most importantly, however, a core group of players remained in place throughout, including not only Chara and Bergeron but also center David Krejci, left wing Brad Marchand, and goaltender Tuukka Rask. "It's comforting as a coach," Cassidy told Fluto Shinzawa of The Athletic in 2022. "These guys were all battle-tested and at each position. Guys who won, played winning hockey, meaningful hockey, good pros, all those things."

And with that strong core leading the way, the Chara-Bergeron Era continued. In Cassidy's first full season as coach in 2017–18, the team collected 112 points while advancing to the second round of the playoffs. The following season (2018–19), the team advanced all the way to the Stanley Cup Final only to fall to the St. Louis Blues in a heartbreaking seven-game series. It was the third time in eight years that the Bruins made the Stanley Cup Final, further attesting to their preeminent position in the NHL.

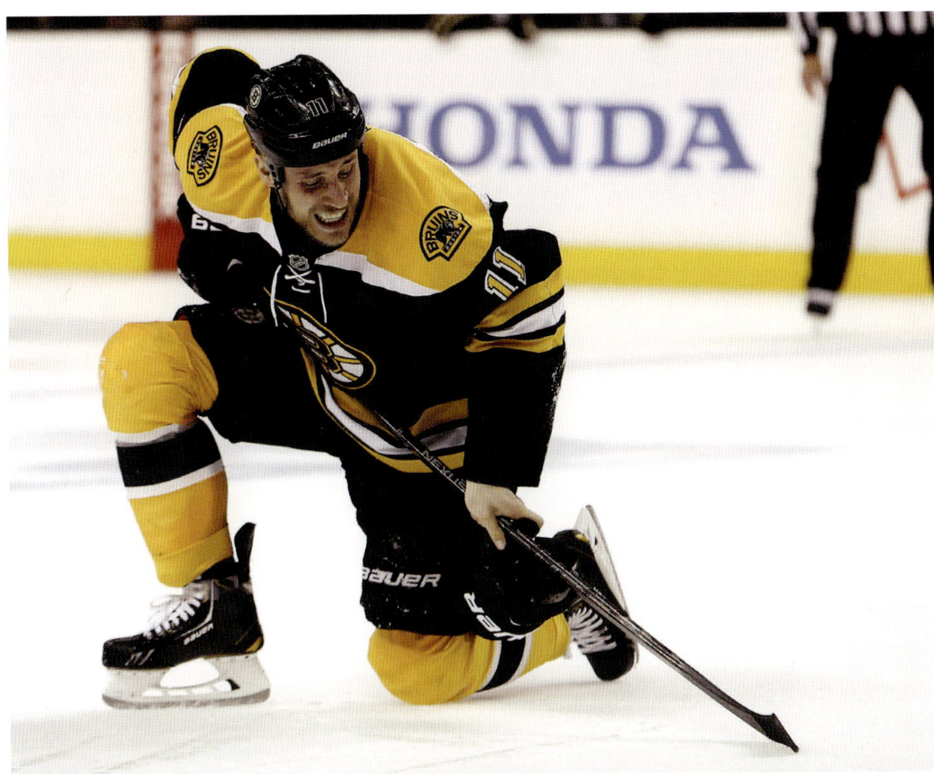

In Game 3 of the 2013 Eastern Conference Finals, Bruins center Gregory Campbell (left) sustained a broken right fibula blocking an Evgeni Malkin slapshot during a Pittsburgh power play. After sustaining the injury, Campbell remained on the ice for the next minute, finishing his shift and helping to kill off the penalty. It epitomized the toughness that has long been a hallmark of the franchise and its players. (Photograph by Bruce Bennett/Getty Images)

Perennial All-Star and eventual Hockey Hall of Famer Jarome Iginla (below) spent one season in Boston (2013–14), ringing up 61 points to help the Bruins win the Presidents' Trophy. In the 2010s, the Bruins made a habit of bringing veteran legends to town to help them with their championship chase, including Iginla, Jaromir Jagr (2013), and Rick Nash (2018). (Photograph by Steve Babineau/NHLI via Getty Images)

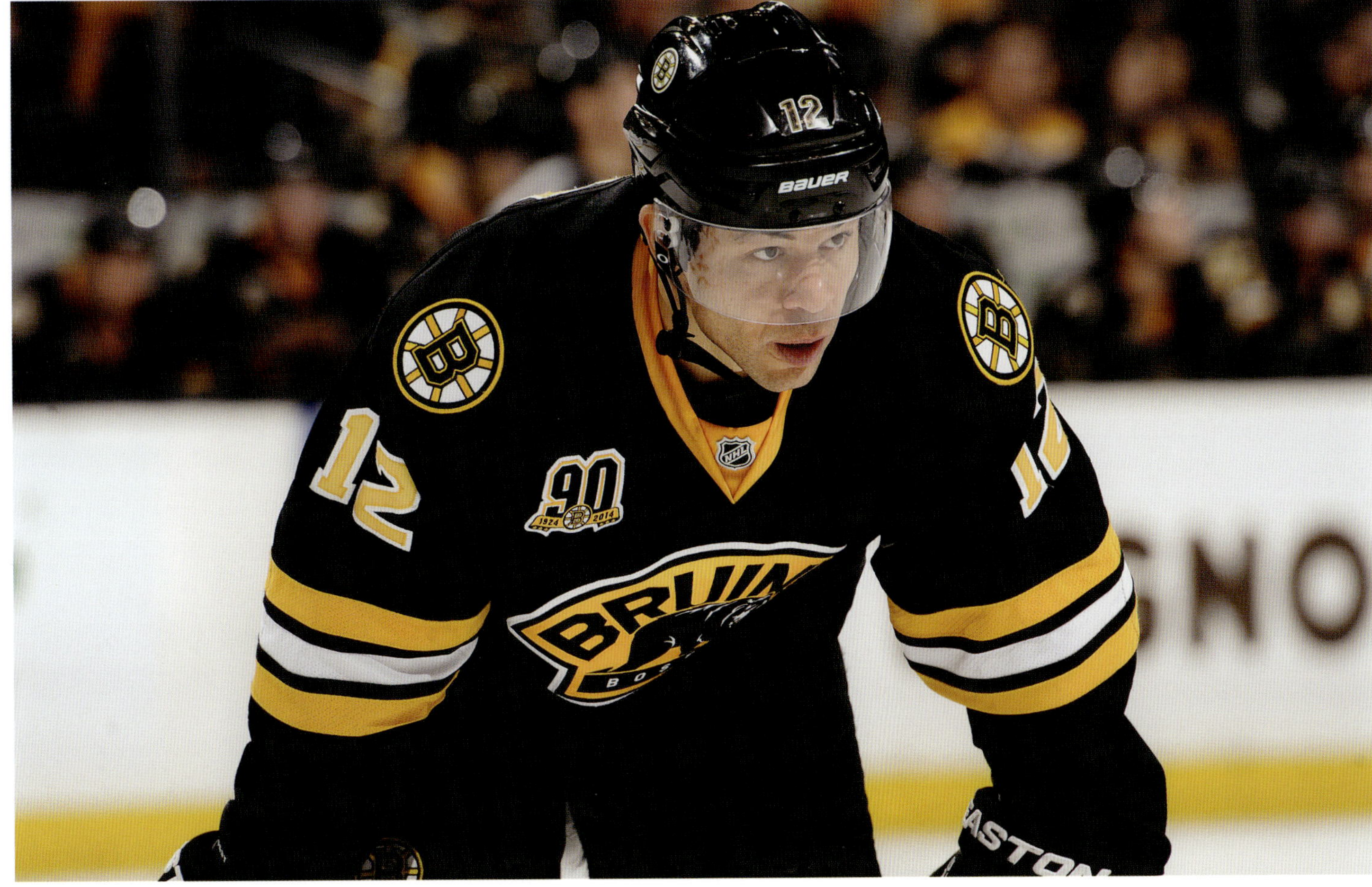

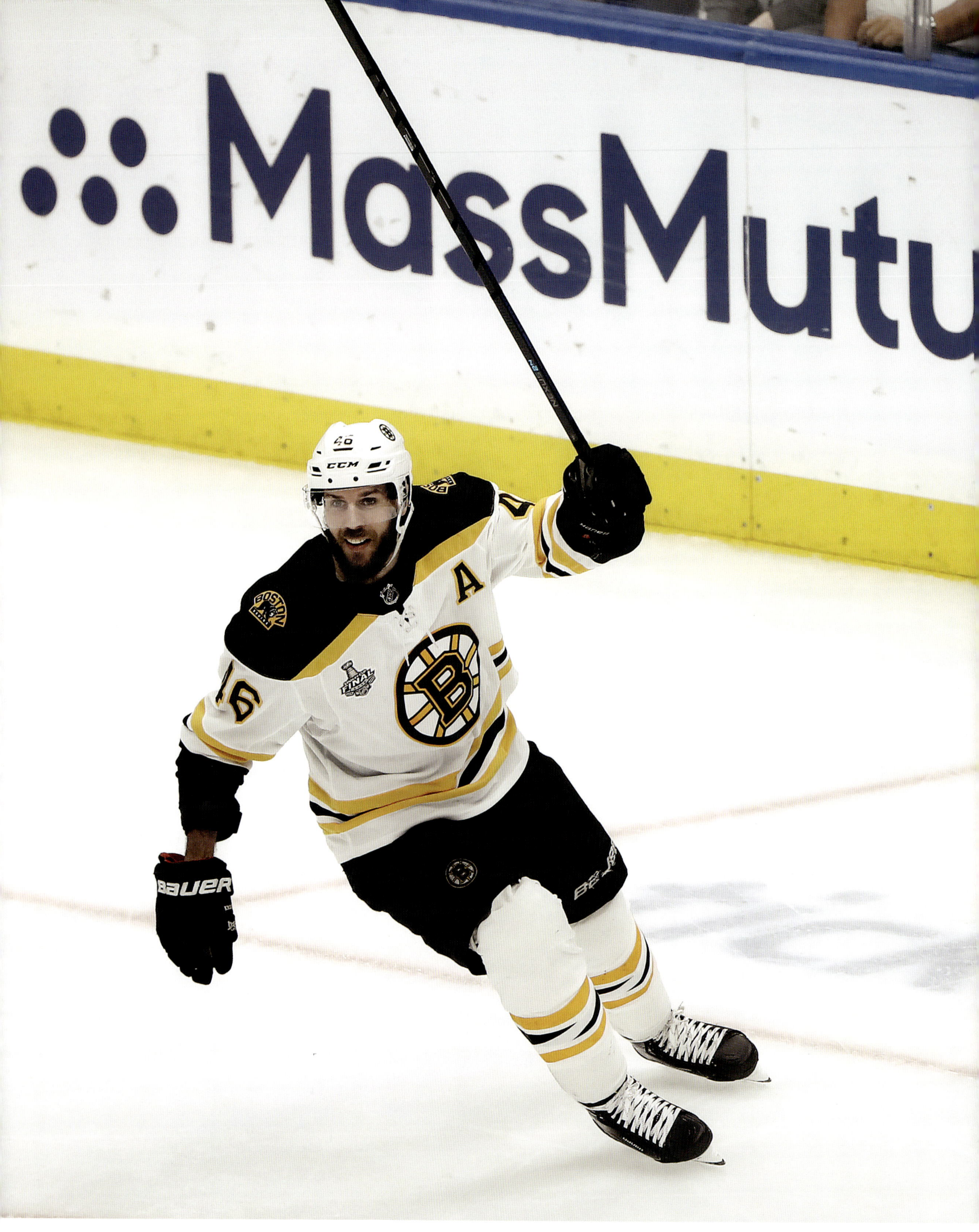
MassMutu
BAUER
CCM
A
46
BOSTON

DAVID KREJCI

DAVID KREJCI has played with the Bruins from 2007 to the present (minus the 2021–22 season, which he spent in his native Czech Republic). It has been a long tenure in Black and Gold—and one filled with distinction.

Let's start with the skills. They are considerable. His most pronounced talents are in the playmaking area, as he possesses a high hockey IQ, excellent vision, and the softest of hands. "Some players have the ability, somehow, to give themselves space, and to create that time that they need to be able to see things," said Tim Thomas in a 2022 interview. "He had a knack for that."

Krejci is more than just a clever passer, however. He is a complete hockey player who can score goals, win faceoffs, and more than hold his own on the defensive end.

And when the chips are down, Krejci is at his absolute best. The statistics here don't lie. During the Bruins' 2010–11 Stanley Cup run, Krejci soared to new heights, finishing as the NHL's leading playoff scorer with 12 goals (including four game-winners) and 11 assists in 25 games. "Playoff Krejci" also led the league in postseason scoring in 2013.

"I think it's more his poise, the way that he just plays the game," said Patrice Bergeron in a 2022 interview. "It is pretty impressive. Usually playoff games get tougher and harder. You have to work for every inch on the ice. He always seems to elevate his game and find ways to be better."

Over time, Krejci has also emerged as a leader with an impact on the next generation of Bruins players. "He's like my big brother," said David Pastrnak in an

Opposite page: Playmaker extraordinaire David Krejci celebrates teammate Karson Kuhlman's third-period goal in the Bruins 5–1 win over St. Louis in Game 6 of the 2019 Stanley Cup Final. It was a gutsy road victory that forced a Game 7 back in Boston. (Photograph by Jamie Squire/ Getty Images)

Below: Rookie Torey Krug (right) greets David Krejci (left) in celebration of Krug's goal in Game 2 of the 2013 Eastern Conference Semifinals versus the New York Rangers. Called up from Providence on an emergency basis during the 2013 Stanley Cup playoffs, Krug shone on the big stage, tallying nine points in 15 games. In his ensuing seven full seasons with the Bruins (2013–2020), Krug averaged nearly 50 points per season as a puck-moving defenseman and the quarterback of the Boston power play. (Photograph by Steve Babineau/NHLI via Getty Images)

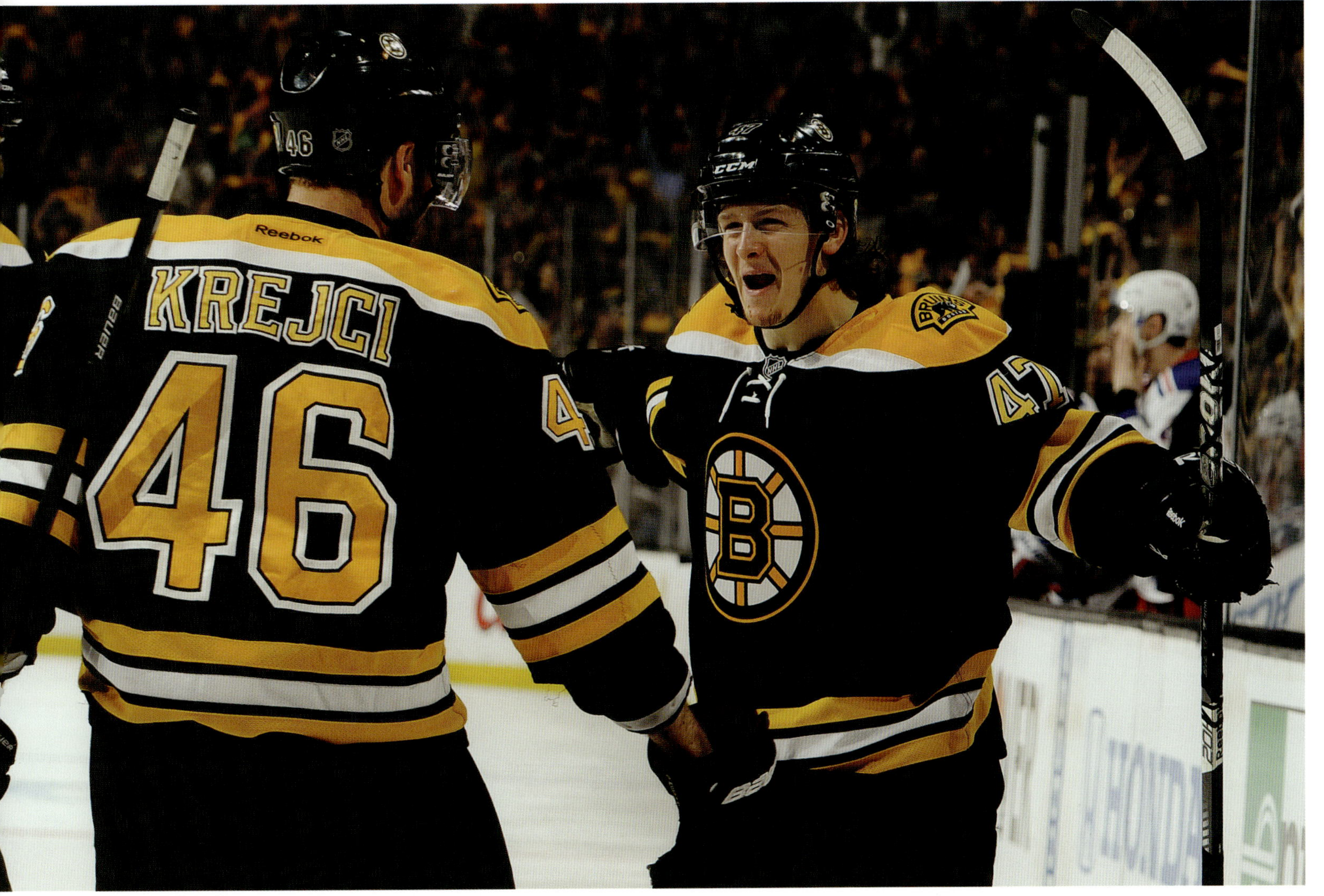

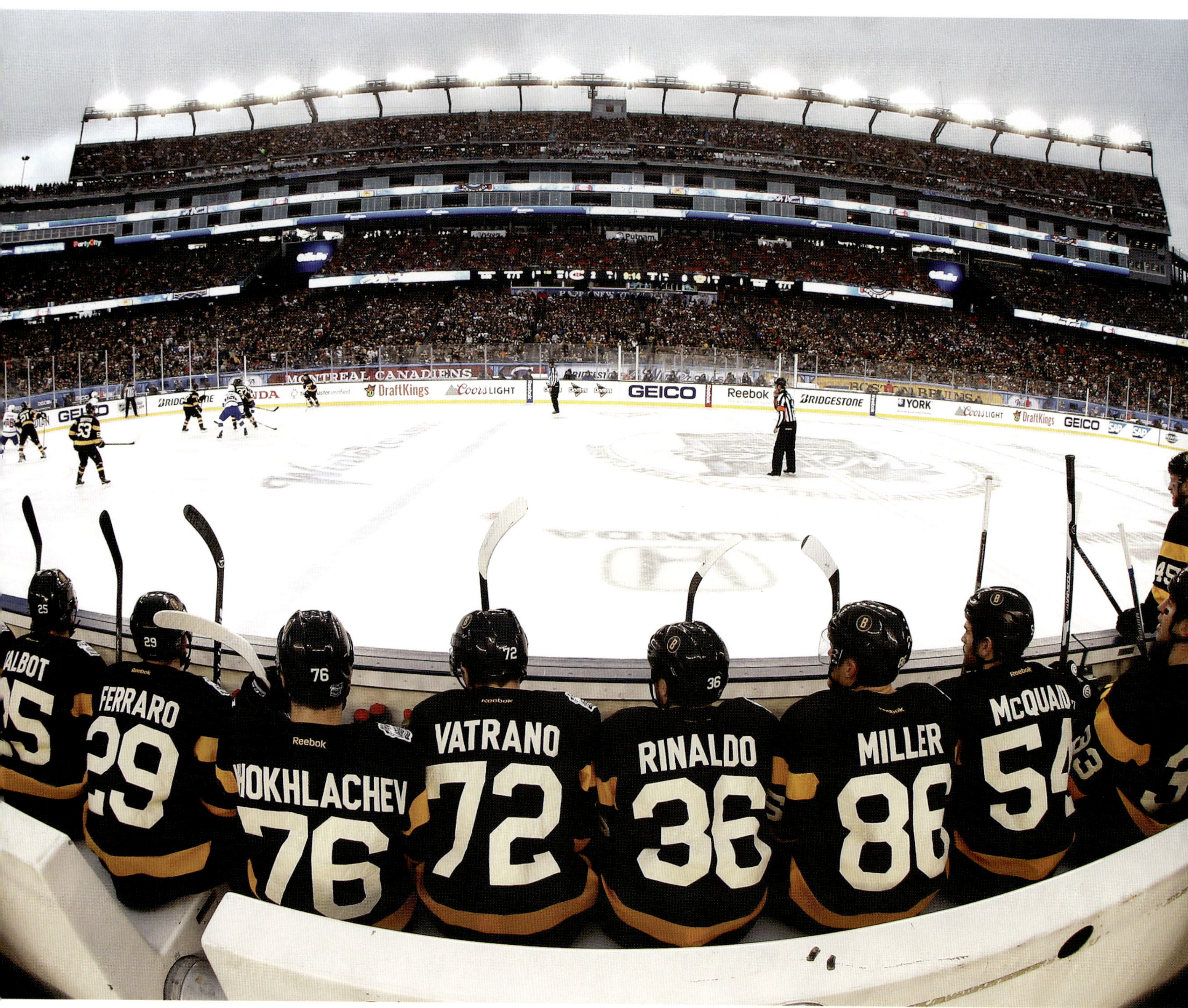

On January 1, 2016, the Bruins appeared in their second Winter Classic at Gillette Stadium in Foxboro, falling 5–1 to the Montreal Canadiens. Their third appearance of the decade in the NHL's marquee regular season game would take place three years later on January 1, 2019, when the Bruins defeated the Chicago Blackhawks 4–2 at historic Notre Dame Stadium. (Photograph by Dave Sandford/NHLI via Getty Images)

interview with David Vautour of MassLive. "He's one of the closest friends I've got. At first, I was idolizing him coming into the league. I was young and learning from him every day.... He helped me grow as a human and as a player."

An even greater appreciation of Krejci developed after he returned to the Bruins in October 2022 from his year away in the Czech Republic. That appreciation grew even greater on January 16, 2023, when he played in his 1,000th game for the Bruins, only the seventh player in franchise history to achieve that feat. Stoic and quiet by nature, the achievement meant a lot to Krejci. "It's obviously a big accomplishment playing for one franchise," he said. "I'm really proud of myself to be able to do that."

It meant a lot to his teammates, too. As Boston forward Pavel Zacha, who grew up rooting for Krejci as a kid in the Czech Republic, told Vautour, "It's fun to see. He's a legend back home. With a thousand games, he's a legend here too."

The final word on Krejci belongs to current Bruins head coach Jim Montgomery: "He makes everyone around him better." Can there be a greater legacy?

TUUKKA RASK

On the weekend of the NHL Draft in June 2006, the Bruins then-interim GM Jeff Gorton shipped Andrew Raycroft to the Toronto Maple Leafs in exchange for the rights to a young goaltender from Finland.

His name was Tuukka Rask. And little did Gorton know that he had just acquired the man who would become the winningest goaltender in the history of the Boston Bruins.

Rask was not shaken by the deal. "[I got] the call I was traded to the Bruins," said Rask. "I thought, 'At least I'm still in the NHL. It's not like they traded me to another league.' I didn't take it as insult. I took it to mean someone wanted me."

Rask's first three full seasons in Black and Gold (2009–2012) were largely spent backing up Tim Thomas. After Thomas left the team in 2012, Rask stepped up to become the No. 1 goaltender. He would remain a fixture between the pipes—durable, consistent, and elite—for the rest of his Bruins career.

Rask was indeed a master at the craft of goaltending. He had it all—size, athleticism, technique, and a makeup that blended a cool demeanor with competitive fire. Confidence was never an issue. "I don't know where that comes from; I guess I was born with it," said Rask in a 2013 interview with the *New York Times*. "But it also comes with having success. At every level I've played, I've had success."

Over his 15-year NHL career spent entirely with Boston, Tuukka Rask set franchise records for regular season games played (564), regular season games won (308), playoff games played (104), and playoff games won (57). Put another way, Rask played a lot—and he won a lot. (Photograph by Emilee Chinn/Getty Images)

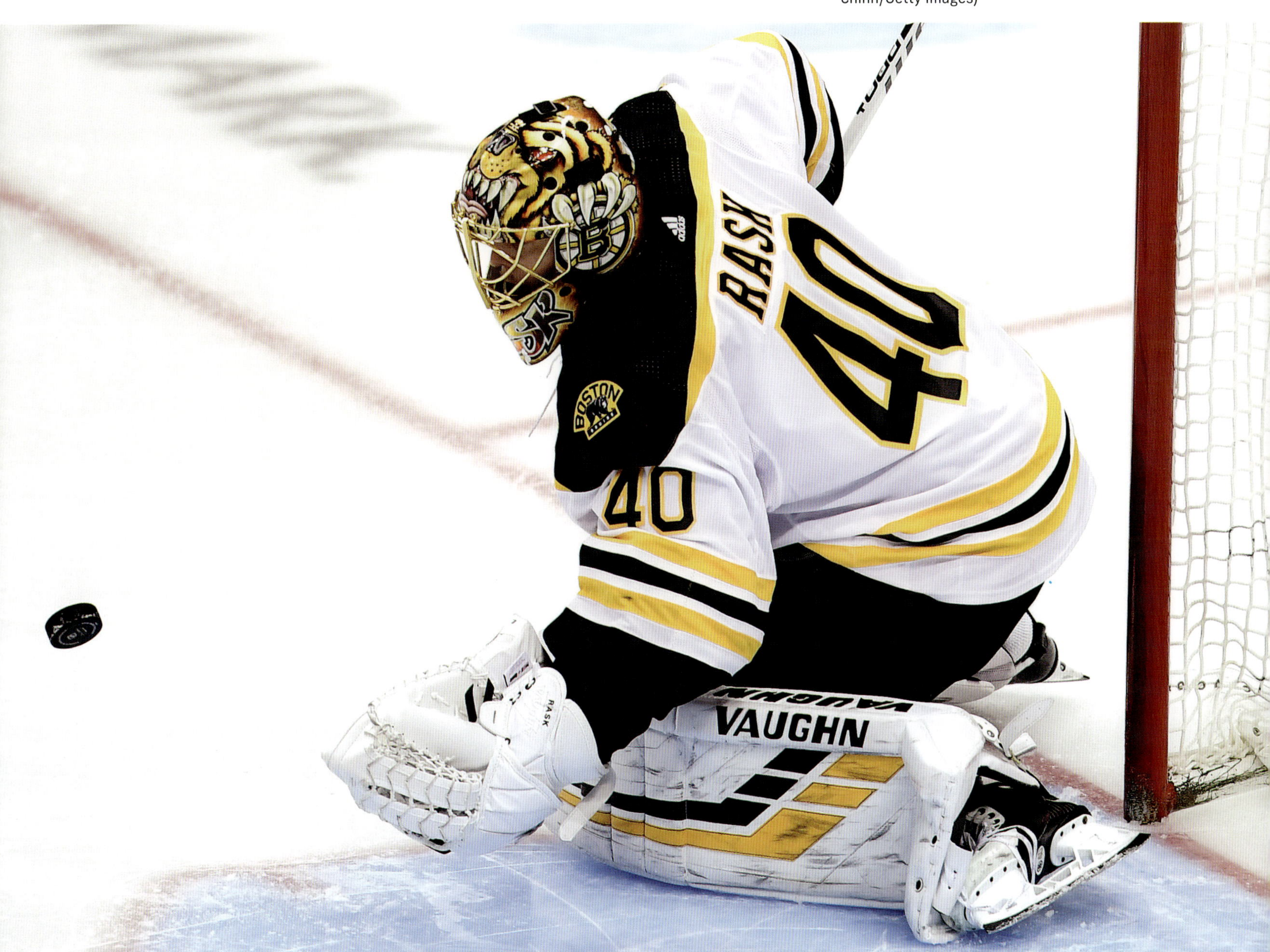

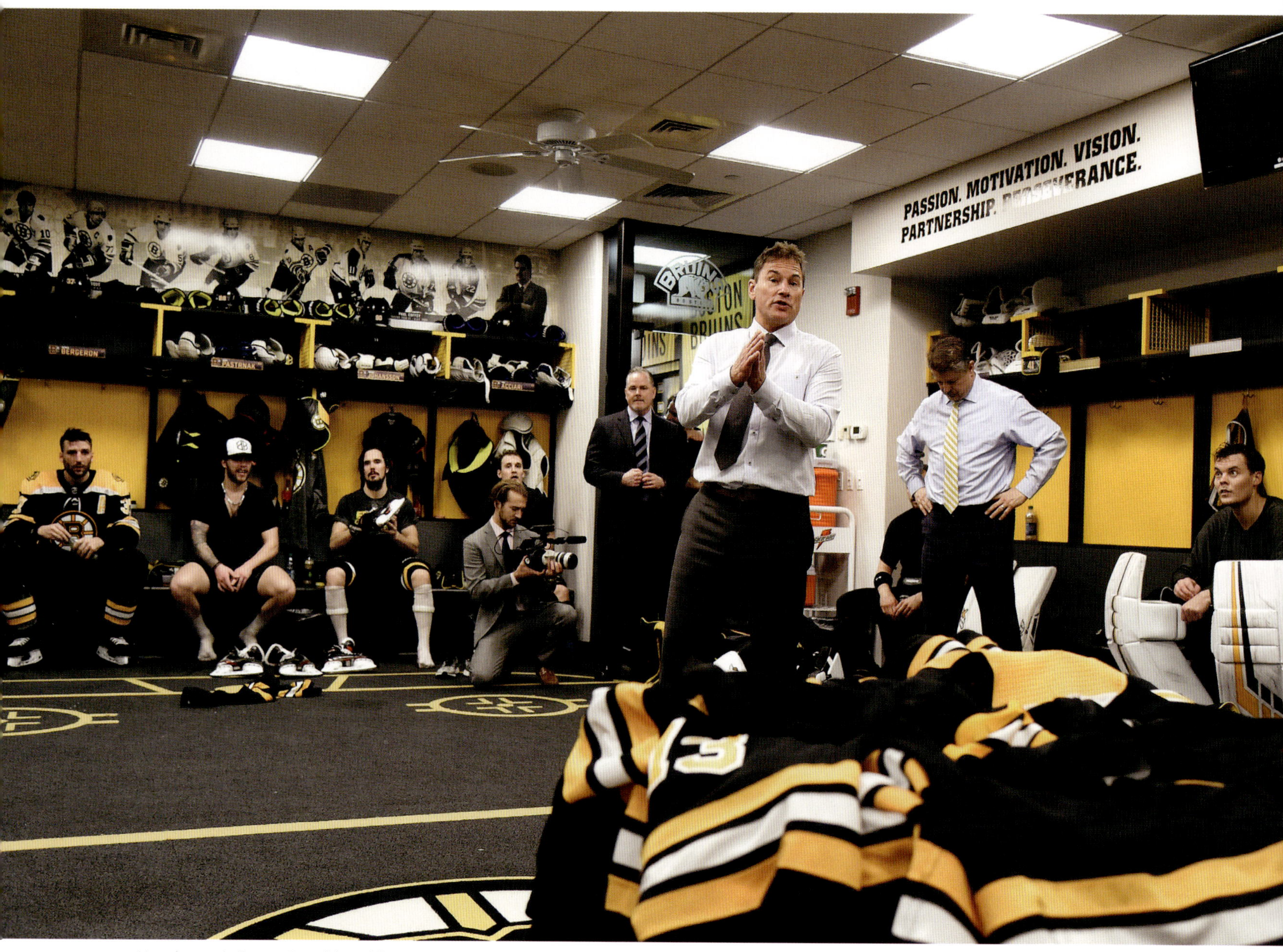

Head coach Bruce Cassidy addresses his players in the locker room prior to a game at TD Garden. In his five-and-a-half seasons as coach of the Bruins, Cassidy recorded a .672 winning percentage, led his team to the playoffs every season (including the Stanley Cup Final in 2019), and won the Jack Adams Award as NHL coach of the year in 2020. (Photograph by Steve Babineau/NHLI via Getty Images)

Needless to say, the Bruins playing in front of him quickly developed a confidence in their netminder. As longtime Bruins defenseman Torey Krug told NHL.com in 2022, "I think having a backbone like him, just how good he was for all those years, it gave us that confidence, and we had nothing to worry about playing in front of him because we knew he was going to show up on a nightly basis."

Rask's finest season came in 2013–14, when he won the Vezina Trophy. His statistics for his 15-year NHL career, all with the Bruins, are eye-popping: 308 wins, a .921 save percentage, and a 2.28 goals against average (GAA). They were even better in the Stanley Cup playoffs, with 57 wins, a .925 save percentage, and a 2.22 GAA.

"Every single night he gave us a chance," Krug said of Rask's play in the playoffs. "Even the games that we didn't deserve, he stood on his head. He was our backstop. He didn't get a lot of the credit he deserved.... It just felt like if you scored two, you probably had a really good chance. Even if you scored one, you had a chance."

"One of the elite goaltenders ever in the NHL, not only with Boston," said former Bruins head coach Bruce Cassidy. That is a conclusion that is hard to refute.

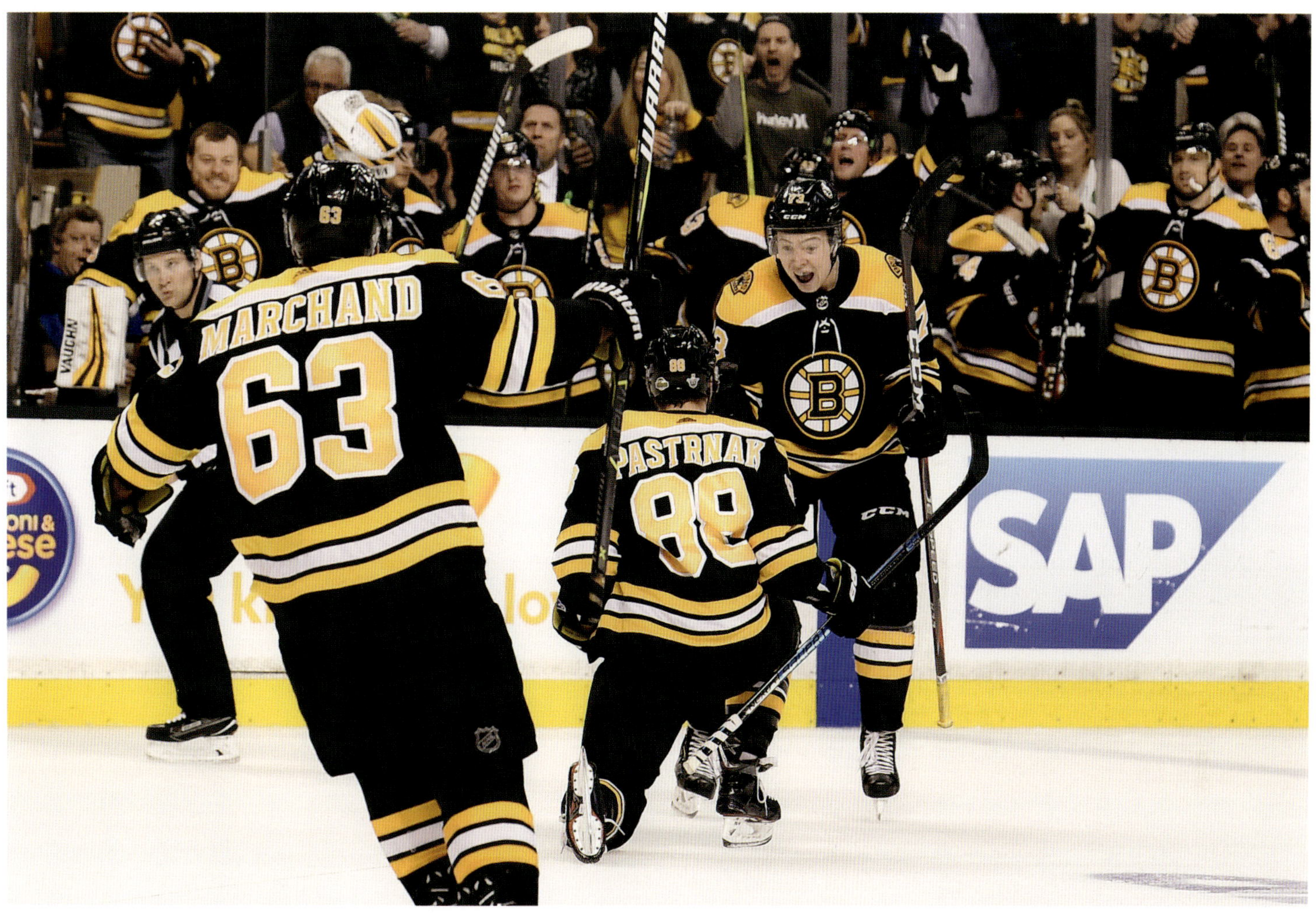

In the latter half of the 2010s, the Bruins infused their roster with young talent to supplement the core players of the Chara-Bergeron Era. Two of the key players in this regard were highly skilled defenseman Charlie McAvoy (right) and goal scorer par excellence David Pastrnak (88). Here, they celebrate a goal against Toronto in the first round of the 2018 Stanley Cup playoffs, along with a key member of that Chara-Bergeron Era core, Brad Marchand (63). (Photograph by Steve Babineau/NHLI via Getty Images)

BRAD MARCHAND

THE EVOLUTION OF Brad Marchand has been wondrous to behold.

At the beginning of his career, Marchand fit a classic hockey archetype—that of "the pest." He made his mark by scrapping, annoying, and agitating. "That's what I had to do to make the NHL," said an unapologetic Marchand in a 2020 *Sports Illustrated* interview. "That was my role."

In just his second season, Marchand shone during the 2011 Stanley Cup playoffs—the Bruins were 9–0 in the playoff games in which Marchand scored. One of those games was the decisive Game 7 against Vancouver, when Marchand came up big, scoring twice to help the Bruins win 4–0 and bring Lord Stanley back to Boston.

The young Brad Marchand was very much a "trick or treat" player—or, as head coach Claude Julien liked to term it, someone who could be a "good brat" or a "bad brat." As Julien explained in a 2012 *Sports Illustrated* interview, "He's a good brat when he stays within the rules and disrupts the other team. He's a bad brat when he takes bad penalties and hurts our team.... He's not a guy who doesn't get it. He gets it. He just slips out of it, and you have to reel him back and spell it out again."

Several years later, though, something changed with Marchand. He cites an international experience as the catalyst—namely, the 2016 World Cup of Hockey, when he won gold while skating on Team Canada's top line along with fellow Nova Scotia native Sidney Crosby and longtime Bruins linemate Patrice Bergeron. "My confidence skyrocketed," Marchand told *Sports Illustrated*. "I always thought I was a decent player. But after that tournament, when you're playing against the best, I knew I could be an elite player."

Andy Brickley of NESN points to the influence of someone else as being critical to the transformation of Marchand: "Bruce Cassidy challenged him and asked him, 'What do you want your legacy to be in this game? Do you want to be a rat, do you want to be a guy everyone hates? Or do you want to be remembered as one of the best players of your era?' And from that point on, Brad decided he wanted to be one of the best players of his era. And that is what he turned into."

The numbers bear out the assertion. Prior to 2016, Marchand averaged 48 points per season. In the last seven years (three of which were shortened by the pandemic or injury), he has averaged 82 points per season. In that time frame, he has been named First or Second Team NHL All-Star on four occasions (2017, 2019, 2020, 2021) and regularly finished in the top 10 in voting for the Hart Trophy as NHL MVP.

Despite his mid-career transformation, Marchand's game still retains some pest-like qualities. As former teammate Tim Thomas observed in a 2022 interview, "I think he enjoys the chaos of hockey games, whether it's the scoring, the momentum swings that a big goal at the right time can do, or whether it's the stick play. I think he just enjoys doing what he does."

So do fans of the Boston Bruins.

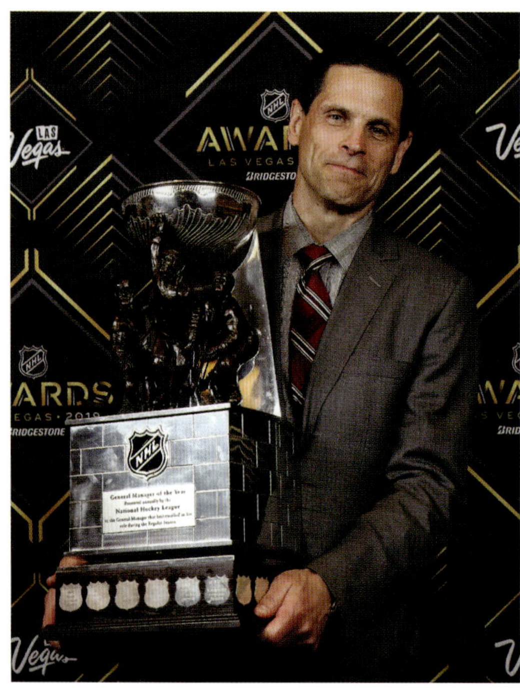

Don Sweeney took home the General Manager of the Year Award during the 2019 NHL Awards ceremony in Las Vegas. The team that Sweeney put together for the 2018–19 campaign blended youth and experience on their way to the Stanley Cup Final versus St. Louis. (Photograph by Maddie Meyer/Getty Images)

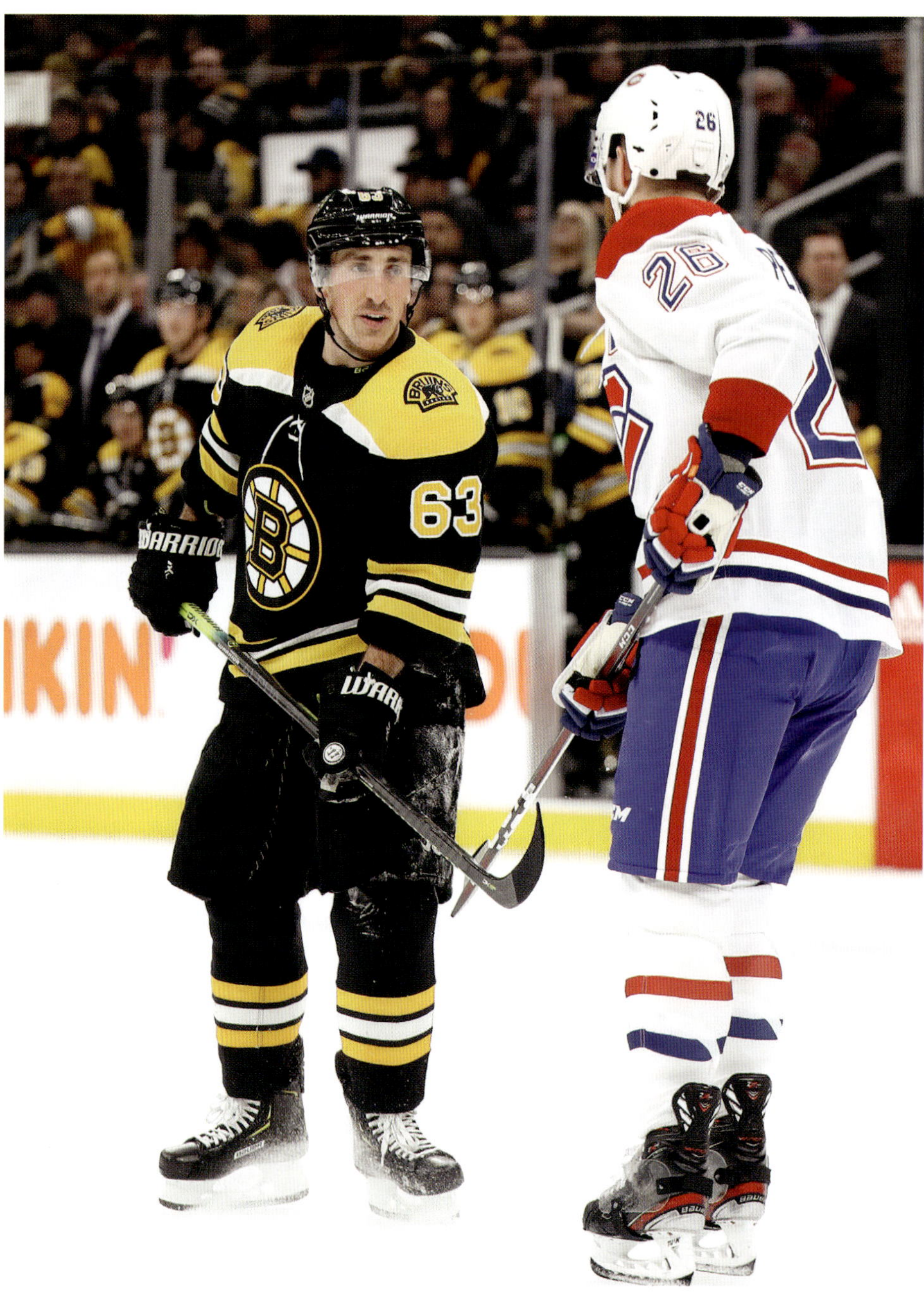

Brad Marchand takes on Jeff Petry of the Montreal Canadiens in a contest at TD Garden in February 2020. The All-Star left winger may be undersized, but he more than makes up for that with skill, determination, and heart. (Photograph by Maddie Meyer/Getty Images)

PATRICE BERGERON

by Matt Porter

THE PROJECTIONS FOR THE 45th overall draft pick in June 2003 were relatively modest. The wisdom of that summer held that the 18-year-old from Quebec City might eventually develop into a solid No. 2 or No. 3 center. Anything beyond that was gravy.

The Bruins have dined quite richly, thanks to Patrice Bergeron's uncommon path to greatness.

This franchise has had dozens of more explosive goal-scorers and a few barrooms' worth of rougher, meaner forces. For all-around excellence over time, however, Bergeron has had few equals.

Like Ray Bourque, he has been effective all night, all over the ice, for two decades. As the heartbeat and conscience of the Bruins, he has followed in the footsteps of the likes of Bourque, Bobby Orr, and Milt Schmidt. He has been Boston's version of Jean Beliveau, with grace and gentlemanly manner beyond reproach, as consistent as a city-square clock when it comes to making the right decision in the public spotlight.

When a 22-year-old Bergeron's battle with concussions left his future uncertain, New England shared in his anguish. When he lifted the Stanley Cup in Vancouver three years later, the region exalted him. Bergeron's appeal has been league-wide, too. He has played for the Bruins in an era where North America was sick of hearing about Boston teams winning—and yet, has anyone ever said a bad word about him over the course of his long career with the Bruins, starting in 2003 and continuing through the 2022–23 season?

He arrived on the scene in the infancy of that Boston sports renaissance, a time dominated by Tom Brady, David Ortiz, Manny Ramirez, Kevin Garnett, and Paul Pierce. With all respect to the GOAT, Big Papi, Manny, KG, and "the Truth," the man the Bruins called "Bergy" has been just as clutch.

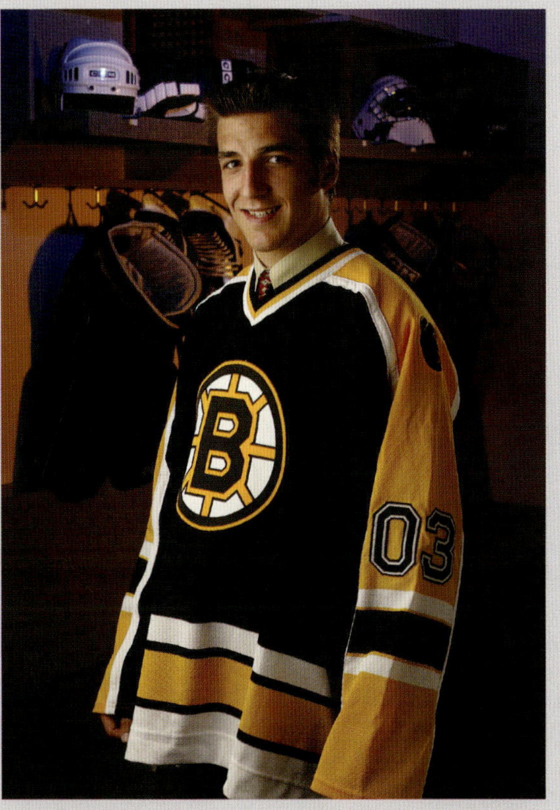

Patrice Bergeron, just 17 years of age, poses in the locker room of the Gaylord Entertainment Center in Nashville after Boston selected him in the second round of the 2003 NHL Draft. He would quickly become a franchise mainstay—and, shortly thereafter, a franchise icon. (Photograph by Robert Laberge/Getty Images/NHLI)

Stand in TD Garden hours before puck drop, listen closely, and you can still hear the echoes of Dave Goucher's radio call:

> *Bergeron! Bergeron! In Game 7! And the Bruins win the series!*

Two years earlier in Vancouver, he had scored two goals in Game 7 of the 2011 Stanley Cup Final to help bring the Black and Gold its first title since the days of Orr. But that playoff masterpiece in Game 7 of the 2013 series against the Maple Leafs, in a game NHL.com ranked as the best game of that decade, was his *pièce de résistance*.

The Bruins finished a three-goal comeback in the final 11 minutes of the third period when Bergeron sent home the tying goal with 51 seconds left in regulation. Moments later, he scored the overtime winner. Maple Leaf Square in Toronto, where those fans had gathered for a watch party, was never the same.

But it has never been about the highlight-reel plays with Bergeron, all the goals and points and trophies, has it?

He has always had that "Bergeron! Bergeron!" show-stopper in him, but he has been the Da Vinci of Detail. He is a crafty playmaker and decisive finisher, but his calling card has been his flawless positioning and dogged checking. He is seemingly always open for a teammate's outlet in the defensive zone, ready to fire a one-timer at the other end.

On the bench, the Bruins chatter "Selke" to each other after Patrice "the Thief" has swiped another puck from an unsuspecting opponent.

No. 37 was among the first of the analytics darlings, a superstar of the streaming age. With the ability to slow down, zoom in, rewind, and rewatch, the subtleties of Bergeron's game have become crystal clear.

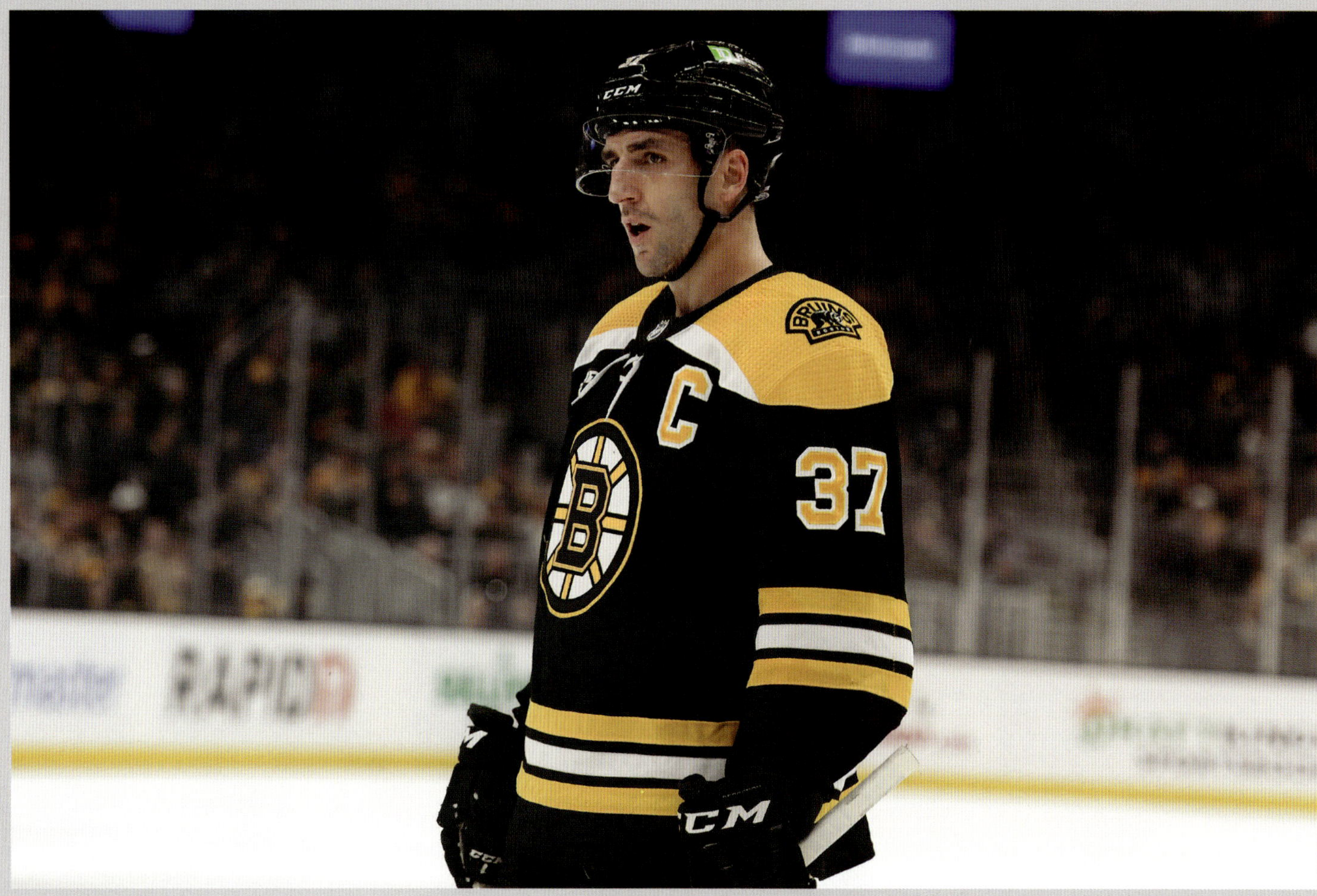

In his 19 years as a Bruin, played over parts of three decades, Patrice Bergeron has displayed a measure of skill, class, and leadership that has branded him as one of the franchise's all-time greats. In addition to winning a Stanley Cup in 2011, he has won six gold medals in every international competition in which he represented Canada, including the Olympics of 2010 and 2014.
(Photograph by Steve Babineau/NHLI via Getty Images)

Brad Marchand is convinced his pal Bergy is the greatest two-way forward ever. He is hardly alone.

In 2003, few saw a Hall of Famer in the making when coach Mike Sullivan's Bruins drafted him in Nashville, though Bergeron, ranked 28th among North American skaters by NHL Central Scouting, had finished second among Quebec Major Junior League rookies in scoring (23-50-73), and put up 15 points in 11 playoff games for Acadie-Bathurst.

At the start of that season, coach Real Paiement had a 17-year-old Bergeron filling Acadie-Bathurst's third-line center slot. Bergeron ended the year as Paiement's go-to guy.

The Bruins expected Bergeron to take a few games of exhibition experience back to the QMJHL—after all, he had spent only one year in that league—but Bergeron suited up for all eight exhibition games in the fall of 2003, signed a three-year rookie deal, and became the third-line center.

The rest is the stuff of Black and Gold legend. He has simply kept making the right play, every night, for 20 years.

Bergeron put up 16 goals and 39 points as a rookie, dominated the AHL during the 2004–2005 lockout, and scored 31 goals and 73 points as a sophomore. The Bruins, aching for a reset, changed the direction of the franchise that summer of 2006.

They signed Zdeno Chara to a megabucks deal and made him captain. Bergeron, 21, was an obvious choice as his alternate. Chara's departure in 2020 officially gave Bergeron the *C*, but he was effectively co-captains with Big Z for most of the 2010s.

Now comfortable speaking English, his second language, Bergeron the leader has felt the weight of the crest. His hope is to leave the Spoked-B in a better place than when he first donned it. Crucial to those efforts are his relationships with the old guard. He has a special bond with Johnny Bucyk, the Chief passing down the knowledge of the 1970s juggernaut. He has picked the brain of Ray Bourque, his fellow French-Canadian superstar, any time he could. He can always lean on Cam Neely, president of Black and Gold passion, for counsel.

In the salary cap era, Bergeron has consistently taken sub-market deals to help the Bruins build a more competitive team. He passes the gravy around before taking his own portion.

When he donned the *A* in 2006, Bergeron was on his way from being a well-rounded but raw young player to becoming a franchise icon. He was going from roster hopeful to the best two-way forward of his generation, with a full trophy case of gleaming Selke Trophies—a record six—international gold medals from the Olympics in 2010 and 2014, and a Stanley Cup (2011) backing that argument.

And it almost didn't happen. Two words (Randy Jones) and one day (October 27, 2007) nearly stopped a promising career in its tracks. The Flyers defenseman's dirty hit from behind broke Bergeron's nose and left him severely concussed. He missed the final 72 games of that season, addled by months of head-pounding, vision-blurring sickness.

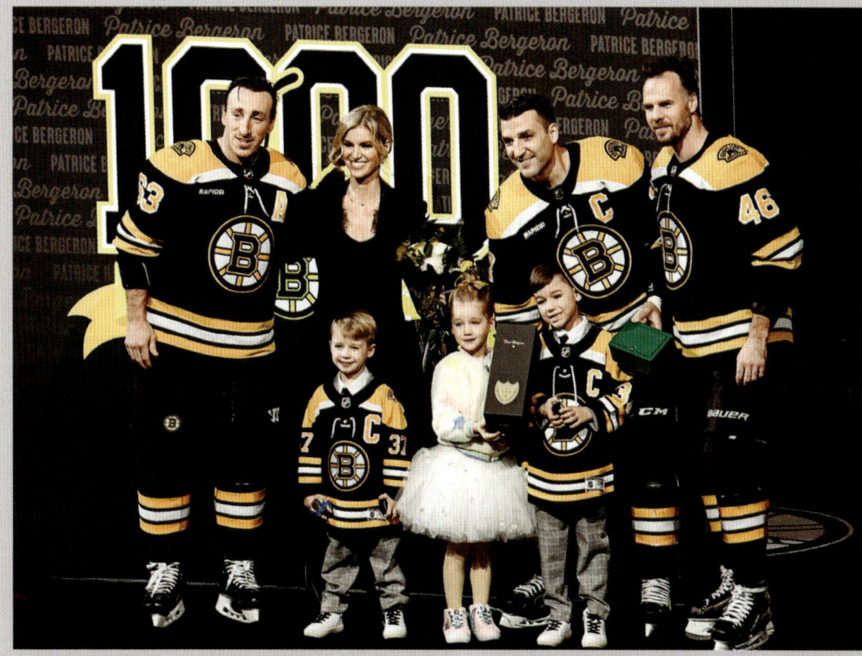

On December 17, 2022, Patrice Bergeron was honored prior to the Bruins game at TD Garden for having scored 1,000 career points. Here, he is shown with longtime teammates Brad Marchand (63) and David Krejci (46), as well as wife Stephanie and children Noah, Victoria, and Zach (left to right).
(Photograph by China Wong/NHLI via Getty Images)

The incident has turned Bergeron into a quiet but fierce advocate for player safety, and has helped force change within the NHL rule book to protect the workforce. It has also made him appreciate every day he's spent in the league. When Bergeron returned to form in the fall of 2009, the Bruins began a run as one of the dominant teams of the next decade, the Batman-and-Robin partnership of Bergeron and Brad Marchand being a primary reason.

They have boasted elements of other great Boston batteries of their trophy-hauling era: the loose confidence of Manny and Papi, the lethal brilliance of Brady and Randy Moss, and the competitive fire of Pierce and Garnett. They have produced some of the prettiest goals of the era, hounding the puck and dancing in the offensive zone. When David Pastrnak arrived as a world-class scorer in the late 2010s, that trio soared.

Bergeron and Marchand have also arguably been the best penalty-killing duo of their day, Marchand setting a club record for shorthanded goals.

Marchand, good as he has been, has readily admitted throughout his career: he would have been nothing without Bergy.

Matt Porter covers the Bruins and NHL for the *Boston Globe*.

BOSTON BRUINS (2010–2019)

Season	W	L	OL	PTS	PTS%	Finish	Playoffs	Coach	Division	Conf.
2009–10	39	30	13	91	.555	3rd of 5	Lost NHL Conference Semifinals	Claude Julien	Northeast	Eastern
2010–11	**46**	**25**	**11**	**103**	**.628**	**1st of 5**	**Won Stanley Cup Final**	**Claude Julien**	**Northeast**	**Eastern**
2011–12	49	29	4	102	.622	1st of 5	Lost NHL Conference Quarterfinals	Claude Julien	Northeast	Eastern
2012–13*	28	14	6	62	.646	2nd of 5	Lost Stanley Cup Final	Claude Julien	Northeast	Eastern
2013–14	54	19	9	117	.713	1st of 8	Lost NHL Second Round	Claude Julien	Atlantic	Eastern
2014–15	41	27	14	96	.585	5th of 8		Claude Julien	Atlantic	Eastern
2015–16	42	31	9	93	.567	3rd of 8		Claude Julien	Atlantic	Eastern
2016–17	44	31	7	95	.579	3rd of 8	Lost NHL First Round	Claude Julien (26–23–6) Bruce Cassidy (18–8–1)	Atlantic	Eastern
2017–18	50	20	12	112	.683	2nd of 8	Lost NHL Second Round	Bruce Cassidy	Atlantic	Eastern
2018–19	49	24	9	107	.652	2nd of 8	Lost Stanley Cup Final	Bruce Cassidy	Atlantic	Eastern

*2012–13 regular season shortened to 48 games due to NHL labor dispute

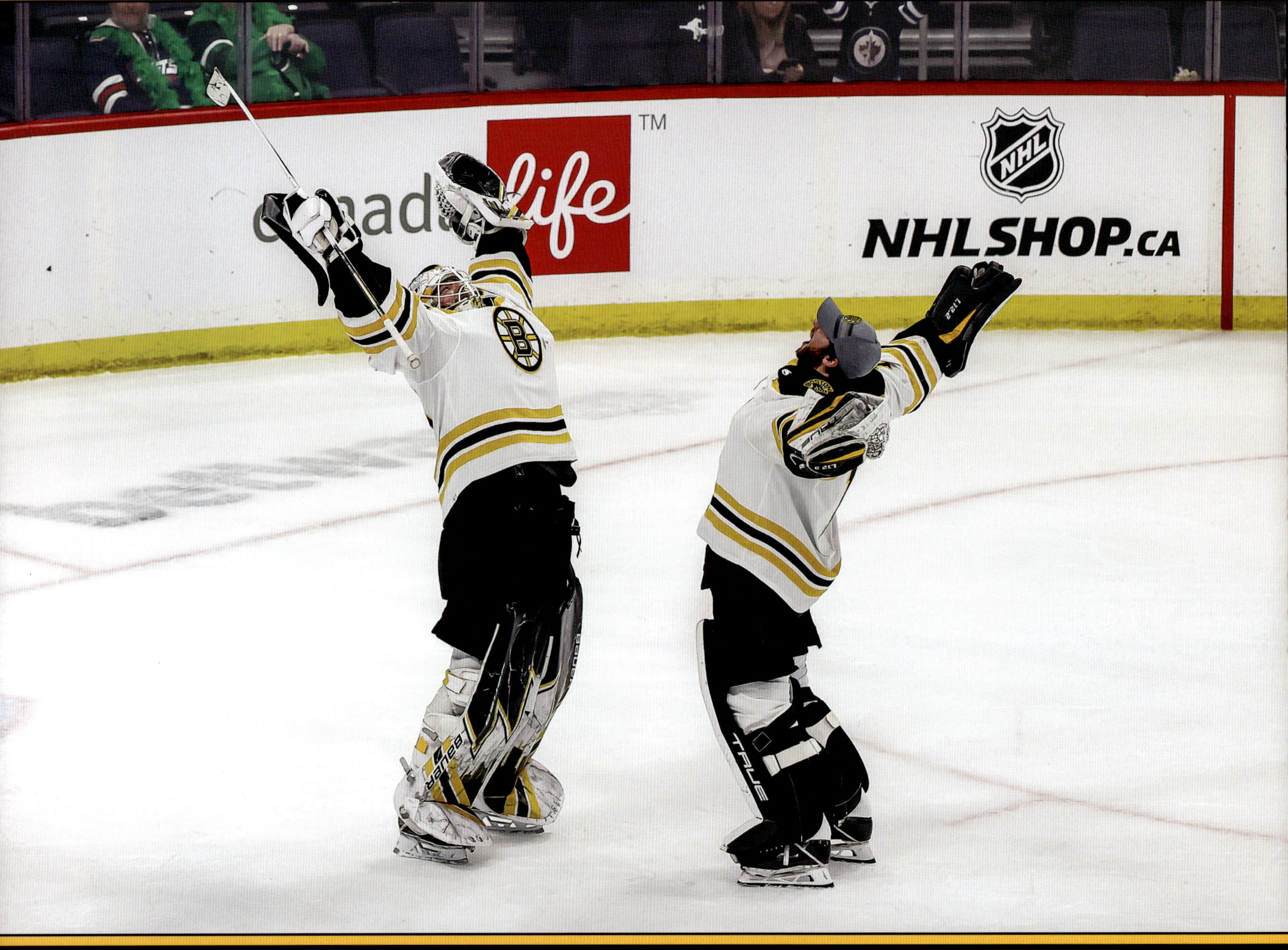

The goaltending duo of Linus Ullmark (left) and Jeremy Swayman engage in their trademark victory celebration after a Bruins win. This was a scene that played out over and over during the 2022–23 regular season—65 times, to be exact. It was a new single-season NHL record for victories—and, of course, for big hugs.

2 0 2 0 s

SOMETHING SPECIAL

I wanted to come back because I still know that I have something left to give.... I want to come back with the Bruins because it's my team. I love the city. I love the team. I love the guys, and I want to make and do something special with them.

—Patrice Bergeron, Bruins captain, prior to the 2022–23 season

On March 10, 2020, the Bruins beat the Philadelphia Flyers 2–0. The victory gave the team 100 points for the season, the best record in the league at the time. With just 10 games left to go in the regular season, the Bruins looked forward to clinching home ice and gearing up for a long playoff run in their quest to win the franchise's seventh Stanley Cup.

Then, over the course of the next 48 hours, the world stopped. Because of the COVID-19 pandemic, the NHL halted the regular season and shortly thereafter declared it to be over. And no one did anything for the next four-and-a-half months. By the time the Bruins and the other NHL teams gathered for the Stanley Cup playoffs in early August, they were playing in "the bubble" in Toronto with no fans in the stands. "We were just playing in a silent building every night," said Boston defenseman Matt Grzelcyk. "It was pretty miserable for a while.... It is tough when you score a goal and you don't really hear anything." The Bruins beat Carolina in the first round but then went out in the second round at the hands of Tampa Bay.

And that is how the 96th season of Boston Bruins hockey ended—in the strangest way imaginable.

Things started to get back to normal the next season (2020–21) when NHL teams played an abbreviated 56-game regular season. The Bruins made the playoffs but again fell in the second round, this time to the New York Islanders. The following season (2021–22) marked a return to full normalcy—but the end result wasn't any better for the Bruins, as they fell to Carolina in seven games in the opening round of the Stanley Cup playoffs.

Then came the 2022–23 season. Prior to the season, the Bruins decided to change coaches, replacing Bruce Cassidy with Jim Montgomery. Captain Patrice Bergeron decided to return for a 19th season in Black and Gold. And David Krejci decided to come back to Boston after a season away playing in his native Czech Republic. Still, expectations were modest.

All expectations ended up being obliterated. The season turned out to be something special.

And no one saw it coming.

From a team perspective, with their jaw-dropping 65–12–5 record, the Bruins made history. They didn't just finish with the best record in the league—they finished with the best record in league history, their 65 wins beating the old record of 62 shared by the 1995–96 Detroit Red Wings and the 2018–19 Tampa Bay Lightning. And their staggering total of 135 points toppled another long-standing NHL record of 132 points set by the 1976–77 Montreal Canadiens.

Simply put, the 2022–23 Boston Bruins were the best regular season team in the history of the National Hockey League.

Individual accomplishments were aplenty. David Pastrnak scored 61 goals, becoming just the 23rd man in NHL history to score 60 or more goals in a season. In the plus/minus category, a trio of Bruins defensemen—Hampus Lindholm (+49), Matt Grzelcyk (+46), and Brandon Carlo (+44)—finished 1-2-3 in the NHL. And Linus Ullmark won the Triple Crown for goaltending, pacing the league in victories (40), goals against average (1.89), and save percentage (.938).

The Bruins would end up receiving a slew of NHL awards at season's end. Ullmark won the Vezina Trophy as the NHL's top goalie as well as the Jennings Trophy along with goaltending partner Jeremy Swayman for fewest goals allowed. Bergeron captured the Selke Trophy as the league's best defensive forward for a record sixth time. And Montgomery took home the Jack Adams Trophy as the NHL's coach of the year. All of the hardware further attested to the regular season dominance of this very special Bruins team.

The dominance unfortunately didn't carry over into the postseason, however. In the opening round of the Stanley Cup playoffs against the Florida Panthers, despite injuries to several key players (including Bergeron, Krejci, and Lindholm), the Bruins took a 3 games to 1 series lead. But then the momentum shifted. The Panthers stayed alive by winning Game 5 in overtime, evened things up by beating the Bruins in a Game 6 shootout, and then prevailed in Game 7 courtesy of another overtime goal, thus capping the comeback and bringing a sudden end to the Bruins' dream season.

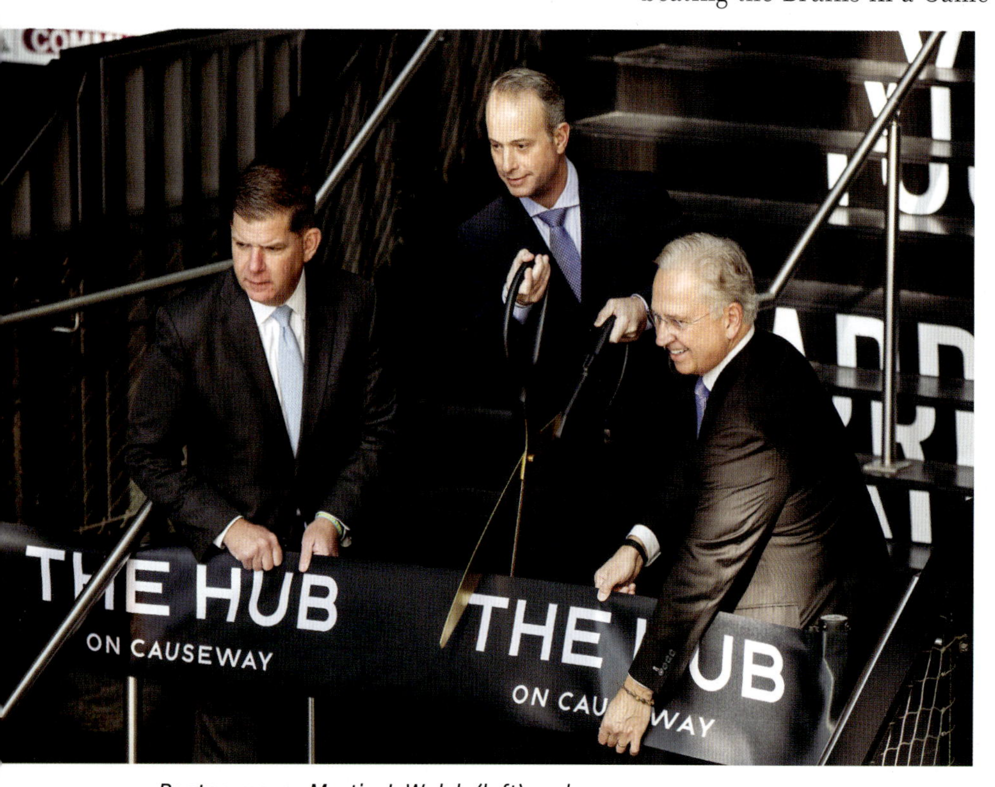

Boston mayor Martin J. Walsh (left) and Boston Properties CEO Bryan Koop (right) flank Boston Bruins CEO Charlie Jacobs (center) at the ribbon-cutting ceremony for the Hub on Causeway in November 2019. Jacobs has now headed up the front office in Boston for the better part of two decades. (Photograph courtesy of TD Garden)

The crushing defeat may strengthen the team's resolve moving forward. There is ample historical precedent. Indeed, past Bruins teams have responded to heartbreaking playoff defeats—in 1971 and 2010, for instance—with a renewed determination that brought about glorious results. Will history repeat itself in the mid-2020s as the team continues its quest to bring the ultimate prize—the Stanley Cup—back home to Boston?

For now, it is clear that the team has a strong core of players, world-class resources, and the very best fan base in the NHL. With such dynamic assets, as well as a rich heritage befitting the NHL's first American franchise, the Boston Bruins head into their second century of hockey with pride, passion, and confident conviction.

CHARLIE JACOBS

Charlie Jacobs began his tenure in the Bruins front office in 2001, arriving with knowledge of the city (having attended Boston College), NHL team experience (having held several positions with the Los Angeles Kings), and even league experience (having served as alternate governor). Ever since, his presence has provided the Jacobs Family's ownership of the team with a constant Boston presence in the front office.

Jacobs has progressed from his initial position of executive vice president to his current position of chief executive officer, retaining the post of alternate governor throughout. Along the way, he has assembled a talented front-office group that has been recognized as one of the best in the NHL and in all of professional sports. It was a tribute to that front office, and Jacobs's leadership, when the Bruins were named by *Sport Business Journal* as the 2012 Sports Team of the Year, based on the criteria of "excellence, growth, creativity, innovation, sound planning, implementation, and outcomes."

In the years since 2012, Jacobs & Co. have built on that momentum by...well, building. One area here involves the substantial improvements made within TD Garden. Back when it was built in 1995, the arena was state-of-the-art. By 2010, that was no longer the case. So, with the backing of his father, owner Jeremy Jacobs, and working closely with TD Garden president Amy Latimer and her team, Charlie Jacobs has presided over a complete reinvestment in the arena. That reinvestment has resulted, over time, in the updating and renovation of every part of the arena, from the locker rooms and back of house to the upper levels of the Garden, where fans now watch the action in new, sleek hospitality spaces.

"The commitment the Jacobs Family has had in really completely revamping the entire building is pretty darn impressive," said Bruins general manager Don Sweeney in a 2022 interview.

Then there is the Hub on Causeway, a $2 billion mixed-use project around TD Garden that involved an upgraded and expanded arena, a hotel, downtown Boston's largest grocery store, a live music venue, and multiple restaurants. The grand opening for the first two phases of the project took place just prior to the pandemic; phase 3 (a 31-story office tower) was unveiled in the summer of 2022. "We're finally here," Charlie Jacobs told the *Boston Globe* at the time. "Almost $2 billion later, a $200 million renovation to the Garden...it's kind of like, pinch myself."

If the Hub on Causeway has been all about galvanizing the neighborhood and improving the game-day experience for fans, then Warrior Ice Arena has been all about the players. Built in conjunction with New Balance Athletics, Inc., the Bruins' new, state-of-the-art practice facility located in Boston Landing opened in September 2016.

As Don Sweeney observed, "That has been a game-changer for the Boston Bruins organization...the amenities that we have now, full-time staff for cooking, for training, for sports performance...[with] the players, from a recruiting tool, from a standpoint of them being comfortable and happy, giving them every resource we possibly can. You know, Cam and the organization and the Jacobs Family just did a phenomenal job getting this thing built in conjunction with New Balance and Warrior."

The sports and business of hockey will no doubt continue to evolve moving forward. With the revamped TD Garden, the Hub on Causeway, and Warrior Ice Arena, Charlie Jacobs and his colleagues in the Bruins front office have all the building blocks in place necessary to meet the challenges.

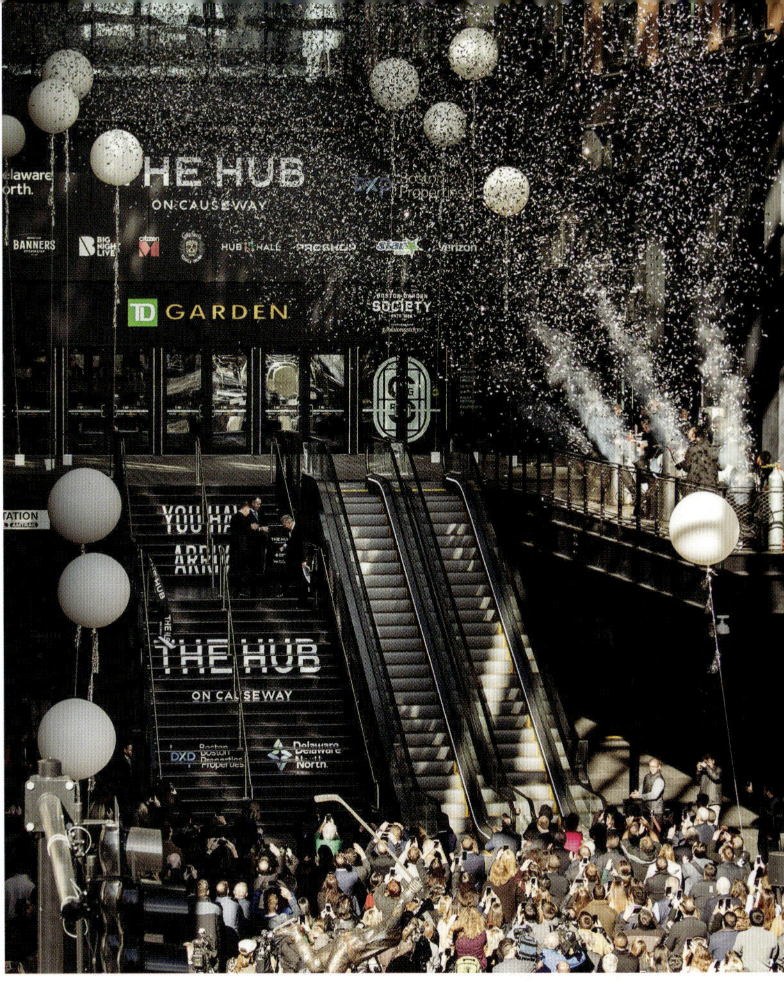

The confetti flies at the ribbon-cutting ceremony for the Hub on Causeway in November 2019. For Charlie Jacobs and the Bruins organization, it was a project years in the making—and one well worth the wait. (Photograph courtesy of TD Garden)

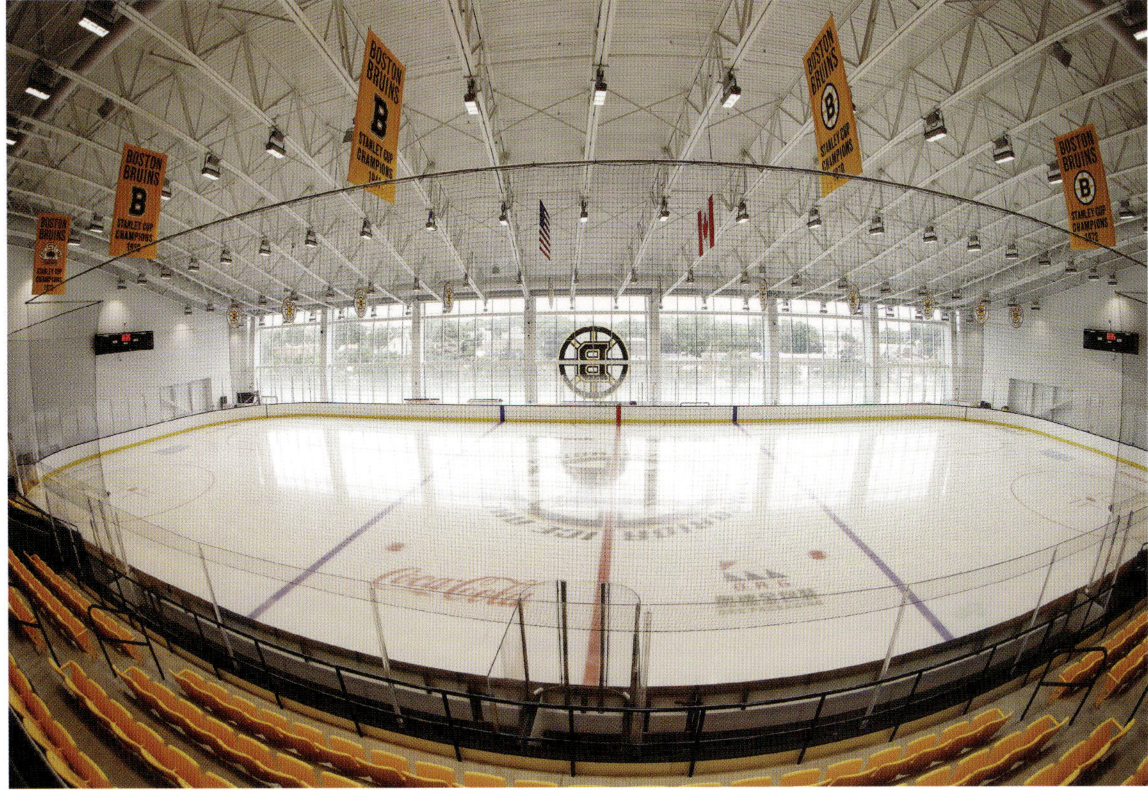

Thanks to their partnership with New Balance, the Bruins now have a state-of-the-art practice facility at Warrior Ice Arena located in Boston Landing. It has emerged as a competitive advantage for the team in terms of recruiting, training, and developing players. (Photograph by Fred Kfoury III/Icon Sportswire via Getty Images)

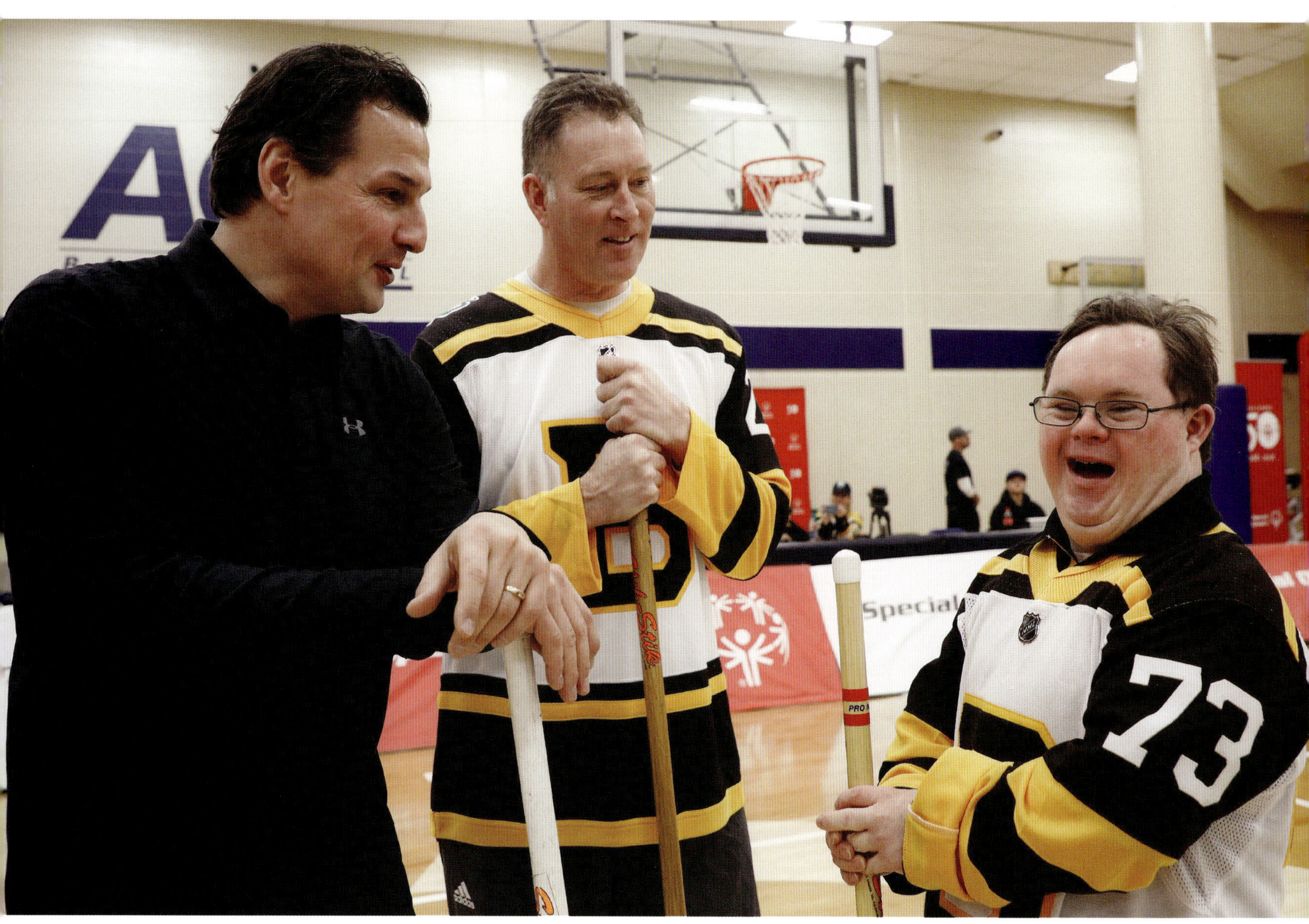

Bob Sweeney (center) connects with former Chicago Blackhawk Eddie Olczyk (left) and participant John Dunleavy (right) prior to the Special Olympics Exhibition Game at the Joyce Center on December 31, 2018, in South Bend, Indiana. As president and executive director of the Boston Bruins Foundation, Sweeney has forged strategic relationships with several leading-edge charities, including Special Olympics Massachusetts. Dunleavy is one of the Special Olympics athletes—as well as a longtime employee of TD Garden. (Photograph by Patrick McDermott/ NHLI via Getty Images)

BOB SWEENEY AND THE BRUINS IN THE COMMUNITY

A PRODUCT OF Acton-Boxborough High School and Boston College, Bob Sweeney achieved a boyhood dream by playing for his hometown Boston Bruins for the first six years (1986–1992) of his 10-year NHL career. He was a very good player on some very good teams, especially the 1988 and 1990 teams that advanced to the Stanley Cup Final against Edmonton.

Sweeney's first act with the Bruins was filled with accomplishments. His second act with the team, helping to lead the organization's charitable efforts as head of the Boston Bruins Foundation, has been even more impactful.

Long before the Boston Bruins Foundation came into existence, the Bruins had a track record of giving back in the community—something that Sweeney himself recognizes. As he noted in a 2022 interview, "The thing that really resonates with me with the Bruins and the community is the leadership from years back, whether it was Milt Schmidt, Fernie Flaman, or the Chief, and to Terry O'Reilly, Wayne Cashman, Ray Bourque, Rick Middleton.... It's like, okay, this is what you're supposed to do. You gotta go here, you gotta go there. And I think that really resonated all the way to Zdeno Chara and now Patrice Bergeron. The torch has been passed."

Bergeron confirms the commitment to the community that he and scores of Bruins have embraced through the years. "I talk a lot about connections with the game of hockey," said Bergeron. "For me, it's what I'll remember the most. But those connections off the ice, with the charitable work and my Patrice's Pals program and all the other stuff that we do with the Boston Bruins Foundation, those are the things that are really important. Those are the things that make a real impact."

The fact that the Bruins have an especially strong alumni group (which has been led through the years by the likes of Johnny Bucyk, Rick Middleton, and, currently, Frank Simonetti) helps facilitate strong community involvement. So does the team's dedicated community relations group, led by longtime senior director of community relations Kerry Collins.

And so does the Boston Bruins Foundation. Founded by Charlie Jacobs soon after he arrived in Boston in the early 2000s, its mission is to assist charitable organizations that demonstrate a commitment to enhancing the quality of life for children and their families throughout New England. Since its inception in 2003, the Boston Bruins Foundation has contributed more than $54 million to New England–based charitable organizations.

Jacobs continues to serve as chairman of the Boston Bruins Foundation. Sweeney came aboard in 2007, switching over from running the alumni group. "I had a good meeting with Charlie and said I wanted to do more with the organization," said Sweeney. "I was going to come on board as the director of Youth Hockey, but then there was an opening with the Foundation.... Charlie thought I would be better off doing the Foundation, which I did."

Sweeney started as director of development before quickly ascending to his current positions of president and executive director of the Boston Bruins Foundation. Under his leadership, the Bruins have forged high-impact partnerships with charities such as Special Olympics Massachusetts. "I've enjoyed it," said Sweeney. "We do so much in the community, and it is a great feeling to give back. It's something that I take a lot of pride in."

As well he should.

Charlie Coyle meets with youth hockey players before the game against the Chicago Blackhawks at TD Garden in March 2022. The Bruins acquired the Boston University product in February 2019, and the big, sturdy center quickly emerged as an anchor for the third line. As a native of Weymouth, Massachusetts, Coyle has a special appreciation of the importance of the Bruins giving back to the community. (Photograph by Steve Babineau/NHLI via Getty Images)

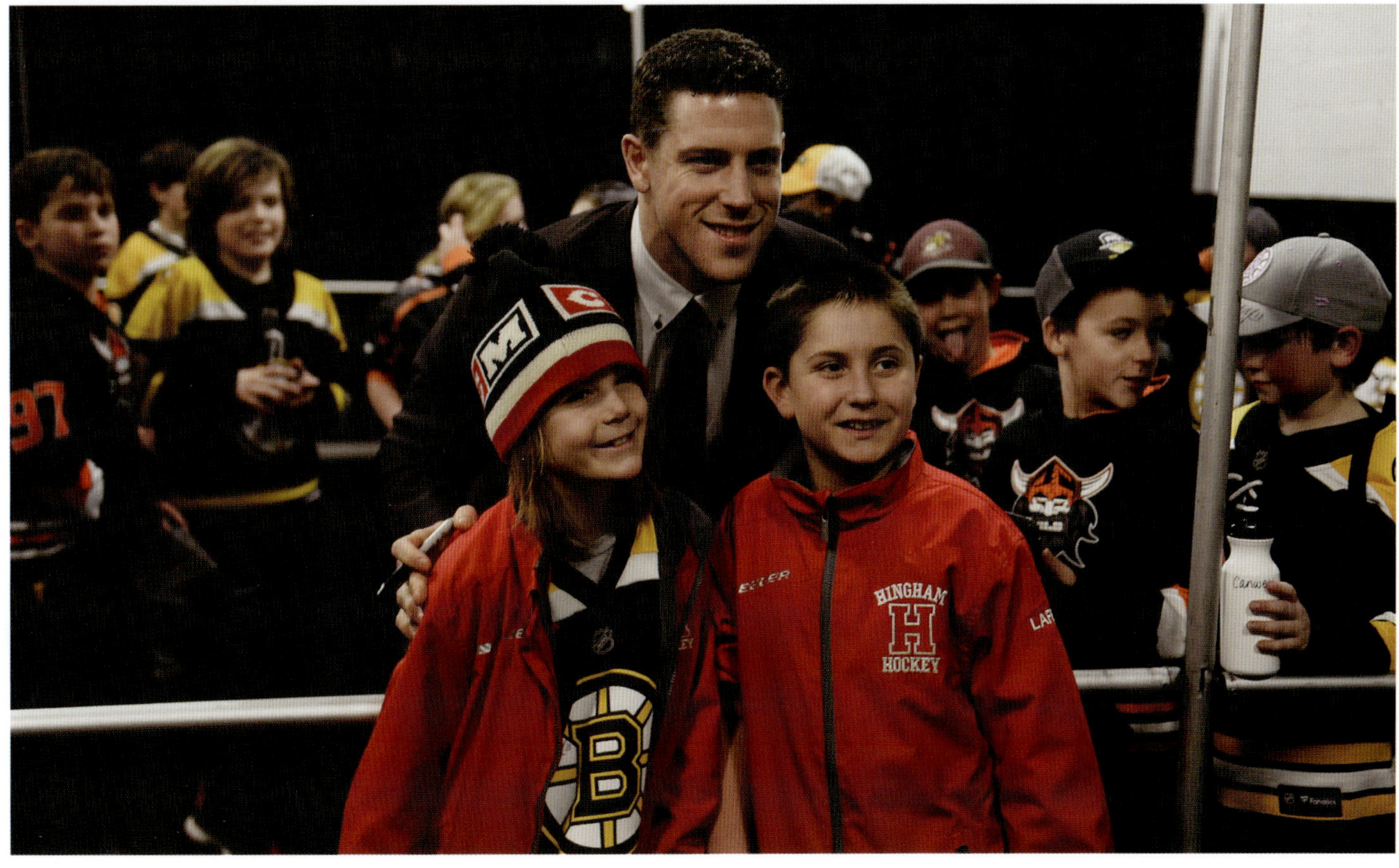

MATT GRZELCYK

EVEN THE BEST screenwriter would be hard-pressed to match the real-life Hollywood tale of Boston Bruins defenseman Matt Grzelcyk.

Raised in nearby Charlestown, Grzelcyk literally grew up in and around TD Garden as his father and brother, both named John, have worked as members of the Garden's famed Bull Gang, the crew responsible for switching the arena back and forth from Garden ice to the parquet floor of the Boston Celtics, often under extreme time constraints. John Sr., in fact, has been a member of the Bull Gang since 1968—27 years in the old Boston Garden, 28 years in TD Garden—55 years in all (and counting).

Matt Grzelcyk grew up hanging around TD Garden, often skating on the ice on dark days and befriending the likes of Ray Bourque.

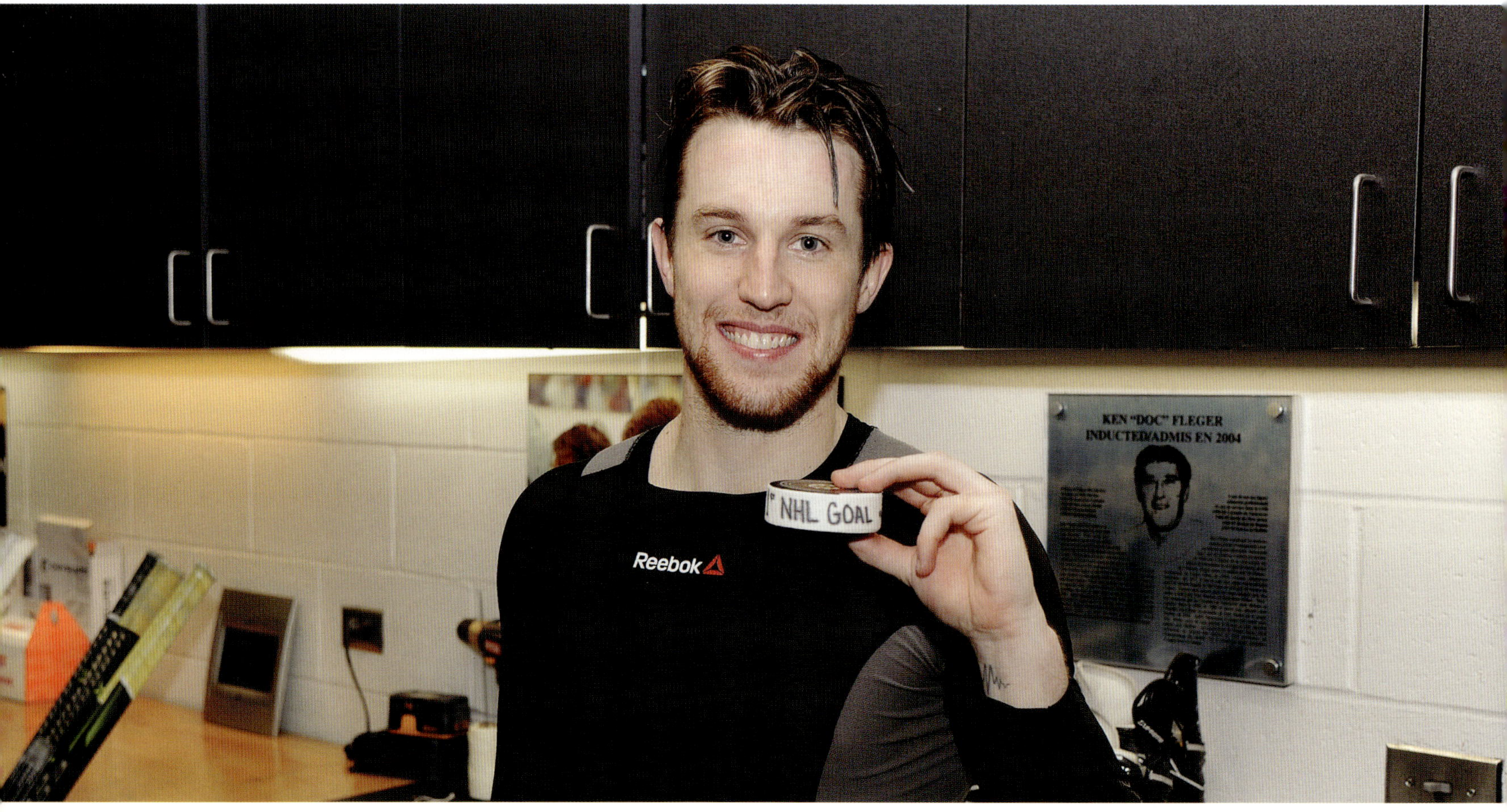

Charlestown native Matt Grzelcyk celebrates his first NHL goal following the Bruins 4–3 victory over the Pittsburgh Penguins in November 2017. Grzelcyk soon became a fixture in the Bruins lineup, repeating a classic tale of "local boy makes good." (Photograph by Steve Babineau/NHLI via Getty Images)

Amid a development path that took him from Belmont Hill School to the captaincy of Boston University, he was selected by Boston in the third round of the 2012 NHL Draft. Following a minor-league apprenticeship in Providence, Grzelcyk made his Bruins debut in December 2016. He was back and forth for much of the next two seasons before landing in Boston for good during the 2018–19 season. "Going into my second year, I think that's kind of when I decided that I wasn't going to take no for an answer," said Grzelcyk in a 2022 interview. "I'm not going to take going down there [to Providence] for another year as an option. I wanted to make it happen."

Grzelcyk indeed made it happen, earning regular playing time while skating in front of his hometown fans. "It is a super surreal feeling," he said. "It is something that I don't think I have kind of fully grasped yet.... Obviously, your goal is to make it to the NHL and play there one day, but to play in front of your friends and family, I think it comes with a lot more pride and responsibility at the same time.... It is something I always dreamed about and am very fortunate that it came true."

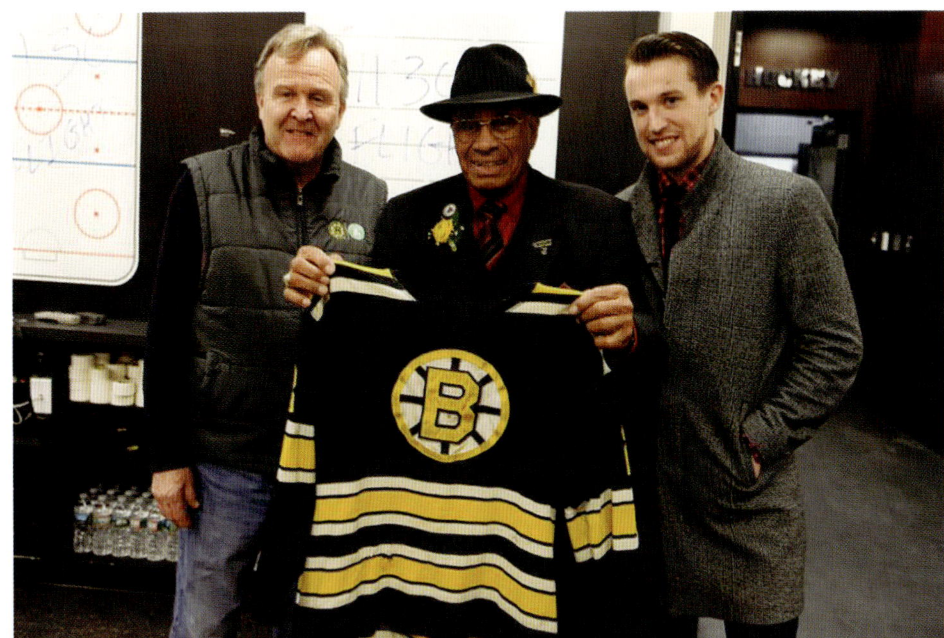

Longtime TD Garden Bull Gang member John Grzelcyk, Bruins legend Willie O'Ree, and Bruins defenseman Matt Grzelcyk (left to right) stand together in the Bruins dressing room. The Grzelcyks have just presented O'Ree with a No. 22 jersey that he had worn back in the early 1960s while skating with the Bruins. Somewhat incredibly, the jersey had hung in the closet of the Grzelcyks' Charlestown home all these years. As Matt Grzleyck said of O'Ree, "It was pretty cool to see how moved he was.... It was super cool, not just to hand him the jersey but to meet him in person and have a conversation with him. Whenever he is around the room, it puts a smile on everyone's face." (Photograph by Steve Babineau)

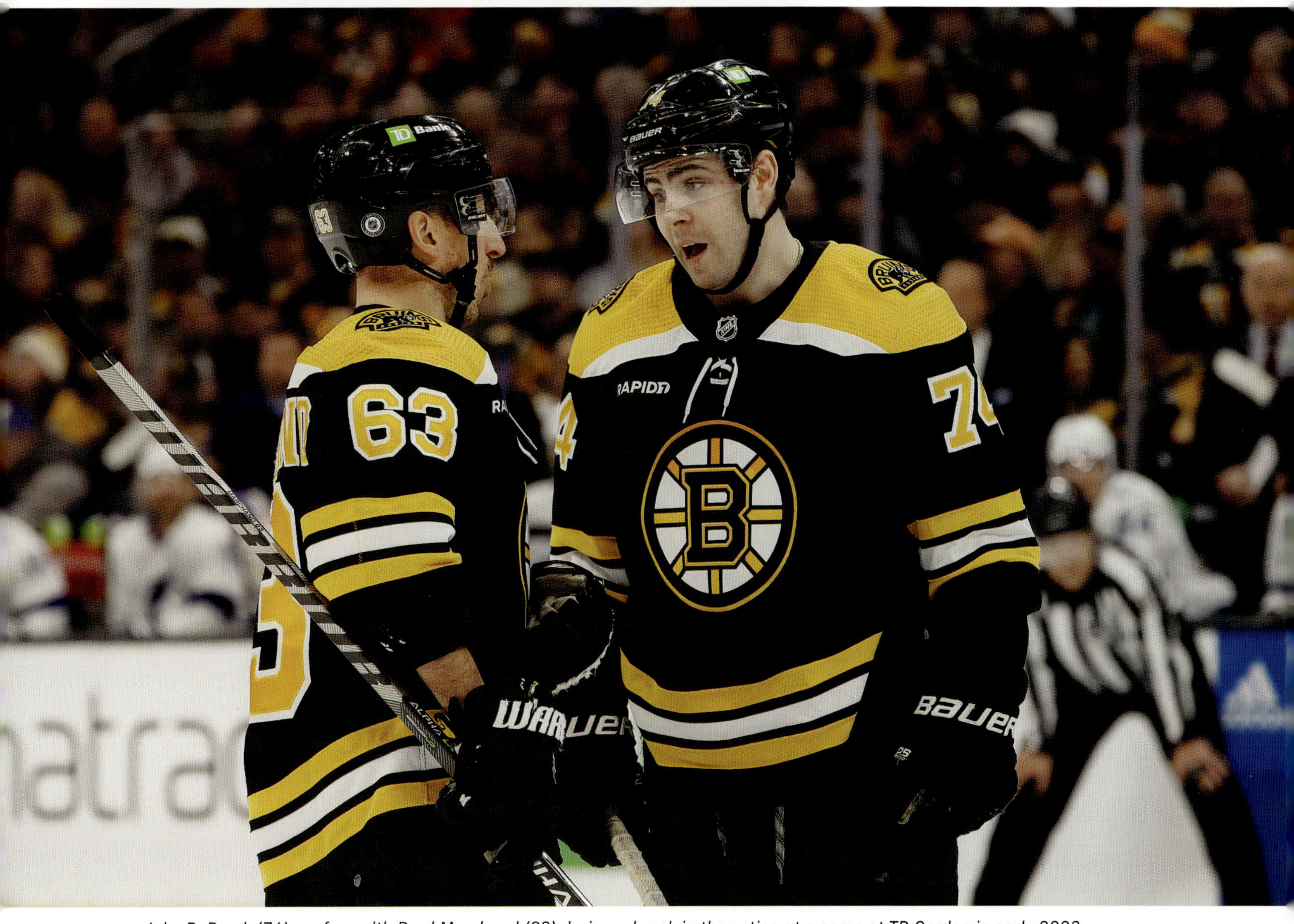

Jake DeBrusk (74) confers with Brad Marchand (63) during a break in the action at a game at TD Garden in early 2023. Boston selected the speedy DeBrusk in the first round of the 2015 NHL Draft. He grew to become a key contributor for the Bruins, someone capable of scoring goals in bunches. DeBrusk has scored 25 or more goals in a season three times (2019, 2022, and 2023). (Photograph by Richard T Gagnon/Getty Images)

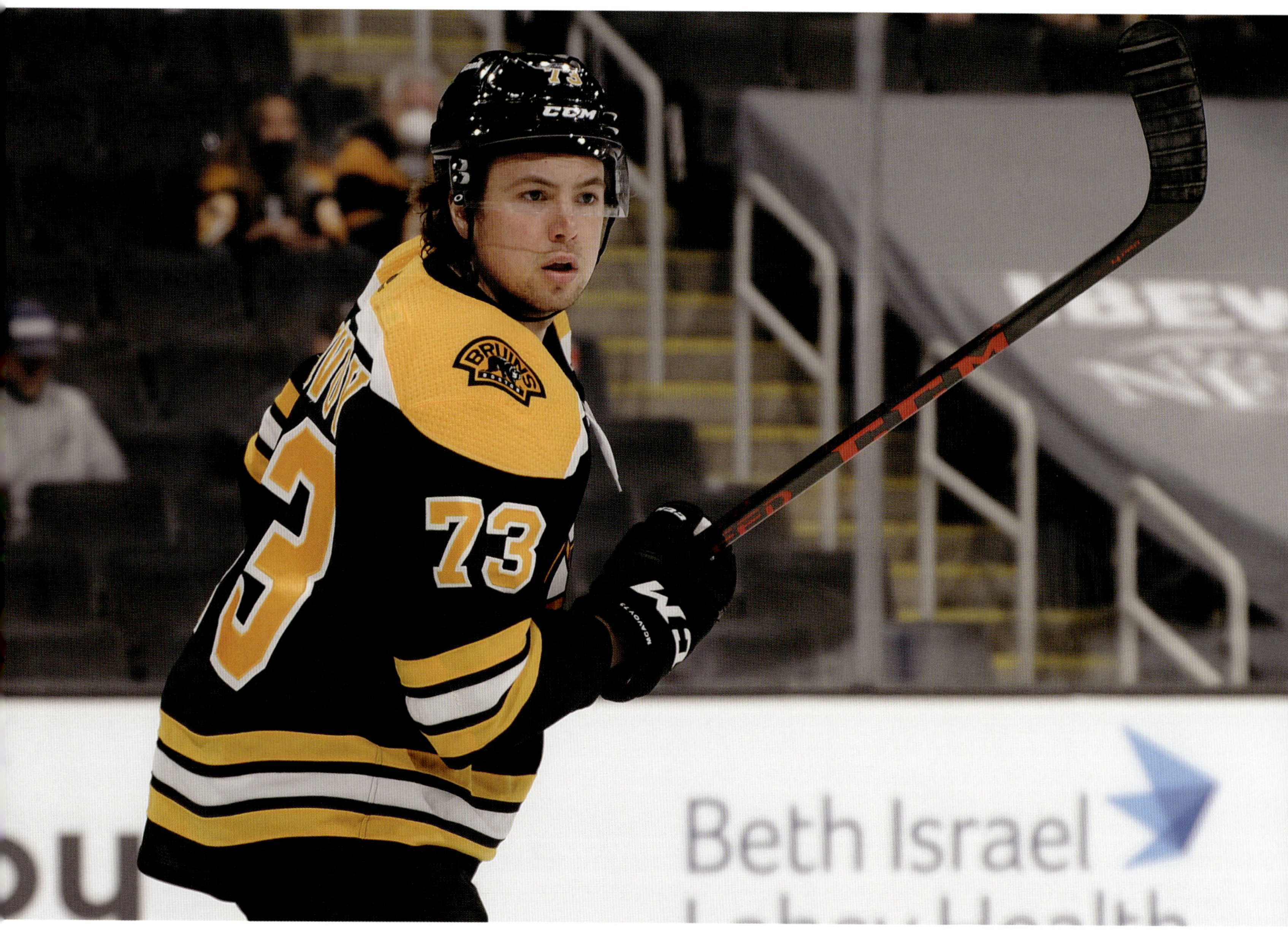

Long Island native Charlie McAvoy played just four minor league games in Providence before making his debut with the Bruins in the 2017 Stanley Cup playoffs. He is Boston's best homegrown defenseman since Ray Bourque and widely recognized as a potential future Norris Trophy winner. (Photograph by Steve Babineau/NHLI via Getty Images)

CHARLIE MCAVOY

THROUGH THE YEARS, the Bruins have been blessed with a succession of elite NHL defensemen. This series of "Bluebloods of the Blueline" began in black and white with Eddie Shore, Lionel Hitchman, and Fernie Flaman, and has continued in living color with Bobby Orr, Brad Park, Ray Bourque, and Zdeno Chara.

And now, there is Charlie McAvoy.

The most conspicuous characteristic of McAvoy's game is the abundant confidence he displays on the ice. Fearless, he pushes the action forward while never forgetting to mind the store. He is one of a handful of players whose style is immediately recognizable from a distance. Among his more prominent fans is Bobby Orr, who has praised his work ethic and skill set.

Ray Bourque is another member of the McAvoy Fan Club. "I think he's there," he told Matt Porter of the *Boston Globe* in 2021. "You show flashes as a young guy; the potential's there. I think the consistency came a lot more last year in his game. That's very encouraging to see. If he holds that consistency, he's going to be one of the top players at that position for many years to come."

A native of Long Island, McAvoy matriculated to Boston University in the fall of 2015. He played the 2015–16 season for the Terriers as a 17-year-old, the youngest player in Division I hockey. He showed enough skill and talent to convince the

Bruins to select him with the 14th overall pick in the 2016 NHL Draft. In the spring of 2017, McAvoy turned pro. It was not an easy decision.

"I remember being so terrified," McAvoy told Porter. "I didn't know if I could do it. Even leaving college was such a jump. I was just a mess. Once you sign, something's torn away—so permanently. There were a lot of tears, a lot of sad goodbyes with friends. But when I got to [Providence, home of the Bruins' AHL affiliate], it was like something clicked. I felt like I belonged."

Just days later, McAvoy made his debut with the Bruins in the 2017 Stanley Cup playoffs. It was immediately clear that he belonged at that level, as well. He has since emerged as one of the top defensemen in the NHL and a perennial Norris Trophy finalist.

In October 2021, McAvoy inked a long-term deal that will keep him in Black and Gold through the 2029–30 season. "Charlie, he's embraced Boston," said Bruins president Cam Neely at the press conference announcing the signing. "He went to college here. I think he likes the city, loves the sports environment, loves our fan base. Playing in front of a packed house every night is certainly something special."

For his part, McAvoy expressed both gratitude and hunger. "I think every year in the league you try to take a step," he said. "It's a humbling league. Nothing's ever easy. But I think just as far as development and growth, every year you want to take that step where the game looks like it's slowing down in a way that you know your plays, you know all your reads, you know all the things that allow you to have success.... I know I have so much to give, so much to go, and I want to grow into the very best I can be. There's no complacency. There's where I am now and where I feel I can get to. And every year, I just want to continue to take strides."

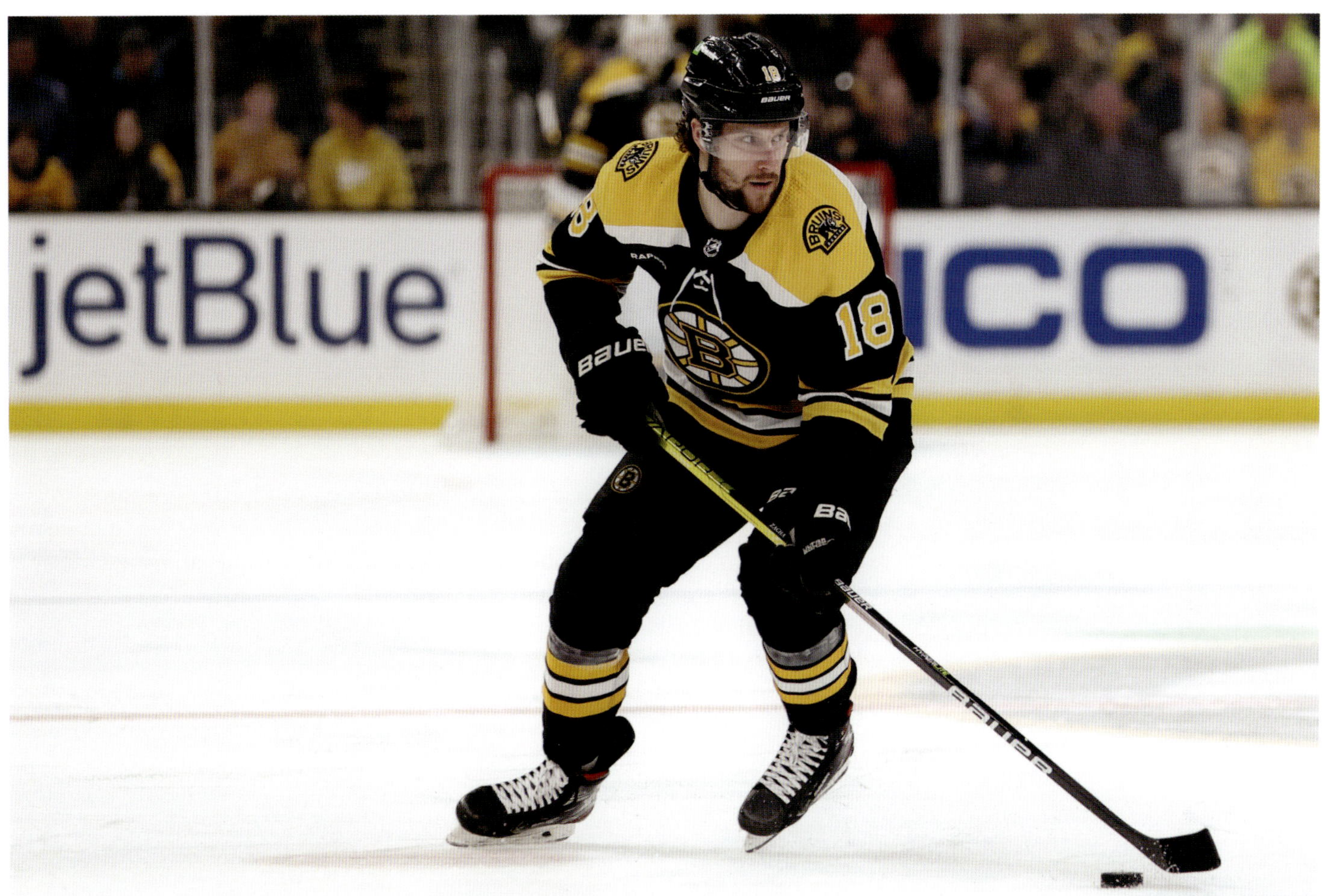

The Bruins acquired forward Pavel Zacha prior to the 2022–23 season—and the former top prospect ended up delivering in a big-time way. Skating for much of the season on a line with fellow Czech countrymen David Krejci and David Pastrnak, Zacha finished fourth on the team in scoring with 21 goals and 36 assists. It was a breakout season for the tall, rangy center—and one that bodes well for the future. (Photograph by Maddie Meyer/Getty Images)

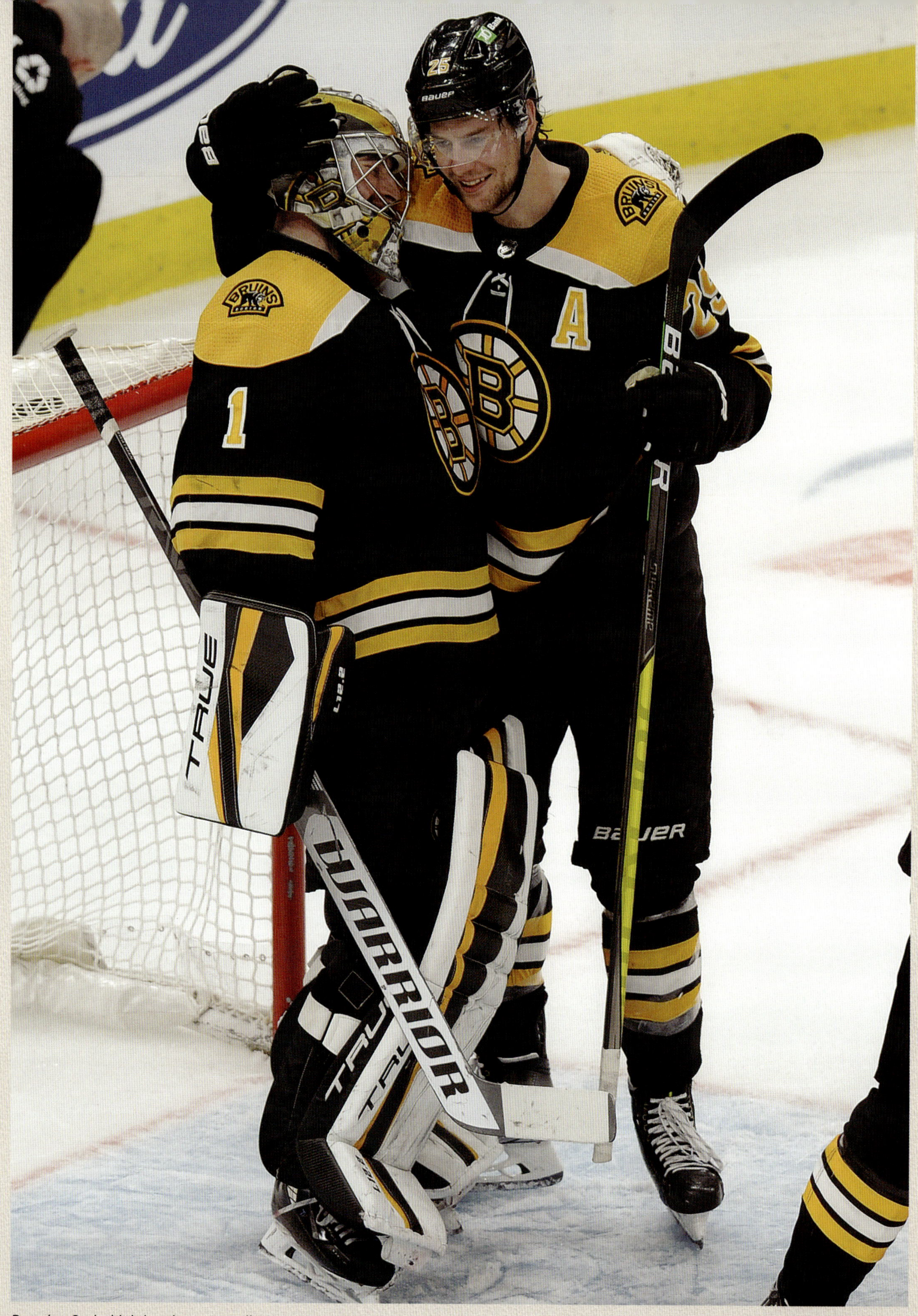

Brandon Carlo (right) embraces goalie Jeremy Swayman after a Bruins victory over the Penguins in April 2022. The 6'6" Carlo established himself as a hulking presence on the Boston blueline after debuting with the team in 2016—a "defenseman's defenseman" who excels at patrolling the slot and shutting down opposing forwards. Swayman, part of the Bruins goaltending rotation since 2021, has been just one of the netminders who have been grateful to have Carlo playing in front of him. (Photograph by Steve Babineau/NHLI via Getty Images)

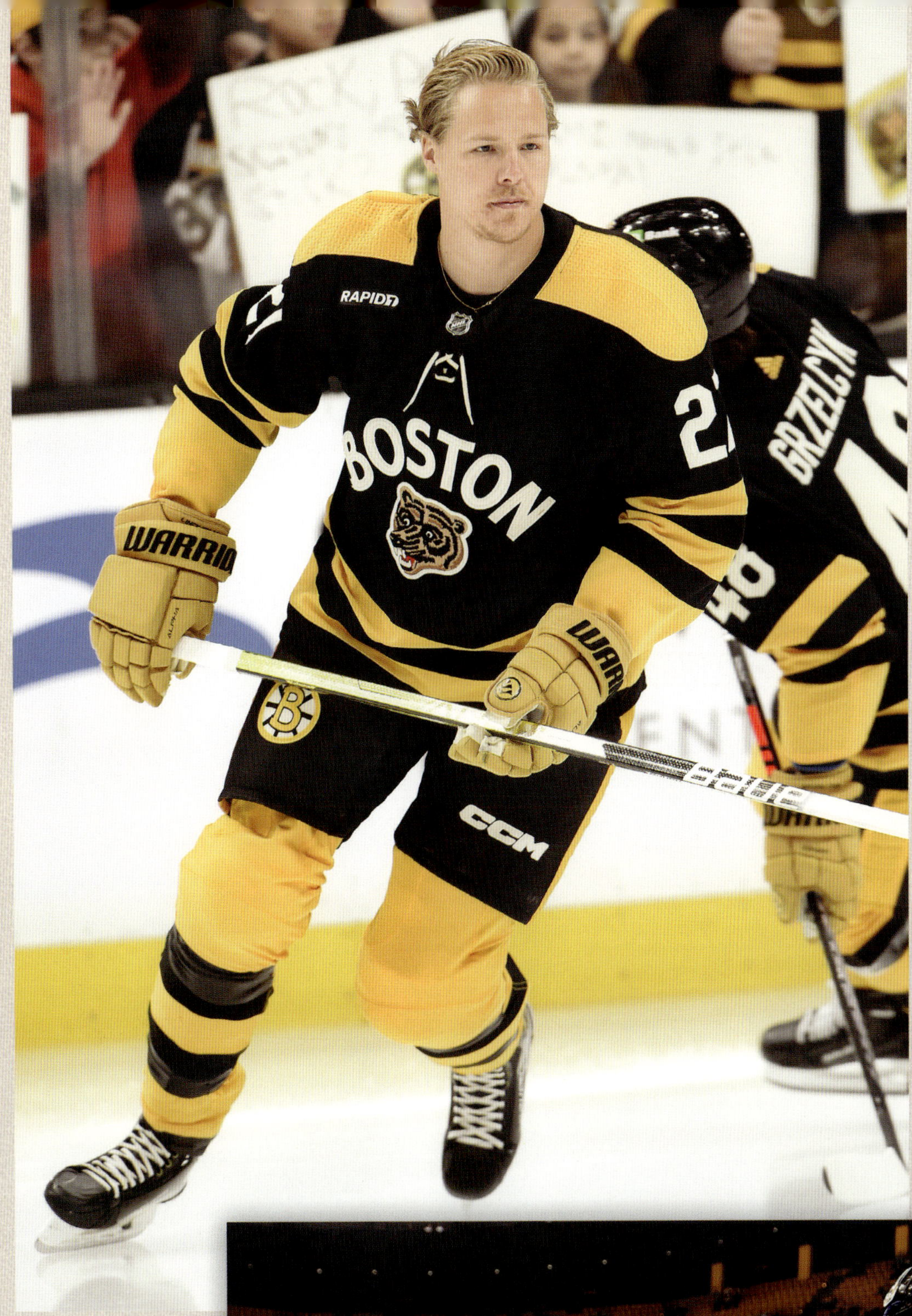

Acquired via trade from the Anaheim Ducks in March 2022, Hampus Lindholm (left) has emerged as a star and fan favorite while skating for the Bruins. In 2022-23, his first full season in Boston, the native of Sweden rung up 53 points (10 goals, 43 assists) while leading the entire NHL in the plus/minus category (with a +49 rating). He is an elite NHL defenseman. (Photograph by Steve Babineau/NHLI via Getty Images)

A popular, "stay at home" defenseman, Adam McQuaid (below) played nine seasons for the Bruins (2009–2018). Here, he greets Liam Fitzgerald (known as "The Fist Bump Kid") prior to an October 2017 game at TD Garden. In August 2021, Don Sweeney brought McQuaid back to the organization as player development coordinator. Back in 2007, Sweeney had conceived, organized, and run the team's first off-season Development Camp. "Adam McQuaid is doing that in our organization now," said Sweeney. "He was part of that first development camp that I ran. Sometimes it comes full circle..." (Photograph by Steve Babineau/NHLI via Getty Images)

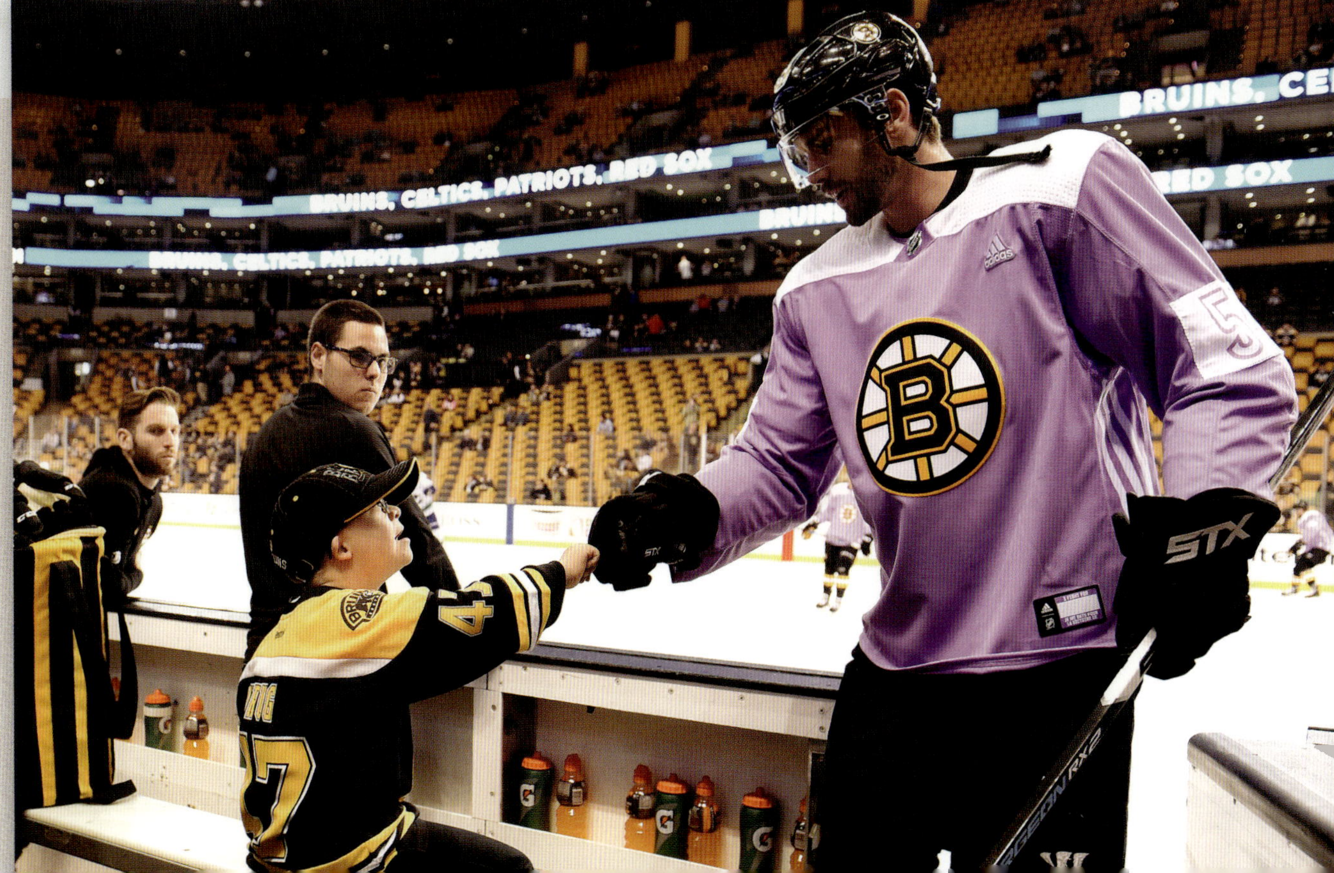

DAVID PASTRNAK

In the final analysis, the object of the game of hockey is to put the puck into the net.

Few do it quite as often, or quite as well, as right wing David Pastrnak. Even though he is just entering his prime years, he has already scored more than 300 career goals (301, to be exact), only the ninth man in Bruns history to do so.

Ironically, Pastrnak always thought of himself as more of a playmaker than a goal scorer, noting in a 2019 interview, "[I wasn't] a scorer growing up as a young player.... Everybody loves to score, but since I was a kid I always loved to prepare the goals for the other guys."

Whether he qualified as a goal scorer or playmaker, the Bruins knew they were getting a talented player when they selected the native of the Czech Republic in the first round of the 2014 NHL Draft. Pastrnak spent much of his first two seasons shuttling between Providence and Boston. While with the Bruins, he usually played on the third or fourth line.

In 2016–17, Pastrnak had his breakout season, scoring 34 goals with 36 assists. Teammates were impressed. "His goal scoring is pretty phenomenal," said defenseman Brandon Carlo in an interview with SI.com. "He finds pucks in and around the net all the time. He has a phenomenal shot.... He's been great so far this year, and I don't expect him to slide at all."

Chosen with the 25th overall pick in the 2014 NHL Draft, right winger David Pastrnak has blossomed into one of the greatest goal scorers of this generation—and in NHL history. (Photograph by Frederick Breedon/Getty Images)

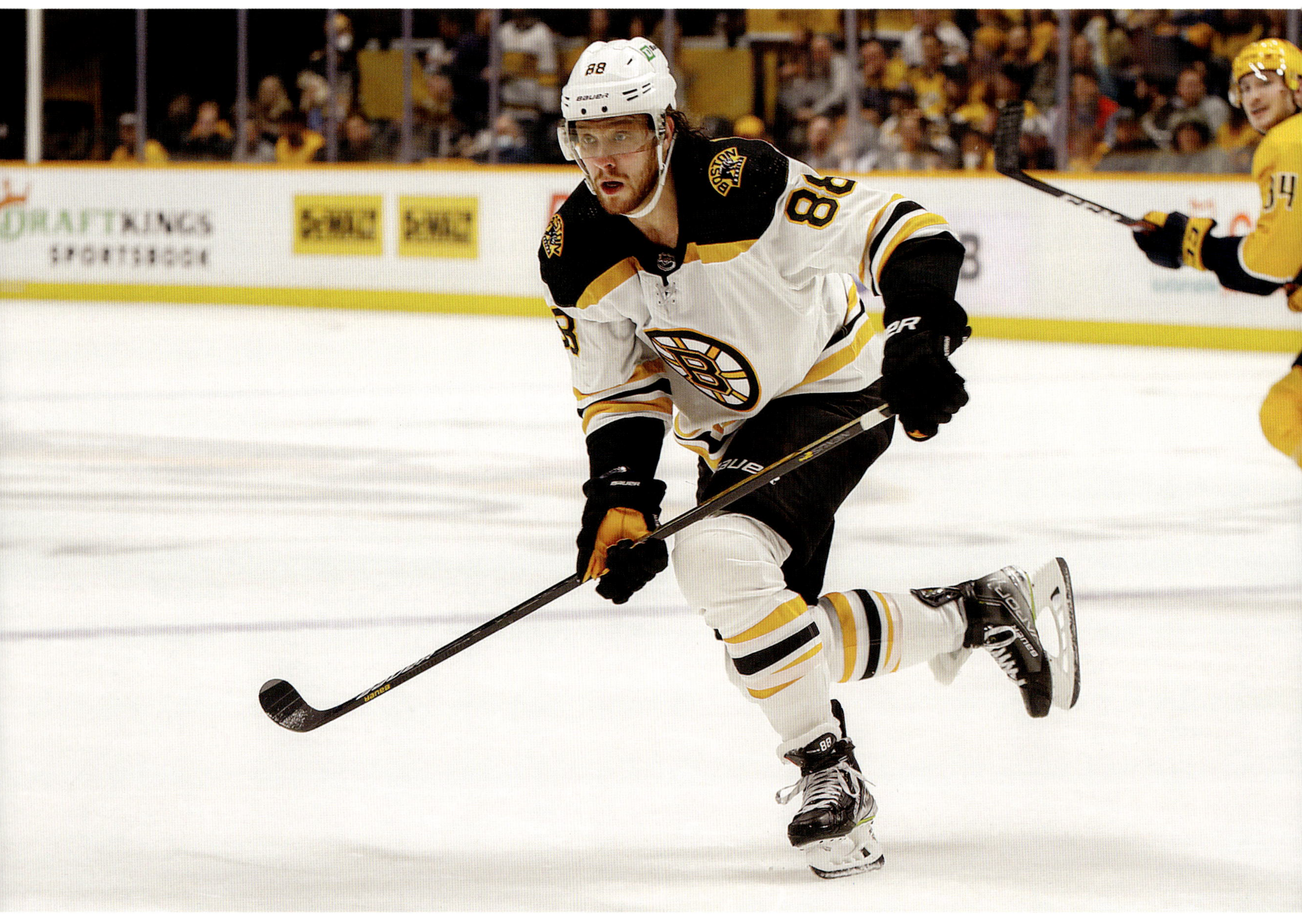

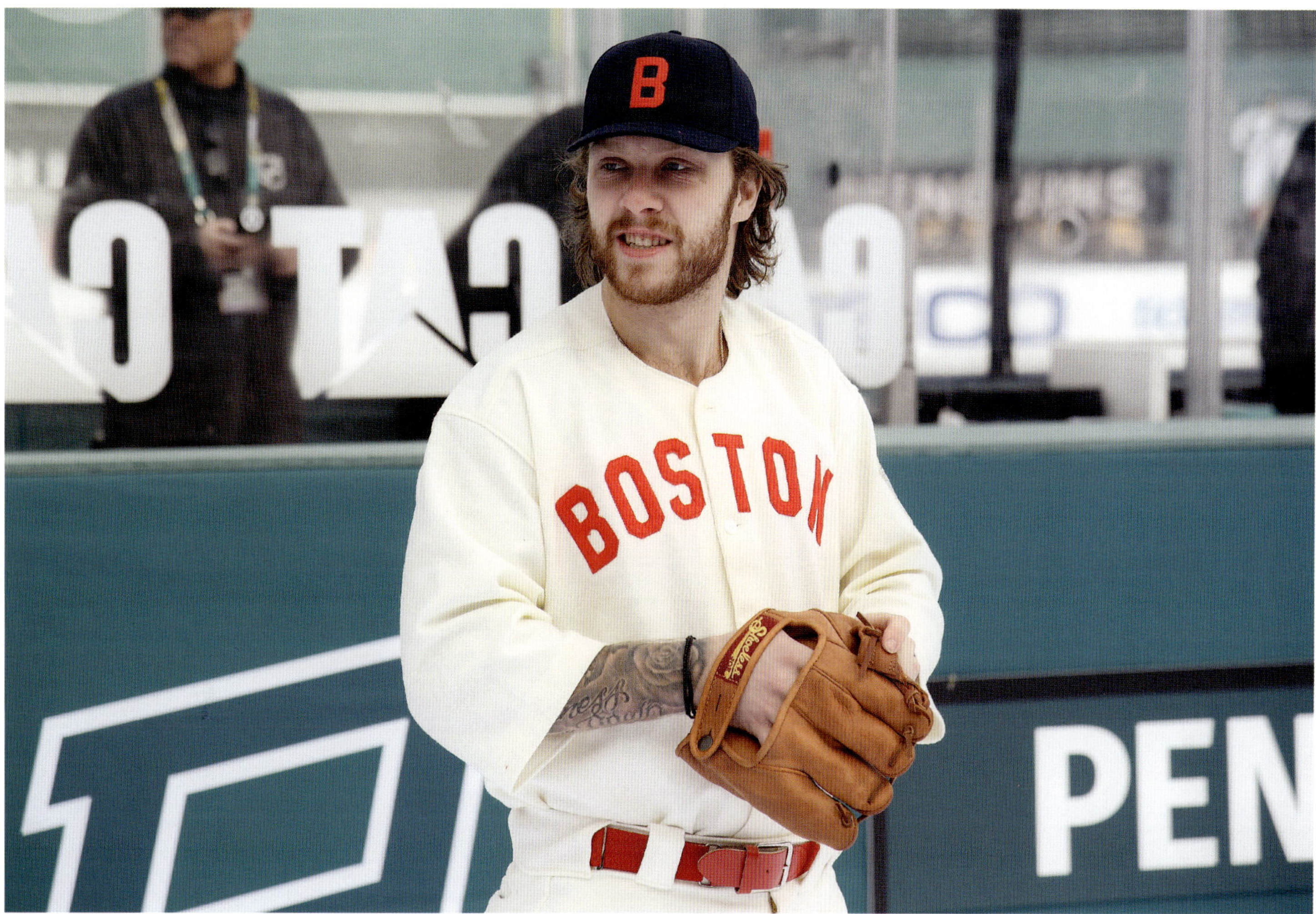

David Pastrnak has an upbeat, infectious, and endearing personality. Here, he plays catch at Fenway Park prior to the 2023 Winter Classic. If the Red Sox are in the market for a new lefthanded reliever, the Bruins would prefer that they look elsewhere. (Photograph by Steve Babineau/ NHLI via Getty Images)

Carlo was correct, as Pastrnak put up seasons of 80 and 81 points in 2018 and 2019, respectively. He took things to a new level in the pandemic-shortened 2020 season, scoring 48 goals with 47 assists.

By that time, the personality of "Pasta" had emerged in full bloom. Off the ice, his sartorial flair includes a wide selection of wildly colorful suits. It reflects his infectious joy at all times, not unlike that displayed by other Boston sports icons such as David Ortiz and Rob Gronkowski.

"I just love his air of confidence," said Bruins coach Jim Montgomery in an April 2023 interview with the *Boston Globe* shortly after Pastrnak signed a long-term deal that will keep him in the fold through 2030–31. "It's a jovial confidence. He makes others want to be around him, and be at the rink, because of his attitude. He doesn't have a lot of bad days, and that's an infectious attitude over the course of a long season.... That's why he's Pasta."

Montgomery has also studied the art and mastery of Pastrnak as a goal scorer—and has observed that it has a lot more to do with his trademark shot, the stationary one-timer from the left circle. It's also about his ability to "read opponents' joints," cut against the grain, and use change of pace and subtle movements to create space.

"He's kind of like Pedro [Martinez] was on the mound," Montgomery told the *Globe*. "First time [you're] up at bat, he's going to set you up with a fastball, then here comes the curve, and all of a sudden he's going inside and high. He sees how they're trying to defend him, defensemen and goalies, then he adjusts."

Pastrnak put it all together during the 2022–23 season, exploding for 61 goals. He became just the second player in Bruins history (after Phil Esposito) and the 23rd man in NHL history to achieve the 60-goal milestone.

What does the achievement mean? "It means you're an elite goal scorer," said Montgomery. "I mean elite, elite as there is."

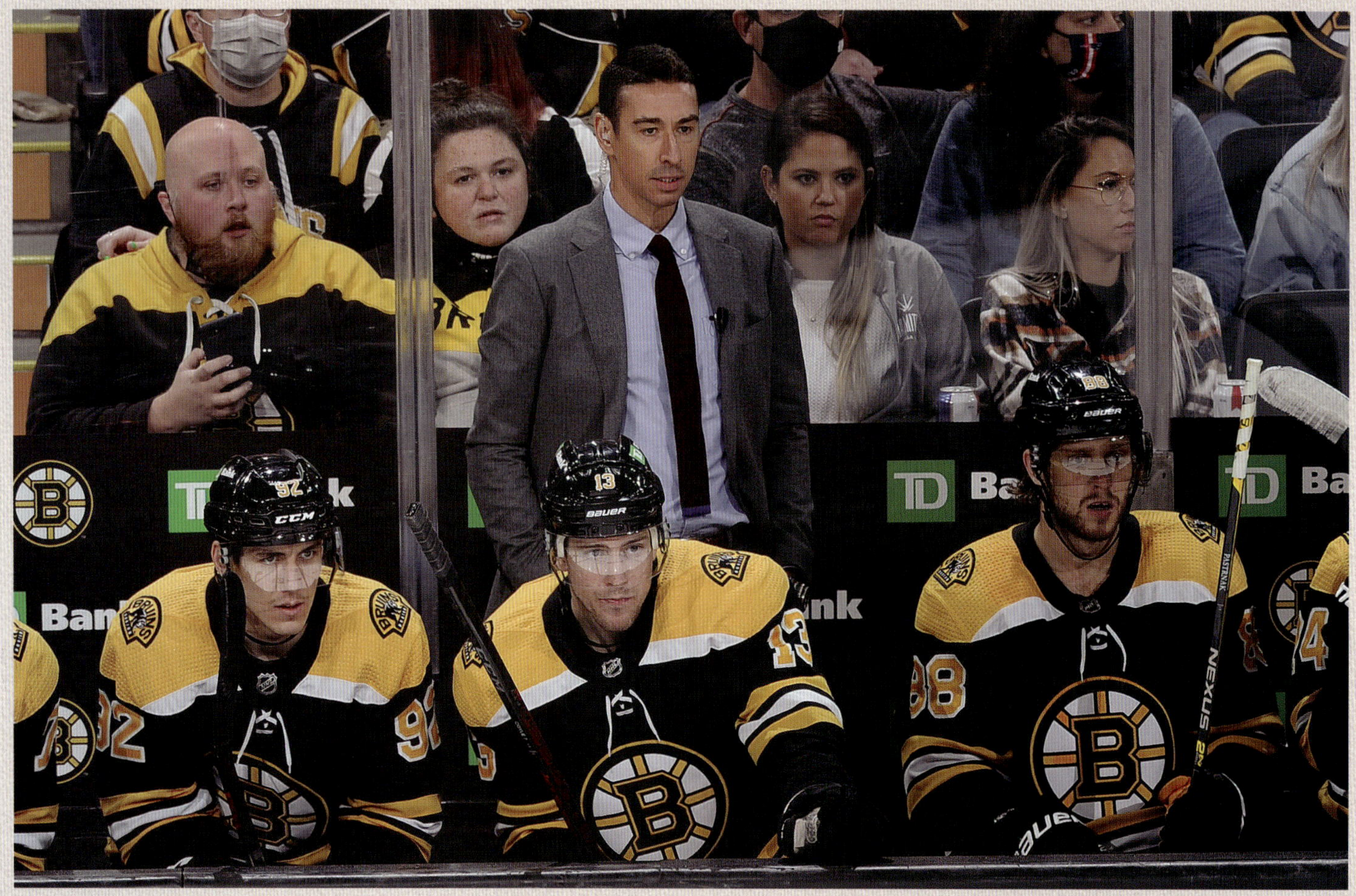

One of the heroes of the 2011 Stanley Cup championship team and a smart, respected player throughout his six-year tenure with the team (2011–2016), Chris Kelly returned to the Bruins organization as player development coordinator in 2019. Two years later, in 2021, he was promoted to assistant coach. Kelly continues to serve the Bruins in that capacity along with two other former NHL players, John Gruden and Joe Sacco. (Photograph by Steve Babineau/NHLI via Getty Images)

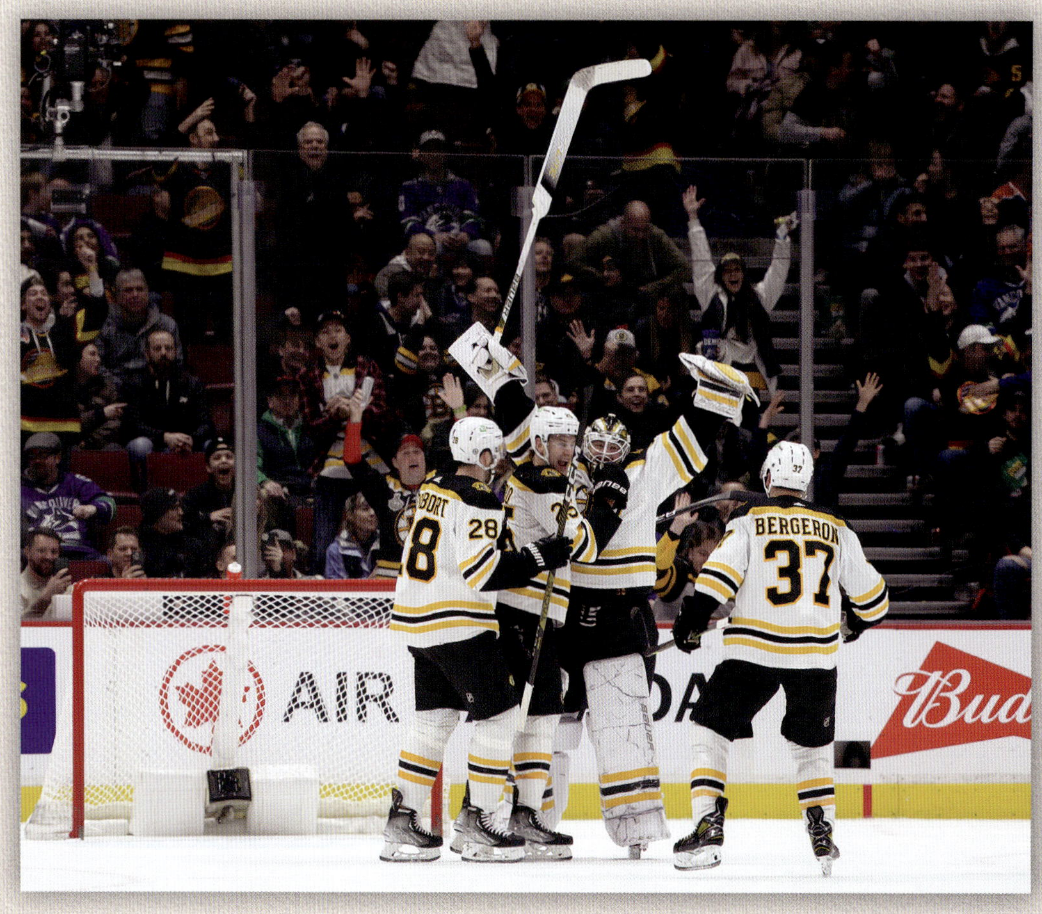

On February 25, 2023, with less than a minute remaining in a game against the Vancouver Canucks at Rogers Arena, Bruins goaltender Linus Ullmark launched the puck the length of the ice to score an empty-net goal that sealed Boston's 3–1 victory. In so doing, he became the first Bruins goaltender in franchise history (and just the 13th goaltender in NHL history) to score a goal in a regular-season game. Here, Ullmark celebrates with teammates Derek Forbort (28), Brandon Carlo (25), and Patrice Bergeron (37). He was still ecstatic after the game. "It's hard to describe what I'm feeling right now.... I have to digest it," he said. "I'm just so bloody happy." (Photograph by Derek Cain/ Getty Images)

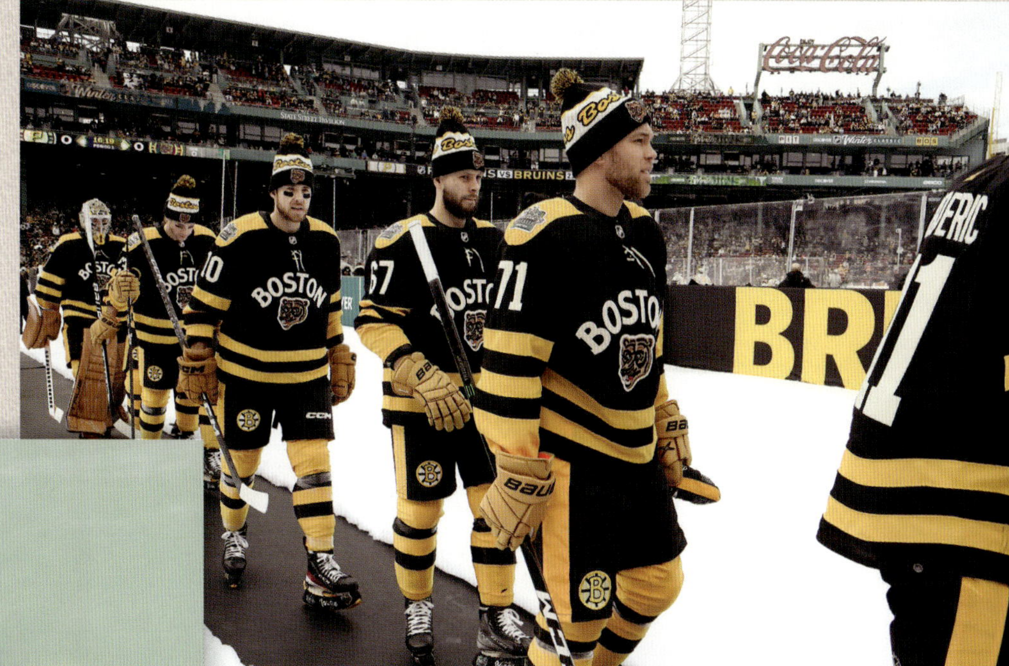

A conga line of Boston Bruins—(left to right) Jeremy Swayman (1), Charlie Coyle (13) , A.J. Greer (10), Jakub Zboril (67), Taylor Hall (71), and Trent Frederic (11)—make their way to the Fenway Park ice surface ahead of the 2023 Winter Classic between the Bruins and the Pittsburgh Penguins. (Photograph by Brian Babineau/NHLI via Getty Images)

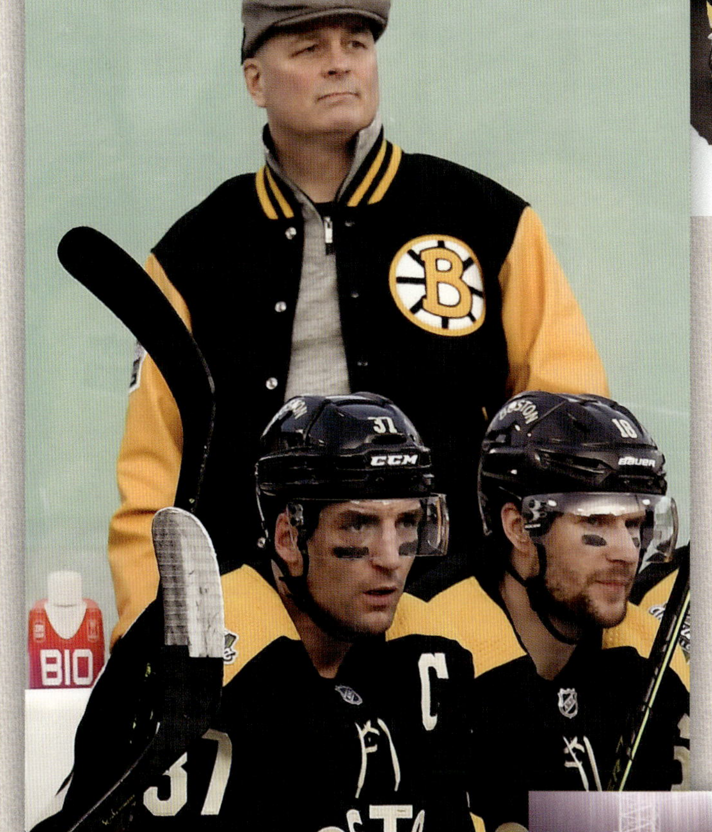

Jim Montgomery (left) was Boston's new man behind the bench for the 2022–23 season. After a standout career at the University of Maine, "Monty" played six NHL seasons. His previous NHL coaching stops prior to coming to Boston included Dallas (as head coach) and St. Louis (as an assistant). All that was a prelude to his first season in Boston, when his team won an NHL record 65 games. Here, Montgomery surveys the action during the 2023 Winter Classic at Fenway Park. (Photograph by Brian Babineau/NHLI via Getty Images)

The Bruins (right) pose for a team photo on the Fenway Park ice after they beat the Penguins 2–1 in the 2023 Winter Classic. The big hero in the third period was Jake DeBrusk, who pumped home two goals while playing through injuries. The victory sent everyone home happy—including, of course, Blades, the longtime Bruins mascot. (Photograph by Brian Babineau/NHLI via Getty Images)

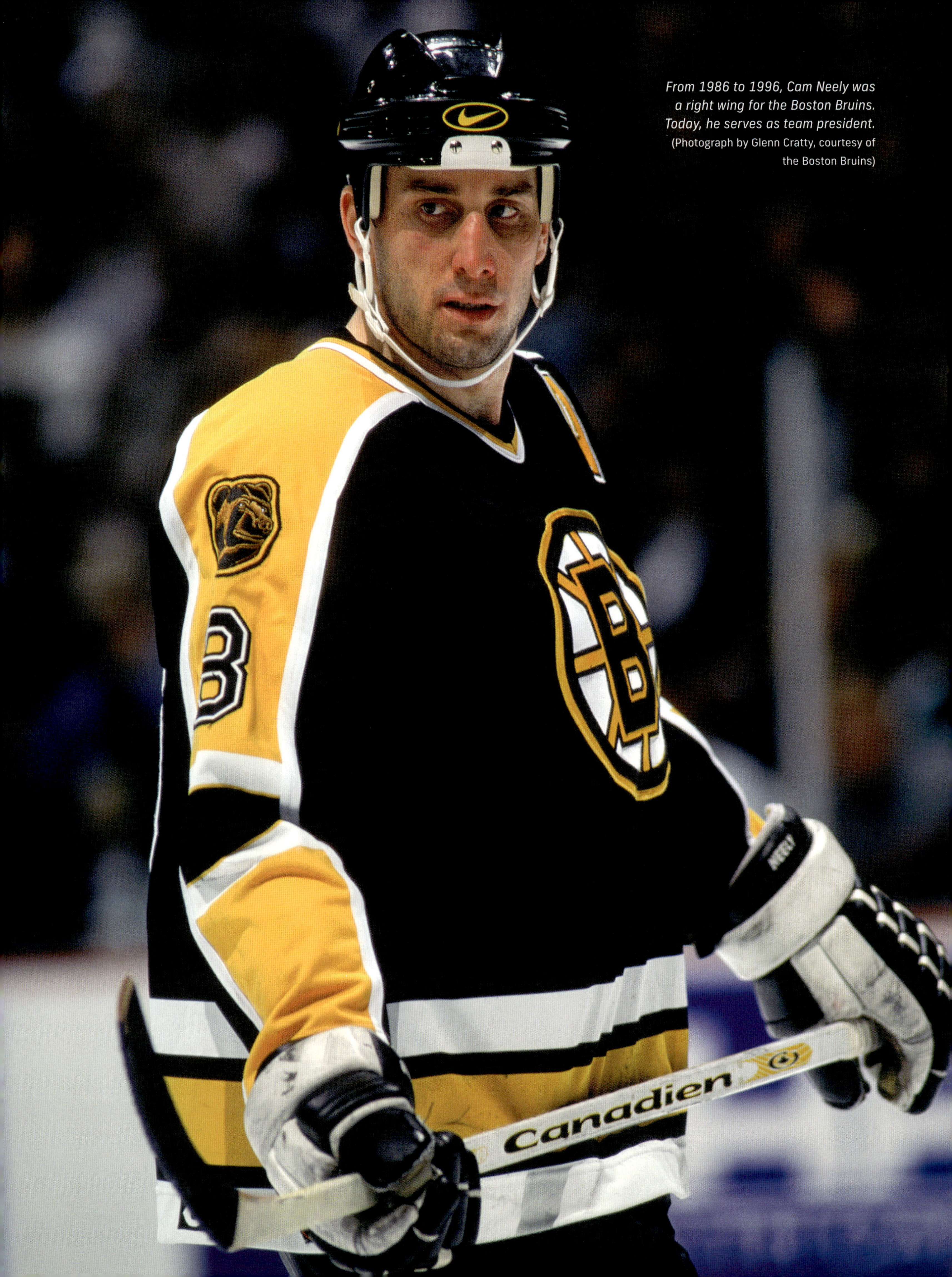

From 1986 to 1996, Cam Neely was a right wing for the Boston Bruins. Today, he serves as team president. (Photograph by Glenn Cratty, courtesy of the Boston Bruins)

WHAT IT MEANS TO BE A BOSTON BRUIN

By Cam Neely

IT'S HARD TO PUT into words what it means to be a Boston Bruin.

Because being a Boston Bruin doesn't just mean you throw on some hockey equipment, pull a jersey over your head, skate around the Garden a few times, and move on with your life.

No, being a Boston Bruin is your life. For life.

Sure, there are countless professional sports teams across North America—and the world—with impressive histories, rabid fan bases, and athletes that bond together like family.

But here in Boston, hockey—and the Spoked-B—just means something more. It's not only passion and commitment and enthusiasm. It's different.

It truly is in our blood.

We eat, sleep, and breathe it. Every game, every practice, every event. We live it every hour of every day all year long, even when Causeway Street goes quiet for the summer.

My own personal history with the Bruins shows just how special it can be to become part of this franchise. When I arrived here from Vancouver, a town with a storied hockey history of its own, I couldn't have imagined what it would mean for my family and me. It truly changed my life. It was my 21st birthday when I got the call from my sister while I was at the gym—there were no cellphones back then!—that I was headed to Boston for the 1986–87 season. My career was at a crossroads. I was struggling to get ice time with the Canucks and wasn't quite sure what a move across the continent would mean for me.

Admittedly, I was a bit down as I contemplated such a huge change. But I remember a call with my friend Michael J. Fox, who loved the Bruins growing up. He knew I was uneasy and made sure to reassure me, telling me that transitioning to an Original Six team, especially Boston, was going to be great for me.

He wasn't wrong.

My main goal when I arrived in town was to solidify my career with a fresh start. But I couldn't have imagined what was in store.

I spent 10 amazing years here as a player, and the memories are endless. I don't know if I could've played in a better building. The energy at the old Boston Garden, the way the fans were on top of you...it was one of the best feelings to be able to play in that environment every night. The way I played fit perfectly into what this blue-collar town expects out of its players, and there's no doubt I fed off that.

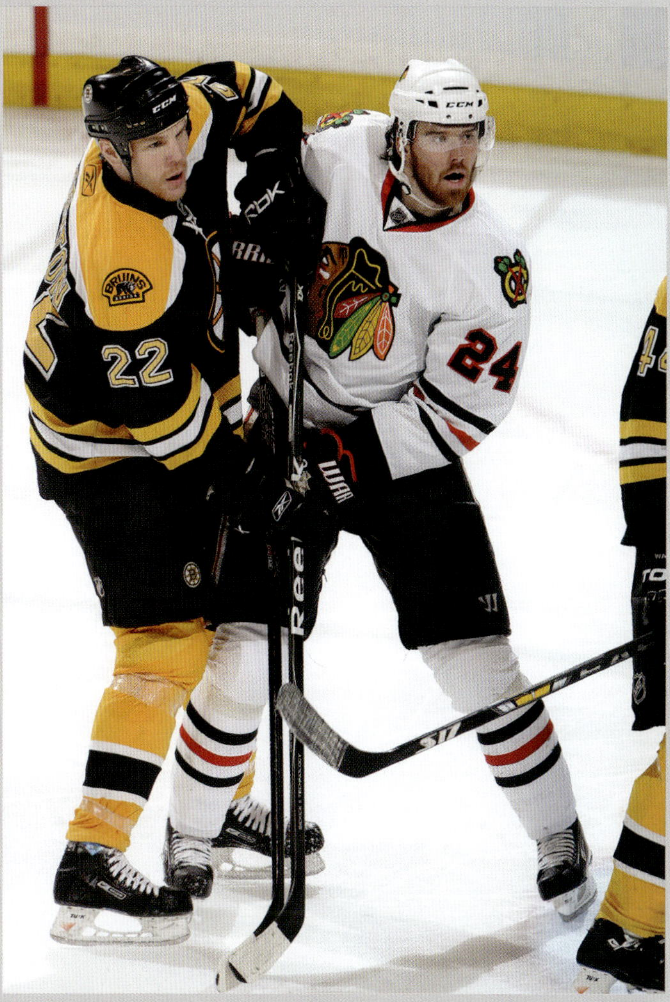

Shawn Thornton on what it means to be a Boston Bruin: "The DNA, the epitome of a Bruin is team first, unselfish, hates to lose more than they like to win, will sacrifice themselves for a win, whether that is physically, a fight, blocking a shot..." (Photo by Steve Babineau/NHLI via Getty Images)

After my career, I was privileged to be inducted into the Hockey Hall of Fame—and have my No. 8 raised to the Garden rafters, which I believe is the greatest honor a player from an Original Six team can receive.

And, of course, there were so many special moments and seasons along the way, including the 50-goal season in 44 games in 1993–94. But the one that stands out above the rest is when we finally beat Montreal in the 1988 Stanley Cup Playoffs after 45 long years. It was only the second round, but to finally break the drought—which we heard about over and over again—made an impact here that left us blown away. I'll never forget when we returned to Boston and landed at Logan Airport and saw thousands of fans there waiting to celebrate us. We knew it was a big deal before that—but to see the passion first-hand made us understand that it was an even more significant accomplishment than we had realized.

It's moments like those that allow you to grasp how fortunate you are to play in a place like this.

So, while my time on the ice was cut short, I knew when I hung up the skates in 1996, I never wanted to leave. Yes, British Columbia will always be where I'm from. But this place, some 3,000 miles away, has become home.

Nearly 30 years after I retired, I've remained here with my family, as I've taken on a second career with the team—and the community—that means so much to us. The way this place has embraced us and the Cam Neely Foundation through the Neely House and Comics Come Home is simply incredible.

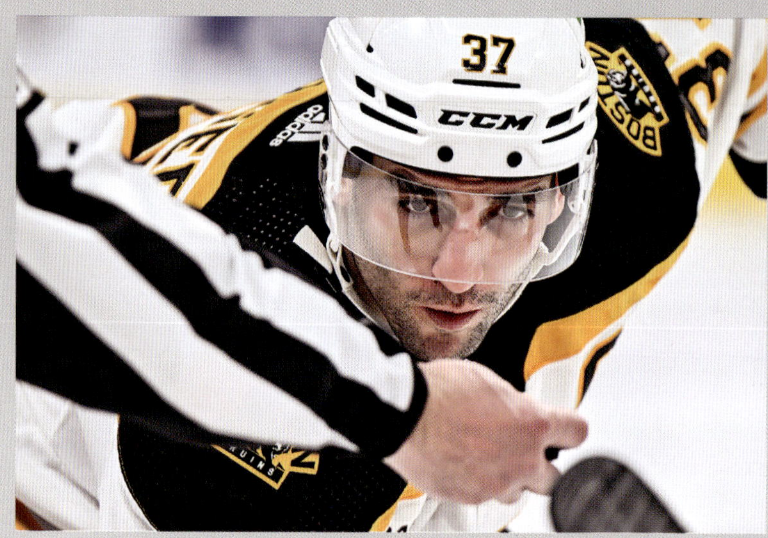

Patrice Bergeron on what it means to be a Boston Bruin: "It just has a special place in my heart. I've spent more than half my life now in Boston, being part of the Boston Bruins organization. I have a lot of pride and joy. It's not something that I take lightly. It's something I'm proud of and I want to be a good role model, obviously for kids, and represent this organization the best that I can." (Photograph by Minas Panagiotakis/Getty Images)

It has been an honor to remain with this organization and be part of so many memorable teams, including one that won the Stanley Cup, while watching a new generation of Bruins players follow in the footsteps of so many legends who came before them to make an indelible impact not only on the ice, but on this region.

And that is what makes being a Bruin such a singular experience.

Yes, there is immense pride when you pull that sweater on, but it's not just your hockey accolades that get remembered here. It's what you did to make Boston a better city and New England a better region. It's how you make people feel, it's how you connect with them on a personal level, it's how you become family.

In Boston, you don't just come to the rink, jump back into your car after the game and practice is over, and then sit around at home until you do it all over again the next day. You have to embrace being part of the community, especially given the unique ability we have as professional athletes to impact someone's life with even the smallest of gestures.

Here, you become part of the fabric of this city. You get to know your neighbors and the local shop owners and the fans that you pass by on the street. You see them in the North End, or Charlestown, or Southie. Maybe even during a trip to Fenway, or down to the Cape, or up to the mountains. And sure, you may have to absorb a chirp here or there—but that's all part of what makes the Bruins experience.

In the end, if you're a Bruin, you're a Bruin for life. Through thick and thin.

And what could be better than that?

Cam Neely is president of the Boston Bruins.

BOSTON BRUINS (2020–2023)

Season	W	L	OL	PTS	PTS%	Finish	Playoffs	Coach	Division	Conference
2019–20*	44	14	12	100	.714	1st of 8	Lost NHL Second Round	Bruce Cassidy	Atlantic	Eastern
2020–21*	33	16	7	73	.652	3rd of 8	Lost NHL Second Round	Bruce Cassidy	East	
2021–22	51	26	5	107	.652	4th of 8	Lost NHL First Round	Bruce Cassidy	Atlantic	Eastern
2022–23	65	12	5	135	.823	1st of 8	Lost NHL First Round	Jim Montgomery	Atlantic	Eastern

*Regular season shortened due to pandemic

AFTERWORD

by

CHARLIE JACOBS

LET ME START by saying it's a true honor to serve as CEO of the Boston Bruins during such a tremendous milestone.

Having been around this team since I was a boy, it feels surreal to have the opportunity to lead this franchise in celebrating 100 years—and even more special to be the first U.S. team to do so. This team is about so much more than hockey—we're about bringing people together. We're about teamwork. We're about making an impact in our community. We are privileged to be part of the heartbeat of our great city on and off the ice.

As demonstrated throughout this book, our team's rich history reaches far beyond the walls of TD Garden. It has been our mission to leave a positive impact in our community, our city, our region, and the league. The Boston Bruins Foundation is also hitting a milestone this year—20 years. In that time, the Foundation has raised more than $54 million to assist charitable organizations that demonstrate a commitment to enhancing the quality of life for children and families throughout New England. I'm incredibly proud of what we've done so far and what we will continue to do for the next 100 years to come.

It is also very special to see the Hub on Causeway project completed and our neighborhood revitalized just in time for our centennial celebration. The Hub on Causeway took over a decade from concept to reality and has brought a hotel, grocery store, office and apartment buildings, and major renovations to TD Garden. It is important to my family that our loyal fanbase have a state-of-the-art arena and surrounding area that come to life every event day.

Looking forward, our goal is to continue growing. We want to continue to bring our city, state, and region together through the power of sport.

Thank you to every single fan who has embraced the Black and Gold—we quite literally wouldn't be here without you.

Cheers to the next 100 years of Boston Bruins hockey!

Charlie Jacobs is CEO and alternate governor, Boston Bruins and TD Garden.

ACKNOWLEDGMENTS

THE AUTHORS extend thanks to the many individuals who contributed to the creation of this book.

Thanks to Jeremy Jacobs for writing the Foreword that starts this book off in such grand fashion. Similarly, thanks to Charlie Jacobs for writing the Afterword that closes it out in a similar vein—and for the faith that he showed in entrusting us with this project more than two years ago.

Thanks to Cam Neely for his support and for contributing the essay in the final chapter that tied everything together.

Thanks to Glen Thornborough for leading the team at the Boston Bruins and TD Garden that drove the creation of this book.

Three members of that team deserve special mention for their contributions to this book. Brian Codagnone conducted more than 20 interviews with Bruins alumni for this book while also providing creative assistance. Andrea Mazzarelli made enormous editorial and project management contributions far too many to list. And Samantha McGraw went above and beyond on a consistent basis and on multiple fronts. Without Sam's vital contributions, this book may never have happened.

Other members of the internal team who helped make it all happen include Fred Bunker, Laney Byler, Lily Calary, Carley Cavallaro, Hailey Clements, Mark Majewski, Tricia McCorkle, Brandon McNelis, Molly Phalan, Connor Powell, Jordan Salisbury, Bryan Simmons-Hayes, Sean Sullivan, and Janice Trybus. Special thanks to Hilary Gorlin, Katie Gorman, Heidi Holland, and Eric Russo for their editorial contributions and to Shannon Torgerson for her sage advice and wise counsel.

Thanks to John Dellapina and Gary Meagher of the NHL for their editorial assistance and Steve Garabedian of NESN for his general assistance, especially with respect to his interviews with Patrice Bergeron, Bobby Orr, and Tim Thomas.

Thanks to the other Bruins players and alumni who graciously agreed to be interviewed for this book, including Ray Bourque, Andy Brickley, Johnny Bucyk, Don Cherry, Phil Esposito, Matt Grzelcyk, Ken Hodge Sr., Eddie Johnston, Don Marcotte, the late Don McKenney, Rick Middleton, Cam Neely, Willie O'Ree, Terry O'Reilly, Brad Park, Derek Sanderson, Ed Sandford, Harry Sinden, Rick Smith, Bob Sweeney, Don Sweeney, Shawn Thornton, and Eddie Westfall.

Thanks also to the late Milt Schmidt and the late George Owen. The interviews that they gave a long time ago allowed us to include their voices in this book, too. We are glad that we could.

Thanks to those individuals, talented and accomplished, who contributed the incisive essays contained in this book on various aspects of the proud history of the Boston Bruins: Commissioner Gary Bettman, Steve Conroy, Kevin Paul Dupont, Michael Farber, Karen Guregian, Steve Hardy, Michael Hiam, Christopher Lydon, Leigh Montville, Matt Porter, and Eric Zweig.

The wonderful Bruins books written by Dale Arnold, Steve Babineau, Pam Coburn, Fred Cusick, John Devaney, Phil Esposito, Dick Grace, Ted Green, Matt Kalman, Kerry Keene, Jeff Miclash, Willie O'Ree, Bobby Orr, Stewart Richardson, Derek Sanderson, Fluto Shinzawa, Rob Simpson, Harry Sinden, Kevin Vatour, Tom Whalen, and, last but not least, hockey maven Stan Fischler all proved indispensable to this volume. So did the archival pages of the *Boston Globe* and *Sports Illustrated*.

Thanks to Getty Images, the Library and Archives of Canada (LAC), the Boston Public Library, and The Sports Museum for providing much of the imagery that graces this book as well as to the various individuals at various institutions who helped in that regard, including Andy Krause from Getty, Cedric Lafontaine from LAC, and multiple folks at the NHL, including Jessica Johnson, Kelley Lynch, Susan Cohig, Conal Berberich, and Jennifer Kallas. And our great gratitude also goes to Steve Babineau, Brian Babineau, the late Leslie Jones, the late Al Ruelle, and all the other talented photographers responsible for these remarkable images.

Over several decades our Bruins guru and go-to hockey expert Harvey McKenney has provided tremendous assistance and insight. Likewise, Howie Sylvester, producer of the Bruins radio broadcasts, has also been a huge help. Thanks also to Jim Bednarek, Casey Blossom, John Brooks, Amy Latimer, Kathryn Maynes, Carlton "Mac" McDiarmid, Matt Pepin, Joe Preston, and Bill Swift for helping in varied, sundry, and invaluable ways. Extra special thanks to Laura Krotky for putting up with one of us in particular over the last six months.

And, finally, many thanks to the Triumph editorial team of Noah Amstadter, Jesse Jordan, and Alex Lubertozzi for producing such a beautiful volume, one that truly befits the rich heritage of the NHL's first American franchise on the occasion of its centennial celebration.

Richard A. Johnson
Rusty Sullivan
June 2023

BOSTON BRUINS ALL-TIME ROSTER

(Alphabetical by Last Name, Through the 2022–23 Season)

Player	Seasons
George Abbott	1943–1944
Noel Acciari	2015–2016, 2018–2019
John Adams	1972–1973
Rick Adduono	1975–1976
Kenny Agostino	2017–2018
Jack Ahcan	2020–2022
Johnathan Aitken	1999–2000
Andrew Alberts	2005–2008
Gary Aldcorn	1960–1961
Bobby Allen	2006–2008
Jason Allison	1996–2001
Bill "Red" Anderson	1942–1943
Earl Anderson	1974–1977
Dave Andreychuk	1999–2000
John Arbour	1965–1966, 1967–1968
Bob Armstrong	1950–1962
Scott Arniel	1991–1992
Jamie Arniel	2010–2011
Barry Ashbee	1965–1966
Brent Ashton	1991–1993
Steve Atkinson	1968–1969
Oscar Aubuchon	1942–1944
Alex Auld	2007–2008
Don Awrey	1963–1973
P.J. Axelsson	1997–2009
Pete Babando	1947–1949
David Backes	2016–2020
Ace Bailey	1968–1973
Scott Bailey	1995–1997
Mike Bales	1992–1993
Murray Balfour	1964–1965
Stan Baluik	1959–1960
Darren Banks	1992–1994
Ralph Barahona	1990–1992
Marco Baron	1979–1983
Dave Barr	1981–1983
Marty Barry	1929–1935
Eddie Barry	1946–1947
Ray Barry	1951–1952
Matt Bartkowski	2010–2015
Jim Bartlett	1960–1961
Shawn Bates	1997–2001
Bobby Bauer	1935–1942, 1945–1947, 1951–1952
Ken Baumgartner	1997–1999
Red Beattie	1930–1938
Bob Beckett	1956–1958, 1961–1962, 1963–1964
Clayton Beddoes	1995–1997
Bob Beers	1989–1992, 1996–1997
Steve Begin	2009–2010
Yves Belanger	1979–1980
Ken Belanger	1998–2001
Matt Beleskey	2015–2018
Harvey Bennett	1944–1945
Bill Bennett	1978–1979
Bobby Benson	1924–1925
Paul Beraldo	1987–1989
Bryan Berard	2002–2003
Patrice Bergeron	2003–2023
Daniel Berthiaume	1991–1992
Tyler Bertuzzi	2022–2023

Player	Seasons
Phil Besler	1935–1936
Sam Bettio	1949–1950
Nick Beverley	1966–1967, 1969–1970, 1971–1974
Paul Bibeault	1944–1946
Craig Billington	1994–1996
Jack Bionda	1956–1959
Dick Bittner	1949–1950
Byron Bitz	2008–2010
Anders Bjork	2017–2021
Don Blackburn	1962–1963
Bob Blake	1935–1936
Zdenek Blatny	2005–2006
Anton Blidh	2016–2022
John Blue	1992–1994
John Blum	1983–1986, 1987–1990
Brandon Bochenski	2006–2008
Gus Bodnar	1953–1955
Andrew Bodnarchuk	2009–2010
Leo Boivin	1954–1966
Ivan Boldirev	1970–1972
Buzz Boll	1942–1944
Marcel Bonin	1955–1956
Dennis Bonvie	2001–2002
Buddy Boone	1956–1958
Bill Boucher	1926–1927
Fred Bergdinon	1925–1926
Ray Bourque	1979–2000
Chris Bourque	2012–2013
Paul Boutilier	1986–1987
Johnny Boychuk	2008–2014
Yank Boyd	1931–1932, 1942–1944
Brad Boyes	2005–2007
Nick Boynton	1999–2006
John Brackenborough	1925–1926
Bart Bradley	1949–1950
Tom Brennan	1943–1945
Rich Brennan	2002–2003
Andy Brickley	1988–1992
Archie Briden	1926–1927
Frank Brimsek	1938–1943, 1946–1949
Ken Broderick	1973–1975
Wade Brookbank	2006–2007
Ross Brooks	1972–1975
Adam Brown	1951–1952
Wayne Brown	1953–1954
Sean Brown	2001–2003
Josh Brown	2021–2022
Gordie Bruce	1940–1942, 1945–1946
Ron Buchanan	1966–1967
Johnny Bucyk	1957–1978
Billy Burch	1932–1933
Eddie Burke	1931–1932
Charlie Burns	1959–1963
Randy Burridge	1985–1991
John Byce	1989–1992
Gordie Byers	1949–1950
Lyndon Byers	1983–1992
Jack Caffery	1956–1958
Charles "Moose" Cahill	1925–1926
Herb Cain	1939–1946

Player	Seasons
Norm Calladine	1942–1945
Wade Campbell	1985–1988
Gregory Campbell	2010–2015
Carter Camper	2011–2012
Jack Capuano	1991–1992
Jim Carey	1996–1998
Paul Carey	2018–2020
Wayne Carleton	1969–1971
Brandon Carlo	2016–2023
Jordan Caron	2010–2015
Bobby Carpenter	1988–1992
Connor Carrick	2022–2023
George Carroll	1924–1925
Bill Carson	1928–1930
Billy Carter	1960–1961
John Carter	1985–1991
Anson Carter	1996–2000
Joe Carveth	1946–1948
Jon Casey	1993–1994
Wayne Cashman	1964–1965, 1967–1983
Colby Cave	2017–2019
Peter Cehlarik	2016–2020
Ed Chadwick	1961–1962
Murph Chamberlain	1942–1943
Art Chapman	1930–1934
Zdeno Chara	2006–2020
Gerry Cheevers	1965–1972, 1975–1980
Don Cherry	1954–1955
Dick Cherry	1956–1957
Denis Chervyakov	1992–1993
Tim Cheveldae	1996–1997
Real Chevrefils	1951–1959
Art Chisholm	1960–1961
Stanislav Chistov	2006–2007
Dave Christian	1989–1991
Jack Church	1945–1946
Dean Chynoweth	1995–1998
Rob Cimetta	1988–1990
Dit Clapper	1927–1947
Gordie Clark	1974–1976
Patrick "Nobby" Clark	1927–1928
Sprague Cleghorn	1925–1928
Connor Clifton	2018–2023
Paul Coffey	2000–2001
Les Colvin	1948–1949
Roy Conacher	1938–1942, 1945–1946
Wayne Connelly	1961–1964, 1966–1967
Brett Connolly	2014–2016
Harry Connor	1927–1928, 1929–1930
Lloyd Cook	1924–1925
Bud Cook	1931–1932
Bun Cook	1936–1937
Carson Cooper	1924–1927
Carl Corazzini	2003–2004
Norm Corcoran	1949–1950, 1952–1955
Mark Cornforth	1995–1996
Joe Corvo	2011–2012
Murray Costello	1954–1956
Alain Cote	1985–1989
Maurice Courteau	1943–1944
Geoff Courtnall	1983–1988
Billy Coutu	1926–1927
Bill Cowley	1935–1947
Charlie Coyle	2018–2023
Jim Craig	1980–1981
Jack Crawford	1937–1950
Lou Crawford	1989–1990, 1991–1992
Dave Creighton	1948–1954
Terry Crisp	1965–1966
Tommy Cross	2015–2017

Player	Seasons
Keith Crowder	1980–1989
Bruce Crowder	1981–1984
Wilf Cude	1931–1932
Craig Cunningham	2013–2015
Bill Cupolo	1944–1945
Brian Curran	1983–1986
Austin Czarnik	2016–2018
Mariusz Czerkawski	1993–1996, 2005–2006
Byron Dafoe	1997–2002
Kevin Dallman	2005–2006
Nick Damore	1941–1942
Harold Darragh	1930–1931
Cleon Daskalakis	1984–1987
Kaspars Daugavins	2012–2013
Pinkie Davie	1933–1936
Lorne Davis	1955–1956, 1959–1960
Murray Davison	1965–1966
Jake DeBrusk	2017–2023
Norm Defelice	1956–1957
Matt DelGuidice	1990–1992
Armand "Dutch" Delmonte	1945–1946
Ab G. DeMarco	1942–1944
Ab T. DeMarco	1978–1979
Nathan Dempsey	2006–2007
Cy Denneny	1928–1929
Bill Derlago	1985–1986
Bob Dillabough	1965–1967
Rob DiMaio	1996–2000
Gary Doak	1965–1970, 1972–1981
Brian Dobbin	1991–1992
Clark Donatelli	1991–1992
Ted Donato	1991–1999, 2003–2004
Ryan Donato	2017–2019
Dave Donnelly	1983–1986
Shean Donovan	2006–2007
Gary Dornhoefer	1963–1966
Doug Doull	2003–2004
Peter Douris	1989–1993
Aaron Downey	1999–2000
P.C. Drouin	1996–1997
Luc Dufour	1982–1984
Lorne Duguid	1935–1937
Woody Dumart	1935–1942, 1945–1954
Dale Dunbar	1988–1989
Darryl Edestrand	1973–1978
Pat Egan	1943–1949
Gerry Ehman	1957–1958
Todd Elik	1995–1997
Dave Ellett	1997–1999
Mikko Eloranta	1999–2002
David Emma	1996–1997
John Emmons	2001–2002
Hap Emms	1934–1935
Aut Erickson	1959–1961
Grant Erickson	1968–1969
Loui Eriksson	2013–2016
Phil Esposito	1967–1976
Claude Evans	1957–1958
Bill Ezinicki	1950–1952
Glen Featherstone	1991–1994
Andrew Ference	2006–2013
Tom Fergus	1981–1985
Lorne Ferguson	1949–1952, 1954–1956
Brian Ferlin	2014–2015
Manny Fernandez	2007–2009
Peter Ferraro	1998–2000
Landon Ferraro	2015–2016

Player	Seasons
Guyle Fielder	1953–1954
Marcel Fillion	1944–1945
Tommy Filmore	1932–1934
Brian Finley	2006–2007
Eddie Finnigan	1935–1936
Dunc Fisher	1950–1953
Tom Fitzgerald	2005–2006
Fernie Flaman	1944–1951, 1954–1961
Reg Fleming	1964–1966
Ron Flockhart	1988–1989
Justin Florek	2013–2014
Steven Fogarty	2021–2022
Nick Foligno	2021–2023
Dave Forbes	1973–1977
Mike Forbes	1977–1978
Derek Forbort	2021–2023
Yip Foster	1931–1932
Dwight Foster	1977–1987
Norm Foster	1990–1991
Hec Fowler	1924–1925
Jimmy Franks	1943–1944
Matt Fraser	2013–2015
Trent Frederic	2018–2023
Frank Fredrickson	1926–1929
Jesper Froden	2021–2022
Harry Frost	1938–1939
Art Gagne	1929–1930
Pierre Gagne	1959–1960
Simon Gagne	2014–2015
Johnny Gagnon	1934–1935
Dutch Gainor	1927–1931
Perk Galbraith	1926–1934
Garry Galley	1988–1992
Don Gallinger	1942–1944, 1945–1948
Bruce Gamble	1960–1962
Bert Gardiner	1943–1944
Cal Gardner	1953–1957
Ray Gariepy	1953–1954
Armand Gaudreault	1944–1945
Brendan Gaunce	2019–2020
Jean Gauthier	1968–1969
Jack Gelineau	1948–1951
Jean-Guy Gendron	1958–1961, 1962–1964
Gerry Geran	1925–1926
Ray Getliffe	1935–1939
Barry Gibbs	1967–1969
Doug Gibson	1973–1974, 1975–1976
Jeannot Gilbert	1962–1963, 1964–1965
Gilles Gilbert	1973–1980
Andre Gill	1967–1968
Hal Gill	1997–2006
Mike Gillis	1980–1984
Brian Gionta	2017–2018
Jonathan Girard	1998–2003
Art Giroux	1934–1935
Jean-Paul Gladu	1944–1945
Matt Glennon	1991–1992
Warren Godfrey	1952–1955, 1962–1963
Roy Goldsworthy	1936–1938
Bill Goldsworthy	1964–1967
Sergei Gonchar	2003–2004
Fred Gordon	1927–1928
Lee Goren	2000–2001, 2002–2003
Butch Goring	1984–1985
Bob Gould	1989–1990
Bob Gracie	1933–1934
Thomas Gradin	1986–1987
Teddy Graham	1935–1937
Rod Graham	1974–1975

Player	Seasons
Ron Grahame	1977–1978
John Grahame	1999–2003
Benny Grant	1943–1944
Terry Gray	1961–1962
Red Green	1928–1929
Ted Green	1960–1969, 1970–1972
Travis Green	2003–2006
A.J. Greer	2022–2023
Seth Griffith	2014–2016
Lloyd Gronsdahl	1941–1942
Michal Grosek	2002–2004
Lloyd Gross	1933–1934
Don Grosso	1946–1947
John Gruden	1993–1996
Bob Gryp	1973–1974
Matt Grzelcyk	2016–2023
Paul Guay	1988–1989
Bill Guerin	2000–2002
Bep Guidolin	1942–1944, 1945–1947
Ben Guite	2005–2006
Jonas Gustavsson	2015–2016
Jeff Hackett	2002–2003
Matti Hagman	1976–1978
Jaroslav Halak	2018–2021
Taylor Hall	1987–1988
Taylor Hall	2020–2023
Doug Halward	1975–1978
Red Hamill	1937–1942
Zach Hamill	2009–2012
Dougie Hamilton	2012–2015
Ken Hammond	1990–1991
Brett Harkins	1994–1995, 1996–1997
Happy Harnott	1933–1934
Hago Harrington	1925–1926, 1927–1928
Smokey Harris	1924–1925
Henry Harris	1930–1931
Ed Harrison	1947–1951
Jim Harrison	1968–1970
Garnet Hathaway	2022–2023
Erik Haula	2021–2022
Greg Hawgood	1987–1990
Chris Hayes	1971–1972
Jimmy Hayes	2015–2017
Paul Haynes	1934–1935
Don Head	1961–1962
Fern Headley	1924–1925
Eric Healey	2005–2006
Andy Hebenton	1963–1964
Danton Heinen	2016–2020
Lionel Heinrich	1955–1956
Steve Heinze	1991–2000
Murray Henderson	1944–1952
John Henderson	1954–1956
Jay Henderson	1998–2001
Josh Hennessy	2011–2012
Gord Henry	1948–1951, 1952–1953
Jim Henry	1951–1955
Jimmy Herberts	1924–1928
Phil Hergesheimer	1941–1942
Matt Herr	2002–2003
Matt [Hervey] Block	1991–1992
Obs Heximer	1932–1933
Wayne Hicks	1962–1963
Andy Hilbert	2001–2004
Mel Hill	1937–1941
Dutch Hiller	1941–1942
Randy Hillier	1981–1984
Floyd Hillman	1956–1957
Larry Hillman	1957–1960

Player	Seasons
Lionel Hitchman	1924–1934
Shane Hnidy	2007–2009, 2010–2011
Ken R. Hodge	1967–1976
Ken D. Hodge	1990–1992
Ted Hodgson	1966–1967
Jeff Hoggan	2006–2008
Benoit Hogue	2001–2002
Nick Holden	2017–2018
Flash Hollett	1935–1944
Ron Hoover	1989–1991
Pete Horeck	1949–1951
Nathan Horton	2010–2013
Bronco Horvath	1957–1961
Marty Howe	1982–1983
Bill Huard	1992–1993
Brent Hughes	1991–1995
Ryan Hughes	1995–1996
Cameron Hughes	2019–2021
Joe Hulbig	1999–2001
Ivan Huml	2001–2004
Matt Hunwick	2007–2011
Paul Hurley	1968–1969
Jamie Huscroft	1993–1995
Bill Hutton	1929–1931
Dave Hynes	1973–1975
Gord Hynes	1991–1992
Al Iafrate	1993–1994
Jarome Iginla	2013–2014
Frank Ingram	1924–1925
Ted Irvine	1963–1964
Matt Irwin	2015–2016
Brad Isbister	2005–2006
Richard Jackman	2001–2002
Stan Jackson	1924–1926
Percy Jackson	1931–1932, 1935–1936
Walter Jackson	1935–1936
Art Jackson	1937–1945
Busher Jackson	1941–1944
Jaromir Jagr	2012–2013
Craig Janney	1987–1992
Roger Jenkins	1935–1936
Bill Jennings	1944–1945
Eddie Jeremiah	1931–1932
Frank Jerwa	1931–1935
Joe Jerwa	1931–1934, 1936–1937
Jeff Jillson	2003–2004
Marcus Johansson	2018–2019
Norm Johnson	1957–1959
Tom Johnson	1963–1965
Aaron Johnson	2012–2013
Chad Johnson	2013–2014
Nick Johnson	2013–2014
Eddie Johnston	1962–1973
Greg Johnston	1983–1990
Stan Jonathan	1975–1983
Ron Jones	1971–1973
Bob Joyce	1987–1990
Joe Juneau	1991–1994
Joe Junkin	1968–1969
Milan Jurcina	2005–2007
Tomas Kaberle	2010–2011
Walter Kalbfleisch	1936–1937
Petr Kalus	2006–2007
Max Kaminsky	1934–1936
Steven Kampfer	2010–2012, 2019–2021
Jakob Forsbacka-Karlsson	2016–2017, 2018–2019
Martins Karsums	2008–2009

Player	Seasons
Alexei Kasatonov	1994–1996
Ondrej Kase	2019–2021
Steve Kasper	1980–1989
Doug Keans	1983–1988
Duke Keats	1926–1927
Don Keenan	1958–1959
Jarmo Kekalainen	1989–1991
Chris Kelleher	2001–2002
Chris Kelly	2010–2016
Joonas Kemppainen	2015–2016
Forbes Kennedy	1962–1966
Sheldon Kennedy	1996–1997
Phil Kessel	2006–2009
Alexander Khokhlachev	2013–2016
Dmitri Khristich	1997–1999
Anton Khudobin	2011–2013, 2016–2018
Darin Kimble	1992–1993
Keith Kinkaid	2022–2023
Lloyd "Deed" Klein	1928–1932
Joe Klukay	1952–1955
Gord Kluzak	1982–1991
Bill Knibbs	1964–1965
Fred Knipscheer	1993–1995
Mike Knuble	1999–2004
Chuck Kobasew	2006–2010
Pavel Kolarik	2000–2002
Russ Kopak	1943–1944
Joona Koppanen	2022–2023
Doug Kostynski	1983–1985
Andrei Kovalenko	2000–2001
Steve Kraftcheck	1950–1951
Skip Krake	1963–1964, 1965–1968
David Krejci	2006–2021, 2022–2023
Torey Krug	2011–2020
Mike Krushelnyski	1981–1984
Ed Kryzanowski	1948–1952
Karson Kuhlman	2018–2022
Arnie Kullman	1947–1950
Jarno Kultanen	2000–2003
Sean Kuraly	2016–2021
Orland Kurtenbach	1961–1962, 1963–1965
Zdenek Kutlak	2000–2001, 2003–2004
Dmitri Kvartalnov	1992–1994
Gus Kyle	1951–1952
Antti Laaksonen	1998–2000
Leo Labine	1951–1961
Guy Labrie	1943–1944
Blaine Lacher	1994–1996
Dan LaCouture	2005–2006
Daniel Lacroix	1994–1995
Bobby Lalonde	1979–1981
Joe Lamb	1932–1934
Myles Lane	1928–1930, 1933–1934
Robert Lang	1997–1998
Steve Langdon	1974–1976, 1977–1978
Josh Langfeld	2005–2006
Al Langlois	1965–1966
Guy Lapointe	1983–1984
Martin Lapointe	2001–2004
Drew Larman	2009–2010
Bonner Larose	1925–1926
Guy Larose	1994–1995
Reed Larson	1985–1988
Matt Lashoff	2006–2009
Marty Lauder	1927–1928
Jakub Lauko	2022–2023
Jeremy Lauzon	2018–2021
Dominic Lavoie	1992–1993
Brian Lawton	1989–1990

Player	Seasons
Hal Laycoe	1950–1956
Curtis Lazar	2020–2022
Jeff Lazaro	1990–1992
Larry Leach	1958–1960, 1961–1962
Reggie Leach	1970–1972
Steve Leach	1991–1996
Jay Leach	2005–2006
Pat Leahy	2003–2006
Rich Leduc	1972–1974
Grant Ledyard	1997–1999
Brian Leetch	2005–2006
Guillaume Lefebvre	2009–2010
Tommy Lehmann	1987–1989
Mikko Lehtonen	2008–2010
Bob Leiter	1962–1966, 1968–1969
Moe Lemay	1987–1989
Reggie Lemelin	1987–1993
Bill Lesuk	1968–1970
Pete Leswick	1944–1945
Vinni Lettieri	2022–2023
Normand Leveille	1981–1983
Tyler Lewington	2021–2022
John-Michael Liles	2015–2017
Matt Lindblad	2013–2015
Par Lindholm	2019–2021
Hampus Lindholm	2021–2023
Ken Linseman	1984–1990
Howard Lockhart	1924–1925
Ross Lonsberry	1966–1969
Jim Lorentz	1968–1970
Ross Lowe	1949–1951
Milan Lucic	2007–2015
Morris Lukowich	1984–1986
Harry Lumley	1957–1960
Pentti Lund	1946–1948, 1951–1953
Vic Lynn	1950–1952
Peaches Lyons	1930–1931
Lane MacDermid	2011–2013
Parker MacDonald	1965–1966
Craig MacDonald	2003–2004
Joey MacDonald	2006–2007
Duncan "Mickey" MacKay	1928–1930
Fleming Mackell	1951–1960
Craig MacTavish	1979–1984
Mikko Makela	1994–1995
Dean Malkoc	1996–1998
Troy Mallette	1996–1997
Phil Maloney	1949–1951
Ray Maluta	1975–1977
Eric Manlow	2000–2002
Cameron Mann	1997–2001
Ray Manson	1947–1948
Sylvio Mantha	1936–1937
Paul Mara	2006–2007
Brad Marchand	2009–2023
Don Marcotte	1965–1966, 1968–1981
Frank Mario	1941–1942, 1944–1945
Nevin Markwart	1983–1988, 1989–1992
Daniel Marois	1993–1994
Gilles Marotte	1965–1967
Mark Marquess	1946–1947
Clare Martin	1941–1942, 1946–1948
Frank Martin	1952–1954
Pit Martin	1965–1967
Marquis Mathieu	1998–2001
Joe Matte	1925–1926
Wayne Maxner	1964–1966
Alan May	1987–1988
Norm McAtee	1946–1947

Player	Seasons
Charlie McAvoy	2016–2023
Tom P. McCarthy	1960–1961
Tom J. McCarthy	1986–1988
Sandy McCarthy	2003–2004
Trent McCleary	1996–1997
Bob McCord	1963–1965
Brad McCrimmon	1979–1982
Ab McDonald	1964–1965
Shawn McEachern	1995–1996, 2005–2006
Jack McGill	1941–1942, 1944–1945, 1946–1947
Dan McGillis	2002–2004
Bert McInenly	1933–1936
Marty McInnis	2001–2003
Jack McIntyre	1949–1953
Zane McIntyre	2016–2017
Walt McKechnie	1974–1975
Greg McKegg	2020–2021
Don McKenney	1954–1963
Johnny "Pie" McKenzie	1965–1972
Andrew McKim	1992–1994
Kyle McLaren	1995–2002
Marc McLaughlin	2021–2022
Scott McLellan	1982–1983
Mike McMahon	1945–1946
Sammy McManus	1936–1937
Peter McNab	1976–1984
Adam McQuaid	2009–2018
Pat McReavy	1938–1942
Marty McSorley	1999–2000
Harry Meeking	1926–1927
Dick Meissner	1959–1962
Larry Melnyk	1980–1983
Andrej Meszaros	2013–2014
Glen Metropolit	2007–2008
Nick Mickoski	1959–1960
Rick Middleton	1976–1988
Mike Milbury	1975–1987
Al Millar	1957–1958
Mike Millar	1989–1990
Bob Miller	1977–1981
Jay Miller	1985–1989
Kevan Miller	2013–2021
Colin Miller	2015–2017
Herb Mitchell	1924–1926
Mike Moffat	1981–1984
Sandy Moger	1994–1997
Doug Mohns	1953–1964
Carl Mokosak	1988–1989
Steve Montador	2008–2009
Andy Moog	1987–1993
Dominic Moore	2016–2017
John Moore	2018–2022
Ian Moran	2002–2006
Bernie Morris	1924–1925
Jon Morris	1993–1994
Derek Morris	2009–2010
Jim Morrison	1951–1952, 1958–1959
Doug Morrison	1979–1982, 1984–1985
Shaone Morrisonn	2002–2004
Joe Morrow	2014–2017
Mike Mottau	2011–2012
Alex Motter	1934–1936
Mark Mowers	2006–2007
Joe Mullen	1995–1996
Ron Murphy	1965–1970
Gord Murphy	1991–1993, 2001–2002
Joe Murphy	1999–2000
Glen Murray	1991–1995, 2001–2008
Brantt Myhres	2002–2003
Anders Myrvold	1996–1997

Player	Seasons
Riley Nash	2016–2018
Rick Nash	2017–2018
Mats Naslund	1994–1995
Andrei Nazarov	2000–2002
Cam Neely	1986–1996
Ray Neufeld	1988–1990
Al Nicholson	1955–1957
Eric Nickulas	1998–2001, 2005–2006
Graeme Nicolson	1978–1979
Kirk Nielsen	1997–1998
Kraig Nienhuis	1985–1988
Chris Nilan	1990–1992
Jim Nill	1983–1985
Petteri Nokelainen	2007–2009
Peter Nordstrom	1998–1999
Joakim Nordstrom	2018–2020
Jack Norris	1964–1965
Jeff Norton	2001–2002
Tomas Nosek	2021–2023
Hank Nowak	1974–1977
Michael Nylander	2003–2004
Adam Oates	1991–1997
Ellard "Obie" O'Brien	1955–1956
Dennis O'Brien	1977–1980
Mike O'Connell	1980–1986
Chris Oddleifson	1972–1974
Jeff Odgers	1996–1997
Fred O'Donnell	1972–1974
Sean O'Donnell	2001–2004
Billy O'Dwyer	1987–1990
Rob O'Gara	2016–2018
Harry Oliver	1926–1934
Murray Oliver	1960–1967
Krzysztof Oliwa	2002–2003
Paul O'Neil	1975–1976
Jim "Peggy" O'Neil	1933–1937
Willie O'Ree	1957–1958, 1960–1961
Terry O'Reilly	1971–1985
Dmitry Orlov	2022–2023
Bobby Orr	1966–1976
Colton Orr	2003–2006
Gerry Ouellette	1960–1961
George Owen	1928–1933
Clayton Pachal	1976–1978
Samuel Pahlsson	2000–2001
Daniel Paille	2009–2015
Aldo Palazzari	1943–1944
Brad Palmer	1982–1983
Eddie Panagabko	1955–1957
Jay Pandolfo	2012–2013
Grigori Panteleev	1992–1995
Bernie Parent	1965–1967
J.P. Parise	1965–1967
Brad Park	1975–1983
Dave Pasin	1985–1986
David Pastrnak	2014–2023
George Patterson	1933–1934
Davis Payne	1995–1997
Allen Pedersen	1986–1991
Barry Pederson	1980–1986, 1991–1992
Pete Peeters	1982–1986
Johnny Peirson	1946–1954, 1955–1958
Scott Pellerin	2001–2002
Pascal Pelletier	2007–2008
Jeff Penner	2009–2010
Cliff Pennington	1961–1963
Bob Perreault	1962–1963
Jim Peters	1947–1949

Player	Seasons
Garry Peters	1971–1972
Jim Pettie	1976–1979
Eric Pettinger	1928–1929
Gordon Pettinger	1937–1940
Rich Peverley	2010–2013
Harry Pidhirny	1957–1958
Jacques Plante	1972–1973
Willi Plett	1987–1988
Ray Podloski	1988–1989
Bud Poile	1949–1950
Dan Poliziani	1958–1959
Poul Popiel	1965–1966
Peter Popovic	2000–2001
Jack Portland	1934–1940
Paul Postma	2017–2018
Corey Potter	2013–2014
Marc Potvin	1994–1996
Felix Potvin	2003–2004
Dave Poulin	1989–1993
Benoit Pouliot	2011–2012
Petr Prajsler	1991–1992
Jack Pratt	1930–1932
Babe Pratt	1946–1947
Dean Prentice	1962–1966
Wayne Primeau	2005–2007
Sean Pronger	1999–2000
Andre Pronovost	1960–1963
Claude Pronovost	1955–1956
Brian Propp	1989–1990
Joel Prpic	1997–1998, 1999–2000
Jean Pusie	1934–1935
Bill Quackenbush	1949–1956
Max Quackenbush	1950–1951
John Quilty	1947–1948
Stephane Quintal	1988–1992
Tyler Randell	2015–2016
Bill Ranford	1985–1987, 1995–1997
George Ranieri	1956–1957
Tuukka Rask	2007–2022
Jean Ratelle	1975–1981
Jake Rathwell	1974–1975
Matt Ravlich	1962–1963, 1971–1973
Andrew Raycroft	2000–2006
Terry Reardon	1938–1941, 1945–1947
Marty Reasoner	2005–2006
Mark Recchi	2008–2011
Gord Redahl	1958–1959
Wade Redden	2012–2013
George Redding	1924–1926
Dick Redmond	1978–1982
Dave Reece	1975–1976
Larry Regan	1956–1959
Dutch Reibel	1958–1959
Jeremy Reich	2006–2008
Dave Reid	1983–1988, 1991–1996
Ed Reigle	1950–1951
Mike Reilly	2020–2023
Dan Renouf	2022–2023
Stephane Richer	1992–1993
Barry Richter	1996–1997
Vincent Riendeau	1993–1995
Pat Riggin	1985–1987
Jack Riley	1935–1936
Zac Rinaldo	2015–2016
Bob Ring	1965–1966
Vic Ripley	1932–1934
Brett Ritchie	2019–2020
Nick Ritchie	2019–2021

Player	Seasons
Al Rittinger	1943–1944
Wayne Rivers	1963–1967
Jamie Rivers	2001–2002
Doug Roberts	1971–1974
Gordie Roberts	1992–1994
Maurice Roberts	1925–1926
Bobby Robins	2014–2015
Nathan Robinson	2005–2006
Randy Robitaille	1996–1999
Earl Roche	1932–1933
Eddie Rodden	1928–1929
Jon Rohloff	1994–1997
Dale Rolfe	1959–1960
Brian Rolston	1999–2004, 2011–2012
Roberto Romano	1986–1987
Paul Ronty	1947–1951
Bobby Rowe	1924–1925
Andre Roy	1995–1997
Jean-Yves Roy	1996–1998
Gino Rozzini	1944–1945
Kent Ruhnke	1975–1976
Paul Runge	1930–1932, 1935–1936
Vladimir "Rosie" Ruzicka	1990–1993
Michael Ryder	2008–2011
Sergei Samsonov	1997–2006
Martin Samuelsson	2002–2004
Derek Sanderson	1965–1974
Ed Sandford	1947–1955
Charlie Sands	1934–1939
Craig Sarner	1974–1975
Miroslav Satan	2009–2010
Glen Sather	1966–1969
Philippe Sauve	2006–2007
Maxime Sauve	2011–2012
Gordon "Tony" Savage	1934–1935
Andre Savage	1998–2001
Andre Savard	1973–1976
Marc Savard	2006–2011
Terry Sawchuk	1955–1957
Kevin Sawyer	1995–1997
Dave Scatchard	2005–2006
Peter Schaefer	2007–2008
Paxton Schafer	1996–1997
Tim Schaller	2016–2018
Chuck Scherza	1943–1944
Bobby Schmautz	1973–1980
Milt Schmidt	1936–1942, 1945–1955
Jack Schmidt	1942–1943
Clarence Schmidt	1943–1944
Joe Schmidt	1943–1944
Werner Schnarr	1924–1926
Ron Schock	1963–1967
Danny Schock	1969–1971
Jim Schoenfeld	1983–1984
Al Secord	1978–1981
Tyler Seguin	2010–2013
Dennis Seidenberg	2009–2016
Zachary Senyshyn	2018–2021
Jeff Serowik	1994–1995
Eddie Shack	1967–1969
Evgeny Shaldybin	1996–1997
Sean Shanahan	1977–1978
Gerry Shannon	1934–1936
David Shaw	1992–1995
Normand Shay	1924–1926
John Sheppard	1933–1934
Gregg Sheppard	1972–1978
Jack Shewchuk	1938–1943, 1944–1945
Allan Shields	1936–1937

Player	Seasons
Steve Shields	2002–2003
Jack Shill	1934–1935
Bill Shill	1942–1947
Bruce Shoebottom	1987–1991
Eddie Shore	1926–1940
Babe Siebert	1933–1936
Jordan Sigalet	2005–2006
Jonathan Sigalet	2006–2007
Dave Silk	1983–1985
Charlie Simmer	1984–1987
Don Simmons	1956–1961
Al Simmons	1973–1974, 1975–1976
Frank Simonetti	1984–1988
Al Sims	1973–1979
Alf Skinner	1924–1925
Petri Skriko	1990–1992
Peter Skudra	2000–2001
Jiri Slegr	2003–2006
Louis Sleigher	1984–1986
Don Smillie	1933–1934
Alex Smith	1932–1934
Reginald "Hooley" Smith	1936–1937
Des Smith	1939–1942
Kenny Smith	1944–1951
Floyd Smith	1954–1955, 1956–1957
Dallas Smith	1959–1962, 1965–1977
Rick Smith	1968–1972, 1976–1980
Barry Smith	1975–1976
Brandon Smith	1998–2001
Reilly Smith	2013–2015
Gemel Smith	2018–2019
Craig Smith	2020–2023
Bryan Smolinski	1992–1995
Vladimir Sobotka	2007–2010
Carl Soderberg	2012–2015
Tom Songin	1978–1981
Spunk Sparrow	1924–1925
Bill Speer	1969–1971
Irv Spencer	1962–1963
Ryan Spooner	2012–2018
Frank Spring	1969–1970
Martin St. Pierre	2008–2009
Drew Stafford	2016–2017
Steve Staios	1995–1997
Fred Stanfield	1967–1973
Allan Stanley	1956–1958
Paul Stanton	1993–1994
Pat Stapleton	1961–1963
Vic Stasiuk	1955–1961
Yan Stastny	2005–2007
Oskar Steen	2020–2023
Phil Von Stefenelli	1995–1996
Lee Stempniak	2015–2016, 2018–2019
Phil Stevens	1925–1926
Mike Stevens	1987–1988
Kevin Stevens	1995–1996
Shayne Stevenson	1990–1992
Doc Stewart	1924–1927
Nels Stewart	1932–1935, 1936–1937
Ron Stewart	1965–1967
Bob Stewart	1971–1972
Jim Stewart	1979–1980
Alan Stewart	1991–1992
Cam Stewart	1993–1997
P.J. Stock	2001–2004
Anton Stralman	2022–2023
Red Stuart	1924–1927
Brad Stuart	2005–2007
Mark Stuart	2005–2011
Jack Studnicka	2019–2023

Player	Seasons
Jozef Stumpel	1991–1997, 2001–2003
Marco Sturm	2005–2010
Malcolm Subban	2014–2015, 2016–2017
George "Red" Sullivan	1949–1953
Mike Sullivan	1997–1998
Max Sutherland	1931–1932
Ron Sutter	1995–1996
Niklas Svedberg	2013–2015
Jeremy Swayman	2020–2023
Bob Sweeney	1986–1992
Don Sweeney	1988–2003
Tim Sweeney	1992–1993, 1995–1997
Don Sylvestri	1984–1985
Jordan Szwarz	2017–2018
Maxime Talbot	2014–2016
Rob Tallas	1995–2000
Dave Tanabe	2005–2006
Jamie Tardif	2012–2013
Mikhail Tatarinov	1993–1994
Bob Taylor	1929–1930
Billy Taylor	1947–1948
Tim Taylor	1997–1999
Chris Taylor	1998–1999
Skip Teal	1954–1955
Petr Tenkrat	2006–2007
Orval Tessier	1955–1956, 1960–1961
Mats Thelin	1984–1987
Michael Thelven	1985–1990
Tim Thomas	2002–2012
Dave Thomlinson	1991–1992
Tiny Thompson	1928–1939
Cliff Thompson	1941–1942, 1948–1949
Nate Thompson	2006–2007
Bill Thoms	1944–1945
Joe Thornton	1997–2006
Shawn Thornton	2007–2014
Mattias Timander	1996–2000
Jarred Tinordi	2020–2021
Rick Tocchet	1995–1997
Hannu Toivonen	2005–2007
Zellio Toppazzini	1948–1951
Jerry Toppazzini	1952–1954, 1955–1964
Bill Touhey	1931–1932
Graeme Townshend	1989–1991
Patrick Traverse	2000–2001
Zach Trotman	2013–2016
Marty Turco	2011–2012
Gordon Turlik	1959–1960
Tony Tuzzolino	2001–2002
Linus Ullmark	2021–2023
Urho Vaakanainen	2018–2022
Rogie Vachon	1980–1982
Carol Vadnais	1971–1976
Darren Van Impe	1997–2001
Dennis Vaske	1998–1999
Frank Vatrano	2015–2018
Kris Vernarsky	2002–2004
Jim Vesey	1991–1992
Terry Virtue	1998–1999
Daniel Vladar	2019–2021
Chris Wagner	2018–2023
Ben Walter	2005–2007
Mike Walton	1970–1973, 1978–1979
Wes Walz	1989–1992
Aaron Ward	2006–2009
Don Ward	1959–1960
Dixon Ward	2000–2001
David Warsofsky	2013–2015
Grant Warwick	1947–1949
Joe Watson	1964–1967
Tom Webster	1968–1970
Cooney Weiland	1928–1932, 1935–1939
Eric Weinrich	2000–2001
John Wensink	1976–1980
Glen Wesley	1987–1994
Eddie Westfall	1961–1972
Blake Wheeler	2008–2011
Trent Whitfield	2009–2012, 2011–2012
Kay Whitmore	2000–2001
Dennis Wideman	2006–2010
Jim Wiemer	1989–1994
Archie Wilcox	1933–1934
Barry Wilkins	1966–1967, 1968–1970
John Wilkinson	1943–1944
Burr Williams	1934–1935
Tommy Williams	1961–1969
Wally Wilson	1947–1948
Gord Wilson	1954–1955
Ross "Lefty" Wilson	1957–1958
Landon Wilson	1996–2000
Tommy Wingels	2017–2018
Hal Winkler	1926–1928
Chris Winnes	1990–1993
Eddie Wiseman	1939–1942
Bob Woytowich	1964–1967
Andy Wozniewski	2009–2010
Ken Yackel	1958–1959
Stephane Yelle	2008–2009
Jason York	2006–2007
C.J. Young	1992–1993
Pavel Zacha	2022–2023
Rob Zamuner	2001–2004
Greg Zanon	2011–2012
Joe Zanussi	1975–1977
Jakub Zboril	2018–2023
Jeff Zehr	1999–2000
Alexei Zhamnov	2005–2006
Sergei Zholtok	1992–1994
Sergei Zinovjev	2003–2004
Rick Zombo	1995–1996